PARTY PATRONAGE AND PARTY GOVERNMENT IN EUROPEAN DEMOCRACIES

COMPARATIVE POLITICS

Comparative Politics is a series for students, teachers, and researchers of political science that deals with contemporary government and politics. Global in scope, books in the series are characterized by a stress on comparative analysis and strong methodological rigour. The series is published in association with the European Consortium for Political Research. For more information visit www.ecprnet.eu

The Comparative Politics series is edited by Professor David M. Farrell, School of Politics and International Relations, University College Dublin, Kenneth Carty, Professor of Political Science, University of British Columbia, and Professor Dirk Berg-Schlosser, Institute of Political Science, Philipps University, Marburg.

OTHER TITLES IN THIS SERIES

Parliaments and Coalitions
The Role of Legislative Institutions in Multiparty Governance
Lanny W. Martin and Georg Vanberg

When Citizens Decide
Lessons from Citizens Assemblies on Electoral Reform
Patrick Fournier, Henk van der Kolk, R. Kenneth Carty, André Blais, and Jonathan Rose

Platform or Personality?
The Role of Party Leaders in Elections
Amanda Bittner

Political Leaders and Democratic Elections
Edited by Kees Aarts, André Blais, and Hermann Schmitt

The Politics of Party Funding
State Funding to Political Parties and Party Competition in Western Europe
Michael Koß

Designing Democracy in a Dangerous World
Andrew Reynolds

Democracy within Parties
Candidate Selection Methods and
Their Political Consequences
Reuven Y. Hazan and Gideon Rahat

Party Politics in New Democracies
Edited by Paul Webb and Stephen White

Intergovernmental Cooperation
Rational Choices in Federal Systems and Beyond
Nicole Bolleyer

The Dynamics of Two-Party Politics
Party Structures and the Management of Competition
Alan Ware

Cabinets and Coalition Bargaining
The Democratic Life Cycle in Western Europe
Edited by Kaare Strøm, Wolfgang C. Müller, and Torbjörn Bergman

Party Patronage and Party Government in European Democracies

EDITED BY
PETR KOPECKÝ, PETER MAIR,
AND MARIA SPIROVA

UNIVERSITY PRESS

Great Clarendon Street, Oxford, OX2 6DP,
United Kingdom

Oxford University Press is a department of the University of Oxford.
It furthers the University's objective of excellence in research, scholarship,
and education by publishing worldwide. Oxford is a registered trade mark of
Oxford University Press in the UK and in certain other countries

© Petr Kopecký, the estate of Peter Mair, and Maria Spirova 2012

The moral rights of the authors have been asserted

First Edition published in 2012

Impression: 1

All rights reserved. No part of this publication may be reproduced, stored in
a retrieval system, or transmitted, in any form or by any means, without the
prior permission in writing of Oxford University Press, or as expressly permitted
by law, by licence or under terms agreed with the appropriate reprographics
rights organization. Enquiries concerning reproduction outside the scope of the
above should be sent to the Rights Department, Oxford University Press, at the
address above

You must not circulate this work in any other form
and you must impose this same condition on any acquirer

British Library Cataloguing in Publication Data

Data available

Library of Congress Cataloging in Publication Data

Data available

ISBN 978–0–19–959937–0

Printed in Great Britain by
MPG Books Group, Bodmin and King's Lynn

Links to third party websites are provided by Oxford in good faith and
for information only. Oxford disclaims any responsibility for the materials
contained in any third party website referenced in this work.

Preface

This book has been long in coming. Back in April 2006, Petr Kopecký and Peter Mair organized a workshop at the Joint Sessions of the European Consortium for Political Research in Nicosia entitled 'Political Parties and Patronage'. This book is in many ways the outcome of what began at that meeting. The workshop discussions led to the formulation of our research agenda, selection of cases among the European democracies, and the recruitment of the core of the contributors to this volume. We are very grateful to all twenty-two participants of that workshop for their contributions and stimulating comments.

Our approach to understanding and measuring party patronage was initially developed for a comparative study of party patronage in new democracies. This pilot study began in January 2004 and focused on five new democracies: Argentina, Ghana, Bulgaria, the Czech Republic, and South Africa. The study laid the basis for the analytical framework taken in this book. It has also led to several studies published parallel to this volume. We would like to thank Gerardo Scherlis Perel for his contribution to devising our initial approach to the subject, and for its brilliant application to the case of Argentina.

It is still hard to believe that after collecting data on Bulgaria and the Czech Republic, we managed to convince thirteen other country teams to apply our methodology without any major changes, engage in quite demanding data collection, and write excellent analysis, all in the period of about three years. It did take some organizational effort and planning and three additional workshop meetings in Florence and Leiden. But all this means that we now have a consistent comparative analysis of party patronage in fifteen democracies. We are very grateful to the whole team of contributors for their efforts.

Various institutions have supported us financially along the way: a VIDI grant (Innovational Research Incentives Scheme) from the Dutch Organization for Scientific Research (NWO) provided the resources for the original study in the five new democracies, and the basis for this volume as well; the European University Institute provided financial support for one of the additional meetings that we held. The execution of the country studies was financed by additional grants acknowledged, where appropriate, within the individual country chapters.

We are also grateful to all our colleagues who helped us organize the interviews with 647 experts in the fifteen countries, and of course to the experts themselves. None of this would have been possible without the cooperation of this latter group, who gave us their time and shared their knowledge about patronage appointments in their respective countries. We would also like to acknowledge the insightful assistance of several research master students at Leiden University, who are, by the publication of this book, already establishing their own academic careers: Yvette Peters, Edward Koning, Kristian Voss and Joost Waterborg.

The last thing is the hardest for us to write. Peter Mair's untimely death, which occurred shortly after we submitted the volume to the press, deprives us of the possibility to share the moment of publication with him. Anybody who has ever worked with Peter will recognize instantly that this volume would not have been the same without his contribution. Without him, the time that we spent on this project would also not have been filled with so much fun and joy. We dedicate this book to his memory.

Petr Kopecký and Maria Spirova, Leiden,
October 2011

Table of Contents

List of Figures   ix
List of Tables   xi
List of Abbreviations   xiii

Part 1: Studying Party Patronage

1. Party Patronage as an Organizational Resource   3
Petr Kopecký and Peter Mair

2. Measuring Party Patronage Through Structured Expert Interviews   17
Petr Kopecký and Maria Spirova

Part 2: Party Patronage in Europe

3. Party Patronage in Austria: From Reward to Control   31
Oliver Treib

4. 'A Tradition We Don't Mess With': Party Patronage in Bulgaria   54
Maria Spirova

5. Give Me *Trafika*: Party Patronage in the Czech Republic   74
Petr Kopecký

6. Party Patronage in Denmark: The Merit State with Politics 'On the Side'   92
Carina S. Bischoff

7. Party Patronage in Germany: The Strategic Use of Appointments   121
Stefanie John and Thomas Poguntke

8. Party Patronage in Greece: Political Entrepreneurship in a Party Patronage Democracy   144
Takis S. Pappas and Zina Assimakopoulou

9. Party Patronage in Hungary: Capturing the State   163
Jan-Hinrik Meyer-Sahling and Krisztina Jáger

10. Party Patronage in Iceland: Rewards and Control Appointments   186
Gunnar Helgi Kristinsson

11. Party Patronage in Ireland: Changing Parameters   206
Eoin O'Malley, Stephen Quinlan, and Peter Mair

12. Party Patronage in Italy: A Matter for Solitary Leaders   229
Fabrizio Di Mascio

13. Party Patronage in the Netherlands: Sharing Appointments to Maintain Consensus   250
Sandra van Thiel

14. Appointments to Public Administration in Norway: No Room for Political Parties?   272
Elin Haugsgjerd Allern

15. Party Patronage in Portugal: Treading in Shallow Water   294
Carlos Jalali, Patrícia Silva, and Diogo Moreira

16. Party Patronage in Spain: Appointments for Party Government   316
Raúl Gómez and Tània Verge

17. Party Patronage in the United Kingdom: A Pendulum of Public Appointments   335
Matthew Flinders and Felicity Matthews

Part 3: Conclusion

18. Conclusion: Party Patronage in Contemporary Europe   357
Petr Kopecký and Peter Mair

Appendix 1: Procedure for Data Aggregation and Common Indicators   375
Appendix 2: Questionnaire for the Expert Interviews   376
Appendix 3: Institutions Covered by the Analysis in Germany   378

Bibliography   382
Index   411

List of Figures

2.1	Map of a generic state	22
3.1	Motivations for party patronage in Austria	45
3.2	Qualifications of appointees in Austria	46
3.3	Patronage power	46
4.1	Percentage of respondents who believe that political appointments happen never, sometimes, and often in 2000 and 2005, in Bulgaria	60
4.2	Motivations for party patronage in Bulgaria	63
4.3	Qualifications of appointees in Bulgaria	66
5.1	Motivations for party patronage in the Czech Republic	84
5.2	Qualifications of appointees in the Czech Republic	86
6.1	Institutions in the minister's portfolio—the agency model (an ideal type)	95
6.2	Party roles in Denmark	106
6.3	Motivations of patronage in Denmark	108
6.4	Qualifications of appointees in Denmark	110
7.1	Germany: relevant actors for appointments within federal ministries	130
7.2	North-Rhine Westphalia: relevant actors for appointments within ministries	133
7.3	Motivations for party patronage in Germany	137
7.4	Qualifications of appointees in Germany	138
8.1	Motivations for party patronage in Greece	155
8.2	Qualifications of appointees in Greece	156
9.1	Selectors of political appointees in Hungary	179
9.2	Qualifications of appointees in Hungary	181
9.3	Motivations for party patronage in Hungary	182
9.4	Distribution of jobs between government and opposition parties in Hungary	183
10.1	Motivations for party patronage in Iceland	201
10.2	Qualifications of appointees in Iceland	202

11.1	Motivations for party patronage in Ireland	220
11.2	Qualifications of appointees in Ireland	222
12.1	Types of respondent	233
12.2	Range and depth of party patronage, by level of government	237
12.3	Motivations for party patronage in Italy	238
12.4	Qualifications of appointees in Italy	239
12.5	Sharing of patronage appointments in Italy	241
13.1	Motivations for party patronage in the Netherlands	264
13.2	Qualifications of appointees in the Netherlands	265
14.1	Importance of parties as such to patronage in Norway	283
14.2	Motivations for party patronage in Norway	284
14.3	Qualifications of appointees in Norway	286
15.1	Reach and depth of party patronage, by institutional type	306
15.2	Reach and depth of party patronage, by policy area	307
15.3	Motivations for party patronage in Portugal	308
15.4	Qualifications of appointees in Portugal	310
15.5	Party patronage style	312
16.1	Political appointments in Spanish public administration	320
16.2	Motivations for party patronage in Spain	324
16.3	Qualifications of appointees in Spain	325
16.4	Sharing of patronage appointments among parties	330
17.1	Motivations for party patronage in the United Kingdom	346
17.2	Qualifications of appointees in the United Kingdom	348
18.1	Motivations for party patronage, European averages	362
18.2	Qualifications of appointees, European averages	365
18.3	The index of party patronage in fifteen European democracies	367

List of Tables

1.1	Overview of different concepts related to patronage	8
2.1	Type and number of respondents	25
3.1	The index of party patronage in Austria	37
3.2	The role of the party in appointments	38
3.3	Range and depth of patronage, by policy area and institutional type	39
4.1	The index of party patronage in Bulgaria	58
5.1	The index of party patronage in the Czech Republic	80
6.1	The index of party patronage in Denmark	103
7.1	Employees in the German civil service	124
7.2	The index of party patronage in Germany	128
7.3	The index of party patronage in North-Rhine Westphalia	129
8.1	The index of party patronage in Greece	150
8.2	Range and depth of party patronage by institutional types in Greece	150
8.3	Dimensions of party patronage: a qualitative synopsis	153
8.4	Summary of chief characteristics of political patronage in Greece	159
9.1	The index of party patronage in Hungary	171
10.1	Change in the use of patronage over the last 15–20 years	192
10.2	The index of party patronage in Iceland	193
10.3	Role of parties in strategic and less strategic sectors	200
10.4	Who decides within the party?	203
10.5	Do governing parties share with the opposition?	204
11.1	The index of party patronage in Ireland	216
12.1	Number of general government institutional units under the ESA95 (S.13) methodology (2008)	232
12.2	The index of party patronage in Italy	234
12.3	Range of party patronage in Italy	235
12.4	Depth of party patronage in Italy	236

12.5	The evolution of party patronage in Italy	243
13.1	The index of party patronage in the Netherlands	257
13.2	Formal appointment procedures in NDACs and executing institutions	258
13.3	The index of party patronage, per sector	259
13.4	In political parties, who is in charge of appointments?	267
13.5	Changes in appointment practices	269
14.1	The index of party patronage in Norway	280
14.2	Scope and reach of party patronage in state institutions in Norway	281
15.1	Party goals and nature of patronage	298
15.2	The index of party patronage in Portugal	304
15.3	Party patronage practice, by institutional type and policy area in Portugal	306
16.1	The index of party patronage in Spain	323
16.2	Top-level political appointees and advisers (1999–2008)	329
17.1	The index of party patronage in the United Kingdom	344
18.1	Party patronage in different types of institutions	370
18.2	Party patronage in different policy areas	371

List of Abbreviations

ABD	(*Algemene Bestuursdienst*) the Senior Civil Service bureau (Netherlands)
AFM	Financial Market Authority (Netherlands)
AGCOM	Italian Communications Regulatory Authority
ÁK	State Treasury (Hungary)
ÁKK	State Debt Management Agency (Hungary)
ÁNTSZ	National Public Health and Medical Officer's Service (Hungary)
ÁPEH	Tax Office (Hungary)
ASEP	Council for Personnel Selection (Greece)
ÁSZ	State Audit Office (Hungary)
BAFIN	Federal Financial Supervisory Authority (Germany)
BCP	Bulgarian Communist Party
BNetzA	Federal Network Agency (Germany)
BSP	Bulgarian Socialist Party
BZK	Home Office (Netherlands)
BZÖ	Alliance for the Future of Austria
CDA	Christian Democratic Party (Netherlands)
CDS-PP	Party of the Democratic Social Centre—Popular Party (Portugal)
CDU/CSU	Christian Democratic Union/Christian Social Union (Germany)
CEE	Central and Eastern Europe
CGPJ	General Council of the Judiciary (Spain)
CIDE	Centro do Investigación y Docencia Económicas, Mexico
CiU	Catalan Convergence and Union Party (Spain)
CNB	Czech National Bank
CPA	Commissioner for Public Appointments (UK)
CPANI	Commissioner for Public Appointments for Northern Ireland
CPAS	Commissioner for Public Appointments in Scotland
CQ	Commissioner of the Queen (Netherlands)
CSM	Higher Council of the Magistracy (Italy)
CSPL	Committee on Standards in Public Life (UK)
ČSSD	Czech Social Democratic Party (Czech Republic)
CU	Christian Union (Netherlands)
D66	Democrats 66 (Netherlands)
DC	Christian Democrats (Italy)
DEI	Public Power Company (Greece)
DESA	Department of Economic and Social Affairs (Bulgaria)
DG	director general

DnA	Labour Party (Norway)
DPADM	Division for Public Administration and Development Management (Bulgaria)
DPS	Movement for Rights and Freedoms (Bulgaria)
DR	Public Broadcast Organization (Denmark)
EEKH	Office of Authorization and Administrative Procedures of the Ministry of Health (Hungary)
EI	executing institution
EU	European Union
FDP	Free Democratic Party (Germany)
FFG	Austrian Research Promotion Agency
FKGP	Independent Smallholders (Hungary)
FPÖ	Freedom Party of Austria
FrP	Progress Party (Norway)
FWF	Austrian Science Fund
GERB	Citizens for the European Development of Bulgaria (Bulgaria)
GIS	Government Information Service (Ireland)
GL	Green Left (Netherlands)
H	Conservative Party (Norway)
HRM	human resource management
IKA	Social Insurance Organization (Ἴδρμα Κοινωνικῶν Ἀσφαλίσεων) (Greece)
INE	Institute of Labour (Greece)
IPSA	International Political Science Association
IU	United Left Party (Spain)
JAAB	Judicial Appointments Advisory Board (Ireland)
JABS	Judicial Appointments Board for Scotland
JAC	Judicial Appointments Commission (UK)
KDNP	Christian Democratic People's Party (Hungary)
KDU-ČSL	Christian Democratic Union—the People's Party (Czech Republic)
KEHI	Government Control Office (Hungary)
KISZ	communist youth organization (Hungary)
KrF	Christian People's Party (Norway)
KSČM	Communist Party of Bohemia and Moravia (Czech Republic)
KSH	Statistical Office (Hungary)
LAC	Local Appointments Commission (Ireland)
LSA	Bulgarian Law on the State Administration
LCS	Bulgarian Law on the Civil Servant
LMP	'Politics Can Be Different' (Hungary)
LPF	Pim Fortuyn List (Netherlands)
MÁV	Hungarian Railways
MDF	Hungarian Democratic Forum
MFB	Hungarian Development Bank

MIÉP	Hungarian Justice and Life Party
MNB	Hungarian National Bank
MP	member of parliament
MSZMP	Hungarian Socialist Workers' Party
MSZP	Hungarian Socialist Party
NBH	National Security Office (Hungary)
ND	New Democracy Party (Greece)
NDACs	non-departmental agencies and commissions
NDPB	non-departmental public body
NDSV	National Movement Simeon the Second (Bulgaria)
NGO	non-governmental organization
NHS	National Health Service (UK)
NIJAC	Northern Ireland Judicial Appointments Commission
NKA	National Cultural Fund (Hungary)
NPM	New Public Management (Netherlands)
NRW	North-Rhine Westphalia (Germany)
NSA	Norwegian State Administration Database
NSD	Norwegian Social Science Data Services
NSDAP	National Socialist German Workers' Party (Germany/Austria)
NZa	Dutch Health Care Authority
OAED	Greek Manpower Employment Organization
ÖBB	Federal Railways Company of Austria
OCPA	Office of the Commissioner for Public Appointments (UK)
ODS	Civic Democratic Party (Czech Republic)
OECD	Organisation for Economic Co-operation and Development
OEP	National Health Insurance Fund Administration (Hungary)
OF	Civic Forum (Czech Republic)
ÖGB	Austrian Trade Union Federation
OIT	National Council of Justice (Hungary)
OMV	Austrian energy company
ORF	Austrian Broadcasting Company
ORTT	National Radio and Television Commission (Hungary)
ÖVP	Austrian People's Party
PASC	Public Administration Select Committee (UK)
PASOK	Panhellenic Socialist Movement (Greece)
PCE	Communist Party of Spain
PCI	Italian Communist Party
PCP	Communist Party (Portugal)
PESY	regional health systems in Greece
PNV	Basque Nationalist Party (Spain)
POE-OTA	Greek Federation of Municipal Workers
PP	People's Party (Spain)
PR	proportional representation

PS	permanent secretary
PS	Socialist Party (Portugal)
PSD	Social Democrat Party (Portugal)
PSOE	Spanish Socialist Workers' Party
PSZÁF	Financial Supervisory Agency (Hungary)
PvdA	Labour Party (Netherlands)
PVDD	Party for the Animals (Netherlands)
PVV	Party for Freedom (Netherlands)
RAI	Radiotelevisione Italiana (public service broadcaster) (Italy)
RLA	Regional and Local Administration
RSZVSZ	Protective Service of Law Enforcement Agencies (Hungary)
SDS	Union of Democratic Forces (Bulgaria)
SER	Socio-economic Council (Netherlands)
SG	secretary general
SGP	Political Reformed Party (Netherlands)
SOE	state-owned enterprise
Sp	Centre Party (Norway)
SP	Socialist Party (Netherlands)
SPD	Social Democratic Party (Germany)
SPÖ	Social Democratic Party (Austria)
SPSS	Statistical Package for the Social Sciences
SV	Socialist Left (Norway)
SZ	Green Party (Czech Republic)
SZDSZ	Alliance of Free Democrats (Hungary)
SZW	Ministry of Social Affairs and Employment (Netherlands)
TAE	Merchants' Insurance Fund (Ταμείο Ασφάλισης Εμπόρων) (Greece)
TD	member of parliament in Ireland
TEBE	Professionals' and Craftsmen's Insurance Fund (Ταμείο Επαγγελματιών και Βιοτεχνών Ελλάδας) (Greece)
TLAC	Top-Level Appointment Committee (Ireland)
UCD	Union of the Democratic Centre (Spain)
UDF	Union of Democratic Forces (Bulgaria)
UN	United Nations
V	Liberal Party (Norway)
VVD	People's Party for Freedom and Democracy (Netherlands)
WFD	Westminster Foundation for Democracy (UK)

Part 1: Studying Party Patronage

CHAPTER 1

Party Patronage as an Organizational Resource

Petr Kopecký and Peter Mair

INTRODUCTION

The aim of this volume is to explore the practices of party patronage in contemporary European democracies. The exercise of political patronage in the political world is not a new phenomenon, of course. It is usually conceived of as a form of particularistic exchange, between patrons and clients, which has existed in both traditional and modern societies, in both democratic and non-democratic regimes, in various types of organizations, and on the local, regional, national, and even supranational level. Party patronage as such is also not a new phenomenon, but has been distinguished from political patronage more generally, in that the party, rather than an individual political leader, serves as the 'collective' patron in the exchange relation. In the European context, for example, access to patronage resources has sometimes helped to provide party leaders with the means to initially build, and later maintain, party organizations, by means of distributing 'selective incentives' (Conway and Feigert, 1968; Panebianco, 1988; Müller, 1989) to party activists and party elites in exchange for organizational loyalty or other benefits. Party patronage has also helped parties to develop clientelistic networks as a means of maintaining their electoral support (e.g. Mainwaring, 1999; Blondel, 2002; Hopkin, 2006; Kitschelt and Wilkinson, 2007).

In this volume, we distinguish patronage as an *organizational resource* from patronage as an *electoral resource*. While most of the attention in the literature has been on the latter (for two most recent accounts see Piattoni, 2001a; Kitschelt and Wilkinson, 2007), we consider the former as an increasingly important element of party organizational development and of party government. Indeed, it is this distinction between two different understandings of party patronage, including the systematic conceptual and empirical attention that we devote to patronage as an organizational resource, that sets our volume apart from most of the existing literature on patronage and clientelism, and on party organizations and party government.

This introductory chapter provides a theoretical and conceptual background to the entire volume. We first briefly review the literature that associates patronage with electoral strategies and resources. We show that party patronage so understood is defined as a form of particularistic exchange between the party on the one hand, and a supporter or a group of supporters on the other hand, in which state resources, or privileged access to those who control state resources, are traded for political support within the wider society. We also point out that the generic label of party patronage often hides important variations on particularistic exchanges, namely clientelism and brokerage. Much in line with the existing literature, we argue that these traditional forms of patronage are likely to be in decline in contemporary European democracies.

The second section of the chapter elaborates on our own perspective on party patronage as an organizational resource. We show that patronage so understood is usually defined as a power of parties to appoint people to positions in public and semi-public life. By doing so, we disentangle party patronage from traditional exchange politics, instead placing it in the context of a modern multilevel governance system, as the parties' organizational resource and as one of the sinews of party government. We then provide several arguments contending that patronage as an organizational resource is likely to become an increasingly important strategy through which parties in contemporary democracies try to ensure their organizational survival and success. At the same time, we argue that such patronage might increasingly become less identifiable with partisanship in the traditional party government sense of the term. We finish our introductory chapter by specifying the research questions that are addressed by the volume and by each of the empirical chapters, and outlining the rest of the book.

PATRONAGE AS AN ELECTORAL RESOURCE

As understood in most literature, patronage involves an exchange of various public goods for electoral support. It is usually assumed to involve a more or less dyadic relationship between a party (or politician) on the one hand, and a supporter or group of potential supporters on the other, whereby the parties use their own resources, or resources to which they gain privileged access in public institutions or other arenas, in order to cement political support within the wider community. A wide range of goods can be used for such purposes, such as when a particular public industry is located in a particular district, when a public housing project is placed in a particular part of town, when teachers, or taxi drivers, or other groups of voters are offered particular benefits in exchange for political support or endorsement at a coming election, or when loyal party members gain en masse preference when it comes to filling positions in the public sector. In poor or rural settings, even such simple goods as packets of pasta or small financial gifts could be used to secure the vote. In other words, patronage here represents a form of linkage politics—a mechanism through which individual politicians or parties obtain electoral support in exchange for selectively distributing (mostly material) benefits through state institutions.

It is with this understanding of patronage that the term *clientelism* is most closely associated. The patrons, who are the parties or politicians, have clients, who are voters or potential supporters, with the link between the two being vertical and dyadic, characterized by unequal status in power between those involved in the exchange, and being only slightly different from the sort of patron–client relationships that are also found in the economically underdeveloped and politically traditional settings. The key difference here is that the traditional clientelistic linkages are characterized by personalized, face-to-face exchanges between a powerful person, usually a landlord or local notable, and individuals or groups, typically poor peasants, who display high levels of deference towards their patrons (for an insightful account of one such system, see Gibbon and Higgins, 1974). In contrast, the more modern version of clientelism, known for example from the machine politics in the US cities (see Scott, 1969), depicts relatively impersonal exchanges in which a bureaucratic organization, the political party, becomes the key agent in distributing the material and other rewards to clients that are already far less dependent on, and less identified with, their patrons (see also Weingrod, 1968, Caciagli, 2006; Hopkin, 2006).

In some cases, however, the phenomenon approximates more to *brokerage* than to patronage as such. The key difference here is that, unlike the patron, the broker does not directly own or control his own resources, but acts as an intermediary between those who do own or control the resources, principally the state and the bureaucracy, and those who require those resources, who are usually found amongst the urban or rural poor. The politician gains benefit by being reputed to be able to negotiate benefits for those who would otherwise be denied them. Politicians as brokers are valued for their expertise and know-how, and, as Komito (1984: 174) noted in the Irish case, for their 'ability to monopolize and then market their specialist knowledge of state resources and their access to bureaucrats who allocated such resources' (see also Boissevain, 1969; Blok, 1969; Abercrombie and Hill, 1976; Bax, 1970; Clapham, 1982).

Both clientelistic and brokerage linkages between politicians and voters have been shown to be particularly important in rural and less economically well-developed regions, as well as in political systems in developing countries, and it is precisely this form of linkage which is assumed to be challenged by modernization, on the one hand, and by the development of the mass party organization, on the other. The traditional literature dealing with these themes is rich and extensive, and need not be detailed here (see, for example, Weingrod, 1968; Graziano, 1976; Shefter, 1977; Eisenstadt and Roniger, 1980; Eisenstadt and Lemarchand, 1981). Suffice it to note that the individualized processes of vertical integration and mobilization associated with patron–client ties are seen to be undermined by the forms of horizontal mobilization and integration promoted by class politics and cleavage structuring. Conversely, it has also been argued that cleavage structuring is itself impeded by the disaggregating effects of clientelism (Hazelkorn, 1986). Either way, as mass electoral alignments take shape, the scope for individually based networks of supporters becomes more limited.

Second, as the mass party itself takes over from pre-modern and cadre parties, and as appeals based on programmes and ideology replace those based on more personalized political representation, it also becomes more difficult to sustain patron–client links, and especially to build a distinctive clientele. Third, as polities modernize and professionalize, meritocratic systems of advancement become more acceptable and widespread, and hence objective rules, exams, and qualifications replace favours, friendships, and networks in the process of career building. Here too, then, the scope for patronage becomes limited, in this case as a result of a shortage of supply—there is simply less available to distribute within the patronage system.

Fourth, as economies modernize, local markets, especially in poor rural areas, become better integrated into larger regional, national, or even supranational units. The members of these initially isolated communities thus enter into commercial and social ties with persons in other places, which, in turn, diminish demand for patrons and brokers to advance their interests at the centre. Finally, as societies also become richer and more educated, the demand for particularized benefits or favours is likely to diminish, while citizens also become more confident of their own ability to deal with the bureaucracy. In this sense, citizens begin to handle their own affairs more effectively, and have less need of a patron or a broker to work on their behalf.

All of this implies a more or less secular process, whereby clientelism and brokerage practices are steadily eliminated in favour of more conventional patterns of linkage based on collective representation and accountability. The clientelistic linkages characterized by direct exchange of material benefits are gradually replaced by programmatic linkages characterized by indirect compensation of voters through policy packages offered by political parties. Indeed, one of the key agencies in this process is the emerging mass party, which encourages horizontal rather than vertical integration, and which promotes the provision of universal rather than particularistic benefits. This is not to suggest that patronage practices are inevitably eliminated with the advent of the mass party. On the contrary, as Shefter (1994) and others (Sotiropoulos, 1996; Kristinsson, 1996; Warner, 1998; Golden, 2003) have shown very effectively, mass parties have also been known to adapt these practices as a means of ensuring their own electoral survival. Indeed, as Kitschelt (2000) argues, while there are clear trade-offs between programmatic and clientelistic linkages, the two modes of representation are compatible with each other up to a certain point in any competitive electoral setting. What this does suggest, however, is that these practices become more difficult to sustain in the era of the mass party, and are likely to prove more exceptional than conventional. In modern polities, the argument runs, the bias operates against patronage.

Recent developments in the patterns and processes of European politics have now led some scholars to a partial rethinking of this familiar expectation, however. With the emergence of often weakly structured parties and party systems in many newly democratizing polities, for example, and with the continued favouring of personalistic ties in those systems in which voters are expected to choose between competing candidates as well as between competing parties, clientelism can take on a fresh impetus (Kitschelt, 2000). It can also be argued that the declining intensity of ideological differences between parties in many modern democracies may even encourage a recrudescence of clientelistic links at the grass-roots level, at the same time as it encourages at the top a process that Poguntke and Webb (2005) have identified as one of more personalized presidential-style leadership. Moreover, and somewhat paradoxically, it has also been argued that precisely because modernization promotes an increase in the spread and scope of professional qualifications, it may also eventually encourage a return to clientelism. The greater the number of qualified personnel that becomes available, for example, the more difficult it is to select on the basis of objective criteria alone, and hence more personal, ad hoc, or ad hominem factors can acquire increased weight. Among the many postdocs with publications who apply for a tenure-track position in a Department of Political Science, for example, references, networks, and sheer personal charm can often prove more decisive than formal qualifications in making the final selection.[1] It is for these reasons, as well as due to the continuous relevance of clientelism in many non-European polities and areas, that studies of party patronage as an electoral resource still constitute an important area of the literature on party politics and on political behaviour (see, for example, Martz, 1997; Gordin, 2002; Walle, van de, 2003; Golden, 2003; Calvo and Murillo, 2004; Tavits, 2009; Kitschelt, 2000).

PATRONAGE AS AN ORGANIZATIONAL RESOURCE

For the purposes of this chapter, and for the purposes of the volume as a whole, we are less interested in patronage in this sense. That is, we are less interested in patronage as an electoral resource, and more concerned with patronage as an organizational resource. When it is understood as an organizational resource, party patronage represents a form of institutional control or of institutional exploitation that operates to the benefit of the party organization. Patronage in this sense is less a form of vote gathering or a means of establishing loyal clienteles, and more a strategy to build parties' organizational networks in the public and semi-public sphere. Patronage in this sense can best be considered as (one of the forms of) party–state linkage(s), rather than as a party–society linkage (see van Biezen and Kopecký, 2007).

Empirical studies of party patronage as an organizational resource have usually revolved around the distribution of jobs within the state (see, for example, Sorauf, 1959; Wilson, 1973; Goldston, 1977; Müller, 1989 and 2006b; Bearfield, 2009), and we also follow this tradition here. More specifically, we define party patronage as the power of political parties to appoint people to positions in state institutions; we consider the scope of this patronage to be the range of positions distributed in this way.

One of the principal concerns of this volume is therefore with Hans Daalder's (1966) notion of the 'reach' or 'permeation' of parties within the state. In this particular case, we are concerned with the question of how far within a given political system the allocation of jobs and other important public and semi-public positions is at least partly controlled by political parties. These positions include, for example, posts in the central state administration or the core of the civil service, but also positions in public sector companies and their governing boards, universities, advisory committees and commissions, quangos and other regulatory bodies (for more details see Chapter 2).

It is important to emphasize that patronage so understood is related to, but theoretically and empirically distinct from, *corruption* and from *clientelism*, the two concepts with which it is most often equated in the popular as well as academic discourses. Table 1.1 summarizes these important differences along several key dimensions. (For similar conceptualizations see the chapters on Iceland and Portugal in this volume.) The distinction with corruption, understood here to be an illegal use of public resources (public decisions) for financial gains, is particularly important, for while there may sometimes be popular opposition to the exercise of party patronage, the distribution of state and semi-state positions at the discretion of a party need not necessarily be seen as corrupt or illegitimate, and in fact is often quite overt and above board. Indeed, it is the open and above board type of appointment that is of greatest interest to this volume (see Chapter 2 for

TABLE 1.1 *Overview of different concepts related to patronage*

	Patronage	Clientelism	Corruption
State resource	Jobs in state institutions	Subsidies, loans, medicines, food, public sector jobs	Public decisions
Party goal	Control of institutions; reward of (organizational) loyalty	Electoral support	Financial resources
Recipients	Anybody	Party voters	Companies, entrepreneurs
Legal status	Legal or illegal	Legal or illegal	Illegal
Crucial question	Will you work for me?	Will you vote for me?	Will you give me a bribe?

Source: adapted from Kopecký, Spirova, and Scherlis (2008) and Scherlis (2010)

more details about the type of appointments we investigate). That said, it is also clear that patronage and corruption may in practice closely follow one another, as for example when patronage appointments are made for the purpose of providing private kickbacks or in return for bribes. In a similar vein, patronage is an important supporting condition for the survival of systemic corruption, in that it is through the appointment of bureaucrats and other state personnel loyal to party politicians that operations designed to place checks on the activities of politicians are often effectively covered up.

The distinction between patronage and clientelism (i.e. patronage as an electoral resource) has already been underlined, but it is perhaps useful to emphasize once again that, by definition, clientelism is a far more penetrating phenomenon than party patronage, reaching larger numbers of people, covering a wider range of exchanges, and including a greater range of state resources that are the subject of these exchanges. As in the case of corruption, however, there is often also a close relationship between patronage and clientelism. Patronage is the first, and more or less inevitable, step in the emergence of clientelism, since it is mainly due to their ability to control positions in the state administration and in other public and quasi-public agencies that parties are able to distribute divisible goods to their constituencies. In other words, parties that do not control state agencies will hardly be in the position to develop large-scale clientelist exchanges or to favour specific constituencies through legislation or the allocation of funds. In this sense, patronage is a necessary, but obviously not a sufficient, condition for clientelism.

That patronage and clientelism are often considered coterminous also relates to the fact that the distribution of state jobs had in some cases in the past been used on a mass scale for electoral purposes—as, for example, was the case in post-war Italy or in the era of American city machines. However, most modern polities, certainly in contemporary Europe, are probably best characterized as having 'too few jobs and too many votes'; consequently, the use of patronage as a way of directly securing electoral support is unlikely to be a very feasible strategy in either an organizational or a financial sense. Indeed, at the extreme, when jobs are handed out as a form of vote- or support-gathering, or as a form of exchange, the availability of patronage positions is likely to fall far short of the expected demand, and hence the positions are also likely to be highly valued. When patronage functions as a form of organization-building, on the other hand, it may sometimes be difficult for the party to fill the positions which it regards as necessary for its survival (see, for example, Sundberg, 1994). In the studies that follow in this volume we will see this frequently.

The buying of votes is of course only one of the reasons why parties might try to distribute positions in the public administration. In addition to, or alongside, the vote-buying strategy, party patronage may also serve a variety of entirely different ends. It can, for example, serve as an intra-party organizational resource in the hands of the leadership, which is used to reward (or punish) elected officials or to promote intra-party cohesion and organizational loyalty (cf. the use of the notion of 'selective incentives' by Conway and Feigert, 1968 and Panebianco, 1988). Positions in public institutions and enterprises represent valuable resources in the form of salaries, contacts, prestige, and information that can be used for such purposes. Another key reason for parties to seek to secure access to non-elective offices within the state might also be the control of policy design and implementation, or what is referred to in the German literature as *Politikpatronage*.[2] Rather than being solely an instrument for rewarding organizational or personal loyalty, patronage here should be seen as part of party government (see also Blondel, 2002; Meyer-Sahling, 2006c), and as a means of governing rather than just a means of generating favours. By staffing the state with trusted individuals, political parties can make their policies flow more effectively, can be better informed, and can thereby enhance their policy-making capacity and reputation. In this sense, party patronage offers some of the glue that is needed for what Tony Blair liked to call 'joined-up government'.

It should be clear from the above that our understanding of party patronage as an organizational resource is analytically distinct from the traditional understanding of patronage as exchange or linkage politics. It should also be obvious that treating party patronage as one of the sinews of party government means that we consider it as an important phenomenon in its own right. For example, no consideration of the 'partyness of government' (Katz, 1986) or the development of cartel parties (Katz and Mair, 1995) can be complete without empirical reference to patronage as an organizational resource. However, it is also our contention—and we develop this argument in the following section—that there are reasons to expect that patronage as an organizational resource is becoming of increasing relevance to contemporary political parties. In other words, patronage might no longer be just a normal part of intra-party organizational activities and of government formation processes, as it has always has been, but might rather offer an increasingly valuable resource with which parties can seek to ensure their organizational survival and success in contemporary political systems.

FROM PARTY GOVERNMENT TO THE PARTY AS NETWORK

There are at least three reasons why we see a strong stimulus towards patronage as an organizational resource. The first one relates to the changing nature of party organizations. Party organizations in developed democracies have been far from static, and over the twentieth century have progressed through a variety of forms and stages, from the elite party in the early part of the century, through the mass party, the catch-all party, and later the cartel party (Katz and Mair, 1995; 2002). Other models of party have also been mooted in recent contexts, including the modern cadre party, the business firm model, and the media party (see, respectively, Koole, 1994; Hopkin and Paolucci, 1999; Krouwel, 2006). But while this plurality of models tends to suggest a growing diversity among organizational types, most analysts are agreed that one of the key organizational developments of the past quarter century has been the shift in the party centre of gravity from society to the state. That is, from a dominant mass party era, in which party organizations were strongly rooted within civil society and during which they laid great emphasis on their representative role, parties have now begun to take their principal terms of reference from within the political institutions, and have begun to define themselves primarily as governors and managers of the polity. Interestingly, parties in developing democracies appear to have passed up the stage of mass party development altogether. In many of these new democracies of Southern and Eastern Europe, Latin America, and sub-Saharan Africa, and from the very onset of democratization, political parties have often been characterized by their relatively weak social anchoring on the one hand, and their strong presence within the state institutions on the other (e.g. van Biezen, 2003; Mainwaring and Scully, 1995; Salih, 2003; van Biezen and Kopecký, 2007).

Whether in developed or developing democracies, therefore, the parties have become primarily parties of the public office, or, as van Biezen (2004) has elegantly put it, they have begun to serve as public utilities. This also clearly implies that these parties are now more likely to have a need for patronage than when they are organizations of mass integration. As modern parties lose their traditional grounding within the wider society, patronage can become a key resource in anchoring the party presence within the political system and in controlling flows of communication. Through patronage, and through the appointment of party personnel to key agencies and institutions, parties can hope to gain an oversight of the likely demands posed to political leaders, as well as of the likely policies and programmes that are needed to meet these demands. In this sense, patronage can also serve as the basis for a powerful network of communication between policy-making sectors, expressed both vertically and horizontally. Patronage can therefore compensate for otherwise decaying grass-roots organizational networks (see also Peters and Pierre, 2004a: 286–7).

Moreover, it is important to emphasize again that, in this context, patronage is also likely to serve a different purpose. Rather than being a means by which networks of support are sustained or rewarded—rather than being directed at the electorate of the party or at the activists' bases of the party—patronage is for contemporary parties a mode of governing, a process by which the party acquires a voice in, and gains feedback from, the various policy-making forums that characterize modern multilevel governance systems. Patronage in this sense constitutes one of the sinews of party government rather than being a means of distributing spoils. It belongs to the activities of the party in public office rather than to those of the party on the ground. Indeed, the relative unimportance of the party on the ground in intra-party mechanisms of patronage control is something that is frequently highlighted in many of the country studies presented in this volume.

The second reason why patronage as organizational resource is likely to be stimulated relates to the changing nature of party competition, and in particular to the declining intensity of ideological differences between parties in modern democracies. Kitschelt (2000) has argued that declining relevance of ideology in party competition will lead to the reappearance of clientelistic links at the grassroots level. This may well be so. But our contention is that it is even more likely to stimulate a tightening of parties' reach and control within the state and semi-state sector via political appointments. In the absence of clear ideological demarcations, parties are likely to distinguish themselves from one another on the basis of their policy performance (as opposed to promises), their governing competence, and their managerial experience. In other words, governments are more likely to compete on the basis of how they will do something rather than on what they will do—the latter being likely to reflect a more consensual commitment across the mainstream. This is where patronage as an organizational resource becomes important: as a key mechanism for creating organizational networks of personnel which combine some degree of political or personal loyalty with at least a modicum of technical expertise, and which are capable of placement in key decision-making institutions once parties acquire office.[3]

At the same time, it is also clear that this type of party competition appears to undermine party government in the traditional sense of the term. The conditions for party government may be summarized as requiring: first, that parties win control of the executive as a result of competitive elections; second, that the political leaders of the polity are recruited by and through parties; third, that parties offer clear policy alternatives; fourth, that public policy is determined by the parties in the executive; and finally, that the executive is held accountable through parties (Mair, 2008a: 225–6; see also Katz, 1987). If parties no longer offer clear policy alternatives and lack the autonomy to effectively determine the course of public policy during their incumbency, and if accountability mechanisms are undermined through increased delegation and agencification, then party government becomes reduced to a procedural mechanism for ensuring the election of office-holders and the recruitment of personnel. Parties in these circumstances then lose their sense of ideological purpose, and become instead networks of elites that are bound together by the need to win elections and organize public office.

Patronage as a key mechanism of elite recruitment is then also likely to look different than in a traditional party government, something that is frequently highlighted in the chapters assembled in this volume. It is not so much a practice that is oriented towards a particular partisan purpose, but rather a mechanism by which the party leadership, or individual elements within the party leadership, can ensure the provision of safe pairs of hands in key corners of the policy-making process. It is also a practice that is oriented towards effective communication within increasingly complex decision-making environments, with the party's people, or the leader's people, providing the glue or the dovetailing that can facilitate 'joined-up' government.

This also implies that the stimulus towards this form of patronage has further been enhanced by widespread processes of privatization and marketization, on the one hand, as well as by the huge expansion in the number of agencies and non-majoritarian institutions that have now been given responsibility for the formulation, implementation, and regulation of public policy. In other words, the third reason for the increased importance of patronage as an organizational resource can be seen in the changing nature and growing complexity of decision making and of policy-making processes. The delegation of power from the core executive towards non-governmental institutions has already been aptly described by the burgeoning literature on new forms of 'governance' and 'delegation' (see, for example, Peters, 2002; Thatcher and Stone Sweet, 2002). If parties are to retain their grip on policy making, even if only indirectly, then it is likely that they will need to exert influence on the form and composition of these bodies. As governance becomes more dispersed, parties therefore have a greater need for an organizational network that can reach through to the different levels and arenas. Decision making may no longer be hierarchical, in the traditional party government sense of the term, but this makes it even more pressing for parties to seek to achieve coherence through their appointments policies and through their organizational networks.

This is also what Papadopoulos (2003: 476) highlights, when he emphasizes how a plurality of viewpoints need to be organized through a system of 'cooperative policy making' in order to avoid the risk that complexity might lead to ungovernability. 'At various levels', he argues, 'institutions, procedures or forums typical of "governance" are created (such as policy networks, roundtables, intergovernmental conferences and expert committees), the major aim of which is to produce coordination by transcending the parochial attitudes of sectoral or territorial interests.' Parties can obviously play a crucial role in effecting this sort of coordination or cooperation. Indeed, this is precisely where the emerging significance of the 'party as network' can be seen (Scherlis, 2010), involving a role within governance which is quite different from the traditional role associated with parties, and with the mass party in particular, whereby a closed organization with a fixed programme would seek to implement its ideas by winning control of the commanding heights of a hierarchical system of government. It is for this reason also that we contend that patronage is of growing importance to contemporary parties.

KEY RESEARCH QUESTIONS OF THE BOOK

This book seeks to combine two important perspectives. On the one hand, we wish to restore attention to the unnecessarily neglected topic of party patronage, while casting it in a more contemporary light and relating it more closely to the field of party government rather than exchange politics—hence our focus on patronage as an organizational resource rather than on patronage as an electoral resource. Second, we wish to explore the role of parties in contemporary policy-making processes, not in the sense of the familiar 'do parties matter?' literature, which is more concerned with the impact of party preferences on policy outcomes, but rather in the sense of the management and organization of policy- and decision-making—hence our empirical focus on parties' ability to control appointments within the institutions of the state. This means also linking two developing literatures: that on governance and that on changing models of party. Our chief concern is with the role of parties in twenty-first century democracies, and with the way in which they organize and act within the institutions of modern governance. The study of patronage as an organizational resource offers an important avenue for further exploring this concern and for filling it out with some substantial empirical data.

In order to address our general concerns, we have formulated several research questions that are systematically treated in this volume.

- *What is the level of party patronage in each political system?*

As said above, party patronage is defined in this volume as the power of parties to appoint people to positions in public and semi-public life. The scope of the patronage is then considered to be the range of positions distributed in this way. Consequently, the first specific concern of the volume is to establish how far, in a given political system, the allocation of jobs and other important public and semi-public positions is in the gift of, or is controlled by, political parties. It is important to note that we are not only concerned with the scope of the patronage as such, but we are also interested in mapping out the precise institutional location of patronage appointments within each political system. This includes not only the core of civil service, but also institutions that are not part of the civil service but are under some form of state control, such as public hospitals, various regulatory agencies and commissions, and state-owned companies (for more details see Chapter 2).

- *What motivates political parties to engage in patronage appointments?*

As indicated above, there are several theoretical reasons why parties or politicians might like to appoint people within the state. The two basic motivations involve a desire to control state institutions, by appointing like-minded individuals to them, usually in order to ensure formulation and implementation of policies compatible with a party's or politician's aims; and a desire to reward the party or politician's supporters, activists, or even friends and family. Each of these motivations is linked to our distinction between patronage as an organizational resource and patronage as an electoral resource: the desire to control should logically play a predominant role in the former, while the latter should be more closely associated with the desire to reward. It is therefore very important to explore the motivations of parties to engage in patronage appointments and also examine more closely the kind of people who are the subject of party appointments.

- *What is the role of political parties in making patronage appointments?*

As will be apparent in most chapters in this volume, the term 'party patronage' is fraught with difficulties because in practice it is hard to distinguish whether an appointment is made by the party, or by an individual politician (for an interesting conceptual treatment of this problem see the chapter on Iceland). Indeed, a vast majority of appointments in modern states are officially done by individual politicians (usually the ministers) and, in that sense at least, party patronage rarely exists. The key question is: to what extent is the party involved when the minister makes the appointment—i.e. is it the party that is the principal and the minister that is the agent, or the other way around? The third specific concern in this volume is therefore to establish whether parties possess internal mechanisms of coordination and control so that politicians in office merely appoint whoever the party proposes, or whether, conversely, individual politicians appoint from within their own networks of candidates and are relatively unconstrained by their own parties.

- *To what extent are patronage appointments shared among the (mainstream) political parties?*

This specific question explores the extent to which party patronage is exercised in a 'majoritarian' as opposed to a more 'consensual' manner or, in other words, whether the appointments include only the party(ies) in government or also opposition parties, or even some other organized groups and political actors. When patronage is proportional or consensual, even if this is usually only within the mainstream, it tends not to be seen as important. Hence, countries in which such patronage is practised, as in the Netherlands for example, are sometimes treated as if no patronage exists, with only majoritarian or highly partisan patronage tending to register in comparative research. One of the principal goals of this volume and of our approach is to act as a corrective to this tendency, and this has also helped to guide our case selection.

PLAN OF THE BOOK

These four research questions, together with the theoretical focus on patronage as an organizational resource defined in terms of appointments, constitute the guiding analytical framework of this volume, which is systematically adopted in each individual chapter. The chapters that follow consist of case studies of 15 contemporary European democracies, presented in alphabetical order (for more information, see Chapter 2). Each country chapter provides detailed empirical analyses of party patronage that address each of our four research questions. In addition to this empirical analysis of patronage, each country study starts[4] with two lines of important background information: concerning the traditional reach of the parties in that society, on the one hand, and the civil service traditions, on the other. The former refers to the position of political parties within the polity and provides an answer to the question of how strong and how relevant parties in each country have traditionally been in societal terms. The latter refers to the country's bureaucratic traditions in general and the relationship between parties and bureaucracies in particular, providing an answer to the question of how far parties in each country have been able to interfere in the recruitment of personnel to the state. While the first piece of background information offers an analysis of the overall position of parties in the society, the second part highlights the capacity of parties to control state institutions and government apparatus. Indeed, with this book, and for the first time, these two elements are brought together systematically and comparatively. It is also for the first time with this book that party patronage is analysed using robust empirical evidence based on a specific research approach. This method, together with the corresponding empirical indicators and aggregate measures, is explained in detail in the following Chapter 2.

NOTES

1. See Abercrombie and Hill, 1976: 423–4: 'Proessional careers show how patronage ... is a central facet of an institution which is sometimes thought to be dominated by the principles of technical competence and achieved status ... Professions' monopoly supply situation and control over their internal affairs throw great power into the hands of elders, who control the career prospects of juniors in ways which are often *independent of the market* ... The sponsorship of junior academics by senior professors is helpful at least, and more often essential, at each career stage.' We would like to thank Nicole Bolleyer for drawing our attention to this reference.
2. The two other terms, *Herrschaftspatronage* and *Versorgungspatronage*, refer to, respectively, patronage as an electoral tool (i.e. clientelism) and patronage as an internal reward strategy. We would like to thank Philip Manow for this reference. See also Manow, 2002.
3. At an extreme, of course, this form of political competition may prompt politicians to give up on policy-solving altogether and to delegate their authority to non-elected experts, who might be seen to have a better claim to deal with the technicalities of modern public policy (see Vibert, 2007).
4. The data are available at http://www.socialsciences.leiden.edu/politicalscience/research/research-data/party-patronage.html.

CHAPTER 2

Measuring Party Patronage Through Structured Expert Interviews

Petr Kopecký and Maria Spirova

INTRODUCTION

The introductory chapter has suggested several key research questions that guide this volume in its attempt to study party patronage as an organizational resource in contemporary European democracies. Do parties actually engage in patronage practices, and how far and how deep do they reach into the state institutions to make patronage appointments? What motivates parties in making these appointments? What is the role of the party in this process, and how do parties make these appointments? And, finally, do parties share appointments among each other? In that sense, the introductory chapter has addressed the 'why' and 'what' questions central to the research inquiry. This chapter addresses the remaining central question of any research undertaking, i.e. the 'how' question. Studies of patronage have long suffered from the lack of reliable measures and sources of data that would allow for wider cross-national comparative analysis and help to provide answers to interesting questions with a much higher degree of assurance than has hitherto been the case.

This book uses the approach to studying and measuring patronage developed by Kopecký, Scherlis, and Spirova (2008) and originally applied to new democracies.[1] This chapter provides an overview of this method and research approach in detail. We first situate our approach for measuring patronage among already existing ones. We stress from the outset that our review focuses on existing studies of patronage as an organizational resource, defined in terms of appointments. We thus leave aside attempts to empirically account for clientelistic practices, pork-barrel politics, and of course corruption.[2] We then provide an overview of our own approach, focusing both on the construction of the questionnaire that we used and the way we conducted expert interviews. Finally, we describe the data collected and the three key indicators used by each of the individual country chapters. This chapter thus provides an essential backdrop for reading and interpreting the empirical evidence collected by our country teams and presented in each case study chapter.

EXISTING APPROACHES

The study of patronage—understood as party appointments in the state institutions—is not a new undertaking. There are numerous studies of individual or comparative cases that have been carried out in the context of both established and new democracies. They fall within four broad categories of research.

The first one—the *patronage recipients survey* approach—focuses on the potential recipients of patronage appointments, and uses interviews with a somewhat large group of party members and voters to estimate the extent of patronage in single countries. For example, Burstein (1976) interviewed 732 voters from Haifa, asking if they got some help from a party to get a job or to solve some other problem; he used this data to assess the scope of party patronage in Israel. Similarly, Müller (1989) used opinion polls and interviews with Austrian party members across time to estimate the scope of patronage appointments in Austria. A similar approach has been used by Li and Walder (2001) in their study of patronage in China, and by Pappas (2009b) in his investigation of the nature and mechanics of party patronage in Greece.

This method of estimating the extent of patronage clearly gets to the heart of the issue by asking the respondents if their party affiliation was in any way connected to getting the jobs they have. However, the approach might also produce biased estimates of how big the phenomenon is, as it includes only a small fraction of the potential recipients of patronage appointments. Patronage appointees do not need to be limited to party voters or members—as was argued in the introductory chapter, parties might seek appointees from all sections of society, not just from their own ranks. For example, ministers might be inclined to tap their own networks of professional colleagues and friends, rather than recruit exclusively from among their fellow party members. In addition, despite their evident values, surveys of this nature are logistically difficult to administer in a comparable way across countries, and do not offer very precise estimates.

A second approach—the *career pathways analysis*—focuses on the career paths of a smaller group of potential patronage recipients (top ministerial officials, for example) and looks at their professional and political backgrounds to determine the role of political parties or a political connection in appointing them. Some of these studies propose a clear separation between a partisan and a professional (or career) appointment (Meyer-Sahling, 2008; Sikk, 2006), while others permit for each appointment to have elements of both (Kristinsson, 2006). This method allows for the composition of comparable indicators across countries and certainly is a valid way to study the phenomenon of a party's political appointments. However, it relies on the assumption that you can easily separate the 'political' motivation from the rest, and hence discounts appointments made by the political party that are not considered 'political'. In fact, and in line with our understanding of patronage as an organizational resource, we expect that many

Measuring Party Patronage Through Structured Expert Interviews 19

party appointments will be professional in character (see also Chapter 1). Finally, the career pathways studies do not allow for an estimation of the range and depth of the practice as they are limited to small groups of civil servants at the top levels of the administration.

To estimate patronage practices on a bigger scale, a third approach—the *aggregate indicators* one—uses several aggregate quantitative indicators as proxy estimates for patronage appointments. These usually relate to the size or growth of the state administration and have included the share of public employment, the size of the state administration, the share of temporary appointments in the administration, or the percentage of total expenditure allocated to personnel spending. Gordin (2002), Manow (2006), and Remmer (2007) for example, conceptualize patronage as the level of job growth in the high-level bureaucracy and measure it as the percentage of total expenditures allocated by the central government and ministries to personnel spending. In a similar vein, Brusco, Nazareno, and Stokes (2005) use municipal spending on personnel as a proportion of total budget per year to estimate the extent of patronage at the local level, while O'Dwyer (2004 and 2006) and Gwiazda (2008) use the increase in the absolute number of positions in the state administrative personnel at the national level as a proxy measure of party patronage. Grzymala-Busse (2003) has also used the share of state administration employment out of total employment and its absolute numbers to estimate the particularistic behaviour of political parties. Finally, Ferraro (2006) used the proportion of temporary personnel compared to permanent personnel to judge the extent of political appointments.[3]

These purely quantitative measures are relatively accessible and can be utilized easily in different contexts. They are also excellent for comparative purposes, be that temporal or cross-national analysis. The most obvious problem that studies using this approach share is that the proxies might not reflect the extent and nature of patronage practices, as they measure different aspects of the rate of employment in the state administration. They focus on how many people are employed, a figure that might be influenced by more than just the ability and likelihood of parties to make appointments. Institutional reform, economic situation, international factors such as EU integration and NATO membership, as well as domestic actors such as trade unions, syndicates, lobbies, and professional corporations are examples of factors that might independently influence the number of people working for the state. Conversely, patronage might be occurring even if there is no noticeable change in the size of the administration, with appointments being made through the replacement of existing personnel rather than through the addition of new positions. At the extreme, it is even possible that the most patronage-ridden administrations would be those that are shrinking in size, in that the reforms needed to cut the size of, or spending on, administrative units might require the support of politically loyal bureaucrats. In addition, these studies are usually limited to the central administration or ministries, and thus ignore a large proportion of the public sectors (regulatory agencies, state-owned enterprises, state services, etc.) in which a large proportion of the patronage appointments might be.

A final approach—which we characterize as *expert estimates*—has been developed by Geddes (1994). In *Politician's Dilemma*, Geddes combines several indicators into an 'Appointment Strategy Index', which estimates the extent to which the executives use competence rather than partisanship or personal loyalty as the basis for making administrative appointments. The index is a count of the negative answers to eight separate questions that capture quite different realities, such as the criterion (competence or partisanship) for choosing the finance minister and the presence or absence of scandals about partisan appointments in the press. Based on detailed information about each country and government, the index allows for comparisons across space and time. However, even in this approach the incidence of partisan appointments that are not overtly political risks being neglected. In a somewhat similar vein, Müller has also compared and ranked several western European countries on the extent of their patronage practices by using secondary sources and experts' opinions (Müller, 2000).

Overall, the most problematic issue in the research on patronage to date has been its failure to provide a measure that allows for a reliable estimation of the actual scope of patronage practices and that is also useful for cross-country comparisons by being generalizable beyond a specific country or institutional context. Given how complex patronage appointments are, their scope can hardly be captured by figures such as number of jobs or ministerial spending or equated with the level of corruption. In-depth interviews and analysis of career paths provide good insights into patronage appointments, but are very limited in their scope and difficult to replicate in different contexts. These approaches are also unable to investigate the motivations and mechanics of patronage appointments, features that we regard as an integral part of the patronage that we analyse in this volume.

STRUCTURED EXPERT INTERVIEWS

In our book we are interested in estimating the range and depth of patronage appointment, as well as their motivations, mechanics and dynamics. To achieve this, we develop our own approach using data from in-depth interviews with 641 experts in fifteen countries. There are two major features that distinguish this approach from similar studies:[4] the first one is that we clearly delineate the areas of the state where patronage appointments might happen, and which, thus, interest us. The second one is the nature of our interviewees, interviewers, and the interviews themselves. Our interviews were conducted by country research teams, face to face, with people who are experts in a specific substantive area. The interviews follow a

Measuring Party Patronage Through Structured Expert Interviews 21

set protocol of eleven questions, but also allow the possibility for detailed discussion of the practices of patronage. In this way, the data can be coded and aggregated to produce quantitative measures, but also used for a more qualitative and rich analysis of the intricacies of patronage practices in each country. Our approach uses elements of Geddes' approach (1994), and that of Kristinsson (2006) and Meyer-Sahling (2008) already discussed in this chapter. We also come close to the work of De Winter (2006), who scrutinizes patronage practices in different areas of the Belgian public administration on the basis of formal rules and previous research. However, we attempt to study patronage in a more systematic manner (than De Winter), using a broader definition of the 'state' (than Meyer-Sahling and Geddes), and in a way that would allow us to carry out the research in numerous country settings.

Mapping out the state

As the first step in our research strategy we create a generic model of the state. This helps us to delineate the areas where patronage appointments can and do happen. Here we borrow from Peters' (1988) comparative work on public administration. He argues that to compare the public administration sectors across countries one can use several approaches, including comparing the size of the public administration in different settings, comparing public administration according to different policy areas, and comparing different organizational structures of the administration. We have chosen to combine these approaches by firstly dividing the state by the types of policy areas. The state can of course be divided into nearly infinite numbers of policy areas. However, for comparative and analytical purposes, we have chosen to include the following policy areas: Economy, Finance, Judiciary, Media, Military and Police, Foreign Service, Culture and Education, Health Care, and Regional and Local Administration, presented graphically in Figure 2.1.

These nine policy areas represent, we argue, the 'classic' state area, and while they are not exhaustive of the modern state they fulfil several other important criteria. They are present in every country and they are diverse enough to represent a good sample of the various functions of the state. Importantly, they can be considered as 'classic' policy areas which might be of particular interest to political parties.[5]

We further subdivide each policy area by the types of institutions that represent it. We include three different types of institutions:

- ministerial departments (i.e. the core civil service)
- non-departmental agencies and commissions (NDACs) (i.e. regulatory and policy advising and devising agencies, sometimes called quangos)
- executing institutions (i.e. institutions involved in delivering services and provisions, or in production).

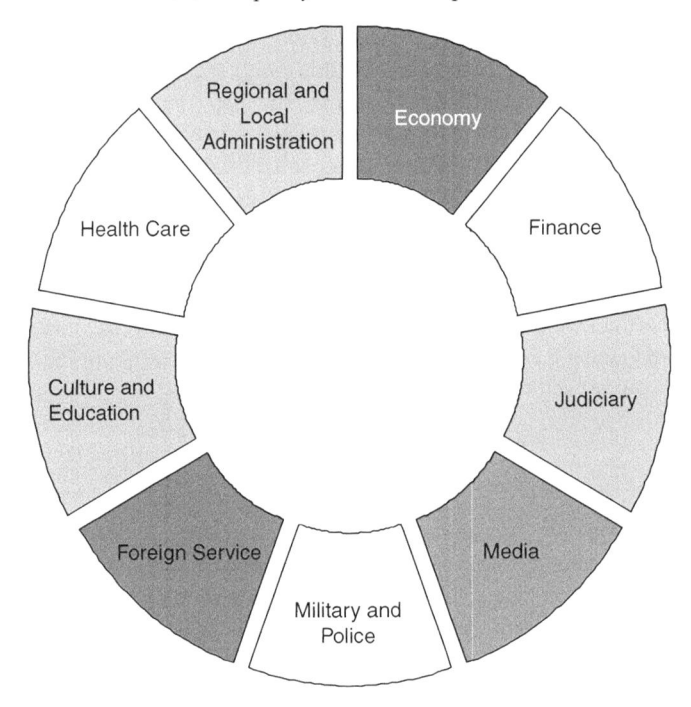

FIGURE 2.1 Map of a generic state

This is an important conceptual and empirical addition to the subdividing of the state into nine policy areas, in that it allows for comparisons of patronage practices across institutional types and enables us to test propositions such as whether patronage practices are more widespread among regulatory agencies than within the core of the civil service. Indeed, given the literature on new forms of governance and the evidence of increasing agencification and administrative fragmentation (see Chapter 1), it is of crucial importance that we focus our investigation not just on the core of civil service, as is routinely done in most studies of patronage, but that we also look at the two other types of institutions that are part of the modern state.

The final caveat here concerns the territorial subunits of the state. We do not include 'political institutions' (e.g. cabinets, parliaments, presidential staff) in our generic model of the state. We assume these institutions are per definition subject to party patronage. We do, however, include Regional and Local Administration (RLA) as one of our policy areas. The RLA is of course not a policy area as such, and is likely to be a substantial area in terms of both institutions and personnel. We define it to include both the institutions of regional and local self-government and the regional and local-level bodies of the institutions in all other eight policy areas. Thus, for example, the regional offices of the police, the tax collection agency, the education inspectorates, or the health care administration are part of the RLA area.

There are several reasons for this decision. First, and especially in decentralized countries, this level of government is very important for the state itself, and will thus be subject to the patronage appointments by the political parties (see especially the chapters on Austria, Germany, and Spain). Further, given the sometimes big differences between party politics at the national and local level, we can also expect patronage appointments to follow different logics. Both inter and intraparty dynamics might be different at the local level: the governing parties might be different; even in the case of the same party controlling national and local governments, different party strata might be in control of the political process at the local level; and finally, the practice of patronage might be faced with different social constraints, given the local nature of the process. Understanding the process of party appointments at this level thus becomes of crucial importance for a comprehensive assessment of patronage in contemporary democracies.

Country selection

This generic map of the state then allows us to carry out the research in various country settings and engage in comparative analysis. In this present volume we study fifteen European democracies: Austria, Bulgaria, the Czech Republic, Denmark, Germany, Greece, Hungary, Iceland, Ireland, Italy, the Netherlands, Norway, Portugal, Spain, and the United Kingdom. We do not see this group of countries as a sample, but rather as a selection of countries ranging across both Northern and Southern Europe, Eastern and Western Europe, and across both large and small democracies, and new and old democracies. It also includes the analysis of polities in which there has been a strong tradition of patronage and clientelism, such as Greece, Ireland, and Italy, as well as those in which patronage is normally deemed irrelevant or non-existent, such as Denmark and Norway. The approach can of course be, and in fact has already been, applied in other country settings as well (Scherlis, 2010; Kopecký, 2011).

The policy areas and institutional types for every country are represented by a defined list of institutions. Each country research team drew the respective map of state following the general protocol and determined the institutions to be included in each policy area and institutional type. To ensure consistency and cross-country comparability of both policy and institutional types, a training meeting was held early on in the research time frame to guarantee that similar institutions were not classified in different areas and that researchers applied consistent criteria in these classifications.[6]

Expert interviews

The basis of our data collection in each country consists of interviews with respondents familiar with one (or more) of the nine different policy areas. As suggested by Kitschelt and Wilkinson (2007), 'surveys among small panels of experts' might resolve some of the problems of studying clientelism and patronage in comparative settings, including the grey nature of these phenomena, the consequent reluctance of participants in the process to identify it as such, and different cultural interpretations. However, relying on experts or elite interviews for data collection is not without methodological problems. Although they can provide an invaluable wealth of details and insider information, the objectivity of the respondent in reporting data might pose challenges for the validity and reliability of the research (Dexter, 1970: 125; Putnam, 1973: 18). There is no doubt that respondents inject their own experience, ideas, and value judgements into their responses. In addition, some of them may have limited knowledge or selective memory of what has happened in the past, making their opinions about distant events problematic (Dexter, 1970: 119–38).

There are several ways in which we verified and validated the information received from experts. First of all, local research teams conducted the interviews in each country, and invested the equivalent of about two months of fieldwork into the research. Researchers familiarized themselves with the formal and practical situation of patronage in each political setting in order to be able to validate the information received and interpret it within the contextual understanding of patronage and its practice. This is in contrast to other expert surveys in which the survey is administered by post, telephone, or Internet, and where the local expertise is not necessarily put into context.

Further, we selected our respondents carefully. The basic criterion was that they had experience and expertise in (usually) one of the policy areas, and that they were open to considering and evaluating the extent of patronage (as defined by us) in that policy area. Unlike other expert surveys, we in fact avoided experts who are researching patronage per se. Instead, we aimed at getting several different perspectives on the phenomenon and thus included not only several (five in most cases) experts per policy area, but also brought in experts of various backgrounds. Table 2.1 reports the number of respondents by policy area and respondent type. They include academics, who studied each of the policy areas; current or retired civil servants who were open to our investigation and had experience in the specific field; analysts who work for the NGO sector in the particular area; journalists who report on it; and finally, and relatively rarely, party officials and politicians. This variety of perspectives allowed us to estimate the extent of party patronage in each specific policy area and to avoid the particular biases—whether in terms of under or overestimation—that one dominant perspective tends to produce. These criteria were applied consistently, to the extent possible, across all the countries.[7]

Measuring Party Patronage Through Structured Expert Interviews

TABLE 2.1 *Type and number of respondents*

Policy area	Academics	Civil servants	NGO experts	Journalists	Party officials	Others	Total
Economy	15	28	11	5	9	7	75
Finance	14	31	8	7	4	4	68
Judiciary	22	18	8	2	6	12	68
Media	12	13	9	16	6	9	65
Military and Police	14	32	9	2	7	9	73
Health Care	15	20	11	1	11	11	69
Culture and Education	22	29	4	3	7	5	70
Foreign Service	15	32	7	4	10	1	69
Regional and Local Administration	22	19	19	2	13	9	84
Total	151	222	86	42	73	67	641

The experts were asked to answer several closed-ended and several open-ended questions that reflected the research questions specified in the introductory chapter (a sample questionnaire is included in Appendix 2). However, given the face-to-face nature of the interviews, even the closed-ended questions allowed for additional clarification and discussion, in addition to the immediate, assessment-related objective of each question. The information received from our respondents was judged for consistency with data reported by other respondents, and with information available through primary and secondary sources. In addition, as suggested by Dexter (1970: 15–127), the use of local teams brought in an understanding of the position of the respondent in the political system, or administrative or party hierarchy, and their political experience, which allowed the research teams to estimate the level of reliability and plausibility of the information received.

COMMON INDICATORS

The expert interviews have provided us with a wealth of data on the practice of patronage in the fifteen countries included in this volume. The interviews have been transcribed and the data on the closed-ended questions coded for use in Statistical Package for the Social Sciences (SPSS) format. We have also composed three indicators of the extent, motivations and character of patronage that each of the country chapters reports, in addition to other, country-specific indicators.

The first one is the *index of party patronage*. The index is calculated using the median values for the range and depth of patronage in each of the nine policy areas and three institutional types. The values of the question on the range of patronage appointments reflect whether respondents believed appointments happened in some (1), most (2), or all (3) individual institutions in each of the institutional arenas in each of the policy areas. The values of the question on the depth of appointments reflect whether respondents believed that these happen on the top managerial level (1),[8] middle level (2),[9] or lowest level (3).[10] Because of the ordinal nature of the data, we use the median score as a measure of central tendency (Healy, 1999: 78). This leads to one potential problem, which is that if the five answers per observation vary substantially, the median might hide this variation. However, major disagreement among the respondents is itself unusual, and where it does occur we have chosen to follow the dominant opinion, which the median does represent.[11] The exact procedure for calculating the index is described in Appendix 1.

Overall, the index is presented in standardized values with a range of 0 to 1. A value of 1 indicates that patronage practices approximate a full overlap of party and the state, and a value of 0 indicates no party politicization of the state. However, in order to interpret the actual values of the index as calculated and reported here, it might be useful to interpret some sample values. A value of around 0.65 (see the chapter on Greece) should be interpreted to mean that parties appoint in most institutions at all levels of the administration; a value of around 0.4 (see the chapter on Spain) means that parties appoint in most institutions at top and middle level; and a value of 0.1 (see the chapter on the UK) that parties appoint in a limited number of institutions at only the top level.

The second common indicator is that reflecting the dominant *motivations for patronage* appointments, and simply reports the proportion of respondents giving possible categories of answers. Following the theoretical discussion in the introductory chapter, we see the motivations for patronage as being dominated either by a desire to reward members and activists (reward function), control various aspects of the policy-making process and institutions (control function), or a combination of the two (both rewards and control). Respondents were asked to choose the dominant motivation among the three categories but could also choose 'other' as an option and clarify their answer.

The third indicator is on the *characteristics of people* who are appointed to the patronage positions, and reflects existing understandings of why people might get jobs in the state administration (Kristinsson, 2006, Meyer-Sahling, 2006c and 2008). Respondents were asked to say which one(s) of the following three applied: professional experience, political allegiance, or individual connections. Again they could report 'other' characteristics as long as they clarified the meaning. The indicator in this case reports the percentages of respondents that mentioned each of the possible categories.

CONCLUSION

We argue that our method of semi-structured, face-to-face interviews with a larger number of respondents presents several advantages over existing studies of patronage. The existing approaches have either only been applicable to one country (or party) case or have greatly limited the scope of potential patronage by focusing on a number of state institutions only. Proxy indicators used, such as the public employment numbers or public employment expenditure, are not only misconstrued as indicators of patronage but might also greatly over or underestimate the real phenomenon.

As the following chapters will demonstrate, the face-to-face interviews conducted by country research teams have allowed us the in-depth investigation necessary to grasp the fine details of the practice of patronage in each country. At the same time, the use of a structured questionnaire and a multitude of respondents gives the confidence to aggregate the results into several quantitative indicators. This allows us to compare trends in patronage across countries and to investigate various aspects of patronage in specific substantive areas.

NOTES

1. For other research outputs using this method see Scherlis (2010), Kopecký (2011), Kopecký and Spirova (2011).
2. Studies on these topics include: (clientelism) Kitschelt and Wilkinson (2007), Piattoni (2001a); (pork-barrel politics) Tavits (2009); and (corruption) Treisman (2007), Golden and Chang (2001), and della Porta and Vannucci (1999).
3. Similar approaches have been used by Calvo and Murillo (2004) and Greene (2010). Going even further, Manow (2002) and van Biezen and Kopecký (2007) have used several variations of the widely available corruption indices compiled by Transparency International to approximate the extent of rent-seeking behaviour, including patronage. However, given our discussion of the conceptual differences between corruption and patronage in Chapter 1 and the highly contested ability of the corruption indices themselves to capture the real as opposed to perceived levels of corruption, this approach is clearly not suited to the purposes of this present volume.
4. The data are available at http://www.socialsciences.leiden/edu/politicalscience/research/research-data/party-patronage.html.
5. In each individual country, other, additional, areas might be very important for the understanding of patronage practice. While, for comparative purposes, our common indicators are limited to these nine substantive areas, individual country chapters might also include discussion of the additional ones.

6. The 'maps of state', including all individual institutions included in the analysis for each country, are available from the editors of the book.
7. 28 interviews were conducted in Austria, 41 in Bulgaria, 42 in the Czech Republic, 42 in Denmark, 40 in Germany, 45 in Greece, 40 in Hungary, 45 in Iceland, 47 in Ireland, 45 in Italy, 51 in the Netherlands, 44 in Norway, 47 in Portugal, 45 in Spain, and 45 in the United Kingdom—a total of 647 interviews for the whole volume.
8. This level includes positions such as ministers, deputy ministers, and political cabinets, which are assumed to be patronage appointments, but also state or permanent secretaries in the ministries, directors of NDACs, and members of the governing boards of the executing institutions.
9. This level includes positions such as section directors, heads of departments, national directors, general directors, coordinators, heads of directorates in the ministries; managers of lower-level sections in the NDACs, and managers in the executing institutions.
10. The lowest level includes positions such as experts, specialists, secretaries (administrative), cleaners, drivers, and security guards in the ministries and various employees in the NDACs and executing institutions.
11. Why experts might disagree to varying degrees in each of the observed cases is a separate question, which is not discussed presently.

Part 2: Party Patronage in Europe

CHAPTER 3

Party Patronage in Austria: From Reward to Control

Oliver Treib

INTRODUCTION

Austria was traditionally considered a country marked by high levels of party patronage (Müller, 1989, 2006b: 189).[1] However, this assessment rests on a conception of party patronage that differs significantly from the one used here. While we conceive of party patronage as the power of political parties to appoint people to positions in public or semi-public life, Müller's understanding is much wider, also covering clientelistic practices of exchanging material benefits (subsidies, tax reliefs, access to jobs and public housing, etc.) for political support (votes, party membership, party activism).

It is true that clientelistic practices by the two major parties, the Social Democratic Party (SPÖ) and the People's Party (ÖVP), were formerly widespread in post-war Austria, in particular in the area of public housing. According to an article published in the German weekly, *Der Spiegel*, in 1965, a person living in a public apartment building in SPÖ-led Vienna would most probably carry a Social Democratic membership book, while somebody living in an apartment building sponsored by the Federal Ministry of Trade, then governed by an ÖVP minister, would be likely to pay membership fees to the Christian Democrats (*Der Spiegel*, 1965: 72). The practice of tying access to public housing to party membership continued until the 1980s. According to an opinion poll conducted among party members in 1980, gaining access to public housing was mentioned as an important or very important reason for joining a party by approximately one-third of all surveyed party members (Müller, 1989: 339). Since the late 1980s, however, these practices of mass clientelism have been in decline. In particular, access to community housing was put on a more objective and transparent basis to prevent political parties from using it as an instrument of clientelism (Sickinger, 2006: 566).

However, there is also evidence suggesting that Austrian political parties traditionally had a tight grip on distributing jobs in the public sector. According to the article in *Der Spiegel* mentioned above, access to public sector jobs in the mid-1960s was firmly controlled by the two major political parties that had been in power since the Second World War. Depending on the party political colour of the ministry in charge of a particular area, jobs were tied to party membership in the SPÖ or the ÖVP. An engineer working in a state-owned steel company in Austria would typically be a member of the Social Democrats, while an army officer would belong to the Christian Democrats, and a member of the traffic police would usually belong to the 'reds', while a village teacher would most probably be one of the 'blacks' (*Der Spiegel*, 1965: 72).

The study by Müller (1989) also contains empirical evidence on the pervasiveness of party patronage until the 1980s. He uses the results of staff representation elections in ministerial departments and their administrative subdivisions as an indicator for the role of party political appointments in the public administration. Indeed, the data indicates that party patronage was a very widespread phenomenon in post-war Austria up until the 1980s. In ministerial departments governed by ministers of the same party for several years, vast majorities of up to 74 per cent of the civil servants and employees voted for representatives belonging to the party of the minister. After a ministry was taken over by the other major party and this new party political leadership was sustained for several years, these majorities were significantly reduced. Also, opinion polls conducted among party members in the 1980s suggest that half of all surveyed party members had decided to join their party in order to gain job-related advantages.

Müller's analysis certainly has the merit of representing the first systematic study on party patronage in Austria. However, it also has its limits. The different types of data he uses are only an indirect indicator of patronage practices. The analysis does not allow any conclusions as to whether there are differences in patronage between different levels of the administrative hierarchy or between different subdivisions of the administration. Neither does it shed light on the motives underlying party patronage. Since the analysis was done more than twenty years ago, it also needs updating to give us an appropriate picture of party patronage in contemporary Austria.

It is the aim of this chapter to fill this gap. It starts out with an overview of the traditional system of Austrian party government and Austria's civil service tradition. Then it reports the main empirical findings of our study on party patronage in contemporary Austria, delineating the range and depth of party patronage, differences between individual sectors, the motivations of patronage appointments, the role of different party political actors in deciding upon appointments, and whether patronage is majoritarian or shared between government and opposition parties. It concludes with a discussion of the main changes in the system of Austrian party patronage since the late 1980s, arguing that the extent of party patronage has not changed dramatically, but the political logic of appointments and the type of people appointed did change considerably.

BACKGROUND

The reach of parties within society

Austria has a long tradition of strong party government. The voting system applied in elections for the first chamber of the federal parliament (*Nationalrat*) is party-list proportional representation. Since 1992, there has been a system of partly open lists, meaning that voters can, in addition to voting for a party list, cast preferential votes for candidates on that list. However, this electoral system still gives political parties complete control over candidate selection, making it virtually impossible to pursue a political career outside of, or without the support of, a political party. This also means that ministers and state secretaries are usually people with a strong party background. The appointment of independent ministers is a very rare phenomenon.

Since the late nineteenth century, the Austrian party system has been structured by the antagonism between the two large parties on the left and on the right: the Socialist/Social Democratic Party on the one hand and the Christian Social Party and its successor, the Austrian People's Party, on the other. Both camps were deeply divided along two strong societal cleavages: the class cleavage, pitting capital against labour; and the religious cleavage, separating defenders of clericalism from supporters of laicism. In the 1930s, this conflict culminated in a civil war between the two sides under the Christian Social Chancellor, Engelbert Dollfuß. As a result of these violent clashes, Social Democracy was outlawed and its leaders had to leave the country or were imprisoned.

After the end of the Second World War, the leaders of the SPÖ and the ÖVP decided to turn conflict into cooperation by agreeing to form a grand coalition government with proportional representation of both sides. This grand coalition system proved to be the dominant form of government in the post-war period. The two large parties cooperated in government between 1947 and 1966, and between 1987 and 2000, and they have been doing so again since 2007. In between, there was a long period of single-party government by the SPÖ (1970–83), and shorter periods of ÖVP single-party government and coalitions between the ÖVP or the SPÖ and the Freedom Party of Austria (FPÖ).

In electoral terms, the traditional dominance of the SPÖ and ÖVP, which during the 1970s regularly received more than 90 per cent of the vote in national elections, has given way to a more balanced system in which the three smaller parties, the Greens, the right-wing populist FPÖ, and its split-off Alliance for the Future of Austria (BZÖ), also play an important role. Since the late 1980s, in particular the right-wing camp has significantly gained electoral support, mostly as a reaction to public criticism of the dominant grand coalition system. In the parliamentary elections of 1999, the FPÖ for the first time won slightly more votes than the ÖVP, with the ÖVP and the SPÖ together receiving no more than approximately 60 per cent of the vote. In the most recent parliamentary elections in

2008, the combined SPÖ/ÖVP share of the vote even plummeted to slightly more than 55 per cent, with the FPÖ receiving around 17 per cent, and the BZÖ and the Greens receiving roughly 10 per cent of the vote each (Pelinka, 2009: 624).

Given the widespread practices of mass clientelism in the provision of public housing and of mass party patronage in the distribution of jobs in the public sector during the post-war period, it comes as no surprise that Austrian political parties have traditionally been marked by very high figures of party membership. The peak of mass party organization was reached by the end of the 1970s, when almost one and a half million Austrians, or almost 28 per cent of registered voters, were members of one of the two major parties. Between the end of the 1970s and 2002, however, the number of party members of the SPÖ and the ÖVP dropped by more than a third. It seems that these losses affect the SPÖ much more severely than the ÖVP. While the latter lost only one in eight members since the end of the 1970s, the SPÖ membership in 2002 was less than half the size of 1979.[2]

The decline of party membership is a general phenomenon affecting many established democracies (Mair and van Biezen, 2001), and it thus needs to be explained by more general processes of societal change in Western countries—changing lifestyles, declining party identification, etc. In Austria, however, it is certainly also a reaction to the waning importance of clientelistic practices in the provision of public housing and, as this chapter will show in more detail below, to the transformation of party patronage in public and semi-public institutions from a mass phenomenon to an instrument targeting primarily leadership positions.

Despite declining electoral support and membership rates, both major parties still have an exceptionally strong societal basis. In 2002, the membership of SPÖ and ÖVP amounted to slightly less than one million, which means that about 16 per cent of the electorate are members of one of the two main parties. This is still by far the highest ratio of party membership among European countries (Mair and van Biezen, 2001: 9).

In addition, both parties are deeply rooted in several societal organizations. The SPÖ has close ties to the Austrian Trade Union Federation (ÖGB), the chief association of trade unions in Austria. Despite declining union membership, the ÖGB still represents approximately one-third of all employees in Austria (Karlhofer, 2006: 466). At the same time, a minority of unions, in particular the union of public employees, belong to the Christian Democratic camp. More important are the ÖVP's tight connections with business interests, in particular with the Federation of Austrian Industries (*Industriellenvereinigung*), which is one of the biggest donors of the ÖVP (Fink, 2006: 453; Sickinger, 2009: 160–70).

There are also close ties between the two major parties and the corporatist system of chambers: the Chambers of Labour, Business, and Agriculture. These chambers operate on the basis of compulsory membership. Each chamber has nine regional organizations, one in each of the nine Austrian provinces (*Länder*), with representative bodies elected by the members in each province and leaderships determined by these elected bodies. Each chamber also has a federal representation. The leadership of the Federal Chamber of Labour and of the Federal Chamber of Business is determined by the respective regional chambers. The Chamber of Agriculture is represented at the federal level by a conference of the nine regional presidents.

Delegates in all chambers are organized according to party lines. In each chamber, there is a Social Democratic and a Christian Democratic faction. Sometimes there are also smaller factions belonging to the FPÖ, the Greens, and the BZÖ. Chamber representation of the ÖVP is organized according to the three traditional 'leagues' (*Bünde*) of which the party consists, with party membership usually being tied to membership in one of these leagues: the Business League (*Wirtschaftsbund*), the Farmers' League (*Bauernbund*), and the League of Blue and White Collar Workers (*Arbeiter- und Angestelltenbund*). The Social Democrats dominate the Chambers of Labour. They hold the majority in all regional chambers except for Tyrol and Vorarlberg, where the Christian Democrats hold the majority, and they control the Federal Chamber of Labour. Conversely, the Chambers of Business and the Chambers of Agriculture are dominated by the respective ÖVP leagues (Pelinka, 2009: 628–30). The ÖVP Farmers' League also has close ties with the Raiffeisen Group, a powerful conglomerate of agricultural cooperatives, banks, and dairy producers (Krammer and Hovorka, 2006).

In addition, there is a wide array of sports clubs, automobile associations, charity organizations, student associations, etc. which have ties to either the Social Democratic Party or the People's Party (Karlhofer, 2001: 345–9; Müller, 2006a: 352–3). Although these ties may have become weaker since the 1970s, there are still distinct Social Democratic and Christian Democratic milieus that reach deep into society.

The administrative tradition

The origins of Austrian administration date back to the eighteenth century, when Maria Theresia, and especially her successor Joseph II, implemented far-reaching reforms to build up a strong, centralized bureaucracy for the Habsburg Empire. These reforms were built upon the principles of hierarchical organization and merit-based appointment and promotion (Müller, 2007a). Austria's administrative tradition thus conforms to what Max Weber later on described as the ideal-typical model of modern bureaucracy (Weber, 1922/1978: 956–1003).

However, after the demise of the Habsburg monarchy in 1918, and in particular under the rule of the Austrofascist regime in the 1930s, the Austrian administration became more and more colonized by members of the Christian Socialist camp. Since social democrats were excluded from the public bureaucracy, the vast majority of civil servants at the time thus belonged to the Conservative camp. Under Nazi rule, many civil servants lost their jobs or were even persecuted because they were Jews, followers of the old regime, or simply supported the idea of an independent Austrian state. Instead, new Nazi partisans were brought in and some of the old civil servants joined the National Socialist German Workers' Party (NSDAP) for opportunistic reasons (Liegl and Müller, 1999: 114; Müller, 2007a: 40).

Under the grand coalition that took office after the end of the Second World War, the Social Democrats in particular feared that the process of denazification would lead to the re-establishment of Conservative dominance in the public administration. To solve this problem, the grand coalition established the so-called *Proporz* system, according to which both governing parties should get a roughly equal share of the jobs in the public sector. With the exception of the army, which the SPÖ sought to turn into a bipartisan organization, the system worked based on the principle of the ministers' personnel autonomy within their sphere of competence—meaning that the ministers of each party would appoint individuals to jobs within their part of the administration dependent on their suitableness to the party. Likewise, jobs in the nationalized industries were divided between both parties. With certain adaptations in phases where only one of the parties was in government, this system of strong party politicization of the state machinery has put its mark on the Austrian public sector until the present day (Liegl and Müller, 1999: 114–16; Müller, 2007a: 43–51). However, as this chapter will show in more detail below, the Austrian system of party patronage has significantly changed its modus operandi.

Following the First World War, the scope of the spoils available to the ÖVP and SPÖ was considerable, especially since post-war Austria used to have one of the largest nationalized sectors among Western industrialized countries (Lauber and Pesendorfer, 2006: 610). The Austrian state owned the Federal Railways Company (ÖBB), the Austrian Post, several large banks, as well as steel, energy, aviation, and tobacco companies. Starting in the mid-1980s, however, all state-owned banks and many of the nationalized companies were (fully or partly) privatized. Nowadays, the last remaining company that is entirely owned by the Austrian state is the Federal Railways Company. In addition, the state holds a majority of the shares of Austrian Post and of the electricity company, Verbund, as well as a minority of shares of Telekom Austria and the energy company OMV.

Today, about 470,000 employees work in the Austrian government sector (Statistik Austria, 2010: 195–6). The federal level makes up about a third of all government employees. The nine provinces employ slightly more than half of all government employees, and the remaining 16 per cent work at the local level. These figures underline the fact that the provinces are important actors in administrative terms. Although they have little legislative power, the provincial administrations are in charge of implementing federal legislation in many areas, in particular with regard to schools and health care.

People working in the government sector are employed on two types of contracts. On the one hand, there are career civil servants with permanent tenure. On the other hand, more and more staff are hired as 'employees under contract' (*Vertragsbedienstete*), i.e. employees with employment contracts under private law and without permanent tenure. Almost two-thirds of all state employees are employees under contract. Most of these work at the regional and local levels, however. In contrast, more than 60 per cent of all employees at the federal level are still career civil servants with permanent tenure, although there has been a far-reaching moratorium on creating new tenured civil service positions in the federal administration since 2000. There are also plans to restrict the status of civil servants with permanent tenure to the core executive functions of the state, such as the Military and Police, or the Judiciary.

Compared to the other countries in our sample, the number of government employees in Austria is relatively moderate. In 2007, only 11.8 per cent of the economically active population in Austria worked in this sector. This is the third smallest government sector after Greece and Germany. The share of employees working in the general government sector in Hungary is almost twice as high as in Austria, and the government sectors of Norway and Denmark are about two and a half times as large as the Austrian one.[3]

EMPIRICAL ANALYSIS OF PATRONAGE

Scope and reach of patronage

Formally, political parties in Austria are able to reach all types of institutions in all sectors analysed.[4] Although the party organizations as such are usually not endowed with the right to appoint people, persons representing political parties, typically the ministers in charge of particular organizational units, are legally entitled to decide upon appointments. In practice, they make wide-ranging use of their patronage opportunities. As Table 3.1 shows, the overall patronage score

TABLE 3.1 *The index of party patronage in Austria*

Policy area	Ministries	NDACs	Executing institutions	Policy area total
Economy	0.67	0.67	0.67	0.67
Finance	0.67	0.44	0.67	0.59
Judiciary	0.67	–	0.11	0.39
Media	0.33	0.22	0.44	0.33
Military and Police	0.67	0.22	1.00	0.63
Health Care	0.67	0.22	0.67	0.52
Culture and Education	0.67	0.00	0.22	0.30
Foreign Service	0.67	0.33	0.22	0.41
Regional and Local Administration	0.67	0.33	0.67	0.56
Total	0.63	0.31	0.52	0.49

of Austria is 0.49 (see Chapter 2 for more details on how this score was calculated). This is the second highest score among all the countries included in our analysis (see the Conclusion of this volume in Chapter 18).

Our interviewees overwhelmingly suggested that these appointments are party political appointments. We asked our respondents about the role of parties in these appointments for each type of institution in each sector (see Table 3.2). In 88.9 per cent of all cases, the answer was that parties play a large role. In 7.4 per cent of all cases, our interviewees considered the role of parties to be small. The remainder pertains to cases where respondents did not answer the question.

Taken together, these results suggest that Austria can still be considered a country with high levels of party patronage. To learn more about the character of party patronage in Austria, it is useful to explore the reach and depth of patronage appointments within the state sector. How many of the public and semi-public institutions are affected by patronage, and how deep down the organizational hierarchies of these institutions does it reach? Table 3.3 presents standardized scores of the range and depth of patronage. The average score of reach is 0.84. This means that patronage affects a very large part of the institutions we studied. Parties appoint people to all ministerial departments and to most non-departmental agencies and executing institutions. In contrast, the average score of depth is much lower, amounting to a value of 0.53. In other words, patronage almost always penetrates the top levels, and to some extent also the middle levels, but almost never the lower levels of public and semi-public institutions.

These data suggest that party patronage in Austria today is a phenomenon that concentrates to a considerable extent on leadership positions rather than reaching down to the level of ordinary employees in the state sector. This finding is in stark contrast to the all-pervasive system of patronage that was built up in the immediate post-war period and was still very much alive in the 1980s (Müller, 1989). The concluding section of this chapter will discuss the reasons for this transformation of Austrian party patronage.

Patronage in ministerial departments

The data show that there are significant differences between different types of institutions. In terms of institutional differences, ministerial departments are most

TABLE 3.2 *The role of the party in appointments*

Percentage of respondents who said that parties have a . . .	Ministries	NDACs	Executing institutions	Total
Small role	–	12.0%	10.7%	7.4%
Large role	96.4%	80.0%	89.3%	88.9%
No answer	3.6%	8.0%	–	3.7%

TABLE 3.3 *Range and depth of patronage, by policy area and institutional type*

	Ministries		NDACs		Executing institutions	
	Range	Depth	Range	Depth	Range	Depth
Economy	1.00	0.67	1.0	0.67	1.00	0.67
Finance	1.00	0.67	0.67	0.67	1.00	0.67
Judiciary	1.00	0.67	–	–	0.33	0.33
Media	1.00	0.33	0.67	0.33	0.67	0.67
Military and Police	1.00	0.67	0.67	0.33	1.00	1.00
Health Care	1.00	0.67	0.67	0.33	1.00	0.67
Culture and Education	1.00	0.67	0.00	0.00	0.67	0.33
Foreign Service	1.00	0.67	1.00	0.33	0.67	0.33
Regional and Local Administration	1.00	0.67	1.00	0.33	1.00	0.67
Total	1.00	0.63	0.71	0.38	0.81	0.59

Average range: 0.84, average depth: 0.53

affected by party patronage. Each and every ministerial department is penetrated by political parties, and in all but one ministry party political appointments cover both the top and the middle levels.[5] At the top of the hierarchy, ministers appoint the members of their ministerial cabinets or bureaus according to party political criteria. The members of these cabinets or bureaus are not career civil servants but political appointees whose fate is directly linked to the political survival of the minister. Although there are differences between ministries as well as between individual ministers, the size of these cabinets has increased considerably since the 1970s (Liegl and Müller, 1999: 102). Currently, the number of people employed in the ministerial cabinets of the federal ministries in our eight policy sectors varies between two (Foreign Ministry) and thirteen (Interior Ministry). The average number of cabinet members is eight.[6]

Apart from that, ministers also appoint the heads of departments (*Sektionschefs*) in their ministries, i.e. the leading positions at the middle level of the ministerial hierarchy. Although there are differences in the extent to which individual ministers actually fill these positions exclusively on the basis of party political affinity,[7] it is safe to conclude that these appointments in general are done on party political grounds. However, heads of departments do not come and go with the minister, but are staffed with career civil servants. Until the mid-1990s, these were permanent positions, which meant that a new minister had to live with the heads of departments of his or her predecessor and could only appoint new people to these positions after one of the heads of department had retired. Inspired by the principles of New Public Management, the new system, which became effective in 1996, provided that appointments to heads of departments and a couple of other senior official positions be made for a fixed term of five years (Liegl and Müller, 1999: 101). This has considerably shortened the party political shadow of history within ministerial departments. Ministers now have many more opportunities to change the personnel of heads of sections according to their party political tastes. At the same time, ministers' powers of reorganization were also strengthened by the new system. While the old system required ministers to provide a job of the same rank to senior officials they wanted to remove from certain positions, the new rules now only require them to make sure that they get another job with adequate payment. Moreover, the ability of civil servants to appeal against ministerial reorganizations was curbed (Liegl and Müller, 1999: 100).

While certainly not all ministers make use of the instrument of reorganization, working instead with their cabinets and using the tool of party political appointments for positions which become vacant when fixed-term contracts come to an end, there are several examples where ministers, usually taking over a ministry that had been headed by another party for several years, employed all available instruments to 're-colour' the senior administrative staff in their ministry. Probably one of the most skilful examples was to be witnessed when the ÖVP minister Ernst Strasser took over the Interior Ministry in 2000. The ministry had been in the hands of the SPÖ for almost the whole post-war period, which meant that virtually all important positions were filled with SPÖ partisans. Within a few years, Strasser completely reorganized the ministry, abolishing old administrative units and creating new ones. Since the newly created positions could be appointed anew, the effect of this reorganization was that Strasser could replace a considerable number of SPÖ officials by civil servants loyal to the ÖVP (Müller, 2007b: 50).

The only restriction a minister has in his appointments is that all positions are subject to a regularized placement procedure. This requirement was introduced in 1989 as a reaction to growing public criticism of patronage practices. The new placement regulations have to be seen against the background of debates surrounding the accession to power of a new grand coalition government in 1987. The SPÖ single-party government (1966–83) had practised a less obvious form of party patronage than the grand coalition during the 1950s and 1960s. Despite making considerable inroads into the formerly 'black' ministries, the SPÖ decided not to fully exploit its patronage potentials, partly because it did not have enough personnel resources to fill all the available jobs. When the grand coalition came back to power in 1987, there was considerable public concern, fuelled by an aggressive anti-*Proporz* campaign of Haider's Freedom Party, that the two parties would return to their old spoils system. The introduction of more formalized placement procedures was meant to appease these criticisms (Müller, Philipp, and Steininger, 1996: 105–6). The concluding section to this chapter will discuss in more detail the role of FPÖ pressure in transforming Austria's patronage system.

According to the new system, jobs in the public administration have to be publicly advertised. Applications are screened by selection committees consisting of four members: two are appointed by the minister, one by the civil service trade union, and a further member comes from the central employee representation, the *Zentralausschuss*, which is usually dominated by trade unionists as well. The committee is chaired by one of the members appointed by the minister. It produces a ranked shortlist of the most promising candidates, which is then put before the minister for a final decision. If the committee is split, the chairman's vote is decisive (Liegl and Müller, 1999: 96–7).

Although this new procedure increased the relevance of professional qualifications in appointments (see below), it did not decisively diminish party influence. First, the job profiles defined in public announcements, especially for more important positions, are frequently tailored to specific party candidates. 'Job offers often come with the photo of the targeted candidate', as one of our interviewees put it. Second, even if the call is relatively open, there is usually a range of qualified candidates from which the committee can choose the person with the best party political fit. In fact, the party groups in the employee representation and in the civil service trade union keep track of the pool of candidates loyal to their party and seek to ensure that 'their' candidate is selected.[8] Third, even if the committee selects somebody the minister dislikes, especially if he or she faces a ministry where the unions of the other party have a majority, he or she is not legally bound by the recommendation of the selection committee. All the minister has to do in that case is inform the employee representation about his or her reason for rejecting the top candidate (Liegl and Müller, 1999: 97).

Patronage in non-departmental agencies

Among the three types of institutions in our study, non-departmental agencies have the lowest overall score of party patronage (see Table 3.1 above). This does not mean that party politics does not play an important role in recruitment decisions, but that it is relatively less important than in ministerial departments and executing institutions. Some non-departmental agencies are considered virtually free of party patronage, and in those agencies where party politics does play a role, it typically covers only leadership positions, i.e. the jobs of directors, members of managing boards and/or members of supervisory boards. External party political influence is usually restricted to these top jobs because party political actors, usually the ministers in charge of the given agencies, do not have a formal say on appointments further down the hierarchy. Some of our respondents mentioned cascading effects from the top to the middle level, meaning that party appointees at the top appoint people according to party political criteria at lower levels of their organizations. However, reports about such practices were restricted to the Economy and Finance sectors, where party patronage in general is particularly widespread.

Among the thirty-seven non-departmental agencies covered by our study, agencies considered to be of strategic importance are more likely to be influenced by party politics than less important agencies. Where economically important decisions are taken, parties are particularly keen to ensure that loyal managers are appointed to leadership positions. This is true for many agencies in the Finance and Economy sectors such as the Financial Market Authority, which supervises the entire banking, insurance, and stock market, the Federal Competition Authority, which monitors compliance with anti-trust regulations in Austria, or the Austrian Industry Holding, which manages the state's shares in nationalized or partly state-owned companies. The same is true for agencies with more important regulatory or supervisory functions in the Media and Health Care sectors or at the provincial level. Party political criteria thus dominate top-level appointments in the Austrian Communications Authority, which is not only the competent authority for broadcasting regulation, but also administers the Austrian federal government's press and journalism subsidies, the Federal Health Agency and Health Austria Limited, two agencies that are key players in implementing controversial cost-containment plans in health care, and the provincial schooling councils, which play a crucial role in selecting candidates for headmaster and teacher positions. In contrast, less important agencies are often left untouched by political parties. This category includes the Austrian Internet Monitor, the Austrian Interior Safety Board, the Study Grant Authority, and, at the regional level, the Federation of Lower Austrian Public Libraries.

In some cases, the strategic importance or unimportance of a particular agency is not obvious. For example, it seems surprising at first glance that the Austrian Science Fund (FWF), an agency administering a considerable share of Austria's research and development budget, is left untouched by political parties. However, the main focus of FWF funding is basic research. Applied research, in contrast, is managed by a different agency, the Austrian Research Promotion Agency (FFG). Given that funds for applied research can be used as an instrument of industrial policy by providing indirect subsidies to certain branches of the Economy or to certain companies, it comes as no surprise that the FFG leadership is controlled by party politics, while the FWF is relatively independent.[9]

Patronage in executing institutions

The extent of party patronage in executing institutions is slightly lower than in ministerial departments, but significantly higher than in non-departmental agencies (see Table 3.1 above). The executing institutions that are most heavily influenced by party political appointments are the armed forces and the police, where appointments according to party political criteria still reach down to the lowest levels. While all of these appointments are formally done by the ministers in charge of the respective sector, there is an interesting overlap of top-down and bottom-up mechanisms behind these appointments. Leadership positions are driven by the ministers in charge, with the aim of gaining control of the sector. At the same time, there is a more clientelistic bottom-up mechanism underlying recruitment decisions at the lowest level of the hierarchy. Local politicians who want to reward a loyal supporter intervene with the minister to ensure that this person gets a job in the army or the police, or will be transferred to another police station or army base. What is party political about these procedures is that they work primarily between local politicians from the same party as the minister. One of our interviewees even described a case where a mayor of a town with army barracks lobbied the minister to ensure that a certain individual would get a job in the catering service of the local barracks.

Also strongly influenced by political parties are appointments in the management of large state-owned companies such as the Federal Railways Company, ÖBB, the state-owned energy company, Verbund, or Austrian Post, as well as management positions in the Austrian National Bank, the Austrian Broadcasting Company (ORF), the Federation of Austrian Social Insurers, and, at the regional and local level, in provincial hospitals, schools, and district authorities or city magistrates. Although the depth of patronage is declining in executing institutions, party influence on appointments in all of these institutions still reaches not only the top managerial level but also the middle level, mostly in the form of a cascading effect where the party appointees at the top appoint further party confidants in positions further down the hierarchy.

Party patronage also affects a number of further executing institutions, although in these cases the influence of parties is restricted to the top level. Judges of the Constitutional Court and the Supreme Court of Justice, members of university boards (one of the three top governing institutions in Austrian universities), the chief editor of the state-owned Vienna Newspaper, as well as ambassadors and permanent representatives are regularly appointed according to party political criteria. Among the few executing institutions that are free of party patronage are ordinary courts, whose judges are selected by independent committees of judges attached to the Supreme Court of Justice and the Courts of Appeal. According to our interviewees, this procedure is based on professional qualifications only, and thus shields the recruitment of judges from party political intervention.

Sectoral differences

Besides variation among different types of institution, there are also relevant differences in the scope and reach of party patronage between sectors. Table 3.1 reveals that Economy is the sector most affected by party patronage, closely followed by Military and Police, Finance, and Regional and Local Administration.[10] At the other end of the spectrum, Culture and Education has the lowest score of party patronage, followed by Judiciary and Foreign Service.

There are two factors that explain this pattern. First, patronage heavily targets institutions that are of strategic importance for political parties, so that they can pursue policy goals they consider of vital importance in electoral terms. This is especially true for the Economy and Finance sectors, but also for many of the institutions under the control of provincial governors, like schools and provincial hospitals. Sectors crowded by institutions that are less important for parties, in contrast, are less affected by party political appointments. This pertains to many institutions in Foreign Service, Culture and Education,[11] as well as the Media and Judiciary sectors. This does not mean that Austrian parties consider courts, TV and radio stations, or schools to be unimportant. It only means that many of the institutions operating in these sectors are not so important and are thus largely ignored by political parties, while the few institutions that do have wide-ranging powers or a potentially significant impact on the public image of the government, such as the Austrian Communications Authority and the public broadcasting company, ORF, in the Media sector, or the Constitutional Court and the Supreme Court of Justice in the Judiciary sector, are heavily affected by party patronage.

Second, some of the patronage-heavy sectors are still marked not only by control-driven appointments of leadership positions but also by more traditional forms of clientelistic patronage, motivated by reward considerations. Our data indicate that this is particularly true for Military and Police, but partly also for Regional and Local Administration and the Finance sector. In these policy areas, all of which belong to the group of sectors most affected by party patronage, we still find traces of the traditional, more clientelistic, system of reward-driven patronage described by Müller (1989), in addition to the now dominant mode of control-driven patronage. As described above, bottom-up appointments aiming to reward partisans are still particularly widespread in the military and the police.

This type of patronage usually targets jobs below the level of leadership positions because it usually involves more people than could be satisfied with the limited number of available top managerial jobs, and it often involves appointees with lower levels of qualifications than those required for many leadership positions. For these reasons, party patronage in sectors that are still partly marked by reward patronage reaches further down the organizational hierarchies than patronage in sectors dominated by control motivations. This increases the overall patronage scores of these sectors.

Motivations and selection criteria

Our respondents overwhelmingly indicated that control is the dominant motive of patronage appointments in Austria today (see Figure 3.1). Almost 80 per cent of our interviewees mentioned control as the dominant motive. Some also said that control and reward was crucial, but no one argued that reward was the decisive motive. The answers highlighting the role of reward in addition to control were concentrated on the three exceptional sectors that were just identified as characterized by reward patronage in addition to control patronage: Military and Police, Finance, and Regional and Local Administration.

The overall distribution of party patronage across the state machinery corroborates the experts' views. Apart from a couple of noteworthy exceptions, patronage

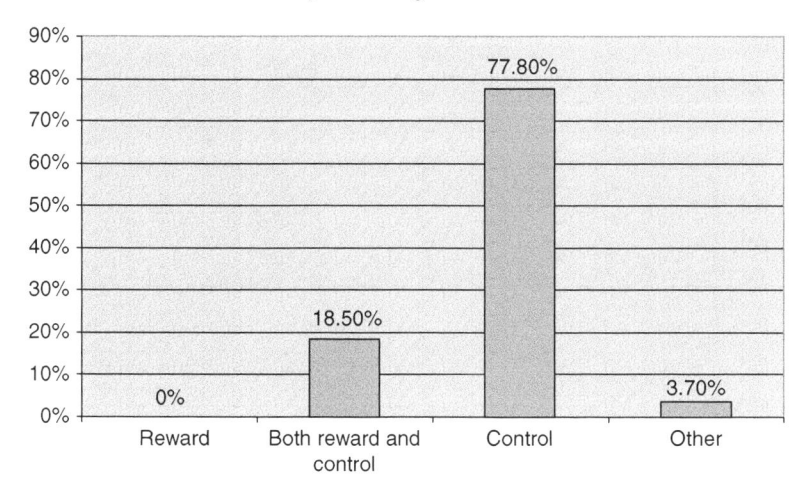

FIGURE 3.1 Motivations for party patronage in Austria

Category	Percentage
Reward	0%
Both reward and control	18.50%
Control	77.80%
Other	3.70%

mostly concentrates on leadership positions and, to some extent, also on influential positions among the middle management. Moreover, agencies and institutions that are considered to be of strategic importance are more likely to be targeted by party patronage than institutions regarded as less powerful.

Concerning the characteristics of successful appointees, our respondents hinted at a mixture of professional qualifications, party political links, and personal ties (see Figure 3.2). Many argued that professional qualification is a crucial prerequisite for being appointed. This is also due to the fact that jobs in the public and semi-public sector nowadays need to be filled on the basis of a public job advertisement. This does not mean, however, that parties cannot influence such appointments. There is usually a range of qualified candidates from which a minister can choose a person who is close to him or her personally or has links to his or her party, or both. Whether personal ties or party links are more important depends on the case at hand and, according to many respondents, is hard to disentangle. What is important to note, however, is that patronage today usually does not involve appointments of people who are not qualified for the job.

In sum, this suggests that patronage is not driven by the goal of finding attractive posts to reward loyal party members but by the objective of finding trustworthy and qualified persons for important management positions.

Who appoints?

As Figure 3.3 shows, patronage is clearly a prerogative of the parties in government. Almost 80 per cent of our respondents argued that patronage is a matter for government parties to decide. In this sense, party patronage in Austria is a

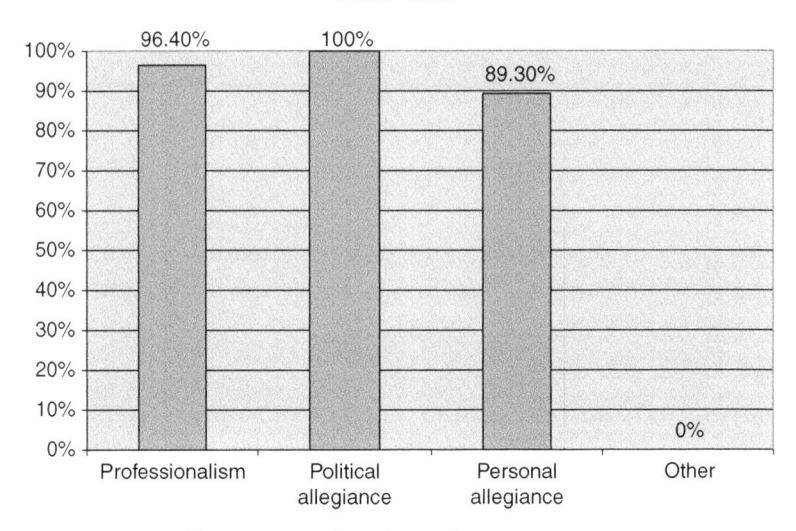

FIGURE 3.2 Qualifications of appointees in Austria

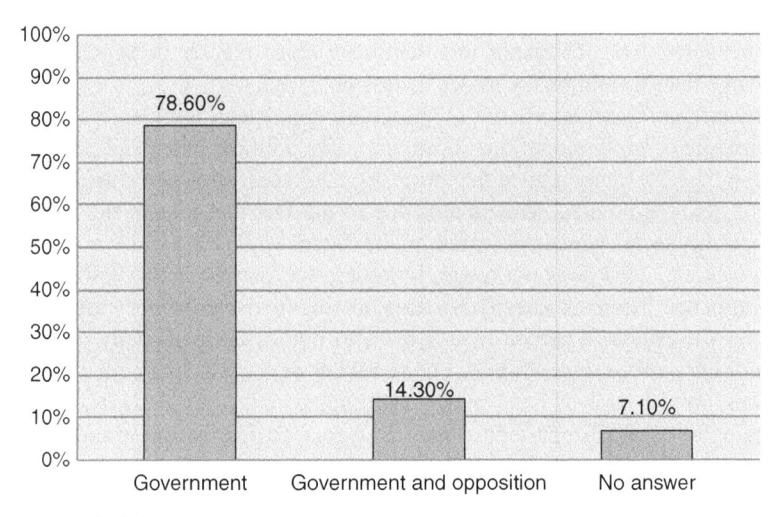

- Professionalism: 96.40%
- Political allegiance: 100%
- Personal allegiance: 89.30%
- Other: 0%

FIGURE 3.3 Patronage power

- Government: 78.60%
- Government and opposition: 14.30%
- No answer: 7.10%

majoritarian phenomenon. At the same time, it needs to be added that grand coalitions have been the dominant form of government since the Second World War. As the traditional logic of patronage under grand coalition governments in Austria was power sharing, balancing, and mutual monitoring between the two major parties, patronage has a certain element of proportionalism between the SPÖ and the ÖVP.

However, the system of proportional patronage between the SPÖ and the ÖVP can only work if both parties remain in power. Patronage practices under the ÖVP-FPÖ (later on ÖVP-BZÖ) coalition in power between 2000 and 2007 clearly suggest that opposition parties do not get a slice of the cake. The ÖVP defended and expanded its sphere of influence, while the FPÖ/BZÖ, despite its long-standing criticism of the party political appointment practices of previous grand coalition governments, did everything to move people from its camp into the available positions under its control. The SPÖ could defend some of its own positions simply because the new government did not have enough time to replace them entirely by ÖVP or FPÖ/BZÖ confidants.

There are only very few exceptions to the general pattern of government-driven patronage. In particular, a number of members of the Austrian Broadcasting Company's governing board (*Stiftungsrat*) are determined by the parties represented in the federal parliament according to their relative strength, which means that opposition parties also get their share. The Austrian provinces, via the second chamber, may also appoint members of the governing board. This provides patronage opportunities for parties that are in opposition at the federal level, but are part of a provincial government. Given that the government appoints the largest group of governing board members, however, it usually has a comfortable majority in the *Stiftungsrat*.

Who are the partisan actors that determine patronage appointments? Our interviews clearly suggest that ministers are the crucial players in party patronage. Almost 80 per cent of our respondents considered the minister in charge of a particular sector to be the key actor deciding upon appointments. In general, ministers have the power to appoint people in institutions under their jurisdiction, and they also make use of this power. This corroborates existing knowledge on the general autonomy of ministers within the Austrian system of public administration (Pelinka, 2009: 614–15). When important appointments are at stake, however, the party chairman of the minister's party also comes into play, and it depends on the standing of the respective minister within the party to decide who gets their way.

In contrast to the federal level, appointments in the Austrian provinces are much less sectorialized. Although provincial governments also have a sectoral structure, there are no separate ministries at the provincial level. The centrepiece of the provincial administration is the Office of the Provincial Government. The Office comprises all administrative functions of the core provincial bureaucracy. It has functional subdivisions, but these are not headed by other members of government but belong to the sphere of responsibility of the governor, who is the head of the provincial government and administration. The key player in provincial appointments is thus the governor, who ultimately decides on all important appointments at this level.

A further departure from the general rule of ministerial patronage powers can be found in the few areas where the government as a whole is responsible for appointments. This is true for ambassadors, for the president and vice-president of the Court of Administration, and for the president and vice-president as well as the majority of the other judges of the Constitutional Court. In these cases, appointments are not determined by the respective ministers alone. Instead, the party chairmen of the government parties also play an important role.

A crucial issue for the functioning of a system of party patronage that is as wide-ranging as the Austrian one is how political parties manage to monitor open positions and keep track of suitable candidates. While the central party offices, or the leagues in the case of the ÖVP, were key in fulfilling these tasks during the 1960s and 1970s, this role has been taken over mostly by the respective party groups in employee representations and in the civil service trade union. They keep an eye on potential candidates and bring their knowledge to bear in the committees that screen the candidates applying for jobs in the public sector. As outlined above, these selection committees always involve a member of the employee representation and a representative of the trade union—usually partisan actors belonging to one of the two traditional party camps.

Especially when a minister takes over a portfolio that has been in the hands of the other party for a long period of time and the employee representatives and trade unionists therefore tend to belong to the opposite camp, the tasks of keeping track of party politically suitable candidates and of ensuring that they are evaluated positively by the selection committees are sometimes also fulfilled by the ministerial cabinets. This was the case, for example, when the ÖVP minister Ernst Strasser took over the Social Democratic Ministry of the Interior in 2000.

At the provincial level, finally, it is usually the so-called '*Landesamtsdirektor*', the top civil servant in the provincial administration, also responsible for human resource management, who is in charge of administering white lists and black lists and ensuring that the right candidates are selected.

In other words, keeping track of personnel with the right political credentials for being appointed has changed from a task managed by the central party offices into a decentralized system run by trade unionists and close political confidants of ministers and provincial governors. This reflects a general shift of patronage powers from the party in central office to ministers and provincial governors.

CONCLUSION: FROM REWARD-DRIVEN MASS PATRONAGE TO CONTROL-DRIVEN ELITE PATRONAGE

The information gathered through our interviews indicates that patronage practices have undergone a significant transformation. More than 70 per cent of our respondents pointed out that party patronage has changed significantly over the last fifteen or twenty years. As outlined earlier in this chapter, party appointments in the post-war period up until the end of the 1980s were a mass phenomenon covering not only leadership positions in public and semi-public institutions, but also ordinary employees in ministerial departments, public authorities, state-owned companies, and other institutions under the grip of political parties. The data presented in this chapter, by contrast, show that party patronage in Austria today primarily targets leadership positions, and to a certain extent also positions in the middle management, of public and semi-public institutions.

This shift from mass to elite patronage goes along with a change in the logic of party patronage. In former times, rewarding loyal party members used to be at least as important as gaining control over important corridors of power. This gave rise to appointments irrespective of professional qualifications, which is seen as one of the reasons why many state-owned companies ran into deep economic trouble in the 1990s. After growing public criticism of the economically ineffective patronage system of former times, more objective and transparent procedures for appointing important positions were introduced, and many of the state-owned companies were fully or partly privatized.

This did not put an end to party patronage in the companies where the state continued to be an important capital owner, but it meant a serious blow to reward-driven mass patronage. Nowadays, professional qualification is generally considered an important precondition for appointments. Parties apply political criteria only in order to select the most suitable people from a pool of qualified candidates. More than half of our respondents explicitly mentioned the increasing importance of professional skills when asked about important changes in party patronage. A number of experts also argued that appointment practices focusing on rewarding loyal partisans have given way to a more control-driven system. At any rate, as shown in Figure 3.1 above, the vast majority of our respondents agreed that control was the dominant motive underlying patronage appointments today.

In sum, the old system of mass patronage, which was at least partly reward-driven, has been transformed into a system of elite patronage, primarily aiming to gain party political control over public and semi-public institutions that are crucial for policy delivery.

A crucial element in bringing about this change was the electoral success of Jörg Haider's right-wing populist FPÖ in the second half of the 1980s (Kitschelt, 2007). After Haider assumed the position of FPÖ party chairman in 1986, he started an aggressive campaign against the patronage-ridden *Proporz* system of the two major parties, the SPÖ and ÖVP. This strategy yielded ample electoral success. The first national election with Haider as FPÖ chairman, the parliamentary election of 1986, resulted in a decisively strengthened FPÖ, which had almost doubled its share of the vote compared to the previous election. Despite the FPÖ success, the two major parties formed a new grand coalition in 1987, and this government constellation remained unaltered for the next thirteen years. This set the stage for an unprecedented electoral upswing of the FPÖ, which continued to thrive on Haider's anti-*Proporz* strategy until it had received almost 27 per cent in the 1999 national election, finishing a few hundred votes ahead of the ÖVP as the second largest party.

Threatened by the electoral challenge of the FPÖ, and pressurized by growing public awareness of party patronage and increasingly critical media reports, the two governing parties started to react. Already in 1989, they introduced a new Appointment Act according to which all jobs in the civil service needed to be advertised publicly and placement decisions needed to be based on professional criteria (Müller, Philipp, and Steininger, 1996: 105–6; Liegl and Müller, 1999: 97). The grand coalition also initiated a process of privatization and de-politicization of state-owned companies to fend off growing public criticism of the ineffectiveness of the party-controlled public sector. The ÖVP in particular adopted an increasingly liberal policy on state ownership (Kitschelt, 2007: 308). Privatization was finally pushed ahead when the FPÖ entered into a right-wing coalition with the ÖVP in 2000.

Some of the former party fiefdoms in the public sector were thus released from the grip of parties through privatization. More important was the growing public criticism of reward-driven appointments irrespective of professional qualifications. Rather than cutting back decisively on patronage altogether, the parties changed their strategy, focusing more on important positions and taking account of public pressure by increasing the role of professional skills in their politically motivated appointments. It is through this defensive process, propelled by the anti-*Proporz* campaign of the FPÖ, that party patronage slowly moved away from reward-driven mass patronage and turned into a system of control-driven elite patronage.

However, it seems that the FPÖ's entry into government in 2000 has decisively weakened the anti-patronage drive in the Austrian party system. Rather than refraining from patronage and pushing its coalition partner to do likewise, the FPÖ, and later on the BZÖ, made full use of the patronage resources offered by their taking control of several important ministerial portfolios (Heinisch, 2003; for a more journalistic account, see Sperl, 2003). One of the ironies of FPÖ/BZÖ participation in government is that it was exactly the FPÖ/BZÖ ministers who received the most public criticism for appointing party confidants with a lack of appropriate professional qualifications. Given the small membership basis of the FPÖ/BZÖ and their lack of government experience at the time, this could hardly have been otherwise. In the eyes of the wider public, however, the scandals surrounding many of the FPÖ/BZÖ appointments clearly indicated that these alleged anti-patronage parties were no better than the former *Proporz* parties, the ÖVP and SPÖ.

Since then, both the BZÖ and the FPÖ have considerably toned down their criticism of patronage practices. As a consequence, the Greens are at present the only major party that is openly critical of patronage practices. Since they are too weak to mobilize a decisive share of the electorate, there is currently much less pressure on the SPÖ and the ÖVP to cut down on their patronage practices than there was fifteen or twenty years ago. Given that the reforms initiated in the shadow of FPÖ mobilization have diminished the likeliness of large-scale scandals due to incompetent appointees, it seems that the current system, although still facing public criticism from time to time, is relatively stable.

NOTES

1. The empirical work summarized in this chapter would not have been possible without the invaluable help of my research assistant, Hannes Biedermann, who conducted and transcribed all the interviews for this study. Some of the empirical findings were presented to a seminar held at the University of Vienna in December 2009. I am grateful for the valuable comments of Wolfgang Müller, Sylvia Kritzinger, and the other participants of that seminar.
2. The party membership figures were taken from Müller (2006a: 347) and Ucakar (2006: 332). To calculate the membership/electorate ratios, figures for the number of registered voters were taken from International IDEA (<http://idea.int>, accessed on 2 April 2010). They were 5,186,735 in 1979 and 5,838,373 in 2002. The other parties in Austria are negligible in terms of membership. In 2004, the FPÖ had approximately 45,000 members (Luther 2006: 374), while membership of the Greens amounted to slightly more than 4,000 in 2005 (Pelinka 2009: 627).
3. Source: International Labour Organization (ILO) labour statistics (<http://laborsta.ilo.org> accessed on 2 April 2010). The available figures on public sector employment collected by the Austrian Statistical Office correspond to the ILO category of employment in the 'general government sector'. This category excludes employment in 'publicly-owned enterprises'. Given that there are no data on Austria for this latter category, all we can compare here is the size of the core government apparatus. In some cases—e.g. in Greece—the rather low figures of employment in this sector would increase significantly if state-owned enterprises were included.
4. The following analysis of patronage practices in Austria is based on 28 expert interviews conducted between May 2008 and April 2010. The empirical work was hampered by severe problems of finding experts with appropriate knowledge who were also willing to give interviews and to talk plainly about the role of political parties in appointments in the public and semi-public sector. We contacted more than 60 potential interviewees. Only 31 of these agreed to give an interview. Three interviews were not included in the analysis since there are serious doubts as to the validity of the information provided. The resulting 28 expert interviews are evenly distributed over the nine sectors, guaranteeing that there are at least three interviews per sector. Although the overall number of interviews is lower than originally intended, we are confident that the information from these expert

interviews provides a reliable picture of party patronage in Austria today. In particular, it should be stressed that the answers of the individual interviewees within each sector are highly convergent. It is thus very unlikely that adding more interviews would alter the picture significantly.

5. The exception is the media sector, which does not have its own ministry. Instead, the small central administration of this sector is attached to the Chancellor's Office. Since December 2008, with the accession of the government under Chancellor Faymann, the media portfolio is held by a junior minister. His administrative staff is concentrated on the Ministerial Cabinet and comprises four employees (source: website of the Chancellor's Office, accessed on 9 April 2010).
6. Source: websites of the federal ministries involved in our study (accessed on 7 April 2010). The count does not include administrative staff. If we add administrative staff, the number of employees is almost twice as high.
7. Apart from the personal styles of different ministers, there are two ministries with a certain tradition of appointing not only partisans but also independents to senior official positions. This is true for the Ministry of Justice because this ministry has often been headed by independent ministers. Likewise, there is a rather strong group of independents within the Ministry of Foreign Affairs (the so-called *Gruppe Ballhausplatz*), which is also represented at the level of senior official positions.
8. This practice was already observed by Müller, Philipp, and Steininger (1996: 107) in the mid-1990s. Our interviews confirm that civil service trade unions and employee representatives still play a key role in keeping track of suitable candidates and ensuring that selection committees recommend them for appointment.
9. Since the FFG is not supervised by the Research Ministry, but primarily by the Ministry of Transport, we did not include it in our study. The non-departmental agencies in research and education thus only comprise the FWF and the Study Grant Authority, both of which are largely independent of party politics. As a consequence, this is the only type of institution in any of our nine sectors that can be considered free of party political appointments. Had we included the FFG, the situation would have been different.
10. Given that Austria is a federal state with nine provinces, we decided to represent the level of Regional and Local Administration by a case study on party patronage in one province: Lower Austria. Lower Austria is the province with the largest territory and the second largest population in Austria. While Vienna, the province with the largest population, has a rather untypical administrative structure because it is a city province, Lower Austria, like most other provinces, is a territorial province with both urban and rural areas. It is also typical for other provinces in that it is marked by a system of proportional party government. The Lower Austrian government is made up of representatives from all parties that have a certain share of seats in the provincial parliament. The number of members in the

provincial government is determined by the relative strength of parties in the provincial parliament. At the time of writing, the Lower Austrian government consisted of six representatives of the People's Party, including the governor (*Landeshauptmann*), two representatives of the Social Democratic Party, and one representative of the Freedom Party.

11. Note that appointments in public schools—which are of considerable strategic importance for Austrian political parties to be able to influence (or thwart) efforts to reform the Austrian schooling system—cannot be influenced by the Federal Ministry for Education, but are in the hands of provincial governors.

CHAPTER 4

'A Tradition We Don't Mess With': Party Patronage in Bulgaria

Maria Spirova

INTRODUCTION

It seems that little has changed in Bulgarian party politics since the beginning of the modern Bulgarian state.[1] Richard Crampton has described the fledgling political parties in Bulgaria in the late 1800s as 'little more than hunting packs in pursuit of patronage' (Crampton, 1987: 40). In 2005, the European Commission observed that Bulgaria was yet to clarify 'the division of responsibilities between the political and administrative levels of the public administration' (European Commission, 2005: 7). The story in between is not much different. Historical accounts describe the extensive party patronage practices of governing parties before the Second World War, accompanied by weak and fragmented parties and a strong royal figure. After the communist takeover of power, this trend found its logical and utmost perfection in the *nomenklatura* system of the Bulgarian Communist Party, which was the perfect example of a complete marriage of party and state. As a result, while democracy brought multiple parties and real contestation of power, it did little to curb the tradition of packing public administration with party supporters.

This chapter starts by situating the contemporary practice of party patronage in the context of the communist legacy and party politics in Bulgaria, and the status of the civil service in the country. It then proceeds to describe the extent and nature of patronage appointments in the 2005–7 period, and to investigate the motivations behind this and the consequences it has for party government in Bulgaria. The main argument of the chapter is that party patronage continues to be highly relevant for the functioning of parties in the country, and that, unlike in most other European countries, it still maintains a somewhat higher function as a reward for party members and activists. While external factors such as the European Union (EU) integration process and NATO membership have managed to constrain the freedom of parties to engage in patronage somewhat, it remains an important organizational resource for contemporary Bulgarian political parties.

POLITICAL PARTIES IN BULGARIA

The Bulgarian party system developed in a polarized environment for most of the 1990s, with the successor of the Bulgarian Communist Party—the Bulgarian Socialist Party (BSP)—and the opposition Union of Democratic Forces (SDS) on the extreme ends of the political spectrum. Founded in 1989 as a single political entity, within which eleven diverse parties maintained separate organizations, the SDS proved fissiparous and soon began to experience a chronic factionalism. A number of smaller political parties struggled for survival between these two poles, the most important of which was the Movement for Rights and Freedoms (DPS), a de facto ethnic party representing the relatively well-mobilized Turkish minority in the country.

The 2001 elections transformed the bipolar nature of the Bulgarian party system with the successful entry of a major new contender, the National Movement Simeon the Second (NDSV). The increasing pluralism of the party system was evident in the results of the 2005 elections, which sent seven parties to parliament and created the most fragmented political situation in the sixteen-year history of Bulgarian democracy, including three new parties and alliances.

By 2006–7, when this research was conducted, only the BSP and DPS appeared to have stable electoral bases and clear links to specific sectors of Bulgarian society. Factionalism and fractionalization continued to plague the rest; at the May 2007 elections for the European Parliament and local elections in October, yet another 'populist party', Citizens for the European Development of Bulgaria (GERB), emerged as a major—and successful—contender for power.

Organizationally as well, the BSP and the DPS maintained a stable and relatively high number of members while the other parties' organizational trends fluctuated substantially. With over 190,000 members, the BSP is the biggest party in the country (membership-wise) and about 26 per cent of its voters are also party members. Similarly, the DPS reports a little fewer than 100,000 members, with 16 per cent of its votes coming from members. The rest of the parties have far fewer members, and while the country as a whole maintains a relatively high indicator of party membership—it is just below the mean and well above the median among the twenty-seven EU countries according to van Biezen, Mair, and Poguntke (2009)—the same study also reports a downward trend in party membership in the country since the early 2000s. The period under investigation was thus characterized by a fragmented party system and individual parties faced with declining membership and loosening links with society.

THE CIVIL SERVICE IN BULGARIA

For most of the 1990s, the state administration in Bulgaria did not enjoy the protection of a special status. Appointments in the ministries and state agencies were governed by the regular Labour Code, which allowed for people to be replaced relatively easily when the need arose. Reform of the civil service, including the introduction of protection from politicization, did not begin until the late 1990s. Just as in other post-communist countries such as the Czech Republic, the reformers of the early 1990s did not consider the institution of an independent civil service among the priorities of democratization. If anything, as argued earlier, politicization was desirable. As a result, legislation regulating the civil service had to wait until 1998–9 to be passed in Bulgaria (DPADM and DESA, 2003). The adoption of this legislation happened, in fact, under the substantial influence of the European Union, which encouraged the reform of the civil service as a preparation for entry (Dimitrova, 2005).

The Bulgarian Law on the State Administration (LSA) and Law on the Civil Servant (LCS) provide for the continuity, professionalism, and political independence of the civil service. Passed by parliament in 1998 and 1999 respectively, they were the first major effort to change the nature and organizational principle of the state bureaucracy, which had been 'frozen' since the 1960s (Georgiev, 1999). The LSA established the structure and basic principles of the Bulgarian executive, defined its functions, and delineated the hierarchy of its positions (Velinova, Bozhidarova, and Kolcheva, 2001). The main goal of the law was to ensure 'vertical and horizontal coherence', a feature that had been lacking until then (Shoylekova, 2004). The LCS established the category of civil servants, and defined their functions and the mechanisms for their selection and dismissal, with the goal of establishing a stable and continuous civil service that was not subject to the whims of the parties in power. The LCS separates civil servants from two other groups within the state administration: political positions and positions regulated by the Labour Code (Georgiev, 1999). The positions that carry out supportive, security, and auxiliary services in the central, regional, and municipal administration are appointed on a basis regulated by the Labour Code and are governed by its regulations.[2]

There is a level of the public administration that is 'political' by law, and the positions within it can thus be considered patronage appointments by default. In Bulgaria, political positions include: the prime minister, deputy prime minister, ministers, deputy ministers and members of their political cabinets, regional governors, and deputy regional governors. These can be appointed and dismissed relatively easily. In an amendment that was clearly implemented to allow for party appointments, the directors of agencies attached to the Council of Ministers were also transferred into political positions in 2001 (Dimitrova, 2002: 185).

It is, of course, difficult to provide an estimate of all positions that this book considers to be potentially patronage positions. As we have defined it, this will include not only the positions which are part of the state administration, including the various ministries, agencies, councils, regional and municipal administrative bodies, but also the employees of state-owned companies, schools, hospitals, museums, theatres, etc. as well as the personnel of the Bulgarian Army, the Bulgarian Police, and other similar services. While numbers for these groups are difficult to come by, the numbers for the state administration are relatively easily accessible.

During 2005–7, which is the period that concerns us here, there were between 90,505 (in 2005), 86,961 (in 2006) and 91,265 (in 2007) employees of the state administration. This number includes all ministries, agencies, councils, and regional and municipal administration as well as the regional and municipal branches of ministries and other national bodies (MDAAR, 2006 and 2007).[3] This represents about 3 per cent of all employment in the country. When all other public sector positions (such as, for example, the employees of the health care, welfare and education systems) are added, public employment in Bulgaria is about 21 per cent of the total employment, or about 680,000 people.

PARTY PATRONAGE IN BULGARIA

The political parties in democratic Bulgaria thus emerged in a polity heavily dominated by the traditions and practices of the Bulgarian Communist Party (BCP) and its successor. The BCP had, in fact, maintained a very well-developed and extensive patronage system through the *nomenklatura* system, basically a database of people who were pre-approved to be appointed to positions within the state structures.[4] And, in fact, the management and leadership positions not only in the state institutions, but also in the economy, the education and health care systems, social services, and cultural intuitions, which were all state-owned and/or operated, were distributed through this system of party patronage par excellence.

As a consequence, when multiple parties emerged and competed for control of the state, they maintained similar practices. In fact, replacing the 'old-timers'— including people in various state institutions such as ministries, schools, and hospitals—became part of the democratization process. The first non-BSP government, the Dimitrov cabinet of 1991–2, began to carry out sweeping personnel changes as part of its 'decommunization campaign': for example, it replaced 260, or about half, of the employees in the Council of Ministers, and 320 employees in the Ministry of Foreign Affairs (Dimitrov, Goetz, and Wollmann, 2006: 183). However, the government was short-lived and this trend could not reach all levels of the state institutions. As the next few cabinets were still either overtly or covertly supported by the Bulgarian Socialists (BSP), the changes they carried out were limited mostly to reverting some of the appointments of the Dimitrov cabinet. When the Union of Democratic Forces (SDS) came to power decisively in 1997, it proceeded to make larger scale replacements in the state structures. In an effort to introduce stronger reforms in all spheres of government, long-term members of the bureaucracy were replaced with younger people with a commitment to reform. The SDS, according to one of our respondents, could not 'implement new policies with old people'.

Party patronage also became useful in terms of attracting members and activists. In the times of economic troubles and insecurity of the early 1990s, positions in the state institutions continued to be desirable, as they provided at least the potential for job security, and thus parties could promise to reward members with such positions. Patronage thus became a necessary element of both reforming the state and building new parties.

The government analysed by this research was a coalition of the BSP, DPS, and NDSV, which in 2005 replaced the NDSV–DPS coalition of the previous period. We expected to find high levels of patronage, not only as part of the tradition of party appointments in Bulgaria, but also because the Socialist Party was the major partner in the coalition and it was, after eight years in opposition, eager to take advantage of its position of power and provide its members and activists with positions at all levels.

The extent of patronage in Bulgaria

Party patronage in Bulgaria, indeed, appears to be extensive: the index of party patronage for the country overall is 0.42. Patronage also appears to be more broad than deep and to be focused mostly in the ministries. The values of the index of party patronage are presented in Table 4.1.

TABLE 4.1 *The index of party patronage in Bulgaria*

Bulgaria	Ministries	NDACs	Executing institutions	Policy area total
Economy	0.67	0.33	0.33	0.44
Finance	0.33	0.50	0.28	0.37
Judiciary	0.67	0.33	0.00	0.33
Media	0.67	0.33	0.33	0.44
Military and Police	0.33	0.33	0.33	0.33
Health Care	0.67	0.44	0.33	0.48
Culture and Education	1.00	0.11	0.44	0.52
Foreign Service	0.67	0.33	0.69	0.56
Regional and Local Administration	0.50	0.33	0.11	0.31
Country total	0.61	0.34	0.32	0.42

In Bulgaria, positions in all ministries are subject to party appointments, but they are mostly limited to the top and middle-level positions. These trends are reflected in a value of 0.61 of our patronage index. Parties that come to power would, naturally, ordinarily replace the minister, deputy ministers, and their political cabinets. In many cases, however, they would also appoint a new permanent secretary of the ministry and replace heads of sections (directors) and, in some cases, people in typically civil service positions such as experts and deputy directors of departments. The ministries that appear to be least prone to suffer from party sweeps after every election are the Ministry of Finance and the Ministries of Defence and Internal Affairs. There, our evidence suggests that appointments happen exclusively at the top level. In the case of the Ministry of Finance, parties have been constrained in their attempt to appoint people to positions by two related factors. One is the centrality of financial reforms in the country and the risks involved in failing at them. Parties have been unwilling to be exclusively associated with control of the financial sector, and have sought to share this with others. In fact, in the 2005–9 Bulgarian government, the finance minister himself was not a party appointment, but an independent choice of the three coalition partners. Second, since 1997, because of the loans the state has taken, the Bulgarian financial sector has been under the close supervision of the International Monetary Fund, which has scrutinized most major decisions taken and policies implemented. As a result, even if parties displayed a desire to replace personnel beyond the legally sanctioned positions, they have had to account for these to this external body, making sweeping party patronage virtually impossible.

The second reason also applies to the Ministry of Defence, and thus partly explains the low levels of patronage in the Military and Police sector. The 1999 Bulgarian entry into NATO has, similarly, provided two constraints on patronage: on the one hand, the personnel of the Bulgarian Armed forces have been cut significantly as part of the military reform associated with NATO membership. And second, the presence of the external layer of authority has made blatant party appointments impossible.

In contrast, the ministries that are the most patronage-ridden are the ones of Culture, of Health Care, and of Welfare. There, parties often reach to the bottom levels to replace technical and service personnel such as secretaries, drivers, and cleaners. The explanation for this is, of course, partly the flip side of the above. These ministries are of little interest to any actors outside Bulgaria—the European Union, for example, has little regulation on social policy or culture policy—and, as a consequence, parties are left free to fill these ministries with their own appointees. Even domestically, they are not of such high policy relevance, making domestic scrutiny of party patronage within them less likely.

In sum, parties in Bulgaria are able to appoint people at the top and middle levels within the ministries, and very rarely reach to the bottom levels of personnel. To further support these observations, Figure 4.1 reports data from a survey conducted by the Bulgarian polling agency, MBMD, in late 2005 and early 2006

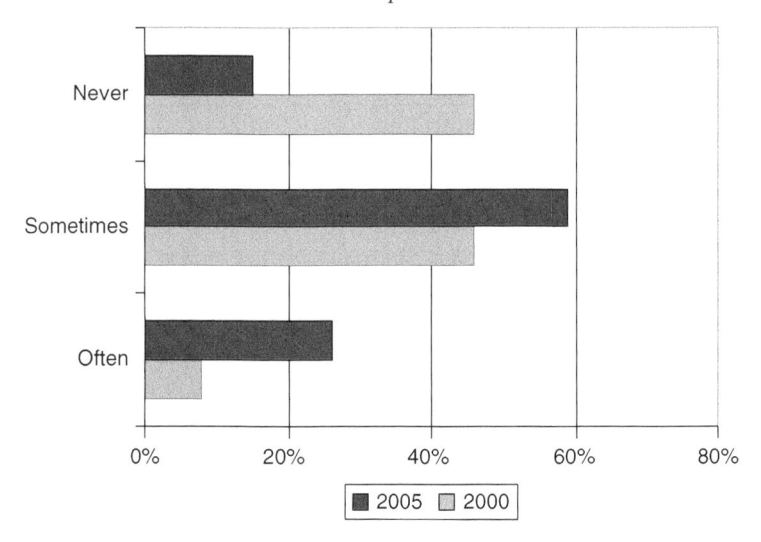

FIGURE 4.1 Percentage of respondents who believe that political appointments happen never, sometimes, and often in 2000 and 2005, in Bulgaria

Source: MBMD, 2005. Survey of the Bulgarian State Administration
<http://mbmd.net/AnonymousActivityPage?param=78cdf2495f4cd92024a61bce5b279ee2>

among a representative sample (N of 922) of the Bulgarian civil service. The data compares answers to the question 'Do you believe that political appointments in the state administration happen often/sometimes/never?' from the 2005 survey to a similar survey conducted in 2000. As the data indicate, in 2005 more than a quarter of the Bulgarian civil service employees believed that political appointments happened often, compared to only 8 per cent who believed so five years before. Only about 15 per cent believed that political appointments did not happen, a decrease from 46 per cent in 2000. Finally, the percentage of respondents who believed that patronage only sometimes reached the state administration had increased from 46 to 59 per cent. Even accounting for accumulation over time, these findings point to the presence of a substantial level of political intervention in personnel decisions among the civil service in 2005.

The second area in which we explore the ability and practice of party patronage is in the institutions that we call NDACs or non-departmental agencies and commissions. These include institutions that are not part of the ministerial structures and have regulatory and consultative functions within each policy area.

The appointment procedures in the ministries are relatively straightforward and easily attributable to political parties—presidents appoint ministers and their deputies, and the latter appoint within the ministries. Appointment procedures in the non-departmental agencies and commissions are not as straightforward, although they are somewhat similar. The leadership positions of most agencies are usually appointed either by the respective minister or the prime minister. These positions in Bulgaria are not part of the civil service, but political. These openly political appointments are thus usually party patronage positions by default, while the people appointed to them are entitled to appoint both the civil service and non-civil service positions in the agencies. In the cases where these positions are civil service, the link to the party in power is more difficult to trace, but even there they present clear opportunities for parties to place people. In the case of regulatory bodies, such as the Judicial Council or the Media Council, the appointment procedure is more complex as the members are appointed by different branches of the government or even by professional organizations. But even there, we can trace most of the appointments to the executive or the legislature, and thus to the political parties—and most often, specifically to the ones in power.

As the results in Table 4.1 suggest, NDACs in Bulgaria are freer of patronage than the ministries. Appointments in them happen, but in fewer institutions than in the core ministerial bureaucracy. They also do not reach as deep as in the ministries—even more so than there, appointments in the NDACs are limited to the top level employees and very rarely reach to the lower levels. The directors of agencies and their deputies are usually replaced following elections, and sometimes these are followed by some changes in positions lower down in the organization, but in general the agencies are not subjected to the wider sweeps that are common to the ministerial administrations.

In terms of sectoral variation, the agencies that are freer of party reach are the ones that belong to the sectors of minor importance. The Culture and Education sector, for example, or rather some of its agencies—such as the National Pedagogical Centre, the Executive Agency 'Academica', or the Executive Agency for Drivers' Education—are neither important for the policy-making process, nor do they distribute large amounts of funds. Parties do not seem to be as interested in appointing in them as they are, for example, in the National Revenue Agency or the Financial Supervision Commission of the Finance sector.

The third institutional area included in the analysis is what we have termed executing institutions. Examples of these institutions include: state-owned companies, national financial institutions, the embassies and consulates, hospitals and schools, museums, and similar state-run entities. The appointment procedures in these institutions still linked to the parties in power, although that link is somewhat weaker. The directors or other top management positions are usually directly appointed by a political figure—such as ministers or mayors, but the positions below them are under the directors' prerogative. In addition, the boards of directors, or boards of supervisors of these bodies are also usually appointed by a linked to the party figure. The boards of directors of state-owned companies, for example, are appointed directly by the respective minister, and as such, expectedly, are subject to party patronage.

Our data indicate that the extent of patronage in the executing institutions as a whole is not as high as in the ministries, but it is pretty close to that in the NDACs:

the index of party patronage for this institutional area is 0.32. Overall, given how removed these institutions are from the seats of political power, this reveals a pretty extensive practice of patronage. The disaggregated data show that a lot of the top-level employees are replaced following a change in power. For example, most directors of hospitals and the members of their boards are replaced, but some highly specialized hospitals are not subject to party appointments because of their high professional and public profile. These include, for example, the Hospital for Emergency Medicine in Sofia. This trend is similar in most sectors. In the state-owned companies, the top management and the boards of directors are usually replaced, as are the chairmen of the national financial institutions, the national theatres, drug commission, and the like. Overall, however, the practice is both narrower and shallower than in the core ministerial bureaucracy or the NDACs. The executing institutions of the judiciary—the courts—seem to be the most devoid of patronage, while the embassies and consulates appear the most reachable by parties, both in terms of the range and depth of appointments.

Overall, party patronage in Bulgaria is extensive: it reaches most of the institutions of the state and reaches quite far down into the ranks of the employees. This is true particularly in the ministerial bureaucracy. Given that there is a law protecting the civil service from arbitrary replacements, the question 'how is this possible?' begs an answer. First of all, personnel changes are often done in a way that does not violate the law. For example, new governments can easily restructure ministries and agencies to eliminate certain positions and create new ones. Toshkov (2003) has described in detail the extensive organizational reshuffles of the Bulgarian ministries and agencies during 1990–2003. While his account does not particularly deal with the personnel changes, it does provide enough evidence to argue that political power allowed the party in power an almost free rein in changing the structures of the Bulgarian executive, including its human resources. Interestingly, he finds a similar core of stable ministries—Interior, Foreign Affairs, Defence, and Justice—that roughly corresponds to the most patronage-free ministries included in our study. In short, people are often not openly fired so new people can be hired in their positions, but their positions are made redundant in a restructuring exercise and the new positions are filled with new appointees. A good example of using restructuring for the creation of new jobs during the period we investigate was the newly created Ministry of State Administration. Officially justified by the need to build a strong bureaucracy because of the EU accession process, according to media reports, the ministry was created specifically to allow for the three parties' demands for positions to be satisfied. Not only did this lead to the deputy minister scandal discussed in footnote 9, but it also created 140 new staff positions, which were filled by the coalition partners (Stanev, 2005).

In addition, patronage appointments can fill vacancies created by purposeful bad evaluations of an employee's performance; by encouraging employees to resign on the urging of somebody at ministerial level; dismissal of employees for violations of the LCS such as participation in the board of a private company or

Party Patronage in Bulgaria 63

tarnishing the image of the state institution; and finally, and most rarely, by transferring an employee to an out-of-country position (*Kapital*, 2006). In fact, some of these actions clearly violate the Civil Service Law. According to media reports, there have been numerous court cases which more often than not reinstall the plaintiffs at their old or similar positions, in many cases leading to the creation of additional staff positions to accommodate both them and the appointees who have already replaced them (*Kapital*, 2006).

The motivations for patronage

In Bulgaria, the motivations behind patronage appointments include, clearly, both the desire to reward loyal members and activists and to control the state and semi-state institutions (Figure 4.2). Overall, 40.5 per cent of our respondents pointed to control as the single dominant motivation, while almost the same proportion (37.8 per cent) thought parties appointed both to reward and control, and about 13 per cent attributed the desire to appoint exclusively to rewarding members. About 8 per cent saw a different motivation as guiding parties in appointing people. While there is some variation according to policy area and institutional location, the more important variation is by the level of appointments within each individual institution. In general, the most important positions—both in terms of substance and location—are motivated by the control function of patronage, while the lower positions are often given as rewards.

The interpretation of the reward motivation is straightforward. Parties in Bulgaria often face a strong demand for patronage from their members, especially in the countryside. As incomes outside the capital, Sofia, are substantially lower,

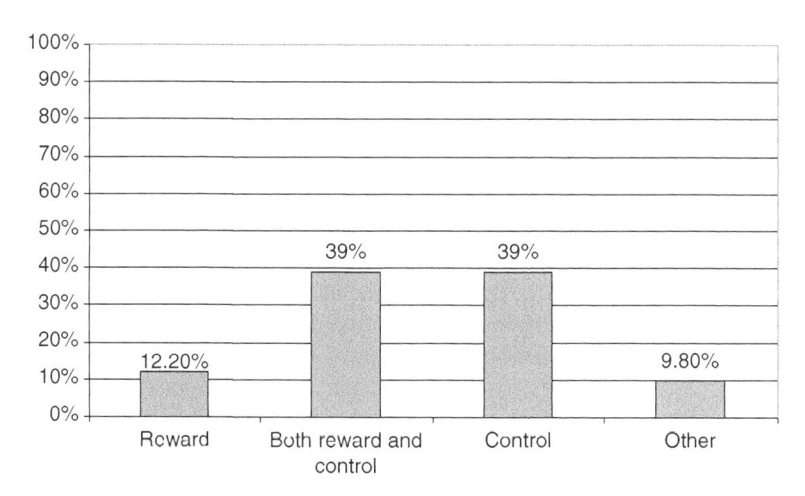

FIGURE 4.2 Motivations for party patronage in Bulgaria

jobs in various state institutions are economically attractive for party members. This was particularly true in the case of the Bulgarian Socialist Party, which has, of course, inherited a strong tradition of patronage from communist times. In addition, when the Socialists came to power in 2005, they had been in opposition for about eight years, which further whetted their appetite for patronage appointments. Finally, as they tend to appeal more to the lower income, rural electorate, their supporters and members also tend to be more likely to desire a position in the regional administration or other state institutions.

However, this is not to say that low-level positions are the only ones given out as rewards. Some high-levels ones—such as board membership in the state-owned companies, positions in the customs office or the agency of post-privatization control, and even certain non-crucial ambassadorships and other positions in the Foreign Service—are also subject to party appointments. In these cases, naturally, the appointees are higher ranking party leaders rather than rank and file members. In these cases again, however, the driving goal is to improve the personal economic situation of the party appointee.

While a lot of the patronage that happens in the Bulgarian state institutions is motivated by a desire to control them, the precise interpretation of what control entails is not as clear-cut. There are at least four control subtypes that are discernible: control of policy-making process, control of the content, control of economic power, and control of corruption.

Parties like to have people that they can trust in positions of authority in the state institutions so that they can trust them to carry out the policies formulated by the government. This position was particularly strong during the late 1990s, when the UDF government of 1997–2001 was faced with the need to carry out sweeping reforms in most of the policy sectors of the state. For these purposes, they also 'need their own people'. Patronage thus became part of the democratization reform in the country. While the 2005 government was not faced with such objectives, we find that situating people in various levels of the state administration so that they can ensure quick and effective policy implementation was a common motivation behind patronage appointments.

In addition, parties also often want to control the direct outputs of the state sector. What is being taught in the high schools in the country, for example, is of interest to the political parties because it has a direct impact on the political dynamics, as one of our interviewees argued. Similarly, the outputs of the state-owned media could be of great consequence in times of elections. Having loyal people in the leadership and governing bodies of Bulgarian national television and radio is seen a political benefit by the parties in Bulgaria.

Further, parties are interested in controlling the major decisions in the economic sectors—not only the state-owned one, but also in terms of regulating the private one. As a result, a lot of the positions in the agencies that regulate the economy—but also agriculture, transport, and infrastructure—were staffed with party appointees who could ensure that the important decisions were also taken with the economic interests of the political parties, or of private companies friendly to them, in mind.

Finally, some patronage appointments in various higher level positions are linked to corrupt practices. For example, membership on the Drug Board, or the commission that distributes radio frequencies in Bulgaria, is seen as a lucrative position because it allows control of access and thus opens the way to corrupt schemes of various kinds. According to one of our respondents, this practice is carried out to such extremes that the absence of accountability and transparency become goals in themselves.

Interestingly, though, parties are often motivated by an altogether other reason—building their own organizations when they disperse patronage. For the new parties this was a particularly powerful motivation, as they had to provide a benefit for their potential members. As the mode-setter in the party system was the Bulgarian Socialist Party, with its tradition of patronage, the newly founded parties had little option but to follow suit in their search for members and activists. The new political and party elites that emerged in Bulgaria are very much a result of this extensive process of state colonization by political parties.

This practice is very much in line with Panebianco's discussion of parties' providing selective incentives such as prestigious positions as a way of securing the elite's interest in preserving the party organization (Panebianco, 1988: 54). We distinguish between this motivation and the typical, classical reward motivation, as the party-building is forward-looking and promises to build loyalty on the condition of access to the state. In contrast, the classical reward function of patronage rewards past loyalty. It appears that in Bulgaria parties in some cases even headhunt—they locate people with good professional standing and then attempt to incorporate them in the party with promises of future powerful and lucrative appointments in the state structures. This practice has been particularly attributed to the Bulgarian Socialist Party and the Movement for Rights and Freedoms. In some cases, such recruitment attempts might be accompanied by expectations that the party appointee will contribute some proportion of their salary or other benefits to the party. The appointment of people in state structures thus becomes a party-building tool in both organizational and financial terms.

The nature of appointees

This picture of extensive patronage practices, driven by the parties' desire to both control the policy-making process and the state institutions and to reward loyal members, is further clarified if we look at what types of people get appointed by political parties. The data on which we base this discussion is presented in Figure 4.3.

Unlike trends in other countries, the political allegiance of the prospective appointees seems to be the most important condition for a person to be appointed

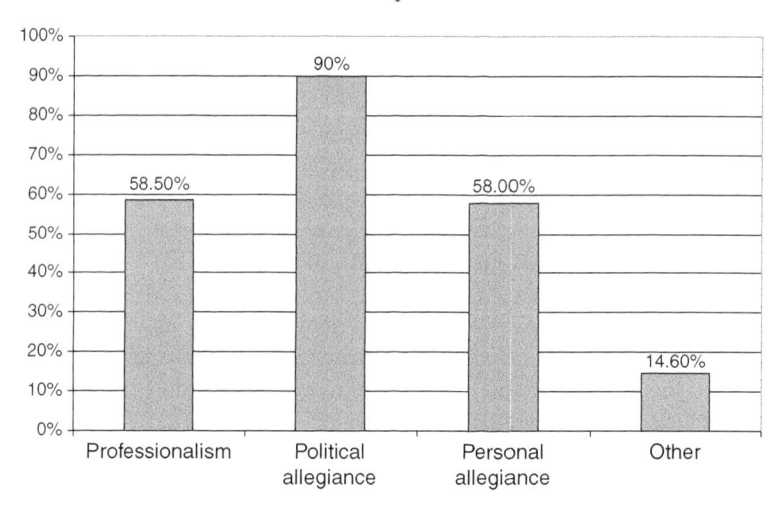

FIGURE 4.3 Qualifications of appointees in Bulgaria

in the state structures. In Bulgaria, jobs in the state administration that are distributed through the party patronage channels are secured through political allegiance. To be a party appointee in the ministries, various agencies, and councils, as well as in the executing institutions, one needs first and foremost to be loyal to the party in power. Party loyalty was given as a characteristic of appointees by more than 90 per cent of our respondents. Interestingly, this is the case for both high-level and lower level positions: at the high level, political allegiance to the party is linked to the appointees' ability to carry out the policy of the party in practice, while at the lower level it is a more of a function of to whom the jobs go. In other words, the party link serves the functions of the control function of patronage at the higher level of positions, and the reward one at the lower level. According to some of the respondents, appointees needed to be politically loyal, but also to lack ambition so that they would do what the 'party wants'.

In some ways linked to this is the low relevance of professional qualifications as a necessary characteristic of the appointees. Only about 60 per cent of our respondents thought that professional expertise played a role in selecting people for patronage appointments—or in other words, just under half of them thought that professionalism played no role in the selection of party appointees to the state structures. Not only is this worrying by itself, but the situation is even worse when we take into account that even when professionalism does play a role it is only as a complementary requirement to that of political allegiance. In the most interesting observation, professionalism was seen as a by-product of party appointments. As people come and go and then come again (as party appointees), they acquire an expertise in their specific sectors of work.

There do appear to be some trends of sectoral, temporal, and party variation. The Foreign Service, the Military and Police, and the Judiciary, for example, are the sectors where professionalism seems to play a real role: there, parties look for experts first, and party loyalists second. This trend has increased with the progress of European integration, which necessitated certain standards of expertise to be respected in the EU-relevant sectors. Finally, according to our respondents, the Bulgarian Socialist Party is the party particularly interested in developing a body of expert party appointees and is also the one that has the most extensive headhunting mechanisms. The Movement for Rights and Freedoms is, in contrast, the party least concerned with professionalism and expertise when making appointments.

In fact, individual allegiance to the appointers is reported to be of as high significance in party appointments as professionalism. About 60 per cent of our respondents thought that it was among the characteristics of the appointees. In some ways, it often proves as important as party links. In some cases, respondents argued, the two overlap as familial and local connections are often transformed into party ones so that one's relatives are also fellow party members. Finally, in Bulgaria other characteristics also play a role: about 15 per cent of the respondents reported one or another 'other' features as relevant in the party patronage game. For example, economic group interests often play a bigger role than political allegiance at local level. Absence of professionalism of any kind—or to put it in the respondents' words, 'mediocrity and fear of initiative'—can also help a person get appointed in the state institutions, while familial links also complement individual allegiances in some cases.

Party mechanisms of patronage

Parties play a key role in making patronage appointments in Bulgaria. As mentioned in the introduction, the country has a long history of a very close relationship between the state and the party, going back not only to the communist era, but even further to the early years of the modern Bulgarian state. As one of our respondents put it, 'patronage is a historical tradition and no party messes with it'. Parties in power feel entitled to take over the bureaucracy whether it is because they do not trust other minded people to execute their politics or because they want to secure jobs for their members and sympathizers. The extent to which parties do so differs only minimally: they all engage in the practice of patronage.

The parties do differ, however, in the manner through which they make the appointments. For example, the BSP has the most sophisticated and extensive mechanism for patronage practices, while in the DPS the process is most centralized, and in the NDSV the process is most subject to professional requirements. In all of the Bulgarian parties, however, the party chairman and the central office play probably a bigger role than in most of the other European democracies studied. As

Dimitrov, Goetz, and Wollmann (2006) have argued earlier, in Bulgaria it is the party chairman who calls the shots in the party. When the party is in power and the party chairman is also prime minister, his or her power extends also into the government of the country. However, unlike in other cases, it is the function of party chairman combined with that of prime minister that gives that person the legitimacy and authority to influence politics.

The patronage practices of the Socialist Party are characterized by several features. To begin with, they have a well-developed system of securing a large pool of potential appointees. This includes not only keeping track of the professional development of their members and activists, but also actively headhunting people from professional circles and universities and offering them a place in the party and promises of future posts in the state institutions. Further, the process of selecting appointees is subject to the intra-party dynamics. As the party has been made up of several distinct ideological and personal factions, the distribution of patronage is also subject to this struggle. For example, appointments in the Foreign Service were made by the presidential lobby in the party, while the Economic and Police sectors, for example, were dominated by the party factions of Rumen Ovcharov and Rumen Petkov.[5] Finally, positions at the local level are often controlled by the regional party headquarters, creating a clear divide between the more reward-oriented patronage of the local party leaders and the more policy-driven appointments of the national leadership.[6] As a result of these trends, the patronage appointments reflect the nature of the BSP and can be considered the product of the most diverse but also most strictly controlled party mechanism.

The patronage practices of the party of the Turkish minority are also party-controlled, but much more centralized around the leadership of the party chairman, Ahmed Dogan. Since the party is focused on recruiting and appointing individuals who are members of the minority, it uses a different strategy to ensure that it has enough people to place in the state structures. The DPS recruits young people from the Turkish minority and educates them in order to have its own pool of personnel. This practice is very much in line with the DPS' nature as an ethnic party and its well-disciplined and unified membership. Parallel to this, the distribution of positions is very much in the hands of the central party leadership and its chairman. This practice was, in fact, most pronounced in the agricultural sector, which, for cross-country comparison purposes was not included in our analysis. Since the majority of the Turkish minority is engaged in agriculture, the Ministry of Agriculture was given to the DPS in both the 2001–5 and the 2005–9 governments. The party proceeded to staff the ministry and its agencies, including offices such as the local forestry departments, with people who belong to the party and the minority, to the most extreme level. Appointments there reached far down into the ranks of the state administration and into most institutions. In fact, it was the possibilities that the patronage appointments created for the build-up of clienteles around the EU agricultural subsidies distributed by the ministry and the agencies that created the massive problems between Sofia and Brussels during 2007 and 2008 and led to the freeze on all funds for agricultural programmes for Bulgaria. For the purposes of the DPS, however, these extensive state–party links seem to have served their purpose: the membership of the party almost doubled during its time of governmental tenure (from 58,000 in 2003 to more than 95,000 in 2006), and by 2007 included about 12,000 ethnic Bulgarians as members, indicating that membership of the DPS was a pathway to a professional career (*Mediapool*, 2006; *Business Post*, 2007).

In the case of the NDSV, the party of the Bulgarian ex-monarch, which rose quickly to power in early 2001, the supply of patronage appointees was the biggest challenge to the party as it had not established party structures in the country. As a result, the recruitment of people to staff the state institutions was done ad hoc, which allowed, in fact, for professionalism to play a bigger role (at least in some cases), as prior experience became more significant than party membership. The choice of appointees remained, according to our respondents, not in the hands of the party chairman but in those of the informal party leader (at the time) and Bulgarian Prime Minister Simeon Saxe-Coburg-Gotha.

In the SDS, patronage appointments during its tenure in government (1997–2001) were coordinated in the National Council of the party, although Party Chairman Kostov also had a leading role in controlling them. As one of our respondents put it, 'the media commission in the party [SDS] was stronger and more influential than the media commission in the Parliament'.

Overall, Bulgarian parties keep a close check on who gets a job in the state institutions. They have developed different mechanisms for building a party pool of suitable individuals and maintaining this check. In some cases, these include quite extensive networks and methods (in the BSP and DPS), and in others appointments have been more ad hoc. However, the party influence has almost always been centred on the personality of the party leader and chairman, sometimes extending to the party leadership. What we do observe in Bulgaria, I would argue, is the dominance of the party over individual politicians in terms of controlling this process. However, this does not mean that individuals do not play an important role in the party. On the contrary, some of the Bulgarian parties are very heavily centred on a certain personality. However, to become a patronage appointee, one cannot just be a friend of a minister or the local party leader. Some form of party identity and allegiance seems to be a necessary condition for being appointed to the state apparatus.

'Winner takes all' patronage

While the Bulgarian survey did not include a particular question on the sharing of patronage appointments, our data allow for some observations. In the period that we studied (2005–9), Bulgaria was governed by a coalition government of three parties. Patronage appointments were distributed very strictly according to a formula that reflected the strength of each party in parliament.[7] With the exception of one ministerial position (Finance),[8] no positions were given to non-partisans or other parties.[9]

The way the top political positions were distributed among the coalition partners, while not particularly questionable from a party government point of view, was indicative of the trends in the whole administration. 228 'political' positions (including ministerial positions, deputy ministers, regional governors and their deputies, as well as the chairs of the parliamentary committees) were split up strictly among the three parties, with the ratio at all levels approximating 8:5:3 as closely as possible.[10]

The parties used various ingenious mechanisms to achieve the proportionality. For example, two ministries (Economy and Energy) were merged into one; one (Sport and Tourism) was downgraded into an agency, and one extra ministry (State Administration) was created (Klisurova, 2005). The number of deputy ministers was increased in a way that allowed the positions to be split according to the '8:5:3' ratio, or its reduced form, 3:2:1, and for the DPS to receive a deputy minister in every ministry (Litova and Klisurova, 2005). Similarly, the number of deputy regional governors was also increased. Overall, the distribution of appointments among the partners resulted in the creation of twenty new deputy ministerial positions and fifty-three new deputy gubernatorial positions (Stanev, 2005).

The positions of heads of agencies—twenty-three of them directly attached to the Council of Ministers and around forty under the jurisdiction of individual ministries—were also subjected to patronage appointments. As a result, the heads of around sixty-three agencies were up for grabs in the second stage of appointments distribution among the coalition partners in 2005. The difficulties of maintaining the balance of the coalition while preserving most of the NDSV and DPS appointees made these negotiations particularly acrimonious. In addition, some of these agencies—and the agency 'Customs' is a particularly good example—are subjected to 'many and diverse political and economic interests', making them extremely important to control (*Kapital*, 2005). Finally, the coalition partners laid claims to specialized agencies from the point of view of the sectoral interests of their electorates. The DPS, for example, whose electorate is mainly engaged in agriculture, sought to control most of the agencies with relevance to that sector. The distribution of these positions took about a month, and became symbolic of the emerging divisions among the coalition partners and their shared thirst for control of the state institutions.

As the 8:5:3 'principle' was part of the coalition agreement on which the cabinet was formed, it achieved a somewhat mythical status and its spirit was carried over into the positions in the civil service and local administrations as well. As the data reported earlier described, party appetites reached further and deeper than the formal structure allowed them to, while the opposition did not participate in the distribution of the appointments in any shape or form. Of course, as time went on, the parties themselves started to experience fragmentation, and some of the 'party' appointees, particularly those of the NDSV, became more 'opposition' appointees, but this was more of a function of the nature of Bulgarian parties than of the method of patronage distribution.

CONCLUSION

Overall, the practice of party patronage in Bulgaria is extensive. Parties feel entitled to replace people at various levels of the state institutions once they are in power. This practice has a long historical tradition in Bulgaria: since their establishment in the late nineteenth century, Bulgarian parties have always seen patronage as one of the legitimate benefits of being in power. This historical trend has, if anything, only been reinforced by the post-1989 democratization process, when the need to replace the old bureaucracy with a new, reform-oriented one was popularly accepted as part of the rebirth of Bulgarian democracy.

This trend has hardly been circumscribed by any legal means. The principle of an independent bureaucracy is still fighting its way into the Bulgarian political reasoning. While legislation to reform the state administration and introduce a unified civil service was introduced in the late 1990s, it has achieved limited success in ensuring the permanency of the central ministerial bureaucracy and other civil servants. Whether to ensure smooth policy implementation, to get the rascals out, or to get jobs for 'our people', parties do reach into the state institutions to appoint individuals way beyond what is formally allowed.

Nevertheless, an important constraint on this practice has been the European integration process. Not only has the EU been an important advocate for the reform of the state administration in the country, but it has also indirectly intervened to circumscribe the practice of patronage in particular policy areas. By requiring professional and transparent policy-implementation processes, Brussels has managed to limit the free rein of political parties to appoint with no respect to due process, at least partially. This trend is mostly visible in policy areas such as Finance and Military and Police.

Constraining patronage has proven difficult, however, not only because it is part of the historical tradition, but also because, for the Bulgarian parties emerging in the early 1990s and 2000s, access to state jobs became a valuable tool for attracting and keeping members. Some of the Bulgarian parties actively headhunt and attract partisans with promises for secure, even if badly paid, jobs. Patronage appointments, at least during the 2005–9 period, provided further access to channels for clientelism and corruption for the political parties. Control of major decision-making positions led to control of funds distribution and other similar benefits, a problem that became widely acknowledged and reflected in the EU's treatment of Bulgaria in 2007–8.[11]

This extensive rent-seeking became problematic for the parties from an electoral standpoint. The three-party coalition was voted out of office decisively in 2009 and replaced by a minority government of a newly founded party, GERB, which focused its electoral campaign on fighting the evils of the BSP–NDSV–DPS coalition, and particularly their corruption, clientelism, and patronage. Of the three parties, only the DPS managed to maintain its seats in parliament, while the other two suffered major losses. Thus, it appears that, from the standpoint of the individual parties, the patronage circus of the last few years had proven counterproductive and in the case of the NDSV, suicidal.

NOTES

1. I would like to thank all my Bulgarian colleagues who participated in this survey and, in particular, Rumyana Kolarova for her invaluable help in the set-up of the fieldwork.
2. The political positions are also formally appointed as Labour Code positions.
3. There were several parallel trends of development in the numbers employed in the state administration during this period. One was the general attempt to decrease the number of employees in the bloated state administration inherited from the communist regime. However, at the same time, new positions, and in some cases new institutions, had to be created in order to accommodate the increased volume of work related to EU accession. Finally, as decentralization accelerated during the early 2000s, and more governmental functions were transferred to the regional and municipal governments, there was a transfer of personnel within the state administration as well. Thus, all in all, the number of positions to be distributed remained relatively stable, with about 5 per cent yearly changes in each direction (MDAAR, 2006 and 2008).
4. For a detailed discussion of the patronage systems in communist times, see Georgiev (2008: 68–75).
5. On the Bulgarian Socialist Party, see Spirova (2008).
6. Indicative of the divisions in the BSP in relation to the practice of patronage, in his address to the 46th Congress of the Bulgarian Socialist Party, held in December 2005, Prime Minister and Party Chairman Stanishev warned his 'comrades' that they should not expect the party to reward them by giving them jobs in the administration of the state, because a state 'should not be run with politically loyal staff but with professional people' (Stanishev, 2005).
7. The BSP–NDSV–DPS coalition was in control of 70 per cent of the seats in parliament. Of these 171 seats, 82 (or 48 per cent) were controlled by the BSP, 53 (or 30 per cent) belonged to the NDSV, and 34 (or about 20 per cent) were controlled by the DPS. The 8:5:3 ratio thus reflects pretty strictly this distribution.

8. The positions in the financial sector, as already indicated, were also subject to the most limited party interests.
9. The exceptions were, of course, the parties that were part of the BSP electoral alliance. The Socialist Party has a long tradition of forming broad alliances with 'centre-left' parties of different natures—including social democratic, green, ethnic Roma, and patriotic parties. The number of alliance members has ranged from a low of five (in 1997) to a high of nineteen (in 2001). At the 2005 elections, the BSP's electoral alliance had eight members whose demands for patronage appointments had to be satisfied. As a result, some of the deputy ministerial positions were 'given' to the BSP alliance partners: two of the deputy ministers in the Ministry of State Administration, for example, came from two separate allies of the BSP (Trifonova, 2005). Although the Bulgarian Social Democrats and the Bulgarian Communist Party had demanded these positions, they had trouble filling them with qualified members. The appointment of Ms Bozhka Lukic, reportedly a hairdresser with a questionable university education, to the position of deputy minister became symbolic of the 'unprincipled deals [struck] for the distribution of positions among members of the governmental coalition' (Trifonova, 2005). Similar problems of expertise put the reasoning behind the appointment of several other deputy prime ministers into question as well.
10. The BSP got 46 per cent, the NDSV got about 31 per cent, and the DPS around 22 per cent of the political positions (Litova and Klisurova, 2005).
11. For a discussion of this treatment, see Spirova 2009.

CHAPTER 5

Give Me *Trafika*: Party Patronage in the Czech Republic

Petr Kopecký

Countries have their own distinct popular discourse and terms when it comes to patronage.[1] In the Czech Republic, there are two expressions that are popularly used to refer to it: *trafika* and *klientelismus*. *Trafika* is literally a small stand or kiosk that sells newspapers, cigarettes, and other small goods. Under the Austro-Hungarian Empire, when the state held a monopoly on the sales of tobacco products, licences to run these small shops were given to the war veterans to reward them for their services to the Empire. Following the First World War, the newly established Czech Republic (then Czechoslovakia) carried over these Empire practices to reward its own disabled war veterans. In its more contemporary popular incarnation, *trafika* denotes a practice of handing out state jobs to politicians for their services in political life. These jobs include lucrative positions in the executive bodies of state-controlled companies, usually provided to ex-ministers or important party donors. But they can also involve less demanding positions in public administration, for example some of the ambassadorial posts, handed out to prominent party activists or party faithfuls. Given the focus on appointments in this volume, the popular term used by the Czechs then obviously comes very close to its subject matter.

Klientelismus is popularly used with reference to practices of collusion between politicians or bureaucrats on the one hand, and (economic) lobby groups on the other hand, in which the objects of exchange are usually state contracts, handed out for individual monetary gains. *Klientelismus* is, in that sense, just another popular term for corruption and, as such, is seemingly less relevant for this chapter and the book than the phenomenon of *trafika*. However, there is no proper understanding of Czech patronage without at least some understanding of *klientelismus*. For clientelistic networks are widely seen as being cemented by dubious political appointments whereby, for example, lobby groups force politicians to appoint their own particular person in the state, or when politicians systematically place appointees in institutions to cover up their personal, or their party's, questionable practices. Under the communist regime, similar clientelistic elite networks were referred to as *nomenklatura*: a hierarchical system of privileged classes instituted and managed by communist parties on the basis of political criteria.

The central argument of this chapter is that popular discourses overestimate the weight of *trafika* and, perhaps to a lesser degree, also that of *klientelismus* in Czech politics. I will demonstrate that party patronage in the Czech Republic is neither particularly pervasive nor predominantly supposed to reward partisans with state jobs. I will do so by first outlining the key features of the Czech parties and party systems, as well as those of the country's civil service. This background section will be followed by detailed considerations of scale and depth, motivations for party patronage practices, as well the intra and interparty dynamics of this phenomenon. The conclusion also explores the implications of the observed patterns of patronage for our understanding of party and party government performance in the country.

PARTIES AND THE PARTY SYSTEM

More than two decades after the momentous events of 1989, the relevance of political parties for the Czech political system can be little doubted. Overall, if one examines the functioning of democracy in the country, the political party—in all relevant aspects—is an important variable to look at. Czech politicians and their parties have gradually been able to impose a party government order on society; there is consequently relatively little independent political authority exercised beyond the party reach (see Kopecký, 2006b; 2007). The Czech party system—best characterized as moderate pluralism (see, e.g. Toole, 2000; Hloušek, 2010)—is also generally seen as one of the most stable in the post-communist region (e.g. Deegan-Krause and Haughton, 2010).

The origins of the Czech party system date back to the early 1990s in Federal Czechoslovakia, when the electorally dominant but ideologically diverse opposition movement—Civic Forum (OF) in the Czech Republic and the Public against Violence in Slovakia—started to disintegrate into a number of distinct parties. It was at that time that, in the Czech part of the Federation, the now dominant Left–Right divide started to crystallize and replace an amorphous cultural conflict centred on the communist/non-communist divide. The elite which eventually seized power in OF formed around a group of liberal economic technocrats, led by the founder of the Civic Democratic Party (ODS), Václav Klaus, who largely succeeded in framing the social and political conflict in terms of a struggle for allocation of economic resources. Several studies show that party system competition in the Czech Republic is of a one-dimensional nature, with the dominant conflict consistently structured along a socio-economic dimension (Huber and Inglehart, 1995; Markowski, 1997; Evans and Whitefield, 1998; Kitschelt et al., 1999).

The one-dimensional nature of party competition does not mean that the same parties have represented the dominant socio-economic conflict. There have been changes, sometimes quite dramatic, in the electoral fortunes of individual parties, as well as several splits and mergers between political parties. However, the fragmentation of parties has gradually decreased. Now the same parties are accounting for the largest share of votes. The Czech parties have also eventually come to coalesce into two blocks, with ODS being the main party on the right, and the Czech Social Democratic Party (ČSSD) the key player on the left. Two other parties, both with long organizational histories dating back to the pre-communist times, have also been the mainstays on the political scene: the Communist Party of Bohemia and Moravia (KSČM) on the left, and the centrist Christian Democratic Union—the People's Party (KDU-ČSL). Indeed, it is only the numerically rather small conservative right which, though consistently represented in the parliament by various formations (since the 2010 elections by TOP09), has seen major organizational instabilities and discontinuities. The same applies to the Greens (SZ), which were part of the governing coalition at the time the research for this chapter was carried out.

The relative stability of the Czech parties and party systems is, to a very large extent, institutionally induced. Much like in the rest of Eastern Europe, the anchoring of Czech parties within society is relatively weak. The precise nature of the weak social roots of the parties has been documented elsewhere and need not concern us in great detail here (see, e.g. van Biezen, 2003). Suffice it to say that it can be seen in a variety of indicators, such as relatively low levels of party identification and party attachments among voters, modest numbers of party members, continuing popular disdain towards parties, low voter turnout, and weak links between parties and collateral organizations. Even taking into account some important cross-party variation, these indicators all point in the same direction across the entire party spectrum.

Much in contrast to this weakness on the ground stands Czech parties' procedural strength or, in other words, their strong position within the institutions. If one looks closely at the two decades of democratization in the country, the intentions of the political elites to manipulate the institutional structures to reduce the uncertainty of the environment in which their parties reign are striking. The numerous modifications to constitutional, electoral, parliamentary, and other legal norms since 1992 show a rather consistent trend to adopt rules conferring to parties a leading institutional position and, within these rules, a trend to adopt institutional devices which protect the privileges of the established parties against potential newcomers. The bickering around the adoption of new civil service regulations, to which I will turn below, is just one example of such institutional engineering; the other relevant examples include a very generous system of state party financing (e.g. Krnáčová, 2006), and a strong version of proportional representation (PR) in the electoral system (e.g. Kopecký, 2004). Taken together, the institutional structures of the Czech state provide for a system where party strength plays a crucial role, and where parties, as opposed to individual politicians or other organizations, are the principal managers of the governmental and administrative structure.

The fact that KSČM is considered a party with no coalition potential, together with relatively modest vote/seat shares of the election winning party (either ODS or ČSSD), has often made it difficult to form and sustain governments. The governments are nearly always either coalitions of three parties (ODS, KDU-ČSL, and the Greens (SZ) at the time of this research) or single-party minority governments; they tend to have fragile support in parliament and often unite partners with weak policy connections. This has brought the country a series of unstable governments, somewhat paradoxical considering the relative stability of the party system itself. What is relevant in the context of this chapter, however, is the fact that, as a result of the governmental instability, none of the Czech parties or coalitions of parties has enjoyed a sustained period in office. In that sense, none of the relevant political actors, perhaps with the exception of the centrist KDU-ČSL, which has played a pivotal role in most post-communist governments, has had an opportunity to develop a monopoly on government, its ministries or any other state institutions.

CIVIL SERVICE TRADITION

To understand the current civil service, and in particular the lack of specific civil service code or legislation, one has to appreciate the changes brought to the organization of the state by the communist regime shortly after its inception in the post-Second World War period. The communists, who came to power in 1948, first revolutionarily purged the state in order to strip it of its worst 'class enemies', and then gradually moulded the state apparatus to their liking by appointing new ideologically screened cadres into the administrative ranks. By doing so, the communists more or less completely destroyed the civil service system dating back to the Austro-Hungarian Empire, of which the Czech lands were part until the establishment of the independent Czech(oslovak) state in 1918. The administrative structures under the communist regime were subordinated to the will of the ruling party, and the entire state apparatus became the instrument for implementing social and economic programmes according to the socialist blueprint. Importantly, getting a job in any significant position within the state required a 'clean political profile' and authorization by the communist party organs. Indeed, by establishing parallel party and administrative structures at all levels of state administration, and by subordinating the latter to the former, the communist elite and its *nomenklatura* possessed an effective mechanism of control over the administrative staff.

The legal pretext for a high level of political interference in the state administration was provided by the legislation implemented in 1966 (e.g. Kotchegura 2008). From that year, employment in ministries and other central state institutions became governed by the Labour Code, and thus no longer by special civil service legislation, as was the case during the First Republic (1918–39). The Labour Code abolished the distinction between public sector employees (like teachers, doctors, or factory workers) on the one hand, and civil servants on the other hand. This had effectively downgraded the special position and protection that civil servants had enjoyed under the imperial Civil Service Rules dating back to 1914.

The end result was not just a highly politicized administrative management of the state, but also a near complete erosion of the popular standing of bureaucracy in the eyes of the population. As a matter of fact, the state bureaucracy has probably never enjoyed a strong popular standing. Although the state itself was bureaucratized and administratively well developed even before the advent of the First Republic, the bureaucrats had always been seen in a bad light. Under the Austro-Hungarian Empire they were considered vassals in the service of foreign powers; after independence, they came to be seen as pedantic and unfriendly individuals, more loyal to their political masters than to the citizens that they were supposed to serve. Indeed, much of the best satire and prose coming from that period of time, including the works of Karel Havlíček Borovský, Franz Kafka, or Jaroslav Hašek (with his *Good Soldier Švejk*), revolves around such bureaucratic characters. Needless to say, the communist period only further intensified popular distrust of the administration so that, by the time the authoritarian regime came to an end in the late 1980s, the state and its institutions were engulfed in a serious crisis of trust.

The post-communist Czech constitution, agreed upon in 1992, contains a provision for special civil service legislation. This might appear to signal a willingness of the post-communist elites to reform the state administration and restore public confidence in the institutions of state. However, more or less the identical Labour Code that had governed the civil service during the communist period has also been in use for over two decades of democracy. Consequently, Czech politicians enjoy a high level of discretion in appointment of personnel in the ministries; they can relatively easily initiate organizational restructuring of ministries; they also enjoy practically free hands in appointments to a vast majority of non-departmental agencies and commissions (NDACs), as well as to the majority of the executing institutions under state control.

Several successive governments in the 1990s promised to initiate new civil service legislation (e.g. Verheijen and Kotchegura, 2000; Meyer-Sahling, 2006a; Dimitrova, 2005). However, it was not until 2002 that a Civil Service Act was agreed upon in parliament. There were political parties, most notably the ČSSD, which had initially supported the administrative and bureaucratic reform. On balance, however, the new Civil Service Act was largely agreed because of pressure from the EU during the accession negotiations. The domestic political will to fundamentally reform the civil service is still largely lacking and, as a result, the 2002 Civil Service Act has been subject to numerous further amendments and, to the present day (the end of 2010), never enacted in practice.

There are numerous reasons for the reluctance of Czech politicians to implement the Act, which would have provided for a career-based civil service with its own employment, recruitment, and promotion procedures, and autonomy from politicians. Some of these relate to ideologically motivated differences in the visions for state management among the Czech political parties (see, e.g. Štička, 2006); however, reminiscent of popular attitudes, Czech politicians too share the deep-seated distrust of bureaucrats and their administrative competence. In the early 1990s, such attitudes were motivated by the association of the state administration and its staff with the previous regime; it resulted in rather chaotic personnel changes, especially in the army and the police, as well in the successive waves of organizational restructuring in many institutions. Somewhat ironically, as the party system has eventually evolved and settled into its current bipolar and heavily adversarial pattern of competition, politicians' distrust of administrative staff has possibly deepened even further. Few party leaders will nowadays perceive (top) civil servants and other state managers as 'old structures', a euphemism used to denote bureaucrats with communist service history. However, being appointed by and loyal to the previous government counts these days as a far more serious threat than having a communist past.

The size of the public administration itself has not changed too dramatically in the last two decades: according to the Czech Statistical Office, in 1995 there were about 277,000 people employed, of which about 125,000 were in central state administration (ministries and other central offices), and 66,000 in regional and local administration (the rest of the figure is mainly employment in social security). For relative measures, the country has a population of about 10.5 million people, of which about 4.8 million are economically active. In 2008, public administration counted nearly 295,000 employees, of which 105,000 worked in central and 88,000 in regional and local administration. The relative shift in size between central administration on the one hand, and regional/local on the other hand, in comparison with the mid-1990s can be attributed to the implementation of decentralization reforms in the early years of the twenty-first century.

EMPIRICAL ANALYSIS

It is arguable that a particular combination of organizationally and procedurally strong parties with an environment lacking—to borrow from Shefter (1994)—domestic 'constituency for bureaucratic autonomy', arguably constitutes a strong basis for potentially a vicious circle of politicization of the state. Party patronage can be expected to be relatively high in the Czech Republic because parties that were, from the outset of democratization, strongly positioned to make use of the state for their own purposes face relatively little legal and cultural constraints to actually doing so. Politicization of the Czech state is, in fact, routinely lamented by scholars (e.g Grzymala-Busse, 2003; O'Dwyer, 2006) and political analysts alike (e.g. Štička, 2006; Outrata, 2007). Apparently, *trafika* is a relevant phenomenon in this recently emerged democracy.

Scale and depth of party patronage

Table 5.1 presents the index of party patronage as reported in all the other chapters in this volume. In the comparative perspective (see the concluding chapter), the Czech Republic represents the European mean in terms of the scope and depth of party patronage, suggesting from the outset that politicization of the state is neither absent nor particularly pervasive. What becomes immediately striking when looking at the Czech data is a fairly uniform and consistent pattern of politicization in the ministries. The ministries in general are the subject of more party patronage than either the NDACs or the executing institutions. The ministries are, in other words, the most politicized type of institution within the Czech state, irrespective of the particular policy area. In practice, this means that top-level positions—certainly ministers, but also state secretaries (which are, somewhat confusingly, referred to in English translations of the Czech term as deputy ministers)—are practically all subject to political appointments.

Each ministry has about four to five deputy ministers. In addition, ministers form their own cabinets, staffed with up to seven advisers, which are also political appointees. They change routinely with the arrival of a new government, or even of just a new minister. The deputy ministers are also habitually replaced with cabinet changes; indeed, there is an unwritten rule that deputy minister positions

TABLE 5.1 *The index of party patronage in the Czech Republic*

Policy area	Ministries	NDACs	Executing institutions	Policy area total
Economy	0.67	0.22	0.22	0.37
Finance	0.67	0.22	0.00	0.30
Judiciary	0.67	0.33	0.11	0.37
Media	n/a	0.33	0.33	0.33
Military and Police	0.67	0.33	0.11	0.37
Health Care	0.67	0.11	0.11	0.30
Culture and Education	0.67	0.11	0.11	0.30
Foreign Service	0.67	0.00	0.11	0.39
Regional and Local Administration	0.67	0.33	0.17	0.39
Total	0.67	0.25	0.14	0.34

are divided proportionally among the coalition parties, so that at least one deputy minister nominated by the other party(ies) serves under each minister, acting as a watchdog for that party within the ministry. However, it is also the case that the survival rate among deputy ministers is far higher than among the advisers. There are deputy ministers, for example in highly specialized positions in the Ministries of Finance or Economy, who have survived not only a change of minister (during cabinet reshuffles), but also a change of government following elections.

At the opposite end of the continuum, i.e. the clerical and other low-level jobs in the support apparatus of the ministries, political appointments are virtually non-existent. According to the respondents, ministries dominated by KDU-ČSL might be a partial exception to this (see below), in that the party is known to have appointed some of its members and sympathizers to low positions in the ministries that members from other parties would most likely find unattractive. However, the second, or the middle-level, positions within the ministries, involving heads of sections and divisions and their deputies, present a different story. The personnel in these jobs are not as routinely changed as deputy ministers. Yet, according to our respondents, heads of important sections in ministries, such as those who make decisions concerning investments or strategic financial decisions, or heads of sections which are (known to be) hostile to a particular minister, will also be replaced by a more politically sympathetic appointee.

It should be emphasized that mechanisms of patronage within the ministries differ quite significantly depending on the level of appointment. The deputy ministers and members of ministerial cabinets are sacked directly at the will of the minister, and their contracts allow for that. In the case of heads of sections, and despite the relatively weak protection offered by the Labour Code, the minister is obliged by law to comply with a lengthy procedure to get rid of a surplus employee. The termination of contract can be done only on the basis of employees' incompetence, which has to be demonstrated; heads of sections can also be dismissed because their job disappears following reorganization. In both cases, the minister faces a certain hurdle and potentially politically difficult situation. As a result, the unwanted heads of sections are in practice either marginalized within their departments or transferred to another formally comparable post, and thus pressured to leave without the minister or deputy minister ever taking a direct action. As one respondent remarked, 'it is possible to liquidate a bureau-crat in this way within about three to twelve months'. The ministerial advisers often play a key role in these processes by, for example, ostensibly taking over the tasks that belonged to section heads.

In contrast to the pattern of patronage that is similar to all ministries, the NDACs fall into three categories. The first category is represented by various advisory councils and commissions, such as the Government Advisory Councils for Human Rights, for Roma communities, and for national minorities (all in Judiciary), or the Government Commission for Church–State Relations (Culture and Education). Members of these institutions are appointed directly by government, usually for a fixed period of time. The majority of appointments are clear cases of party patronage. Only politically sympathetic 'experts' will be chosen for these jobs, even though some individual ministers are an exception and do select commissioners from a wide range of political colours and opinions.

Politicization of appointments is less pervasive in the second category of NDACs, which comprises of institutions that are organizationally related to ministries, such as nearly all NDACs within the Finance and Economy sector. Patronage is possible via the relevant minister, but in practice it happens only in strategically important agencies, such as the Czech Consolidation Agency or the Medicines Commission. Given the technical expertise required for most of these appointments, politicians face high natural constraints. At the same time, if an agency becomes the subject of intense party interest, patronage can be quite insidious and perpetual. Frequent changes of the top management of Czech Invest, started in 2007 by the ODS-nominated Minister of Economy by sacking the agency's director, is a good example of such pervasive patronage practice.

The third group of NDACs concerns institutions where the right to make appointments is shared between several institutions, like the media commissions, or where appointment procedures are clearly spelled out and where politicians thus enjoy less discretion in making appointments, like for example within the military and police intelligence services. In all cases, patronage appointments do happen, but they demand major political craft. Good examples of this are three important media commissions, and especially the Council for Czech Television (see Šmíd, 2000). According to the law, the fifteen members of this council, which has far-reaching powers over the management of Czech state TV, are elected by parliament on the basis of nominations from civil society organizations. In practice, given the huge importance of TV broadcasting for political parties, the politicians try to influence nominations at the stage when they are discussed within the civil society organizations so that instead of vetoing 'independently chosen candidates' they can then only endorse their proposed list.

The element common to party patronage in all NDACs is that it normally reaches only the top-level employees, e.g. the councillors, directors, or CEOs. This, together with the fact that not all NDACs that were part of our survey are the subject of party patronage, explains the much lower total value of patronage index for NDACS (0.25) in comparison with the ministries (0.67).

The index shows even lower values (0.14) for the executing institutions. They comprise a rather heterogeneous group of institutions, but here also it is the norm that if party patronage happens, it does so only at the top level. Some of the jobs in the executing institutions can be lucrative, in terms of salaries or prestige, and these will be subject to patronage on a regular basis. The examples include non-executive boards of state-owned companies or some foreign embassies. It should be emphasized here (see also discussion below) that quite a lot of patronage that happens in these institutions is more personal than party political, in the sense that it is the friends and allies of a particular politician rather than people with a distinct partisan purpose that get appointed to these jobs.

However, in contrast to ministries and most NDACs, a very large number of executing institutions in the Czech Republic are governed by their profession, like most courts, the army and the police, or the fire brigade (each with their own service code). The top management of some others, like the Czech National Bank (CNB), or Czech TV and Czech Radio, are appointed by other institutions (the president in the case of CNB). Most of these executing institutions are thus virtually unreachable for party politicians. As a result, political appointments in them are very rare, as also reflected in the data. If party appointments happen, they do so via the political influence in the appointing institutions (e.g. media and media commissions).

This all said, it is important to point out a difference between the national level on the one hand, and the regional and local level on the other hand. The data in Table 5.1 do indicate that, looking at policy area differences, regional and local level administration is somewhat more affected by patronage than institutions in other policy areas. Our respondents, including experts in policy areas other than regional and local administration, stressed this difference during the interviews. A somewhat higher level of patronage in the regional and local administration is largely driven by executing institutions in that policy area. The regional and local councils, a subnational equivalent of ministries, more or less mirror the national pattern of patronage in the central administration. The Regional Council Commissions, i.e. the regional NDACs, also follow the national pattern, at least in that party patronage will happen only in the politically more significant of the commissions, such as those dealing with strategic planning, European funds, or housing.

However, since the Czech EU accession and corresponding wave of state decentralization reforms (see Novotný, 2004), regional and local administrations have also assumed control over a large number of institutions providing social and other services, such as hospitals, schools, or housing corporations. Given that hundreds of such institutions and organizations fall under the regions and municipalities, political parties, with their relatively thin presence on the ground (see above), can hardly cover all those positions: as one respondent remarked, 'parties are so weak on the ground that almost each and every member can have a state job or other state position if they want to'. Clearly, regional and local politicians have an absolutely free hand in making appointments into these institutions, in no small part because regional politics is less scrutinized in the media than national politics. Politicians also control budgets, which are often filled from sizeable EU regional funds, which are given to these institutions. As a result, the changes of (boards of) directors in the important municipal companies and utilities, as well as heads of regional hospitals, are often politicized. This is even more so with the overseeing boards of the municipal companies: they are specifically composed of regional and local deputies and councillors, who get paid for carrying out the board functions, and who consequently often serve on more than one of these boards. Company

CEOs are happy for deputies to be present on boards because that way they can effectively lobby for higher company budgets.

All in all, the overall picture on the regional/local level is, in the words of one interviewed expert, 'politicization and corruption which is far more brutal than on the national level', or, in the words of another expert, 'reminiscent of "city boss" politics from the past'. This also involves clientelistic practices such as when private sector companies take control of local party branches (and thus of important local decision makers) by either providing campaign and other 'representation' funds to politicians, or by forcing their own employees to become members of a local party chapter (known in the country as the phenomenon of 'dead souls'). It should be stressed that in comparison with the national level, personal and even family contacts are far more important in the appointment process than anything that might be considered partisan or party-controlled. In addition, rewarding friends, or friends of friends, is often seen as the most important motivation when regional and local politicians make appointments. In that sense, Czech regional and local politics looks more clientelistic than the national politics. In that sense also, regional and local party patronage appears more traditional, geared towards rewards and rents, than the control-driven patronage that dominates at the national level.

Motivations for party patronage

Indeed, looking at the data in Figure 5.1, it is apparent that with 65 per cent of the answers control dominates as the most important motivation for patronage

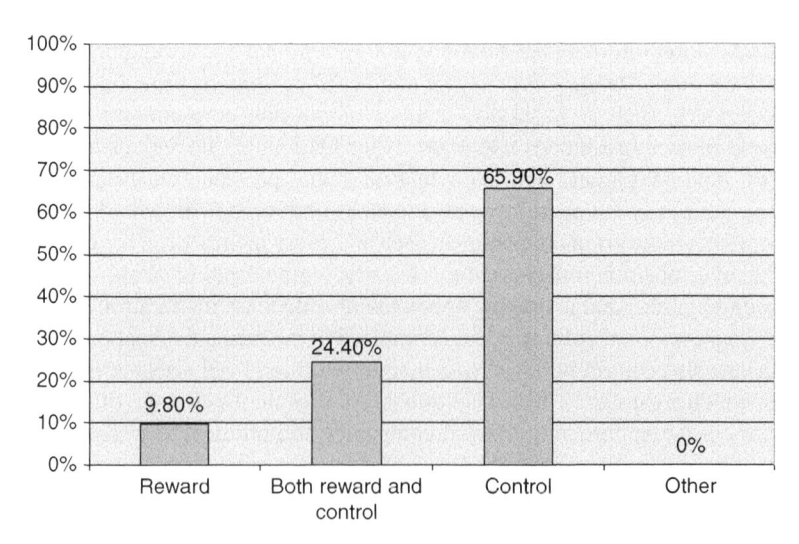

FIGURE 5.1 Motivations for party patronage in the Czech Republic

appointments. In contrast, reward on its own is a relatively insignificant category, with close to 10 per cent of the answers. If reward plays an important role, then it is in combination with control purposes. As said above, the patterns in regional and local administration are more reward-orientated, according to the interviewed experts.

Even if reward plays a relatively insignificant role in motivating party patronage, it is relatively clear what the reward entails, and also in which of the institutions that were part of our survey reward-driven appointments are most often made. The national state institutions that were routinely mentioned in the interviews were governing (i.e. non-executive) boards of state-owned companies, or companies in which the state has a significant share, such as the energy giant ČEZ, the famous Budvar brewery or Czech Airlines. Also mentioned were the Czech embassies and consulates with their ambassadorial posts, even though the share of those Foreign Service institutions where parties make appointments does not exceed about 20 per cent of their total number, according to the experts. The reward will typically be ex-post orientated; that is, the appointees will be 'paid' for their past services to the party, such as when a former minister obtains an ambassadorial post or a position in the EU administration. Less typical, but no less important, are appointments for future services, such as when MPs are given jobs on the non-executive boards of companies in order to cement their party loyalty. It is important to emphasize that, on the national level, reward-driven appointments are almost exclusively elite-level rewards; party activists, let alone ordinary party members, will not, with the partial exception of KDU-ČSL (see below), be beneficiaries of this sort of party patronage.

The dominant motivation for party patronage—the control of institutions—deserves a more detailed analysis in order to fully appreciate the political dynamics that are in play here. Control involves, in the first place, an attempt to influence policy making, coordination, and implementation. The ability to tune key sections of ministries, as well as some of the NDACs (e.g. the Medicines Commission) and executing institutions (e.g. key state-owned companies), to party (or ministers') policy preferences and agendas via appointments is clearly deemed very important in the context of the heavily polarized Czech politics and in the context of persistent mutual distrust between politicians and bureaucrats. Party appointments are also deemed instrumental to ensure political coverage of, and information gathering from, certain institutions, even if parties do not have immediate policy objectives in them. The standard practice of nominating deputy ministers in 'hostile' ministries (see above) is a great example in this respect. The partisan patronage on the national level is, in this sense, a systemic consequence of party government functioning in a specific political context. In all likelihood, only the emergence of greater trust between politicians and civil servants, as well as among the politicians themselves, would lessen the incentive for incoming ministers to engage in relatively extensive patronage games that are motivated by these policy and party political considerations.

However, it is clear from the survey that 'control of institutions' also involves motivations that have less to do with the legitimate pursuit of a party's programmatic goals, and more to do with the grey area of party financing, personal enrichment of individual politicians, and questionable lobbying practices for which the country's politics is, justly or unjustly, quite notorious. The patronage appointments that are the case in point here include political takeovers of institutions such as the now defunct Czech Consolidation Agency—a bank-like agency that was set up in 2001 to deal with crisis management of key enterprises, banks, and insurance companies. It also includes appointments to most of the energy sector regulators. Allegations are rife that control of these institutions via appointments has been instrumental for the realization of parties' clientelistic networks. Frequent attempts by politicians to reach into police secret services and anti-corruption units can be seen in a similar vein, as an attempt to control institutions that can unveil and penalize the existence of parties' shady activities. It is hard to judge the scale of such activities, and hence the relative importance of 'control for corruption' within the overall control category. The experts were, however, in agreement that these clientelistic practices are less of a problem on the national level than on the regional and local levels.

The regional/national level contrast appears, again, also when one looks at the qualifications of appointees. At country level, Figure 5.2 demonstrates that a political link appears as the single most mentioned requisite for a candidate to get a state job, closely followed by a professional qualification. On the regional level, however, the personal link, which is the least important on the national level,

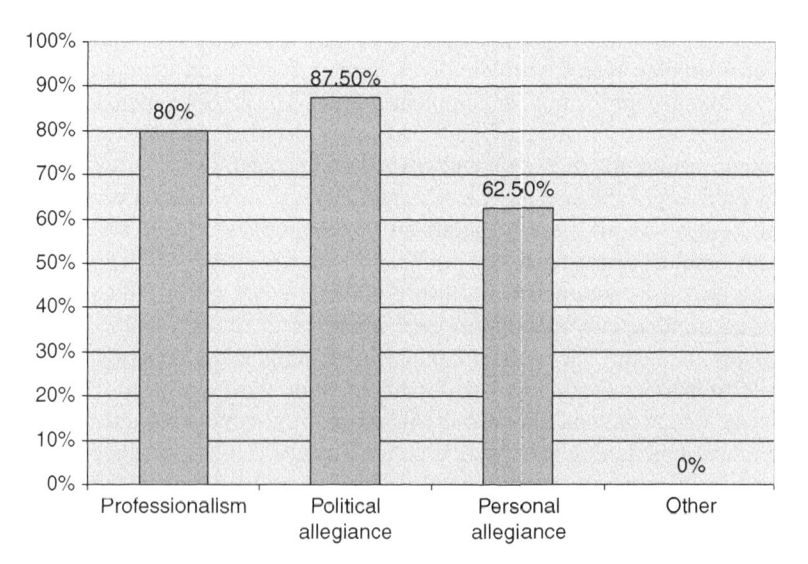

FIGURE 5.2 Qualifications of appointees in the Czech Republic

plays a far more important role, according to the respondents. Their answers suggest that a personal allegiance, either a direct personal friendship or a recommendation via a close acquaintance, will count first in the eye of an appointer. If that friend is politically rightly connected, either being a member of the same party or having a proven track record of cooperation with local administrations of a certain political colour will not be seen as a necessary, but rather as an enabling, condition; professional qualification is something that will be merely hoped for by those that make the appointment on the regional and local levels.

In contrast, a politically connected professional—somebody with 'responsive competence' (Suleiman, 2003: 215)—is probably the best term to describe the crucial combination of allegiances required for getting a job on the national level. A relevant professional qualification will be a necessary, but by no means a sufficient, condition for candidates to get a job which is subject to partisan patronage. In a country with a fair degree of formalism, proper qualifications might often be seen as satisfied by the candidate holding a degree or school diploma in a corresponding policy field. But increasingly, as the experts suggested, the subject of examination will also be a wider professional career, general managerial experience, and the candidate's communication skills. This in no small part relates to the fact that key appointments in the country are more and more scrutinized by the media, which will only be happy to point out candidates' shortcomings in any of those professional competences that go beyond the educational degree.

The media scrutiny, together with parties' weak recruitment capacities (see below), also means that 'political allegiance' cannot be equated with party membership. This is an important point. There is no doubt that Czech parties would like to possess a sizeable pool of candidates ready to take over the positions that are available to them, but the reality is that parties often tread in shallow waters when recruiting for an office. In a country where partisanship in general is seen in a negative light, job candidates themselves will be keen to publicly emphasize their distance from political parties. As a result, political allegiance, which has obtained such high mention in our survey, most often denotes sympathy with the party's programmatic aims, or even just the same policy preference as that of a particular minister or appointed director, rather than a commitment in the more traditional party government sense.

Parties and patronage

Considering their relatively weak organizational presence on the ground, it should come as no surprise that, in general, Czech parties do not display an overflow of suitable candidates for appointive positions. If patronage as described in the conventional literature is a demand-driven phenomenon, it is certainly a supply-driven phenomenon in the contemporary Czech Republic. The parties are actually hardly in a state to fill all the jobs that are available to them. For some of the smaller or newer parties in government, such as the Greens (SZ) at the time this research was carried out, the problem with finding suitable candidates (read 'politically connected professionals') is so urgent that they struggle to nominate even just deputy ministers according to the proportional principle agreed in coalition negotiations. In other words, once such small parties have filled the parliamentary benches and their ministries, all of which are key political positions, there is hardly anybody left to be considered for the bureaucratic and managerial appointive positions.

The weak social anchoring of parties is probably the most important factor in explaining the supply-driven nature of patronage in the country. That many state jobs are not professionally very attractive—certainly not in combination with the public scrutiny and hence the loss of personal privacy that will now follow most important appointments—only adds to parties' misery. It is interesting to note, in this context, that even the two big Czech parties—ODS and ČSSD—do not perform particularly well in terms of party patronage relative to their political and electoral strength. In fact, viewed in patronage terms, the two parties represent something of a paradox. The Social Democrats have long tried to establish an intraparty mechanism of elite recruitment, centred on various policy commissions and expert groups coordinated by the party in central office. However, ČSSD has been persistently seen, in the media as well as by our experts, as the party that lacks cadres and that suffers from the shortage of suitable aspirants for public offices. In contrast, the Civic Democrats have never invested heavily in recruitment, with most 'expertise' gravitating loosely around its shadow cabinets and their likely-to-be ministers. Yet, chiefly because of the party's strong support within the country's economic and cultural elites, ODS has always fared better than ČSSD in staffing the government and the administration when in the position to do so.

These differences notwithstanding, common to all Czech parties is that party patronage (on the national level) is to a very large extent the prerogative of the party in public office. Furthermore, it is chiefly the ministers that are making most appointments, often tapping into their own personal networks rather than party networks, in a fashion that is not particularly strongly coordinated, even within the party in public office. The ministerial positions, appointments to key foreign abroad missions, and to the key EU institutions are likely to be discussed within the narrow party leadership, or between the leadership and the parliamentary party, surely also among the coalition partners. However, the party as such, be that the central office, the congress, or even the wider party executive that includes representatives of the regions, barely constrains the party leadership in choosing candidates, let alone pushing for candidates of its own. Patronage is, in this very important aspect, rather unpartisan in the Czech Republic. Indeed, it is not uncommon to observe that it is the party that emanates from patronage, rather than that patronage emanates from the party, in the sense that some of the politically connected professionals that are placed by parties in important state offices become courted by the party leadership. Some of these well-performing people eventually decide to join the party and pursue their career in politics, guaranteeing a renewal at the party elite level that would otherwise be hard to obtain in the standard bottom-up intraparty process.

The Christian Democratic Union (KDU-ČSL)—a small party that was a mainstay of most post-communist governments until 2010—is an exception to the elite-dominated patronage of most Czech parties. Owing to its long organizational history and strong presence on the ground in several provinces, the party's leadership has always faced demands from within the organization for state jobs at all levels. These demands were routinely satisfied by Christian Democratic ministers, so much so that absence from government (and since 2010 also from the parliament) has been seen as a political disaster. Still famous is the utterance of the former KDU-ČSL leader, Miroslav Kalousek, during one of the government's crises in the early 2000s, that the state would lose 300 employees if the Christian Democrats left the government. Given its similar organizational history and style, the Communist Party (KSČM) would in all likelihood follow a similar pattern if the party was invited to join the government.

An invitation to join a governing coalition—something that is unlikely to happen to KSČM on the national level in the foreseeable future—is a necessary condition for any Czech party keen to take advantage of patronage. Parties that are part of the governing coalition carve up the vast majority of appointments between themselves, in a rather majoritarian manner. A bipolar pattern of party competition reinforces this dynamic—Czech parties do not keenly endorse administrators that were appointed by previous coalition governments. However, one clear consequence of parties' weak capacity to recruit candidates for appointive positions is that the majoritarian principle which characterizes the interparty relations rarely results in radical sweeps of the state administration after the elections. The positions that are deemed important in policy terms, especially in the ministries (i.e. deputy ministers and ministerial cabinets), are swept relatively quickly according to the coalition agreements; this also happens with jobs in other institutions if the responsible minister brings about a new, radical policy agenda, or if the person concerned was the subject of political controversy under the previous government. With a great number of other jobs, however, the replacement is relatively slow, usually following a vacancy; it is also increasingly common that well-performing CEOs and other directors with demonstrated political links to the previous government will simply not be replaced. In addition, the overall effect of majoritarianism is mediated by the fact that national governments are frequently of different (a combination of) colours compared to coalitions formed at regional/local level. It might occasionally irritate national party leaderships that their own regional and local branches join in subnational governments with national arch-enemies. The net effect is that there is no major Czech party, including the Communists, without at least some access to party patronage.

Are the party patronage practices and patterns described above different from the early post-communist period? Has there been any important change in this area of politics? There was no apparent consensus among the interviewed experts concerning this question, certainly with respect to potential changes in the scale and depth of party patronage. It seems that the index of party patronage reported in Table 5.1 might not have been all that different if the survey was performed a decade or two ago. There is no way to judge precisely. However, consistent with the patronage analysis presented above, experts often pointed to a 'higher sophistication' and to 'less overt forms' of contemporary party patronage, underscoring serious constraints that Czech parties face when taking on appointments. To an inside observer it might appear that the same type of people get appointed again and again; indeed, scandals concerning incompetent or corrupt political appointees abound in the country. However, the fact that there are media outlets that do practically nothing else than scrutinize candidates for all sorts of political and appointed positions means the politicians have increasingly been forced to at least follow some rules and procedures to avoid hostile reactions from the journalists. Party political appointments do and will occur in the Czech Republic, but the days of unstructured cleansing that, for example, characterized the de-communization period in the early and mid-1990s is gone for good. Patronage these days requires political craft.

CONCLUSIONS

The evidence presented in this chapter suggests that popular perceptions overestimate the importance of *trafika*—a euphemism standing for party patronage practices—in Czech politics. This is certainly so if one examines closely the partisan capture of institutions on the national level. Party patronage is relatively widespread inside most ministries, frequently involving more than top-level appointments. But party appointments get fewer when looking at NDACs and executing institutions, where for the most part only strategically important state offices get the attention of politicians. Importantly, the dominant motivation for parties to engage in patronage practices is not their need to satisfy partisans and party supporters with jobs, as the term *trafika* implicitly assumes, but rather to control institutions that are seen as important in terms of policy creation, control, and implementation. Indeed, most state jobs are probably not attractive enough to become a potential source of 'constituency clientelism'; in addition, the activists' basis in most Czech parties is too thin to constitute a significant demand side for old-style patronage. Even on the elite level, where most patronage happens, Czech parties are in fact hard pressed to fill the positions that are available to them, and more often than not have to appoint non-partisans to these jobs.

Klientelismus, though not the main subject of this analysis, seems also to be a relatively overestimated phenomenon in light of the evidence presented above. It is overestimated not in the sense of its existence—it certainly does exist—but more in terms of the role the parties play in the establishment and coordination of these networks. Clientelism is widespread on the regional and municipal level, but is of a personal nature, much like most of the patronage. To be sure, party labels are also very important here, for it is nearly impossible to reach elected office in the Czech Republic without competing on one of the party lists. But once politicians reach office, their own parties constrain them very little in the process of personnel selection. Personal contacts and politicians' own elite networks are frequently more important as a source of recruitment than the party itself. This is certainly true for the regional and local levels. But even on the national level, the individual politicians, mostly the ministers, enjoy a near free hand in the recruitment of personnel for appointed positions.

These patterns of party patronage raise important questions about the performance of party government in the country. I have argued elsewhere that the *partyness of society* is relatively weak in the Czech Republic, much like in most of the post-communist space (Kopecký, 2006b; 2007). In that sense, party government has always missed one of its key fundamentals, despite the fact that (national) elections continue to be conducted in predominantly partisan terms. Indeed, the claims for the existence of party government in the country have always been based on the observance of parties' strong procedural and institutional roles or, in other words, on a strong *partyness of government*. This foundation of party government still stands: there is no alternative to parties in terms of the organization of public office and leadership in key areas of public policy. Governments are formed and dismissed by parties; most ministers also come from within the parties. Patronage at the top level is mainly exercised in order to translate parties' programmatic commitments to real policy outcomes. However, building networks of power to achieve all these aims is quite non-partisan, as this research shows, with parties as organizations playing no meaningful role in the coordination of appointments or in the recruitment for those appointments. Government in that sense looks more *ministerial* than *party*. Even more, ministers sometimes also use these networks of power for their own political purposes rather than for the benefit of their party organization. Party government, in short, looks like a strangely hollow entity in the contemporary Czech Republic.

NOTES

1. In addition to colleagues who participated in the research project leading to this volume, I would like to thank Petra Guasti and Radka Dudová for their helpful comments on this chapter. I would also like to thank Vladimíra Dvořáková and Lukáš Linek for helping me with the organization of the fieldwork research for this chapter.

CHAPTER 6

Party Patronage in Denmark: The Merit State with Politics 'On the Side'

Carina S. Bischoff

INTRODUCTION

Comparative studies need 'negative' cases as well as 'positive' ones to generate viable explanations of the outcomes of interest.[1] Although the type of systematic comparative evidence harnessed by this Europe-wide study has not been available before, there was much to suggest that Denmark would be at the negative end of the patronage scale. The Danish reputation in international organizations and academic research suggests that its system of appointments in state institutions is predominantly merit-based. So why do this study? On the one hand, politics is an ever-moving object, and reports on political influence on appointments date back to the 1990s (Knudsen, 1997; Jensen and Olsen, 2000; Christensen, 1999). Given the challenges facing parties competing for power in a complex modern society, it would not be surprising if old ways had been replaced by new. On the other hand, the focus in earlier studies is on the civil service at departmental and NDAC level, and much less at the level of executing institutions. This study is designed to assess practices at all levels of the state and therefore to give an indication of where practices conform to or deviate from prior expectations. The data used are no doubt sufficiently accurate to answer the large comparative questions asked here, and provide a solid basis for the comparative ranking of countries on scales of patronage. However, the interviews naturally do not exhaust the need for detailed information on practices in particular sectors and institutions.

DENMARK AND ITS POLITICAL SYSTEM

Denmark is a small country with a population of just over five million. Its thriving open economy places it as the sixth richest country in Europe in 2010 (OECD,

2010). From the second decade after the war, its public sector expanded at very high rates (Christoffersen, 2000). This has left Denmark ranking among the highest in the world when it comes to taxation levels, public employment, and welfare provision. Government revenues and expenditures account for over half of the GDP—a level that is matched only by its Nordic neighbours (OECD, 2010). The public sector presently employs just under 30 per cent of the workforce, of which social protection,[2] health service, and education account for more than 75 per cent (Danmarks Statistik, 2010). Denmark is a unitary state with a comparatively high degree of decentralization to the regional and local levels (Christoffersen, 2000: 31; Andersen, Christensen, and Pallesen, 2008: 250). The levels of government are not constitutionally determined, and both the units and functions of the regional and local levels have been subject to changes (*Indenrigs- og SundhedsMinisteriet*, 2004).[3] Following the most recent reform in 2005, the subnational level now comprises ninety-eight municipalities and five regions, which raise around one-third of the total state revenue and are responsible for more than half of the expenditures[4] (*IndenrigsMinisteriet*, 2007). Politically, it can be defined as a constitutional monarchy with a parliamentary form of government. It has a working multiparty system with coalition governments, regular alternation, and a strong tradition of broad collaboration on policy. Negative parliamentarism, combined with the absence of large dominant parties, has made minority government the norm. Denmark has had few and short-lived majority governments in the post-war period (Damgaard, 2003). Until the 1970s, the party system was highly stable—even frozen—with the four old parties alternating in government and dominating representation of the electorate in parliament. The so-called earthquake election of 1973, however, not only doubled the number of parties, but also increased the ideological polarization of the party system as parties on both the extreme left and right were strengthened. In the following decades, ideological polarization has waned, while the number of parties has also declined to the eight that are currently represented in parliament. The electoral system is proportional, with a low legal threshold of 2 per cent, which ensures a fair representation of parties in parliament and permits representation of small parties. The electorate tends to divide the vote quite evenly between the coalitions of right- and left-wing parties that compete for government office, with neither ever winning a comfortable majority (Damgaard, 2003: 150). Replacing a coalition of centre-left parties that had held government from 1993, a right-wing coalition of Liberals and Conservatives formed a government in 2001. This government relied on the Danish Folk Party as its stable collaborator in parliament.

The formal organizational bases of most parties resemble the mass party model, although observers have commented on strong trends towards centralization of power in the leadership, resembling catch-all or cartel party types (Bille, 1997; Pedersen, 2003). Also, as elsewhere in Europe, the membership of political parties has diminished sharply since the 1960s, and presently just around 4 per cent of the voting population are party members (Kosiara-Pedersen, 2010). The principal means of solving this challenge has been the institution of generous state funding for parties, while efforts to recruit new members—even once by means of a joint campaign—have so far had less tangible results (Bille, 1997; Pedersen, 2003; Bille et al., 2003: 23). The electorate's party identification is not very high, but the relatively high level of vote switching does not signify a widespread dissatisfaction with the parties either (Andersen, 2004; Nielsen, 2002). Several studies show that Danes have comparatively high levels of trust in the political system. The levels of institutional trust are among the highest in Europe.[5] However, the level of trust varies across institutions. Justice and law enforcement score highest, while political institutions such as parliament and political parties are at the lower end of the scale (see Hansen and Beck Jørgensen, 2009).

What practices of patronage—if any—might be expected on the basis of features of the Danish political system, as outlined above? While I will return to a discussion of possible causes of the outcomes at the end of the chapter, it is worth highlighting here some of the salient traits that could have implications for patronage practices. The minority status of most governments, combined with close competition and regular alternation in office, implies that parties in office have faced constraints in exercising control over the state. This might dampen their ability to change the status quo, and possibly hinders party efforts to colonize the state. The tradition of cooperation and consensual-style politics could, on the other hand, be expected to give rise to patterns of sharing patronage positions among parties, and opposition control could give rise to sharing rather than restraint in party appointments. The large, universal welfare state naturally provides ample opportunity for patronage as well as incentives to seek to control it. High levels of managerial competence are necessary, however, as most Danes are directly affected by state institutions (childcare, health, education, elderly care, etc.) and charges of mismanagement could therefore have significant consequences at the polls.

GOVERNMENT AND STATE INSTITUTIONS

When a royal decree ended absolute monarchy in Denmark in 1848, a hierarchical model of ministerial government—inspired by the French system—was simultaneously introduced (Knudsen, 1997: 36). The new model was embodied in the new constitution of 1849, which heralded a new era of constitutional monarchy and eventually led to democracy in the modern sense of the term when parliamentarism was finally instituted in 1901. The hierarchical model signified a concentration of authority as well as responsibility with the minister rather than a collegiate body (§13–15 of the constitution). The constitution confers the power to determine the number of ministers and ministries on the prime minister, who also delineates the content of ministers' portfolios (§14 of the constitution). In practice, the number of ministers and ministries, as well as the specific area of competence falling under their jurisdiction, has varied over time, but currently there are eighteen. In practice, Danish government is 'party government' (Jensen, 2002). The position of prime minister is held by the leader of the largest party in the coalition, and typically ministers are members of parliament as well as prominent figures in the parties that form the coalition. More rarely, ministers are recruited from the 'outside', but following such appointments the expectation is that the new ministers will build a base in the party and run for a seat in parliament.

The minister has a dual role. Firstly, he or she has a political role as a member of the cabinet, and typically also of the parliament. Secondly, the minister is the administrative head of a hierarchical ministry, and as such he or she has the formal authority to issue instructions to civil servants. Moreover, the minister also has a wider authority to direct any business falling within his or her portfolio and to intervene personally in decisions related to it. The general legal framework formally provides ministers with a fairly free hand in taking action within their areas and relatively few constraints. It also follows, however, that ministers can be held politically responsible by parliamentary majority for any decision or problem arising within his or her portfolio (see Nissen et al., 2010; Christensen, 2004; Finansministeriet, 1998a; Ministeransvarlighedsloven, 1964).

The ministries fall directly under the ministers' authority. There is no general blueprint for their organization, and the pattern has changed over time. Since the 1960s, however, the typical organization resembles the 'agency model' (see Figure 6.1). In this model, there is a ministerial department, which functions as a secretariat to the minister. The department is responsible for provision of the advice and information the minister needs as a member of government, and to handle relations with parliament. The cases handled are of a general nature and the focus is on issues that are presumed to be of interest to the minister. Another important function of the department is public relations. The actual implementation of regulation, administration, and management of policies, as well as concrete

Organizational diagram of the state administration

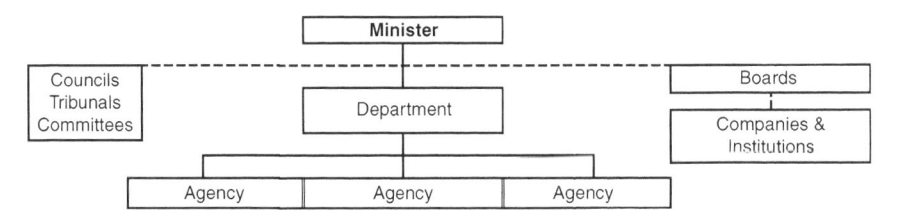

FIGURE 6.1 Institutions in the minister's portfolio—the agency model (an ideal type)

handling of cases, is generally the work of agencies (*styrelser og direktorater*) (Figure. 6.1), or in particular cases by councils, foundations, or tribunals that are not subordinate in the ministerial hierarchy. The typical ministry consists of one department and several agencies reporting to the minister through the department. There is considerable variation in the allocation of tasks, however. Size of department also varies. Some departments are large and handle policy-related tasks and oversee agency business. Others have small departments—to serve the minister—while agencies are entrusted with policy analysis and planning, drafting bills, and answering parliamentary questions (Finansministeriet, 2004: chapters 3–4). The precise allocation of tasks and responsibilities is open to modification at any moment, even on an ad hoc basis by the minister, reflecting the authority to organize his or her 'own house' (Knudsen, 2000).

Ministers' portfolios and spheres of influence do not stop at civil service institutions (departments and agencies), however. They also include a number of 'arm's length' institutions that do not fall under the minister's direct instructional competence. Parliament may delegate decision-making competence to bodies outside the ministerial hierarchy, such as boards, councils, commissions, committees, or tribunals (*bestyrelser, kommissioner, udvalg, råd nævn*). However, as Christensen comments, 'even in these cases it is rare to find a minister entirely deprived of authority', as the minister will 'still keep his powers as holder of that body's budget and the authority to make key appointments and decide its organizational structure' (Christensen, 2006: 999). The type of quasi-independent bodies that include committees, commissions, councils, and administrative tribunals can of course also be established at the initiative of the minister or the government itself. In this way, ministers are able to draw on expertise outside the ministries to monitor policy areas, develop policy proposals, administer grants, perform judicial functions and the like. The lack of a clear relationship between the titles of such quasi-independent bodies and their functions makes it difficult to describe them systematically (Knudsen, 2000). In overviews they tend to be lumped together—also with boards—in spite of significant differences in status and function. The number of such bodies also varies considerably from one sector to another. At the modest end, the Ministry of Defence reports appointing just five councils, while the Ministry of Foreign Affairs reports having thirty-eight boards, councils, and committees under its wings, and the Ministry of Culture has as many as sixty-six (Ministry homepages, 2010).[6] Not long after the current right-wing government took office in 2001, the prime minister revealed intentions to reduce the role and number of auxiliary institutions.[7] Although over 130 bodies were abolished shortly after, new ones have been appointed since. According to experts, there are no indications that their numbers or roles have diminished under the current government (*Ugebrevet A4*, 1 February 2010; *Information*, 28 December 2004).

Production or service organizations are a completely different set of institutions which also fall outside the ministerial chain of command. In 2003,

Denmark registered twenty-two companies of which the state was a shareholder. Only one of these was completely state-owned. These numbers represent a drop of some 50 per cent from 1993, when the state still held shares in forty-seven companies. This indicates a trend towards liberalization of public ownership. However, the low number of companies partly owned by the state is partly explained by the fact that a high number of 'productive or service organizations' are placed within the public administration, rather than being constituted as companies outside the government's sphere (Finansministeriet, 2004).[8] The companies that operate within the ambit of the state administration are found in the areas of property, business and export promotion, culture, and research, and fall under the responsibility of the minister of the relevant portfolio. The share-holding companies operate mostly in the areas of transport and infrastructure and services, but also include energy, finance, and other sectors. However, where the latter used to be placed under the relevant sector ministries, government has moved ownership to the Ministry of Finance since 2001. In terms of management of the companies, ownership and relationship to the state clearly matters. For the state-owned company, the minister can—and does—get involved in business decisions in the company.[9] For companies of which the state owns shares, the main influence is exerted through the general assembly, where the board is selected. Day-to-day running of the business is left to the top management of the company, which is selected by and responsible to the board. In earlier times, civil servants could serve—and often did—as members of the boards. Since 2004, however, this practice has changed, and as a rule no civil servants serve in this capacity. Companies that are part of the administration are obviously closer to the government, since the formal right to appoint its board or top manager belongs to the minister. However, the official policy is that the same norms of leadership that apply to companies of which the state merely owns shares are also valid for the state-run companies, even though the legal guarantees are not the same. In many cases, the competence to appoint is shared with other actors, such as major interest organizations, and in a few cases with parliament itself.[10]

As indicated by this brief overview, the organization of the Danish state places government ministers in a unique position of power over the apparatus of the state. As government ministers in Denmark are agents of the political parties rather than independent politicians, the structure opens a door to influence over the state for the political parties. On the face of it, the potential for influence on personnel and modus operandi appears to be greatest in the ministries themselves (departments and agencies). Although by no means out of reach to ministers, the auxiliary as well as executing institutions are not as immediately subordinate to their dictates. One might therefore expect that party patronage would be stronger in ministries than elsewhere, but, as the following sections will demonstrate, nothing could be further from reality.

POLITICAL APPOINTMENTS IN THE STATE?

Data and methods

In addition to the forty-two sector interviews, three experts were interviewed about general aspects of public employment and appointment decisions. This was done to complement the information provided by sector experts. Initially, respondents were selected to include high-ranking officials at department, NDAC, and executing level within the state, as well as politicians and independent experts (academics and journalists). However, after the initial round of interviews, it was found that respondents who did not have direct work experience in the civil service, or had not served in relevant institutions, did not have sufficient knowledge of the practice of appointments to be able to answer detailed questions. Some were therefore excluded. Most of the interviews (thirty-eight) were with current or former civil servants in departments, agencies, and executing institutions. Since it was not uncommon for the interviewees at NDAC or the executing level to be uncertain of practices at the levels above them, most respondents were selected at the department level. Although not part of the comparative design, the environmental sector was added in the Danish case, since initial expert interviews indicated that appointments there might follow different patterns from those found elsewhere. For the sake of comparability with the other countries, the results for this sector are not included in the summary scores presented in the tables, but are presented separately.

As evidenced by the map of the state, not all relevant institutions and bodies are included in the study. The institutions described above as auxiliary institutions are not directly included in the coding scheme. The decision to omit this group from coding was prompted by the following three considerations. Firstly, many of these bodies are ad hoc rather than of a permanent nature. Including them in a coding scheme that places them vis-à-vis permanent institutions of the state therefore creates a problem of comparability. Secondly, in terms of their functions, they can be identified in all three levels of the state, but the big differences in status as well as appointment practices between these and the main civil service and executing institutions mean that joint coding would give a muddled picture and describe neither type of institution very well. Finally, it is simply difficult to find respondents who have knowledge about appointments to such bodies in general. A different research design would therefore be needed to identify features of current practice. Rather than introducing uncertain estimates and codes, it was therefore decided to describe appointments to such bodies in a separate section.

Formal and informal constraints on the right to appoint

At first glance, there would appear to be few obstacles in the way of a minister wishing to shape the civil service according to partisan lines. According to the

Statute of Civil Servants,[11] the competence to hire all civil servants resides with the King,[12] which in practical terms refers to the government and the relevant minister. The law on ministerial responsibility also confers wide powers on ministers in the direction of affairs within their portfolio, as mentioned above, but they can—and do—delegate their competence to others (Knudsen, 2000; Christensen, 2004). Interestingly, several senior civil servants interviewed expressed uncertainty regarding the exact extent of the minister's competence in relation to hiring decisions in the civil service, due to a strong practice of delegation (see further below). In strictly formal terms, however, such delegation could be revoked at any time and in relation to particular cases. When it comes to appointments to boards of companies or councils, committees, or tribunals, a legal competence to appoint key members—though frequently not all members—clearly resides with the minister. Interestingly, this competence has not been subjected to generalized delegation (Knudsen, 2000). Finally, while the law does not permit parties to make appointments to offices in the state directly, there is nothing to prevent ministers from consulting political parties when exercising the right to appoint.

Personnel decisions do not operate in a legal void, leaving them to the whim of ministers, however. The most direct legal constraint on exercising ministerial authority in personnel decisions lies in the statute prohibiting discrimination in the labour market.[13] The law stipulates that an employer may not discriminate against employees in questions of employment, transfers, promotions, demotions, dismissal, or salary. The statute moreover excludes personal political convictions from the list of criteria that can have a legitimate bearing on personnel decisions. However, the law is not a watertight barrier against party political considerations in employment per se. If an organization's purpose would be defined as specifically political—as for instance the secretariat of a political party—the above does not apply. By implication, if offices—or specific jobs—in the public sphere can be defined as having a political purpose, partisan criteria could be used in personnel decisions. To date, such a redefinition has only been formally applied to the position of 'special adviser' (*særlig rådgiver*) to ministers, and therefore the general discrimination act applies to all other positions in the state (Finansministeriet, 1998a). Finally, with respect to the employment and dismissal of civil servants specifically, these are considered administrative decisions, and as such the statute of public administration[14] and the general principle of legality[15] apply. This principle entails that personnel decisions must be based on objective criteria relating to the position in question, the overarching principle being that the most qualified applicant must be chosen for any position (Gammeltoft-Hansen et al., 2002: 203–9). Allowing partisan criteria to play an explicit role in hiring civil servants would therefore require a change in law. The statute of discrimination as described above also applies to companies (public or private). Local government has its own individual sets of regulations, but these largely contain the same regulations as the statute of civil servants (Gammeltoft-Hansen et al., 2002: 164).

The nature of the contracts offered to staff also limit the freedom of ministers. In this area, however, there have been clear developments towards the use of more flexible terms of employment in the bureaucracy. In the middle of the last century, civil servants were almost as difficult to get rid of as judges, and particularly top civil servants were—until recently—difficult to dismiss (Nissen, 2000: 7). The situation today is much more flexible, as ministers can dismiss civil servants on a discretionary basis (Knudsen, 2000; Christensen, 2001). Protection is primarily financial—either through substitute appointments or a period of payment followed by pension. Moreover, an increasing number of employees in the bureaucracy are offered another type of contract (*overenskomstansatte*) that is more flexible. Moreover, in 1975 a new clause was specifically added to contracts of top civil servants, which made it easier to move them to other ministry departments. One indication that this discretionary authority is indeed used can for instance be found in the number of years civil servants remain in their positions. For the top-level jobs in the civil service this has more than halved, from around twenty years in the 1940s to eight or nine years in the 1980s (Knudsen, 1997: 22).

In addition to the constraints given by laws governing the labour market, the freedom of ministers to appoint within their portfolio is also limited by a kind of 'peer approval'. Important positions at departmental, agency, or executing level require the approval of the government Employment Committee. Like other government committees, the operational guidelines, functions, and membership are not described by law, and proper documentation about its 'modus operandi' is hard to come by (Knudsen, 2000). The description here is based on an interview with Karsten Dybvad,[16] who functioned as the committee's secretary in the period 2005-10, and on information provided by other civil servants (including four permanent secretaries).

The practice of having an internal government committee dealing with public appointments dates back to at least the 1970s. The members of the committee include the prime minister and leader(s) of the other party(ies) in the governing coalition, irrespective of the specific ministries they head, the minister of finance,[17] and possibly other prominent government ministers.[18] As is the case for other government committees, access to or information on matters related to committee work is not shared with opposition parties. A list, which is updated as new institutions arise or change, specifies which jobs require the approval of the committee. The procedure prescribes that ministers who recommend a candidate for a position appear before the committee to explain their choice.[19] For positions at the executing level the requirement is similar, but such positions are on the agenda for three consecutive meetings instead of just one. This is the norm for all civil servants except the permanent secretary, which is on the agenda for at least two meetings.[20] It is plausible that the more open base of recruitment to positions outside the civil service makes opportunities to recommend unsuitable candidates more difficult to prevent. This would explain the fact that such positions are on the agenda for more meetings.

Dybvad stressed that the main function of the committee is to 'create transparency internally in the government' and to serve as a permanent reminder of the criteria for appointments, since 'in the final analysis, you have to be able to stand up and defend your choice before the committee'. Undoubtedly, it can be seen as a direct constraint on individual ministers' freedom to appoint. However, Dybvad underlined that the authority of the deciding minister to appoint is not generally called into question. Other permanent secretaries had the same experience and none could (or would) mention instances where a recommendation had not been followed. One permanent secretary said: 'I have never heard that changes have been made after presentation in the committee. It would indicate poor administrative procedures indeed.' Confronted with Knudsen's report of examples, under the previous left-wing government, of individual ministers getting their appointees rejected in the committee (Knudsen, 2000), one civil servant stated that it depends on the type of position in question. Personally, he did not have knowledge of a case where a minister's recommendation for a position in the civil service had not been followed. However, disagreements over appointments to boards of companies or chairpersons in permanent councils, committees, or the like were not unheard of, and ministers could have their recommendations overturned.

In any case, as many appointees may stay in the designated positions for much longer than the appointing ministers, it can be argued that the government has an interest in weeding out candidates selected for their relationship to the incumbent minister rather than for their professional qualifications. Top positions, most notably the permanent secretary, naturally generate more interest from the leadership of the government, and when a change is contemplated, the minister is expected to advise the committee that a process of finding a new candidate is to be initiated. The implication is clearly that while the minister's opinion obviously counts, it is not the only weight in the scale. Dybvad commented that 'the PM could change the government tomorrow and while he recognizes the importance of the relationship between the incumbent ministers and the [permanent secretary] in question, it also has to be the right person for the job who can function more universally'.

The overall impression is that by demanding that ministers justify their choices of candidates in front of their colleagues, the committee counterbalances individual predilections and criteria in the process of appointments. For appointments in the civil service, the role of the committee appears to be confined to the pre-recommendation stage. For other appointments, ministers' candidates may be contested at the meetings, even if this is not the typical scenario. Given the absence of input from opposition parties, it is naturally difficult to see how the committee can safeguard against political bias in appointments. While denying that such considerations play a role in appointments in the civil service, Dybvad did not exclude the possibility that political considerations play a role in the appointment of board members to executing institutions. Emphasizing that the overriding principle of board appointments remains professional qualifications, and that he does not himself have direct knowledge of political considerations playing a role, he says that 'for many positions on boards, there has been a bit of a tradition... that there is a certain political balancing at play... it is the government that appoints every time and the government could say that we don't care about earlier principles in this respect, but it doesn't... it is the politicians themselves that balance these matters. It is a Danish tradition.' This perspective is supported by the results of some of the sector interviews described below.

Scope and reach of appointments

Before presenting the findings with respect to the scope and reach of appointments in practice, it is necessary to include a few comments on the coding. It was not always easy to decide which of the alternatives would be more appropriate given the dichotomous choice of *yes/no* in answer to the question 'do parties (people linked to them) appoint individuals?'. The choice I made in this respect called for a clear choice of which positions to consider when dealing with the departmental level, on the one hand, and on the other on how to interpret the answers given. Firstly, at the departmental level, there is one position—that of special adviser—which the minister decides independently. Moreover, the top civil servants interviewed also made it clear that the minister played a definite role in the choice of staff for his secretariat, although here the process is led by the permanent secretary. If these positions were included, the code for all ministries would be 'yes', regardless of the degree to which the minister was seen to influence other appointments in the department. I therefore decided to exclude these positions from consideration in the coding. Since top-level positions at all levels are filled at the direct recommendation of the minister, it can be argued that the answer in these cases is 'yes, the minister appoints'. However, unless respondents believe the minister actually exerts an independent influence on the choice of candidate, the code of 'no' is chosen in answer to the question whether the minister appoints. This strategy for coding is designed to allow for the differences in response between respondents' evaluations on the extent to which ministers are seen to play an active role in appointments, or simply rubber stamp recommendations.

The analytical results of the scope and reach are summarized in Table 6.1. As is evident from the table, the overall conclusion with respect to both scope and depth of political involvement in appointments is that it is very limited in Denmark. Before dwelling on specific aspects of the use of appointment powers at the three levels, it is important to comment on what the different scores signify in substantial terms.

With respect to depth of appointments at all three levels—ministerial, NDAC, and executing institutions—the result of the interviews is quite unambiguous. Ministers' interest in personnel matters is confined to the top management, and interference below that level is not common. At both NDAC and executive levels,

TABLE 6.1 *The index of party patronage in Denmark*

Policy area	Ministries	NDACs	Executing institutions	Policy area total
Economy	0.00	0.00	0.33	0.11
Finance	0.33	0.00	0.33	0.22
Judiciary	0.00	0.00	0.00	0.00
Media	n/a	0.00	0.33	0.17
Military and Police	0.33	0.03	0.03	0.13
Health Care	0.33	0.22	0.00	0.19
Culture and Education	0.33	0.06	0.22	0.15
Foreign Service	0.33	n/a	0.33	0.33
Regional and Local Administration	0.33	n/a	0.00	0.17
Total	0.23	0.04	0.18	0.16
Environment	0.33	0.11	0.11	0.19

Note: Regional and Local Administration refers only to the municipality of Copenhagen. Environment is not included in the total scores

none of the respondents said that they knew of instances of ministerial interference below the top level. The agency directors interviewed—eight in all—were adamant about the point that decisions related to staff below their level were theirs to take, and indicated that ministerial interference in those decisions was unheard of. For departments, the overall impression given was similar, even if some respondents indicated that ministers might take an interest in and influence important middle management appointments (office heads). This was not seen as common practice, however. The practice of delegating decisions to the permanent secretaries, heads of sections and offices was described as a strong norm.

The range of appointments reveals an overall pattern of interference at department and executing level, while the agency level in the summary codes appears almost untouched by ministerial interference. These results have to be interpreted with some care. Firstly, at the departmental level, most respondents claimed that the minister only plays a determinant role in the selection of the permanent secretary (PS). As one respondent said: 'the procedure for hiring the Permanent Secretary is separate. The minister never interferes in any of the other positions... he never comes to the interview or anything.' The minister's right to select the PS is generally recognized. For example, in 2005, following a government reshuffle, the new minister of education brought the PS from the Ministry of Integration, which he had headed until then, with him to the Ministry of Education. The respondents who spoke of this event all commented on this as a highly unusual step to take. However, none of them seemed to perceive it as an illegitimate move. Permanent secretaries do not come and go in a predictable pattern, following a change in ministers, however, even if studies suggest that a large majority leave office before retirement.[21] In three sectors (Economy,

Culture, and Justice), the current permanent secretaries were employed by the previous centre-left government, i.e. before 2001. When coding the current practice with respect to appointments, two of these three sectors are therefore the only ones where the codes indicate that ministers do not actively use their powers. This is because most respondents in Economy and Justice did not believe the minister played much of a role in other top-level appointments. For positions immediately below the PS—section chiefs—the result of the interviews was more ambiguous. Some ascribed an independent role in the process of candidate selection to the minister, while others thought the role was more akin to 'rubber-stamping' candidates proposed by the PS (and the selection committees). The latter perspective was clearly prevalent among interviewees in most areas, except Foreign Service, and Culture and Education, where several interviewees indicated a more active role for the minister in selecting the top management of departments. It is interesting to note that in two cases there is a clear discrepancy between the ministerial role as described by the PS and by civil servants in the same department on the question of power over appointments. Where the latter tended to put less emphasis on the part played by the minister, the PS indicated a more active dialogue concerning potential candidates—although none mentioned instances of disagreement. No doubt the fact that the process of handling applications and interviewing candidates is done according to set procedures and handled by the PS contributes to explaining this difference. The minister is generally not visible to civil servants in this process. In fact, many heads of agencies, as well as top civil servants in departments, were not actually sure what role the minister had played in their own appointments.

Respondents also in some cases described strong differences in the level of involvement of particular ministers. The explanation most emphasized for the differences was 'time in office' of the minister, although personality differences were also mentioned. As one civil servant, who had at first outlined a modest role for the minister, said: 'but honestly, when a minister has occupied the office for many years, then you have a minister who is intimately acquainted with the staff and therefore also interferes'. The longer their time in office, the better the minister 'knows the house' and consequently has independent opinions on potential candidates for top jobs. In the areas of Culture and Foreign Affairs, the longevity in office of the recent ministers was specifically mentioned by respondents as a reason for more active involvement on their part.[22] The implication would seem to be that more frequent alternation in government or government reshuffles helps preserve the norm of a 'division of labour' between politicians and civil servants with respect to appointments in the civil service. This division of labour was mentioned repeatedly, as for instance:

> 'the employment of civil servants is the responsibility of the PS. I have no experience [of] any serious infringement on this.'

'the employment of civil servants is something the Permanent Secretary heavily controls. It is a very important management instrument and I believe all top civil servants are aware of this.'

However, where the minister was seen to play a part and to influence outcomes, it is important to stress that the choice is generally constrained to choosing between front-runners in a selection process, and only rarely involves proposing specific civil servants for the top jobs.

Finally, for the local level, only the municipality of Copenhagen was included in the study. The results for this municipality indicate that the mayors and committees of representatives of the political parties have a say in top appointments at departmental level, but also that in these cases it is a similarly constrained choice that is made.

At the NDAC level, agency directors are recommended to the government employment committee by the responsible minister, and in light of this the low scores for involvement at this level seem odd. Again, here, the permanent secretaries who have direct knowledge of the selection process all indicated that they discuss the potential candidates with the minister and that the minister plays an active role—even if it is constrained by a process led by the PS. In one instance, an agency director mentioned that he knew that the responsible minister had personally called his former employer to get an assessment of his performance. However, he portrayed this more as an act of validation of the recommendation made by the PS than indication of a minister who is active in the selection process. This type of behaviour would, however, seem to indicate an active role for the minister, and in this light the very low scores for interference seem at odds with this and similar remarks made by others. However, most respondents across all the areas believed that the PS was the more important person in this process and cast ministers in a passive 'rubber stamping' role. It is possible, therefore, that the very low summary scores in Table 6.1, which are based on the median response in each sector, may somewhat underestimate the role played by the minister in selecting candidates.

At the executing level, the type of institutions covered is diverse, ranging from courts to enterprises and museums. Perhaps not surprisingly, sector differences with respect to how the political level is involved in appointments emerge from the interviews. On the one hand, in the areas of Finance, Economy, Culture and Education, and Foreign Service the interviewees tended to agree that ministers make active use of their appointment powers. The competence to appoint to boards or directors resides with the minister, and it is not a competence ministers are inclined to delegate to the civil service. The process described by most respondents involved in such appointments indicated that lists of potential candidates are submitted by the civil servants and that the minister actively selects from them. Some respondents indicated that ministers actively add names to the list, but more described that the selection was made from names submitted by civil servants. However, the difference between the two scenarios may not be great, as a few civil servants described how the minister's preferences were taken into account when identifying potential candidates. With respect to the Judiciary, the respondents agreed that the minister's role was not active, while for the sectors of Military and Police and Health Care there were differences between respondents' answers. Most portrayed the minister's role as passive with respect to appointments to executing institutions, although a few indicated that the minister plays an active role in a few or even most appointments. Finally, for the Municipality of Copenhagen, the interviews described an absence of formal competence as well as practice of appointments at the level of executing institutions.

As Table 6.1 indicates, the results found for the sector of the Environment were not found to differ substantially from the other sectors. The early expert interviews cited a few ministerial top appointments made more than a decade ago, which were generally perceived as partisan and highly unlikely to occur in other sectors. Being a 'young' ministry, it was possible that the pattern of a merit civil service had been less resilient here. However, although respondents mentioned the same top appointments as 'dubious', we did not find evidence that a different style had been established. The differences seemed to be confined to a few appointments in the past.

In conclusion, with respect to the depth of appointments, it is clear that only top positions at all three levels are influenced by the political heads of sectors. The role played by politicians in filling positions in the civil service seems very moderate, however, and largely limited to choosing between front-runners selected by civil servants. When it comes to executing institutions, the role is much more pronounced as powers tend to be used rather than delegated. There is clear variation in the extent of involvement across sectors and institutions, however.

The role of parties, motives, and selection criteria used in appointments

The answer given with respect to the role of parties in appointments was predominantly negative (see Figure 6.2). Even so, it is still important to differentiate

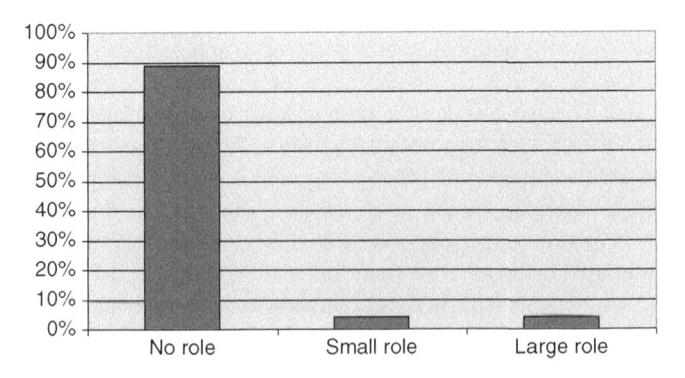

FIGURE 6.2 Party roles in Denmark

between the levels. At departmental and NDAC level, none of the respondents believed that parties played any role in the decisions taken. The relatively few respondents who indicated that parties do play a role in appointments in state institutions therefore referred to the executing institution level. Moreover, the positive answers were confined to the sectors of Culture, Economy, and Media. For the latter, both parliamentary and ministerial appointments to the board of the Public Broadcast Organization (DR) are political. For the area of Economy, not all agreed that parties matter, but one respondent clearly indicated that parties may be heard: '[The shortlist] can be changed completely—and that can be after conversations with the parliamentary group of the party or the parties behind the accord.' Similar statements were given with respect to boards in the area of Culture, although one respondent professed ignorance of exactly how it works: 'I have a feeling that it is discussed with the minister's party ... but I don't know exactly where the minister's inspiration comes from.' Another respondent in the same area was more confident: 'there is a political tradition with respect to the positions the minister has the right to fill, then they will oftentimes consult the spokespersons of the opposition: do you have a good suggestion for who might be relevant for this board? ... in this way you include the different parties ... Denmark is after all a consensus society.'

Parties, as organizations represented by others than ministers or mayors, thus appear to play a limited role. As expected, they are not present when it comes to civil service appointments, but neither do they seem to be a strong force when it comes to directly influencing appointments to executing institutions (other than the broadcasting organization). However, a few respondents in two of the sectors directly state that parties play a role, and indicate that partisan interests are balanced in the appointments as also indicated by Dybvad.

With respect to the motives behind appointments, the majority pointed to motives other than control or reward. However, caution with respect to coding would be in place here, as the meaning of 'control' is perhaps interpreted differently here than in the other case studies. The motive to control was taken to mean the wish to have a specific political agenda carried out by appointing a particular individual who shared such preferences. If the motive is to have an institution that is run competently, this is not seen as a control motive as such.

As Figure 6.3 shows, reward is never mentioned as a normal motive for appointments, whereas control is. Where ministers are seen to play a role in appointments at department and NDAC level, the dominant answer pointed to the interest in having well-functioning institutions rather than the ability to control the institution in policy terms. It should naturally be observed that these two levels fall directly under the ministerial hierarchy, and loyalty of civil servants towards the agenda of any minister is therefore implied. In other words, where ministers can instruct directly, the emphasis in appointment decisions is on professional merits, as subsequent obedience to partisan agendas appears to be taken for granted.

108   Carina S. Bischoff

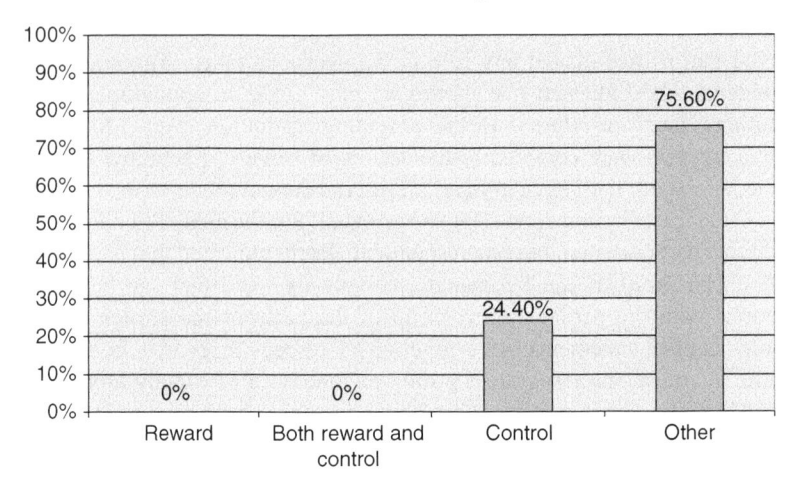

```
100% ┐
 90% ┤
 80% ┤                                                    75.60%
 70% ┤
 60% ┤
 50% ┤
 40% ┤
 30% ┤                                    24.40%
 20% ┤
 10% ┤    0%          0%
  0% ┴──────────────────────────────────────────────────────────
        Reward    Both reward and      Control            Other
                     control
```

FIGURE 6.3 Motivations of patronage in Denmark

The distinct impression, based on these interviews, is also that the political heads would have little cause to worry about the loyalty of employees, whatever their personal views. The socialization of Danish civil servants into faithful servants of their political masters appears to be extremely effective. Unprompted, one civil servant after another depicted a strong ethos of service and loyalty in the civil service (cf. below). Not only are obstructions of the minister's agenda regarded as illegitimate, but the ability to proactively further the minister's goals without waiting for instructions is seen as part of the job. Some selected statements may illustrate this:

> We have a tradition that civil servants know when they are in this role, it is the minister's politics they have to carry out.
> We live with changing governments. We simply change the hard disc.
> I cannot simply wait for the minister to ask for a strategy in this or that area, but I should be able to see where the minister needs to act.
> There is a socialization amongst us... you do not speak critically about your politicians because... you just don't.

Although this research is not aimed at uncovering attitudes in the civil service, it was difficult not to be convinced that civil servants have internalized strong professional norms that make control by partisan appointments largely unnecessary.

A small anecdote related by one of the agency heads in the course of the interviews illustrates the point. He described how a newly appointed right-wing minister's strong initial scepticism towards the civil servants had dissipated quickly after his instatement in office. Since the ministry had expanded significantly under the long-lasting leadership of the former left-wing minister, the expectation was that staff changes would be necessary. A few days after his instatement in office, however, he had joyfully exclaimed that the staff of the ministry all seemed to belong to his own party. To this remark, a political colleague had replied, 'yes, and last week they were all left wing'. The Danish civil servants could in this sense be called 'professional turncoats'. The idea that they have to leave their own convictions on the doorstep and serve different political agendas is strong. The top civil servants also emphasized, however, that their advisory positions also entailed 'speaking their minds' and occasionally arguing against the minister's proposals, as part of the package of giving political advice. Serving a minister was clearly not seen as simply echoing his or her opinions.

At the level of executing institutions, one could argue that the control aspect should be more relevant, as these are typically 'arm's length' institutions, outside the minister's direct instructional competence. However, most respondents resisted the word 'control' and spoke instead of the interest in having well-functioning boards and institutions as the motive for using appointment powers. Only about one in four respondents mentioned control, and these were mostly limited to the areas of Media, Culture, and Economy. It is interesting to observe that in the area of Culture, a motive that was mentioned was the need to balance appointments among parties of government and opposition. As one top civil servant said, 'it is neither control nor direct reward, it is more a question of getting political life to run smoothly'. Reward was only mentioned once in connection with ambassadorial posts, but here it was mentioned that it was rare, rather than emphasized as a norm. The fact that ambassadorial posts are given to career civil servants and not open to politicians also makes it difficult to use them as political rewards. When the motive of reward was brought up, almost all respondents seemed to believe this would be a dangerous strategy, which could easily backfire on the government.

Finally, with respect to the selection criterion employed, the dominant answer for departments and NDACs was 'professional qualifications', as shown in Figure 6.4. With one exception,[23] none of the respondents believed that either party affiliation, political beliefs, or personal affiliation with the minister played a role. In the category of 'other' criteria, the most frequently mentioned criteria were 'personal chemistry' and 'trust'. This was also most frequently indicated as the reason for ministerial involvement in the first place, since the close working relationship is seen to require that the minister and the civil servants 'get along'. In addition, other criteria mentioned included considerations for the representativeness of the civil service of society at large, for example by including concern for gender balance.

Unlike in Norway and Sweden, where the top management of ministries is politically appointed and leaves office at a change of government, the non-political character of the whole civil service has been retained in Denmark. This is not to say that such changes have not been proposed by politicians from time to time, but

110   *Carina S. Bischoff*

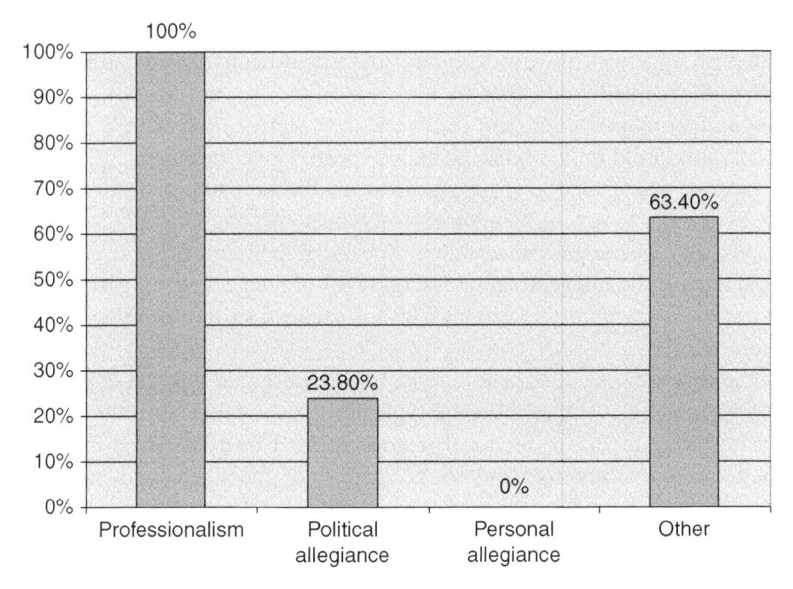

FIGURE 6.4 Qualifications of appointees in Denmark

Bar chart showing: Professionalism 100%, Political allegiance 23.80%, Personal allegiance 0%, Other 63.40%.

until now these attempts have been unsuccessful (cf. below). Finding this avenue blocked, it might be natural to expect ministers to appoint more political allies under the guise of professional criteria. This is clearly not the case, however. As one top civil servant said:

> As yet, I don't believe we have seen a minister who proposes a party political candidate. The system depends on a level of seriousness in the government employment committee so I do not think it would pass. I also believe that government recognizes that there is a day after them. There is nothing formally preventing them from hiring a party political Permanent Secretary, but they just don't.

The minister's role in appointments at this level is generally seen to be detached from the role as partisan. A permanent secretary described the intervention of changing ministers as follows: 'I do not experience that different criteria apply according to whether a social democrat, a conservative, or a liberal occupies the office. It is a question of his job as head of the administration.' Similar statements were given by other civil servants: 'I have never heard that any of the ministers that I have served undertake the slightest interest in what kind of political convictions people might have.' On the other hand, civil servants may also choose to be discreet about personal convictions. As one respondent expressed: 'our civil servants are relatively skilled at keeping it hidden so it doesn't shine through where they belong'. Another said: 'if you are at chief level you are better off not being explicit about your own political views'.

However, although many mention that having a clear public profile is definitely not an advantage for advancement to top positions, personal convictions—or indeed active involvement in politics—is not completely off-limits for civil servants. Perceptions on the matter appear to vary, as the following statements illustrate:

> Typically none of our colleagues has a political profile. They don't. Of course there are exceptions, but then it is completely legitimate and legal to be a party member... but there is a tradition in this house that it cannot influence your professional work.
>
> I know civil servants here who run for political parties—and not necessarily for the right-wing.
>
> Most staff here are politically involved. Many are party members.

In a few instances, it was mentioned that the political heads might see it as an advantage to have a person with a different political background from their own, to get a different perspective and strategic advice. Although there were different portrayals of how politically involved civil servants are, none of the respondents believed political conviction was a factor to be reckoned with in employment decisions. Rather, the ability to 'think politically' and advise on political strategy was universally mentioned as an integral part of the professional requirements for top jobs.

All respondents were asked to mention cases where the political neutrality of appointments could be or had been called into question, and one case that was typically mentioned was the appointment by the former left-wing government of a permanent secretary who had a background in the labour organizations before entering the civil service. The leader of one of the largest opposition parties at the time, Fogh Rasmussen, heavily criticized this move as a clear break with the principle of non-partisan appointments. However, when Fogh Rasmussen won government power a few years later, the same civil servant not only retained his position but was eventually promoted to serve as permanent secretary to the prime minister. In other words, the case most frequently mentioned as 'borderline' turned out to be rather uninteresting in the sense that this particular 'partisan' PS served governments of both persuasions.

These findings are also supported by an earlier comprehensive study of recruitment and dismissal patterns for top civil servants, where it was found that hardly any agency heads or permanent secretaries have a background in political interest organizations, and it is virtually unknown for them to come from private business or local government (Christensen, 1999). Interestingly, it was also found that those who did have a background in political interest organizations were actually selected from the opposition or from interest organizations not in the government's own base of support. Moreover, for permanent secretaries the period in office is clearly shorter if the appointing and dismissing ministers belong to the same part of the political spectrum, and it makes no difference whether they come from the left or the right. There is a clear tradition of selecting permanent secretaries who have advanced within the ministerial system, thus also reducing the opportunities for selecting on political criteria without breaking with established norms concerning qualifications required for the job.

At the executing level, respondents clearly emphasized strong professional qualifications as the most important criterion. Many indicated that the risk of scandals in appointing incompetent people overrides any potential gains. However, political profile was also mentioned by some 30 per cent of the respondents as a supplementary consideration. This was found by several respondents to play a role in the areas of Culture and Media, and also by some in the area of Economy. There were not many who believed that party membership as such plays a role, and instead the considerations refer to a more broad ideological profile of the candidate. Exceptions to this could be found in Culture and Media, however, where a specific example was mentioned of board positions being shared between representatives (in this case mayors) of different parties: 'positions on boards are not just given to partisan colleagues but you also take others so that it is not party political, but there is something for everybody . . . but not always. There are also boards where party politics plays no role.' A civil servant in the area of Economy said:

> [Political affiliation] plays a role, but informally. It is not something that is openly discussed. It is not party affiliation as such, but the minister knows where different business people stand politically. One could say that . . . right now it is not a problem because most business people are not very far from [the minister's] camp.

Somewhat surprisingly, personal affiliation is not a normal way to obtain positions, according to the respondents. As one respondent said: 'we try to avoid the networks that could be associated with VL-groups [discussion groups for top leaders in the private and public sectors] to avoid that the minister gets into trouble for having appointed someone who is in their network . . . it is just a bad case in the media'. This should not be taken to mean that it never occurs, however. Several could mention individual cases where they knew this had occurred, but it was not viewed as normal practice. However, being known to the minister (and not in a critical role) is a different matter. Many mention that this might often be advantageous when positions are to be filled.

Auxiliary bodies: councils, committees, commissions, and administrative tribunals

The somewhat politically 'chaste' relationship between politicians and the civil service described above does not extend to all bodies that fall under the minister's area of competence. There are many more autonomous bodies under the minister's jurisdiction, whose functions vary from monitoring developments in different policy areas or providing policy advice on specific issues, to passing judgements on cases put before them (Knudsen, 2000; Albæk, 2004). Although these institutions were not included in the coding—as explained earlier—the picture would be incomplete without some description of practices in this area. As mentioned, ministers enjoy powers of appointment to such bodies, although this power is often shared with other actors (e.g. major interest organizations), depending on the type of body. There is no clearly defined relationship between title and function in the Danish system, which makes classification and subsequent description difficult. This lack of clarity may also create a situation where ministers are less constrained in appointments than they would otherwise be. In an interview, Knudsen, Professor of Public Administration, stated that, 'Contrary to most other EU countries, in Denmark there is no clear-cut understanding of what the different bodies [councils, committees, commissions, etc.] work with. This gives the ministers considerable leeway to decide when it comes to appointments' (*Information*, 30 December, 2004).

When this group of administrative bodies was mentioned during the interviews, the vast majority of the respondents claimed that ministers actively use their appointment powers. Moreover, for a majority of the respondents, political profile was also seen as a salient criterion in addition to strictly professional criteria—although never as the only criterion. A selection of representative statements illustrates this point:

> [Political profile does not matter] to the employment of civil servants or judges or judicial chairpersons, but you can well imagine an advisory organ, that you would put a political angle on as a minister.
>
> You can find some who have the same ideological convictions when we speak of councils or committees—but when we enter the agencies and departments, there is nothing to put your finger on.
>
> We have these ad hoc councils, where it might be someone who has a vision of schools that accords with the minister's, and that can be a reason [for the appointment].
>
> It is part of the ordinary political process when you appoint to councils and committees etc.... these people are selected on their qualifications, network, and political profile.
>
> I am not sure that we would select as chairman to one of our councils or committees a member of the Socialist Party. I don't think so. We would rather choose a former conservative or liberal, something or the other.

Respondents typically differentiate between the bodies that provide policy advice—on an ad hoc or more permanent basis—and those that have administrative or judicial functions. In the former case, many say that political criteria are more likely to play a role, while in the latter the emphasis is on professional qualifications. For policy advisory bodies the minister typically either selects people whose ideological profile is close to their own, to get a result that resonates with their own policy preferences, or on the contrary selects people who represent different political visions in order get a proposal that will have an easy passage through parliament. One PS commented: 'the practice of placing some issues outside your own scope of action and [getting] somebody to work with some complicated questions somewhere, who can then come and tell you what to think about things. That is actually a very convenient "deflector" for the political system.' Moreover, a former minister explained: 'typically commissions and committees are appointed... to develop new proposals or plans. They can often be composed to reflect a certain ideological orientation, but the opposite can also be the case. That is, to select people with different political positions so that the proposal is easily passed by parliament afterwards.' For more permanent bodies, the evidence was more conflicting, as some mentioned that political criteria play a role and others insisted that only professional criteria were relevant. The differences may well reflect the fact that practices vary across the specific auxiliary institutions, but they naturally also reflect differences in experience of the respondents and their willingness to share.

Although systematic academic research on appointments to boards, commissions, councils, and similar bodies is missing, the subject has not escaped public attention. The war declared on 'expert tyranny' and 'opinion leaders' acting through such bodies, by the centre-right government in 2002, generated media interest in monitoring developments in the area. Media reports based on expert interviews and independent research indicate that the role of these bodies in policy making has not diminished in recent years. The perspectives given on appointment practices are similar to those given by interviewees in this study. That is, they are not aloof from political concerns (e.g. *Ugebrevet A4*, 3 May 2010; *Berlingske Tidende*, 22 November 2007; *Politiken*, 22 July 2010). Commenting on the actions of the current government, Professor Sonne Nørgaard said that there never was a real attempt to dismantle these bodies: 'What we saw was a confrontation with the experts appointed by the social democratic government that the right-wing government could not live with. What we see now is an expansion of commissions, which are established for political rather than factual reasons' (*Berlingske*, 22 November 2007). In 2004, one of the Danish national newspapers investigated whether political bias could be detected in the new appointments made by the government. They found that of the twenty-two people who had known political affiliations and received over 50,000 Dkr. annual remuneration for their work, only three were associated with opposition parties (*Information*, 28 December 2004). Similar indications of bias were found by the newsletter of the largest national confederation of trade unions, LO, in 2010. They mapped 1,221 government-appointed members of policy advisory councils, committees, and commissions from 2001 to 2009, and found a strong over-representation of business interests compared to trade unions (22 per cent versus 6 per cent of the positions) (*Ugebrevet A4*, 1 February 2010). While these studies do not present the full picture of political bias in appointments (for instance, the extent to which the centre-right government has reappointed people originally appointed by the centre-left government is not considered), they do support the expert statements that such appointments have a political slant.

The information provided by interviewees in this study, combined with experts' statements and research by media organizations, thus clearly indicates that political concerns play a role in appointments to the auxiliary institutions. Differences in the status and functions of such bodies make it difficult to get a precise overview of the nature and extent of this influence, however.

DISCUSSION OF RESULTS: WHY SO LITTLE PATRONAGE?

The findings of the study show that parties do not have an impressive grip on the state apparatus in Denmark. Evidence of party patronage is scant indeed. Within the bureaucracy proper, there are no signs that politicians apply partisan criteria when staff are hired or fired. At the level of executing institutions, there are indications that the political profile of candidates for top jobs sometimes plays a role and that partisan balancing is a key factor. But these are far from consistently applied, universal criteria. It seems that membership or other direct affiliation with parties does not improve the chances of getting top jobs in any of these institutions. Often quite the opposite is the case, as appointing politicians want to avert accusations of political cronyism in the media. Naturally, as in any system, there are exceptions, but the stories told by experts were consistent in their portrayals of the 'big picture'. This big picture applies to the main institutions of the state. What doesn't come out in the main arena slips through the cracks, however. There is ample evidence of politically motivated appointments 'on the side'. Political criteria play a role in appointments to auxiliary institutions including numerous boards, councils, committees, commissions, and the like. Not all such bodies are affected, however, and the influence is not pervasive. It was beyond the scope of this study to give a systematic account of the practices in relation to these bodies.

Against the backdrop of these findings, one might ask: are Danish parties amateurs in the art of power games, or is there some sort of rationality behind their 'ascetic' behaviour? 'Danish political parties are quite amateurish', said one civil servant in the course of the interview. The remark was prompted by his observation that interest organizations systematically put pressure on ministers to make appointments (outside the civil service), but that parties never seemed to get into the game at all—not in any systematic fashion, at least. The question is, why is that? What can explain the dominance of merit and the low level of partisan influence on appointments in the main public institutions? In this section, I will briefly discuss some of the possible causes of this particular outcome that were alluded to earlier in the chapter.

First, the absence of political appointments in the civil service may have historical path-dependent causes. At the first change of power after the institution of parliamentary democracy in 1901, the liberal party (Venstre) inherited a civil service that was closely affiliated with the conservative party associated with the monarchy (Højre). Although formal power to effect changes in personnel now lay with Venstre, their hands were tied by the scarcity of sufficiently educated elites among their own ranks, capable of replacing the existing administrative elite. When the first social democratic government took power in 1924, they faced similar constraints. According to Knudsen, the new political elites chose instead to work with the administration and establish Weberian ideals of a neutral civil service detached from the political elite (Knudsen, 1997: 12–13). The separation of political and administrative elites became a pattern, which characterizes Danish government to the present day. Political and administrative career paths intersect only on rare occasions, unlike in countries such as France where exchanges between political and administrative elites are normal (Gallagher, Laver, and Mair, 2006: 162–3). Patterns of this nature may be interrupted by extraordinary events or crisis situations, however. De-legitimization of the civil service occurred in several European countries as a result of association with a non-democratic regime or due to extensive collaboration with alien occupying forces. This could serve as a critical juncture and lead to extensive changes in the administrative personnel. However, as Knudsen argues, Denmark has not experienced a crisis of this nature that could justify a change of path (Knudsen, 1997). The strong norms of non-partisanship in the state institutions have therefore survived. These norms are apparent in political debates and media coverage, as well as in the civil service itself (Christensen, 2004; Knudsen, 2002).

A second type of explanation is related to the strength and stability of governments. On the one hand, the ability of governments to carry out their political agendas can be curbed by the presence of veto points. The more veto points in a system, the more difficult it is to change the status quo (Tsebelis, 2002). The Danish system has few institutional veto points, being a unitary state with (since 1953) a unicameral parliamentary system. However, there are many veto-actors in the multiparty system, where coalition minority governments have been the norm. Particularly, the prevalence of minority governments in Denmark can be seen as an obstacle for governments wanting to politicize the civil service, as opposition parties are unlikely to support such an agenda. On the other hand, stability in the parties that control governments can also be an important factor. As mentioned in the empirical analysis, several civil servants mentioned that longevity in office has an effect. Ministers who have been in office for longer tend to get more involved in decisions related to staff, rather than leave this to the civil service itself. A structured comparison of changes in the organization of the civil service in Denmark, Norway, and Sweden lends support to the notion that the number of veto-players and government stability matter (Larsen, 2003). Both Norway and Sweden had similar civil service traditions to the Danish, but introduced political civil servants at the top of the ministerial systems in the post-war period—in Sweden more so than Norway. Larsen argues that differences in stability and majority status of government in the three countries go a long way to explaining the differences observed (Larsen, 2003: chapter 5). In the light of this, Larsen furthermore suggests that it was no coincidence that the initiation of the process leading to the introduction of politically appointed 'special advisers' in 1993 coincided with the first majority government in twenty-two years in Denmark (Larsen, 2003: 75).

The third type of explanation draws on the potential costs and benefits of politicizing appointments in a competitive political system. If parties want to strengthen their own organizations and control over the state by making politically motivated appointments in the civil service or executing institutions, they have to consider the potential costs. It can be argued that the relatively strong electoral competition in Denmark, with regular alternation of parties in office and opposition parties that are rarely far behind in the polls, constrains government and reduces its tolerance to charges of corruption and other scandals (Grzymala-Busse, 2003; Gabriella and Jackman, 2002). Combined with strong norms opposing such practices and media eager to blow the whistle on cases of mismanagement or cronyism—partisan or personal—it may well make the potential costs outweigh the benefits of engaging in such strategies. This argument finds support in this study, where many respondents explicitly mentioned the threat of 'bad press' as a motive for being careful not to make appointments that could subsequently be criticized. In political systems where governing parties enjoy a more comfortable majority and where takeover by the opposition is a more distant threat, politicians can more easily discount such costs. One could also speculate whether there would be any real benefits to political appointments in the present situation. Since the Danish electorate—and workforce—is weakly identified with individual parties, party membership is low, and the party system polarization is weak, appointing people on the basis of party affiliation may well be a blunt instrument to achieve greater control of state institutions. Party affiliation may simply be a weak predictor of behaviour. It is also notable that in the cases where respondents mentioned that the political views of candidates mattered, party membership was hardly ever mentioned, while the broad ideological orientation of the candidates in question was. A former minister remarked during one of the interviews that experts and professionals are generally not interested in being active party members. So, even if demand were present, supply of loyal professional partisans might not be.

In addition to the structural causes discussed above, it is also possible to identify a role for actors in explaining the outcomes. Since the 1960s, leading members of government have on several occasions expressed their intentions to strengthen the political support for ministers by introducing models such as those in Norway and Sweden. However, these initiatives have been actively opposed by the civil service. The fact that such models would preclude merit civil servants from advancing to the highest offices in the ministries undoubtedly explains their position. But even if the civil service has worked effectively against such proposals, it is unlikely that the outcome can be attributed to their actions alone, since other changes in the organization of the civil service have, on several occasions, been implemented against their wishes (Christensen, 2000: 99). However, it is plausible that the introduction of flexible contracts giving more power to ministers in matters of personnel, along with strengthening of the political advisory functions of the civil service, has gone a long way towards meeting politicians' demands. The term 'integrated counselling' is used to describe the expectation that top civil servants have to be capable of advising ministers on matters related to political strategy as well as on substantial policy issues (Christensen, 2004; Salomonsen, 2003: 421; Finansministeriet, 1998a, 2004). Top civil servants see it as an integral part of their job to give political advice and do not perceive this to be in conflict with their roles as neutral civil servants, as described earlier. Although wishes for political appointments at the top are occasionally raised by individual politicians, reforms of the present system are not currently on the political agenda (for an overview of the Danish debate, see Larsen, 2003: 86–99).

It is naturally difficult to assess the relative importance of the causes discussed when there is only one case to refer to. And, quite plausibly, it is the combination of factors rather than any single one that explains the remarkable resilience of the merit bureaucracy in Denmark. However that may be, there are no signs of imminent changes in the system.

NOTES

1. I would like to thank the following people for their valuable input and assistance with the research for this chapter: Tim Knudsen for general advice on the project, as well as valuable comments on earlier drafts of this chapter; Søren Mollerup Rasmussen, Jacob Riiskjær, and Thomas Holmgaard for valuable research assistance; and Søren Mollerup Rasmussen, Birgitte Mortensen, Birgitte Vestgaard, and Helle Aagaard for assistance with interviews.
2. This category mainly includes care for elderly people and children.
3. The latest two major reforms were the reforms of 1970 and 2007, which among others reduced the number of municipalities from 1300 to 275 and then 98, and the number of counties from 25 to 14, and then to 5 at present.
4. The local and regional levels have a wide range of responsibilities in the areas of health, social affairs, childcare, education, employment, business services, transport, traffic and roads, nature and environmental planning, and culture.
5. Denmark, together with Iceland and Norway, showed the highest score in institutional trust, while Spain and Italy showed the lowest (Finansministeriet, 1998b).

6. The Ministry of Finance lists twenty-one, the Ministry of Justice forty, the Ministry of Health fifty-one. The precise number was not reported by the Ministries of Business and Economy or Ministry of Education.
7. The declaration was made in the New Year Speech by the prime minister in 2002.
8. The figure is low compared to the neighbouring countries Sweden and Norway, where the figures were 55 and 79 respectively in 2003. However, the Ministry of Finance in a recent report concludes that extent of public ownership in Denmark and the other Scandinavian countries would be roughly the same if the latter were constituted as proper companies as is the case in the other two countries (Finansministeriet, statens aktieselskaber, 2004).
9. In its report, 'State Share-Holding Companies', the Ministry of Finance (Finansministeriet, 2004) writes: 'there appears to be a common recognition that the Minister in charge of the ownership must necessarily be involved in certain business-related decisions' (chapter 2).
10. Parliament itself also enjoys some appointment powers to some institutions, including the boards of the public service broadcast corporations and the National Bank.
11. Lov om tjenestemænd: LBK no. 531, 11 June 2004 (reference to Danish Civil Servants Act).
12. Reference to the King in Danish law is to be interpreted as a reference to government (Gleerup, 2002: 22)
13. Lov om forbud mod forskelsbehandling på arbejdsmarkedet m.v.: LBK no. 1349, 16 December 2008 (reference to Danish Act related to differential treatment in the labour market).
14. Forvaltningsloven: LBK no. 1365, 7 December 2007 (reference to Danish Act related to public administration).
15. The principle of legality entails that decisions made by a public authority must adhere to laws and that decisions must be based on sources of law (Gammeltoft-Hansen et al., 2002:170).
16. Karsten Dybvad was the Permanent Secretary in the Ministry of State from 2005 to 2010 and secretary to the government Employment Committee in this period.
17. The Ministry of Finance is responsible for the personnel policies of the state, and the minister is therefore a natural member of the committee.
18. The membership in spring 2010 was Lars Løkke Rasmussen (PM, Leader of Liberal Party), Lene Espersen (Minister of Foreign Affairs, Leader of the Conservative Party), Claus Hjort Fredriksen (Minister of Finance, Liberal Party), and Brian Mikkelsen (Minister of Business and Economy, Conservative Party).
19. The minister is also expected give an overview of the other front-runners considered for the position, although the confidentiality of applicants puts certain limits on this.
20. At the first meeting, it is mentioned which positions are open and some suggestions for candidates are given and others are invited to give an opinion, but decisions are always postponed to a later meeting.

21. Eighty-five per cent of the permanent secretaries are early leavers, i.e. they leave before the retirement age of 65 and have not died in office (Christensen, 1999).
22. The former Minister of Culture, Brian Mikkelsen, served in that capacity from 2001 to 2008, while the former Minister of Foreign Affairs, Per Stig Møller, served from 2001 to 2010.
23. This was an independent expert, who commented that Ministers may choose persons who share their political view for the policy area in question independently of how their general political beliefs are.

CHAPTER 7

Party Patronage in Germany: The Strategic Use of Appointments

Stefanie John and Thomas Poguntke

INTRODUCTION

Political parties are the central actors in the political process of Germany.[1] They control access to virtually all (if not all) political offices in the Federal Republic, they occupy a central role in the process of interest intermediation and, last but not least, they are the unrivalled actors in the electoral process on all but the local levels. In other words: anyone who wants to get elected to an elected assembly above the local level needs to work through a political party because they control the nominations and determine the positions on (overwhelmingly) closed electoral lists. To be sure, there has been a very modest erosion of the party monopoly, in that electoral lists have become more open in some *Länder* (federal states) through the introduction of open lists or multi-member constituencies, but there are also countervailing developments in local politics where political parties seem to be acquiring a stronger position in many cases. Hence, anything but a considerable influence of political parties on the recruitment process in public and semi-public institutions would be a surprise, and political parties have often been accused of using their power of patronage beyond reasonable proportions. However, assumptions should not be mistaken for empirical facts, and this chapter sets out to determine how strong this partisan influence really is, how much has changed over time and, above all, who are the central actors in this process. In so doing we need to keep in mind that German parties are essentially federations of *Land* party organizations (Poguntke, 1994). The autonomy of *Land* and even constituency party organizations is very considerable. As a corollary, the power of national party leadership groups largely depends on their anchorage in *Land* party organizations, and this means that intraparty dynamics are characterized by a complex interaction of vertically and horizontally fragmented party arenas, which also want to secure their influence over personnel decisions.

The strong role of parties in the political process is mirrored by a considerable over-representation of state employees and civil servants among the party membership. While about 11.6 per cent of the German workforce[2] was employed in the public sector in the year 2000, the German parties counted between 28 per cent and 42 per cent of public sector employees among their ranks in 1998 (Biehl, 2006: 283). Even though these figures exclude a considerable, and growing, share of pensioners among German party members, this means that parties are very likely to find suitable candidates for posts in the public sector among their own members. At the same time, there is a considerable incentive for ambitious public employees to join a political party as this might improve their career prospects. These brief remarks indicate that we need to first provide a brief overview of the structure of the German state before we turn to the empirical analysis of party patronage, as it constitutes the institutional opportunity structure for political appointments.

THE GERMAN STATE

German federalism is characterized by a unique distribution of competences between three political levels: federal (*Bund*), *Land* (*Länder*), and local (*Städte und Gemeinden*). More precisely, the bulk of the competences are shared between the federal and subnational levels, but each political level also has exclusive competences—for instance, the federal government in Foreign Services or the *Land* governments in education policy. One has to keep in mind, however, that the distribution of competences does not follow the logic of policy areas but of specific functions. As a result, each political level might hold exclusive and shared competences in one policy area. Federal and subnational levels are also linked by the so-called *Vollzugsföderalismus*, which means the responsibility of the subnational administration for implementing federal law. Hence, ministries at the *Land* level have a dual capacity, since they not only govern their territories but also fulfil the day-to-day administrative tasks induced by federal law.[3] Additionally, this multilayered German administrative structure means that the local level is politically largely independent from the *Land* and federal levels (except for the general legal supervision). More precisely, higher political levels have no direct influence on the appointment of positions that are under the jurisdiction of local authorities.

The federal public administration is composed of federal ministries and several federal authorities (*Bundesbehörden*). The latter are subject to legal control and general supervision by the appropriate federal ministry and are mainly responsible for specific regulative and service functions. Moreover, a multitude of public law institutions (*Anstalten und Körperschaften des öffentlichen Rechtes*) are located at the federal level, such as the Federal Employment Agency or social insurance agencies. These institutions are under the legal control of the appropriate federal ministry, but they cannot interfere directly with their internal business, including personnel or management decisions (Bogumil and Jann, 2009: 96). The structure of the public administration at the *Land* level is quite similar. However, as each *Land* organizes its public administration independently, the number of institutions varies between the *Länder* (Bogumil and Jann, 2009: 97).

The size of the civil service in Germany has exploded in the years between 1950 and 1990. Since then, all administrations have been compelled to implement successive rounds of personnel reductions. As a result, the ratio of public employees to inhabitants in 2007 is similar to the one in the sixties (Bogumil and Jann, 2009: 114). Table 7.1 shows the number of civil service employees at the different levels, and clearly indicates the tendency of cutbacks. Furthermore, the distribution of employees between levels clearly reflects the distribution of administrative tasks between them. The separate statistics for direct and indirect public service are the result of the different legal status of the institutions involved (see note b to Table 7.1). In most cases, institutions categorized as 'indirect public service' execute federal competencies, while the bulk of public administration rests with the *Länder* and the municipalities.

German administrative tradition is strongly Weberian in that the civil service is conceptualized as a neutral instrument that follows a bureaucratic and legal rationality (Derlien, 2003). Access is strictly according to qualification and talent, and careers are regulated through criteria of seniority and qualification. In short, Germany has a strong tradition of a neutral career civil service characterized by permanent, often tenured, employment and a high degree of legal regulation and codification. It needs to be added, however, that the shift towards the principles of 'New Public Management' has eroded some of these principles. Firstly, the seniority principle has lost its overriding importance and careers are more subject to performance criteria, even though the actual implementation of the reforms seems not to have gone very far. Secondly, and most importantly, there is a drive towards replacement (whenever possible) of civil servants (*Beamte*) by public employees. In East Germany, for example, some *Länder* no longer employ teachers as civil servants.

There is a very thin layer of so-called political civil servants only at the top of ministerial hierarchies, who are explicit political appointees in that they can be sent to temporary retirement without any substantive reasons.[4] More precisely, political cabinets (ministerial spokesperson, personal assistants), secretaries of state, and heads of departments in federal ministries are political appointees. As already mentioned, the *Länder* organize their public administration individually, which includes also decisions about the number and positions of political appointees. For example, North-Rhine Westphalia (NRW), which we have chosen for our case study (see below), has fewer political appointees than the federal level. They include the chief of the prime ministerial office (*Chef der Staatskanzlei*), secretaries of state (but not heads of ministerial departments), presidents of

TABLE 7.1 *Employees in the German civil service (thousands)*

	Total[a]	Direct public service						Federal Railway Fund	Indirect public service[b]
		Total	Territorial authorities				Associations of communes		
			total	federal	Land	local			
1996	5,276.5	4,813.9	4,634.5	533.2	2,429.9	1,671.5	67.8	111.6	462.6
2000	4,908.9	4,420.9	4,277.5	502.0	2,273.3	1,502.2	69.8	73.6	488.0
2007	4,540.6	3,761.2	3,657.6	474.2	1,948.2	1,235.1	55.2	48.4	779.4

Source: Statistisches Bundesamt, 2008: 594

[a] Employees in the civil service are civil servants, judges, employees, and workers. Minor part-timers (*geringfügig Beschäftigte*) are not included.

[b] According to their legal status, specific non-departmental agencies and commissions (NDACs) and executing institutions (EI) from different sectors like economy, social services, and research are defined as indirect public service. More precisely, here employees of the German Central Bank (*Deutsche Bundesbank*), Federal Employment Agency (*Bundesagentur für Arbeit*), social insurance agencies, and legally independent public institutions (e.g. public research and development organizations) are included.

administrative districts (*Regierungspräsidenten*), the president of the Department of Constitutional Protection (*Verfassungsschutz*), the government spokesperson (*Regierungssprecher*), and chiefs of police. Until 2000, the attorney general (*Generalstaatsanwalt*) was also a political appointee.[5]

The role of political parties in German public administration has been highlighted by different research traditions. First, the legal discipline mainly views party influence in public administration with a legal-normative perspective and regards party patronage as illegal discrimination (Klieve, 2003; Kloepfer, 2001, 2002; Wichmann, 1986). From this perspective, it is assumed that the public service underperforms as a result of personnel decisions that are not exclusively guided by the principles of seniority and qualification (among others von Arnim, Heiny, and Ittner, 2005; Krusekamp, 2004). Even though the literature cites anecdotal evidence of party patronage, a systematic and quantifiable analysis of party patronage is largely absent in this body of literature. Second, research on public administration focuses on the politicization of the bureaucracy. Here, party political recruitment of top bureaucrats and the political preferences of civil servants are systematically measured by quantitative analysis of biographical data (Derlien, 2001) and several surveys amongst civil servants (Derlien, 2001; Derlien and Mayntz, 1988; Ebinger and Jochheim, 2009; Mayntz and Derlien, 1989; Putnam, 1976; Schwanke and Ebinger, 2006). These studies find an increasing degree of public sector politicization, also perceived by civil servants themselves. Since this research tradition is merely interested in administration and its performance, it does not investigate the motives and behaviour of political parties themselves. Other authors ask whether a change of government produces any changes in the number and quality of positions in federal or *Land* administrations (Manow, 2005; Manow and Wettengel, 2006a, 2006b). Using quantitative time series analysis, they look for pre-election (*Versorgungspartronage*: reward) and post-election (*Herrschaftspatronage*: control) partisan effects in public recruitment and promotion, indicated by a change in the number of employees. This macro perspective, however, is blind to patronage mechanisms that have no effect on the overall number of employees. To sum up, all of these perspectives struggle with explaining whatever they find. Hence, we have chosen a different path by looking at the extent of and actors in party patronage across the state and semi-public institutions and by investigating the motives that guide public appointments.

EMPIRICAL ANALYSIS

Data and the design of the empirical analysis

As mentioned above, federalism is one distinctive feature of the German state that finds its expression in (a) shared and separated competences between the federal government, *Land* and local governments; (b) the specific administrative structure (*Vollzugsföderalismus*); and (c) the structure of party organizations. Hence, a complete picture of the nature and extent of party patronage in Germany would have required the inclusion of local, *Land*, and national levels of the state machinery. Ideally, we would have covered all the German *Länder* as so much of the state machinery is under the control of *Land* governments and the *Länder* have quite different traditions and party political histories. In addition, a considerable portion of public administration is under the control of local government.

As this would have been a major project in its own right, the empirical study concentrates on the federal level and the *Land* of North-Rhine Westphalia as a case study of the *Land* level. This choice has two advantages: first, North-Rhine Westphalia is by a considerable margin the largest German *Land*, which means that we are in fact covering a considerable portion of the *Land* administration and, second, there was a complete governmental turnover in 2005 when power went from a red–green to a Christian–Liberal coalition. This is an almost ideal test situation, as the change of government is sufficiently recent to be present in interviewees' memories and sufficiently far back to allow us to gauge the effect of a change in government on party patronage.

Due to the above-mentioned political independence of local authorities from the other political levels, a considerable portion of the state apparatus is not systematically included in the research for reasons of feasibility. Nevertheless, in some policy areas our analysis is informed also by information that we obtained on practices in local politics. Our data are based on forty-two expert interviews[6] (for detailed information on methodology and selection of experts see Chapter 2 in this volume). This leaves us with the question as to how we actually operationalize party patronage. In the overwhelming majority of cases, the formal power to appoint lies with *party* politicians. Hence, the distinction between ordinary appointments and personnel decisions which contain an element of party patronage is not always very clear. Yet, our interviewees had no difficulty in identifying cases in which additional considerations beyond the actual professional qualification had influenced personnel decisions. To be sure, this is not always related to party membership per se. As we will see below, aspects of personal loyalty and trust are also important but they are considered to be part of the phenomenon of party patronage because they are dependent on the relationship between the *political* leadership and individual appointees.

In line with the cross-national comparative research design, German public and semi-public institutions were grouped into three institutional categories for each policy sector (for detailed information see Chapter 2 in this volume). The first, self-explanatory category, 'Ministries', refers to ministries at the federal and *Land* levels. The second institutional type combines 'non-departmental agencies and commissions' that fulfil regulatory or advisory policy functions. Strictly speaking, no German regulatory institution works independently of the appropriate ministry. They are, at the least, controlled by contract management, and as a result there are virtually no agencies in Germany (Döhler, 2007: 13).[7] Having said this, national and *Land* authorities show some characteristics of an ideal model of an agency (Döhler, 2002: 274–5; Pollitt et al., 2001), and we therefore included them in our research design. Institutions involved in delivering public goods and services are covered under the third category, 'executing institutions'. The number of executing institutions at the federal and *Land* levels is relatively small because much of this service provision falls under the remit of local authorities.

The admittedly crude description of the German state structure clearly demonstrates the very complex institutional setting, with numerous public and semi-public institutions. As a result, our interviewees could not always report on all institutions within a given policy sector. Furthermore, some policy sectors could not be covered as we did not manage to find appropriate experts. The military service, for example, presented itself as a closed club, while media experts pointed to the common knowledge through public news coverage. Contacted experts on the cultural sector emphasized that appointments of museum directors or theatre managers, for example, were normally not politically induced and therefore rejected an interview (see Appendix 3 for detailed information on the institutions covered).

Strictly speaking, our analysis uses specific institutions as units of observation, while our unit of analysis is party behaviour within these institutions. We generalize from many individual observations to a general pattern of party behaviour. While we are confident to generalize in this way, we obviously cannot claim that all institutions in individual policy subsectors are penetrated by parties in the same way. In other words, we have identified a general pattern of party patronage in the state, but there may be (institutional) islands not reached by political parties or reached differently.

The overall picture of party patronage in Germany

In our country study we included the comparison between the scope and practice of party patronage in three different institutional types. Scope is defined as the legal power of party politicians (or even political parties) to appoint individuals to positions in the institutions that are included in our research. Practice means that party politicians actually use their legal competencies, in that they are involved in the appointment of individuals. In addition, we distinguish between range and depth of party patronage: range refers to the horizontal extension of party patronage, which may extend to some or all institutions in each institutional arena; depth indicates the vertical extension in that we are investigating how far 'down' within organizational hierarchies party political considerations have an impact on recruitment and promotion. It is important to keep in mind that these measures do not reflect the frequency of party patronage. For reasons of comparability we do not attempt to measure precisely *how often* party patronage occurs on a certain level of the departmental hierarchy or in certain institutions.

The dimensions 'range' and 'depth' are combined in an index of party patronage (for technical details see Chapter 2 in this volume). Table 7.2 shows our results for practice of party patronage in Germany. For the sake of comparability with the other country studies the index refers to the practice of party patronage at the federal level, while data on the *Land* level are aggregated under the policy area 'regional and local administration'. As a result of the distribution of competencies in the German federal state, some cells are empty. More precisely, the federal state has no competences for Media, educational policy, or the police. Additionally, the local level is mostly responsible for executing institutions in the Health Care sector. Other cells contain no information due to the above-mentioned lack of expert interviews.

As many competences are located at the *Land* level, Table 7.3 disaggregates the entry for 'Regional and Local Administration' of Table 7.2, providing a detailed account of the practice of party patronage in North-Rhine Westphalia. Again, some cells are empty as the *Land* level has no competences, e.g. in Foreign Service.

Obviously, the numbers indicate similarities and differences between both levels, which require a more detailed discussion. In the next section, we will first present patterns of practice of party patronage in ministries at both levels, followed by a discussion of the relevance of NDACs for partisan political appointments. This is followed by a more detailed view on party patronage in executing institutions and its differences across policy sectors.

TABLE 7.2 *The index of party patronage in Germany*

Policy area	Ministries	NDACs	Executing institutions	Policy area total
Economy	0.67	0.11	0.00	0.26
Finance	0.67	0.22	0.17	0.35
Judiciary	0.67	n/a	0.50	0.58
Media	n/a	n/a	n/a	n/a
Military and Police	0.67	0.44	n/a	0.56
Health Care	–	–	n/a	–
Culture and Education	n/a	n/a	n/a	n/a
Foreign Service	0.67	n/a	0.33	0.50
Regional and Local Administration	0.75	0.22	0.26	0.46
Total	0.68	0.25	0.21	0.43

Data: Calculation based on 42 interviews
n/a: not applicable (no institutions at the federal level)
–: missing data

TABLE 7.3 *The index of party patronage in North-Rhine Westphalia*

Policy area	Ministries	NDACs	Executing institutions	Policy area total
Economy	1.00	–	0.44	0.72
Finance	0.67	–	0.56	0.61
Judiciary	0.83	n/a	0.11	0.47
Media	–	–	–	–
Military and Police	0.67	0.33	0.22	0.41
Health Care	0.67	—	0.11	0.39
Culture and Education	0.67	0.11	0.11	0.30
Foreign Service	n/a	n/a	n/a	n/a
Regional and Local Administration	–	–	–	–
Total	0.75	0.22	0.26	0.46

Data: Calculation based on 20 interviews
n/a: not applicable (no institutions at the federal level)
–: missing data

PATTERNS OF PARTY PATRONAGE: THE REAL STORY BEHIND THE PATRONAGE INDEX

Ministries at federal level

At the federal level, the minister is senior to all employees in his or her ministry; this means that the minister has the legal power to appoint all individuals in the ministry. As mentioned above, the legal competence of ministers to hire and fire civil servants based on political considerations is very restricted as it concerns only a thin layer of political appointees. Recruitment and promotion in ministries are prepared and controlled by the ministry's personnel department in cooperation with heads of relevant departments. Furthermore, the staff council for civil servants (*Personalrat*) has a legal right to be involved in personnel decisions, except for those about political appointees.

Essentially, the analysis of party patronage requires an answer to the question of whether the minister is actually involved in each appointment or whether he or she delegates this task. In general, all federal ministers are directly involved in the selection of their political cabinets and the secretaries of state who, according to our definition, make up the top level of the departmental hierarchy. The same usually applies to the appointment of heads of departments (*Abteilungsleiter*). In most cases, ministers (or their secretaries of state) are also involved in the selection of heads of directorates (*Unterabteilungsleiter*), and sometimes they directly decide about heads of divisions (*Referatsleiter*); all other decisions are delegated to the responsible lower-level heads who act in collaboration with the personnel department. It should be kept in mind, however, that nearly all personnel decisions (except for those of political appointees) require the involvement of the personnel department.

Figure 7.1 shows the actors who influence appointments in federal ministries. As the data do not distinguish between levels of hierarchy, it should be kept in mind that the relevance of the personnel department is much higher for appointments at the middle and lower levels, where it is identified as the pivotal actor that ensures promotion by professional criteria. The influence of the government only carries weight when decisions about state secretaries, and in exceptional cases about heads of department, have to be made. Partisan networks within federal ministries are particularly interesting: civil servants organize themselves in these networks that are neither linked between federal ministries nor connected to the party organization. Nevertheless loose contacts to the corresponding parliamentary group exist. These networks are used for discussions about strategic questions of the ministerial field of activity, but also for analysing and monitoring promotions within the ministry. If one group notices that its members are disadvantaged, the leader of the network will use his or her relationship to the staff council for civil servants and/or will contact the minister directly. Clearly, direct contact is more promising in cases of congruent party membership, but this does not guarantee that the minister will respond positively to such requests. This indicates that party patronage can also be demand-driven (see Piattoni, 2001c): some interviewees mentioned that civil servants join political parties in anticipation of advantages for their careers, and hence they push for such advantages. Clearly, party patronage has an element of

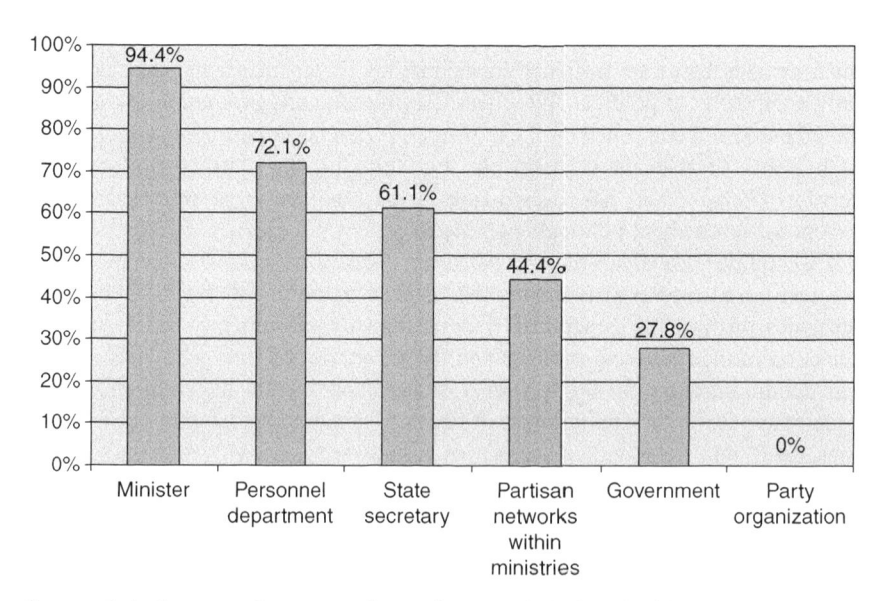

FIGURE 7.1 Germany: relevant actors for appointments within federal ministries

Data: N = 18 (multiple answers)

autopoietic organization, and incoming ministers may face requests from their own camp that they would prefer to ignore.

Overall, in all federal ministries the selection of top-level personnel is at all times based on partisan considerations. Ministers are overwhelmingly party members and always owe their office to nomination by a political party. Federal ministers choose their political cabinet in most cases according to political affiliation and, more importantly, always on loyalty and trust. In other words: the political cabinet of a federal minister is mainly composed of individuals that the minister knows from former working experience, that is, from his or her social and/or political networks. Decisions about appointments of secretaries of state are clearly party political. Finally, ministerial appointments tend to be heavily influenced by the need to satisfy the aspirations of *Land* parties or party factions, which can lead to the appointment of weak ministers (Müller-Rommel, 1997). In such cases, chancellors have frequently ensured that the secretary of state is a strong politician who effectively takes over much of the political management of the department. Generally speaking, a strong minister will not tolerate strong secretaries of state, while a weak minister's only chance for political survival may be to leave most important decisions (including personnel decisions) to the secretaries of state.

The frequency of party patronage in federal ministries correlates with the level of hierarchy. While party political affiliation often plays a role at the top levels, such considerations become less frequent as we descend the departmental hierarchy. Nevertheless, the relevance of political appointments goes beyond positions reserved for political appointees and is quite widespread among the middle level of the departmental hierarchy (see also Derlien, 2002). Furthermore, the practice of party patronage depends strongly on the leadership styles of individual ministers, while systematic differences between parties could not be found. However, some interviewees pointed out that certain portfolios are more central to a party's ideology than others, and this means that more party patronage will be observable, especially after a change of government. Finally, departmental appointments normally do not follow proportional practices, in that the other major parties regularly get their share of appointments. There are, however, few instances when a minister will do this in order to emphasize that his or her personnel decisions are mainly based on professional qualification. Clearly, this requires a strong political position and a considerable amount of independence from the minister's own party.

The strong impact of ministers' leadership styles on the practice of party patronage means that general conclusions for all federal ministries have to be read with some care. Yet there are some obvious common features. Party patronage is used to ensure that the ministry's top level is staffed with reliable personnel who are trustworthy and loyal and will support the minister's substantive and strategic objectives. This applies also to the heads of departments who are, in the context of this project, regarded as the middle level of the departmental hierarchy even though they are 'political civil servants'. From a comparative perspective, legal opportunities for patronage in Germany reach deeper into departmental hierarchies than in several other countries. This does not necessarily mean that party membership is a precondition for appointment but it is obvious that the heads of department need to share the political and strategic vision of the departmental leadership (for which formal party membership is often a convenient information shortcut). In any case, appointees always need to meet the formal qualifications necessary for employment as heads of departments (top position of the middle level). This is required by German civil service regulation and cannot be bypassed. Finally, the party as an organization seems to play no central role here (see Figure 7.1).

Ministries at Land *level—the case of North-Rhine Westphalia*

While there is variation in detail, the basic administrative structures of federal and *Land* levels are similar. Ministers are also senior to all civil servants in their department but the layer of political civil servants is even thinner than at the federal level. Compared to our results for the federal level, our research yields a somewhat more diverse picture for North-Rhine Westphalia. Even though heads of departments are (unlike at the national level) not political civil servants, they are often selected politically. In other words, party political considerations also play a role for employment and promotion decisions at the middle level of the ministries, and hence the practice of party patronage frequently goes beyond the legal scope. But again, political considerations generally play only a minor or no role for appointments at the lower levels of the ministerial hierarchy.

Furthermore, there is some variation between ministries, in that our interviewees reported very little party patronage in ministries led by Free Democratic Party (FDP) ministers during the Christian–Liberal coalition that was in office between 2005 and 2010. However, no reliable statement is possible as to whether a structural or personnel effect was observed here. It is also worth mentioning that appointments in the Department of School Education (which is exclusively under *Land* jurisdiction) are highly politicized in that they reach deeper down the ministerial hierarchy than elsewhere. Arguably, this is a result of the fact that this policy area is traditionally a contested party political battleground. Finally, other than at the federal level, there are no intraministerial partisan networks, which are sometimes influential in steering departmental careers, while the party organization as such has some influence on political appointments within ministries (see Figure 7.2). The reasons why these friendship circles do not seem to play a role at the *Land* level are not entirely clear. One might speculate that they are simply superfluous because (partisan) networks are smaller and more effective in *Land* politics and need no additional organizational arena. Also, we should keep in mind that we report, strictly speaking, only on the *Land* of North-Rhine Westphalia.

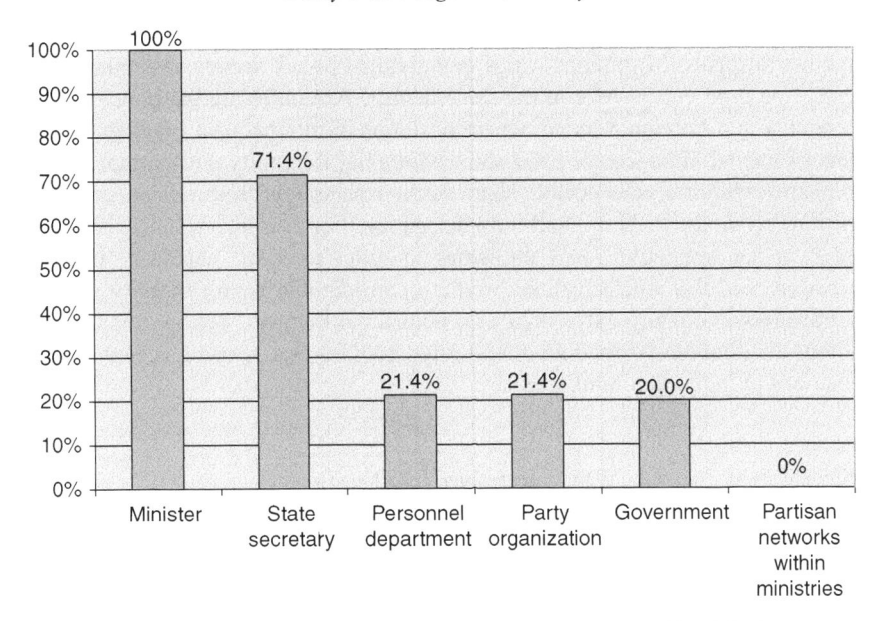

[Figure 7.2 bar chart: Minister 100%, State secretary 71.4%, Personnel department 21.4%, Party organization 21.4%, Government 20.0%, Partisan networks within ministries 0%]

FIGURE 7.2 North-Rhine Westphalia: relevant actors for appointments within ministries
N = 14 (multiple answers)

General mechanisms of party patronage within ministries

We will now concentrate on identical patterns of party patronage within ministries at both political levels.[8] When asked in general terms, 65.7 per cent of our interviewees reported that party political factors play only a small role in departmental appointments, while a mere 22.9 per cent report a large role. Clearly, these results reflect the diverse picture across the different levels of hierarchy. Apart from the positions of political appointees, ministers are very constrained by law when it comes to firing or retiring civil servants. Therefore, interviewees were asked about how party patronage is nevertheless possible. Hence, statements about the range and depth of party patronage summarized in Tables 7.2 and 7.3 represent the practice of party patronage. All ministries at federal and *Land* levels are faced with strict budgetary guidelines and constraints, especially for human resources.[9] Furthermore, all interviewees pointed out that the creation of new positions is not one of the main mechanisms of party patronage, as the budgetary constraints are simply too severe. While this instrument is used in individual cases it is clearly not a job machine for party members.

Hence, incoming ministers are frequently faced with a situation where key positions are occupied by tenured career civil servants who can neither be dismissed nor sent to early retirement. In such cases, reorganization is a frequently used mechanism. Another one is to offer positions in institutions related to the ministry, i.e. positions in agencies, boards, or international organizations. As the number of related institutions varies in individual policy sectors, this mechanism cannot be used everywhere to the same degree. Examples are the policy sectors Economy and Foreign Service, where positions in international organizations or developmental aid agencies offer some additional flexibility. Furthermore, some ministries recruit a considerable share of their personnel from related executing institutions on the basis of fixed-term delegation. For example, teachers or judges work in the respective *Land* ministries in order to inject necessary practical expertise, and this mechanism allows for a considerable degree of party political patronage without any extra strains on ministerial budgets. Yet, all this happens within the confines of specific qualification profiles that regulate access to such positions in individual ministries.

NDACs at federal and Land *levels*

A complex institutional array of non-departmental agencies and commissions (NDACs) can be found at the federal level but not all could be included in our analysis (for details, see Appendix 3). As mentioned in our introduction, federal authorities *(Bundesbehörden)* and independent commissions were included in the analysis. There are two mechanisms through which party politicians can determine senior positions in NDACs: first, in some cases, institutions such as the Bundestag and/or the government simply delegate individuals to top positions, for example to executive boards. In other words, these positions are filled by members (or alternates) of the delegating institution. Second, ministers have rights of appointment. This includes heads of federal authorities that are under their supervisory control, for example the Federal Networking Agency or the German Council of Economic Experts *(Sachverständigenrat)*. Both legal mechanisms (delegation and appointment) apply only to positions at the top level, i.e. the heads of federal authorities. All other positions in such federal authorities are under the exclusive control of the respective chief executives, and political parties do not normally attempt to interfere with their independence. Our analysis of NDACs in North-Rhine Westphalia includes only a few institutions, but the mechanisms observed are identical.

As delegation does not involve appointment to permanent positions, but *ex officio* memberships, our analysis concentrated on appointment mechanisms. There are no significant differences between federal and *Land* levels. In general, proposals for appointments are prepared within the responsible ministry, where the relevant department mainly considers the professional qualification of candidates. Hence, experts emphasize the influence of the minister and the ministries.[10] Party political considerations nevertheless play a role in the selection of heads of federal or *Land* authorities in the following manner: when an appointment to a single top position of a federal or *Land* authority, this needs to be made, i.e. whenever there is an opening for a single top position of a federal or *Land authority,* this position will normally go to a qualified person who is a member (or sympathizer) of the minister's party. Whenever more positions need to be filled at the same time (and this may involve several authorities), it becomes likely that the logic of proportional representation will come to bear. This will normally only involve the two large parties (i.e. Christian Democratic Union/Christian Social Union (CDU/CSU) and Social Democratic Party (SPD) at the federal level) but when smaller parties are in government and sufficient numbers of positions are available they may also get their share. Experts clearly highlight that only appointments for the top positions can be politically motivated and that this happens very often. Below this hierarchical level, however, almost no political appointment happens. Hence, the scope and practice of party patronage are equal.

Executing institutions at federal and Land *levels*

The research objective, namely to compare party patronage across different policy sectors, meant that a highly varied range of executing institutions were part of our empirical investigation. For example, schools and local energy companies are included, as well as implementing organizations responsible for carrying out the development policy information and education work of the Ministry for Economic Corporation and Development. Hence, the legal right to appoint individuals to these institutions varies depending on the legal status of the executing institutions. To put it in very simplistic words, the legal power to appoint is highly related to ownership structure. Whenever the state is (partially) an owner or stockholder of companies or organizations, for example, the appropriate ministry or ministries delegate individuals to the respective supervisory boards. Additionally, the important role of the local level for providing public services needs to be emphasized again. Schools and publicly owned banks (*Sparkassen*), for example, are part of the local responsibility for public service provision.

Practice of party patronage depends greatly on the particular conditions in individual policy sectors that influence the operation of executing institutions. To give some examples: formerly state-owned companies at federal and subnational (i.e. *Land* and local) levels face new constraints since they have been privatized during the last decade. Also, banks at all levels are working under new conditions as a result of the liberalization that was induced by European integration. Hence, federal ministries, for example, just delegate individual civil servants to supervisory boards of companies where the state is still a significant shareholder. Access to any other position in companies like Deutsche Telekom AG or Deutsche Post AG does not happen and is not intended. These companies are no longer part of strategic partisan considerations, i.e. neither for control nor reward or 'job machine' reasons, and party patronage has decreased a great deal.

Even though the above-mentioned conditions are the same for companies and banks at subnational levels, the practice of party patronage is more prevalent here compared to the federal level. There are several indications that partisan considerations play a role in the composition of executive boards at this level. Nevertheless, it needs to be kept in mind that party affiliation (or ideological closeness to a specific party or politician) for those boards is only an added value. First of all, the professional qualification is the main selection criterion.[11]

Executing institutions in the judiciary are all courts at federal and *Land* levels. Top positions in federal courts are subject to the logic of proportional representation. This method has been applied unchanged for decades. In the *Land* of North-Rhine Westphalia, the number of positions within the judicial authorities and courts where party patronage played a role has decreased, even though the incumbent minister can influence the appointment of top positions (i.e. court presidents). This seems to be the result of the change of government. In any case, access to the judiciary depends on the necessary professional qualification and neither the minister nor the *Land* party organization influences any appointment or promotion of ordinary judges.

As discussed above, no experts about Culture were interviewed, but the results on the Education sector are quite interesting. Nearly all the experts emphasize the high influence of party affiliation on the selection of heads of schools, especially due to the attractive salaries for those of grammar schools. However, the Christian–Liberal *Land* government passed a new school law in 2006, which has removed the power to appoint heads of schools from local administration and elected assemblies. Instead, a so-called school assembly composed of teachers, parents, and schoolchildren (older than 16 years) decide on the top positions in schools upon nomination by (*Land*) school authorities (*Schulaufsichtsbehörde*). Although the local administration can refuse approval, a tremendous loss of its original power can be attested. In terms of party patronage, the (local) party political influence was greatly reduced. Even though these shared competences of appointment between school authorities, local administration, and school assemblies (with school authorities having the final say) are quite common in most *Länder*, this cutback of local political power is quite unique. Only one other *Land* (Saxony-Anhalt) decided recently to withdraw the participation right of local administration in decisions about heads of schools.

WHAT MOVES PARTY PATRONAGE IN GERMANY?

Motivations

Eschenburg (1961) argued that control and reward are the major motivations for party patronage. However, our research clearly shows that aspects of control are far more important than reward, which is never mentioned as the sole motivation

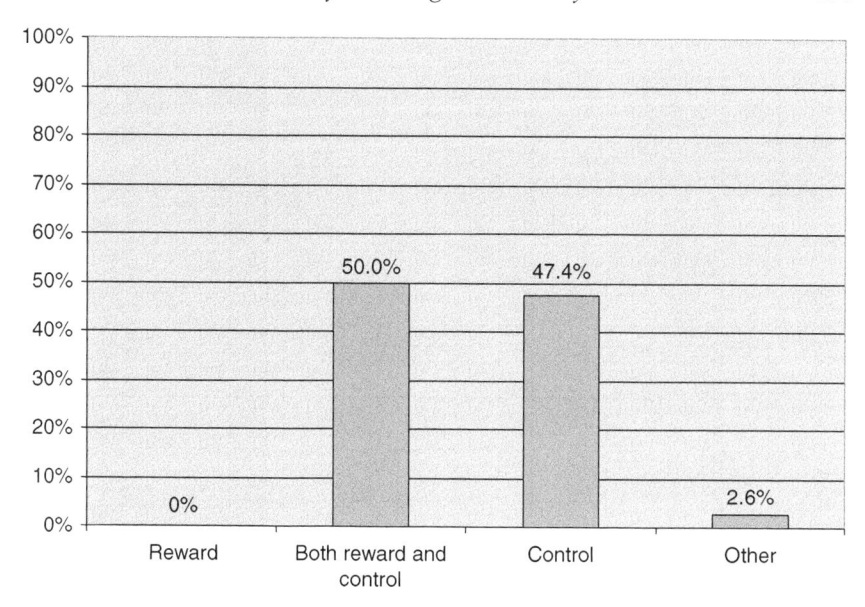

FIGURE 7.3 Motivations for party patronage in Germany
N = 42; Question: What are motives for party patronage? (multiple answers)

driving appointments (see Figure 7.3). Furthermore, when asked to choose 'which motive is the most important one?' nearly 74 per cent of our interviewees mention control, whereas only 5 per cent identify reward as the most important and 9.5 per cent say that both carry equal weight (N = 42). We have learned from our interviews that party affiliation functions as an information shortcut which indicates that the person chosen is likely to be trustworthy and to share partisan policy objectives.

Supplementary to reward and control, power was sometimes mentioned as one reason behind party patronage, especially at the local level.[12] Job appointments secure power within the administration and within the party organization. In addition, control over resources secures job appointments and facilitates business rewards, for example in the sector of road building, and hence influence beyond the administration proper. Beyond that, appointing members of a minority party ensures common voting in cases of unstable majorities. Astonishingly, the loyalty generated in this way persists for any length of time.

Unsurprisingly, the personal qualifications of successful candidates closely correspond to the motivations driving patronage appointments. Overall, personal allegiance (mainly trust and loyalty) and political allegiance were mentioned as the central motives for ministers appointing individuals for top and middle-level positions in ministries and for top jobs in NDACs (see Figure 7.4). Loyalty and trust are important since the minister depends on civil servants to implement his or

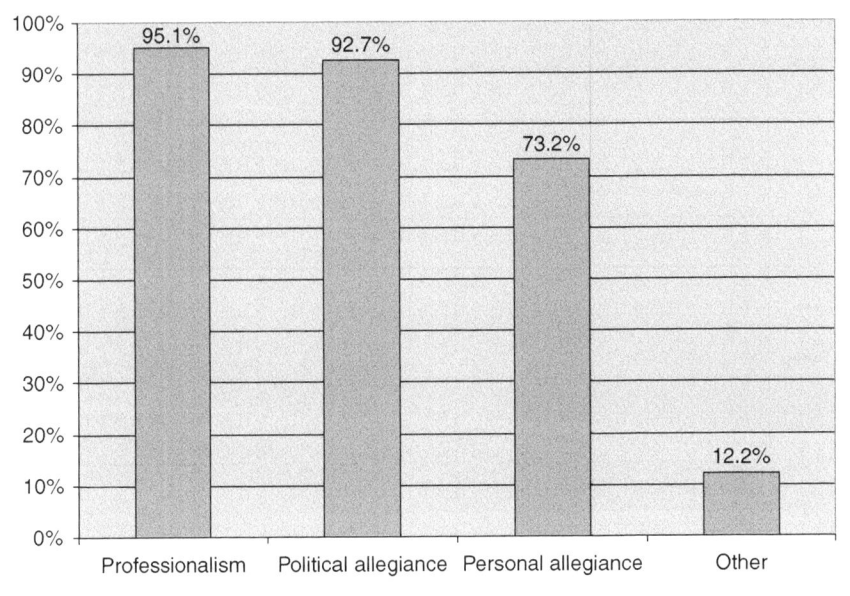

FIGURE 7.4 Qualifications of appointees in Germany

- Professionalism: 95.1%
- Political allegiance: 92.7%
- Personal allegiance: 73.2%
- Other: 12.2%

her political objectives and handle confidential internal information. Political allegiance may not necessarily require party membership but a broad agreement with the minister's political visions. Political and personal allegiance, however, are mostly combined with professional qualification. When ministers and their political parties want to achieve their political objectives through effective control of ministries and their related institutions they need to rely on professional qualification. Hence the latter is highly relevant for nearly all political appointments. In times of high media attention to ministerial workflows, no minister wants to run the risk of negative media exposure resulting from unprofessional work by his department because personnel recruitment disregarded professionalism on political grounds. Moreover, due to liberalization of the common European market, nowadays *Land* and local banks, as well as companies owned fully or partially by the state, need to 'survive' in the market. That (new) market competition implies an increased demand for professional management.

Actors

Clearly, our analysis of what moves party patronage in Germany would remain patchy without a discussion of the kinds of actors (collective or individual) who are operating the levers of appointment procedures. We have already seen that senior politicians like government ministers or secretaries of state are central actors in party patronage, as they hold the legal power of appointment. Yet this does not exclude the possibility that political parties as organizations also play a role in the process. Some interviewees mentioned personnel databases compiled by political party organizations at *Land* and federal levels, which are designed to provide an overview of human resources within the party organization and so should facilitate strategic employment. However, it was also reported that they are rarely used in an efficient manner. By and large, ministers and secretaries of state are also de facto the most important actors for partisan appointments within ministries and associated NDACs. This corresponds to our findings that trust and loyalty are highly relevant selection criteria when it comes to choosing individuals for top positions.

However, there are several avenues for party political influence on the decisions made by ministers or their secretaries of state. The above-mentioned political party networks within federal ministries are important for articulating demands for promotion by public employees vis-à-vis ministers or secretaries of state. At least members of the SPD, CDU, and FDP are organized in every federal ministry. Again, they are neither linked with each other across ministries nor with the party organization. The role of the party central office seems to be fairly small as no interviewee mentioned any involvement of the federal party central office in individual appointments, while there is some role for it in *Land* politics. Parliamentary groups sometimes lobby for specific personnel decisions. More precisely, such requests by Bundestag parliamentary groups tend to come from working groups (*Fraktionsarbeitskreise*). At the *Land* level, the chairs of *Land* parliamentary groups will often make concrete demands concerning senior positions. Overall, the influence of parliamentary groups and their leadership is much higher at the *Land* than at the federal level.

The effectiveness of such requests by party political networks, however, strongly depends on the specific leadership style of individual ministers, in that some may want to make sure that they are responsive to party political considerations while others (often those with greater political clout) choose to put 'state before parties' by ignoring such pressures.

When we look at key actors for executing institutions and NDACs, the picture does not change fundamentally, even though it becomes difficult to identify a general pattern of party patronage here as ownership and appointment mechanisms of executing institutions vary considerably across political levels. Nevertheless, we have found that in cases of proportional representation (e.g. for executing institutions in the Economy and Foreign Service and for NDACs) not the party central office but individual members of the government, the ministerial hierarchy, or the parliamentary group seem to have a strong influence on personnel decisions.

Overall, this highlights one of our main general findings in that party patronage in Germany is largely the result of strategic decisions by different individual party politicians at different levels of the state, and not by a coordinating party body like the party central office. In other words: individual party politicians try to pursue their goals (be it securing their office or implementing policies) through creating a supportive and loyal network using their power of appointment. However, these decisions are rarely driven primarily by party political considerations as other motivations, institutional logics, and actors serve as important counterweights.

CHANGE OVER TIME

The development of party patronage over time varies considerably between the three institutional types, policy areas, and political levels. Hence, there is no single answer to the question whether party patronage has become more prevalent over the past decade. Nearly half of our experts maintain that the relevance of party patronage has not changed over time, while about a third observed less party patronage and a few interviewees report a higher relevance (approximately 16 per cent).[13] In particular, experts on federal institutions see fewer changes in the frequency of party patronage than those on the *Land* level. Apart from the rather *Land*-specific reform of the education system, the liberalization of the financial and economic sectors is an important explanation in this context. This EU-induced push towards liberalization has had a stronger impact on *Land* and local levels, where many banks and service providers were affected, while it concerned only a limited number of companies at the federal level. Hence, the practice of party patronage has declined because privatization has simply removed organizations with very considerable manpower from political control. Traditionally, post, telecommunications, and railways have been important targets of party patronage. Now, only the railways are still under state control but increasingly act under market constraints, and this extends to much of the recruitment to top positions.

When it comes to a possible shift in the relative weight of motives guiding party patronage, our results are somewhat ambiguous. While most of our interviewees maintain that little has changed, others emphasize that the need for political control has become a more prominent factor in driving patronage appointments. Overall, many factors interact, including the personality of the minister, a possible previous change of government, and, importantly, the greater relevance of professionalism. The latter is reflected in a trend towards a more prominent role for professional qualification when appointees are selected, while loyalty and party political congruence have remained important criteria. Finally, our interviews show that the influence of party political considerations in personnel affairs on the middle and lower levels were gradually reduced by the implementation of a catalogue of criteria for recruitment and promotion within government departments[14]—even though party patronage has remained observable.

Additionally, a changing relevance of a specific political issue may induce changes in party patronage patterns. If a policy area becomes moved to the centre stage of political awareness by political events, like domestic security in the age of terrorist threats, the relevant minister is likely to monitor appointments in relevant NDACs much more closely than previously. Overall, however, little has changed for NDACs. Qualification has always been important, but the top job regularly required political compatibility.

CONCLUSION

Our research on party patronage in Germany yields a complex and multifaceted picture. Arguably, the most important findings are that there is considerable variation across policy sectors and types of state institutions and that parties as organizations play only a fairly minor role in the process. The top echelons of departmental hierarchies (and this includes the top of the middle level) are clearly under the control of ministers, who are always party political animals even though they may in rare cases not be party members. Here, our results confirm earlier studies (Derlien, 2001; Ebinger and Jochheim, 2009; Manow, 2005; Schwanke and Ebinger, 2006). However, and this is where we depart from the thrust of most of these earlier studies, this does not necessarily mean that ministers (or their closest collaborators) look first at party affiliation when they recruit to top positions. Our research highlights the importance of a range of other criteria that drive personnel decisions. Party membership may be a strong indicator of loyalty here but there are other, equally strong considerations like personal networks. Furthermore, professional qualification is essential, and its importance has grown over time. In other words, there clearly is patronage at the top level of ministries but it is not always *party* patronage in a narrow sense. Furthermore, actual practice depends a lot on the individual minister's approach, and he or she may not always consider primarily 'party friends' (a frequent synonym for 'foes' in German political vernacular) when top positions need to be filled. There may even be situations when an incoming minister needs to fend off requests by partisan networks in federal ministries of his or her own party, in cases where he or she wants to 'break the mould' of the party political penetration of the department. Last but not least, there are very strict legal constraints that ensure that recruits have the required levels of qualification.

Once we go down to the middle level of hierarchies the scope for direct patronage is limited as a result of budgetary constraints. In other words, there are simply no additional jobs to be filled, which means that ministers need to resort to reorganizing their departments in order to ensure that strategically important divisions are led by trustworthy and loyal civil servants.

In sum, party politicians are firmly in control of considerable parts of the civil service, but parties are not cohesively coordinated actors when they do so. This applies to the top positions in non-departmental commissions and agencies and executing institutions, and to a much larger degree to the core machinery of government. It is very difficult to find non-party civil servants beyond the upper half of the middle level of departmental hierarchies. However, this is not primarily the result of a centrally coordinated strategy by political parties wanting to 'colonize the state' (see for example von Arnim, 2004; von Arnim, Heiny, and Ittner, 2005). To be sure, the considerable ideological and, above all, regional fragmentation of German political parties would stand in the way of any such strategy. The structure of the German state is closely mirrored by party structures, and local and regional parties eagerly guard their autonomy in personnel decisions. Hence, political parties resemble opportunity structures for political careers, which are used by ambitious civil servants who have learned that it is better to be a member of an opposition party than not to be a party member at all. In other words, the motivation of rewarding party members through promoting their civil service career is not a dominant force driving party patronage. Here, patronage has a considerable demand side element in that middle-level civil servants use their party membership as a resource in their efforts to further their own career. It follows from this that party patronage is also not used primarily as a mechanism to recruit party members.

Having said this, we need to emphasize that procedures and motivations are different at the top levels. Here, party affiliation plays an important role but it is not the only criterion. When it comes to choosing close collaborators within ministries or chairs of NDACs or EIs, party affiliation is an important information shortcut when assessing the likely loyalty of a potential appointee. Even more important is a common way of thinking about the general direction of the specific NDAC or EI. This is not only ensured by party affiliation but also by ideological closeness. Again, there is fairly little influence of party qua organization on such recruitment processes, even though individual senior parliamentarians and/or parliamentary working groups may make their preferences known. Since power rests primarily with *Land* party organizations it is not surprising that we find somewhat more involvement of party actors in North-Rhine Westphalia than in Berlin.

To conclude, at the top level, party patronage in Germany is an expression of party government in that party politicians try to control strategically relevant sectors of the state machinery through personnel decisions. However, these decisions are not exclusively driven by party affiliation. First and foremost, they are motivated by the need of ministers to build a team of loyal collaborators that will facilitate the successful pursuit of strategic objectives. In some cases, they may even go against the mainstream of the party of the minister. From this perspective, party patronage has a significantly individualized component in Germany.

NOTES

1. The fieldwork for this study has been funded by a German Research Foundation grant (no. PO 370/7-1).
2. Own calculation based on Statistisches Bundesamt, 2008: 78, 594.
3. To give an example: while the federal ministry in Berlin is mainly concerned with legislation, the 16 *Land* ministries of justice control the bulk of the juridical system.
4. Given the generosity of German pension regulations, this is hardly a disciplinary measure.
5. For more detailed information, see the Constitution for North-Rhine Westphalia, articles 37 to 40.
6. In total 71 experts were contacted, from which 47 agreed to a face-to-face interview or an interview by telephone. Interviews were conducted between October 2008 and March 2010. Five interviews are not included in the analysis, either because the information obtained was not of sufficient quality compared to other interviews or because the information did not fit in the analytical framework of our sectoral analysis. Nevertheless, the latter are useful for understanding mechanisms and for the final qualitative evaluation.
7. Currently only two German agencies can be identified, namely the Federal Network Agency (BNetzA) and the Federal Financial Supervisory Authority (BAFIN).
8. N = 35; residual category 'different answer'.
9. Pension payments for civil servants at federal level, for example, are no longer covered by a common line in the federal budget but directly linked to individual ministerial budgets. As a result, every civil servant who is retired early directly impacts on the ministerial budget, and hence the instrument of early retirement is likely be used more carefully.
10. Additionally, beyond the partisan dimension other actors are relevant for those appointments, e.g. trade unions, business associations, or particular companies.
11. Overall, 36.4 per cent of interviewees attest that parties play a small role, while 42.4 per cent of interviewees highlight a large role for parties in these appointments (N = 33, residual 'different answer').
12. This is coded in Figure 7.3 as 'others'.
13. N = 42.
14. Note that there is no common selection criteria catalogue for employment and promotion that is used in all federal ministries. Each ministry has developed its own catalogue and proceedings for personnel affairs.

CHAPTER 8

Party Patronage in Greece: Political Entrepreneurship in a Party Patronage Democracy

Takis S. Pappas and Zina Assimakopoulou

INTRODUCTION

In early 2010, Greece went effectively bankrupt and had to sign a financial bailout deal with the European Union and the International Monetary Fund. Among that major crisis' several culprits, political patronage undoubtedly topped the list. For decades, political parties had enjoyed the power to appoint individuals to positions in the public sector, with two ominous long-term consequences: the excessive growth of the country's civil service and the continuous increase of the public sector wage bill. Greece thus presents as a model of patronage democracy in the European context. This chapter analyses the workings, mechanics, and logic of patronage in contemporary Greece by political parties that used it to outbid each other while at the same time leading the country into major crisis.

The term *patronage democracy* has been used by Kanchan Chandra to describe 'a democracy in which the state monopolizes access to jobs and services, and in which elected officials have discretion in the implementation of laws allocating the jobs and services at the disposal of the state' (Chandra, 2004: 6). As the same author further explains, the key aspect of such a democracy 'is not simply the size of the state but the power of elected officials to distribute the vast resources controlled by the state to voters on an *individualized* basis, by exercising their discretion in the implementation of state policy' (ibid.). When substituting 'state' in the foregoing definition with 'party in office' we feel that we get an apt description of the workings of political patronage in contemporary Greece—hence our labelling it a 'party patronage democracy'. Although patronage has been a permanent feature of Greek politics since the transition to party democracy in 1974, it became particularly pronounced during the 1980s and, since then, continued intensifying. The time frame used for the present analysis is the decades of the 1990s and 2000s, a period also marked by a major attempt to curb patronage by establishing a party-independent authority and making it responsible for the recruitment of civil service staff. To the extent, however, that that experiment went half-awry, this analysis also points to the persistence of patronage politics in Greece, as well as the limits of future attempts at curbing it.

The chapter proceeds as follows: the next section points to the role of political parties, party competition, and politicized state as the necessary parameters of understanding patronage in contemporary Greece, and also brings into the analysis a major attempt made for restricting it. The third section analyses the dimensions of patronage and, more specifically, its scope and reach within the state, while the fourth section is about the workings and logic of patronage as it takes issue with the motives, selection criteria, spoils-sharing, and the (lack of) mutations of this phenomenon in contemporary Greek politics. A final section contains the main findings and conclusions from the empirical investigation of patronage politics in Greece.

THE (RESISTANT) FRAMEWORK FOR PATRONAGE

Political patronage has been a time-honoured feature of Greece's political system. The earliest studies of this phenomenon were made by pioneering anthropologists and ethnographers like John Campbell (1964), whose fieldwork focused on mountainous communities in northern Greece and showed that patronage was an intrinsic characteristic of social and political exchanges at local level. Soon thereafter, political scientists and sociologists found out that clientelism was a quite pervasive phenomenon in post-war politics (Meynaud, 1965); some of them even went so far as to pretty much reduce their overall analysis to clientelistic practices and the ethos those practices tended to produce (Legg, 1969). Progressively, however, the study of political patronage became more fine-grained. George Mavrogordatos (1983, 1997), for instance, distinguished between 'traditional clientelism' and 'machine politics' (for similar views, see Landé, 1977; Günes-Ayata, 1994), in which 'the political loyalty and identification of voters benefits the party as such, rather than individual politicians' (Mavrogordatos, 1997: 2). Christos Lyrintzis, focusing specifically on contemporary Greek politics, has coined the term 'bureaucratic clientelism' to describe a distinct type of patronage that 'consists of systematic infiltration of the state machine by party devotees and the allocation of favours through it [and] characterized by an organized expansion of posts and departments in the public sector and the addition of new ones in an attempt to secure power and maintain a party's electoral base' (Lyrintzis, 1984: 103; also see Mouzelis, 1978; Spanou, 1996). To this day, as an ongoing comparative expert survey on citizen–politician linkages has shown, each of the two major parties in Greece pursues patronage in the form of public employment, but also by offering advantageous policy entitlements to targeted social categories (Kitschelt, 2009). As with other countries, no understanding of political patronage in Greece can be possible unless we bring into analysis its two constitutive components—the strong political parties and the politicized state—to which we now turn.

Ever since Greece's transition to pluralist politics in 1974, parties have played crucial roles in organizing the public space, aggregating social demands, socializing the citizens, and, in short, creating what has been termed a 'party democracy' (Pappas, 1999; also cf. Voulgaris, 2001). As major pillars of the pre-authoritarian regime became either discredited (the army) or abolished (the monarchy), political parties became in Greece the focal points of new democratic politics that, now vested with new legitimacy, were to organize the polity in a both democratic and rationalized way. The major parties that emerged in the new pluralist environment were the centre-right New Democracy (ND) and the (initially Marxist but soon to metamorphose into) centre-left Panhellenic Socialist Movement (PASOK). The turning point was the elections of 1981, which PASOK won by a landslide, thereafter creating the conditions for two decades of almost uninterrupted rule. That election also signified the transformation of the multiparty system that had existed in Greece for three decades into a classic two-party system (Pappas, 2003)—that is, a system in which 'the existence of third parties does not prevent the two major parties from governing alone, i.e. whenever coalitions are unnecessary' (Sartori, 1976: 186). Since 1981, PASOK and ND have competed against each other for the absolute majority of seats and the winner has always been able to govern alone. With only two exceptions (in the 1993 and 2000 elections), alternation in power has occurred regularly after each party has served two terms in office. The predominance of parties, in conjunction with the solidification of two-partyism, has given rise in recent decades to political polarization (Kalyvas, 1997; Pappas, 2009a), which often peaks around election times. Political competition thus often takes the form of a near zero-sum game between the two rival parties over the spoils to be gained from capturing the state.

Polarized competition in a two-party system is, of course, only one side of the patronage coin; the other side is statism, that is, the expansion of the state in all areas of public life, which thus becomes 'a major aspect of Greek political culture, not only as an ideology and practice... but also as a core social expectation' (Spanou, 2008: 152). The Greek state, far from resembling Weber's rationalized public administration system based on universalistic rules, has to this date four characteristics that, put together, create an ideal environment for the development of patronage politics: a tradition of state centralism; the large size of public administration and its extensive control over key sectors of the national economy; the overt politicization of its functions; and the lack of autonomy of the bureaucracy, which thus becomes subordinated to political authority.

State centralism, first, has a long pedigree in Greece as is associated with the pre-industrial pattern of development in this until recently homogeneous country that was motivated by a large public sector. This tradition has deeply affected politics which, to this date, is characterized by centralism, bureaucratization, and legalism. Second, with regard to size, the Greek state is today reputed as offering employment, whether on a permanent or temporary basis, to approximately one million individuals.[1] Besides being the largest employer, the Greek state has always aimed at asserting economic control over strategic sectors of the economy. Such state expansion has slowed down since the early 1990s, when privatizations were initiated by the then ND government and continued under both PASOK and ND, thereafter alternating in power. Even so, to this date 'government control on public corporations remains the heart of the matter' (Spanou, 2008: 157). The third characteristic of the Greek state is the predominance of party political loyalty rather than individual merit for both recruitment and promotion in the civil service hierarchy. As an author specializing on the topic asserts, 'Greek public administration is top-heavy and politicized. Every ministry has an overabundance of political appointees who aid the minister and who supervise and, at times, supplant top civil servants' (Sotiropoulos, 2004a: 15, 14). The fourth characteristic of the Greek state is the bureaucracy's lack of autonomy and its subservience to political elites. A wave of creating 'independent authorities' that began in the 1990s and continued into the following decade was intended precisely to reinvigorate the status of the civil service vis-à-vis central political authority.

Although never a dormant phenomenon, party patronage in post-authoritarian Greece became particularly prominent after PASOK's 1981 accession to power (Pappas, 2009b). Under PASOK, as numerous studies have shown, the public sector increased in size and most of its posts were filled with party appointees so that, at the end, 'PASOK subordinated the state in a surprisingly quick way' (Sotiropoulos, 1996: 116; Pappas, 2009a). Patronage politics, to be sure, anything but subsided after PASOK was succeeded in power in 1990 by its rival ND. Under pressure from its own electorate for precious state jobs and other state-related benefits, and despite an effort towards state reform through privatizations (Pagoulatos, 2005), party patronage remained the order of the day. In 1993, when PASOK once again returned to power, it had become quite obvious to everybody that patronage had got out of hand and that it should be contained. This led the government to establish in 1994 (Law 2190) the Supreme Council for Personnel Selection (*Ανώτατο Συμβούλιο Επιλογής Προσωπικού*, ASEP), an independent authority intended to be the watchdog over the hiring of civil service staff. Not subjected to supervision by the government or other administrative authorities but only to parliamentary control according to established rules of procedure, ASEP is run by a president, two vice-presidents and twenty-one council members who are elected by the Conference of the Speakers of Parliament. Its chief responsibilities are, first, to choose through written examinations and a predetermined grade system the permanent staff of the broader public sector and, second, to control the lawfulness of staff appointment procedures followed by core state and state-supervised agencies of the public sector. Since its foundation, and despite certain disadvantages 'in terms of slowness, legalism and rigidity' (Spanou, 2008: 164), ASEP has provided for the first time in contemporary Greek politics the most important mechanism for control of civil service appointments. At the same time, however, established political parties at both central and local levels and individual political entrepreneurs alike have developed at least four ways to get around it and continue their traditional patronage practices:[2] setting exemptions from ASEP's jurisdiction; recruiting personnel on the basis of renewable, fixed-term contracts; promoting the privileged gaining of work experience through temporary employment in state-funded programmes, which is then used to meet the criteria set by ASEP; and, finally, utilizing the personal interview with candidates.

More analytically:

(a) *Setting exemptions from ASEP.* With time, a large number of important areas of public administration became exempted from ASEP's controls. These exemptions can be grouped into three broad categories: first, state appointees with specific qualifications acquired through formal training, as are judges and coroners, public hospital doctors, university professors and researchers, armed forces personnel, the diplomatic corps and foreign policy experts, the clergy and other church personnel; second, the core staffs in an ever-increasing number of independent authorities and regulatory agencies (of which more later), as well as the staffs of certain state areas falling under the jurisdiction of top polity organs such as the Presidency of Republic, the Greek Parliament, the Legal Council of State, the National Intelligence Services; and, third, an assortment of special categories of appointees similarly falling outside ASEP's controls such as the National School of Public Administration graduates, journalists, and the numerous staff who are regularly transferred to better posts within the state, often as special advisers and experts.

(b) *Renewable fixed-term work contracts.* Another way to circumvent ASEP has been through the extensive supply of temporary but renewable fixed-term work contracts ($συμβάσεις$ $εργασίας$ $ορισμένου$ $χρόνου$) which lie outside ASEP's control. Such work contracts had been offered by state agencies (particularly hospitals, the local and regional administration, etc.) in order to cover personnel needs that are 'not permanent or lasting', but have both a defined beginning and a defined end (Law 2527/1997). In reality, however, this practice became overused for patronage purposes, let alone its many other advantages for the state employer: contract employees received low salaries and worked at irregular hours with no public insurance and only partial protection by the labour law, while the state retained the right for dismissal at any time without compensation (ASEP 2003a, 2003b, 2005, 2007, 2009; Greek Ombudsman 2006: esp. 46, 49). In some state areas (e.g. hospitals, universities, and research centres), and in particular municipalities and the various enterprises they may set up, temporary work contracts tend to be the rule, thus circumventing the ordinary process of tenured recruitment.

(c) *Privileged gaining of work experience.* Such experience is acquired through participation in (mostly EU-funded) apprenticeship programmes and has the advantage of adding extra points to candidacies for tenured civil service jobs via the ASEP-controlled procedure. These programmes, of which the most well known is the so-called 'Stage' scheme, are coordinated by the Greek Manpower Employment Organization (OAED), within the framework of the common European policy for fighting unemployment, for promoting vocational training and lifelong learning but in reality have been used extensively by both PASOK and ND governments as antechambers for full state employment. In practice, candidates for tenured state jobs use the experience gained through the Stage or similar programmes for gaining extra points (which, after twenty-four months of apprenticeship, may amount to 50 per cent) to be added up with the other ASEP criteria.[3]

(d) *The personal interview.* This criterion for appointments in the public sector was introduced as supplementary to the existing ASEP criteria (Law 3320/2005) and for the purpose of 'evaluating the candidates' personalities, as well as their potential in relation to the new positions'. According to the new law, any state institution could organize interviews with candidates, either in cooperation with ASEP or by itself. The interview weighs heavily (up to 40 per cent) in the final evaluation of the candidates but, significantly, there is no provision for keeping minutes. Under the last ND administration (2004–9), the practice of candidate interviewing was spread to many state institutions and other organizations, which include the Municipal Police and the Rural Police, the Fire Brigade, the Public Power Company (DEI), the Piraeus Harbour Organization, the Professional Privates and the prison guards, and the general secretary of Fiscal Policy (Ministry of Economy and Finance).

THE DIMENSIONS OF PATRONAGE POLITICS

As with all chapters in this volume, to examine the scope and reach of patronage we have divided the Greek state into three domains: ministries, non-departmental agencies and commissions (NDACs) and executing institutions. Unlike other chapters, however, we have decided to collapse the last two domains into one, which we will refer to as the 'extra-ministerial' domain, because the differences that have been observed between NDACs and executing institutions are relatively small when compared to the much more significant differences between the ministerial and the extra-ministerial domains.

As depicted in Table 8.1, patronage is pervasive in Greece in both ministerial and extra-ministerial domains. The relatively low scores observed in the areas of Foreign Service and Military and Police in the ministerial domain are due to the fact that both appointments and promotions here depend mostly on examinations and seniority. Patronage scores are overall lower in the extra-ministerial domain, but still remain high by European standards.

Scope of patronage may be further analysed as range (i.e. the number of institutions affected by it) and depth (i.e. the number of levels within each institution permeated by patronage), both of which score exceptionally high in Greece (Table 8.2). What follows in this section is a qualitative analysis of our empirical findings with a focus on how exactly recruitment of personnel takes place in the Greek state's three domains, each of them examined at all levels—top, middle, and bottom. These findings are summarized later on in Table 8.3.

Within the ministerial domain, first, at top level all positions are distributed through political appointment. In typical fashion, shortly after a government turnover or major reshuffle, the prime minister appoints the ministers, alternate ministers, ministers without portfolio, and deputy ministers. He also appoints the members of his political bureau, as well as the heads of three important bodies that fall under his own jurisdiction: the General Secretariat of Government, the General

TABLE 8.1 *The index of party patronage in Greece*

Policy area	Ministries	NDACs	Executing institutions	Policy area total
Economy	1.00	0.22	0.44	0.56
Finance	1.00	0.22	0.44	0.56
Judiciary	0.83	0.44	0.11	0.46
Media	0.67	0.00	1.00	0.83
Military and Police	0.22	0.22	0.44	0.30
Health Care	1.00	1.00	1.00	1.00
Culture and Education	1.00	0.67	0.67	0.78
Foreign Service	0.22	1.00	0.44	0.56
Regional and Local Administration	0.67	0.00	0.67	0.67
Total	0.73	0.54	0.58	0.62

TABLE 8.2 *Range and depth of party patronage by institutional types in Greece*

	Ministries	NDACs	Executing institutions	Policy area total
Range	3	2	2	0.78
Depth	3	2	2	0.78

Note: Data represent median values of all nine policy areas for each institutional level. Values for range: 1 = in a few institutions; 2 = in most institutions; 3 = in all institutions. Values for depth: 1 = at one level; 2 = at two levels; 3 = at all levels. For the method of score calculation, see Di Mascio et al., 2010.

Secretariat of Communication, and the General Secretariat of Information. Ministers, in turn, also have ample opportunity for appointments within their respective areas of responsibility. They first of all appoint their secretaries general (γενικοί γραμματείς), who are either recruited from within the ministry hierarchy (as is the case in the Ministry of Foreign Affairs) or, more often, chosen from outside the ministry (and even from outside the civil service). Ministers can also institute, by joint decision with the prime minister, special secretariats (ειδικές γραμματείες), and appoint revocable employees to head them; they also appoint the boards of directors in the agencies, corporations, and other institutions that are supervised by their respective ministry. The bulk of appointing at top ministerial level occurs within the political bureaus of ministers, alternate ministers, and deputy ministers.[4] Interestingly, the President of Republic also appoints his own people in the (not particularly overstaffed) various offices and services of the Presidency, and the same is true with regard to the President of Parliament. As for mayors, depending on the size of their municipality, they also maintain political offices staffed by their own appointees.

Still remaining at top level, but now shifting focus onto the NDACs and the executing institutions that comprise the extra-ministerial domain, the vast majority of state corporation directors, chief executives, and boards of directors are all *direct* political appointments. All such top management positions are in the full discretion of the government and filled upon political criteria. There are only a few but important exceptions, of which the most important is perhaps the appointment of the heads of the 'independent' and regulatory authorities, which are decided by the Conference of the Speakers of Parliament. The fact that those appointments are made after at least the two major parties have reached consensus ensures their non-partisan character.[5] Other exceptions include the appointments of chiefs in the military and police, the presidents of the major courts, as well as the senior diplomatic corps. In all those cases, the twin formal preconditions of advancement to top level are seniority and merit. It is not unusual, however, that governments try to sidestep those criteria and promote to top positions individuals who are politically friendlier to them. One such example was the decision of the PASOK government in 1998 to omit several judges of the Council of State from regular promotion to positions of vice-president, to the advantage of two younger and, presumably, more politically reliable ones (Alivizatos, 2001: 90). Quite similar is the case with appointments at the top of the military and the police, where hierarchically senior officers may be honourably discharged so as to make room for others who are lower in the hierarchy but politically closer to the party in government.

Personnel appointment procedures at the middle and bottom levels within either the ministerial or the extra-ministerial domains are remarkably similar. At middle level, first, although most posts are earned through regular advancement within the civil service hierarchy, personnel selection on the basis of party affiliation is also fairly common. Civil service personnel at this level include directors general (γενικοί διευθυντές), directors (διευθυντές), and heads of sections (τμηματάρχες). Promotion to the post of director general depends on the decision of a council, permanently seated at the Ministry of Interior and consisting of seven members appointed by the Minister of Interior: one senior judge, two university professors, a judge at the Council of State, two general directors from the ministries of Interior and Economy, and the president of ADEDY, the civil servants' union (Civil Service Code, art. 158 §1). Promotions to the posts of director general and head of section, however, depend largely on departmental councils (υπηρεσιακά συμβούλια), which are set up in each ministry according to unmistakably party political logic. Each such council has five members: three ministry directors, who are directly appointed by the minister, and two representatives of the ministry employees, who are elected by labour unions. Evidently, in what appears to be common practice, 'by appointing friendly directors to the council the minister can influence the selection of heads of directorates and of sections in the ministry. These directors tend to be of the same political persuasion as the minister' (Sotiropoulos, 2004a: 21).

A particular aspect of party patronage, which is widespread especially at the middle but also the bottom level of public administration, concerns transferring civil servants to better (and better paid) state positions. Such employee movements can take three forms: temporary interorganizational transfer (απόσπαση); permanent intraorganizational relocation (μετάθεση); and permanent interorganizational transfer (μετάταξη), which in essence amounts to a new tenured appointment. Since such transfers need not be sanctioned by ASEP, most of them are made on the basis of party (*and* union) affiliation or personal networking. They are also quite extensive. Considering, for instance, that each parliamentary deputy (of whom there are 300) and each ministry secretary general (whose numbers amount to several dozen) is allowed by law to transfer to his or her political bureau up to four civil servants, one understands that there must be a certain pool of party affiliated *and* personally connected civil servants who are transferred to better positions after every change of government or cabinet reshuffle. Personnel transfers are also common in many areas of the broader state. To give just one example, from the 7,000 individuals hired in the period 2004–9 to serve in hospitals as nursing and paramedical personnel, almost 3,000 were quickly transferred, either temporarily or permanently, to better state posts (Karanatsis, 2009).

At the Greek state's bottom level, and in the absence of unified legislation, personnel is distinguished into two categories, tenured and contracted. Tenured staff include those occupying organic positions in the Greek public administration (including the local government). According to the Civil Service Law (art. 12 §1), the recruitment of such personnel is based on yearly programming by the Ministry of Interior and depends on successful performance in written nationwide examinations supervised by the ASEP. In parallel, however, there is also a large number of contract employees 'who are hired on looser procedures and criteria, and often claim their incorporation into the permanent public workforce' (Spanou, 2008:

162). Contract employees are further distinguished into three specific categories: employees on renewable fixed-term contracts (συμβασιούχοι εργασίας ορισμένου χρόνου); employees with work contracts lasting for the duration of specific projects (συμβάσεις έργου); and seasonal workers (εποχικό προσωπικό). Most, if not all, of these categories enter the state through party patronage channels.

Having so far established the extensiveness and permeability of patronage in Greek politics (summarized in Table 8.3), the remainder of this section is a brief analysis of the logics of party patronage, mostly from the supply side, at the three levels of the Greek state. Beginning in reverse order at bottom level, patronage is sought after by individuals trying to gain (preferably tenured) access to the broader public administration area. Since in most cases such entry is regulated by strict ASEP procedures, state job aspirants exert pressure on parties and various political entrepreneurs alike to either circumvent ASEP in ways we have already seen or to expand the public sector by the creation of new institutions and agencies explicitly placed outside of ASEP's jurisdiction. When no tenured positions are available, or when obtaining them is impossible, party political patrons revert to the solution of massively offering opportunities for contracted work. This is particularly evident in state-owned corporations but also, and more importantly, in local and regional administration, where elected officials are often able to offer numerous temporary work contracts. When pressure mounts from the armies of state employees working on renewable contracts for either a fixed term or for the duration of a specific project, governments are often obliged to grant them tenure,[6] as happened, for instance, when, shortly after the 2004 elections, the government turned the renewable contracts of nearly 33,000 employees into open-ended ones (Presidential Decree 164/2004).

At the middle level of state administration, chiefly thanks to a rigid system of hierarchical promotions along public sector ranks, the demand for patronage to specific social categories becomes weaker. Typically at this level, state employees seek two things: first to climb the ladder of hierarchy in as fast and unobstructed a way as possible and, second, to get transferred across administration departments or sectors, whether temporarily or permanently, to positions with better working conditions and higher remuneration. Examples of such highly sought after posts

TABLE 8.3 *Dimensions of party patronage: a qualitative synopsis*

	Ministerial	Extra-ministerial[a]
Top	Full patronage	Extensive patronage
Middle	Mostly hierarchical advancement, yet large room for patronage	
Bottom	Extensive patronage, except where ASEP controls entry into state	

[a] For their many similarities, 'extra-ministerial' includes both the NDACs and executing institutions

include the Ministry of Economy (where even a janitor's salary is reputedly higher than a university lecturer's), the various services of the Greek Parliament (for a lighter workload, high salaries combined with lower taxation, and proximity to the corridors of power), most public corporations (for the many extra benefits added to regular salaries), but also posts for police officers guarding foreign embassies (for the extra pay they receive). Demand is particularly high for temporary interdepartmental transfers to political bureaus of government members, either as administration and secretariat staff or as advisers and experts. The best way for middle- and bottom-level civil servants to achieve these ends is by affiliation to the governing party *and* through personal networking. Labour unions can also exert significant pressure in favour of individuals either directly affiliated to them or known to be supporters of the party each represents.

Promotion to the top level of public administration is practically out of reach for career bureaucrats and open only to party appointees. In the extra-ministerial domain, there is opportunity for advancement from middle to top level only for certain professions, especially in the sectors of Judiciary, Military and Police, Education, and the Foreign Service. In all those sectors, however, advancement to top level seems to be as closely linked to patronage as to individual merit.

At the top level of public administration, demand for patronage is particularly evident among high-ranked professionals who either seek to advance beyond the post of ministry director or, more simply, nurture political ambitions. Among the most prominent professional categories vying for positions at this level one finds academics, technocrats (such as lawyers and civil engineers in the past, and environmentalists more recently, and economists at all times), the omnipresent journalists, labour union leaders, and even artists. Competition at this level concerns well-paid positions at the top of the state, both in the ministerial and the extra-ministerial domains.

THE WORKINGS OF PATRONAGE POLITICS

For most interviewees, patronage appointments are made for *both* controlling public institutions and rewarding party and political loyalty; among the rest, only about one out of four believed that control is the only motive for patronage, while less than 20 per cent thought reward the only motive (Figure 8.1). However, from the detailed qualitative analysis of our cases emerges a more nuanced picture that points to the existence of an interesting pattern: control becomes more pronounced for patronage appointments at the state's top and middle levels, while the reward function is evident mostly at its bottom and middle levels.

First, at top state level, ministers, deputy ministers, ministry secretaries general, public corporation managers, top executives, and boards of directors are appointed to exercise control on behalf of their respective appointers with regard to decision

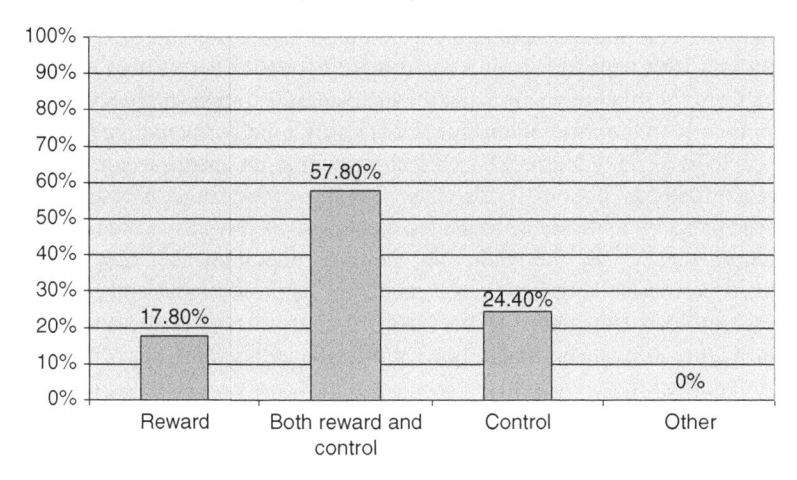

FIGURE 8.1 Motivations for party patronage in Greece

making, policy implementation, and the flow of state resources in large sectors of public administration. To a large extent, this happens because in practice policy making tends to depend on the priorities set by individual ministers rather than on detailed policy programmes drafted by parties while they are still in opposition. Therefore, incoming ministers seeking to pursue their own policy programmes usually appoint to key state positions falling under their jurisdiction people who they can keep under tight personal control. To illustrate by example, to implement her or his distinct policy programme, each of the three successive ministers of education under ND rule during 2004–9 had to replace all previous cohorts of same-party appointees with new ones owing their personal allegiances to the new minister. The same was true in Health Care and other ministries.

Conversely, most of the appointments at the bottom level seem to be motivated by the reward function of patronage. Temporary workers in public administration, service employees in regional and local administration, and lower administrative or other staff in hospitals, schools, or public corporations are offered jobs as a reward for their party allegiances or personal loyalty to individual politicians. A particular case of patronage-as-reward is the allocation of state jobs according to geographical origin, as is the case with whole groups of people from a particular geographical region appointed en masse to some organization controlled by their compatriot minister. Finally, at the middle level of public administration there seems to be a mixture of motivations for both control and reward. Control is, however, more evident with regard to appointments made mostly in the extra-ministerial domain (e.g. journalists at various state posts), whereas reward becomes the dominant motive with regard to intrastate transfers of staff.

The foregoing pattern becomes nonetheless somewhat blurred when specific areas are examined in closer detail. So, even at the top level, reward appears to be a strong motive for political appointments in the sectors of Foreign Service (both at various ministry departments and some highly sought after foreign embassies), Health Care (hospital directors), and the local administration (probably due to the predominance of family relationships at this level). Finally, the motive for appointing people (especially journalists and technicians) in the media sector, whether at central, middle, or bottom levels, seems to be reward either for services (i.e. publicity) already rendered or in the prospect of such services in the future.

Turning now to the motivation for political appointments, there was near-universal consensus about at least a modicum of professional competence and political and party allegiance as the basic requirements for state sector appointments (Figure 8.2). Again a high portion of respondents (63.6 per cent) believed that, in addition to the previous two requirements, the personal allegiance of the appointees to those appointing them is also of crucial importance. Finally, a smaller but still significant portion (33.3 per cent) suggested other requirements such as trade union membership, but also some quota system that seems to tacitly exist in public sector appointments for accommodating candidates of the smaller parties, particularly those of the left.

Since professionalism and political allegiance are constant, the requirement of personal allegiance emerges as the most important one. Indeed, from both interviews and the empirical investigation of many institutions and public organizations, we found that people at the state summits tend to know each other relatively well and, in several cases, to be related by family ties.[7] From the qualitative analysis of interviews, however, two different patterns become apparent. Appointments at the top level, first, depend predominantly on personal networking, often

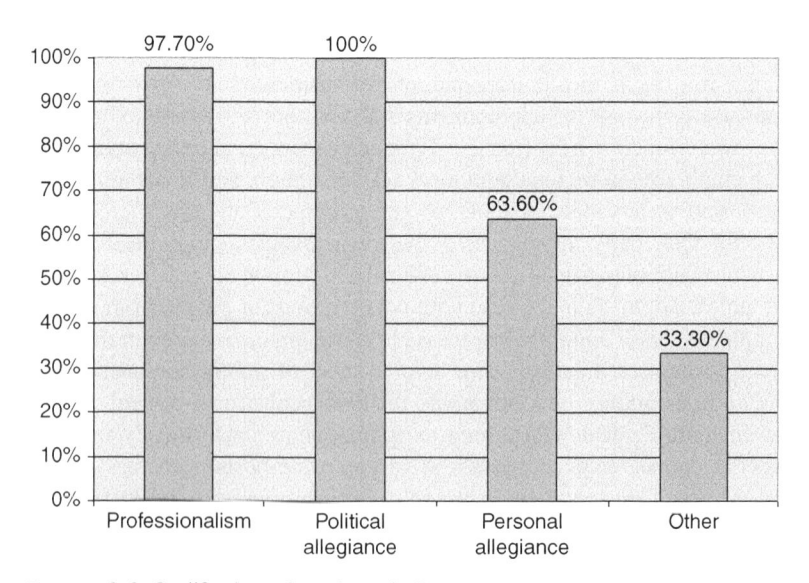

FIGURE 8.2 Qualifications of appointees in Greece

in ways that are unrelated to professional expertise.[8] This is to say that appointments at this level are made from within overlapping circles of candidates that are physically proximate to top party patrons. What is important in this respect is belonging to particular power networks and the ability of political legerdemain rather than professional expertise. This also explains the all too common circulation of the same political appointees among high political posts during any government's life.

Things are somewhat different at the bottom and middle levels of the state, where appointments are determined mostly by a combination of personal and party allegiances. Most of the ways that have been used to circumvent ASEP, like entry in state-funded programmes or the personal interview, are designed to facilitate the preferential treatment of party members, political friends, and personal acquaintances. This is particularly evident in the media sector and at the local administration level, where patronage still resembles in some cases traditional clientelism. Journalists and media specialists win privileged positions (for instance, in embassies, boards of directors, or the Radio-Television Company) through personal networking and, quite often, irrespective of party affiliation. Elected mayors, on the other hand, tend to offer posts to people they know personally and who are known affiliates to the party standing behind the mayor. Finally, irrespective of state level, candidates' membership in trade unions or smaller parties may be a strong criterion of admittance into the public sector, although usually in combination with personal allegiance. This raises the issue of patronage spoils sharing.

Are the opposition parties eligible for appointing their own people in state positions, and to what extent? The general pattern that emerges here is that sharing in the spoils increases the furthest one moves away from the top state positions. Top positions are in fact off limits for members of the opposition parties in both the ministerial and, to a lesser extent, the extra-ministerial levels. The only exceptions are either when some individual at the top is determined to appoint on merit; when no candidates affiliated to the governing party are readily available, as may sometimes be the case in regional executing institutions (e.g. hospital directors); or, as already explained, when some quota system has been informally agreed for the representation of opposition in various boards of directors, 'independent' authorities, or even some core state areas (as is the case with the Greek Parliament staff, the majority of which is appointed in proportion to the strength of each political party). Another exception concerns the media sector, thanks to both its extreme politicization and the fact that a large proportion of top journalists and other media people are affiliated with the left.

Moving to the middle level of public administration, sharing in the spoils depends primarily on one's belonging in informal networks controlling the appointment system. As for appointees belonging to networks that are removed from power, they are often transferred to disadvantageous positions (the so-called 'state's freezer') while new ones take their former positions. Finally, spoils sharing is more common at the bottom level of appointments in the public sector and, more particularly, in the local administration. The reason for this is, quite obviously, the importance of interpersonal relations at this level and of course the great number of posts that have to be filled.

Finally, as expected given that the framework of patronage in Greece has remained stable, all interviewees underlined the strong continuity of patronage practices during the last two or three decades, as well as the great similarities in the employment of such practices by either of the two major parties once in office. During those decades, the main elements of party and political systems in Greece have remained essentially unaltered: two major parties regularly alternating in power, both thriving on the uninterrupted expansion of an overpoliticized state. Asked about the reasons for such a remarkably ubiquitous practice, our interviewees offered three explanations: the limitations of the Europeanization project in Greece; the failure of extensive market liberalization; and the absence of a bold administrative reform specifically addressing the issue of party patronage.

FINDINGS AND CONCLUSIONS

Shortly after PASOK's electoral victory in 2000, new Health Minister, Alekos Papadopoulos, a prominent party veteran with a solid reformist record, set out to reorganize Greece's health care system. The centrepiece of the proposed reforms was the establishment throughout the country of seventeen 'regional health systems' (PESY) aimed at improving efficiency and quality in the provision of health services. The core of this reform was 'to shift the power base of the hospital boards, the majority of which was composed of government-appointed members and representatives of the hospital unions' to regional administrators and hospital managers, who were now made responsible for planning each region's health system (Mossialos and Allin, 2005: 429). The law establishing the PESY was passed early in 2001 and, promptly, the minister appointed regional administrators and hospital managers. Not long thereafter, under the combined attack of several stakeholders, the attempted reform failed to materialize. Civil servants in both the ministry and the hospitals, as well as hospital doctors, stood against the reform because it undermined their influence on new personnel appointments; the same happened with party politicians, who, long accustomed to influencing 'individual appointments in hospital boards, no longer had political connections with some of the regional [administrators] and hospital managers who were directly accountable to the Minister of Health' (ibid.: 437).

The following is the experience of such a regional health administrator. Our interviewee, a doctor by profession with political sympathies to PASOK but no formal affiliation to the party organization, was in 2001 personally appointed by

TABLE 8.4 *Summary of chief characteristics of political patronage in Greece*

State level	Patronage type	Range	Appointees	Motives	Criteria	Spoils sharing
Top	Political appointments	Full	Individuals	Control	Political/personal networking	No
Middle	Within-state transfers	Extensive	Individuals	Control/reward	Varies	Some
Bottom	Temporary work contracts/transfers	Extensive	Individuals/groups	Reward	Personal/party loyalty	Yes

the minister to administer one of the recently established PESY. Her regional unit was an electoral stronghold of ND, then the major opposition party, and included four hospitals. Upon assuming her tasks, the new regional director staffed her office with people of her own choice through temporary internal state transfers and, with the minister's approval, appointed new hospital directors. Although she acknowledged that her preference was to appoint PASOK-affiliated directors, availability was low, with the result that three out of the four hospital directors chosen belonged to ND. Given their diverse party sympathies, it came as no surprise to the new regional health administrator that some of the hospital directors were not particularly cooperative. Her biggest surprise, however, was the outright hostility displayed by PASOK's local organizations for fear of losing control over appointments at the bottom and middle levels of the regional health system. When our administrator had made it clear to the local party entrepreneurs that she meant to restrict appointments, the party organization declared open war against her and sabotaged the reform. As the case of our interviewee was certainly not unique, the reform eventually failed at national level and Papadopoulos was replaced in the Health Ministry by a new person who was more prone to patronage. Within days of his appointment, and as a new national election was forthcoming, the new minister requested (through his secretary general) from our regional administrator the transfer of selected personnel from hospitals to other, more privileged posts. Our regional administrator refused and gave up her position. As she reported, the new administrator, with only three months to go until the election, arranged at least thirty public employee transfers to better state posts. Meanwhile, reform of the health care system was altogether abandoned.

The foregoing case contains all the components of party patronage politics as exercised in contemporary Greece (and summarized in Table 8.4). First, patronage in contemporary Greek politics is both extensive and pervasive. In point of fact, it is hard to find any state sector that is not deeply permeated by political patronage.[9] Patrons not only use all the opportunities they have legally created, but they also try to twist the law so as to expand their chances of patronage, as is clearly shown by the various ways used to circumvent the ASEP. Patronage includes appointments to top state jobs, preferential promotion within the civil service, and the offering of temporary positions in the public sector. Patronage, furthermore, has to be understood in relation to three structural characteristics of the post-authoritarian Greek political system:

(a) the predominance of parties in the polity and the creation since 1981 of a two-party system in which the significant parties have regularly alternated in office
(b) the intense polarization of political competition that has been used by the major parties in order to both rally their supporters and, once in power, fully exploit the state resources
(c) the politicization of the civil service, in conjunction with its lack of autonomy from party political authority.

To the extent that parties dominate a winner-takes-all political system, the state is up for grabs by the party that wins elections and the spoils ready to be distributed to party supporters, voters, and other affiliates.

Second, patronage is particularly evident at the bottom and top ends of the public administration area, but also flourishes at the middle level in the form of preferential intrastate transfers. At the bottom level, each party has tried while in office to allow into the state the largest number of individuals possible. This has led to the inflation of the civil service, either through the hiring of large numbers of state employees or through the creation of new state institutions and agencies in order to absorb the surplus labour force. As successive governments have brought into the state new masses of employees on the basis of party patronage criteria, the Greek state has come to look like a sedimentary rock, each layer of which represents a particular geological period.

Turning to the top level, almost all appointments in both the ministerial and the extra-ministerial domains are political, and in the vast majority of cases their duration equals the longevity of either the party in office or the appointing minister's stay in the cabinet. The only exceptions to this rule are a few high-ranked positions associated with specific terms, and the heads of the 'independent' and regulatory authorities. Patronage is also clearly evident at the middle level of public administration and includes preferential promotion within the civil service, as well as transfers to privileged in-state positions.

Third, and perhaps most important, is the fact that patronage is not produced by political parties acting as unitary actors. It is rather prompted by political entrepreneurs that thrive inside the two major parties, which, despite their commonly loose organizational structures and blurred ideological positions, are destined to alternate in office. A two-way logic seems to develop: the parties need those entrepreneurs who, through developing patronage networks, bring in voters, and the political entrepreneurs need the parties, especially when in office, for offering them access to state-related spoils. There is, however, an unintended consequence. Party entrepreneurs in both of the major parties may exercise as strong an opposition to same-party fellow politicians as to the adversary party. As for the smaller parties, they take part in patronage politics only in some sectors (e.g. the media or higher education institutions, where the left is relatively strong) or in proportion to the strength of the unions that represent them.

NOTES

1. That the real number of public employees in Greece is a matter of contention is due to the fact that data about the size of the Greek public sector are scant and often unreliable. According to recent official figures (Greek Ministry of Interior, 2009), by the end of 2006, the *core* public sector (i.e. ministries, local and regional administration units, and other state institutions governed by either public or private law) employed on a permanent basis 375,004 individuals. To this figure must be added another approximately 336,000 individuals who were permanently employed in the military, the public security corps, the coastguard, the public education system, the judiciary, medical staff in the public health and social security funds systems, the clergy, the Foreign Office and the Post Bank (ibid.: 11). Furthermore, to the total of approximately 711,000 permanent civil service staff, we should add a large number of employees hired on renewable fixed-term contracts, which remains unidentified. For instance, between March 2004 and December 2006 no less than 92,287 people were reported to have been offered such contracts (*Eleftherotypia*, 1 April 2007). Most of them were hired by the Ministries of Interior (36,112 persons), Education (4,159 persons), and Rural Development (451 persons, many of whom were hired in 2006, allegedly to cover emergent needs arising from the spread of bird flu in the country), but also by several social security organizations such as IKA (Social Insurance Organization (Ίδρυμα Κοινωνικών Ασφαλίσεων)), TEBE (Professionals' and Craftsmen's Insurance Fund (Ταμείο Επαγγελματιών και Βιοτεχνών Ελλάδας)), and TAE (Merchants' Insurance Fund (Ταμείο Ασφάλισης Εμπόρων)). Local administration was also an important area for hiring people on short-term contracts as, according to the president of the Greek Federation of Municipal Workers (POE-OTA), in October 2009 there were about 15,000 such individuals working in them (*Kathimerini*, 22 October 2009). Roughly estimating, therefore, the number of all public sector employees to approximate one million, their percentage is a stunning 21.8 per cent of the active workforce, which in 2009 was 4.5 million (INE, 2009: 179).
2. This recalls V. O. Key's (1935) five methods of evasion of civil service laws used during patronage appointments in early twentieth-century US cities, which included several ways of manipulating the selection process, either through the movement of promotion and personnel or, more simply, by fixing examination results.

3. By October 2009, it was estimated that about 23,000 individuals were employed under the Stage scheme, of whom 8,000 were in local administration (Kopsini, 2009).
4. As specified by law (1558/85), (i) each minister's bureau may consist of nine positions, five of which are occupied by *revocable* administrative employees and four by 'special advisers and special assistants', who, usually, do not belong to the civil service; (ii) bureaus of alternate ministers and ministers without portfolio consist of eight positions each, of which five are reserved for revocable employees and three for special advisers; and (iii) deputy ministers' bureaus have six positions each, of which four are occupied by revocable administrative employees and two by special advisers.
5. The real independence of those authorities from party controls is of course an altogether different matter. As several authors have correctly remarked, everything seems to depend on their leaders. Witness, for instance, the case of the Greek Ombudsman, where the 'hard work and ingenuity' of both the first leader and his successor has so far made the institution one of the great success stories in Greece, which comes in sharp contrast to the National Council for Radio and Television which, at least during its initial phase of operation, remained subservient to the Minister of Press and Media (a post abolished in 2004 by ND), who had to approve all the Council's decisions (Eleftheriadis, 2005: 324).
6. Cassese (1993) uses the term 'titularization' to describe the process of hiring short-term contract personnel to meet immediate needs in the public sector, only to have those temporary positions made permanent in politically opportune times.
7. To give an example, many of the people who staffed public corporations and other state agencies during ND's more recent government were in the same age cohort (mid- to late forties), had common political experiences (most originated from within ONNED, ND's youth organization), had studied in the same country (Great Britain), and had personal relationships to Costas Karamanlis, ND's leader and prime minister.
8. Let it be noted, however, that professional criteria are more evident in those state sectors where advancement to the top requires examinations in combination with seniority, as in the Foreign Service, Military and Police, the Judiciary, as well as in Education.
9. Fully aware of this fact, even university freshmen have come to accept that obtaining a university degree is a necessary but far from sufficient requirement for getting a state job. The majority of them are fully convinced that, to get such a job, one needs the sponsorship, or at least the intermediation, of some party-affiliated patron.

CHAPTER 9

Party Patronage in Hungary: Capturing the State

Jan-Hinrik Meyer-Sahling and Krisztina Jáger

INTRODUCTION

Party patronage in Hungary has received a considerable amount of attention in debates in both comparative politics and comparative public administration. There is general agreement that party patronage exists in Hungary, but it is contested how important it is and how Hungary compares to other countries, in particular in Central and Eastern Europe. Comparative politics research has examined party patronage in the context of studies of party formation and party–state relations in Central and Eastern Europe. Both Grzymala-Busse (2007) and O'Dwyer (2006) classify Hungary as a case of low patronage.[1] By contrast, comparative public administration research has stressed that the position of Hungary in comparison to other post-communist countries has changed over time. Initially, Hungary was classified as a front-runner in the area of administrative reform, in particular, thanks to the passage of the 1992 Civil Service Act, which created conditions for the departyization of the state after the exit from communism (Meyer-Sahling, 2001; Dimitrova, 2005). More recent research on the state of the civil service in Hungary after EU accession has been more sceptical. It shows that the politicization of the civil service is higher in Hungary than in most other new member states from Central and Eastern Europe (Meyer-Sahling, 2009; World Bank, 2007).

This chapter re-examines party patronage in Hungary. It confirms recent research that stresses the importance of party patronage for public sector governance. We argue that political parties reach into all institutional domains (ministerial bureaucracy, non-departmental agencies, executing institutions such as state-owned enterprises) and into all policy sectors studied in this volume. For the Hungarian case, we therefore speak about the capture of the state by political parties. Yet the chapter finds important differences in the way parties intervene in the staffing of policy sectors. Three patterns of patronage are distinguished.

'Captured sectors' (Media, Health Care, Foreign Service, Regional Administration) are characterized by an overall high degree of patronage and a decline in the relative importance of patronage as the distance from the political leadership of government ministries increases. That is, patronage is most important for the ministerial bureaucracy and least important for executing institutions, while non-departmental agencies take an intermediate position. Second, 'partially disciplined sectors' (Finance, Economy, Military and Police) are characterized by an intermediate degree of patronage but the partial insulation of non-departmental agencies from party intervention. Finally, 'partially insulated sectors' (Judiciary, Education and Culture) are characterized by a low degree of patronage—by Hungarian standards—and the minimal importance of patronage for executing institutions.

Party intervention in personnel policy in public administration was of course a hallmark of the 'real-existing socialist administration'. Party involvement remained widespread after transition to democracy despite efforts to establish a separation between politics and administration. This chapter further argues that, over time, party patronage has become more important in Hungary. The stabilization of the party system in Hungary has hence been accompanied by an increase rather than a decrease in party patronage. In fact, party patronage might have contributed to the stabilization of the main political parties and their relationships to each other. Yet the entrenchment of parties in the public sector by means of patronage cannot prevent major electoral backlashes, as recently illustrated by the outcome of the 2010 parliamentary elections.

The chapter is divided into three parts. The first part outlines the main features of governments, parties, and the party system in Hungary. It then discusses the Hungarian tradition of civil service governance, in particular with regard to the politicization of the civil service. The second section forms the main part of the chapter. It analyses the scope and the processes of party patronage in Hungary. The third part, the conclusion, discusses the trajectory of party patronage in Hungary since transition to democracy and examines the implications of the findings for party government in Hungary.

PARTY SYSTEM AND CIVIL SERVICE TRADITION

Hungary belongs to the first wave of post-communist countries that joined the European Union in 2004. Between 1990 and 2010, Hungary held six national elections. The elections in 1990, 1994, 1998, 2002, and 2010 produced wholesale changes of government between the left and the right of the political spectrum. After the first democratic elections in 1990, a government was formed by a centre-right coalition consisting of the Christian-conservative Hungarian Democratic

Forum (MDF), the agrarian Independent Smallholders (FKGP) and the Christian Democratic People's Party (KDNP).

The second election held in 1994 led to the first return of the former communist party to power. The Hungarian Socialist Party (MSZP), as the successor of the Hungarian Socialist Workers' Party (MSZMP), formed a coalition with the liberal Alliance of Free Democrats (SZDSZ). During the period in opposition, the MSZP tried to reform itself as a modern-style social democratic party (Ágh, 1997; Bozóki, 1997). Yet the party retained various wings and factions under its broad roof, including neoliberal monetarists, national popular socialists, trade unionists, etc. The 1998 election produced the next pendulum swing back to the centre-right. The coalition was formed by the Alliance of Young Democrats (*Fidesz*), the Smallholders and the MDF. The Fidesz was founded by university students. During the transition period it started as a radical liberal party close to the SZDSZ. After the weak showing at the 1994 elections (7 per cent) and the collapse of the MDF, the Fidesz gradually moved to the centre-right of the political spectrum to become a liberal conservative party (Bátory, 2002; Fowler, 2004). Within a short period of time, the Fidesz has become the dominant party of the centre-right, integrating smaller parties of the right or forming electoral alliances to help them cross the electoral threshold.

The fourth elections, in 2002, led to the return of the socialist–liberal coalition that had already governed the country between 1994 and 1998. The MSZP–SZDSZ coalition was also the first government to win re-elections in 2006, though re-election was secured with a new prime minister after Gyurcsány succeeded Medgyessy in the autumn of 2004. Medgyessy was forced to resign in favour of Gyurcsány, a former leader of the communist youth organization, KISZ, who had become a successful businessman during the post-communist period. Gyurcsány sought to emulate Tony Blair's transformation of New Labour in Hungary. Yet his position was quickly weakened after the 2006 elections. In an internal speech to his party during the preparation of the government programme, Gyurcsány admitted that his government had lied before the elections about the true state of the economy and the public finances. The speech was leaked to the press. It triggered public protests and calls for new elections by the opposition. In the autumn of 2006 the street protests turned violent. The government did not resign, but the credibility and public support of the government parties reached rock bottom. In 2008, the SZDSZ left the coalition but continued to support the minority government led by Prime Minister Gyurcsány. In 2009, Gyurcsány resigned from his post to be succeeded by the former Minister of Local Government and Regional Development, Bajnai. The subsequent parliamentary elections of 2010 led to the expected defeat of the MSZP and the return of the Fidesz to government. Victor Orbán became prime minister for the second time. The Fidesz formed a single-party government and gained a two-thirds majority of seats in parliament. The small parties, SZDSZ and MDF, did not cross the electoral threshold but two new parties, the green-liberal LMP ('Politics Can Be Different') and the extreme right-wing Jobbik ('Movement for a Better Hungary') made it into parliament with 7.5 per cent and 12.3 per cent of the vote respectively.

As should have already become clear from this short overview of governments in Hungary, the party system is best characterized as a two-bloc system (Körösényi, Tóth, and Török, 2009). Until 2010, the left was represented by the MSZP and its small partner, SZDSZ. While the LMP has so far not formed any coalition with the MSZP, it can be located on the centre-left of the party system. The right is dominated by the Fidesz. Other small parties of the centre-right largely depend on the support of the Fidesz. Extreme right wing parties have periodically gained popular support. The Hungarian Justice and Life Party (MIÉP) was represented in parliament between 1998 and 2002. It remains to be seen whether Jobbik will be able to establish itself as an additional party on the right of the political scale.

Notwithstanding the outcome of the 2010 elections, the Hungarian parties and party system are typically seen as one of the most stable in Central and Eastern Europe (Lewis, 2006). Yet party organizations remain weak and trust in political parties is low, in particular when compared to other democratic institutions. Party membership is also low. In 2008, the two big parties, MSZP and Fidesz, had 36,000 and 39,932 members respectively (Hungarian Political Yearbook). Taken together, the membership of the parties with parliamentary representation made up less than 1 per cent of the population. Over time, party membership has declined for the MSZP but it was also very low in the early and mid-1990s. The Fidesz, by contrast, has been able to increase its membership from 10,000 in 1996 to almost 40,000 in 2008. To some extent this increase reflects the concerted efforts of the Fidesz to increase its entrenchment in society by setting up so-called 'civic circles' across the whole country.

Membership figures across the country should not be exaggerated as indicators of party entrenchment in society. The MSZP, for instance, continues to benefit from the wide reach of the former communist party into state and society. The MSZMP used to have 800,000 members at the end of the 1980s. Not all of these members should be seen as party believers, since party membership was effectively a necessary condition for career progression in all sectors of state and society. Yet many networks of that time have persisted into the post-communist period and form a natural reservoir of supporters for the MSZP. The Fidesz approach can be seen in this light as a strategy to build popular support even without building a mass party organization. Despite this kind of informal entrenchment in society, it is important to recognize that parties are among the least trusted political institutions in post-communist Hungary.

While the entrenchment of parties in society is informal at best, political parties in Hungary have traditionally had a much closer relationship to the state. In particular, the communist tradition of public administration implies the complete subordination, if not fusion, of party and state (Csanádi, 1997; König, 1992). The communist system institutionalizes the leading role of the communist party.

According to the ideal communist administrative tradition, there is no separation between state and society. Ideally, there is also no separation between state and market, given state ownership of all means of production. The rule of law is subordinated to the will of the communist party and can be bent for the achievement of ideological goals. There is no autonomous civil society but interest associations function as transmission belts of the communist party and its Marxist-Leninist ideology.

Most critically in our context, there are no separations between politics and administration or between party and state (Pakulski, 1986). Recruitment and career advancement are based on political and ideological reliability rather than meritocratic achievements. Promotion to higher positions requires party membership. Senior personnel policy follows the logic of the nomenclature system: that is, the communist party selects and approves appointments to senior positions of the state bureaucracy. From the perspective of patronage studies, the ideal communist system institutionalizes the maximum reach of a ruling party into all sectors and corners of the state.

The communist system in Hungary had gradually moved away from the ideal type. Since the late 1960s, Hungary had liberalized the communist system. Especially economic reform measures led to a communist system that is usually seen as less repressive and less tightly controlled by the communist party (Kitschelt et al., 1999; Schöpflin, 1994). In public administration, initiatives were taken to increase the professional capacity of the state. Meritocratic criteria gained importance in the selection and promotion of administrative personnel (Balázs, 1993; György, 1999). Yet the basic principles of communist public administration, in particular the need to demonstrate basic political commitment to the communist party and its ideology, remained intact until the collapse of communism in 1989.

The transition to democracy created a break with the communist tradition of organizing the state. The establishment of multiparty constitutional democracy implied the elimination of the leading role of the communist party from the constitution, the introduction of free elections, and multiparty competition. Administrative reform was an important element of the transformation process, for party and administration had to be disentangled and public administration had to be brought under the rule of law. In this context, Hungary passed an Act on State Secretaries in 1990, shortly before the investiture of the first democratic government, in order to formalize a separation between the political and the professional, permanent part of the executive. In 1992 Hungary adopted a new Civil Service Act. The Act aimed to establish a professional civil service that upholds democratic values and is politically neutral and impartial. The Civil Service Act covers employees of the state administration at central, regional, and local level, as well as the employees of local self-governments. This includes approximately 100,000 civil servants and has remained relatively stable over time. Additional legislation was adopted to cover employees in the public sector such as doctors, nurses, and teachers. Specialist legislation was later adopted for judges and armed bureaucrats such as soldiers, police officers, customs officers, etc. Civil servants, civilian public servants, and armed public servants amount to approximately 800,000 employees (*c*.20 per cent of the labour force). The number was lower after the passage of the 1995 so-called Bokros package, an austerity programme for the consolidation of public finances, but it increased again in subsequent years.

The effects of the legal reforms that were passed in the 1990s on the depoliticization of public personnel policy have been contested. Most research in the area of public administration argues that the formal legal frameworks incorporate many possibilities for executive politicians to politicize the civil service (Meyer-Sahling, 2006b; Gajduschek, 2007). This finding is especially relevant for the study of party patronage in Hungary. As we will see in the next section, the high degree of political discretion that is provided by formal rules governing public personnel policy provides ideal conditions for parties to make appointments to state institutions.

SCOPE AND PROCESSES OF PARTY PATRONAGE IN HUNGARY

The scope of party patronage

The literature on party patronage in Central and Eastern Europe tends to assume that the mere presence of laws and regulations establishes breaks on the ability of parties to make political appointments in the public sector (Grzymala-Busse, 2007). This volume shows that this assumption is not tenable, and the Hungarian case is no exception to this finding. Instead, it is more appropriate to assume that the ability of parties to make political appointments depends on the degree of political discretion that is built into legislation (Meyer-Sahling, 2006b). Political discretion is higher if legislation assigns the authority to make appointments to a political rather than a non-political actor. Moreover, the degree of political discretion depends on the standards and procedures such as professional qualifications that decision makers have to follow.

From the perspective of political discretion, formal rules and regulations create few limits for political parties to make appointments in the public sector in Hungary. Procedures differ with regard to the type of political actor who is in charge of making appointments and with regard to the entry criteria that appointees have to meet. But there are only very few institutions that eliminate political discretion over the appointment of personnel, for instance by delegating the appointment authority to professional bodies rather than political actors. Let us first look at the ministerial bureaucracy and then at non-departmental agencies and commissions (NDACs) and executing institutions (EIs).

For the ministerial bureaucracy, there are no differences between ministries and hence between policy sectors. Ministers are selected by the prime minister and appointed by the president of the republic. Below the minister, executive branch ministries are led by one senior state secretary and three to five specialist state secretaries who oversee distinct policy areas within the jurisdiction of the ministry. Senior state secretaries are selected by the prime minister in cooperation with the relevant minister and appointed by the president of the republic. Specialist state secretaries are selected by the minister and appointed by the prime minister. In addition, ministers have ministerial cabinets that are staffed with political advisers. The top positions in the ministerial bureaucracy are therefore clearly classified as political appointments.

Below the top level, the Hungarian ministries distinguish heads of departments, deputy heads of departments, and heads of divisions. They constitute the middle management in the ministerial bureaucracy. They are formally classified as senior civil servants covered by the Civil Service Act. They have to hold a university degree and have to pass a specialized examination within one year after their appointment unless they have a degree in law, political science, or public administration. Formally, the minister assigns civil servants to the position of head of department, deputy head of department, or head of division.

The lower level of the ministerial civil service can also be reached by political parties but the access is less direct. The Civil Service Act distinguishes different types of civil servants based on their level of education. Higher civil servants, for instance, must hold a university degree. Only administrators and civil servants in blue-collar positions can be appointed without having to meet specific entry criteria. The authority to make appointments rests with the specialist state secretary as the head of a branch of departments within the ministry. In practice, this authority is usually delegated to department heads. The allocation of decision-making powers to a political appointee, i.e. the specialist state secretary, implies that party patronage can cascade downwards to the bottom of the ministerial hierarchy. The general access of political parties to the ministerial bureaucracy is therefore relatively unrestricted. Political discretion is high with regard to the top of the ministries, while politicians face a range of standards and procedural constraints when seeking to make appointments below the top positions.

Most of the personnel employed in NDACs are also covered by the Civil Service Act, though the procedures for the appointment of top-level personnel are usually specified in the statutes that establish the institutions in the first place. As in the case of the ministerial bureaucracy, parties can make appointments to almost all of these institutions. The differences stem from the appointment procedure and hence the degree of political discretion. We identified more than twenty different procedures, which can be lumped together in three groups. First, most appointments to central agencies are the prerogative of executive politicians. The main players are the ministers of executive branch ministries. Alternatively, the minister proposes but the prime minister makes the actual appointment, as is the case for the Hungarian Energy Office. In several cases, such as the Hungarian Patent Office and the Statistical Office, the prime minister has unilateral authority to make appointments. In others, such as the Hungarian Competition Office, the prime minister proposes the candidate, while the appointment is officially made by the president of the republic.

Second, parliament can be involved in a variety of ways in the appointment process. In several cases, parliament adds transparency to the process—for instance, the head of the Hungarian Tax Office is selected and appointed by the Minister of Finance but he or she needs to pass a hearing in the Budgetary Committee of Parliament before the appointment becomes valid. In other cases, the actual selection authority rests in parliament rather than the executive. For instance, the members of the National Radio and Television Commission (ORTT) are nominated by parliamentary factions and elected by an absolute majority of MPs. Parliament also elects the prosecutor general, the president of the Supreme Court and the president of the State Audit Office.

Third, interest groups and professional associations play a small role in the process of appointing heads of offices, agencies, and executing institutions. In several cases, they participate in the nomination process. For instance, the head of the National Cultural Fund (NKA) and half of the members of the board are appointed by the Minister of Culture and Education, while the other half is appointed by professional associations and institutions from the cultural field. The role of non-political actors is greater in the Education sector and in the Judiciary. For instance, a key body for the governance of the Judiciary is the National Council of Justice (OIT). Its board consists of fifteen members but only three members, the Minister of Justice and two MPs, are politicians, while the others are representatives of the wider judiciary, including professional bodies such as the Hungarian Bar Association.

EIs do not differ much from the appointment procedures that apply to NDACs. Personnel who are employed at institutions such as hospitals, schools, museums, state-owned enterprises, the army, police, the courts, etc. are usually covered by the Public Service Act or by specialized legislation such as the Act on Judges. The procedures for the appointment of top personnel are usually specified in laws establishing the institutions. Executive politicians, particularly ministers, play an even greater role when it comes to the appointment of personnel to these kinds of institutions. Hospital directors, presidents of state-owned banks and enterprises, as well as members of supervisory boards, ambassadors, police and army chiefs, and the heads of many institutions in the artistic sector are the prerogative of the minister of the day. The prime minister is occasionally involved, for instance when appointing the president of the Hungarian News Agency. Parliament also has a less prominent position, though it plays the key role in the appointment of members of the boards of the television and radio corporations. Politicians have least possibilities for direct intervention into personnel policy in the judiciary and in higher education, since self-governing bodies are mainly responsible for appointments. The OIT, for instance, which is a largely non-political body, appoints judges and heads of courts of appeals. Similarly, university rectors are elected by university senates and appointed by the president of the republic, thereby limiting the role of the minister in governing personnel in universities. The small formal role for parties in the appointment procedure does not mean that there is no politics in these kinds of institutions, but political influence is often more subtle and more informal than in other institutions.

In sum, even if formal procedures differ, politicians have the possibility to reach all policy sectors and all institutional domains to make political appointments. The question emerges whether politicians also use their political discretion to make political appointments.

Party patronage in practice

Conceptually, we can distinguish two extreme types of party patronage. First, as discussed above, the communist party state assumes that party patronage reaches all institutions of the state and all positions from the top to the bottom of the hierarchy (Pakulski, 1986; Csanádi, 1997). Ideally, there are no patronage-free areas in the communist party-state. In terms of measurement, the patronage score would equal 1.00. By contrast, the Wilsonian ideal of a clear separation between politics and administration implies that administrative institutions are generally free from political appointments. Politicians engage in the business of politics and bureaucrats deal with the business of implementing public policies (Wilson, 1887). In this case, the patronage score would equal 0.00.

Table 9.1 shows that the Hungarian case cannot be classified as either the party-state type of patronage or the Wilsonian type of (non-)patronage because the overall patronage score of 0.44 reported in the bottom right cell of the table falls

TABLE 9.1 *The index of party patronage in Hungary*

Policy area	Ministries	NDACs	Executing institutions	Policy area total
Economy	0.67	0.11	0.67	0.48
Finance	0.67	0.22	0.42	0.44
Judiciary	0.67	0.11	0.00	0.26
Media	–	0.67	0.67	0.67
Military and Police	0.67	0.17	0.25	0.36
Health Care	0.67	0.50	0.33	0.50
Culture and Education	0.50	0.33	0.03	0.29
Foreign Service	0.67	–	0.22	0.44
Regional and Local Administration	0.67	–	0.44	0.56
Total	0.65	0.30	0.34	0.44

more or less between these two extremes. The score brings Hungary closer to the countries with a medium to high degree of party patronage such as the Czech Republic and Bulgaria. It is lower than the score for most southern European countries studied in this volume but higher than the score for most western European countries. The relative position of Hungary notwithstanding, the score of 0.44 requires some additional interpretation. It should not be confused with the understanding that nearly one half of all public sector organizations and positions are subject to party patronage. The score reflects the aggregation of coded expert evaluations. Recalling the calculation of the patronage index outlined above by Kopecký and Spirova (Chapter 2), a score of 0.4 is equivalent to the combined response that (a) 'most institutions in a sector are subject to party patronage' and (b) 'top *and* the middle level of the institutional hierarchy are subject to political appointments'. In other words, a score of 0.4 indicates that the parties have an impressive reach into the staffing of the public sector.

Beyond the aggregate score, the table shows some important variation across institutional domains and policy sectors. First, it shows that the Media, the Regional Administration, and the Health Care sector are coming out with the highest patronage scores. By contrast, party patronage is relatively least important for the Judiciary, Culture and Education, and Military and Police sectors. If Culture and Higher Education sectors were assessed separately, we would have to classify the Educational sector together with the Judiciary at the bottom of the patronage league. By contrast, patronage is much more common in the Culture sector. A similar division concerns the armed services of the military and the police. The police is subject to more political appointments, while the military belongs to the relatively less politicized sectors. Finally, the Financial sector, the Economy and the Foreign Service represent an intermediate group, with scores between 0.48 and 0.44, just at or above the country mean of 0.44.

Second, the bottom row of Table 9.1 indicates that party patronage is more important for the ministerial bureaucracy than for NDACs and EIs. This indicates that the importance of party patronage increases the closer a position is located to the political leadership of executive branch ministries. The aggregate patronage score is higher for EIs than for NDACs but the differences are small. Differences are more evident between NDACs and EIs when looking at individual policy sectors. For instance, in the Finance sector, the Economy, and the Military and Police sector, the patronage scores are much lower for the NDACs in comparison to the EIs and the ministerial bureaucracy. Moreover, it is evident that the Judiciary and the Culture and Education sector have very low patronage scores for their EIs. Instead of distinguishing different degrees of patronage, we therefore suggest that it is more appropriate to distinguish three patterns of patronage for the case of Hungary. We label these patterns 'captured sectors' (Media, Health Care, Foreign Service, Regional and Local Administration), 'partially disciplined sectors' (Finance, Economy, Military and Police), and 'partially insulated sectors' (Judiciary, Culture and Education).

Captured sectors

Captured sectors include the Media, Health Care, the Regional and Local Administration and the Foreign Service. In these sectors, the overall patronage score is higher than the national average and it decreases with increasing distance from the minister. Even if the media is the most politicized sector in Hungary, the features of a captured sector are most evident in the Health Care sector. As in all sectors under study, party patronage in the Health Care sector is more important for the ministerial bureaucracy than for the NDACs and the EIs. The Ministry of Health is known as a very politicized ministry. The senior state secretary, specialist state secretaries, and cabinet members at the top of the ministry are clearly political appointments. The middle level of the ministry is also affected, in particular heads of departments that have special responsibilities for drafting reform concepts and legislation. Party patronage is less relevant for the lower level of the ministry.

The politicization of the Ministry of Health hardly differs from other ministries. The high average but minor variation among patronage scores indicates that the ministerial bureaucracy is generally captured by political parties. In most ministries, it is common that both the top and the middle management are subject to political appointments. Greater differences can often be found within the ministries rather than between them. The policy departments tend to be more frequently targeted by political appointments than departments such as legal affairs and budgetary affairs. To some extent this can be explained with regard to the specialized administrative expertise that the officials of these departments are required to demonstrate. Until recently, it was also typical to find international relations departments, and especially EU affairs departments, to be more professional and hence subject to fewer political appointments. This phenomenon is typically discussed under the heading of 'islands of excellence' that emerged during the EU accession process (Goetz, 2001). Interestingly, our research indicates that EU affairs departments and generally policy departments with great exposure to the EU are increasingly the target of political appointments. This development could be the result of reduced adaptive pressures from Brussels after accession, as well as the discovery of EU policies by national political parties. In particular, the distribution of EU funds through the regional development councils has attracted the interest of political parties, and as a result political appointments to these bodies have become increasingly 'normal' over the last few years.

By contrast, our research shows that the lower level of the ministerial bureaucracy is only rarely subject to political appointments. The most typical appointment at this level concerns drivers and secretaries who follow the minister from his office in parliament to his new office in the ministry. But this kind of patronage is commonly accepted. Otherwise, one can find favouritism and informalism in the recruitment process but political considerations tend to play a relatively small role at this level. There was wide consensus among our interviewees that appointees who are well connected to a political party or network are unlikely to accept jobs below the level of department leader because both the authority and the financial reward that come with the job are not sufficiently attractive (Meyer-Sahling, Vass, and Vassné, 2012). At the middle level, it is therefore not surprising to find that political appointees tend to be relatively young, because the job at the level of department head can work as an excellent (political) career springboard.

In comparison to the ministerial bureaucracy, the patronage scores for the Health Care sector are lower for NDACs and the EIs. Among the NDACs, there are several agencies, such as the National Public Health and Medical Officer's Service (ÁNTSZ), the Health Insurance Supervisory Authority, and, more recently, the Office of Authorization and Administrative Procedures of the Ministry of Health (EEKH), that are subject to political turnover and party patronage. The difference in patronage score between the Ministry of Health and the NDACs in the Health Care sector are mainly the result of the greater depth of politicization in the ministerial structure. In the agencies, most observers agreed that political appointments are limited to the top of the institutions. The patronage score for the Health Care sector is marginally lower for the EIs such as state hospitals, the National Health Insurance Fund Administration (OEP), various services such as the National Blood Transfusion Service and the National Emergency and Ambulance Service, and a considerable number of research institutes in the periphery of the Ministry of Health. For the EIs, the minister has far-reaching appointment powers, which are also used in practice. Yet again the appointments are concentrated at the top of the institutions. The new appointees may initiate further personnel changes but the political leadership of the ministry would usually not get involved in these decisions.

In comparison to the Health Care sector, party capture differs for the Media, the Regional Administration, and the Foreign Service because only two of the three institutional domains were subject to investigation. For the Media, we covered only NDACs and EIs, since there is no specific line ministry responsible for the management of the media. Yet it is fair to argue that parties have also captured the equivalent of ministerial structures. The press offices and media relations units that work for the prime minister and for individual ministers are usually among the most politicized units of the ministerial bureaucracy. The overall patronage score for the media must hence be seen as underestimated.

Looking more closely at the NDACs and the EIs in the Media sector, we find that, similar to the Health Care sector, there are no NDACs that can be regarded as free from party patronage. Appointments to the National Radio and Television Commission (ORTT) and to the Public Broadcasting Fund are inherently political. It is mainly politicians or media experts of the parties that take jobs in these bodies. Political parties developed an interest in the media right after transition to democracy. The proportional representation of seats on the relevant media bodies goes back to the transition period when the then government and opposition parties agreed on a power-sharing deal. The first president of the public broadcasting agency was affiliated to the SZDSZ, which at that time was the largest opposition party. Perennial conflict between the government, then led by MDF politician, Antall, and the public media was the consequence, and certainly nurtured the understanding among political elites that political control of the media is of utmost importance.

The Media also comes out with the highest patronage score for the EIs. The Media sector presents a special case among EIs because parliament plays a central role in the appointment process. The radio and TV corporations are each governed by two bodies, the presidency and a board of trustees. The presidency is nominated by the factions represented in parliament and the chair is nominated by the senior governing party. The first deputy president is nominated by the main opposition party. The board of trustees also includes delegates of civic organizations such as the churches, the national cultural and educational organizations, the social partners, the organizations of journalists, etc. It is widely known that the civic organizations have been co-opted by political parties, leading to yet more opportunities for party patronage. Moreover, the politicization of the public media has spilled over into the private sector, which makes it increasingly difficult to access information that is not politically biased in one way or the other.

Party patronage in both the Regional Administration and the Foreign Service follows the general pattern of captured sectors but it also displays sectoral particularities that set them apart from the Media and Health Care sectors. For instance, in the area of Foreign Service, the patronage score is much higher for the ministerial bureaucracy than for EIs such as embassies and missions to international organizations such as the UN, NATO, the EU, etc. The Ministry of Foreign Affairs has traditionally experienced a larger degree of personnel turnover than other ministries due to inter alia the regular posting of officials to embassies and missions abroad. Political affiliation also plays a very important role in landing promotions and postings to attractive locations. Yet appointees have usually come from within the diplomatic corps or they are part of a wider corps of foreign and security policy experts. In many respects it appears that both political camps, the left and the right, have developed their own reservoir of diplomats and foreign policy experts. As a result, political appointments by the political leadership may reach deep into the ministerial hierarchy and they certainly reach embassies and missions, but the politicization of the Foreign Service has remained largely bounded within the foreign policy sector.

Recently this pattern was challenged by the Gyurcsány government, which appointed several successful businessmen, usually with close affiliation to the prime minister and the MSZP, to important ambassadorial posts. There is hence a sense that party capture of the Foreign Service increased during the Gyurcsány years. The influx of private sector managers who have close contacts to the MSZP and the SZDSZ is a recent trend that can also be observed in several other sectors such as Health Care and Culture, while it has been traditionally important for the Finance and Economy sectors. The growing importance of private sector managers as a category of political appointees is closely related to the ascendance of successful businessmen such as Ferenc Gyurcsány and János Koka to senior positions in political parties and government.

Partially disciplined sectors

The partially disciplined sectors differ from captured sectors in two respects. First, the average patronage score is at an intermediate level. Second, and more important, patronage is lower in the NDACs in comparison to both the ministerial bureaucracy and the EIs. The partially disciplined sectors include the Economy, the Financial sector and the Military and Police. With regard to the ministerial bureaucracy, these three sectors do not differ much from the other sectors discussed so far. By contrast, they differ to a considerable extent from the captured sectors with regard to the much larger proportion of patronage-free NDACs. In the Finance sector, our interviewees identified above all the State Audit Office (ÁSZ) as one of the least politicized NDACs in Hungary. Agencies such as the State Debt Management Agency (ÁKK) and the State Treasury (ÁK) are also seen as less political, while there is less agreement on the role of political appointments to the Financial Supervisory Agency (PSZÁF) and the Tax Office (ÁPEH). Yet even the Finance sector includes several offices that have traditionally been subject to tight political control by means of appointments, for example the Statistical Office (KSH) and the Government Control Office (KEHI), which is the government's instrument for internal financial control.

The less politicized agencies of the Finance sector share the feature that they operate at the interface with the private sector. Policy failures in this area, it is widely understood, would be extremely costly for the Hungarian government. The exposure to the private sector and the integration into the international financial markets seems to reduce the willingness and/or the ability of parties to make political appointments to these agencies. A similar pattern can be found in the Economy sector. The Competition Office, for instance, stands out as a largely depoliticized agency. By contrast, political appointments have traditionally been important with regard to the Energy Office.

At first glance, the Military and Police sector is unexpected in the group of NDACs with a low patronage score. Both the army and the police are large bureaucracies that do not face private sector competition. Moreover, there have regularly been scandals in Hungary that concern the leaking of classified material and the use of intelligence information to discredit political opponents. Most recently, the Minister for National Security during the Gyurcsány government, Szilvásy, had to resign because he was accused of ordering the surveillance of telephone conversations related to a firm that was close to the Fidesz. Ironically, the firm itself comes from the security sector and rumour has it that it sought to gain information from the security services on behalf of the Fidesz. Offices and agencies dealing with national security aspects and secret intelligence are therefore among the most important appointments that political parties make. Unsurprisingly, the National Security Office (NBH) is a very politicized body. Yet several other relevant offices that we surveyed for the Police and Military, such as the Protective Service of Law Enforcement Agencies (RSZVSZ), the National Disaster Recovery Directorate, and the Office of Immigration and Nationality, are much less affected by party patronage.

The three partially disciplined sectors are also similar with regard to the relatively high importance of party patronage for EIs. In the public sector economy and in the Finance sector there are a large number of state-owned banks and other state-owned companies that are under tight control of governing parties thanks to political appointments. The Hungarian Development Bank (MFB), the Hungarian Railways (MÁV), and the Lottery serve as prime examples of party patronage. Even the Hungarian National Bank (MNB) is not free from political appointments, despite the international norm that central bank independence is required in order to gain credibility in the eyes of international investors and to keep inflation low (McNamara, 2002). During the last eight to ten years the government has used its political discretion to appoint the governor of the central bank and several members of the monetary policy committee. These appointments have had spillover effects, leading to yet more political appointments inside the bank.

The bureaucracies of the Military and Police are less politicized than the state-owned companies and banks of the Finance and Economy sectors. The differences are largely a result of the kind of institutions that constitute the EIs in this sector. State-owned companies in the defence sector are typically subject to as much party patronage as companies in the Finance and Economy sectors. Moreover, political appointments to the top of the national police organization have traditionally been important, but political influence is said to have increased significantly after the violent street protests of 2006. By contrast, party patronage plays a smaller role in the Hungarian army. Moreover, both the police and the defence sector include several institutions that are relatively free from party patronage, such as the national defence university and the police college. Party patronage in the Military and Police sector is therefore very diverse. It includes some institutions that are largely free from political appointments and others that are subject to deep politicization.

Partially insulated sectors

The third pattern of patronage concerns partially insulated sectors. They are distinguished from the former two patterns in that the overall patronage score is relatively low and the EIs are, by and large, free from party patronage. This pattern is relevant for the Judiciary and, with qualifications, for the Culture and Education sector. The Judiciary comes out as the sector with the lowest patronage score for its NDACs and for its EIs. In particular, the National Council of Justice (OIT) stands out as a relatively apolitical body. The OIT, as outlined above, is headed by the president of the supreme courts. It includes judges, representatives of the bar association, the minister of justice, and a few MPs. The limited political influence on the OIT and its office is also reflected in the practice of personnel selection.

The patronage score for the Judiciary is especially lowered by the minor importance of political appointments to the EIs of the sector, in particular the court system. Senior judges are selected and appointed by the OIT. The personnel system for judges largely follows the logic of a closed career system, which implies that senior judges have already served for many years before gaining an appointment to the top of the hierarchy. This is not to say that there is no politics involved in the Judicial sector. Interviewees pointed out that the system of promotions and appointments for judges is far from transparent, leading to problems of nepotism and risks of capture by parties and even organized crime. Moreover, the prosecutor's office has been subject to political pressure since the period of the Orbán government. The status of the courts and prosecutor general as a largely patronage-free zone in the future can therefore not be taken for granted.

The Culture and Education sector fits the label of partial insulation from party patronage much less well than the Judiciary. As mentioned already above, party patronage differs for the two subsectors. Differences can be identified for both the NDACs and the EIs. The National Cultural Fund (NKA), in particular, is seen as subject to many political appointments among the NDACs in this sector. The staffing of the administrative office of the Fund is very much influenced by the minister of culture and education. The minister, and the president of the fund as the trustee of the minister, also have great influence over the composition of the board of the Fund. Cultural institutions can delegate their members but the minister can veto the appointments. Moreover, membership is limited to three years. Bearing in mind that the MSZP–SZDSZ coalition had been in office for six years at the time of research, our observers explained that the NKA had become a politically fairly homogeneous body close to the centre-left. The relatively low patronage score for the Culture and Education sector is therefore mainly the result of offices in the higher education sector such as the National Accreditation Office and the Rectors' Conference, both of which are relatively unaffected by party patronage.

The main reason for classifying the Culture and Education sector as partially insulated stems from the curiously low degree of party patronage in higher education institutions as part of the EIs in this sector. University rectors, for instance, are elected by the university senates and appointed by the president of the republic. Appointments to these posts are largely free from meddling by education ministers. Yet good relations with the ministry are important for the universities, so the political arithmetic cannot be fully ignored during the selection process. Moreover, universities are one of the most important parking grounds for political appointees who have lost their position after their party has been voted out of office. In other words, the governance of the higher education sector has retained a remarkable degree of political independence, while the views of its personnel are much less independent.

Selection of political appointees

The party patronage literature does not pay particular attention to the mechanisms through which political appointees are selected. Müller (2000) is therefore justified in asking whether appointments are taken by the party in central office or the party in public office, that is, politicians in government positions. Figure 9.1 shows that the party in central office plays only a secondary role in the selection of political appointees in Hungary because ministers are seen as the dominant decision makers. The prime minister and the wider political party play only a secondary role in the process of selecting appointees. Members of parliament are the least influential in the appointment process, though in the interviews it seemed difficult to clearly distinguish their role from that of the wider party. The category of 'others' refers primarily to mayors at local and regional levels and to semi-professional bodies such as the National Council of Justice, which appoints judges.

The dominant role of ministers requires qualification. First, ministers primarily take appointment decisions at the top of the ministerial bureaucracy, NDACs, and EIs. This reflects the legal basis and their dual role as political and administrative heads of executive branch ministries. Below the top level, ministers are not necessarily the main decision makers. In the ministerial bureaucracy, the appointment authority is mainly delegated to specialist state secretaries and heads of departments. In NDACs and EIs, the authority is delegated to the heads and deputy heads of the respective institutions. Second, ministers are not alone in taking

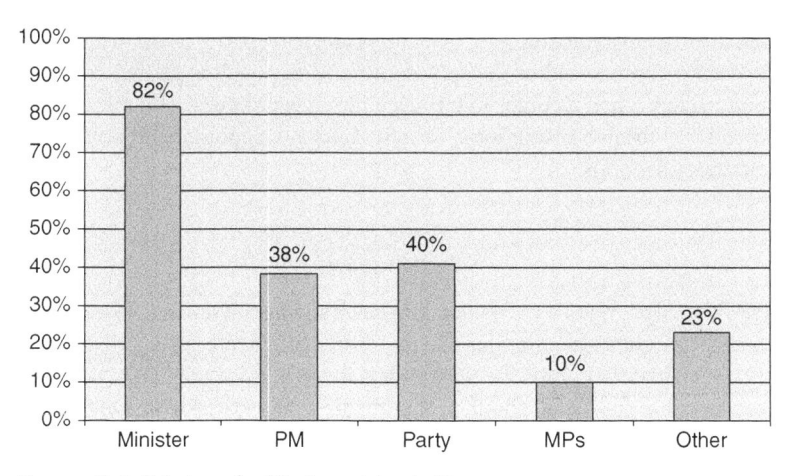

FIGURE 9.1 Selectors of political appointees in Hungary

appointment decisions. It is more common that the minister together with his or her close advisers agrees on the minister's appointees. In fact, the advisers in the background of a minister tend to play a very important role in the search for and identification of suitable appointees.

Third, the roles of ministers, the prime minister, the party, and MPs in the selection of appointees should not be seen as mutually exclusive, because in many cases ministers have to share their appointment authority with the prime minister, the party, or both. The prime minister, for instance, has important formal powers over the appointment of state secretaries and specialist state secretaries. But there are also important sectoral differences, which are rooted in politics rather than in formal rules. In sectors such as Foreign Service, Finance, Economy, Military and Police, it is common to observe the intervention of the prime minister. For instance, finance ministers have traditionally been weak in Hungary, which has facilitated prime ministerial influence (Greskovits, 2001). By contrast, in foreign affairs, prime ministerial influence has fluctuated over time. During the first socialist-liberal government, prime minister Horn kept a close eye on personnel policy in the Foreign Service. He knew the sector very well, as he was the foreign minister of the last socialist government before the transition to democracy. During the second socialist-liberal government, the pendulum swung to the foreign minister. Prime minister Medgyessy was not a party member, while foreign minister Kovács was the leader of the MSZP. Kovács was known for his very proactive approach to personnel policy. Often he intervened down to the level of head of division. During the Gyurcsány years it was again the prime minister who was seen as more influential in personnel policy than the foreign minister.

MPs and the party tend to play a background role in relation to both ministers and the prime minister. They are often involved in 'proposing' appointees to ministers and their advisers. Yet their influence remains limited because the authority of the minister, and in some areas the prime minister, to take appointment decisions is largely uncontested. An important exception is the Media. In this sector, senior figures within the governing and opposition parties are the main decision makers when it comes to the selection of appointees. The role of parties is reinforced by formal institutions, which delegate appointment powers to the parliamentary factions.

Selection criteria

Having identified ministers as the key actors when it comes to appointment decisions, the question emerges as to what criteria are used to discriminate between candidates. Figure 9.2 shows that there is no dominant criterion but it is more suitable to speak about a combination of criteria that matters for the selection of appointees. In particular, professional skills and political loyalty tend to go together. Political loyalty was mentioned by almost all interviewees

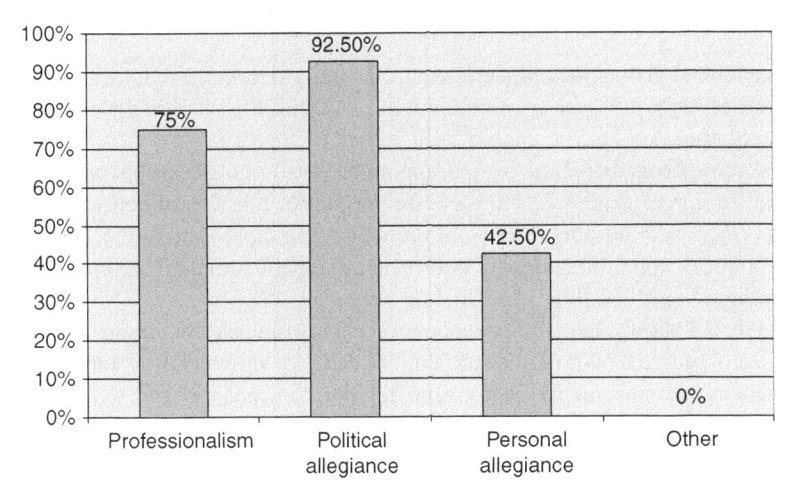

FIGURE 9.2 Qualifications of appointees in Hungary

as a key selection criterion. It is comparable to a necessary condition that all appointees need to meet before they can be considered eligible for selection. By contrast, candidates without an identifiable political affiliation struggle to advance beyond the middle ranks of the ministerial bureaucracy, NDACs, or EIs insofar as they are subject to party patronage.

Professional skills were also mentioned as a selection criterion for the large majority of policy sectors. The importance of professional expertise indicates that political loyalty alone is usually not enough to land a job as a political appointee. Ministers do not like to appoint officials who lack subject expertise unless they can be sure that the work of the appointee is largely inconsequential for policy making and implementation. The interviews suggest that professional knowledge is relatively more important in sectors that rely on specific skills such as Finance, the Economy, Health Care and the Judiciary.

Personal connections are secondary selection criteria relative to professional expertise and political loyalty. The major exception is the Regional and Local Administration. At the regional and local level, personal networks and relations tend to be more relevant than party connections and professional skills. Moreover, the Judiciary has been identified by our interviewees as an area that is subject to relatively little political influence, but professional expertise is often paired with personal connections and even accusations of nepotism. Yet the distinction between political and personal connections is not always clear-cut. The selection of political appointees is usually not filtered by a central institution such as the prime minister's office or the central party organization, so informal relations between appointer and appointee prior to the actual appointment are very common.

182 Jan-Hinrik Meyer-Sahling and Krisztina Jáger

The purpose of appointments

As mentioned above, the classic literature on party patronage assumes that political parties offer political appointments in exchange for services rendered to the party (Shefter, 1977). The appointment is then seen as a reward for a service that has already been delivered by the appointee. By contrast, comparative public administration research tends to focus on the control function of political appointments (Page and Wright, 1999b). In particular, principal-agency theory assumes that political appointments can reduce a principal's problem of controlling a bureaucratic agent (Calvert, Moran, and Weingast, 1987).

Figure 9.3 shows that political appointments in Hungary are primarily made for the sake of political control. Political control can take various forms. First, political appointees are specifically responsible for the coordination and control of the policy-making process. In particular, the preparatory stage of the policy process allows political appointees to influence the contents of legislation in accordance with the programme of the party or more specifically the minister. Second, political appointees are specifically charged with the control of policy implementation. According to our interviewees, in almost all sectors political appointees influence the allocation of licences, permits, contracts, and financial subsidies. In the Media, broadcasting licences would be handed out. In the Culture sector, funding for the organization of exhibitions, competitions, festivals, etc. would be provided. In the area of EU fund management, contracts and financial support are granted by regional development councils. The list of examples quickly indicates that political appointments have created considerable risks of corruption in the public sector.

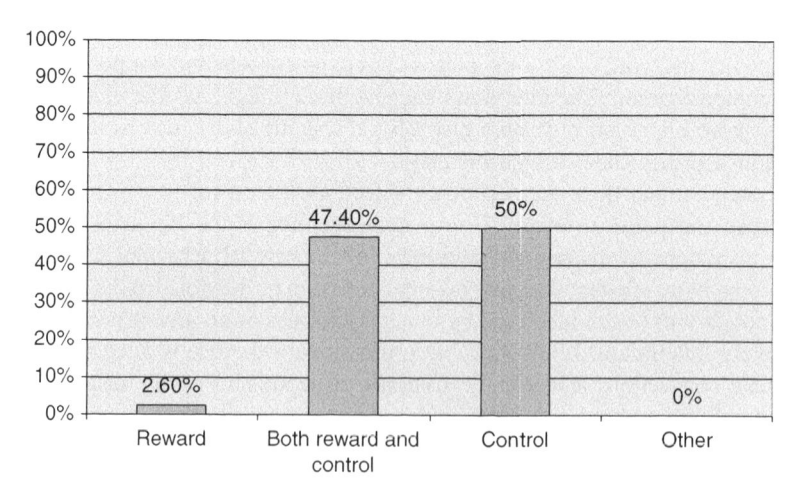

FIGURE 9.3 Motivations for party patronage in Hungary

Party Patronage in Hungary 183

Third, we learned that political appointees are specifically dealing with the control of information flows. In the area of foreign policy, for instance, prime ministers can benefit from the appointment of loyal supporters in order to stay in the loop and to pre-empt the activities of the foreign minister if they so desire. Fourth, control can take the form of co-option, when political opponents are given appointments in order to buy their silence or even their collaboration in selected areas. We found that co-option occurs frequently in the financial sector when financial experts from competing wings within the governing parties, as well as experts close to the opposition parties, are silenced with an appointment to the managing boards of state-owned banks and enterprises.

Even if control comes out as the most important motivation behind political appointments, we have to recognize that appointments also have a reward function in many sectors. Several sectors, such as Foreign Service, Finance, the Economy and the Media provide islands of reward in the EIs. In Foreign Service, for instance, it is possible to earn an appointment to an ambassadorial post. Appointments for the sake of reward are also regularly made to boards of state-owned banks and enterprises. The assumption in these cases is typically that the appointee has a less strategic role to play in the process of policy making and implementation.

Jobs for the opposition

Finally, Figure 9.4 shows that party patronage in Hungary follows largely a majoritarian, winner-takes-all principle. Governing parties typically reserve the spoils for themselves. Opposition parties only have access to a small number of

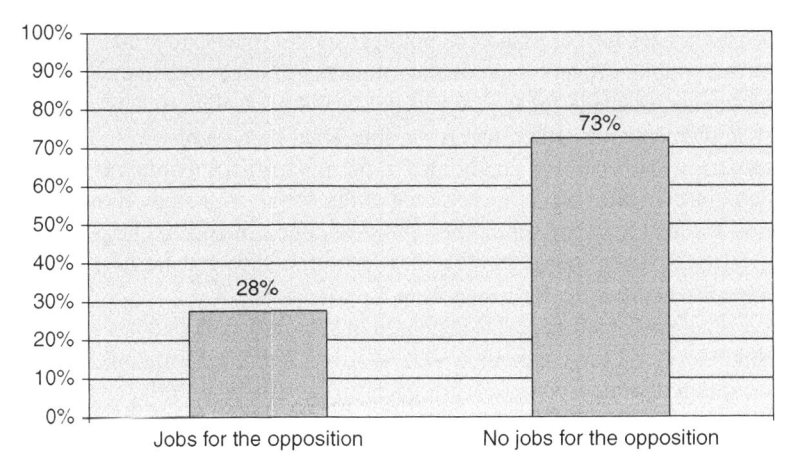

FIGURE 9.4 Distribution of jobs between government and opposition parties in Hungary

policy sectors and only under specific conditions. In the Media, the proportional representation of government and opposition parties is ensured by law. The president of the Hungarian broadcasting commission, ORTT, is an affiliate of the senior governing party, while the first deputy president is a delegate of the largest opposition party. Proportional representation is also ensured with regard to nomination to the governing boards of television and radio corporations. In a few other sectors, such as Foreign Service, Finance and the Economy, affiliates of the opposition have areas in which they can 'survive' while their party is out of office. Strategically less important embassies and the boards of state-owned companies provide settings in which opposition affiliates may be kept in their posts but their influence on decision making is minimal. These kinds of EIs were also mentioned above as 'islands of reward', in that the control of policy making and implementation was not necessarily the main purpose of political appointments.

CONCLUSION

This chapter has examined party patronage in Hungary. It has shown that parties reach all sectors of the state, but the degree and the patterns of patronage vary across policy sectors. In particular, we identified 'captured sectors' with a high degree of party patronage, such as the Media, Health Care, the Regional Administration and Foreign Service; 'partially disciplined sectors' such as Finance, the Economy and the Military and Police, which maintain patronage-free areas among NDACs; and 'partially insulated sectors', such as the Judiciary, and Culture and Education, that are characterized by a relatively low degree of patronage and by keeping their EIs largely free from political appointments.

The chapter has further found that political appointments are primarily made by the party in public office—in particular, ministers of executive branch ministries. Appointments are made for the sake of politically controlling policy making and policy implementation rather than rewarding loyal party supporters. Yet political loyalty is a near necessary condition for promotion and appointment to senior positions in the state, while professional skills are an important complementary criterion for the choice of appointees. Political appointments are largely reserved for governing parties unless formal rules institutionalize a share of positions for the opposition parties as, for instance, in the Media sector.

Over time, party patronage has increased in Hungary, though it has always been at a high level. During transition and shortly after the formation of the first democratic government, efforts were made to depoliticize public administration and hence to reduce the influence of parties on appointments. These attempts did not succeed. The Antall/Boross government (1990–4) started to repoliticize the appointment and selection of public sector managers during the second half of its term in office. The election victory of the socialists in 1994 led to the dismissal of appointees associated with the Antall/Boross government and the return of many officials from late-communist governments. At this point, patronage politics in Hungary had adapted to democratic conditions and had regenerated itself. Subsequent government alternations followed the same script. Appointees of the departing government were dismissed. Then the vacancies were taken by appointees close to the incoming governing parties. Over time, the scope of political appointments has increased in width, by including more and more institutions, and in depth, by slowly creeping down the institutional hierarchies.

Party patronage has hence become a key feature of political life in Hungary. The two main political camps have created their own reservoirs of experts and activists who are ready to move into public office when their bloc of parties comes into government. Patronage plays an important role with regard to the political control of the policy process in a competitive and polarized political environment. It has also been important for the stability of the main parties on the left and the right. Parties have acted as gatekeepers for careers in the public sector and for the provision of public goods, thanks to their control of the policy process by means of political appointees. This stabilization has come at a price, as patronage increases the risk of corruption in the public sector and hence increases popular distrust in political parties. In fact, patronage strategies run the risk of being self-defeating because they further decrease the legitimacy and trust of the public in political parties and as a result nurture populist challenges of the establishment. The outcome of the most recent elections in 2010 provides a good illustration of this dynamic. Yet party patronage is deeply entrenched in Hungary and it is unlikely to disappear, regardless of the parties that are present.

NOTES

1. This classification has been contested by both Haughton (2008) and Meyer-Sahling (2006a).

CHAPTER 10

Party Patronage in Iceland: Rewards and Control Appointments

Gunnar Helgi Kristinsson

INTRODUCTION

Political appointments serve two distinct functions. One is to reward party supporters and the other to control the state (Kopecký and Scherlis, 2008). Patronage may occur for other reasons, as in the case of nepotism and corruption, but the political functions of such patronage are coincidental. Reward and control appointments are different in many respects, even if they may coexist, and they are dealt with differently in the theoretical literature.

The reward function of political appointments is a feature of many traditional patronage systems, where the parties reward supporters in an exchange relationship between political parties and the recipients of clientelistic services[1] (Piattoni, 2001a). Clientelism, according to Shefter (1994), developed only where administrative elites were weak during the instigation of democratic politics. Where bureaucratic elites, on the other hand, were sufficiently strong to establish a 'constituency for bureaucratic autonomy', as Shefter puts it, mass politics took a different turn. In such cases, aspiring political entrepreneurs could mainly offer ideological or programmatic rewards for the efforts of party members. Put differently, patronage developed where democratization preceded bureaucratization, but was blocked where bureaucracy developed prior to democratization.

Some political appointments, however, aim at control rather than rewards. Peters and Pierre (2004b) maintain that the reason politicians devote increasing attention to securing control of the bureaucracy has to do with the weakening of traditional control mechanisms through administrative reforms in recent decades. Managerial reforms in the civil service have, according to this view, 'freed major parts of the public sector from direct ministerial control' (Peters and Pierre, 2004b: 7). But politicians are still held accountable for policy, irrespective of the loss of control which they have suffered. Hence, ministers find that 'they need civil servants who are in agreement with their stances and who are personally loyal, if not necessarily partisans' (ibid.). As Mathieson et al. (2007: 10) put it, 'the objectives of political involvement in senior appointments are usually politically responsive policy and implementation, rather than patronage in the form of jobs to party faithful or family members'.

The two theories of appointments, rewards and control, are not necessarily contradictory in all respects, and there is no reason to think that frequent use of rewards patronage excludes the possibility of control appointments, or vice versa. There is an interesting disharmony, nonetheless, in the way they treat bureaucratic autonomy. In rewards theory, bureaucratic autonomy is a decisive factor preventing the development of patronage on a large scale whereas in control theory political appointments occur as a consequence of too much bureaucratic autonomy. While it is possible that further specifications might resolve the apparent contradiction, in their present form the two theories provide contradictory predictions, at least with regard to the higher echelons of the civil service.

They also provide very dissimilar interpretations of the functions of political appointments for the political parties. Rewards theory sees patronage as building material for political parties. Patronage provides part of the incentive for party members to contribute to party work. According to Shefter, the decisive phase of mass political mobilization was a 'critical experience' which subsequently determined the use of patronage in the relevant polity. Once established, there is no political force able to hold back the temptations of party politicians to use jobs and other public sector values to reward their supporters. Control theory, on the other hand, largely ignores the demand for patronage. Mathieson et al. (2007: 10) rather optimistically claim that 'other mechanisms, particularly transparency' will prevent the wider use of patronage for particularistic purposes. The question is, however, whether political appointments can realistically be restricted to the fine purpose of maintaining democratic control. If Shefter is right, once the political coalition for bureaucratic autonomy is broken, the gates to the bureaucracy are likely to open not only to control appointments but to other types of political appointments as well. The gates are basically protected, not by regulations or technical arrangements, but by a political coalition in favour of bureaucratic autonomy.

The problem with Shefter's account, however, is that it stops after the initial mobilization of democratic mass politics without considering the impact which different organizational forms may have on patronage. Political parties have undergone major changes after the initial phase of mass mobilization (cf. Katz and Mair, 1995) and may no longer rely on large numbers of party activists to the same extent. Evaluations of the attractiveness of rewards patronage may have changed accordingly.

The prevalence of clientelism and patronage in Icelandic politics has been the subject of several attempts at interpretation by political scientists (e.g. Kristinsson 1996, 2001; Indriðason, 2005). The present chapter attempts to untangle the complex story of patronage and political appointments in Iceland using the tools of rewards and control theory. We begin by tracing the development of reward patronage in Iceland through an account of how the modern state and parties took shape in the country. We then go on to describe the main results of the forty-five-strong expert survey conducted in Iceland in 2008 with regard to political appointments and their role in Icelandic politics. Other relevant material is also considered. Finally we sum up the conclusions of the study and place them in a wider context.

BACKGROUND

The Icelandic state emerged from the Danish kingdom in stages between 1874 and 1944. Major steps on the way included separate constitutions in 1874, Icelandic Home Rule in 1904, formal sovereignty in 1918, and the dissolution of the union in 1944. Icelandic separatism was based primarily on cultural differences where the Icelandic language played a key role, although other social interests also had an effect. The form of government adopted by the Icelandic state was to a great extent modelled on the Danish one, which continues to influence Icelandic legislation and administrative thinking in many ways. This applies to the constitution (although a president has replaced the king in the Icelandic one) as well as the administration, which is based on weak collegiate authority in the cabinet, ministerial government, and a formal merit system of public appointments.

The administration of Iceland was until 1904 part of the Danish bureaucracy. The tug of war between crown and parliament took the form of a dispute between bureaucrats representing foreign rule and popularly elected parliamentarians representing the nation. The introduction of parliamentarism and Home Rule in 1904 brought reorganization of the administration, as control of the state passed into the hands of domestic politicians. While the politicians undoubtedly applied their newfound powers of appointment with favouritism and political bias, there is nothing to indicate that large-scale patronage was introduced at this point. The parties at this time existed only in parliament.

The weak state which emerged with Home Rule, however, was easily susceptible to clientelism once the parties realized the potential value of mass organization and clientelism. This began to take place during the 1920s, when a minority government of the Progressive Party made some highly controversial appointments. In fact, Reykjavík doctors tried in 1930 to have a government minister committed to a mental asylum, so infuriated were they by his style of appointments. The minister in question, however, saw himself as something of an organizational innovator, as he later explained:

> I brought two innovations to organized politics: to meet moves made by our opponents with an alliance which could win, if at all possible. Secondly, to

attract supporters by distributing positions of influence and prestige between fellow workers while taking none for myself. Much of the Progressive Party's success over a quarter of a century was due to this tactic. (Jónsson, 1952: XLIX)

The Conservatives (Independence Party from 1929)—the party of officialdom and the establishment in Iceland—strongly criticized early attempts by the Progressives to make use of appointments for party purposes. The rural Progressives, however, were permanently in power from 1927 to 1942 (alone or with others) and in a position to shape the administration during a critical phase in its development. Before long, the Independence Party decided, with characteristic pragmatism, that if you can't beat them you join them. It established party machines in its local strongholds, such as Reykjavík, competed for access to financial services, licences, and other favours on behalf of the business community, and made partisan appointments to public sector jobs. Similarly, the relatively small (by Nordic standards) Social Democrats did not stay outside the sharing of favours for long. After their first taste of power, in 1934, they quickly gained a reputation as patronage-seekers with regard to public appointments to a no lesser extent than the other parties. Only the Socialists, an outsider party in Icelandic politics, never quite managed to become part of the patronage and clientele system, and had to rely instead on their supporters to do party work without the offer of material rewards.

The four parties which emerged out of the mobilization phase of Icelandic party politics during the 1930s quickly established a near monopoly of political representation during the Second World War and its aftermath. Most spheres of society became party politicized, including foreign trade, banking, literature, housing, retail trade, and jobs in government. The press was party political, and while the national radio remained formally neutral it served under a political watchdog committee which greatly limited its scope for initiative in agenda-setting. The occasional fifth party managed a breakthrough prior to the 1980s (one in 1953 and another in 1971) but quickly disappeared again, leaving little behind.

Organizationally, the Icelandic parties were neither the typical European mass party described by Duverger (1976) nor the patronage party machines described by Epstein (1980) in the American context. They presented a hybrid formation of class-based mass parties and patronage machines where social class, pressure group politics, and patronage networks combined to form well-functioning organizations which were based partly on material incentives and partly on class interests and/or ideological conviction.

The membership organizations proper were part of a wider organizational network in which party activities outside the Althingi (the national parliament of Iceland) took place. The party newspapers played a central role in all cases, as did a hybrid of interest group organizations, local governments, and businesses which had ties to the parties. In the case of the Social Democrats and Socialists it was, above all, the unions which mattered, but the Conservatives also began during the late 1930s to pay attention to the organization of their working class followers. The Progressive Party had close ties to the rural cooperative movement, which under its protection became a major business operation in various branches of trade and industry during the interwar period. The Independence Party, on the other hand, had a strong basis in the business community and the employer organizations. All the parties were deeply entrenched in local government with their different local strongholds which often served as training grounds for future leaders.

In the networks of party workers, local governments, organized groups, and businesses which formed the basis of the parties there was inevitably strong demand for the services and benefits controlled by the increasingly assertive Icelandic state. The general shortage which prevailed during the Great Depression and the rationing which followed strengthened this demand in the 1930s. But there was a supply-side story as well. A politically weak bureaucracy and failure to create a 'constituency for bureaucratic autonomy' allowed the parties to penetrate the administration in search of favours for their supporters.

Patronage became increasingly contested in Icelandic politics from the 1960s onwards. Four linked developments played a role here. In the first place, with the liberalization of the economy, underway since the 1960s, the business community preferred to manage on its own, without too much intervention from political parties. This eventually led to the decline of the cooperatives (which were more dependent on the state), privatization in the financial system, and a more liberal regulatory regime. Professionalization in the labour market was a second development which undermined the traditional hold of the parties, not least in the large public sector professions which grew with the advent of the welfare state. With increasing professionalism, the use of patronage became politically more risky because of the adversity it created, and in many cases the cost would outweigh the benefits. In the third place, various developments in the media market led to the partial replacement of party-controlled media with privately run media, while party newspapers went out of business, especially during the 1990s. The Independence Party made a serious attempt at maintaining its media advantage but succeeded only partly after it had alienated some of its business supporters (Kárason, 2005), and created a constitutional crisis (in 2004) when it tried to ban concentrated media ownership which would have put the main firms they considered hostile out of business.

Finally, the professionalization of politics and campaigning made the part previously played by party volunteers less important than before. Private contributions to the parties were granted tax exemptions during the early 1990s and government subsidies were at the same time growing significantly. The parties increasingly hired professionals to plan election campaigns based on relatively capital intensive methods, such as television advertising. They still kept highly inflated membership files, which as a rule expanded greatly during the party primaries (introduced around 1970), but the role of the membership, except for the primaries, increasingly became that of onlookers.

During the era of unrestrained clientelism, patronage appointments were used primarily as a reward to those who had proven themselves worthy. They were the spoils of power and a currency in which people's worth to the party could be measured. Thus, the scope of patronage was wide and its reach deep. The problem was that formally the Icelandic bureaucracy was based on the assumption of merit rather than patronage, with tenured positions and relatively generous pension entitlements. Political appointees would usually outlast the politicians who put them in place, because as long as they respected minimal standards of conduct they were well protected by civil service legislation. New political masters were unlikely to get rid of political appointees but could to a certain extent bring in their own people by creating new jobs or by replacing older employees when they retired.

The practice of political appointments was common knowledge, even if the politicians making them invariably denied the political connection, cooking up arguments to suit the case as they went along. The politically controlled media might make some criticisms, but since all parties were guilty of similar practices (except to a certain extent the left socialists, who were in opposition much of the time) the critical sting of the discussion was blunted.

There are winners and losers under patronage. It distributes value to those who have the right political connections at the expense of those who don't. Non-merit appointments are particularly damaging to those who have invested in professional or bureaucratic careers and from that point of view should have the competitive edge. During the 1960s and 1970s, increasing dissatisfaction with patronage and clientelism in general led to some discussion of the role of parties and criticism of 'party rule' (*flokksræði*) in Icelandic politics—more or less all challengers to the traditional four-party system have made a point of attacking party rule. Political appointments have become more risky and much less common at lower levels in the public sector.

A series of reforms during the past two decades have been introduced to create a stronger regulatory framework and greater efficiency in the public sector. These include the introduction of an ombudsman for administration (1987), a Public Administration Act (1993), Transparency in Government (1996), and a new Public Employment Act (1996). To enhance efficiency the government, at the same time, subscribed enthusiastically to New Public Management (Kristmundsson, 2003). For the first time, public administration became the subject of comprehensive reform policies, and hence many of our respondents were optimistic that real change had taken place since the 'bad old times' of unlimited patronage (see Table 10.1).

There seems little doubt that the overall use of patronage has declined over time. Survey material from 2006 among public employees indicates that 32 per cent

TABLE 10.1 *Change in the use of patronage over the last 15–20 years*

Substantial change	84%
Not substantial change	16%
Total	100%
(N)	(44)

know examples of non-merit appointments in their agencies in the last two years, compared to 39 per cent in 1998 (Kristmundsson, 2007).

SCOPE AND REACH OF PARTY PATRONAGE

Ministerial government, a basic principle of public administration in Iceland, means that cabinet ministers are both the political and administrative masters of the civil service. Administrators serve the state through the agency of individual ministers. Since the cabinet in practice rarely infringes upon the right of ministers to control their administrative sectors, they have wide formal and real powers to steer the civil service as they see fit. The law, however, limits their power of appointment in two ways. On the one hand there are, since 1996, limits to the downward reach of ministerial appointments, to which we will return below. On the other hand, the law also, in some cases, grants a certain degree of autonomy to agencies, usually through the establishment of a board with specific powers, including those of appointing the agency head. Such independent agencies are established by an act of parliament, and although they are not reachable by the ministers directly the representatives on the agency board in some cases have direct or indirect links to the parties.

The state administration is usually seen as a two-layered one. The higher layer contains the ministries, where 2–3 per cent of state employees work, who basically form the policy and administrative units around the ministers. The lower layer consists of the state agencies, which may be divided into non-departmental agencies and commissions (NDACs) and executing institutions (although such a distinction is not usual in Iceland), which all adhere under particular ministries. Most NDACs are fairly small. They account for just over 10 per cent of state agencies but in terms of relative manpower they are much smaller. Some of the executing institutions are regional offices for particular functions at their ministries, but there is no integrated regional state administration in the country. Below the state level, however, there is the municipal level, which consists of seventy-seven local governments, accounting for roughly a third of public consumption.

TABLE 10.2 *The index of party patronage in Iceland*

Policy area	Ministries	NDACs	Executing institutions	Policy area total
Economy	0.44	0.22	0.22	0.30
Finance	0.11	0.22	0.22	0.19
Judiciary	0.22	0.00	0.44	0.22
Media	0.22	0.33	0.17	0.24
Military and Police	0.22	0.22	0.44	0.30
Health Care	0.44	0.22	0.22	0.30
Culture and Education	0.17	0.11	0.06	0.11
Foreign Service	0.22	0.33	0.11	0.22
Regional and Local Administration	0.17	0.11	0.22	0.17
Total	0.25	0.20	0.23	0.23

In principle, all the ministries and almost all agencies are reachable by the political parties through the appointment of ministry staff and agency heads, usually by the relevant minister (see Table 10.2). In some cases (e.g. in judicial appointments) the minister acts on the advice of evaluation committees but is not necessarily bound to follow their advice and in practice sometimes goes against their conclusions. Autonomous agencies are usually governed by boards, but the boards themselves are often appointed by the ministers. According to an estimate from 2000, 14 per cent of Icelandic state agencies are autonomous and an additional 8 per cent consist of various commissions, which often enjoy a large degree of autonomy (Ministry of Finance, 2000).

Although formally the scope of political appointments is broad, the actual impact of political considerations is contested. The legal understanding is that politicians (usually ministers) should play an active role in appointments to ministry posts and agency heads but apply meritocratic criteria. The extent to which they do so, however, is debated. Many respondents believe that politicians apply partisan criteria in most institutions, but equally many believe they seldom do so.

For a new minister entering the ministry the immediate problem is, above all, that of taking control. Some manage to make promising bureaucrats part of their personal network but others look beyond the ministry. The small size of the state administration (with approximately 22,000 employees) should have the effect of simplifying control, but does so only to a limited extent. Lack of organizational coherence at both the ministry and agency level, together with the relatively large number of small organizations, actually makes control rather difficult. Local government does not simplify matters, with units ranging from fewer than one hundred inhabitants to 120,000 and corresponding variability in administrative and service capacity.

The twelve Icelandic ministries are small—usually with between 20 and 120 employees—but the ministers are administratively in charge of the subordinate agencies as well. With one exception (ministerial assistants) the employees of the ministries are formally non-political and expected to remain in their jobs after the minister eventually has to leave. The ministerial assistants, on the other hand, must leave their posts when a new minister comes into office.

Apart from using the permanent ministerial staff that they inherit, there are three strategies available to the ministers for taking effective control. In the first place they may rely on the ministerial assistants, who are typically (and increasingly) young party members with little professional or bureaucratic experience. They serve liaison functions, public relations functions, and to some extent act as special advisers. Some ministers hire more than one assistant (despite the formal maximum of one) but usually not more than two (Kristmundsson, 2005).

Secondly, some ministers use various kinds of special advisers and consultancy firms for the formulation of policy. These are often hand-picked, replacing to some extent the advisory role of the permanent administration. In some cases the consultancy firms also play a role in campaigns during elections (although paid from a different account).

Finally, the ministers may use the non-political positions within the ministries and elsewhere to establish or strengthen their personal network of reliable agents, nested within the formal bureaucratic one. According to the Public Employment Act, it is obligatory to advertise public positions except in specific areas (Foreign Service, formerly Central Bank directors). One respondent gave the following description:

> The process is often like this: you advertise and if you have already decided who is to get the job then you only advertise in the government Gazette, which nobody reads and then you don't have to worry about too many applications. So you have two options: a low profile advertisement if you have already decided—but you can also go through this usual agency hiring process where the agency is used for preliminary elimination. Then, when you have a group of about three applicants left, the minister and Permanent Secretary decide jointly who gets the job.

Ministers seem increasingly to feel that they should be able to choose their permanent secretaries rather than simply accepting the ones chosen by their predecessors. Getting rid of permanent secretaries is easier since the Civil Service Act of 1996 abolished life tenure (which of course makes them less permanent) and the Ministry Act in 2007 increased the possibilities of transfers without advertisements within and between departments. In 1990–2005 there were twenty-eight appointments to the position of permanent secretary in Iceland, half of which could be considered political appointments (Kristinsson, 2006).

Through a revision of the Public Employment Act in 1996 the power of appointment in the agencies—which had formally been in the hands of the minister—was given to the agency heads. The power to appoint agency heads, however, remained in the hands of the minister, unless otherwise stated in the relevant legal acts, and the power of appointment within the ministries remains in the hands of the ministers. The passing of the Act reduced the downward reach of ministers to some extent, although they were by this time not very actively involved in the appointments of lower-level employees in any case. They can, of course, still apply indirect pressure with regard to lower-level appointments. Our respondents' evaluation of the impact of parties on appointments at different levels indicate that 95 per cent think parties have an impact at the highest level, 32 per cent at the middle level, and 9 per cent at the lowest level. This, of course, does not mean that 95 per cent of highest-level positions are distributed by the parties. As we have seen, there has been a considerable reduction in the number of positions which they distribute. What is does show, nonetheless, is that the parties are not only involved at the highest level of the administration, where the control motive may be strongest, but remain active to a certain extent at the lower levels.

> They [the politicians] control the top layer. Clearly. They have less influence at the middle level. But I have seen things happen also at the level of the ordinary employee which are clearly connected to the political parties. They have never been prepared to let go completely. Sometimes things have to be arranged.

POLICY SECTORS AND POLITICAL APPOINTMENTS

Our data, based on five interviews in each policy sector, allows for very limited statistical manipulations. The interviews, along with previous research, however, allow us to make qualitative evaluations of the role of patronage in different parts of the state.

The Financial sector

The Financial sector played an important role in Icelandic clientelism through state-run banks governed by boards elected by the Althingi and bank directors who were usually de facto chosen for their political reliability. Privatization of the banking sector in 1998–2003 would have created problems for the parties had they not already abandoned mass clientelism to a significant degree. Nonetheless, the ruling Independence Party and Progressive Party were highly sensitive to the political connections of the new groups of owners, and a precondition for the privatization of the banks was that owner groups acceptable to the two parties were involved (Rannsóknarnefnd Alþingis, 2010). For similar reasons, they were sensitive to the way in which the regulatory agencies were governed, including the Financial Supervisory Authority, the Competition Authority, and not least the Central Bank. The political forces kept their hold on these through appointments of agency heads and boards. One respondent put it like this:

> It is obvious that the political parties have been interested in a lot of these agencies, beginning with the Central Bank, the Housing Financing Fund where the director is a fine fellow, someone who used to be minister of health, and before that worked in a bank in the provinces. The student loan fund is directed by someone who is, I mean, an economist, a professional of sorts, who used to be a ministerial assistant, but of course is a known member of a certain political party... The leadership of the Central bank is political.

Political interference with the privatization of the banks and appointments to the regulatory agencies was widely criticized after the bank crash in 2008 (which incidentally led to partial renationalization of the Financial sector). Since its foundation in 1961, the Central Bank was governed by three directors appointed by a minister and a supervisory board elected by parliament. The three directors were not formally political appointees, but in reality their positions were regarded as party property: one for the Independence Party, one for the Progressive Party, and the third usually the Social Democratic Party. Out of seventeen Central Bank directors between 1961 and 2009, only two were without party associations—one of them a temporary replacement. Eight were former ministers. One designates his period in the bank as the most relaxed in his life (Eggertsson, 2000: 378). To some extent the Central Bank served a similar function to that of the Foreign Service (see below), as a retirement home for leading politicians. The potential for influence was there, nonetheless, especially after the independence of the bank with regard to monetary policy was written into the new Central Bank Act of 2001. This became a major issue in the early months of 2009, when the government made clear that the politically appointed chairman of the board of directors, former prime minister, Oddsson, who had been prime minister in 1991–2004, did not enjoy its confidence. The government actually had to change the Central Bank Act to have him removed.

Media

The Media is another sector of strategic importance that has been at the centre of political attention for a long time. During the 1980s the electronic media market was liberalized and a private TV station, Channel 2 (Stöð 2), appeared alongside the national radio and television. Groups close to the Independence Party appear to have made a determined attempt to establish control of a sympathetic medium in the electronic media market in the wake of privatization. In the mid-1990s they lost control of Channel 2 to businessmen who had fallen out with the party leadership (Kárason, 2005). From that time, according to a number of commentators, the party paid increasing attention to the national radio and television.

In 1995 the Minister of Education (Independence Party) appointed the former Mayor of Reykjavík (Independence Party) as director of the agency. At the same time it was felt within the agency that the party was increasingly active in supplying it with reporters, often first as temporary replacements and later as full reporters. This applies in particular to the television newsroom, where appointments are usually much more controversial than in the radio newsroom (as may be seen, for example, by looking at the way votes were distributed in the Radio Council). This created a sense of professional resentment within this agency, that—despite everything—enjoys greater confidence among the public than other news agencies. Despite some political interference, as one respondent explained, there are still standards that must be met:

> Usually they don't hire completely unqualified people to these jobs but rather if there are two qualified they choose the one with the correct political colours. Although there are examples to the contrary . . . [complete incompetents are] usually not hired in the media sector. It would be too obvious.

In 2005 the situation finally boiled over when a new executive for the radio newsroom was to be hired by the director of the agency. A candidate who seemed less qualified than other applicants was chosen for the job—supposedly for political reasons. After strong protests the new executive resigned from the post and the appointment of a replacement was generally considered a victory for professionalism. Later in the year the director of the agency left his post and became an ambassador.

In 2007 the agency was changed into a limited company, although fully owned by the state. Our interviewees seem uncertain what effect this will have on political appointments. The company, however, does have a board with political appointees, which hires the director, who in turn hires other employees.

The judicial system

The arguments for and against strategic political appointments may apply with variable strength in different contexts. Where important considerations of impartiality and credibility are involved, however, there are strong arguments in favour of agency autonomy (Majone, 2001; OECD, 2002). Thus, whatever the arguments for control appointments may be in different policy sectors, such arguments must be particularly fragile in the case of the judiciary. Several of the Icelandic cases where concerns have been raised concerning undue political influence in appointments have to do with such jobs, including the appointment of two Supreme Court judges in 2003 and 2004. Traditionally the appointments of Supreme Court judges have not been much politicized, but after the court found several important legislative acts unconstitutional in the late 1990s and early 2000s, the strategic value of positions on the court increased significantly, as some of our respondents pointed out.

> They want to influence and control how the judiciary works; which decisions are reached has become increasingly important. We have recent examples where the Supreme Court has declared legislation from the Althingi non-constitutional, first in the quota ruling, which of course was a very political issue, and then in the so-called invalids ruling where the court decided that reducing payments to invalids was non-constitutional. There is no doubt that the politicians want to influence the judiciary so that it will shy away from decisions and leave the Althingi completely in charge... I am certain this lies behind this. Then there are also personal considerations, they want to place friends and family in comfortable positions, like the examples show.

Regional administration

Our respondents in regional government represented mostly influential people in local government. They were, on the whole, sceptical concerning the widespread belief that patronage and nepotism thrive at the local government level, especially under their own rule. In some cases they were willing to believe that their political opponents might resort to such measures.

> The Independence Party built Reykjavík as a patronage system; you could not get a job as a garbage collector except by registering to the [IP-controlled] Vörður union. This culture permeated the system; there was no one working in the Town Hall who was not an IP supporter.

But there was also scepticism concerning the use of patronage:

> I wouldn't want to do something like this in my municipality. We need all the talent we can get and we can't afford people who aren't doing a good job.
>
> You have four years and if you get a difficult official then maybe you won't get a lot done in these four years... but you also have to keep the supporters happy.

Some of the respondents from local government were defensive and felt that widespread beliefs in political appointments at the local level were exaggerated. A survey conducted in 2009 shows that 79 per cent of the public believe that nepotism, personal contacts, and political patronage play an important role in their municipality, compared to 38 per cent of council members. Interestingly enough, however, 73 per cent in the council minorities agree with the public, which indicates the extent to which political appointments are a contested issue also at the local level (Kristinsson, 2010).

The smaller local government areas, according to some of our respondents, are more susceptible to political appointments than the larger ones (which were represented in our study).

> According to the Local Government Act [article 56] the elected representatives have the final say in appointments. They appoint the Mayor [and] department heads I think in all cases, but at lower levels it varies by municipality. In the smallest ones, where everything is discussed in the council, they appoint teachers. The representatives are involved at every stage. In the larger ones the officials are entitled to make appointments and the political representatives are not necessarily part of the appointment process although they are in a position to decide (and they sometimes do) but in the smaller ones they do the interviews.

The Foreign Service

The Foreign Service is a particularly illuminating case with regard to the strategic argument for patronage because we are less dependent on subjective evaluations there than in other policy sectors. Ambassadorships are highly valued posts in the civil service for the personal rewards associated with them rather than their strategic importance for the political parties. There are two roads to becoming an ambassador, one through a bureaucratic career and the other through political connections. Ambassadors either rise from the ranks of the bureaucracy or else they get their positions through the patronage of the Minister of Foreign Affairs.

During 1990–2009, forty-two people were made ambassadors in the Icelandic Foreign Service. Of these, twenty-three had bureaucratic backgrounds, while nineteen came in through the patronage of the minister. Although bureaucratic politics played a role in some of the bureaucratic appointments they were basically compatible with merit criteria. The others usually had no experience in the ministry (or one or two years in a few cases). The non-bureaucratic appointments fall into three groups. Some applied to close administrative co-workers of the ministers in question who received their posts in reward for their services. A second group consists of the ministers' own party fellows, some of whom were former ministers but others simply wished for a change of job or needed taking care of in one way or another. Finally, there are several cases where the foreign ministers solved occupational problems in other parties—often even the opposition parties—by their appointments. It is primarily the former leaders of the opposition parties who could expect such appointments. The appointment of former opposition party leaders to ambassador posts is an instance of collective insurance, whereby the political elite takes care of its own, irrespective of old differences. But it is doubtful if these would take place if the political cost of such appointments were substantial.

TABLE 10.3 *Role of parties in strategic and less strategic sectors*

	Strategic sectors	Less strategic sectors
Parties play a great role	62%	51%
Parties play small or no role	38%	49%
Total	100%	100%
(N)	(42)	(49)

Note: Strategic sectors include Finance, Media and the Judiciary, while non-strategic ones include Economy, Military and Police, Health Care, Education and Culture. Not included are the Foreign Service, which has an ambivalent position, and Regional Administration. Each respondent was asked for their opinion on ministries, NDACs, and executing institutions, which means that potential N is three times the actual number of respondents.

Other sectors

The remaining sectors of Education, Economy, Health Care, and Military and Police[2] are probably of smaller strategic importance to the parties than the Judiciary, Media, or the Financial sector. To the politicians responsible for these sectors, however, political control remains important. There is a slight tendency for the more strategic sectors to have more political appointments, according to our data, but the difference is not statistically significant (Table 10.3).

MOTIVATION OF THE PARTIES

The relative impact of the rewards and control according to our respondents is seen in Figure 10.1.

Despite the declining relevance of rewards to the parties, they remain part of the motivation for political appointments in Iceland. Half our respondents mentioned a mixture of control and rewards, while a third mentioned only control and far fewer (16 per cent) mentioned only rewards. Adding up, we find that 84 per cent mentioned control while 66 per cent mentioned rewards.

> To the extent that [political appointments] occur, their purpose is to strengthen the minister himself and his political position. Occasionally the politicians may wish to reward someone for their support, but I think that is becoming much rarer. That was the old way.

The great majority of respondents thought that appointees, as a rule, fulfilled the minimum requirements of a job:

> Yes, there are political connections but I haven't seen ministers (at least recently) appointing people who don't fulfil the minimum requirements... you don't just take some clown and put him in there just because he is a Progressive or similar.

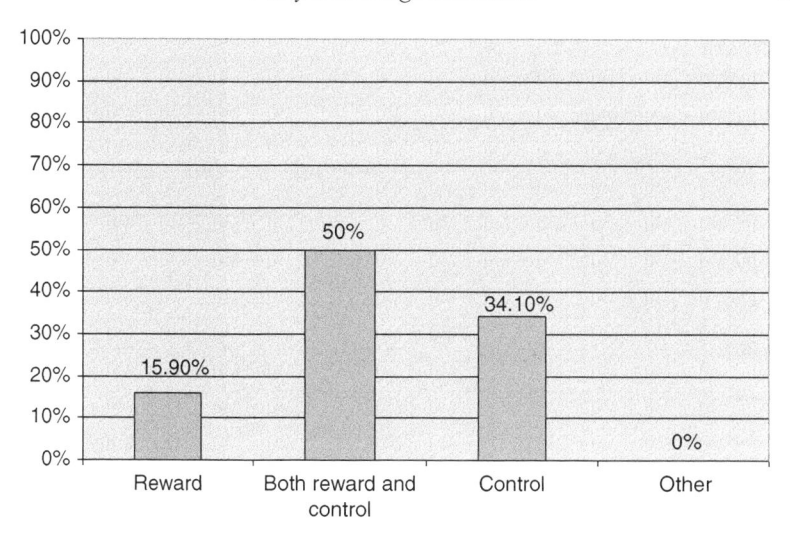

FIGURE 10.1 Motivations for party patronage in Iceland

Bar chart showing: Reward 15.90%, Both reward and control 50%, Control 34.10%, Other 0%.

Usually people meet the minimum standards. But sometimes the standards are designed to fit individual applicants.

In answer to an open question concerning the qualities of appointees we got the following responses. The great majority of respondents (80 per cent), according to Figure 10.2, maintain that appointments are compatible with professional criteria (although only a third think they are the only criteria). A majority (59 per cent) also think political criteria play a role, but they are seldom the only factor. Fewer (21 per cent) believe in a personal connection, and given the small size of the political system they are, perhaps, surprisingly rare. The personal factor, nonetheless, is important as we shall see.

A DECENTRALIZED AND PERSONAL SYSTEM OF APPOINTMENTS

Political appointments in Iceland are to a great extent decentralized and informal compared to some other patronage systems. When evaluating the role of parties in the scope and reach of political appointments, as in Table 10.2 above, many respondents were ill at ease because, as they pointed out, the parties as such usually do not play a great role. Hence, the role of political appointments may be underestimated in the table. Political appointments usually take place through personal networks rather than the party hierarchy or party apparatus.

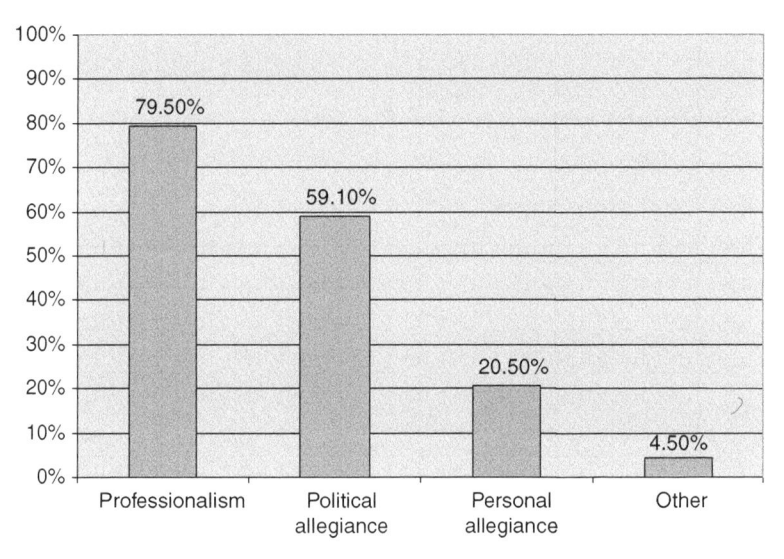

FIGURE 10.2 Qualifications of appointees in Iceland

When asked who, within the parties, makes the decisions on political appointments, 75 per cent mentioned either ministers or ministers and leaders (see Table 10.4). Leaders were mentioned by 40 per cent, either alone or with ministers. The meaning of 'leaders' may be subject to some speculation in this context (local or national, broad or narrow sense) and the distinction between ministers and leaders is not very clear. Party leaders can usually influence appointments, even if they play no formal role. But on the whole the role of individual ministers is crucial.

The decentralized nature of political appointments in Iceland is partly the result of ministerial government with highly autonomous ministers, and partly of the decentralized nature of the Icelandic political parties. Membership organizations no longer play the same role for the parties as they used to. Campaigns can be run without relying on a large number of foot soldiers to distribute pamphlets, attend meetings, or mobilize potential voters on election day. The role of the membership has to some extent been taken over by public relations specialists, advertising agencies and the media in general. Yet the Icelandic parties boast membership figures which are (relatively speaking) almost without parallel in present day democracies (for comparative data, see Scarrow, 2000). According to a poll conducted in 2009, 26 per cent of the voters are party members—and the figures published by the parties are even higher (Kristinsson, 2010, 2007). High membership figures in the Icelandic parties partly reflect the low cost of membership. Some members have never in their lives attended party meetings and never paid any kind of fees to the parties. Most of them do very little party work or none at all, and the majority designate themselves as inactive (Kristinsson, 2010). Usually,

TABLE 10.4 *Who decides within the party? (% of respondents)*

Elected representatives	7.5%
Party managers	2.5%
The mayor	5.0%
Ministers	45.0%
Leaders and ministers	30.0%
Leaders	10.0%
Total	100.0%
(N)	(40)

they will remain on the party files despite total inactivity unless they specifically ask to be removed—but since membership makes no specific claims on them, the incentive to do even that is low.

It is, above all, the introduction of the primaries as the main method of candidate selection since the 1970s that has inflated the party membership files and increased the dependence of individual politicians on their personal networks of supporters. At the time of such contests, the membership files of the parties tend to swell, as candidates mobilize their supporters from within and outside the party. The right to vote in the primaries is often (or even usually) not restricted to party members, (although a declaration of support for the party may be called for), but since membership makes no financial or other demands on the voters, it is relatively easy to recruit them on a single occasion like this. Candidate selection is no longer confined to party activists and the party institutions, but has been transferred to the broader arena of quasi-members or non-members, an ill-defined group of people who may flood the parties on irregular occasions but take no part in their activities in between. Politicians, as a result, lead a less sheltered life than before.

The maintenance of personal networks requires the recruitment of supporters on a personal basis and often access to funds as well. Personal supporters may put pressure on individual politicians for rewards, and hence the personalized networks have to some extent replaced the old party patronage networks as the source of rewards patronage in Iceland. Access to funds, however, became increasingly important to both individual politicians and the parties from the 1980s, with increasing professionalism in party campaigns (e.g. the use of consultancy firms) and commercial advertising (including television commercials since 1987). Little was known until recently about private contributions to parties and politicians, which remained entirely unregulated until 2007. State subventions, however, had been rising for some time; in 2000–5 alone they rose by 31 per cent (Prime minister's report 2005: 3–4; Björnsdóttir, 2006). In 2007, a rather strict regulation of political finance emerged. This was further strengthened after the banking crisis of 2008, which was partly blamed on too close a relationship between business and the political community.

Control appointments may also play a role in the personal networks of ministers, as already indicated. Gaining effective control of the policy sector for which they are responsible is often an individual endeavour where the party is of limited help, although the recruitment material often (but not always) comes from the party organization. Such informal control networks of different ministers from the same party may interconnect, but the 'principal' is usually the minister rather than the party.

SHARING

Political appointments to a certain extent serve the function of reducing the risks of a political career. Political careers are not only risky; they can be expensive as well for those who have to compete in many closely contested primaries. Leading politicians often expect to be taken care of when they retire from politics. And active politicians have an obvious interest in maintaining the tradition, since they may end up in a similar position themselves at some point. Patronage of this kind is not confined to party fellows (Table 10.5). It takes place across party boundaries, and even leading opposition politicians may gain from patronage of this kind.

There are well-recognized rules regarding this type of patronage. It has mainly been confined to the Foreign Service and the Financial sector, although it may take place in other policy sectors as well. In the Foreign Service the former leaders of political parties and former foreign ministers have usually been able to obtain ambassadorial posts, irrespective of which party holds the post of foreign minister. Foreign ministers, however, have also been able to reward their personal networks of co-workers and even friendly members of different parties. In the financial sector there used to be well-recognized quota systems for the distribution of bank directorships and board positions, but during the expansion and subsequent fall of the Financial sector following its privatization this order disintegrated.

CONCLUSION

The use of political appointments in Iceland has gone through quite substantial changes in recent decades. They are increasingly used for strategic purposes, to

TABLE 10.5 *Do governing parties share with the opposition?*

Share	44.2%
Don't share	55.8%
Total	100.0%
(N)	(43)

control the public sector, while their use as rewards has declined, especially at the lower levels of the administration. A tidy change, however, from rewards to control is not what we have seen. By accepting control appointments it may be difficult to maintain the kind of political alliance for bureaucratic autonomy which is needed to fight against rewards patronage. Hence, what we see at the higher levels of the Icelandic administration is a mixture of control and rewards patronage. Political appointments to non-strategic posts (e.g. in the Foreign Service) and at lower levels of the administration are also more common than would be expected on the basis of control considerations alone.

Political appointments usually do not mean hiring total incompetents to positions which they have neither the education nor experience to fill. Appointees usually fulfil the minimum professional requirements for the job. But often they are not the best qualified among the applicants, according to merit criteria, and in this sense they lead to a less efficient administration than might otherwise have developed. This is the opportunity cost of political appointments.

Control theory casts political appointment in a semi-legitimate role, namely that of securing political control over the bureaucracy. Patronage can make policy more responsive to the demands of democratically elected representatives. The counterargument, as put by Müller (2000: 157), is that 'these appointments may turn out to be an obstacle to party government if they are permanent and the government passes from one party or coalition to another'. Political appointments, in some cases, may actually hinder effective political control of the administration more than strengthen it.

In the greatest policy disaster in modern Icelandic history—the bank crash in October 2008—political appointments played an interesting role. The competence, credibility, and loyalty of the administration are, according to the subsequent Parliamentary Commission of Enquiry, open to doubt, and this played a role in the turn of events (Rannsóknarnefnd Alþingis, 2010). The effectiveness of control appointments in creating an efficient bureaucratic system may in this case be subject to some doubt. Not surprisingly, perhaps, an impartial and meritocratic bureaucracy has been among the political priorities of the reform work since the crisis, and in May 2010 an independent committee appointed by the prime minister recommended that the involvement of ministers in appointments be restricted (Starfshópur forsætisráðuneytisins, 2010).

NOTES

1. The term patronage in this chapter is reserved for appointments, while clientelism refers to the distribution of a broader range of values within the context of mass politics.
2. Iceland has no military forces, but the coastguard is included here with the police.

CHAPTER 11

Party Patronage in Ireland: Changing Parameters

Eoin O'Malley, Stephen Quinlan, and Peter Mair

INTRODUCTION

In 1950 a government elected at least in part on an anti-corruption agenda suffered a major crisis. The 'Battle of Baltinglass' (as it became known) involved the transfer of the right to run the local post office on the retirement of the postmistress. Convention would have dictated that the position would stay within the family, and the niece of the outgoing postmistress applied to take it over. The Minister for Posts and Telegraphs and local Labour party TD (i.e. MP), James Everett, was to make the decision. Departmental advice was that it should stay within the family, although as the niece was not a blood relation of the original postmistress, there was no requirement for this to happen. Everett decided to transfer the running of the post office to the son of a former Labour councillor (a local government representative) who was personally close to Everett. This caused problems within the minority coalition government, as one independent TD threatened to withdraw support from the government and another government party TD resigned from the party, as did a senior Labour party figure. Everett eventually relented and the niece of the retiring postmistress was given the right to run the post office, but not before it had caused a serious split in one of the coalition parties.

This story illustrates two aspects of party patronage in Ireland. First, that such patronage exists, or has existed in the past, and second that it is politically sensitive and not always accepted. That said, it may have been more acceptable in the past than now, and possibly also more widespread. Donogh O'Malley, a senior Fianna Fáil politician in the 1960s, suggested that, all else being equal, a state job would be given to a supporter of Fianna Fáil over a supporter of Fine Gael (Mills, 2005: 34). Though controversial at the time, it is unthinkable that a minister would utter these sentiments now, publicly at least.

One of the main generalizations about politics is that it concerns the allocation of resources, including patronage resources. Indeed, in the Irish case, it has been contended that the dominance of Fianna Fáil is in part due to the loyalty it engenders in its members and followers, with 'longevity in government afford [ing] it greater access to sources of patronage' (Weeks, 2009: 148). As the historian F.S.L. Lyons (1973: 585) once observed, 'power generates its own momentum in a country like Ireland, where patronage has always had an important function in government, [and] to be in office is a great help towards staying in office'. Those sources of patronage, used here in the sense of patronage as reward, tended to relate to the provision of state jobs, but could also include the particularistic delivery of public services in housing, health, and education. The assumption here is that the delivery of such goods afforded a political gain that could come in a number of forms, benefiting the party in terms of how it runs its organization, wins votes, develops policy, recruits members and elites, or, more simply, generates popular loyalty.

The parties also obviously benefit from those patronage appointments that are used not for reward as such, but to help control and steer public policy. These are also controversial, however. Fine Gael was criticized extensively in the early 1980s when members of the key advisory group around the then Fine Gael Taoiseach (prime minister; pl: Taoisigh), Garret FitzGerald, began to benefit from appointments to state boards or were awarded public contracts (e.g. O'Byrnes, 1986: 278–9). The Labour party was routinely accused of 'jobbery' and nepotism when it introduced a new type of political aide (programme managers) to oversee the programme for government and increased the number of other advisers and aides—sometimes disparagingly known as 'bag carriers'—when it formed a coalition with Fianna Fáil in 1993. The Labour party claimed that, given its experiences in government in the mid-1980s, these appointments were necessary to ensure the effective delivery of policy and control of the administrative system. Subsequent governments have expanded these types of appointments, as well as those to the greatly increased range of public agencies and boards that have been created in recent years, leading one recent report on problems of accountability in Irish government to complain of a lack of transparency and of partisan partiality in the public appointment process (Clancy and Murphy, 2006; see also below). However, as we also see below, while this sort of patronage appointment is potentially extensive and is reachable by parties, it is not always under the control of the party as such. Rather, a good deal of discretion is afforded to the individual ministers, who actually make most of the political appointments. Moreover, when those appointments have an electoral/political impact, it may be to the benefit of the individual minister rather than to that of the party.

THE REACH OF THE PARTIES

The Irish party system was dominated by two large, programmatically similar centre-right parties, each with a heterogeneous base of support.[1] The system grew out of a split within the nationalist elite in the early 1920s and a subsequent civil war. The traditionally largest party, Fianna Fáil, though emerging from the side that lost the civil war, has come to dominate the state, first coming to office in 1932, and then going on to be in government for sixty of the last seventy-eight years. For most of this period it governed as a single party, rejecting coalition 'on principle', but since 1989 it has changed strategy and is now open to forming alliances with other parties. It has never governed with Fine Gael, the party that emerged from the other side of the civil war split and that is currently the main opposition party. Affective loyalties have weakened significantly since the 1980s (Marsh, 2006). Indeed, voters are likely to be attracted to the personal characteristics of candidates as much as their party label, if not more so (Marsh, 2007), a feature that is also fostered by the intraparty competition for votes that follows from the use of the single transferable voting system in multi-member districts.

Party membership levels are low—at just 2 per cent, membership levels are among the very lowest in western Europe, and are less than half the EU average (van Biezen, Mair, and Poguntke, 2012)—although it is also the case that many people who are not members of the parties will campaign for particular candidates at election time. In terms of organization, Irish parties are now much less embedded in the local communities than was the case in the early post-war decades. They rarely have local branch buildings, but rather rely on the use of a local pub or hotel for meetings. Only individual TDs have permanently staffed offices in constituencies. Many candidates are expected to bring resources to the party in terms of their electability and may also need to point to their ability to raise funds and to bring in their own organization, especially door-to-door canvassers. Candidates can no longer rely on a group of party canvassers who would assist any candidate from that party. Constituency parties can then come to be dominated by local notables whose eventual retirement or departure noticeably weakens the party organization.[2] This also means that in electoral terms the parties are moving closer towards a franchise model (Carty, 2004): organizationally empty vessels with brand labels that are useful for marketing the candidate, and with standardized promotional material which the party cedes to potentially successful candidates in return for a willingness to support the party when elected to parliament. In this sense, the formal boundaries of the parties are becoming less and less apparent, and hence it becomes more and more difficult to determine who is in the party and who is not. This also impacts on the parameters of patronage, such that being the recipient of patronage is sometimes more important than the possession of a formal party card in determining who might be deemed to be a party member.

Party Patronage in Ireland 209

At national level, political parties are central to directing public policy in Ireland, and a variety of major shifts in public policy have flowed directly from decisions made by the party in government. The parties themselves have also undergone their own dramatic policy shifts, both in government and in opposition. Almost all such changes, however, whether in party policy or government policy, occurred without having much discernible impact on the grass-roots support of the parties. Indeed, one of the most remarkable features about Irish politics was how fundamental changes in state and party policy were accompanied by long-term stability in aggregate electoral outcomes. When Labour and Fine Gael moved to the left in the 1960s, for example, the one with a claim that 'the 70s will be Socialist', the other with a commitment to a 'Just Society', their new direction was often ignored by local parties and local candidates, many of whom carried on as before. When Fianna Fáil went from being a protectionist to a free trade party in the 1960s, it scarcely caused a ripple in the party organization, and when it later moved from defending traditional morality to advancing the cause of social and cultural pluralism, this seemed to have almost no electoral or organizational cost.

What this broad picture suggests, and what has been amply attested in much of the literature on Irish politics, is that policy competition has mattered little in accounting for variation in the support base of the parties. Indeed, it was not until the early 1980s that Irish parties began to issue election programmes on a routine basis. Party competition is in this sense a two-level game. At the local level, candidates compete by emphasizing personal appeals and by promoting local interests. At national level, and in the Dáil, these same candidates have traditionally lined up dutifully behind whatever policy is being promoted by their party leaders, leading to a level of voting discipline in parliament that is one of the highest in contemporary Europe.[3] There has also been a traditional system of payoffs, whereby the party in power distributes resources to the local level that can help ensure the successful re-election of its candidates, and hence also ensure their continued loyalty in the voting lobbies. As has been frequently documented by many observers of Irish politics (e.g. Chubb, 1963; Bax, 1976; Carty, 1981), all of this has offered ample scope for the exercise of brokerage and clientelism, and hence for reward-oriented patronage.[4]

At national level, policy making is strictly partisan, at least in institutional terms, and one of the most important aspects of the relations between party and government in Ireland is the complete occupation of government by the parties. Opposition parties are able to exert very little influence and are treated with disdain by those in office. Within government, on the other hand, the party cedes almost all control of policy to the ministers, and beyond these ministers the party as an organization has almost no voice in policy control. Moreover, and until recently, the party in government and its ministers have been obliged to work through a neutral civil service that has been traditionally independent of party politics. As we shall see below, this obviously narrowed the scope for patronage appointments at senior levels, and hence limited the capacity for patronage as control. Nor did there seem much demand for such patronage, at least in the past. In the first place, there was little alternation in government, and Fianna Fáil dominated the state through decades and through generations. This also led to a process of mutual adaptation with the institutions of the state in which, on the one hand, the bureaucracy absorbed the values of the long-dominant party and, on the other hand, the party came to rely on the bureaucracy for policy initiatives and innovation, and could even begin to think of that bureaucracy as a branch of the party as much as a branch of government.[5] Second, the bureaucracy was highly qualified and contained an exceptional degree of competence. Given the lack of other outlets for social mobility in a long underdeveloped economy and the poor state of private sector employment, the bureaucracy (and the church) attracted some of the best and the brightest of Irish society. This also meant that the civil service became an important source of policy advice and innovation for governing parties, and particularly for the dominant Fianna Fáil, whose TDs, and even some of whose ministers, were often uninterested in this side of politics.

This, then, marks the second relevant feature of the Irish case: while there were always many incentives to maintaining an extensive system of patronage as reward, as we have seen, there were relatively few incentives or opportunities to develop a system of patronage as control. In other words, and at least in its more traditional mould, the party organization dispensed patronage resources in order to attract voters and reward loyal members, but it relied for its steering capacity on the resources, ideas, and initiatives of the state bureaucracy, which itself was seen in neutral Weberian terms.

PATRONAGE AS REWARD AND PATRONAGE AS CONTROL

We can anticipate that both of these features might have changed in recent years. To begin with, it is likely that both the demand for and supply of rewards from the patronage system have declined. There are three principal reasons for this. First, while low-skilled jobs in the gift of local politicians might have been a focus for party competition in the bleak years of the 1950s, 1960s, and even the 1980s, this was less likely to have been the case when set against the opportunities available in a flourishing private sector during the boom years in more recent decades. Indeed, by the early 2000s (but now no longer so), as one of the experts interviewed for this research project pointed out, the problem was not finding low-skilled jobs for an available pool of labour, but finding workers to fill these jobs in the first place. Second, while much of the local patronage was 'imaginary' (Sacks, 1976; Komito, 1984)—in the sense that politicians claimed personal responsibility for the delivery of services which were in fact normally available through conventional state agencies—this practice clearly became less tenable when confronted with the demands of more educated voters and with the greater availability of information on rights and facilities. Third, and not least as a result of the growing power of the media, both nationally and locally, patterns of local politics have changed, in that many of the grievances that now concern citizens are those that are more likely to lead them to band together in action committees and lobby groups than to seek redress through the dispensation of individual favours,[6] and this militates against the effectiveness of patronage as a reward mechanism. That said, interesting evidence in Suiter and O'Mally (2012) suggests that this form of patronage is still visible, with individual ministers being likely to favour their own constituencies when channelling the capital funds at their disposal—whether for building sports centres, new schools, or new roads.

At the same time, the demand for patronage as control is likely to have grown, and this is the third feature that we need to underline in the Irish case. Three principal reasons can also be cited here. First, for reasons common to most of its European neighbours, the Irish system of governance has become much more complex and fragmented in recent years, not least as a result of the enormous growth in the number and influence of delegated agencies (see also below). To gain control of government in this context is therefore likely to impose on political parties the need to make a number of key coordinating political appointments, particularly when the complex of agencies and authorities itself appears as 'an organizational zoo'[7] and when the parties in government might be expected to act as keepers. Second, since the late 1970s, parties in competition in Ireland have begun to lay substantially more emphasis on their policy commitments and on their potential programmes for government. The differences between these programmes may not be very pronounced, particularly during the period of economic boom and effective political consensus, but the programmes themselves have received considerable flagging by the parties, including the publication of sometimes substantial election manifestos. Party websites have also devoted considerable attention to policy statements. Given this new emphasis, therefore, it is unlikely that the parties can continue to rely primarily on the bureaucracy for both ideas and management in public policy—rather, they will require their own sources of information and their own sources of input, as well as their own ways of controlling performance. This inevitably enhances the demand for patronage as a control mechanism. Moreover, and for much the same reasons that the parties now place much more emphasis on policy, there is also a much greater concern from both the public and the media with the policy performance of government. There is, in this sense, a far greater concern with both accountability and output legitimacy (MacCarthaigh, 2005), referring here to both policy outputs and procedural outputs and performance. Third, as government formation processes have become more open and more competitive, it becomes imperative for the different parties in government to stake their claims—not only against the opposition and hence the likely challengers, but also against their own partners in government. Indeed, it was for this reason that Labour broke new ground by introducing its programme managers and 'bag carriers' in 1993 (see above). In sum, we can expect that an emphasis on patronage as reward will have given way to a new emphasis on patronage as control.

THE CATHOLIC CHURCH AS PATRON

Before leaving this discussion, however, there is one other aspect of patronage that needs to be highlighted and which has always lain largely outside state and party control. This is the system of patronage that is exercised by the Irish Catholic Church, which has always been intimately involved in determining the parameters of social policy making over the years, particularly with regard to health, education, welfare, and cultural policy making (see Whyte, 1980). This involvement was also strongly institutionalized. For example, a number of the state's major hospitals began as voluntary institutions run by religious orders, and while these were later incorporated into and funded by the public health system, the church nevertheless retained a key voice in their management and direction. The Church also had a strong voice in both teacher training colleges and the university sector, effectively controlling professorial appointments in key areas including ethics and politics, psychology, education, sociology, and metaphysics in the 'Catholic' University College Dublin (Garvin, 1998; see also Cooney, 1999). In secondary education, largely financed by the state, the majority of schools were run by religious orders, as were the so-called industrial or approved schools that catered for neglected or delinquent children, and from which a flood of stories of sexual and physical abuse has recently emerged (see Arnold, 2009). In primary education, even through to today, the Church is 'patron' to 90 per cent of schools, a system which allows the local bishop to appoint the principal teachers, nominate two of the eight members of the board of management, and approve all appointments and dismissals of teachers (Flynn, 2010).[8]

The details of this state within a state are unimportant in this context, of course. But even this incomplete list offers a good indication of the extent to which the state both funded and shared its authority with an autonomous institution which, in turn, had control over a huge network of patronage appointments, almost all of which would be classified in terms of control rather than reward. This also implied that a whole sector of conventional state activity was closed off, either wholly or partially, from the possible exercise of patronage by the government and the political parties. In other words, and this is the fourth feature of the Irish case that needs to be emphasized, areas that might normally serve as domains of patronage for political parties in advanced welfare states instead formed part of the reserved domain of the Irish Catholic Church, and hence were kept at one remove from the political parties.

IRELAND'S BUREAUCRATIC TRADITION

When the new Irish state was founded in 1922, it inherited and went on to maintain much of the organization, personnel, ethos, and work practices of the former British bureaucracy. In this way it followed the Northcote-Trevelyan reforms in the UK which sought to introduce a professional, non-partisan, career civil service and to limit patronage by using open competition for posts (Fry, 2000: 17). The new state set up its own Civil Service Commission and a Local Appointments Commission (LAC) to administer appointments at national and local levels. The LAC, which had no British predecessor, caused some controversy because of its interference in appointments normally made at the local level. Given that the new state had been born into a civil war, there was some expectation that the victors would reward its demobilized soldiers. But the new government's commitment to non-partisan recruitment seemed genuine. Indeed, the organizing committee of the then governing party, Cumann na nGaedheal, complained that 'the Organization's influence on government policy and its power to affect patronage has been negligible, if not nil' (cited in Daly, 1997: 128).

This commitment to a Weberian, non-partisan civil service has been maintained throughout the state's history, and has been jealously guarded by the civil service itself. Legally, however, civil servants would appear to be in a tenuous position, as all appointments are technically made by ministers or the government, and civil servants, in theory, could be removed by the minister for certain vague offences, including underperformance. In reality, civil servants enjoy a security of tenure that a monarch would envy. The security of these 'permanent and pensionable posts' made them highly sought after, particularly as Ireland was economically underdeveloped. Recent legislation (Public Service Management (Recruitment and Appointments) Act 2004 and Civil Service Regulation (Amendment) Act 2005) reduces the *de jure* ministerial control, and gives greater personnel management functions to secretaries general (the senior civil servants in each department). As such there is little or no potential for political interference in the recruitment and promotion of civil servants at any grade. There were a small number of cases where ministerial advisers had been recruited into the permanent civil service, causing some disquiet. However, this avenue was later closed off by the Ethics in Public Office Act 1995. Promotion within the civil service was traditionally though seniority in a department, but since 1984 a Top Level Appointment Committee (TLAC) recommends candidates for senior appointments on a more meritocratic basis, and allows ministers some discretion. Some civil servants, noticed by ministers, are fast-tracked, but these are not partisan appointments in the strict sense of the term, since civil servants are not allowed to engage in party or electoral politics. Moreover, since many of these people have later also been favoured by ministers from other parties, it is more likely that they attracted notice because of particular talents. That said, the idea of a non-partisan, career-based civil service is challenged somewhat by the fact that, at senior levels, these are intelligent people with an interest in policy. Moreover, given the long-term dominance of Fianna Fáil, fears have always been expressed about the effective impartiality of the civil service, and it was this issue that was cited by Labour when introducing its programme managers in the 1990s (see above).

The civil service itself only constitutes a small part of the public service in Ireland (OECD, 2008: 22). Civil servants primarily work within government departments (though there are a small number of exceptions). Outside the civil service a much larger number of people work in public sector institutions, representing about 15 per cent of the total workforce. State spending is lower than in most OECD countries—34.4 per cent of GDP compared to an OECD average of 42.7 per cent (OECD, 2008: 52), though this may underestimate the real level of government spending since Ireland's GDP is inflated by high levels of foreign direct investment.

Given the tradition of using patronage as reward at the local level, we might also expect that patronage appointments would be common where this is practically possible. Komito (1985: chapter 9) alleged that access to state jobs was a scarce resource 'rarely wasted on the broad mass of citizens...rather reserved for personal supporters and party activists'. His research, based on practice in the early 1980s, claimed that many low-level jobs in the broader public sector were then subject to patronage, even where officials formally controlled the process. By now, however, the Civil Service Commission and Local Appointments Commission are likely to have succeeded in removing party patronage in the appointments they used to control. These agencies were merged and expanded in 2004, when a Commission for Public Service Appointments was set up. This sets clear guidelines for recruitment to public sector bodies, and has expanded the number of posts it covers. Introducing this legislation to the Senate, the minister, Tom Parlon, claimed that it would ensure that an already patronage-free system would become even more secure from political interference (Seanad Éireann, June 30, 2004, vol. 177 col. 479).

EMPIRICAL ANALYSIS OF PATRONAGE IN IRELAND

Scope and reach of patronage within the state

Without exception, ministers have the legal authority to make appointments in their departments.[9] The tradition of a non-partisan civil service, however, means that the parties' scope for appointments within them is limited. Though, technically, ministers make most appointments within their departments, they have very little scope to effect partisan appointments. An exception to this was at the very lowest levels in departments, as these were not established civil service positions and so open to party members. Jobs such as porters, messengers, and cleaners were available to ministers, and according to some respondents used for party political purposes, i.e. hiring party loyalists. However, most of these functions are now tendered to private contractors, reducing the potential for party patronage, and Ireland's economic modernization has meant that such appointments would not be an advantage, given the ready availability of similar low paid/low status posts in the private sector. At the higher level, ministers still have scope for appointment. As noted above, ministers have some discretion at this level and are given a choice of appointees for the most senior positions in a department. Even then, however, ministers are more likely to choose people they know and feel they can work with, and even though some ministers might have a sense of the policy approach of the candidates, party affiliation as such cannot play an overt role.

Ministers do have a direct role in the appointment within their ministries of ministerial advisers. Most ministers, other than the Taoiseach, Tánaiste (deputy prime minister), and party leaders, are limited to appointing two advisers. These are sometimes policy experts in the field of the minister's portfolio, but, as can be seen from the fact that advisers usually follow ministers from one department to another in the event of a reshuffle, often they are not. Most are political advisers—political associates from the minister's party but usually with a closer allegiance to the minister than the party. Special advisers are normally well paid, and those appointed have previously served as constituency operatives for the individual minister or have been employed in one form or other by the party. This is also a source of patronage, since, in addition to the more senior appointments, ministers can make appointments at lower grades to their constituency offices. Each minister will have about five or six staff including a personal assistant, a personal secretary, and clerical staff at the constituency office. These are in addition to the staff in the minister's private office in the department, staffed by civil servants, but much of their work involves dealing with constituents' queries. More generally, the picture in this regard tends to be the same across all ministries (Table 11.1). Healthcare which has been a particularly sensitive policy area in recent years, and which has also gone through rapid administrative reorganization, scores on the high side. The economic area, where civil service expertise is extremely well protected, ranks at the lower end.

The number of advisers a Taoiseach, Tánaiste, or party leader can appoint is not specified but it is usually around five. Party leaders in government also have access to press advisers through the Government Information Service (GIS). The party leaders' appointments and press advisers will be expected to work closely with the party head office. None of these appointments, however, is given any executive or statutory functions, and the appointees are now barred from being made established civil servants and must leave office with the relevant minister. Nor can all of these appointments be classified as patronage appointments with a party political end, as such, in that some ministers appoint civil servants as their ministerial

TABLE 11.1 *The index of party patronage in Ireland*

Policy area	Ministries	NDACs	Executing institutions	Policy area total
Economy	0.22	0.33	0.30	0.22
Finance	0.33	0.22	0.28	0.28
Judiciary	0.33	0.56	0.67	0.52
Media	0.33	0.33	0.22	0.30
Military and Police	0.33	0.11	0.22	0.22
Health Care	0.50	0.42	0.33	0.42
Culture and Education	0.33	0.22	0.22	0.26
Foreign Service	0.33	0.33	0.33	0.33
Regional and Local Administration	0.42	0.22	0.22	0.29
Total	0.36	0.29	0.31	0.32

advisers and some appointees are genuine policy experts with no obvious party connection. They are still party—or ministerial—patronage appointments, of course, but often not driven by a partisan purpose.

Outside the ministries, there has been a widespread growth in the number of both non-departmental advisory and executing agencies, and these are also open to partisan and personal patronage. In 1927 there were three non-departmental agencies (Dooney and O'Toole, 2009: 259), and four decades ago Devlin (1970) referred to 80 such agencies. More recent research fails to agree on an exact number of agencies, mainly because of definitional issues, but there is agreement that the number of agencies has increased exponentially in the last twenty years. McGauran, Verhoest, and Humphreys (2005) put the number at 601. Tasc, a left-wing think tank, refers to 'over 450' such agencies (Clancy and Murphy, 2006). Fine Gael, the main opposition party, conducted research which estimated that there were 445 national state agencies, over 200 of which had been created in the previous ten years (Fine Gael, 2008). These figures refer to those agencies with a statutory basis that are permanent. In addition, many other temporary bodies exist with some short-term function, often to write a report or advise a minister on a policy issue.

Each of these statutory agencies was created by legislation which sets out how each of them would be staffed. In nearly all cases responsibility for staffing is devolved to a chief executive, who must abide by the strict regulations governing public appointments. The chief executive is usually chosen by a board, and it is the appointments to these boards which afford ministers most discretion and where patronage is most likely to be seen. Many smaller agencies have one or more directors/commissioners/regulators appointed directly by ministers, though often on the advice of the Commission for Public Service Appointments.[10]

The purpose of the board of an agency is to set the long-term direction and strategy of the agency, and to oversee its operation. Appointees to boards undergo virtually no scrutiny, and the only obligation that ministers face when making these appointments is that they are published in *Iris Oifigiúil*, a little-known gazette for state announcements. Sometimes these announcements are published in the Irish language and the names of appointees are Gaelicized, thus making oversight even more difficult. There is no formal role for the Oireachtas (parliament) to oversee appointments, nor are there usually requirements for formal qualifications or relevant experience. Appointments are normally for five years. Though rarely published, the remuneration for these non-executive appointments varies greatly, with the fees paid to members of boards usually being set by the relevant minister, and requiring the consent of the Minister for Finance. The legislation on each agency usually states that the minister makes appointments, on the approval of the Minister for Finance, but more recently, as a result of Social Partnership, the minister gifts many of the appointments to interested 'social partners'.

Establishing the exact number of appointments available to a minister or government is difficult because there is no register of agencies and only a limited requirement to publish details about appointments. The Tasc research (Clancy and Murphy, 2006) refers to 5,000 appointments, but this is an overestimate as it extrapolated from the departments with most appointments available to them. Fine Gael (2008: 15), the main opposition party, has calculated that some 2,416 people have been appointed to serve on the board of a state agency on the direct nomination of government ministers. These do not include appointments that are formally made by a minister on the nomination of non-governmental bodies such as NGOs, charities, or universities. Equally, the figure does not include some local appointments, which are also important for party patronage. However, at lower levels of non-departmental agencies and commissions (NDACs) and executing institutions, ministers are not perceived to have a great deal of influence, and, with the exception of the Judicial and Economic arenas, these generally score lower than the ministries in the figures in Table 11.1. We can perhaps conclude that ministers have control over temporary non-executive appointments, but do not appoint people to permanent or full-time posts, except at the highest levels. Increasingly, these latter appointments are made by open competition, though in some cases ministers retain the power to choose without a competition. Again, it must be emphasized, we are referring here to individual ministers rather than to the party or government as such. Nonetheless, to the extent that these nominations are seen to be politicized, they become a partisan issue. In July 2010, a senior Fine Gael figure pledged that his party would replace the membership of every state board within six months of coming to office, and that it would give the new members 'a clear letter of appointment setting out their duties, and requiring them to be approved by the Oireachtas' (*Irish Times*, 24 July 2010).

For some senior appointments, the government as a whole makes a recommendation to the president, who formally appoints. Senior officers in the military and police, judicial appointments, and the governor of the Central Bank must first be agreed at cabinet. Appointments to the Judiciary, which have traditionally been highly partisan, and which sometimes go to former politicians, differ in that they now go through a Judicial Appointments Advisory Board (JAAB). The JAAB gives the impression of depoliticizing the process, but as it gives seven names to the government for each appointment, the government retains effective control of appointments. It is also free to ignore these names and offer a post to someone who was not part of the open competition, on the condition that it advertises this fact in *Iris Oifigiúil* (see McAuley et al. 2012).

Role of the party

When we ask ourselves about the role of the party we must immediately think of what we mean by 'the party'. Parties are not unitary actors, and in this case one element of a party could work against another. Obviously, as ministers to a large extent make the appointments that are relevant here, and ministers are all party members,[11] party does have a role. But to what extent is this a centralized and coordinated process, designed to maximize the benefit to the party organizationally and in terms of policy delivery? Or to what extent is it simply a matter of the individual ministers acting in their own interests? The headquarters of Irish political parties are under the direct control of the party leader, and do not act to represent the interests of, say, the party membership. Moreover, for a party in government the party headquarters tends to have little policy input, though it may provide a secretariat and research support for a senior figure in the party who coordinates the process of writing the election manifesto (Garry and Mansergh, 1999). Hence, although we can see the potential for party influence, and do see political influence in many senior state appointments, most interviewees believed that there was little input from the party qua party.[12] In the course of our research, interviewees were asked about parties' role in three types of appointments: those to departments, to regulatory agencies, and to boards. While parties appear to have much less influence when it comes to departmental appointments compared to the latter two, a common pattern is visible across all sectors: the role political parties play in this process is small. Several interviewees specifically alluded to this and said that rather than political parties being the driving force, it was more likely to be the individual minister, and hence party involvement in these processes was—as one interviewee described it—'much more subtle'. In the vast majority of cases, interviewees said cabinet ministers were primarily responsible for appointments.[13] There appears to be a distinction here, then, between the role of political parties and the role of the individual. While ministers are nearly always members of political parties, their appointments are not necessarily driven by the party. The process is such that ministers are given almost complete autonomy in this area. It appears that civil servants will often suggest lists of names to ministers, and ministers may offer other names that they would like to see appointed. Certainly not all appointees are partisan, and often we see that serving and former civil servants are prominent on the boards of many agencies. Some appointments may have to go before the cabinet for discussion in cases where the responsibility for appointment lies with the government (e.g. judicial appointments and senior executive appointments in the army/Garda Siochána (police)). But even when it comes to these appointments, the relevant minister will suggest the appointment for the cabinet to discuss, and in many if not most cases the cabinet will accept the minister's proposal. Sometimes there will be lobbying by colleagues in government or on the backbenches for the inclusion of certain names, and, depending on who is doing the lobbying, it may be desirable to accommodate these requests, as ministers, to some extent, depend on good relations with cabinet colleagues and backbenchers for support for legislation.

Ministers also appear to use their autonomy in part to reward political supporters, very often from their own constituency. This is suggestive of what Laver and Shepsle (1994) called *ministerial government*, especially where there is only one party in government. But coalition, now the norm in Ireland, changes everything, and imposes constraints on patronage as well as everything else. If the appointments process is controlled at all, the party leaders can and do exert some influence, partly to avoid appointments that might cause difficulties in the coalition. Ministers are required to send advance notice of all appointments to the Department of the Taoiseach, where they are logged, and since the mid-1990s they are also obliged to send notice to the other party leaders in government, through their programme managers. Several interviewees alluded to this 'coalition effect', and said that certain appointments would be run past coalition partners before they were formally made by ministers. This obviously enhances the role of party in the process as a whole.

Some ministers may ask party leaders if they wish to put forward nominations for posts, and Taoisigh will frequently take up this offer. But even Taoisigh often appear to act in their own personal interests rather than in the interests of the party as a whole, as was the case with former Taoiseach Bertie Ahern, for example, who appointed a number of close friends who were central to his local party organization. Personal, rather than just party, connections, are therefore important (see Figure 11.2 below)—a case of dinner parties rather than political parties. As one appointee to a board put it, although she was not affiliated to a minister's party, they 'move in the same social circles' and would know each other as a result.

Motivation for patronage appointments

If parties, through ministers, can make public appointments, what motivates the choices ministers make, and whom do they appoint? Popular commentary usually claims that public appointments are an example of 'jobs for the boys' and rewards for 'political cronies'. Furthermore, much of this coverage tends to point to

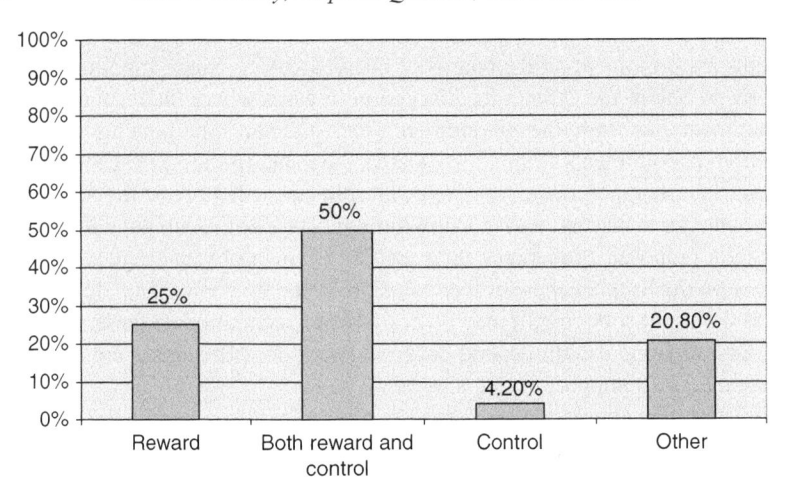

FIGURE 11.1 Motivations for party patronage in Ireland

- Reward: 25%
- Both reward and control: 50%
- Control: 4.20%
- Other: 20.80%

failures by boards to properly oversee the actions of agencies, perhaps leading to the conclusion that ministers are less interested in control or oversight of these agencies but are concerned instead with rewarding political supporters. As noted above, and given the non-ideological nature of Irish party politics, it is less likely that parties see the need to use state appointments to ensure partisan policy goals are achieved, even though all ministers will be keen to enhance policy performance. In this sense, whether a minister would wish to control, or at least remain informed about, the activities of an agency or state company may depend on its political importance and visibility.

Figure 11.1 examines the motivation behind these appointments. Control and reward are seen as the primary driving forces behind patronage. But while control is seen here to play a role in appointments, in our research we heard little from those in agencies that ministers attempt to control or influence the activities of agencies (indeed only 4 per cent of interviewees said control was the sole driving force behind appointments), though they would, as entitled, look for information from the agency. While some sensed that ministers were unhappy with decisions or the focus of an agency, none felt the relationship with the department was improper or that the agency was anything other than independent. In fact it was suggested that it was often the civil service, which had lost direct control of a policy area through the creation of an agency, that was most concerned to gain a voice in the board. As such, we see that civil servants were often quite concerned about how a board was constituted. That said, while a minister would not necessarily be seeking to control an agency, there is, in the words of one former ministerial adviser, 'an eyes and ears element' involved. As one retired civil servant and former secretary general of a government department pointed out, it should not be overlooked that ministers want to see boards and agencies 'function to their maximum utility', in that the minister's own credibility is tied up in the appointment. Again, performance matters.

Motivations appear to vary not across sectors but across levels. Many respondents said that for important state functions, while there was an element of reward and an element of control (or at least oversight), the minister's primary goal for important state agencies was that the agency would be run properly and not cause political headaches. For senior judicial appointments, all respondents agreed that professionalism or ability to do the job was a primary concern and would now (if necessary) override partisan loyalties. For other senior appointments, ministers will wish to avoid being embarrassed by the perceived failures of their appointee. Again, however, the emphasis from our interviewees was on performance rather than partisan programmes. This does not diminish the partisan nature of the appointees, of course; rather, it simply means that any partisans who are chosen for sensitive posts will also be well qualified for the position. Qualifications in this case are not those intended to help push through particular policies; rather they are designed to ensure a more effective performance.

Reward emerges, though, as a primary motivating factor in appointments to agencies and boards, with a majority of interviewees mentioning it either in tandem with control or alone, and a quarter saying reward was the sole reason behind appointments. So if reward is a major goal of such appointments, two questions emerge: how is it rewarding and what is the quid pro quo? Unlike in other countries, patronage in Ireland rarely comes in the form of full-time jobs where the appointment provides the appointee's primary source of income. It was noted above that there is great variation in the fees available to patronage appointees. Some respondents claimed money was not the primary goal, but rather that the appointments offered a number of other advantages, including status. These appointments also offer access to information, contacts, and networks that might prove useful in business or commercial terms. For lower-level appointments such as to the board of a harbour commissioner or to a prison visiting committee, the reward is cruder and more obvious: mileage. Board members receive generous travel and subsistence allowances which mean they can profit from attending a meeting—often making many hundreds of Euros. Though these are probably not important appointments in terms of the control of policy delivery, they can be important for the party organization, or at least for a minister's organizational base at constituency level. There are even cases where the appointees to a harbour commissioner on, say, the south-east coast come from the minister's own constituency in the north-west. These are frequently well-known party activists, often councillors, who profit from the travel allowance, but can hardly have any expertise or interest in the putative object of their appointment.

Figure 11.2 examines the qualifications of appointees to positions. The vast majority of interviewees stressed that at least some of the individuals who are appointed to positions must possess some professional qualification that justifies their appointment. Many pointed out that there will always be enough people on

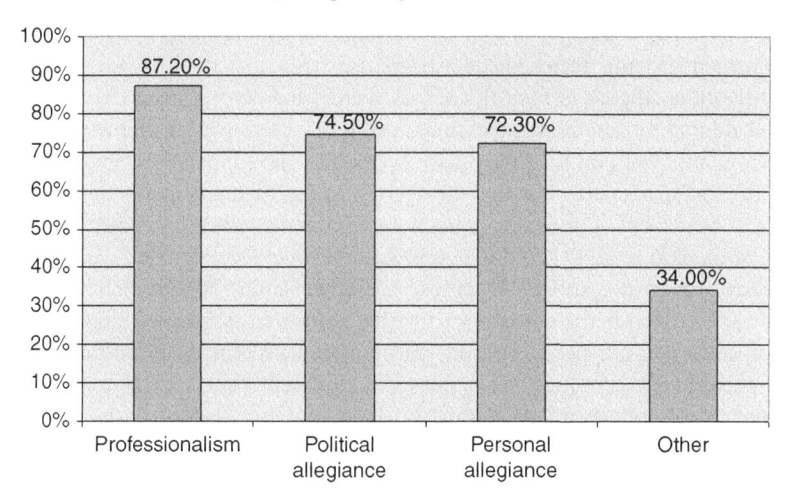

```
100% ┐
 90% ┤  87.20%
 80% ┤            74.50%
 70% ┤                         72.30%
 60% ┤
 50% ┤
 40% ┤
 30% ┤                                        34.00%
 20% ┤
 10% ┤
  0% ┴──────────┬──────────┬──────────┬──────────
     Professionalism  Political   Personal    Other
                     allegiance  allegiance
```

FIGURE 11.2 Qualifications of appointees in Ireland

the board to get the job done, and several said that particular care is taken when choosing the chair of an agency or board, with ministers and departments keen to make sure that they have the appropriate skills to do the job properly. As one former secretary general remarked, 'appointments need to be common sense' and that in the main, appointees must have credibility if the board or agency is to fulfil its obligations.

However, it also appears that a fair number of appointments could be described as purely political—i.e. appointments that come about through personal allegiance with a minister or a political link with a party—with most interviewees mentioning that political or personal allegiance also matters. One interviewee argued that this is a naive question, as any appointment can be justified: anyone could be perceived as qualified for a job if it is framed correctly. He gave the example of the Taoiseach's former partner, who was appointed to the National Consumer Agency without any obvious formal qualifications. Another interviewee, a local county councillor, believes he was appointed to a board by a minister purely because of politics and the appointing minister's fear of his future political ambitions, noting that he had no prior expertise or experience in the area relating to the appointment.

One important point that emerged from many interviews was that personal relations were often more important than party relations in determining appointments, although the two are obviously linked. Ministers tend to appoint people that they know. This is not entirely a surprise. After all, former Taoiseach, Bertie Ahern, openly admitted to appointing people to state boards 'because they were my friends' (RTÉ Six One News, 26 September 2006). But this process trickles further down than the Taoiseach. One interviewee, a former ministerial adviser, observed how one minister during his period appointed several of his canvassers to prominent positions on boards and agencies, and while in some of these cases the people could be considered suitable for the positions, in others they were not and were purely appointed because of the personal link with the minister.

However, a number of respondents did note that there were reasons behind certain appointments other than personal qualifications and political links. Several interviewees alluded to the fact that certain criteria may determine particular appointments, such as gender balance and representation for trade unions and employers, as a consequence of Social Partnership. The 'coalition effect', remarked upon earlier, is also a factor in appointments, with certain appointments being carved up between the parties in a coalition government.

Some former ministers and senior civil servants spoken to in the course of this research claimed that ministers found filling state boards time-consuming, with little end. This claim does not seem plausible in the light of outgoing ministers' behaviour in the interregnum between an election and the formation of a new government, when they usually fill all vacancies, in effect packing the boards. The fact that ministers do this even when the party has not lost power, but when ministers themselves might be moved to different departments, says something about the way in which such appointments are made—for the benefit of the minister rather than the party. In these circumstances and others, ministers appear to act as independent pillars and there is little evidence that the parties as such coordinate patronage appointments.

In sum, although reward may not be the key motivating factor behind appointments, it remains an important consideration. Indeed, it is striking to see the extent that even senior appointments to agency boards and the like are seen by our respondents as a means of rewarding close allies. The use of patronage as reward may have diminished at the local level, but our evidence suggests that it continues to operate as a more selective incentive at more senior levels in the system. When the motive is control rather than reward, on the other hand, the picture that emerges from modern Ireland is rather mixed. In the first place, it sometimes appears that it is the civil service rather than the party or parties in government that is keen to exercise control through the appointment process. This may also have to do with the civil servants' reluctance to see so much of their decision-making power being allocated to independent agencies, and hence may reflect an intention to use appointments to these agencies as a means of keeping policy making within the purview of the departments. Second, to the extent that parties or their ministers are concerned with patronage as control, it is more likely to be about controlling performance and output rather than policies and input. Although policy making can be depoliticized, particularly in good economic times, the decision-making process itself is subject to increasing public scrutiny, and hence those appointed must be able to provide safe pairs of hands. This consideration represents the greatest challenge to patronage as reward. Third, when parties do seek to influence appointments, whether for reward or control, it is often the minister acting on his or her own initiative rather than a party activity as such. Indeed, it is striking to see how much the personalized rather than the party component of the appointment process was emphasized by our respondents. That said, it is also necessary to underline that even when the process is personalized, the appointees themselves are usually drawn from within the wider party hinterland. In this sense, power and access to Power remain closely guarded.

Sharing of patronage appointments among the parties

Ireland provides a clear case of a majoritarian system in the allocation of state appointments accessible to parties, with a substantial majority of our interviewees stating that appointments were mainly government appointments, with few coming from the opposition. Government parties or their ministers make all appointments, and while they have conceded many appointments to the 'Social Partners', these are rarely given to opposition parties. In certain cases, prominent people associated with the opposition parties are given positions, but these are not 'delivered' by their party. Rather, these are often cases where it is important for the government to ensure the appearance of independence in dealing with a sensitive issue. Within government, ministers control appointments to bodies under their aegis, and may consult with cabinet colleagues and especially coalition partners to avoid problems. Opposition parties are completely excluded from this process. Though many parties when in opposition complain about the nature of appointments, thus far there has been no attempt to deviate from the practice. This is partly because when these parties get into government they are anxious to make up for their inability to appoint in the previous term, and this leaves few incentives for reforming current practices. One exception to this pattern, cited by one interviewee, was a recent Minister for Justice coming from the small coalition party, the Progressive Democrats, whose judicial appointments included a number of (opposition) Fine Gael figures. In this case, however, his own party would not have had a sufficiently large network to offer much scope for partisan appointments, while the minister's personal network, building on both his university and professional connections, would have been closely connected to Fine Gael.

Changes in the process over time

The expansion in the number of state agencies has clearly increased the potential for political patronage at one level, but changes in appointments procedures have also reduced the scope for patronage at lower levels. The overwhelming majority of interviewees surveyed in this research regard patronage as having remained the same or as having decreased over the past fifteen to twenty years. Very few claim that there has been an increase. The reason for this is obvious: there is now far more scrutiny of appointments by the media, and this process is helped by Freedom of Information requests.[14] One interviewee pointed out that there has been substantial change in the legal and financial responsibilities that go with being a member of a board, and that the annual reports for each board/agency show how often members attended board meetings and what their contribution was. Another said that ministers are now more wary when it comes to appointments and that ministers now have to make sure 'they will be able to stand over the person's appointment in the worst scenario'. Consequently, more attention is paid to what different individuals bring to the table. Greater transparency, on the one hand, and greater pressure on policy performance, on the other, now count against the traditional tendency towards party favouritism. However, while there are now more checks and balances that have to be considered when making appointments, and that, as one interviewee observed, are designed to ensure 'the best dog jumps the ditch', it is clearly impossible to have a watertight system. There may be fewer jobs for the boys in the Irish patronage system, but one interviewee insisted, 'there is nothing clean about appointments to boards'.

CONCLUSION: THE PARAMETERS OF PARTY PATRONAGE IN CONTEMPORARY IRELAND

Although the scope for party patronage as a strategy for control has greatly expanded in recent years, particularly as a result of agencification and the increased delegation of public policy tasks from the professional civil service to autonomous commissions and advisory bodies, the parties are now obliged to be much more circumspect in how they make appointments. There are two main reasons for this. The first is simply that they can no longer afford to appoint people who are not up to the job. The changes in public administration that have come about under the influence of new public management have led to the creation of a host of new agencies, but they have also resulted in far greater emphasis on performance contracts, performance targets, and efficiency (see, for example, Hardiman and MacCarthaigh, 2008). Moreover, there is clearly more scrutiny of political appointments in the media and through the use of the Freedom of Information legislation. This also makes for less obvious politicking in the appointments process. The second reason for greater circumspection is the declining public acceptability of party patronage, and the parties' fear of hostile coverage from a more active and more critical press. In other words, there is now less public tolerance and admiration for the 'cute hoor' who pulls 'strokes' at the margins of legality (see O'Carroll, 1987). While party patronage as a control strategy might be legitimated more easily than patronage as reward, its use in the Irish case is therefore hampered by its association with traditional clientelism and favouritism. That said, many overtly political appointments continue to be made.

What is also striking about the Irish case is that the involvement of political parties is often indirect and is usually exercised through individual cabinet ministers. Whereas government ministers are nearly always members of political parties, and in some instances make party appointments, our research suggests that personal associations with the minister are at least as important, if not more so. Of course, both sets of contacts overlap. To the extent that family ties and local traditions are important sources of party loyalties, the personal networks of political notables may not always be distinguishable from their party networks. It is also clear from our research that professional qualifications and political considerations are not the only important determinants when making appointments—particularly to boards and agencies. Other dimensions also play a role here, including gender representation, the Social Partnership constraints, and the coalition effect. Opposition parties tend not to be part of this process, however, in that the parties of government tend to get most of the appointments on offer.

The changing and comparatively limited extent of patronage in Ireland reveals a good deal about the changing nature of political parties in the country. Parties in Ireland, we argue, are becoming stratarchical. That is, although there is quite strong leadership control in terms of policy direction, parties at the constituency level increasingly depend on local notables to maintain their organizational strength and have become increasingly autonomous in that regard. Moreover, in the past, when larger numbers of people (foot soldiers) were required for campaigning, rewards were given in low- and medium-status jobs and services. Today, when ambitious politicians have a greater need for the services of policy advisers, public relations consultants, speechwriters, and legal advisers, such rewards are less relevant. Much of the advice required by the politician may be informal, and the advisers themselves may not be members of the party. They are also more likely to be people with permanent and perhaps lucrative jobs, whose rewards, apart from the thrill of political involvement, may come in the form of contacts, contracts, or just recommendations. Patronage of this kind can also work to attract candidates, with those failing to get elected being rewarded in other ways. Lawyers might be given some state work, while others might be appointed to a board that is relevant to their profession. This might also encourage them to keep campaigning.

The absence of strong ideological differences between the parties, particularly in recent years, suggests that there is little demand for partisan patronage for policy implementation purposes. However, as we have emphasized in this chapter, the development of a more critical and demanding electorate and the changing priorities of government have focused much more attention on policy performance and delivery, and here patronage may be increasingly relevant and certainly increasingly constrained. This absence of ideology can also explain why personal relations appear to be so important. Ireland's small size means that the political class lives in a village-like atmosphere and personal relations are very important, perhaps more so than partisan affiliation.

This raises a more fundamental question, however. If personal networks and candidate appeals are more important than party loyalties at local level, and if personal networks and relations are also more important in building networks of power at elite level, then it begs the question as to where the party comes in. When the individual candidates are the key actors at local level, and when the individual ministers are the key actors at cabinet level, there seems little room left over for the party as such. Should the partyness of government increasingly give way to more pronounced ministerial government, and should the partyness of candidate recruitment also give way to a more self-generating bottom-up selection process, this will undoubtedly put the cohesion of the parties in parliament under greater pressure. In these circumstances, parties get squeezed from both sides, and while patronage might remain as important as ever, in terms of both reward and control, it might not be something that is exercised in any meaningful sense by the parties as such.

NOTES

1. See Mair (1987) for a general overview of the development of the Irish parties and the party system.
2. The dismissal of a Fine Gael TD, Michael Lowry, as a minister, his resignation from the party, and the subsequent loss of support for the party in his constituency is a good example of this. In the 2009 local elections, thirteen years after he left, four independent candidates were elected in his constituency, effectively on the 'Lowry' ticket.
3. See Bolleyer (2009) for an extensive evaluation of these processes.
4. The Irish case also reveals parties that, in Kitschelt's (2000) terms, build programmatic and clientelistic linkages at one and the same time: that is, they increasingly emphasize programmatic linkages at national level, particularly where government–opposition relations are concerned, while continuing to emphasize clientelistic linkages within the often depoliticized local constituencies. In the one, patronage can be important as a method of steering; in the other, it serves as a reward mechanism.
5. In 1948, after Fianna Fáil had lost power for the first time in sixteen years, the new government took the extraordinary decision not to allow the Cabinet secretary, Maurice Moynihan, to attend government meetings, on the grounds that he was too close to the previous incumbents. See MacDermott, 1998: 109–10.
6. As, for example, in the sustained local protest against the removal of cancer treatment services from a hospital in Sligo in the north-west of Ireland, the electoral pressure from which eventually led the two local Fianna Fáil TDs to resign the party whip.

7. The term was applied to the Irish case in an OECD report, and is cited by Dooney and O'Toole (2009: 284).
8. In practice, of course, such powers of nomination and appointment were also likely to be shared—or at least negotiated—with local politicians. It is only recently that this aspect of Church control over education has begun to be seriously debated.
9. Because of the size of the country, there are very few policy experts or academics concentrating on the mechanics of each distinct policy area. As a result, many of the respondents to our questionnaire would be better described as elites rather than experts, and sometimes tended to speak more in broad terms than in policy-specific references. However, given the consensus in their responses, we can be quite confident of the validity of the data.
10. In an interview in 2010, the leader of the Labour party explicitly rejected the idea that the membership of state boards should be a matter for an independent commission: 'I think government should appoint the State boards, that is one of the executive functions of government' ('Fine Gael pledges to replace all members of State boards', *Irish Times*, 24 July 2010).
11. There are a small number of exceptions to this. James Dillon was a minister in the late 1940s, despite having resigned from Fine Gael over its policy of neutrality in the Second World War. He later rejoined and went on to lead the party. In 2009, Mary Harney retained her ministerial portfolio even after her party, the Progressive Democrats, dissolved itself.
12. The Green Party has long called for the use of a register of individuals interested in serving on boards, though their entry into government has not immediately resulted in such a process being adopted.
13. The question related to who in the political parties was responsible for appointments.
14. Under the Freedom of Information Acts 1997 and 2003, public bodies are required to publish certain information about themselves and also to make available details of their internal rules, procedures, and interpretations (see <http://www.foi.gov.ie>).

CHAPTER 12

Party Patronage in Italy: A Matter for Solitary Leaders

Fabrizio Di Mascio

INTRODUCTION

Italy constitutes a crucial case for the investigation of changes in patronage practices in contemporary democracies. According to Kopecký and Scherlis (2008), the so-called Italian 'First Republic' was in fact a paradigmatic case of the spread of 'bureaucratic *clientelismo*'[1] characterized by: (a) the distribution of an enormous quantity of posts at all levels of the administration; and (b) the presence of reward as the dominant motivation behind political appointments. Bureaucratic *clientelismo* is held to occur in southern European systems, which share historical developments that produced administrative systems distinct from the Weberian ideal type. Administrative organization and behaviour were shaped by the Napoleonic tradition which was widespread in southern Europe (Peters, 2008). The emphasis on state power over the role of society, which distinguishes this tradition, conforms to the model of 'assisted capitalism' (Sotiropoulos, 2004b). In Italy, the state traditionally promoted economic development through strategies and instruments (protectionism, transfers, subsidies, control of industries) used in a very particularistic way, with a resulting long-term dependence of the weak Italian bourgeoisie on the state preventing distributional particularism from being reformed by the rise of Weberian administrative structures (Amato, 1979). This has produced an administrative system with low institutional capacity, affected by multiple organizational and functional contradictions (Cassese, 1993).

The Italian system has long displayed the features typical of the prevalent southern European bureaucratic model: (a) patronage at the bottom, with patterns of favouritism in the recruitment of low-ranking officials; (b) formalism and legalism complemented by informal shadow governance structures; (c) an uneven distribution of resources, institutional fragmentation, and insufficient mechanisms for policy coordination; and (d) the absence of a typical European administrative elite (Sotiropoulos, 2004b).

An administrative elite equipped with an *esprit de corps* has never formed due to a lack of highly selective recruitment channels. The Italian administrative elite has been described as an 'ossified world' (Cassese, 1999)—elderly and with little professionalization, in which promotions are rewards for age and length of service, without horizontal and vertical mobility, and dominated by the formalism of personnel almost exclusively trained in law. This low level of professionalism allowed the top ministerial bureaucracy to form a pact with politicians of reciprocal self-restraint. This pact was based on an exchange between job security and political power: bureaucrats renounced an autonomous proactive role in processes of policy making, while parties refrained from interfering in the management of careers—the primary preoccupation of a bureaucracy gone 'southern', characterized by a patrimonial conception of public service, dedicated to administrating itself rather than the country. The roots of this arrangement can also be traced back to the key features of the old 'polarized pluralism' (1947–92): tripolar centrifugal competition and a centre occupied by the Christian Democrats (DC) that made any complete alternation of power impossible (Sartori, 1976). Due to the average low duration of unstable coalitions, ministers did not have the time to take control of their departments, and indeed had no motivation to do so either.

'Patronage at the top', a key feature of southern systems, was less extensive in the ministerial domain than in the parallel administration. This consisted of 'a complex and probably unique *mélange* of [parastate] bodies, public agencies and public corporations' (Golden, 2003: 202) marked by an increasing extension and plurality of organizational models. Parties pursued a strategy of colonization (Sartori, 2005) by penetrating all spheres of Italian society with party-nominated appointees. Public organizations thus came under the full control of, or became largely dependent on, the parties' organizational networks entrenched within an overgrown public sector.

This deep colonization of an 'available State' (Di Palma, 1979) created the conditions for the affirmation and reproduction of *partitocracy*, a regime at first characterized by a substantial monopoly of parties over political activity and, later, by the progressive expansion of their power into the social and economic spheres (Pasquino, 1995). The legitimacy deficit of Italy's democracy was compensated for by the organizational strength of its political parties, which dominated the political system (Morlino, 1998). The weakness of public bureaucracies, the interventionist tradition of the state in the economic sector, and the necessity of maintaining a precarious consensus for a regime affected by exclusive legitimation, thus gave relevance to patronage as a crucial resource in the Italian pattern of democratic consolidation.

BETWEEN PARTY SYSTEM CHANGE AND ADMINISTRATIVE REFORMS: ITALY AS A TRANSITIONAL CONTEXT

At the beginning of the 1990s, changes in the international environment shook the foundations of partitocracy: the end of the two-bloc system of international relations sanctioned a definitive erosion of the basis of the systemic polarization that had determined electoral and governmental alliances; and the process of European integration imposed growing constraints on the irresponsible particularistic distribution of material resources (Cotta, 1996). The exhaustion of both the ideological polarization and the material public resources which had fed competition among the old parties accentuated the turbulence in the internal environment. International changes facilitated the launching of challenges to partitocracy by various actors, which provoked an increasing destructuring of the parties and the party system. Between 1992 and 1994, the system became 'atomized', marked by exceptional fluidity and uncertainty as much in party organizations as in their systemic interactions (Di Virgilio, 2006).

It was in 1994 that a new process of consolidation of the party system began. The introduction of new electoral laws providing majoritarian institutional arrangements precipitated the collapse of the old parties and stimulated the consolidation of a new set of competitive interactions. The party system had undergone a radical transformation: most of the parties participating in the 1994 election were either brand new or had been affected by a profound change, with the party system assuming the features of 'fragmented bipolarism' (D'Alimonte, 2005). Systemic atomization was overcome thanks to a new two-level system composed not only of parties but also of pre-electoral coalitions. Alternation in government between pre-electoral coalitions has become the new predictable structure of competition (Verzichelli and Cotta, 2000). If pre-electoral coalitions have provided for the refreezing of the party system, the single party organizations have remained fluid, as is demonstrated by the incessant remodelling of party labels by fissions and fusions. Atomization has been overtaken by change in the party system, but this has left a legacy of crisis among parties as organizations with low levels of institutionalization. The nature of government coalitions is still fragmented and heterogeneous, and this is heightened by the uncertainty of a system where only the bipolar mechanics have been stabilized while the format has remained subject to fluidity.

The collapse of the old parties, which were unwilling to modify a dysfunctional bureaucratic machine, created a unique window of opportunity for administrative reforms that profoundly reshaped three dimensions of the Italian state (Lewanski, 1999). The first of these was a substantial retreat from direct intervention and entrepreneurship in the economy in favour of a regulatory role. Independent authorities were created to regulate liberalized markets, while privatization

TABLE 12.1 *Number of general government institutional units under the ESA95 (S.13) methodology (2008)*

Institutions	N
State (ministries, Prime Minister's Office, fiscal agencies, constitutional bodies)	31
Research bodies	44
Economic bodies (independent administrative authorities, economic activities regulatory bodies, economic service producers, other bodies)	36
Institutions providing cultural services and assistance	61
Total central government	**172**
Regions and autonomous provinces	22
Provinces	104
Municipalities	8101
Producers of health services at local level	283
Economic bodies at local level	436
Institutions providing education, cultural services, and assistance at local level	553
Other bodies	769
Total local government	**10,268**
Social security funds	27
Total	**10,467**

Source: author's elaboration. Data provided by ISTAT (Italian National Institute of Statistics)

processes radically reduced the size of the state and reorganized the remaining public enterprises into shareholder companies controlled by the Treasury.

Up to the late 1980s, Italy had had one of the largest state-owned sectors among Western economies: twelve of the twenty largest non-financial companies were state-owned, and 90 per cent of financial investment was provided by state-controlled banks. The turning point came in 1992, with the advent of a public finance and currency crisis. Privatization in Italy produced the second highest revenues in Europe, after the UK. Real progress has been made since the mid-1990s in reducing the debt-to-GDP ratio, which amounted to 124.8 per cent in 1994. Privatization was a main component of the restrictive budget policy pursued to meet the criteria for joining EMU, and between 1995 and 2000 government spending as a percentage of GDP fell from 52.5 to 46.2. Nonetheless, Italy still has one of the highest debt-to-GDP ratios—amounting to 105.8 per cent in 2008 (EUROSTAT).

The second component of the process of reform was a change in the organizational structure of central administration: organizational flexibility has increased, taking a large share of the regulation of the administrative machinery away from the parliament and into the hands of the executive in order to implement a permanent policy of organizational rationalization (Lupo, 2003). While public management reform reinforced the powers and responsibilities of senior executives in administrative management, this was balanced by a growth in ministerial discretion in the awarding of fixed-term contracts to senior executives who lost tenured positions.

The third dimension of the reshaping of the Italian state was a reform of local government: legislative powers and administrative functions were decentralized; local executives were reinforced, thanks to institutional reforms that introduced semi-parliamentary forms of government; executives acquired wide regulatory powers over local administrative structures; and enhanced organizational flexibility led to a sharp growth in the number of local disaggregated institutions.

After these reforms, local governments represent a larger share of total expenditure (31.3 per cent) than they do of revenue (19.1 per cent), and finance 54.3 per cent of this expenditure through grants and transfers (OECD, 2009). The share of total government staff employed at the central level is still high—it amounted to 58 per cent in 2008. Government employment in Italy as a share of the total labour force amounted to 14.7 per cent in 2007 (Torchia, 2009). Corporatization by local governments has created a wide semi-public sphere composed of local enterprises, which amounted to 4,874 units in 2005 (Citroni, 2009), adding to the already fragmented galaxy of Italian public institutions shown in Table 12.1.

PATRONAGE IN ITALY: AN EMPIRICAL ANALYSIS

The empirical analysis that follows aims to ascertain how far the radical changes of the 1990s have affected the spread, logic, and mechanisms of patronage. The analysis aims to fill a gap in much of the literature, which continues to associate Italy with the old patronage practices that developed in the political-administrative context that was overturned by the crisis of the 1990s. For each policy sector, five experts were interviewed, making a total of forty-five interviews, as shown in Figure 12.1. The respondents were from various backgrounds, ranging from top civil servants, politicians, and academics, to journalists and other specialists with deep knowledge in the policy sectors under investigation.

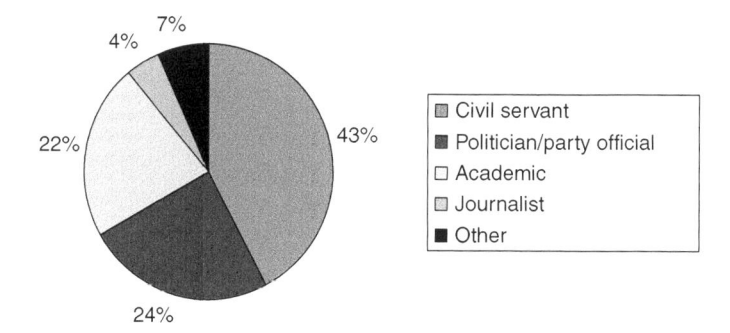

FIGURE 12.1 Types of respondent

Compared to the practices of bureaucratic *clientelismo* of the old partitocracy, the political and administrative changes of the 1990s have altered: (a) the extent of patronage at the central level of government, which has clearly shrunk because external policy constraints have narrowed the state's hold on the economy and reduced the degree of party penetration; and (b) the mechanisms for forming bonds of trust between politicians and appointees, which are no longer governed by party organizations but based on personal networks.

The scope of political appointments: range and depth

Patronage is still pervasive in the Italian public sector. An analysis of formal opportunities for patronage reveals a high level of susceptibility of Italian public bodies to party influence over the distribution of positions. Political appointments are actually allowed by the legal framework for most types of institution in all policy sectors, and parties make use of existing opportunities to fill positions with political appointees. The only institutional subtype that remains formally unaffected by patronage is the executive level for the Judiciary.

Table 12.2 presents an index of patronage scores. It shows that the institutional type where patronage is most pervasive is ministerial departments. These are followed by non-departmental agencies and commissions (NDACs) and executing institutions, which remain less affected.

Data on the range and depth of patronage offer a more differentiated picture across institutional types and policy sectors. Table 12.3 highlights the fact that range values are particularly high at the central level of government—in ministries and NDACs. Lower, but still relevant, is the breadth of patronage in executing institutions, which is due to the presence in this sphere of impermeable organizations operating in policy sectors such as the Judiciary, Education, Foreign Service, and the Military.

TABLE 12.2 *The index of party patronage in Italy*

Policy area	Ministries	NDACs	Executing institutions	Policy area total
Economy	0.67	0.33	0.33	0.44
Finance	0.67	0.22	0.22	0.37
Judiciary	0.67	0.33	0.11	0.37
Media	0.67	0.33	1.00	0.67
Military and Police	0.33	0.33	0.11	0.26
Health Care	0.67	0.33	0.33	0.44
Culture and Education	0.67	0.33	0.22	0.41
Foreign Service	0.67	0.00	0.11	0.39
Regional and Local Administration	0.67	1.00	1.00	0.89
Total	0.63	0.40	0.38	0.47

TABLE 12.3 *Range of party patronage in Italy*

Policy area	Ministries	NDACs	Executing institutions	Policy area total
Economy	3	3	3	1.00
Finance	3	2	2	0.78
Judiciary	3	3	1	0.78
Media	3	3	3	1.00
Military and Police	1.5	3	1	0.61
Health Care	3	3	3	1.00
Culture and Education	3	3	2	0.89
Foreign Service	3	n.a.	1	0.67
Total central level	**0.94**	**0.95**	**0.67**	**0.85**
Regional and Local Administration	3	3	3	1.00
Total	0.94	0.96	0.70	0.89

The relevance of political influence is so low in judicial offices because posts are distributed among the organized factions of the magistracy. The association of the magistracy exploits its own quantitative and qualitative power at the heart of the Higher Council of the Magistracy (CSM), the judiciary's self-governing body, which is the repository of the formal power of nomination. The Education and Culture sector is made less permeable by its legal framework, whereby the complexity and rigidity of formal recruitment procedures protect the state school system from political interference. As for the Military and Police sector, a strictly hierarchical organizational structure contributes to maintaining substantially impenetrable executing institutions, such as in the armed forces and the fire brigade, both of which are composed of professional bodies that privilege technical/bureaucratic rather than political criteria in internal career paths. This is also true for the Ministry of Defence, the only ministerial institution to remain unaffected by patronage. *Esprit de corps* makes political penetration particularly difficult in military institutions, where seniority and bureaucratic solidarity are the guiding criteria in awarding posts. The low level of penetration in the executing institutions of the Foreign Service sector is motivated by the low strategic salience of many of these institutions (consulates and most embassies), which leads parties to concentrate their efforts on a few organizations (permanent representations, embassies, and institutes of culture that operate with strategic partners) that require a strict congruence between the policy orientations of the executive and administrative action. Finally, in the Financial sector, the Bank of Italy continues its tradition of impermeability thanks to the complexity of its institutional mission, which requires posts to be awarded according to strictly merit-based criteria.

Table 12.4 shows that the depth of patronage also varies across the institutional spheres. It decreases in extra-ministerial domains at the central level of government, with political appointments tending to be restricted to the top level of disaggregated institutions.

TABLE 12.4 *Depth of party patronage in Italy*

Policy area	Ministries	NDACs	Executing institutions	Policy area total
Economy	2	1	1	0.44
Finance	2	1	1	0.44
Judiciary	2	1	1	0.44
Media	2	1	3	0.67
Military and Police	2	1	1	0.44
Health Care	2	1	1	0.44
Culture and Education	2	1	1	0.44
Foreign Service	2	n.a.	1	0.50
Total central level	**0.67**	**0.33**	**0.42**	**0.48**
Regional and Local Administration	2	3	3	0.89
Total	0.67	0.42	0.48	0.53

According to the experts, professionalization of the intermediate and lower levels is a necessary condition for the functional autonomy of organizations that have been disaggregated from the ministries in order to be able to operate efficiently in turbulent environments. Limiting politicization to top positions allows disaggregated institutions such as independent regulatory authorities and state-owned enterprises (SOEs) to conserve the high levels of organizational flexibility necessary to remain connected to dynamic transnational networks of economy and governance.

Analysis of the scope of patronage shows that Italian parties cast an extensive net of political appointments over the fragmented administration, and that it is denser in the ministerial centre. Patronage is more pervasive in ministerial departments because of the complexity of policy coordination performed by these institutions, which organize flows of communication between different policy sectors, different levels of government, and between the state and social actors (media and organized interests).

As can be seen in Figure 12.2, local administrations stand out as the heartland of patronage in contemporary Italy, and parties have the capacity to reach all institutions at the subnational level of government. The maximum range score highlights the pervasiveness of local patronage, which was reinforced by the sharp increase in the number of disaggregated institutions. Parties took advantage of the opportunities that the expansion in subnational administration offered to fill the new extra-ministerial organizations with political appointments at all levels. Moreover, the adoption of the enterprise formula in the regional health care systems has not succeeded in depoliticizing local health care authorities, which constitute an arena of massive party rent-seeking. Subnational governments lack professional bodies to hinder the expansion of patronage, since they do not operate in policy sectors characterized by established career paths. In addition to professional reasons, it

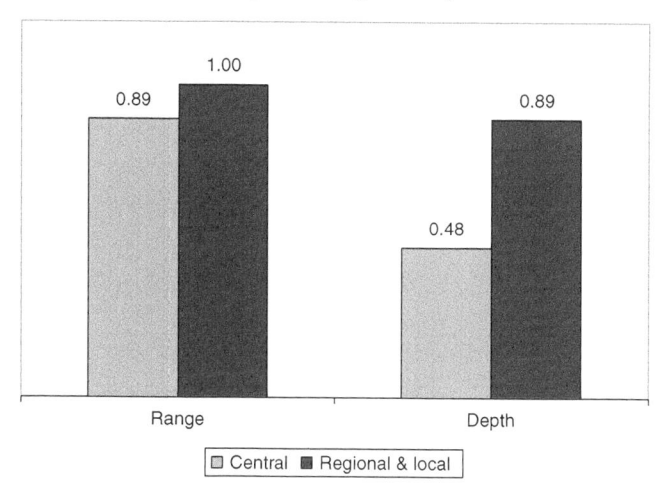

FIGURE 12.2 Range and depth of party patronage, by level of government

must be noted that the feebleness of pressure from the EU for the liberalization of local public service markets allowed subnational governments to extend their hold over local economies, using corporatization to increase the sphere of particularistic exchange which, at the local level, and especially in southern Italy, is clearly broader and deeper than at the national level.

Logic and mechanisms of patronage

According to most of the interviewees, political appointments are made primarily to control public institutions. Figure 12.3 highlights the prevalence of control over reward, despite the high score for 'both reward and control'. Indeed, reward was never cited as the single motivation behind patronage. The logic of patronage in Italy is mainly guided by a desire to allow party governors to control the processes of policy design and the implementation and flow of public resources in all sectors of the central administration. Parties nominate loyal individuals to top strategic positions (senior executives, board members, public corporation managers) in order to render administrative structures more responsive to changes in policy priorities.

Patronage as control at the top is pervasive, and has not been eradicated by the administrative reforms that aimed to rationalize the functioning of the state. Although the reforms reduced the scope of patronage at the top through processes of privatization, they did not trigger a paradigmatic change. They were used instead as opportunities to enhance the flexibility of political control over the administration through the introduction of fixed-term contracts for top positions and the frequent reorganization of public institutions. The permanent policy of

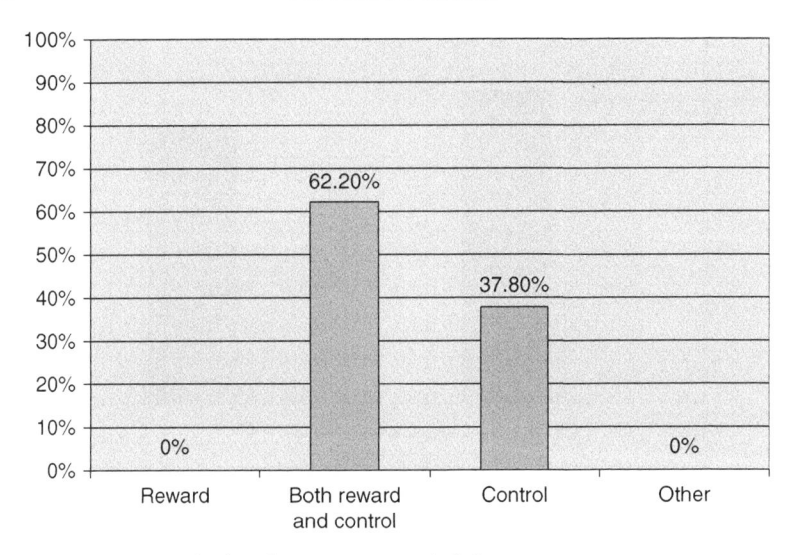

FIGURE 12.3 Motivations for party patronage in Italy

rationalization of administrative structures provoked an expansion of patronage. Both coalitions used arguments for rationalization as an excuse for distributing new positions. Parties in government have transformed the flexibility of the legal framework into an instrument that creates room for manoeuvre in the allocation of administrative positions.

Control of the administration has not only remained widespread, but has become even deeper. There has been an expansion in the swarms of policy advisers and consultants that crowd ministerial cabinets offering specific expertise, flexible support, and unconditional loyalty in the development of policies. The growth of ministerial cabinets as centres of power and communication in the machinery of government increases the imbalance between political control and professional policy advice that marks Italy, where ministers avoid the rigidity of bureaucracy through informal mechanisms of politicization which allow faster and more penetrating control of public institutions.

The exception to the prevalence of control over reward is in the Regional and Local Administration sector, where the experts underline the equal importance of the two motivations. The relevance of patronage as reward in this sector is confirmed by the fact that Regional and Local Administration has the highest scores for depth of patronage. The experts point to the continued relevance of patronage as a mode of exchange of votes for public posts at lower levels, particularly in the south of Italy, where local administrative bodies continue to serve as social shock absorbers.[2] Patronage as a reward for the participation of otherwise inactive activists is widespread in regional and local administrations.

The picture changes at the national level. As the scores on the depth of patronage highlight, in the central administration this form of job allocation is now residual. Parties continue to play a role in the recruitment of lower-level employees in some executing institutions in the Economic sector, for example the postal services, but such interventions are defined as marginal by the experts. Patronage as reward at the national level is therefore restricted to the supply of top positions and intermediate managerial posts to activists and professional politicians, but nevertheless to a lesser extent than that seen in subnational bodies.

The ministerial sphere is particularly relevant for patronage as reward, allowing parties to offer their supporters positions in ministerial cabinets, and to hold intermediate bureaucratic positions open to party friends appointed as 'in-and-outers'. The boards of disaggregated organizations, particularly in the executing institutions of the Economy (SOEs) and Culture and Education (research bodies and companies of the Ministry for Cultural Heritage), constitute the other group of institutions that provide a great many positions for distribution as rewards. To this group must be added RAI (the public service broadcaster), which has been infiltrated at all levels in order to reward activists and party professionals, such as campaign organizers (journalists and media consultants).

The prevalence of strategies of control in appointment processes affects the criteria parties use when selecting appointees. To occupy strategic positions that control resources crucial in processes of policy making, parties are obliged to select individuals with at least a modicum of expertise. As can be seen in Figure 12.4, the professional competence of appointees is a necessary but not a sufficient condition for exercising control over the state.

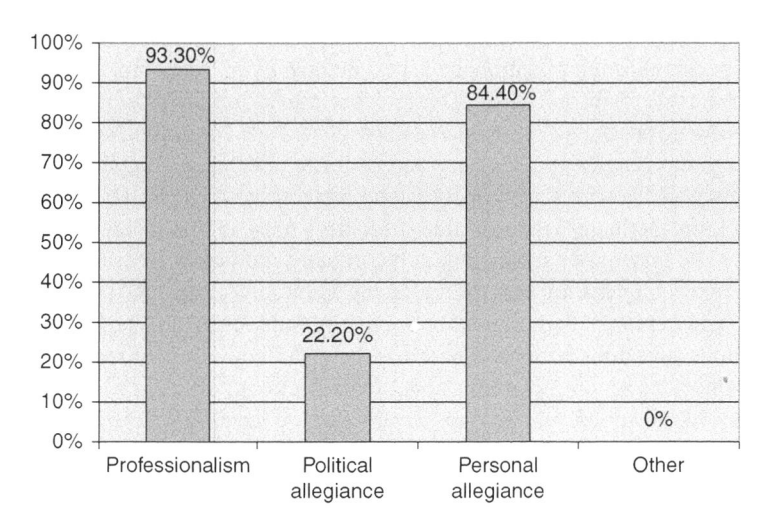

Qualification	Percentage
Professionalism	93.30%
Political allegiance	22.20%
Personal allegiance	84.40%
Other	0%

FIGURE 12.4 Qualifications of appointees in Italy

Parties select appointees that are not only competent and able to manage the processes of policy making, but also loyal, ready to guarantee the responsiveness of institutions to party instructions. Parties recruit personnel that combine expertise and loyalty both to design and implement policy change and to control the particularistic distribution of services—patronage in the widest sense—to their own supporters.

Only candidates that have cultivated a network of personal relations connecting them to party actors are able to obtain the status of being considered trustworthy and obtain positions. Public managers are no longer recruited *through* parties as organizations, but are nominated *by* single party actors that draw on the personal networks embedded in their professional worlds (the public sector, the private sector, academia). The format of the party system affects the formation of links of trust between professionals and parties, as is shown by the low value attached to political links in Italy. Since the crisis of polarized pluralism, catch-all coalitions composed of numerous and fluid parties have alternated in government in Italy. The fragmentation and instability of the Italian party system, resulting from the absence of consolidated loyalties towards the new parties, increases the role of personal ties in the patronage practices of new parties in creating temporary clusters of office holders gathered in catch-all blocs.

The experts underline the collapse of political links as the most important aspect of the qualifications of appointees. In the old polarized pluralism, patronage practices guaranteed the deep segmentation of public institutions according to their political colours: the role of parties as organizations was relevant in entrusting all levels of positions to personnel chosen according to their partisan loyalty. In the new bipolar system, patronage has been transformed into a device for the personalized connection between party leadership and public bodies through the selection of professionally qualified top managers.[3]

The personalization of patronage is best defined by investigating the actors that control the selection processes. The relevant role of ministers emerges sharply, monopolizing patronage in ministerial departments and controlling a large share of patronage in agencies and advisory bodies for relative areas of competence. The ministers with the widest networks of appointments are those for Health, Finance, and Cultural heritage, who are able to control most of the institutions in their sectors. The institutions most open to the influence of actors other than ministers are the executing institutions (SOEs in the Economy sector, RAI in the Media sector, and research bodies in the University subsector) and non-majoritarian institutions (the Constitutional Court and the CSM in the Justice sector, independent authorities in the Economy and Media sectors), which are subject to the division of positions among the leaders of the coalition. The relevance of 'ministers' and 'leaders' in political appointment processes makes it difficult to maintain the distinction between organizational and governmental leadership, because 'the whole leadership of the "new" Italian party system has been recruited

Party Patronage in Italy 241

directly at the top of government without leaving their party responsibilities' (Verzichelli, 2009: 86).

The extreme personalization of patronage has prevented managers from being organized in two compact enemy camps, despite the advent of the bipolar party system. The process of creating personal networks takes place in two phases: in the first, each party governor gathers around her or him, in her or his own personal *entourage,* loyal expert collaborators from the sector of interest; in the next phase each expert from that entourage explores their own personal networks in search of trustworthy managers to whom a position may be given. Party governors therefore acquire the control of institutions through networks largely composed of nodes borrowed from the functional networks of their own closest collaborators. The experts underline the 'loneliness' of party governors, who practice patronage without either close links or support from party organizations, and the ability of appointees, who are skilful in using their personal connections to reach those trusted by the leaders. Intermediation or input by the parties as organizations is the obvious missing element: in fact the experts remarked that parties as organizations play no role in appointment processes dominated by solitary governors. The personal/functional rather than the organizational logic that informs the creation of networks also determines their fluidity: the pragmatism that dominates allows nodes with less intense relations with leaders to skip from one network to another, activating their own personal connections and allowing the two alliances to alternate in government.

Majoritarian and consensual patronage practices

The rather high value of 'jobs for the opposition' in Figure 12.5 is due to the practice of dividing positions between the government and opposition, concentrated in the Media, Justice, Military and Police, and Regional and Local Administration sectors. In the Justice and Media sectors, the distribution of positions in

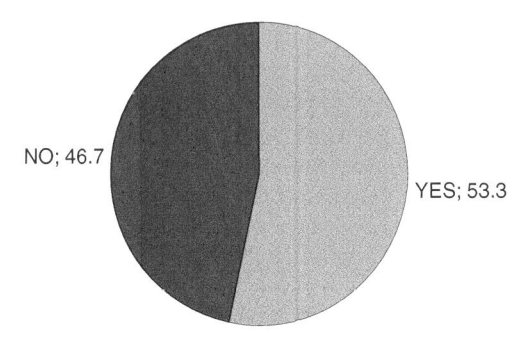

FIGURE 12.5 Sharing of patronage appointments in Italy

non-ministerial institutions among the actors in the party system is proportional, with a correction for the majority. Consensual patronage practices are institutionalized by the legal framework, which assigns the power of nomination to parliament as the arena of cooperation between the majority and the opposition. In the Justice sector, the majority reserves five CSM posts and three constitutional judges for itself, assigning three CSM posts and two constitutional judges to the opposition. In the Media sector, there is an equal division of positions on the AGCOM (independent communications authority) board—four each—while the government retains the choice of the president of the authority, who enjoys wide powers in directing the organization. In the RAI, five members of the board are assigned to the majority and four to the minority, including the president. The majority selects the CEO and the top management positions of the two principal television networks, while the third network is characterized by the prevalent and constant influence of the centre-left coalition. At the intermediate and lower levels, stability prevails and the division of areas of influence among the parties resists changes of government.

The collaboration mechanisms between government and opposition are different in the Military and Police sector. Cooperation between the two coalitions takes place in the specific subsector of the Interior and Police, and assumes the form of sharing rather than a division of appointments. The majority enjoys the power of proposal, while the opposition evaluates the government's proposals and may veto candidates it considers incapable of offering adequate guarantees of impartiality. This sharing of the power of appointment between government and opposition is due to the peculiarity of the sector that controls the administration of elections (the Interior) and manages public order (the Police). Their common interest in the equality of the civil and political rights that feed the democratic process pushes the government and opposition to consult one another and choose personnel loyal to both of them.

In other sectors of the central level of administration, a clear-cut spoils system prevails, with the bipolar structure of competition creating strong pressures towards majoritarian patronage practices. The wholesale alternation in government urges coalitions to acquire exclusive control of the posts that are considered strategic. In Regional and Local Administration, the opposition has easier access to positions. This is particularly the case in the south of Italy, because of the extreme fragmentation of the party systems, characterized by a Balkanization of an extremely personalized representation. In southern Italy, parties are not even able to fulfil the procedural role of expression and support for a government. Southern executives, lacking a coherent parliamentary base, offer patronage opportunities to individual members of the opposition in order to build coalitions of variable geometry that ensure their precarious stability. In central and northern Italy, on the other hand, more structured party systems reinforce the control of the majority over local administrations. In these areas of the country, the opposition is excluded

Party Patronage in Italy 243

from selection processes for strategic positions, but does have regular access to numerous positions on boards of agencies and in local public utilities.

Evolution of patronage practices over time

The collapse of the party system between 1992 and 1994, and the wave of administrative reforms of the 1990s, brought considerable discontinuity to the patronage practices along many of the analytical dimensions examined in this project, as is shown in Table 12.5.

As far as the role of parties in policy sectors is concerned, a clear decline of political control over the Justice sector should be underlined. In the past, cooperation between the old parties in processes of appointment allowed them to exploit the internal divisions within the associated magistracy. The parties were able to influence the selection of magistrates with whom they had formed strong ties. The advent of a strongly polarized party system has provoked a rupture in these practices of exchange on judicial issues between coalitions. The new parties are no longer able to qualitatively increase their quantitative weakness in the CSM through the old consensual arrangements, which have been undermined by fierce polarization.[4]

As for the role of parties in other types of institutions, the traditional relevance of party control over 'parallel administrations' (agencies and executing institutions) remains, a typical trait of the old partitocracy. The politicization of ministries has increased with the introduction of reforms inspired by 'New Public Management', and the resulting temporary nature of positions has served to ensure the loyalty rather than the accountability of senior executives. Contracts are extended and managers are promoted not on the basis of their performance but on the relationship of trust they manage to establish with political leaders, who distribute positions without any procedural curbs on their discretion. Patronage in

TABLE 12.5 *The evolution of party patronage in Italy*

Sectors	From consensual arrangements to polarization:
	Decline of control over judicial offices
Institutional types	Bipolarism and NPM reforms:
	Expansion of patronage in the ministerial domain
Range	Restructuring of the administrative system:
	Decline at central level (privatizations), expansion at local level (corporatization)
Depth	Patronage in retreat under pressures from transnational networks: From deep segmentation to control of top management in extra-ministerial domains
Logic	More control; less clientelism
	Reward still significant, particularly at local level
Mechanisms	Collapse of political link and rise of personalization; growth of head of the executive's influence at all levels; territorialization of subnational patronage

ministerial departments has become a new mechanism of control over policy implementation, replacing the old hierarchical supremacy of the government which was undermined by processes of functional and structural disaggregation. The previously 'ossified world' of the top civil service has now become a 'liquid world', where the precariousness of posts and career progression has generated the individualization of offers of temporary loyalty to the ministers of the moment. An indicator of this politicization of ministries is the growth in senior executive positions as a percentage of ministry personnel. Between 1994 and 2007, the ratio increased from 1.8 to 2.3 (Torchia, 2009), propelled by various legislative interventions of successive governments, which enlarged the quota of posts to be awarded to people from outside ministerial settings and extended the quota of top positions to be filled through the promotion of lower-level managers. In addition, the length of contracts has been reduced.

Patronage as reward has tended to shift to the ministries, while in the First Republic it was concentrated in the executing institutions, particularly in the Economy sector. This difference in the localization of patronage as reward is just one of the aspects of the profound change that has been observed in the executing institutions of the Finance and Economy sectors. Europeanization and globalization have not only notably reduced the extension of the perimeter of the public sector, but they have also caused a qualitative change in patronage practices in the executing institutions, which are now shareholder companies that remain either wholly or partly publicly owned. The Treasury, as the only holder of public shares in these companies, has acquired a concentration of the management power of publicly run companies, which had at one time been spread out, with the intention of guaranteeing a coherent direction of all the decisions regarding them, and of contributing to the recovery in public finances by increasing the value of shares remaining in public hands.

The formal changes in the architecture of power over public institutions have contributed to a transformation in the negotiations between parties over the division of positions. In the First Republic, the dispersion of formal powers of appointment among multiple institutions formalized deeply institutionalized practices of dividing positions, known as *lottizzazione*. The old parties and factions obtained posts in institutions invested with the power of appointment, and consequently in the companies controlled by them, in proportion to their electoral strength and strategic position in the coalition. These practices were possible because the parties both could and preferred to, irresponsibly, finance the inefficiency of public companies. Enterprises and economic bodies were managed by professionals chosen on the basis of their political links and who possessed the only professional quality necessary: the ability to procure the abundant resources that hidden professionals, nominated at high and intermediate levels, arranged to distribute to clients, groups, and hidden donors.

The budget constraints that centralized the formal powers of appointment in the head of the Treasury have made the patronage practices of the Second Republic much more unstable with respect to the old *lottizzazione*. The President of the Council of Ministers and the Minister of Finance have become the dominant actors, in that: (a) they dispose of the power to direct and control companies; and (b) they represent the government in supranational organizations. By controlling the information flows between markets and supranational institutions, the government, and public companies, the President and the Minister for Finance claim and acquire the lion's share of top management posts, thwarting the requests from allied party leaders for a more or less proportional distribution of positions during coalition bargaining. The President of the Council has also extended his own sphere of influence to other important policy-making arenas, such as the intelligence units in the Military and Police sector and the securities regulator in the Finance sector. In the Foreign Service sector, a diarchy of the Minister and the President tends to appear, competing with each other for control over patronage.

The changed global economic/financial context has undermined the role of patronage as an instrument for the mass organizational consolidation of parties through the extraction of resources from economic agencies. After the Italian state's financial crisis and entry into the single currency, patronage was transformed into an instrument for the connection of leaders and shareholder companies through the selection of top managers with professional qualifications, ensuring efficient management. There has been a retreat from patronage at the top levels: since the resources to distribute have become scarce, few hidden professionals and clients remain. Companies have also become more professional at the lower and intermediate levels in order to adapt efficiently to the competitive pressures of globalized markets.

The restructuring of the central level of administration, the changes in the party system, and the introduction of the direct election of heads of local executives have brought noticeable changes to the actors that control the expansion of patronage at the local level. Local executives have become the dominant actors, while in the past the national leaders of the DC and the local party organizations of the PCI (Italian Communist Party) prevailed. In the DC it was the role of pyramidal factions, networks of vertical exchange through which resources from agencies and public companies flowed from centre to periphery, that made local office holders weak and dependent on national leaders (Zuckerman, 1979). The current scarcity of resources at the centre, the expansion of functions and resources for subnational administrations, and the disappearance of the permanent control over the state by the DC as the dominant party have greatly weakened the strength of factional connections.

The legitimacy provided by the direct election of mayors and regional presidents, and the clear reinforcement of executive power over administrative organization have further weakened the factional links. Party system change has facilitated the growth of local post-communist governors, who are no longer controlled by the mass party that disappeared after the fall of communism. Members of the party in government at the local level now have autonomous control of patronage to satisfy local party networks. The head of the executive has become the dominant actor in local patronage processes. However, the rise in the power of subnational presidents does not mean that they can monopolize the distribution of positions, since there is competition from ministers seeking to extend their own networks from local ministerial departments to disaggregated administrations. In the new stratified configuration of Italian parties, subnational bosses offer the national leaders, who dispense patronage at the central level, an organizational base in exchange for non-interference in the implantation of their local committees, fed by public resources.

CONCLUSION: A MATTER OF 'GOVERNMENTNESS'

The empirical analysis has revealed a persistent hold by parties on the Italian administration, and at the same time has highlighted a clear-cut discontinuity in the new parties' mechanisms of control over the state. The wave of administrative and institutional reforms and party system change prevented the return of *colonization* as a specific mode of politicizing the Italian administration, and allowed the formation and reproduction of partitocracy. The extraordinary collapse of the old parties and the reshaping of the state in the 1990s demolished the two most characteristic traits of the partitocratic colonization: the continuously expanding scope and the clear pre-eminence of political links as a criterion for the selection of administrative elites by party organizations.

As for the extent of patronage, the hypothesis of a drop in affluent societies is confirmed (Kitschelt, 2007). In the Italian case of comprehensive *clientelismo*, it was the crisis of old patterns of political competition that allowed the competitive pressures of the new global context of political economy to affect the state. The pressures of new global governance met with no resistance from organizational networks which had been abandoned by parties in the process of disbanding. The exceptional break in the party system opened a window of opportunity for the technocratic elites that had guided the country's entry into Europe by restructuring the state (Sbragia, 2001). The new economic constitution, arising from processes of privatization and liberalization, constituted an exogenous constraint for the new parties, whose patronage practices had to adapt to the culture of macroeconomic stability institutionalized by membership of the European Union (Radaelli, 2002). The more streamlined state, integrated into transnational economic institutional networks, prevented a reproduction of the inflationary tendencies of *clientelismo*.

This study of patronage in Italy has revealed the presence of organizational dynamics typical of parties in new democracies. Such a discovery is unsurprising if we understand the crisis of the 1990s as a regime crisis (Pasquino, 2002) which allowed new parties without institutionalized mechanisms for coordinating the different functional arenas to enter government. As happens in new democracies, the concentration of power in a small nucleus of leaders straddling the roles of party in government and party executive acts as a cohesion-seeking strategy, compensating for the deficit of political loyalty in transitional contexts (van Biezen, 2005). Personal loyalties take the place of procedures such as mechanisms of party integration. The leaders become the only face of the party, since they control the distribution of the institutional resources that form the cement for fluid organizations.

The personalization of patronage in Italy is an indicator of the under-institutionalization of the new parties, which are subordinated to the personal power of their leaders. The organizational weakness of the new parties in government has placed them in a position of dependence on members of the cabinet in the management of patronage. In personalizing patronage, ministers not only reinforce the policy-making ability of the cabinet, but above all they consolidate their power base through access to material public resources, which they manipulate in order to feed the private networks that support their political activity.[5] As in new democracies, in Italy 'political personalities make use of parties for their own ends, rather than act as the leaders of collective organizations of political actions' (Webb and White, 2007: 359). With the new democracies, Italy shares both the generational factors of new parties that are governing without having first institutionalized their own organizational infrastructure, and a weakness of the public administration, from which the private networks of leaders extract resources.

The unbearable financial weight of the 'party governmentness' (Katz, 1986) that characterized the partitocracy has been replaced by the unbearable organizational lightness of the 'governmentness' of new parties. Weak parties constitute an appendage of the personal power of their leaders in government. Patronage practised by the new parties alternating in government has exacerbated the dysfunctions of administrative systems which are still lacking the strong interinstitutional linkages and networks that make a substantial contribution to policy coherence and effective public management (Torchia, 2009). Patronage in Italy cannot guarantee an efficient link between parties and the system of governance, since responsible policy coordination requires procedures and institutionalized networks of communication rather than personal loyalties.[6]

According to Katz, in advanced democracies the political party 'becomes a label by which a group of leaders is known and an organization for coordinating elite activity' (Katz, 1990: 146). The party that no longer fulfils representative functions in society becomes an integrated network of office holders, a stable organizational structure in the governmental process within the state. However, an absence of institutionalization renders Katz's definition invalid for the new Italian parties. They are only able to fulfil the 'labelling function' typical in cases of atomization in the party system.

The new organizations can only be defined as parties in the sense of Sartori's minimal definition: political groups identified by an official label that present at elections and are capable of placing through elections candidates for public office. As Sartori (1976) notes, this definition pays no attention to organizational requirements. In this definition the only cohesive element required is the label that gathers together stable coalitions of office holders and candidates. For Sartori (2005: 15–16), 'before the advent of the mass parties it is proper to speak of "parties" (as stabilized coalitions of leaders) but not of the party system (as being a structured system)'. Western European systems have been structured by the rise of the mass party, which 'resides in the linkage, in the fact that the party is made of its connecting network. The mass party may well remain loose and thus resemble a federation. Still, its constituent units are no longer persons but impersonal agencies; that is, the leaders are no longer above the party' (Sartori, 2005: 15). As underlined by the turnover in party affiliations, which made the political offer particularly fluid after the crisis of pluralized polarism, leaders in Italy have returned to being above the parties. The infrastructure of the new organizations is not the institutionalized connecting network left by the mass parties to the cartel parties in stable systems. It was, instead, personal power that took the place of the connecting network in a context of systemic atomization, in which the party could not stay above the leaders. Nowhere in modern Italy is there the sense of a party that 'both outlasts its leaders and binds them to its logic of inertia' (Sartori, 2005: 12).

As new organizations that emerged after the exceptional crisis of the old system, Italian parties can only function as labels, coalitions of leaders incapable of structuring the actions of elites within governmental institutions through procedural mechanisms. It is the leaders, who control the process of building parties, that prosper as vehicles for professionals who use electoral success for personal profit (Lawson, 2007). Rather than being a device that strengthens pre-existing party networks, as Ware (1996) once identified it, patronage in Italy serves only to strengthen the leaders. The old colonization-oriented parties built extensive networks in a pervasive public sector as systems of organizational occupancy of Italian society. Contemporary political leaders build new parties as labels cemented by institutional resources that feed private networks.

NOTES

1. *Clientelismo*: political patronage or favouritism.
2. On the long life of *clientelismo* in Southern Italy, see Caciagli, 2006.
3. The patronage practices of the Northern League constitute the only exception to the dominant pattern. As a populist party, the Northern League has met with considerable difficulties in recruiting top managers, since professionals have never offered their services to a party perceived as 'not respectable'.

4. For a more detailed overview of the reduction in the politicization of judicial offices, see Guarnieri, 2003. The quantitative weakness of the parties is a result of their political control over only a third of the members of the CSM.
5. As a result, corruption remains systemic, but parties as agents of coordination and the centralized protection of hidden exchanges have declined in importance (della Porta and Vannucci, 2007).
6. Investigation of the Italian case confirms the difficulties of governing efficiently and effectively for new parties in government suffering from organizational underdevelopment (Bolleyer 2008).

CHAPTER 13

Party Patronage in the Netherlands: Sharing Appointments to Maintain Consensus

Sandra van Thiel

INTRODUCTION

Most authors claim that patronage in the Netherlands is either non-existent or highly exceptional (see for example Müller, 2006b; Randeraad and Wolffram, 2001). This chapter will show the opposite. Dutch political parties are actively engaged in influencing appointments in the public and semi-public sectors, a practice that can be partly explained by reference to the Dutch tradition of pillarization and consociationalism (Lijphart, 2007). Political parties always have to cooperate in order to form coalitions and cabinets. This sharing of power extends to sharing appointments, with the result that there is an (informal) system of distribution of appointments between political parties (Baakman, 2004). Political parties have also geared their party organization towards obtaining their 'share' of appointments. In the Dutch tradition, however, this system of distribution is considered to neutralize political differences and competition rather than to increase political power or reward active party members, and it is this which probably explains why (party) patronage has usually been assumed to be absent in the Netherlands.

POLITICAL PARTIES IN THE NETHERLANDS

For a long time Dutch society was divided along vertical lines, or 'pillars', each containing a distinct section of the population, such as Catholics, Protestants, and socialists (Lijphart, 1999). This vertical segmentation superseded class or social status differences. Each pillar had its own newspapers, interest groups, schools, churches, broadcasting companies, trade unions, and political parties. Electoral discipline within the pillars was very strong (Aarts and Thomassen, 2008). Despite the segmentation of society there was a stable political structure. Consensus and compromise were essential to maintain political and governmental stability. This was achieved by politics of accommodation on the part of the pillar elites, and specifically the elites of the associated political parties.

From the 1960s on, a process of depillarization took place. The boundaries between the pillars faded, and new groups and political parties were created. Nowadays, there are five big 'families' of political parties (Andeweg and Irwin, 2005: 48), most of which consist of more than one party: the Christian parties (Christian Democratic Appeal (CDA), Christian Union (CU), Political Reformed Party (SGP)), Liberal parties (People's Party for Freedom and Democracy (VVD), (Democrats 66 (D66)), Socialist or Social-Democratic parties (Socialist Party (SP), Labour Party (PvdA)), Green parties (Green Left (GL), Party for the Animals (PVDD)), and more recently extreme right or populist parties (Pim Fortuyn List (LPF), Party for Freedom (PVV)).[1] In this multiparty system, on average ten political parties are represented in parliament.

Coalition formation

The Dutch electoral system combines extreme proportional representation, party lists, a large number of political parties, and the absence of an electoral threshold. As a result, no single party has ever been able to obtain a majority (Mair, 2008a). Political parties always have to form a coalition cabinet of at least two parties.

Based on the results of the general elections for the lower house of parliament, coalition negotiations are undertaken. Most of the procedures for coalition formation have never been formalized or written down, and most of the process takes place behind closed doors (Andeweg and Irwin, 2005: 111). The Queen appoints an 'informateur', usually a senior party official of the largest party, to discuss possible coalition options with a number of parties. Then, based on the informateur's recommendations about the most likely coalition, the Queen appoints a 'formateur', usually the party leader of the largest party in the preferred new coalition. The formateur leads the negotiations about the policy programme of the new cabinet and the selection of ministers and junior ministers (*staatssecretaris*) from the participating political parties. When the new cabinet is finalized, the Queen will appoint all (junior) ministers and the prime minister.

It is customary that party leaders take a position in the new cabinet, but on occasion individual ones stay on as a member of parliament. All the MPs who take up a position in the cabinet have to give up their seat in parliament; this is known as the principle of dualism. The vacant seat will be taken by the next candidate on the party list, and cannot be reclaimed by a minister after resignation or cabinet termination. The appointment of 'independent' ministers, who are not affiliated with a political party, occurred incidentally only in the

1950s (Baakman, 2004). At the municipal level it is somewhat more common to appoint unaffiliated aldermen.

Party membership

Only relatively few Dutch voters are members of a political party. As a result of depillarization, membership ratios have declined even more (Mair and van Biezen, 2001; DNPP online, Ten Velde and Voerman, 2000). In the 1960s, 6.7 per cent of the electorate held membership cards for a political party. In the 1980s this dropped to about 4 per cent, and by the 2000s the average membership ratio was around 2.5 per cent. Because of these declining membership numbers, it is increasingly difficult for political parties to find enough candidates to carry out political and party functions. Voerman (1995) estimates that the Netherlands holds around 12,700 political and party functions. The number of party members required to fulfil these functions (which represents around 9 per cent of the total number of members) can only just be met—the percentage of party members who actively participate in a party organization is estimated to be about 10 per cent.

Political parties are also plagued by declining societal and electoral support, and increased competition for votes. Electoral volatility went up as a result of depillarization and the advent of new parties (Mair, 2008b). More recently, new populist parties like LPF and PVV have forced traditional parties to copy their restrictive stance on issues like immigration, multiculturalism, and crime in order to maintain electoral support. The differences between parties' viewpoints and ideology have thus become smaller (Oosterwaal and Torenvlied, 2010; Aarts and Thomassen, 2008), leading to a further increase in the competition for vote(r)s.

To conclude, Dutch political parties have a low number of members and a low activist base. This complicates the fulfilment of party and political functions, as well as other functions in the public domain. At the same time, the consensus-based system of coalitions creates a steady flow of appointments to government positions and a need for job opportunities for those who have left such positions.

DUTCH CIVIL SERVICE TRADITION

The Dutch civil service tradition was and is considered to be typically Weberian. Civil servants are expected to be neutral experts, who simply execute the wishes of their political principals ('t Hart et al., 2002; Nieuwenkamp, 2001). However, under the influence of New Public Management (NPM), (senior) civil servants have become 'public managers' who 'run' the government in a business-like way (Noordegraaf, 2000: 37–8). They are expected to be entrepreneurial, innovative, and even risk-taking; to display leadership and operate strategically; to manage networks of public organizations, political actors, interest groups, and citizens; and to be professional managers while retaining a strong public sector orientation or ethos (Pollitt, 2003). As a result, civil servants have become more proactive—contrary to the reactive Weberian civil servant—and thus more visible to parties outside the government. This has led to a blurring of the boundaries between politicians and bureaucrats (van der Meer, 2004).

However, the more proactive behaviour of civil servants has not been matched by an increased accountability of civil servants. The principle of individual ministerial accountability is still dominant in the Dutch politico-administrative system. This mismatch has led to a number of incidents and conflicts ('t Hart et al., 2002), and politicians have been looking for instruments to increase their control over the civil service (van der Meer, 2004). Three of these instruments are relevant to the topic of party patronage and will be discussed below: changes to the legal position of civil servants, the introduction of a unified senior civil service, and the appointment of political advisers.

Legal position of civil servants

According to the Dutch constitution, all Dutch men and women are eligible to be appointed as civil servants. There are no special exams, and the idea of an 'administrative class' is alien to Dutch political and administrative thinking (van der Meer and Dijkstra, 2000). There is very little mobility between political and administrative functions (van der Meer, 2004). This egalitarianism is also reflected in the selection and recruitment system. Personnel management is decentralized (Peters, 2010; van der Meer and Raadschelders, 1999). Ministries, municipalities, and most types of non-departmental agencies and commissions (NDACs) specify their own labour conditions. These can be individual arrangements for an organization, or collective ones for an entire sector, such as the police force or the higher education sector.[2] Regulations for civil servants in ministries, for example, are laid down in two statutes: ARAR (*Algemeen Rijksambtenarenreglement*) and BBRA (*Bezoldigingsbesluit rijksambtenaren*). Distinctions between different functions are expressed in salary scales (with 18 and 19 as the highest, equal to a ministerial salary). This type of 'ranking' has been copied in most parts of the public domain, but with different ranks and intervals.

The Dutch civil service system is generally regarded as a position-based system (PUMA, 2003). Employees are recruited for a function, not for a career (van der Meer and Dijkstra, 2000). Vacant positions are open—through advertisements—to a wide range of candidates, from both the civil service and the private market. However, civil servants are expected to leave one position before they can take on the next. The differences in labour conditions between organizations, combined with the need to terminate prior jobs, are probably important causes of the limited mobility across organizations.

NPM has led to a number of changes in the Dutch personnel system (Peters, 2010; van Thiel, Steijn, and Allix, 2007; Farnham et al., 1996; OECD, 2005; Pollitt and Bouckaert, 2004; PUMA, 2003; van der Meer and Dijkstra, 2000; Page and Wright, 1999a; Wright, 1994). For example, the legal status of government employees has been 'normalized' to make it more similar to private sector arrangements, like a reduction in the permanence of tenure and more opportunities for working part time. Several human resource management (HRM) instruments and policies have been introduced, including policies to increase the diversity of government staff. The pension fund has been privatized. Performance-related pay has been introduced, but on a somewhat haphazard and selective basis. Salaries of top civil servants have been maximized. Furthermore, attempts were made to increase the mobility of civil servants, for example by introducing new trainee programmes, but most importantly by the establishment of a senior civil service.

Senior civil service

The Senior civil service (ABD, *Algemene Bestuursdienst*) was established in 1995 (van der Meer and Raadschelders, 1999). The ABD includes all top civil servants from salary scale 15 upwards (estimated at about 1,500 officials),[3] and was established to improve the management capabilities and mobility of top civil servants. The bureau manages a pool of top civil servants, who are all, formally, employees of the Home Office (*Ministerie van Binnenlandse Zaken*, BZK). The selection and recruitment for all top positions in ministries is handled by the bureau. When a vacancy is advertised, the bureau will provide a list of suitable candidates from their own database, organize the selection and assessment process, and finally nominate a candidate. In the case of the two highest ministerial functions, secretary general (SG) and director general (DG), the minister of BZK has to co-sign the final appointment.

All appointments of ABD members are temporary. Top civil servants are expected to take up a new position every five years (or less in the case of interim management). Mobility has increased slightly since the introduction of the ABD, but it is difficult to say whether this can indeed be attributed to the ABD, as mobility at the top level was already relatively high before 1995 (van der Meer and Raadschelders, 1999; van der Meer and Dijkstra, 2000). However, mobility between the private and public sectors is still very low; the general career pattern of (top) civil servants runs within the civil service and usually within the same ministry—in 90 per cent of cases (van der Meer and Raadschelders, 1999).

The ABD is not an entirely closed circuit; about 10 per cent of job openings are expected to be fulfilled by outside candidates. Furthermore, the bureau has expanded its scope over time to include appointments to international positions and lower-level governments. In 2008, a pilot was started regarding appointments to certain NDACs.

Originally, it was expected that the ABD would contribute to a depoliticization of the civil service. However, one of its objectives is to 'create a unified civil service ethos', which could be construed as a higher degree of compliance with the wishes of the political principal (van der Meer, 2004). Later in this chapter we will see that the expert respondents have very different opinions about the impact and effects of the ABD.

Political advisers

Just like the absence of an administrative class, the ideas of a spoils system and ministerial cabinets are foreign to Dutch government (van der Meer, 2004; van der Meer and Dijkstra, 2000). However, recently the number of political advisers has increased slightly (van der Meer and Raadschelders, 1999). Several ministers—and at local level several mayors and aldermen—nowadays have a single political adviser.

Research into this topic is scarce (but see van der Steen, van Twist, and Peeters, 2009, for an exception). Political advisers are appointed on a short-term basis, no longer than the duration of the ruling coalition. They act as intermediary between the minister and bureaucrats, the party and the media. Although political advisers are appointed as civil servants, they are not part of the government bureaucracy hierarchy. It is the only appointment that the minister can make personally; the grounds for selection are unknown.

POLITICIZATION OF THE DUTCH CIVIL SERVICE

The existence of party political influence on appointments of civil servants is officially denied (van der Meer, 2004; van der Meer and Dijkstra, 2000; van der Meer and Raadschelders, 1999). Following Weber's model of bureaucracy, selection in the Dutch bureaucracy is based on 'neutral competence', training, and expertise (Peters, 2010: 83). However, civil servants will have to work together with or cater to the demands of their political principals. 'Responsive competence' is therefore probably a more important requirement for (top) positions than pure neutrality. In a spoils system, responsive competence is ensured by appointing like-minded civil servants. In a Weberian bureaucracy, responsiveness can be achieved through training and/or by having a representative composition of the civil service.

Most Dutch top civil servants are members of a political party; nowadays many are affiliated with the Labour Party (PvdA), but in earlier times an affiliation with the Christian Democratic Party (CDA) was more common (see van der Meer and Dijkstra, 2000, for an overview). However, van der Meer and Dijkstra's (2000) research suggests that top civil servants generally do not act in (party) political ways. The literature suggests two explanations for this seemingly contradictory finding. First, van der Meer and Dijkstra (2000) state that, at the top, people with different political backgrounds always have to work together, and therefore top civil servants will look for compromise rather than simply pursuing their own agenda. For example, a ministry is usually headed by one minister and one or two junior ministers, all from different political parties, depending on the composition of the ruling coalition. So, even within one ministry, civil servants are faced with the need for compromise and coalition. A second explanation also points to consociational demands, but from a different perspective. This is the need to have all major parties represented, not only in politics (such as in a broad coalition) but also in the civil service and in the wider public sector. This explanation fits with the aforementioned need for a responsive civil service. Both lines of reasoning can also explain why in many cases Dutch ministers appoint top civil servants with a different party political background from their own (van der Meer, 2004: 216–17). A certain mutual understanding of policy problems is considered to be more important than a shared political affiliation. According to van der Meer, the recent appointment of some high-profile candidates—with a strong opinion on certain issues—points to a different type of politicization of civil servants. Civil servants have become policy entrepreneurs, rather than party entrepreneurs (Eichbaum and Shaw, 2010: 204).

To conclude, since the use of political advisers is still very limited in the Netherlands, Dutch civil servants are the most important advisers to ministers. The increased mobility within the civil service due to NPM and the introduction of the Senior Civil Service has raised the number of annual appointments. Officially, there is no room for political influence on these appointments; Dutch civil servants are expected to be neutral and competent. However, many (top) civil servants are members of political parties. Moreover, senior civil servants are expected to be responsive to their political principals and therefore have some degree of political awareness or sensitivity. However, this does not always mean that ministers and their top civil servants belong to the same political party.

SCOPE AND REACH OF PARTY PATRONAGE IN THE NETHERLANDS

Only a limited number of bodies are elected in the Netherlands: the lower house of parliament, twelve provincial parliaments, 430 municipal councils, and twenty-seven water boards. The upper house of parliament (Senate) is elected indirectly,

TABLE 13.1 *The index of party patronage in the Netherlands*

Policy area	Ministries	NDACs	Executing institutions	Policy area total
Economy	0.22	0.22	0.22	0.22
Finance	0.11	0.11	0.00	0.07
Judiciary	0.11	0.11	0.00	0.07
Media	n/a	0.22	0.22	0.22
Military and Police	0.22	0.17	0.00	0.13
Health Care	0.11	0.11	0.03	0.08
Culture and Education	0.11	0.11	0.00	0.07
Foreign Service	0.11	0.11	0.11	0.11
Regional and Local Administration	n/a	n/a	n/a	n/a
Total	0.14	0.15	0.07	0.12

Note: n/a scores for regional and local administration could not be calculated due to a lack of information

by the members of the provincial parliaments. All other public functions are appointed, including mayors and the commissioners of the queen (CQ), who are in charge of a province (Andeweg and Irwin, 2005: 77). Political parties cannot influence appointments directly, as most appointments are the prerogative of individual ministers. Table 13.1 therefore shows relatively low scores for most policy sectors and organizational types. However, the findings of this study will show that indirect influence is exerted extensively and in different ways by all Dutch parties.

Political parties that want to influence appointments have to exert influence on or through ministers, because most appointments to public and semi-public organizations are the prerogative of the parent minister—i.e. the minister who is in charge of the policy sector in which organizations are active. For example, all civil servants are formally appointed by the minister. In practice, ministers are only actively involved in the appointment of top civil servants like directors, directors general (DG) and secretaries general (SG). Lower-level appointments are mandated to the SG. As explained before, appointments of SGs and DGs fall under the ABD procedures and have to be co-signed by the minister of the Home Office.

The minister is also formally responsible for appointments of CEOs and/or members of non-executive boards in 89 per cent of the NDACs in the sample and 65 per cent of the executing institutions. But even when ministers cannot appoint directly, they have a large indirect influence. For example, if the appointment requires a Royal Decision (*Koninklijk Besluit*), the minister will nominate a candidate. This nomination is discussed in the Council of Ministers, after which the Queen will sign the appointment decision. As nominations are almost always followed, a minister still has extensive influence on who is appointed. And in cases

TABLE 13.2 *Formal appointment procedures in NDACs and executing institutions (N = 60 organizations)*

Appointment of CEO (N = 60)		Appointment of members of non-executive board (N = 30)	
Minister of parent ministry	45%	Minister of parent ministry	37%
Board of the organization	31%	Board of the organization	23%
Royal Decision	14%	Royal Decision	40%

when an appointment is the prerogative of the (non-executive) board, the minister is usually involved in or responsible for the appointment of the board members (cf. Table 13.2).

There are two noteworthy exceptions to the ministerial prerogative of appointments. Appointments to the High Council (the highest court) and the Netherlands Court of Audit have to be approved by parliament. These are the only appointments which are directly influenced by political parties.

The Dutch respondents rate the influence of the minister statistically significantly lower than the formal procedures suggest (t-test, $p<.001$). They claim that political influence is exerted most frequently in appointments within ministries (86 per cent of respondents), in the majority of NDACs (76 per cent of respondents), but much less in executing institutions (49 per cent of respondents). This different assessment can sometimes be attributed to a lack of knowledge about specific organizations and their statutes, but more generally these respondents state that the formal role of the minister is no more than a rubber stamp on the nomination or selection of the best candidate—prepared by the administration and/or professional headhunting agencies. According to these respondents, the minister's signature on the appointment decision is only a formality and can therefore not be interpreted as patronage. Moreover, all respondents agree that ministerial influence is limited to top-level appointments only (directors, CEO, DG, SG, boards of NDACs and executing institutions).

The (direct) influence of political parties on appointments is also rated very low by the experts (mean 0.34, in which 0 = no and 1 = yes—cf. Table 13.3 below). More specifically, respondents agree that if political parties can exert influence at all, it is only through appointing ministers and then only if they belong to the same party. Some ministers are more susceptible to such influence than others, according to respondents, but this is more an individual characteristic rather than linked to a specific party background. However, this does not mean that political parties are not interested in appointments; political parties are very interested, but only in certain appointments, in specific (types of) organizations and/or sectors.

SECTORAL DIFFERENCES

There are large differences between sectors in the interest of political parties in appointments, according to the respondents. But even within a sector, not all functions are equally interesting for parties. Some positions and organizations are rated as more politically salient, for example because of the size of the organization (in terms of budget), its visibility (in the media and political debate), its accident-prone nature, or because of its prestige. Important regulatory authorities like the Financial Market Authority (AFM) and the Dutch Health Care Authority (NZa), and long-standing institutionalized advisory bodies like the Socio-economic Council (SER) are highest on the wish list of political parties. Table 13.3 provides an overview of the answers of respondents (not indexed as in Table 13.1). The table shows the varying degrees of political influence in the different sectors. According to the respondents, political parties are most keen to influence in the following policy sectors: Foreign Service and developmental aid, Economy, Regional and Local Administration, Culture and Education, and Health Care. In addition, the interviews revealed that parties' interest is generally limited to top-level appointments. They focus more on organizations that are closer to government. Appointments in ministries attract more attention than appointments in NDACs, which in turn are more interesting to parties than appointments in executing institutions.

TABLE 13.3 *The index of party patronage, per sector (N = 49 respondents)*[a]

	Formal (0–1)	Expert opinion (0–1)	Party can influence (0–1)	Role of parties (0–1)	How many institutions (0–2)	Which level (0–3)
Economy	0.93	0.93	1.00	0.4	2.00	1.00
Finance	1.00	0.67	0.33	0.22	0.78	0.56
Judiciary	1.00	0.67	0.33	0.00	0.87	0.53
Media	1.00	0.33	1.00	1.00	1.67	1.00
Military and Police	1.00	0.54	0.25	0.33	1.11	0.72
Health Care	1.00	0.72	0.72	0.00	0.72	0.72
Culture and Education	0.67	0.75	0.75	0.17	0.92	0.75
Foreign Service	1.00	1.00	0.80	0.53	1.07	0.80
Regional and Local Administration	1.00	0.83	0.50	0.40	0.60	0.40
Overall	0.96	0.67	0.60	0.34	1.05	0.70

[a] Two respondents were interviewed for general background information, not about specific sectors

Economy and Foreign Service

In the case of the Economic policy sector, respondents often refer to the appointment of SER members and the appointment of a number of market regulators like NMA as examples of appointments in which political parties/actors are most interested. In fact, the composition of the SER reflects the power distribution in parliament as far as the Crown Members are concerned; each party has its share of Crown Members.[4] These organizations are all examples of high-profile NDACs.

In the field of foreign affairs, parties are interested in (a) the diplomatic service and (b) the Ministry for Developmental Aid. The diplomatic service is a typical career service, where officials have to rise through the ranks—moving from less interesting posts to more prestigious ones. Candidates all come from a homogeneous, closed, and generally traditional or conservative network, despite recent attempts to diversify (by including more women, and candidates of varying academic and ethnic backgrounds). Outsiders are appointed occasionally, but respondents have mentioned several high-profile examples of appointments of ambassadors or international representatives (with the UN or the EU) as a reward for loyal party members. Career diplomats will not openly express discomfort with such appointments (because of their loyalty to the minister) but such appointments are frowned upon. The reader should note that diplomats are civil servants who have alternating jobs at the ministry and abroad. Formally, the ABD is involved in the top-level appointments (SG and DG), but in practice the pool of candidates is limited to candidates with prior work experience in the ministry and in the diplomatic service. Hence, in the diplomatic service the influence of the ABD over appointments is constrained.

Political parties are also very interested in appointments to development aid organizations because these are overseen by a 'spending' ministry, and money is spent on a good cause. There are few political risks and many political gains in this field. Moreover, the position of the minister of development aid is a prestigious one, according to the respondents, because of its international character.

Broadcasting

Despite the low score for media overall, the broadcasting subsector is reported by many respondents—also experts from other sectors—as the sector with the highest degree of influence by political parties and actors. Broadcasting is a relatively small sector, but it has many remnants of the Dutch history of pillarization; there are several broadcasting associations, most of which are based on ideological and religious convictions. These are private organizations, but funded by the government based on the number of members. The government (i.e. the minister) cannot influence appointments to these private organizations, but one can find many (former) politicians on their boards. According to respondents, the networks of these board members offer access to the political arena and other resources which are considered valuable to the broadcasting company. This type of bottom-up patronage is known as 'patronage from the demand side' (Blakeley, 2001).

The minister is involved in appointments to the public broadcasting company as well as to other NDACs in this sector. In 2000, the Dutch broadcasting sector was reorganized and one new public broadcasting company, NPO, was established. Appointments to the non-executive board of NPO became the minister's prerogative. Before, all broadcasting associations had representatives on the board. The appointment of the CEO became the prerogative of the non-executive board. All respondents agree that the appointment of the most recent CEO of NPO is a typical (and the first) example of a competence-based selection and appointment.

Despite the reduction in the influence of private broadcasting associations and political parties due to the new appointment procedure, political parties remain very interested in vacancies in this sector. Respondents have given several examples of attempts to influence appointments, for example by proposing candidates or trying to find out which candidate(s) had been selected.

Health Care, Education and Culture

In the fields of Health Care, and Education and Culture, respondents report high interest of political parties in appointments. This, however, applies only in the ministry, and not at all or much less in NDACs and executing institutions. This creates a somewhat mixed picture for these sectors (cf. Table 13.3).

In the case of Health Care, another type of 'patronage' seems to be at play as well: the representation of different interests. Several respondents referred to recent appointments of candidates who were selected because of their affiliation with, for example, patient federations, groups of medical professions, welfare or home care organizations, and so on. This kind of 'distribution' of positions is an important instrument in Dutch politics to obtain support (*draagvlak*) for new policies and political decisions, fitting with the tradition of consociationalism. This type of distribution is also applied in the case of appointments to advisory bodies in all parts of the public sector, including, for example, the aforementioned SER (Economic sector).

Similar to the broadcasting sector, the educational sector is characterized by a strong history of pillarization. There is a system of public schools which are governed by the government, and 'private' schools which are governed by private foundations but paid for by the state. As of the late 1980s, the national government has delegated many competencies to municipalities and school boards. Municipalities in turn have turned public schools into local NDACs, to avoid a conflict of interest with their responsibilities for implementing educational policies for all schools in their community (both public and private). Consequently, the Dutch education system is nowadays characterized by a high degree of autonomy for all educational institutions. The influence of the minister and the ministry has diminished over time, including on appointments—that is, in public institutions; they never had any influence on appointments in private institutions. A second characteristic resulting from this history is that religion-based political parties still have strong linkages to religion-based schools and school boards. As in the field of broadcasting, many (former) politicians are members of (non-executive) boards. Earlier, this was referred to as patronage from the demand side (Blakeley, 2001).

The Cultural sector has a very different background from the Education sector; culture has always been a non-political matter. As a result, there has never been much political interest in policies on art and/or cultural institutions, except for financial aspects.

Military, Judiciary, and Finance

According to the respondents, appointments in the Military, Judiciary and Financial sectors are considered the least prone to political influence. In these sectors a career-based system determines one's possibilities to be appointed; one has to have a certain background, prior training, and experience. This precludes appointments of outsiders and appointments for purely political reasons. It also constrains the influence of the ABD on top-level appointments; the pool of candidates is limited to those with prior experience in the same sector.

Examples of appointments in these sectors include the Central Bank, the Prosecution Office and the courts. Members of the judiciary are seldom members of political parties, or at least not openly, according to the respondents. In the military, respondents state that 'it is not your political colour that determines to what position you are appointed, but the colour of your uniform'. This refers to the different colours of the uniforms of the air force, navy, ground forces, and military police.

Regional and local government

At the subnational level, two observations deserve attention. First, a number of positions are elected, like local councils and water boards. Second, in recent years national political parties have lost influence on appointments in municipalities and provinces, but have gained (potential) influence in the water boards. Because of the large size of this 'sector' and the limited number of respondents, it is difficult to draw conclusions about NDACs and executing institutions. The discussion is therefore limited to appointments to the top level of local government.

Provincial and municipal councils are elected directly. Both local divisions of national political parties and local political parties participate in these elections. Based on the results, the largest parties will form a coalition and appoint the executives. At provincial level, executives are referred to as delegates, at municipal level as aldermen. As at the national level, a coalition of at least two parties is always called for to obtain majority support in the council. Executives cannot hold a seat in the council (dualism). At provincial level the delegates and the CQ form the collegial executive; at local level the mayor and aldermen form the collegial executive body.[5]

Like coalition negotiations, the selection of aldermen, delegates, CQs, and mayors takes place behind closed doors. Therefore, it is difficult to obtain hard facts about the influence of political parties. Aldermen and delegates are nominated by political parties. Most of them are members of the political parties that participate in the ruling coalition. In recent years the number of 'independent' aldermen has gone up slightly (estimates vary between 6 per cent and 25 per cent). Mayors and CQs are appointed by Royal Decision and considered to be neutral, even though they usually have a political background, like being a former (junior) minister or MP. National political parties once held a strong influence over the appointment of mayors and CQs. In fact, there used to be a distribution formula for mayoral appointments; based on the number of seats in parliament, parties were 'entitled' to a share of mayoral appointments. However, as of the late 1990s, local councils gained more influence over the selection procedure for CQs and mayors. At local level, a selection and appointment committee is established, consisting of local councillors. They interview and select a candidate, who is then nominated to the minister of the Home Office. National political parties are thus excluded from the procedure. This has already led to a shift in the distribution of mayoral positions, particularly in the four largest cities, Amsterdam, Rotterdam, Utrecht, and The Hague. These positions are no longer distributed between the three largest parties, but dominated by the Social Democratic PvdA.

Water boards are an exceptional form of government, not only because of their task but also because they are one of the very few elected bodies in the Netherlands. Water boards were established from the 1200s onwards to safeguard the country against flooding. Because of this important task, they were given independence from the national administration, so that they could function even in times of war and crisis. There are now twenty-seven water boards, which are responsible for clean tap water and safe waterways in their region. A water board is governed by a board and an executive.

The executives of the water boards are called *dijkgraaf* or *hoogheemraad*; these executives are appointed by Royal Decision. Board members have always been subject to election. At first, only landowners had voting rights. Later on, inhabitants of the region who pay water board levies (*ingezetenenomslag*) were also given voting rights. Most board members were representatives of local government, business, and local or national interest groups. Since 2004, there have been general elections for the water boards. In 2008, national political parties participated in the elections for the first time, but they have a hard time finding candidates to fill water board positions. Voters also show little interest; the turnout in the last elections was a mere 24 per cent. It is therefore too soon to draw conclusions about

264   *Sandra van Thiel*

the influence of political parties on water boards, but the advent of general elections has at least increased the opportunities for patronage.[6]

To conclude, the influence of national political parties—either directly or through their minister—has diminished at the local and regional levels. First of all, this influence never reached any deeper than the top level anyway; the minister of the Home Office is involved in the appointment of the CQ and the mayor, but not in the appointment of executives or the top civil servants (the secretary of a province or municipality). Second, the right to appoint in this 'sector' has been delegated to the authorities at the local level and/or the non-executive boards of organizations. Third, although the introduction of general elections for the water boards has increased the influence of political parties because they can take part in the elections, it has proven difficult to find interested and competent candidates.

MOTIVES FOR PARTY PATRONAGE

Figure 13.1 shows the motives that respondents have mentioned for political parties and political actors to influence appointments. It is difficult to generalize about the motives; most respondents state that for one organization one motive can be important, and in another organization another motive. Hence, the answer 'both reward and control' is the largest category.

Although many respondents mention examples of appointments for reward reasons only, these examples are said to be exceptions. This is reflected in the fact that most respondents mention the same (well-known) examples, for example

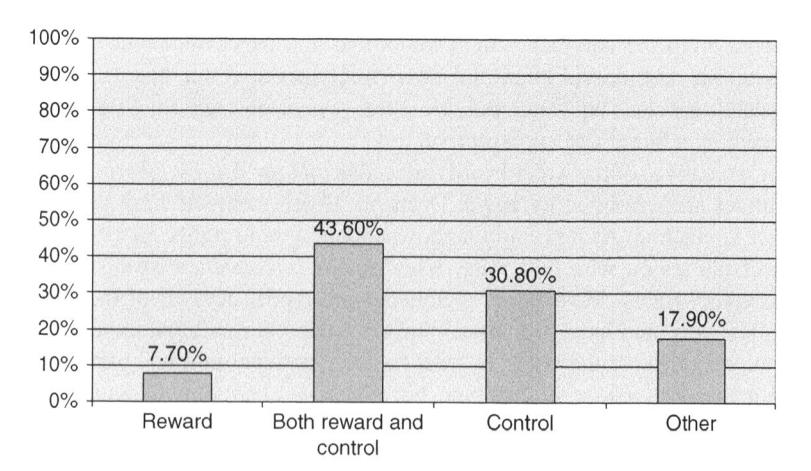

FIGURE 13.1 Motivations for party patronage in the Netherlands

Party Patronage in the Netherlands 265

of a former minister or member of parliament (MP) being appointed as the CEO of an important regulatory authority, or as the mayor of a municipality. Moreover, respondents stress that even in those examples appointees are also considered to be competent, making it difficult to determine which motive was decisive to their appointment.

The single motive that is mentioned most often by the respondents refers to the control that political parties or ministers hope to gain by appointing a trustee to a certain position. Because of the inherent trust in an appointee from the same party, parties and ministers hope to have easy access to information—through the mutual network lines. Also, it is assumed that the appointee will carry out the task in a way that fits with the beliefs or plans of the appointer and/or the political party. However, many respondents also state that it is not uncommon for an appointee to do just the opposite, to demonstrate their independence and disprove that they are appointed because of their political affiliations—because appointees fear that they would not be considered competent. Members of non-executive boards and CEOs will act in the best interest of the organization they serve, rather than in line with the party programme.

Other motives that are mentioned (18 per cent) include, for example, the appointment of personal friends or former colleagues/associates. Again, the implicit trust and familiarity between appointer and appointee is decisive to such decisions. On occasion, respondents mentioned examples of an appointment as 'getting rid' of someone—for example, a minister who cannot get along with a top civil servant may appoint him or her to another position, outside the ministry.

Despite the existence of different motives for party patronage, almost all respondents (96 per cent, see Figure 13.2) agree that the most important criterion

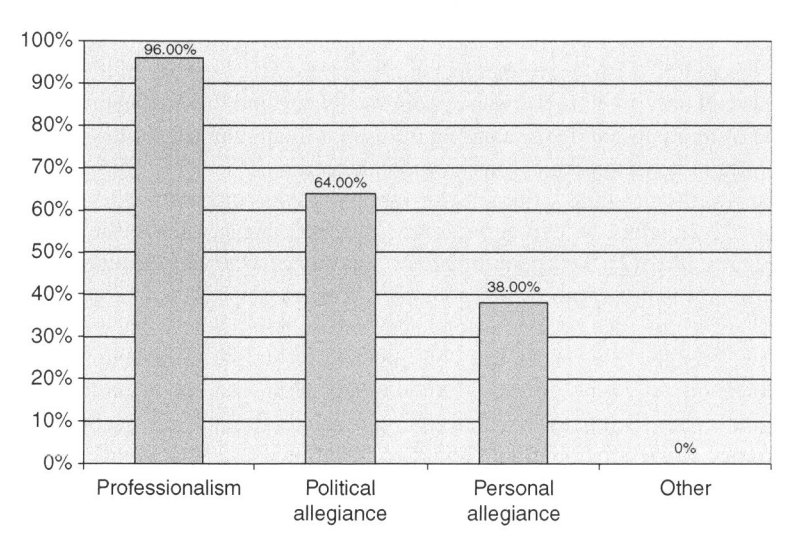

FIGURE 13.2 Qualifications of appointees in the Netherlands

for appointments is competence (professionalism). However, competence can take on different forms. Before the advent of NPM, it referred to substantive knowledge of a sector, and included having network contacts. Nowadays, top-level officials are primarily expected to have managerial skills. About half of the respondents appreciate this change, but the other half consider it to be a change for the worse. The latter half of respondents point to the memory loss of the government, the constant need for (structural) change, and a short-term focus—enhanced by the increased mobility of top-level officials under the influence of the ABD—which leads to the destruction of knowledge, organizations, networks, and traditions, to inefficiency and to poor policy. Respondents who consider the managerialization and increased mobility of civil servants a good development point to the benefits of the influx of new ideas (fresh eyes, innovations) and the improvement in the management of public organizations (application of new techniques, such as performance indicators).

The second most important motive for appointments is political allegiance (64 per cent of respondents). This can take on different forms, but is not necessarily related to party membership. A first form of political allegiance as mentioned by respondents is responsive competence (see above); top-level officials in public and semi-public organizations have to have a degree of sensitivity for political matters to be able to serve their political principal. A second form of political allegiance as mentioned by respondents refers to the fact that many (top) public officials are strongly oriented to and interested in the public cause or the public interest, which is why they want to work in the public sector. This type of allegiance is often related to a specific sector or policy, and was described above as policy entrepreneurship. A third form of political allegiance is party membership. Party membership among top civil servants is quite common (cf. above), but seldom brought out in the open, either by the candidates themselves, or during the selection and assessment procedure. All respondents agree on the prevalence of such discretion. Also, party membership does not always work in a candidate's favour. Not only are pure partisan appointments rare and frowned upon, but in the words of many respondents: a strong minister will appoint candidates *from other parties* to create a system of checks and balances.

The third and final criterion for appointments (personal allegiance, see Figure 13.2) refers to two processes: (1) appointments of former associates/ colleagues; and (2) the appointment of candidates who are 'known' for their performance and viewpoints (cf. policy entrepreneurship). This motive was mentioned by a minority of the respondents, and seldom as a decisive or singular motive. Personal allegiances can contribute to the selection or nomination of a candidate in two ways. First, candidates are selected from a familiar (party) network before being assessed and/or appointed. Second, an appointer gives preference to the most familiar candidate from the shortlist of competent candidates. In both cases, personal allegiances play a role, but only in combination with other qualifications.

To conclude, party patronage is clearly present in the Netherlands. When asked, 91 per cent of the respondents stated that Dutch political parties have a strong tradition of distributing and sharing appointments. However, political allegiances are usually influential in an indirect way, and it is not uncommon for appointer and appointee to belong to different political parties. This fits with the Dutch tradition of consociationalism, in which coalition cabinets seek consensus and societal support to accommodate different viewpoints and/or create internal systems of checks and balances (Randeraad and Wolffram, 2001). The distribution of appointments is most visible in the (representative) composition of advisory bodies and non-executive boards, but also in the appointment of top civil servants.

THE ROLE OF POLITICAL PARTIES

Although political parties cannot influence appointments directly, most respondents mention that parties are very actively engaged in exerting indirect influence. Parties have geared their party organization towards keeping track of vacancies and pushing candidates from their own networks. Table 13.4 shows who—within the parties—is in charge of this task.

Most parties have charged one of their MPs with the task of keeping track of vacancies and selecting potential candidates from the party network. This MP is known as the 'party lobbyist' (43 per cent of the respondents are familiar with this person/function). Originally, the party lobbyist was in charge of selecting and pushing candidates for mayoral appointments. As explained before, during the times of pillarization, political parties had a strict distribution formula for mayoral positions, especially in the four largest cities of the Netherlands (Amsterdam, Rotterdam, Utrecht, The Hague). Depillarization and delegation of appointing powers to local councils have reduced the influence of national parties, and hence of the party lobbyist. This, however, has not meant that parties are less interested in appointments or less active in obtaining their share of appointments. On the contrary, respondents mentioned several examples of (recent) activities by

TABLE 13.4 *In political parties, who is in charge of appointments?*

	Mentioned by number of respondents
Party lobbyist	21 (43%)
Party network	7 (14%)
Spokesmen in parliament	6 (12%)
Minister	5 (10%)
Party leader	3 (6%)
Members of parliament	2 (4%)
Do not know	5 (10%)

the party lobbyist and other party members, including an expansion of lobbying to functions in NDACs and executing institutions. Also, respondents referred to new party initiatives such as making inventories of potential candidates for all kinds of political, party, and public functions, and the creation of talent-scouting committees that assess the capabilities of proposed candidates and interested party members. These examples were not limited to CDA, which is traditionally known as being active on this matter (see below), but also included parties such as the VVD and PvdA.

It is not always clear—including for respondents—which other actors are involved in selecting, nominating, and pushing candidates from the party network (see Table 13.4). The information about vacancies is spread throughout the whole network, at different occasions (meetings). Party leaders, ministers, spokespersons, and individual party members can all contribute to the spread of information, either about upcoming vacancies or about potential candidates. In some cases, candidates take the initiative themselves and approach the party to ensure that they will be supported when applying for a position. In that respect, it is important to note that party members, in particular the party lobbyist, do not only play a role in supporting nominations, but also in discouraging candidates who are not believed to be sufficiently competent for the position or when the distribution mechanism will favour candidates from other parties. In both cases the party will try to discourage candidates to avoid loss of face or reputation, both for the party and for the candidates.

Parties differ strongly in how active they are in this respect, and also how well organized they are in the way they go about it. The Christian Democrat Party, CDA, was mentioned by about one-third of the respondents as the most successful party when it comes to obtaining a share of appointments. There are different explanations for this success. The size and governing tradition of the party were mentioned most often; CDA has the highest number of seats in parliament (until 2010), and has been in office for over eighty years—except in the 1990s, when two consecutive cabinets were formed without CDA. According to the respondents, this absence of power has traumatized the party, and has led to a severe loss of appointment opportunities. As a result, according to these respondents, CDA members have been very active in pushing and appointing candidates from their party since their return to power after 2000. But CDA is also applauded by respondents for being a 'governors' party', which has a strong tradition of supplying good candidates for board and CEO positions. Moreover, CDA is well reputed for its system of keeping track of upcoming vacancies and potential candidates. Other political parties are reported to be less interested and less active, either because party patronage does not fit with their (liberal) viewpoints (e.g. D66, VVD), because their party network is less coherent, or because they are small parties without the resources to supply candidates and/or keep track of interesting positions (e.g. SP, GL). Almost all respondents agree, however, that in the Dutch system no party is excluded from the opportunity to obtain a share of appointments. However, parties do have to be acknowledged by other parties as being trustworthy, i.e. being stable or durable and well organized. New parties such as the SP and PVV will therefore have to wait a while before they can enter into the distributive system of appointments.

The recent expansion and increase in party activities to influence appointments is induced by a number of trends that have reduced the influence of national parties (see Table 13.5). The aforementioned delegation of appointing powers to local-level parties ('decentralization') is mentioned most often by respondents (27 per cent of the answers) as a cause for the reduction in the influence of national parties. A second important trend is the increased professionalization of selection and appointment procedures (13 per cent). The use of headhunting agencies and assessments in the selection of candidates reduces the chances of candidates to be appointed because of their political allegiance. Political parties who push candidates for certain positions will have to make sure that their candidates are qualified and competent, and even then they cannot be certain that they are the best candidate, who will 'win' the selection.

The professionalization of the appointment procedures fits with the rise of NPM (23 per cent). Moreover, because of NPM, the managerial competencies of candidates are becoming more and more important. In the Dutch system, political functions are not always seen as executive or managerial, which probably explains why a number of respondents have said that this has reduced the appointment opportunities for former politicians.

A very recent change in appointment practices is the gender debate. The number of women in top positions in the Dutch public sector is very low. Therefore, the cabinet that was in office at the time of this study (mid-2008 to mid-2009) issued policies to appoint more women. One example is the announcement by the minister of the Home Office that the next police head commissioner had to be a woman, or else the minister would not appoint the nominated candidate. Respondents are generally sympathetic to the debate, although some question the effectiveness of such measures.

TABLE 13.5 *Changes in appointment practices*

	Mentioned by number of respondents[a]
Decentralization of appointments	16 (27%)
Managerialism (NPM)	14 (23%)
Gender debate	9 (15%)
Professionalization of procedures	8 (13%)
Parties have become more active	4 (7%)
More mobility within the sector	4 (7%)
Shorter terms of appointment	2 (3%)
No changes	2 (3%)
Other	1 (2%)

[a] Respondents could give more than one answer

To conclude, Dutch political parties have geared their party organization towards obtaining their share of appointments in the distributive system. The whole party network, but most importantly the party lobbyist, is involved in spreading information about vacancies and candidates. However, it has become more difficult to push candidates for certain positions because appointing powers have been decentralized and appointment procedures have been professionalized. Parties have responded by increasing their focus (also looking into appointments in the semi-public domain) and instruments (new activities like scouting committees).

CONCLUSION

So far, both the academic literature and the formal government story tell us that patronage does not exist in the Netherlands. Competence is said to be the sole criterion for appointments (van der Meer, 2004). And when political allegiances play a role—like in advisory boards—the distribution of appointments between members of different parties is said to serve the accommodation of ideological differences and to obtain societal support for policies and decisions rather than serve party political motives (Randeraad and Wolffram, 2001). The findings of this study show a different picture. Political parties are actively engaged in obtaining their share of appointments and have geared their organization towards this end, most notably by appointing party lobbyists. Exercising influence over appointments is used to gain control by appointing trustees, and sometimes to reward political activists. In both cases, though, competence is required for the candidate to be eligible for an appointment.

There are many opportunities to influence appointments because there are so many appointed positions in the Dutch state and semi-public domain (Andeweg and Irwin, 2005). Most of these appointments are a ministerial prerogative. Political parties can therefore only exert indirect influence by influencing the appointing minister, by spreading information about vacancies in the party network, and by supporting their own candidates. However, there are no guarantees that this indirect influence will be successful. First of all, not all parties are equally active in this respect. Second, ministers are not equally susceptible to influence. Third, appointment powers for a large number of positions have been decentralized out of the reach of national parties. Fourth, selection and assessment procedures have been professionalized, making it more difficult to influence the outcome. And finally, but in the Dutch tradition very importantly, it is not uncommon for ministers to appoint candidates with a different party background from their own. This is explained by the need to share appointments between parties (Baakman, 2004), to maintain consensus, to create checks and balances, and to facilitate (future) coalition formation.

The findings also show that political parties are not interested in all functions; they have clear preferences for appointments to certain sectors (Economy, Foreign Service, Broadcasting) and to certain types of organizations (top civil service, regulatory authorities, advisory bodies). This would suggest that parties become more interested in appointments as positions come closer to the government. The main motive for parties to influence appointments is to obtain control over organizations and/or policy sectors. However, there is some evidence that appointees will often deviate from party lines to prove that their appointment is not the result of patronage, but solely based on competence. Appointments for pure reward reasons are generally frowned upon, although they do occur incidentally.

Recent trends like NPM have negatively affected the possibilities for parties to exert influence on appointments. Parties have responded by increasing both their focus (also looking into appointments in the semi-public domain) and instruments of party patronage (new activities like scouting committees). Whether parties will succeed in maintaining their 'share' of appointments remains to be seen, however, because new parties like PVV and SP will join the distributive system as soon as they prove themselves to be stable and trustworthy political partners.

NOTES

1. It is important to note that the left–right distinction in the Netherlands is not based on conservative versus liberal thinking, but on being more (right) or less (left) opposed to governmental intervention (Andeweg and Irwin, 2005: 59). Thus the liberal party, VVD, is considered a right-wing or conservative party.
2. In 2009, approximately 2.1 million people were working in (parts of) the public sector (Ministerie BZK, 2009).
3. Approximately 35 per cent of the directors of organizations in the Dutch sample are members of the ABD.
4. SER is the official advisory body on socio-economic affairs. The tripartite composition includes representatives of employers' federations, trade unions, and Crown members who represent the government/polity. Interestingly, it is not the Minister of Economics who appoints these members, but the Minister of Social Affairs (SZW).
5. While ministers at the national level have an individual responsibility and can therefore be dismissed individually by parliament, the executives at municipal and provincial level have collegial responsibility. An individual alderman or delegate cannot be forced to resign by the local council, although they can voluntarily leave their position. After resignation or termination of the ruling coalition, they cannot reclaim their seat on the council. The principle of dualism was implemented at local level in 2002 (when it replaced monism).
6. In 2011, the government decided that from 2014 on water boards would be elected indirectly, by the members of the municipal council.

CHAPTER 14

Appointments to Public Administration in Norway: No Room for Political Parties?

Elin Haugsgjerd Allern

INTRODUCTION

Norway has a strong democratic tradition, in which political parties have usually played a vital role, but the power of parties to appoint individuals to positions in public and semi-public life has remained a largely unexplored aspect of government in Norway (Sørensen, 2005; Strøm and Narud, 2006).[1] On the one hand, it has been argued in Norwegian public debate that, historically, political appointments have occurred, and not least during the immediate post-war era known as the 'single party state' (Seip 1963): allegedly, the dominant Labour party tended to give some attractive government posts—like top leader positions of directorates—to party members. On the other hand, comparative scholarly literature has generally viewed Norway as a country where the role of parties, including partisanship, in connection with public appointments has been very limited or non-existent, mainly due to strong and professionalized bureaucratic traditions (see e.g. Müller, 2006b: 189). Yet the argument that patronage is virtually non-existent under such conditions is not empirically well founded, which in turn reflects the undeniable methodological difficulty of studying patronage. This chapter will systematically explore the relationship between party government, bureaucratic autonomy, and appointments to public administration in Norway.

As throughout this volume, the key issue is to what extent, within public administration and semi-public institutions, political parties—*de jure* and de facto—control the allocation of positions. Do relatively tight formal constraints on appointments leave any space for 'party patronage'—for the political parties to appoint individuals, as a tool to enhance their organizational capacity within the state? The empirical section of the chapter is divided into two main parts. The first specific concern is to describe, based on the constitution, relevant laws and regulations, the formal rights of the (parties in) government to appoint to positions in the Norwegian state administration; the second is to map the practice of appointments along the dimensions of scope (range) and reach (depth) by means of the expert survey (presented in Chapter 2). The local administration of two major cities will be included in order to shed light on the relative importance of the national and local levels of the state for political appointments. The state structure of Norway is unitary but formally somewhat decentralized (Lijphart, 1999: 189; but see Østerud, Engelstad, and Selle, 2003: 106ff).

Yet it should be noted that the applied concept of 'patronage' potentially includes appointments made by means of due process and transparency, and it does not presuppose any specific selection criteria (see Chapter 2). The question is first whether public administration is politicized—made political in character—in the sense that politicians actually appoint by undertaking an active choice between candidates. To capture the distinction between further politicization and party politicization, the analysis follows up by distinguishing between the individual minister, the cabinet, and the party as appointing political agents, and by mapping the agents' motivations and selection criteria. I also explore the extent to which appointments are made in a 'majoritarian', as opposed to a more 'consensual', manner. Finally, the chapter examines possible changes in the government's appointment patterns over time, and it concludes by discussing what 'party patronage' might mean in the Norwegian context. My major argument is that appointments to important positions in the state administration are related to government, but less to *party* government in Norway. However, I start by describing the position of parties between society and government and the executive/civil service traditions of Norway to see whether party patronage is more or less likely to exist in the Norwegian case.

POLITICAL PARTIES BETWEEN SOCIETY AND GOVERNMENT

Norway is a small unitary, parliamentary, and multiparty state.[2] The constitution remained silent on parties until 1983 (Heidar, 1991), but the country's party system is usually dated back to the struggle over constitutional reform and parliamentary democracy in the 1880s. Numerous externally created parties emerged, and programmatic party competition for votes developed. By the end of the 1920s, Norway's party system had become a firm structure divided by several cross-cutting cleavages (Rokkan, 1967: 327ff; Valen and Rokkan, 1974). For decades, Norway had one of the most stable party systems in Western Europe, with Labour party majority governments dominating post-war politics. Since the 1960s, the party system has usually comprised two main blocs divided along the left/right axis, but recent political changes have led to new conflict dimensions and a more open and fluid party system (Heidar, 2005: 807–33; Knutsen, 2004). The parties currently represented in the Storting (the Norwegian parliament) are: the Socialist Left (SV), the Labour party (DnA), the Centre Party (Sp), the Christian

People's Party (KrF),[3] the Liberals (V), the Conservatives (H), and the Progress Party (FrP).

All major parties eventually developed large membership organizations, and for a long time played a dominant role in sociopolitical mediation. Norway's parties still enjoy wide-ranging relationships with interest groups, even if they are not as close as in the past (Allern, 2010b). They are also able to control electoral processes and representation—based on proportional representation (PR) in the country's nineteen relatively small multi-member districts—at the local and regional as well as national levels. Candidate selection is the result of closed party conventions, and only in local elections may personal votes be given to individual candidates (Narud, 2008). The level of state subvention of parties is high, and the size of professional party staff has grown significantly in recent decades (Ot prp. no. 84, 2004–5; Allern, 2010a). However, since the late 1970s, aggregate electoral volatility has increased, and since 1990, the seven major parties together have lost more than half of their members (ibid.).

The fact that the government does not need the explicit support of a parliamentary majority (Bergman, 1993: 55–66) has encouraged the formation of several numerically weak governments (Strøm and Narud, 2006: 533)—but firmly organized parties, detailed party manifestos, and a high level of party discipline in the legislature and executive continue to make the executive–legislative relationship work in line with the model of party-based parliamentary government (Jensen, 2000; Strøm and Narud, 2006: 527ff). On the other hand, various governments experienced a growing number of parliamentary defeats in the wake of party system fragmentation, until a majority coalition was again formed in 2005 (Rommetvedt, 2003), and a more fragile chain of delegation and accountability has gradually developed in Norway (Strøm, Narud, and Valen, 2005). To some extent, party government is also weakened by a fairly strong degree of corporatism (Lijphart, 1999: 181), despite decay and increase of lobbyism in recent decades (Rommetvedt, 2005). Overall, Norway's political parties' traditionally strong bridge-building capacity between society and government seems to have declined of late.

THE EXECUTIVE, CIVIL SERVICE, AND POLITICAL PARTIES

Less clear is the institutional position of political parties in, and between, the executive and the civil service. Norway is a constitutional monarchy, but the monarch's duties as head of state are largely representative and ceremonial. The Norwegian cabinet enjoys extensive powers as the Council of State (*Statsråd*). Each cabinet member is usually administrative head of a specific ministry, and may not simultaneously serve as an MP. Individual ministers have final authority in all matters within their ministry's jurisdiction, and are constitutionally responsible for behaviour on their part towards the Storting (Strøm, 1994: 45–6; Strøm and Narud, 2006).

This said, all formal cabinet decisions are made weekly in the Council of State, at which the King is present. More substantive discussions take place, in the King's absence, at the preceding cabinet meetings or during informal cabinet luncheons (cf. Strøm, 1994: 41). Decision making is consensus-oriented, and ministers are expected not to sabotage cabinet decisions.[4] The prime minister's office has expanded over time,[5] and various mechanisms exist to contain 'agency losses' from the cabinet's point of view. Disciplined political parties remain perhaps the most efficient vehicle of oversight and control, and provide significant checks on government. There has never been a non-partisan administration since the introduction of parliamentarism in Norway; cabinets rarely include non-partisan ministers, and party policy obviously matters in cabinet negotiations (for details, see ibid: 50–4). The political staffs of the ministers include 'state secretaries' (*statssekretærer*) appointed by the Council of State, and personal advisers (*politiske rådgivere*) appointed by the office of the prime minister, usually coming from the same party as 'their' ministers.

The degree of political control—by parties—over the civil service is, however, disputed. The cabinet is 'the supreme, collective leadership of the central administration' (Strøm, 1994: 42), and the autonomy of the administration is limited by ministerial accountability (Pedersen and Lægreid, 1999: 353), even though the civil service includes a set of more autonomous and professional agencies (Egeberg, 1998: 5). The size of the political leadership—and its advisers—in the ministries nearly tripled between 1965 and 2005 (Statskonsult, 2007: 10); by 2009, there were sixty-seven political appointees in addition to the twenty ministers. Yet, with the establishment of more autonomous agencies and enterprises over the past twenty years, the degree of decentralization has increased, whereas the number of formal political appointees is still fairly low compared to the number of career civil servants (Christensen, 2005; Christensen and Lægreid, 2009). Moreover, the cabinet and its ministers enjoy few *ex post* institutional enforcement mechanisms over the bureaucracy (see Strøm and Narud, 2006: 545).[6]

Equally importantly, the basic hierarchical model—including *ex ante* control of the civil service through a constitutional prerogative to appoint civil servants—has traditionally not been seen as providing leeway for party patronage in Norway. The subordination of the administration following the introduction of parliamentary government was, as in many Western political systems, combined with the principle of separation of administrative careers from party political influences (Rouban, 2007: 202). Norway's civil service is meant to be professional, non-partisan, and permanent, reflecting the Weberian ideal of administrators as neutral and removed from politics, since 'future political leaderships, potentially originating from a competing political party, have to inherit the existing personnel'

(Egeberg, 1998: 5; see also Strøm and Narud, 2006: 545). The career civil servant has traditionally been a highly educated legal specialist (Christensen and Lægreid, 2009: 954), and the limited number of former political appointees wishing to become civil servants (again) must undergo a 'quarantine period' first (MD, 2005). The informal norms of 'good governance' indicate that the civil service should provide a balance between representing a stable, politically neutral, and impartial expertise on the one hand, and, on the other hand, serving as a loyal secretariat for whatever parties are in office, in addition to protecting legal norms like equality before the law (St. meld. no. 11, 2000–1: 10ff; Christensen and Lægreid, 2002: 98–9). In principle, we can distinguish between state ministers as politicians and as senior civil servants: they are legal heads and thus administrators and specialists, political generalists as cabinet members, and partisans as government representatives of particular parties (Strøm, 1994: 45; Christensen and Lægreid, 2002: 93).

Against this background of strong bureaucratic traditions and professionalized bureaucratic bodies, and as the Norwegian competition for votes is still mainly based on extensive policy platforms, not spoils (Shefter, 1994), Norway is widely seen as a country where the role of political parties in public appointments is very limited or non-existent. Indeed, the Nordic countries, with the exception of Iceland, are often thought to be relatively free of political appointments to public administration (Müller, 2006b: 189). Kopecký and Scherlis (2008) hypothesize that the scope of appointments by parties does not extend beyond the topmost positions in government in Scandinavia. According to Strøm et al. (2006: 661), partisanship plays no role in appointments to civil service positions and only a modest role in appointments to managerial positions in state enterprises in Norway (cf. Egeberg, 1998: 6; Strøm and Narud, 2006: 545, Hanretty, 2010; but see Grendstad, Shaffer, and Waltenburg, 2010).

However, even if it may be disloyal to give politicians advice based on other grounds than impartial expertise, the political role of being a constructive co-player for the minister and the administrative role of being politically neutral may conflict (Jacobsen, 1960; Eckhoff and Smith, 2006: 103–4). In reality, civil servants are not merely technical, apolitical administrators (St. meld. no. 11, 2000–1: 9–13). The various roles of a minister can also be difficult to distinguish from each other, and in recent years more teamwork has developed between politicians and civil servants at the top ministerial level (Christensen and Lægreid, 2002: 109; Statskonsult, 2007). Apparently, 'loyalty' has become more important at the expense of 'neutrality' for civil servants (St. meld. no. 11, 2000–1: 9), and now includes more (pro)active support of the minister, in the wake of, for example, mass media developments and greater emphasis on the ministry's role as secretariat of the executive political leadership (Innst. S. no. 175, 2000–1: 2); Christensen and Lægreid, 2002: 107–10). Interestingly, the proportion of top civil servants with a previous political career is generally low, but it has increased over time (Egeberg, 1998: 9–10).[7]

Hence, the Norwegian political system includes elements of both 'majoritarian' and 'consensus' democracy. Through their constitutional powers of appointment, the party-based cabinet has been able to control the civil servants *ex ante*, and fairly strong parties are able to constrain the ministers' appointments. But questions remain: has the hierarchical political-administrative model made actual political use of appointment powers superfluous, or more widespread? How much room and strong incentives actually exist for political and party political considerations to influence a government's appointments? Partisan appointments may jeopardize government efficiency and electoral support when the meritocratic systems of advancement have become a legal and uncontested norm (see Strøm et al., 2006: 664) and external pressure for bureaucratic autonomy might raise the cost to politicians of emphasizing political considerations (Shefter, 1994). But, as party organizations are weakened, 'delegation' and 'governance' become more widespread; and if external factors widen the grey area between politics and administration, parties and politicians may come to feel a greater need to interfere in appointments to administrative positions, so as to retain their grip on policy making (Kopecký and Mair, 2006: 9–10).

THE EMPIRICAL RECORD

In a long-term perspective, there has been an increase in the number of government officials in Norway. The curve peaked around 1994, and then decayed following a significant decline in the number of administrative agencies. But the number is still significant: as of 2008, there were more than 4,200 regular employees in Norwegian ministries, and about 135,000 in the state administration.[8] At the regional (county) and local (municipal) levels, the number of public sector employees is higher, and in sum, as many as 826,000—about 33 per cent of all Norwegian employees—worked in the public sector in 2008.[9] In addition, there are positions in various types of companies; the Kingdom of Norway owns shares in about eighty different corporations, with state ownership especially strong in the petroleum and hydroelectric energy sectors (NHD, 2008b). However, as we shall soon see, the government is entitled to appoint only to certain key positions in public and semi-public institutions.

Moreover, the focal point of the analysis will be administrative units, not individual positions. We distinguish between ministerial departments (ministries), non-departmental agencies and commissions (NDACs), and executing institutions within nine policy areas.[10] All individual units have been identified through the 'Norwegian State Administration Database' (NSA) of the Norwegian Social Science Data Services (NSD).[11] At the regional/local level, I explore appointment patterns in Norway's largest cities, Oslo and Bergen, municipalities which are not representative of the country's local governments and administrations as a whole, but are readily comparable with the national level, as they embody the characteristics of parliamentary government, and not the Alderman model. They attend to a broad spectrum of tasks, including primary education, primary health care, care for the young and elderly, and a number of other social welfare programmes.

The formal right to appoint, and administrative procedures

According to the constitution, the King—i.e. the Council of State—formally chooses and appoints all senior civil servants of the Crown (*embedsmenn*). A senior civil servant is any government official appointed by the Council of State and installed as a senior civil servant or an official who is temporarily appointed by the cabinet in a senior administrative post of the Crown (*embede*) (Constitution of the Kingdom of Norway: §21; Civil Service Act: §1).[12] These positions include the top-level and mid-level posts in the ministries (from secretary general to deputy director general or principal officer) as well as various key positions outside the ministries—in the Judiciary, the Foreign Service, the Military and Police, the Church of Norway, etc.[13] An ordinary civil servant (*tjenestemann*) is 'any employee of the Civil Service who is *not* a senior civil servant' (of the Crown) (Civil Service Act: §1). As the authority to appoint has increasingly been delegated to administrative top leaders, or a particular collegiate body, or boards of autonomous institutions (Civil Service Act: §5), only a small proportion of all government employees are senior civil servants in this sense today (Eckhoff and Smith, 2006: 94). Even so, the cabinet formally appointed an average of 359 people per year to such positions between 2001 and 2006 (St. meld. no. 10, 2006–7). Moreover, directors—senior civil servants—of ordinary, non-departmental civil service organizations are also usually appointed (*beskikket*) by the cabinet as a whole.

Other (lower-level) civil servants are administratively appointed by ministries, a particular collegiate body, or the board of the institution in question (Civil Service Act: §5).[14] However, members of permanent advisory committees and board members in civil service organizations with extended authority and in government administrative enterprises are often, in practice, also appointed by the Council of State (or individual ministers). Cabinet proposals on appointments are presented by the member within whose competence they fall, and are also discussed during the cabinet meetings and informal luncheons. Members of a few commissions and boards—like the Supervisory Council (*Representantskapet*) of Norway's central bank, the Arts Council of Norway (*Kulturrådet*), and the Broadcasting Council (*Kringkastingsrådet*)—are appointed by the Storting. Government-owned companies, hybrid companies established by special laws, and government limited companies are subject to special regulations regarding appointments, which to a greater or lesser extent may make possible appointments by the minister in charge.[15] In the municipalities of Oslo and Bergen, the power to appoint the top- and medium-level heads of the administrative departments, directors of non-departmental agencies, as well as members of the boards of municipal enterprises and companies, is delegated from the city council (*bystyret*) to the city government (*byrådet*) (Local Government Act; Personalhåndbok for Oslo kommune 2010; Personalreglement for Bergen kommune 2008). Hence, the legal framework allows appointments to key positions by the government in *all* the twenty-six institutional subtypes studied here.[16]

However, political parties as such do not enjoy the legal power to make appointments, and the formal room for genuine (party) political influence seems limited. All decisions regarding appointments are based on thoroughgoing administrative procedures specified in regulations (e.g. Reglement for personalforvaltningen i departementene 1998); such processes usually include public advertisement of vacancies, competitive interview processes, occasionally headhunting firms, and often nomination and/or appointment committees or boards (comprising employee representatives) (Statens personalhåndbok, 2010: ch. 2; Statskonsult, 2004; Civil Service Act: §4). Recruitment and promotion in the civil service are to be non-partisan or apolitical.[17] In both the state and local administration, nominations and appointments should be based on the 'qualification principle' (*kvalifikasjonsprinsippet*)—a principle that has become established through legal usage, administrative usage, and juridical theory, and can be ignored only by means of legal authority (see Civil Service Act: §7, §9, §13 for such exceptions). The main evaluation criteria are formal education, work experience, and personal suitability (for details, see Kroken, 2006).[18] As a general rule, civil servants are appointed on a permanent basis (Civil Service Act: §3), which formally protects against pressure to serve as the minister's political staff (cf. Hanretty, 2010: 84–5).[19] This said, increased use of fixed-term contracts outside ministries allows the government to use its power to appoint more frequently. Also, new special salary agreements for top administrative leaders—including acceptance of transfer if contractual results have not been achieved—may widen the legal room for 'reshuffling' (cf. Christensen and Lægreid, 2002: 110–14; see Statens personalhåndbok, 2010: 2.2.8.1–8.2). Let us now see whether the government actually uses its power to appoint, and what role the political parties play in such decision making.

Scope and reach of appointments by politicians

It cannot be taken for granted that state ministers act as party agents in appointment issues, especially not in systems where the formal room for party political influences is limited. Therefore, the first question is in practice, whether *politicians*—as opposed to bureaucrats—actually appoint individuals to positions in public administration. Answers from five sector expert interviews for each of the sub-policy area units have been recorded (see Chapter 2 for details on the survey material).[20] All respondents were asked to focus on the actions of the red/green coalition of Labour, the Centre Party, and the

Socialist Left Party 2005–9, but often found it reasonable to apply a somewhat wider time perspective. All composite measures aggregating survey results are based on median values. Calculations based on mode and mean showed that the choice of central tendency measure has no significant impact in general, although means yield more variation across sectors. Finally, it should be noted that even though some of the standardized table/figure titles that follow include the term 'party' in addtion to 'patronage', the figures based on Norwegian responses generally refer to the behaviour of politicans as opposed to bureaucrats (see above).

Looking only at the number of 'yes' answers to the question of whether politicians undertake an active choice before a formal decision is made, as a proportion of the total number of institutional subtypes in the state, the score indicates that politicians appoint to key positions in all the twenty-six institutional subtypes studied here.[21] Only a few experts, within a few sectors, think politicians simply rubber-stamp the ranking of candidates proposed by the bureaucrats to entire institution categories (ministries, NDACs, or executing institutions). The composite index of the scope and reach of patronage—presented in Table 14.1— uses individual institutions and organizational levels within the different policy areas as units of analysis. Whereas the scope of patronage refers to whether politicians actually appoint to all, most, or only a few institutions, 'reach' indicates how deeply within each category of institution the cabinet and its ministers may interfere—at one, two, or three levels (top, middle, low). The maximum aggregate score of 1 indicates that politicians appoint to all institutions and organizational levels examined, whereas a value of 0 indicates no such politicization of the state (see Chapter 2 for a complete explanation). The range of answers—i.e. the difference between the highest and lowest reported value for each question—is generally low; any significant differences will be mentioned in due course.[22]

TABLE 14.1 *The index of party patronage in Norway*[a]

Policy area	Ministries	NDACs	Executing institutions	Policy area total
Economy	0.33	0.33	0.22	0.30
Finance	0.33	0.22	0.33	0.30
Judiciary	0.33	0.33	0.11	0.26
Media	n/a	0.33	0.33	0.33
Military and Police	0.33	0.11	0.50	0.31
Health Care	0.33	0.33	0.22	0.30
Culture and Education	0.33	0.22	0.11	0.22
Foreign Service	0.33	0.33	0.11	0.26
Regional and Local Administration[b]	0.33	0.28	0.11	0.24
Total	0.33	0.28	0.23	0.28

[a] Proportional figures based on median values. Maximum possible absolute scores vary as follows: 9 (policy area/ institutional type), 27 (individual policy area sum), 72 (sum ministries), 81 (sum NDACs), 81 (sum executing institutions), 234 (total across policy areas). The Media area has a maximum score of only 18 as it has no separate ministerial department (currently under 'Culture and Education').

[b] The policy area 'Regional and Local Administration' refers only to the administrative units of the two largest cities in Norway: the municipalities of Oslo and Bergen.

According to Table 14.1, Norwegian politicians actually select appointees in about a third (0.28) of the institutional subunits/organizational levels in sum—a share that largely corresponds to, but does not exceed, the formal appointment powers of the government. Also, it is important to emphasize that the threshold applied for 'actually appoint' in this study does *not* equal total control. Norwegian politicians enjoy real veto power, but many respondents stress that due process and predefined qualification criteria constrain the extent to which they influence the early steps of the decision-making processes. A minister might, in theory, change the ranking order of final candidates, signal what kind of candidates he or she would prefer in advance, and, in some cases, even suggest specific names at the beginning of the procedure. But the usual role seems more passive, reshuffling of top leaders in ministries after an election is uncommon, and a minister is expected to take the administration's evaluation seriously and to emphasize professional qualifications.[23] Hence, the power of politicians is based on constrained selectivity. Equally important, sector experts do not fully agree on the extent to which politicians use their right to appoint, beyond making the final choice among candidates, which might reflect that some ministers try to strongly influence appointments, whereas others come closer to 'rubber-stamping' the administration's proposals. According to a few experts, the process of appointing ministerial secretaries general is increasingly being managed by the office of the prime minister.

From Table 14.1 we also see that there is variation in index scores across policy areas and institution categories. But does this variation primarily reflect differences in the scope or reach of political appointments? Table 14.2 clarifies that politicians make appointments to positions in a wide range of state institutions, but not at all organizational levels. The proportional score for scope of about 0.80 suggests that the government reaches into a large majority of Norway's ministerial departments, non-departmental agencies and commissions, and executing institutions. Whereas the reach of such appointments is less extensive across sectors: politicians only appoint in about a third of the possible instances, i.e. the uppermost level of state institutions.

TABLE 14.2 *Scope and reach of party patronage in state institutions in Norway*[a]

	Scope	Reach
Total score: all sectors	63.5	26.5
Max. possible score[b]	78.0	78.0
Proportion (of subtypes)	0.81	0.34

[a] Median scores were calculated for each institutional category in each policy area, added up for each sector, for the whole country, and then standardized.

[b] The maximum possible absolute score is 78, not 81, because for 'Media' there is no separate ministry (belongs under 'Culture and Education').

In the ministries, the top leadership includes the secretary general (*departmentsråd*) (with possible deputy), the director generals (*ekspedisjonssjefer*) of the departments of the given ministry, and usually a head of information. In the NDACs, politicians actually appoint director generals or commission members, whereas positions as senior civil servants (*embeder*) and board memberships are subject to 'patronage'—as defined here—in the executing institutions, according to most sector experts. Many of the latter units are largely autonomous or separate legal entities linked to the state through ownership. In government limited companies where the state owns a majority, a selection committee (elected by the general meeting or corporate assembly) nominates candidates to the board and the general meeting or corporate assembly makes the appointments, but it is assumed that the state minister, as the company's largest owner, is consulted before a proposal is made. However, this does not mean that politicians have entirely withdrawn from the appointment of general managers in former state enterprises. In recent years, we have, for example, seen political turbulence regarding the chief executive for Norway's major oil company, Statoil (Statoil-Hydro from 2007 to 2009) (*Aftenposten*, 2006). A question arising, based on the expert interviews, is whether situations occur in which it is hinted, informally, that the minister will try to change the board if the board does not change general manager.

More detailed analysis shows significant variation across institutional categories. All the ministries examined experience appointments by politicians, according to the experts, whereas fewer of the NDACs (about 0.80) and executing institutions (about 0.60) allegedly do. Policy area differences should be interpreted with caution, but vary between 0.67 (Culture and Education) and 1 (Media) in terms of scope. No marked differences are reported by the majority of the respondents regarding depth of appointments. Hence, the higher overall score of ministries (0.33) compared to other institutional categories, and the relatively low index score of the area Culture and Education (0.22), primarily reflect variation in the scope of appointments. Whereas the former difference might reflect the fact that NDACs and the executing institutions, in contrast to ministries, include some units of lesser importance as seen from a political perspective, the latter variation perhaps indicates that relatively more institutions here are less 'reachable' today: formally, the ministry appoints only a minority of the members of Norway's numerous university and college boards (four out of eleven). However, supposedly, only a few executing institutions experience appointments by politicians within areas as different in terms of formal structure as the Judiciary, Foreign Service, and Local and Regional Administration (Oslo and Bergen).

The role of the party in appointments by politicians

Next, one must ask whether these appointments can be seen as indirectly managed by parties in practice. With party patronage, the party as such must play an important

Appointments to Public Administration in Norway 283

role in political appointment-making by systematically seeking to coordinate public appointments as organizations, for political purposes. Figure 14.1 (N = 35) indicates how the sector experts evaluate the general importance of parties to appointments across sectors and institutional categories, using the individual respondent as the unit of analysis.[24]

On average, more than 90 per cent of those who did have an opinion—33 out of 35 experts—held that the party organization plays only a small role, if any at all: party organizations might in theory propose candidates when a vacancy opens up but do not control governmental administrative appointments through their parliamentary group and cabinet ministers. No significant variation seemingly exists between different policy areas (including Local and Regional Administration). Several experts emphasize that the government is party-based, and the minister is a partisan, but that this is not to say that parties as such exert influence over appointments—and some fear that Norwegian statements might be misinterpreted in an international setting.

Even the 'party in government' plays only a modest role in public appointments, according to the expert survey. In line with the constitutional framework, the interviewees tend to hold that actual appointment-making is mainly the domain of individual ministers, the prime minister, and, in a few cases, the cabinet as a whole, even though appointments are from time to time discussed in public by other 'faces' of the party, the opposition, and trade union leaders (see e.g. *Dagbladet*, 2009). As principals, the prime minister and the cabinet probably enjoy veto power as far as some key positions are concerned, but many

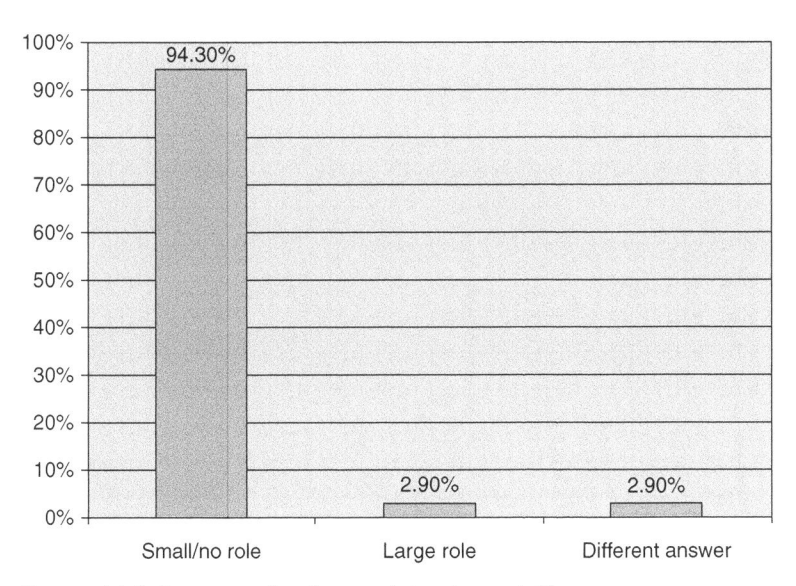

FIGURE 14.1 Importance of parties as such to patronage in Norway.

284   Elin Haugsgjerd Allern

respondents claim that the ministers usually decide on the positions within their purview. Finally, we can also note that to the extent that 'appointments by parties' occur, they involve only the party/ies in government: no sector expert has indicated that appointments are systematically shared by including opposition parties as well. In only very few instances are positions distributed among all parties according to party size or by the Storting itself—as in the case of the health trust and hospital boards,[25] the Broadcasting Council, and the Arts Council of Norway.[26]

Motivations for appointments by politicians

A third dimension is the motivations of politicians for making public appointments: do they use this power to serve goals like maintaining political control of the civil service and reward of partisans? Figure 14.2 (N = 40) shows the motivations underlying such appointments—as perceived and reported by the various sector experts. Whereas 'control' refers to attempts to ensure that the administration follows the various aims and instructions of the government and its ministers, 'reward' denotes appointments used to 'pay' loyal party members and activists.

We see that more than 70 per cent of the experts think that politicians engage in appointments for the wide purpose of control. However, even if many of them refer to efficient policy formulation and implementation, some also argue that politicians hereby look for trustworthy appointees simply 'to prevent administrative mistakes from being made' or because they generally believe in a 'particular type of leadership' in the public sector. Moreover, according to the respondents, increasing the gender balance in public administration serves as a widespread

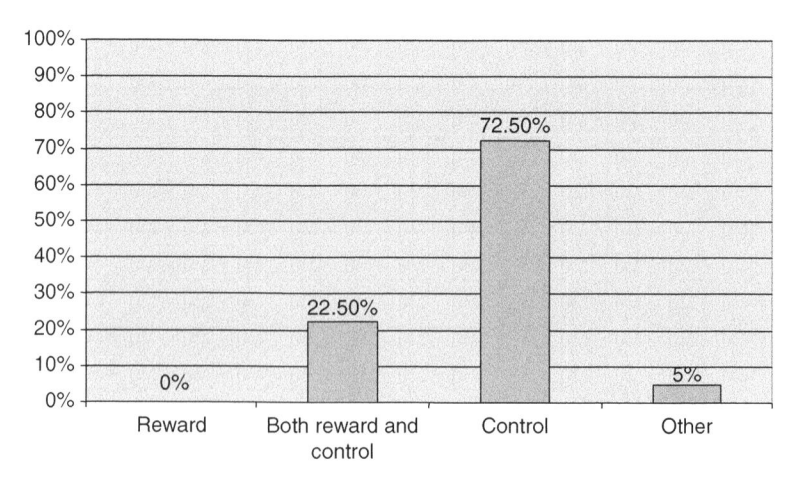

FIGURE 14.2 Motivations for party patronage in Norway

motivation across policy areas and parties, not least within traditionally male-dominated sectors like the Military and Police.

Interestingly, no sector expert responded that appointments are used solely to reward party members or activists by providing them with posts in the core civil service, or on the boards of autonomous institutions, or public or semi-public enterprises and companies. Only about 22 per cent gave the opinion that politicians are motivated by both reward and control. Moreover, those who argue that reward motives do exist tend to see them as occasional additions to the predominant motive of control. For example, it is argued that appointments to company boards may include an element of reward of partisans or individuals with similar policy views. Finally, only two out of forty respondents see 'other reasons' as the major driving forces: for instance, that politicians act out of some sort of 'constitutional necessity', or simply in order 'to provide a link between appointments and the elected bodies of democracy'.

More detailed analysis suggests that some differences might exist between sectors. Control is presented as the sole motive in the Foreign Service, the Military and Police, and in Regional and Local Administration. Appointments as reward are reported only within the areas of the Economy, Finance, Media, Health Care, and Culture and Education, and here mainly in terms of appointments to commissions and boards. Why? One institutional feature that systematically distinguishes the latter state sectors from many others is the high number of autonomous institutions directed by boards. Moreover, according to respondents, the institutions within the older, 'high politics' state sectors like the Foreign Service and the Military and Police have long been known for their strong emphasis on internal, merit-based recruitment. Whereas, for example, Norway's ruling red/green coalition reintroduced in 2006 the rule that a majority of the state's numerous representatives in regional health trust and hospital boards shall be elected politicians.

Selection criteria for appointments by politicians

Finally, we need to examine to what extent partisanship and/or other political links are applied as selection criteria. Figure 14.3 (N = 42) shows the measures allegedly used by ministers and the cabinet in selecting candidates: professionalism, political allegiance, and personal allegiance. 'Professionalism' here refers to qualifications like formal education and administrative experience; 'political allegiance' includes formal party membership, but also party identification and overlapping policy views on particular issues.

When asked about those who have recently been appointed to positions controlled by politicians, across institution categories, all experts claim that 'professional qualifications matter', in line with Norway's formal 'qualification principle'. Nearly 70 per cent also think that 'other qualifications matter'—such as gender, geography, and general political experience. About 50 per cent say that

[Bar chart showing qualifications of appointees in Norway: Professionalism 100%, Political allegiance 52.40%, Personal allegiance 23.80%, Other 69%]

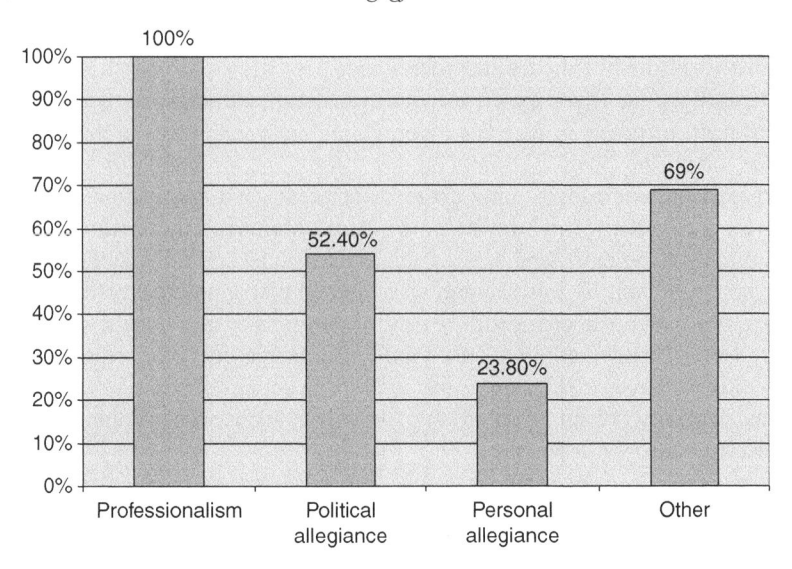

FIGURE 14.3 Qualifications of appointees in Norway

candidates have been appointed on the basis of political ties, whereas one-third indicate that personal connections play a part. More detailed analysis shows that about 48 per cent think that professional qualifications are the only criterion that matters, whereas 52 per cent mention political ties—and 69 per cent 'other qualifications'—in addition to professional qualifications.

In the light of previous research, and the minor role of parties as such, the proportion of experts who argue that political allegiance does matter is surprisingly high. However, these figures might simply indicate that a majority thinks political criteria *occasionally* matter, in *some* administrative branches. Also, to the extent that party membership or policy views count, political ties are almost never reported as the sole determinant of appointments—they are held to tip the balance only in some cases. According to sector experts, sufficient professional qualifications are an almost necessary condition for being appointed in Norway, at least to regular civil service jobs. In the case of commissions and boards, the political profile of candidates is perhaps discussed more openly. A recent example is the much-disputed appointment of the new chairman for Statoil's board in 2007 (*Aftenposten*, 2006). But we certainly cannot conclude that political allegiance usually determines if candidates are more or less equal in professional qualifications.

That said, political experience is, in some cases, seen as a qualification in its own right. For example, in the Foreign Service, appointing former politicians as ambassadors is not unheard of. These might be seen as 'retirement positions' for key figures from the political establishment, and even as rewards for 'long and faithful service' on behalf of a political party. Often they are publicly criticized by trade union leaders as 'legal but disliked' by career diplomats (see e.g. *Aftenposten*, 2008). Nonetheless, the various Foreign Service experts tend to view such appointments mainly as selection of individuals with highly relevant, proven political experience.

More detailed analysis shows that significant differences seemingly exist between policy areas in this regard. Appointments based on political ties are presented as virtually non-existent within the sectors that appear totally dominated by the control motive. No experts on the Judiciary or Military and Police sectors report that appointments are occasionally based on political allegiance. On the other hand, a new study of voting behaviour in the Norwegian Supreme Court (Grendstad, Shaffer, and Waltenburg, 2010) indicates that, even though appointment of Supreme Court justices is usually assumed to be a purely non-political exercise (ibid: 78), political values and attitudes are important determinants of judicial voting (in non-unanimous decisions), and that there is a correlation between the policy profile of Supreme Court judges and the political 'colour' of the government appointing them. Hence, a more subtle political pattern might exist which is hard for observers to detect—like emphasis on the candidates' basic values, or broader understanding of the political system, society, and perhaps contested issues within the judiciary (cf. *Aftenposten*, 2009). But, by and large, the Norwegian judiciary—as well as the Foreign Service and the military—is fairly immune to clear party political influence, according to those interviewed for this study. A common view is that the political leadership would mainly get involved in appointments to the Higher Prosecuting Authority and the Supreme Court. The government seems likely to discuss the total social profile of the Supreme Court: the scope of recruitment—to provide variance in terms of, for example, geography and gender, but not political affiliations. Indeed, the survey generally indicates that political appointments aimed at ensuring control do not necessarily mean appointments based on partisanship or specific policy views.

Change over time: the paradox of professionalization and politicization

A few words can also be said on the experts' perceptions of the long-term development of appointment patterns. Nearly 70 per cent of them say that the role of parties in public appointments has changed over time—at least since the Second World War or the 1960s. Purportedly, the importance of parties—or politicians—has been reduced, across sectors, in three major ways.

First, the cabinet and ministers are said to be less important today in the sense that the share of institutional types 'reachable' for politicians has declined across all sectors. The proportion of ministerial leadership positions has increased since the 1970s (Christensen and Lægreid, 2009: 954), but structural devolution in the central administration has moved several units further away from the government, and greater powers of appointment have also been delegated within the core civil service. The transformation of state enterprises into limited companies has, in particular, made several key positions more difficult for the cabinet to control. Interviewees agree that politicians find it hard to maintain a distance from all autonomous agencies and companies, but they do not tend to think that formal delegation of general power has led parties to reach further into the administration by means of actual influence over appointments.

Second, in relative terms, fewer appointments based on partisanship are allegedly made to regular civil service positions today, even though it seems as if the numerous commissions and boards are among those units where political ties actually play a significant part. It has, for example, been argued that the Labour party tended to give some attractive government jobs to party members in the first decades after the Second World War. The recent emergence of a more pluralistic party system, and more frequent alternations in government, has seemingly shrunk the actual space available for such appointments, as party elites know they are very likely to 'inherit' another cabinet's appointees the next time they come to power.

Third, the significance of the reward motive is seen as having declined during the second half of the twentieth century. Today it is considered less legitimate to appoint party members for 'long and faithful service', according to the interviewees, due to greater formalization and professionalization of appointment procedures. In particular, a greater demand for 'professional' leadership skills is argued to have made it more difficult to use ill-qualified party supporters.

Paradoxically, however, there may also be indications of growing non-partisan politicization of appointments to ministries and agencies in recent years. Echoing Christensen and Lægreid's (2002: 109, 119) thesis that the 'grey area' between politics and administration has grown in the wake of mass media developments, the experts argue that the distinction between the administrative and political top-level ministerial positions has become more blurred, due to intensified political-administrative leadership teamwork, and due to a growing number of public relations officers working closely with ministers.[27] Emphasis on 'efficient administration' across party lines and the recruitment of more social scientists to public administration (Christensen and Lægreid, 2009: 954) may also have stimulated such a development. As a result, some experts argue, having political experience has become increasingly relevant for top-level civil servants—in line with the study concluding that more bureaucrats had occupied central political positions in public office prior to their appointment in the 1970s and 1990s than in the 1930s and 1950s (Egeberg, 1998: 10). This development might, of course, work as a way of appointing party supporters in practice, within a merit-based system. But, over-all, the number of appointments based partly on party affiliation or policy views is argued to have been reduced over time, according to the expert survey.

CONCLUSION

In Norway, the government and individual ministers enjoy the formal right to appoint to positions in public administration, and do make use of this prerogative when key positions fall vacant in a wide range of state institutions across policy areas. This does not mean that the degree of political control is usually strong. But politicians do not only 'rubber-stamp' administrative nominations, according to most sector experts. The hierarchical administrative model has not made political influence over appointments superfluous, but neither is it particularly widespread. According to most experts, appointments by politicians are limited to the important but relatively few leadership or board positions of public and semi-public institutions—and non-departmental agencies and executing institutions seem to be subject to patronage to a lesser extent, in this sense, than ministries in Norway.

Moreover, well-defined legal and administrative rules—designed to ensure significant bureaucratic autonomy—allow, as hypothesized, only scant room for party patronage. Norwegian party elites have had various incentives to politicize the civil service along partisan lines, but they have not sought to compensate for, for example, decline of political parties as societal organizations or structural devolution in public administration by 'penetrating the state' through more partisan appointments. Such appointments are mainly limited to the growing political staff of individual ministers. Even if political parties form cabinets and the party discipline is high, the party unit is but one among several components of government—and the role of parties as organizations in public appointments is reported to be limited. Thus, this study only provides some support to the hypothesis suggesting that parties as such appoint administrative top leaders in Norway (Kopecký and Scherlis, 2008).

True, the party-based cabinet, and not least individual politicians, seem to use public appointments to reward partisans at times, in some sectors—and perhaps the inclusion of more 'low politics' areas such as labour, social inclusion, and public transport in this study would have strengthened this conclusion. The expert survey does not clearly confirm that partisanship plays more than a limited role in appointments to positions in the great number of (partly) state-owned companies (Strøm, Narud, and Valen, 2005: 661), but proximity to the government's policy platform might favour candidates even for regular civil service positions more than traditionally assumed. However, appointments seem mainly to be used by politically accountable leaders as a tool of democratic government: to effectively control public policy through administrative leaders and a potentially manipulative bureaucracy—and then only occasionally, based on party political considerations and selection criteria. The political leadership—and to a limited extent parties—may affect appointments, but apparently not entire careers. The scope available to politicians in terms of appointments is based on constrained selectivity and is argued to have decreased over time.

The reported emphasis on professional qualifications shows that appointments by political leaders, affiliated to parties, do not necessarily imply amateurish administration or a lack of professional competence (cf. Rouban, 2007: 202). Indeed, it seems as if the politicians themselves question the usefulness of—and fear unfavourable publicity due to—appointing (less qualified) party members to administrative positions in the Norwegian context (cf. Shefter, 1994; Strøm, Narud, and Valen, 2005). Also, it could be argued that simple preventive action like avoidance of incompetent and corrupt candidates defined as control in this analysis reflects legal administration more than political goal-seeking. So, even though today's Norwegian government uses appointments to a degree to slightly constrain the autonomy of the civil service in this sense, this does not necessarily mean that in doing this it attempts to implement party platforms. Hence, although Norway may not be relatively free of full-blown political appointments as hypothesized by Müller (2006b: 189), and appointments are, to some extent, used to politicize the public administration despite strong bureaucratic traditions, we may conclude that politicians do not seem to significantly use appointments as a tool for strengthening the party organizational structure within the state.

In turn, this gives rise to a final question: do we need a more nuanced concept of 'political appointments' to grasp the patterns revealed in the case of Norway? In terming all appointments made by politicians 'patronage', and distinguishing only between reward and control, we risk underestimating what might be seen as a separate type of appointment: instances where politicians appoint according to bureaucratic or managerial criteria, purely in line with their administrative role (cf. Allern, Bischoff, and Kristinsson, 2012). As in the case of pure policy control, the politician is likely to appoint someone with strong professional qualifications, but the basic motivation is different. Policy-motivated appointments open up for political links to matter and may therefore—like reward—conflict with the broader concerns of good administration, such as confidence in impartiality.

That said, by systematically distinguishing between politicization and party politicization—the act of appointing, the issue of who appoints, motivations, and selection criteria—this chapter has shown that appointments to important positions within the state administration are related to government, but less to party government. Paradoxically, the number of professional party workers—and the general value of political experience—are increasing, but apparently not the amount of partisan appointees in the civil service. In this way, the Norwegian case clearly illustrates that political appointments entail a delicate balance between 'legitimate' and 'illegitimate' use of political power in the Nordic setting. To the extent that 'patronage' is applied as a networking tool in public administration today, appointments seem mainly to serve individual party-affiliated ministers' aims of political control—not the party organization, and its ideological reform programme as such.

NOTES

1. This chapter has benefited from comments by participants in a seminar at the Department of Political Science, University of Oslo, in the spring of 2010. Thanks are also due to Øyvind Bratberg, Tom Christensen, Morten Egeberg, Knut Heidar, Hanne Marthe Narud, Jo Saglie, and the editors of this volume for useful remarks, and to Anne M. Olsen, Inger Sandvold, and Tommy A. Knutsen for research assistance. I am also grateful for financial support from the Research Council of Norway (FRISAM, project no. 185436) and for valuable help at the early stages of the research process from Erling T. Narum, Paul G. Roness, Eivind Smith, and Hans Robert Zuna. The author has sole responsibility for the contents of this chapter, however.
2. See Strøm and Narud, 2006 for a general description of the political system.
3. *Kristelig Folkeparti* has started to use the label 'Christian Democratic Party' in English (see <http://www.stortinget.no/en/In-English/Members-of-the-Storting/Parliamentary-Party-Groups/>).
4. However, as the number of cases dealt with by the cabinet collectively has allegedly decreased in recent decades due to delegation of authority, Norway has been argued to have moved from the model of cabinet government closer towards ministerial government (Statskonsult, 2003: 58).
5. As of 2010, it includes one 'coordination minister', seven 'state secretaries', and one political adviser. Source: <http://www.regjeringen.no/nb/dep/smk/statsMinisterens-kontor/politisk_ledelse.html?id=897#> downloaded 26 October 2009.
6. But, in recent years, legislation designed for greater scrutiny concerning the administration has strengthened *third-party controls* (Sørensen, 2005: 258–70).
7. In 1996, more than 40 per cent of the ministerial secretaries general (*departementsråd*) had held central political positions (in public office) prior to their appointments—although it should be noted that nearly half of them had been appointed by a government affiliated to another party than their own (Nerland, 1997).
8. Source: Norwegian Social Science Data Services and the Ministry of Government Administration and Reform. The latter figure does not include top leaders, contracted judges, employees paid by the hour and (other) employees with special wage contracts, the Royal household, the Office of the Auditor General, the Office of the Attorney General, the Supreme Court, or separate legal entities like companies.
9. Source: Statistics Norway: <http://www.ssb.no/aarbok/tab/tab-215.html> accessed 11 January 2012.
10. See Roness and Rolland (2010) for an alternative and more detailed taxonomy of the Norwegian public administration.
11. Public foundations have been excluded, as the existing list is not complete, and for the sake of consistency across countries.
12. The term also includes ecclesiastical and military servants.

13. The *Storting* voted in 2012 to grant the Church of Norway greater autonomy, including the right to appoint senior ecclesiastical officials like bishops (even though they will still be employed by the state). See http://www.stortinget.no/no/Hva-skier-pa-stortinget/Nyhetsarkiv/Hva-skier-nyheter/2011-2012/Eadringer-i-Grunnlover-og-kirkeloven/.
14. A state minister might appoint lower civil servants within his or her ministry or delegate this power to the nominating collegiate board (*Innstillingsrådet*), if headed by the secretary general (*departmentsråden*), or to the individual department (Reglement for personalforvaltningen i departementene, 1998).
15. For details on appointments to boards in the various types of companies, see Act Relating to Limited Liability Companies §20, NHD, 2005; NHD, 2006; NHD, 2007; NHD, 2008a.
16. For more details on appointment procedures in the Judiciary and the Foreign Service, see Grendstad, Shaffer, and Waltenburg (2010), Innstillingsrådet for dommere (2009) and Reglement for personalforvaltningen i utenrikstjenesten med kommentarer (2003).
17. Civil servants may have political assignments or positions, but administrative officials employed in government ministries, the Supreme Court, and in the diplomatic or consular services cannot simultaneously serve as elected MPs (Constitution: §62).
18. In 2005, the Storting approved a significant revision of the Public Service Act initiated by the non-socialist Bondevik II coalition government; the revision included simplification of nomination procedures and inclusion of the 'qualification' principle'. However, in 2006, the new law was reversed by Jens Stoltenberg's first red/green coalition government (Eckhoff and Smith, 2006: 94).
19. For exceptions, see The Constitution: §23.
20. Forty-five sector experts, covering five predefined categories, were carefully identified based on a variety of sources, but I have interviewed more civil servants and NGO experts than politicians, academics, and journalists, as the former are better informed or likely to speak more candidly about the subject than the latter. Moreover, most of the top civil servants (mainly director generals) and politicians (former ministers or state secretaries) surveyed had just changed positions or left office and could therefore probably talk rather openly about the government's general practice of appointments. The NGO experts are mainly current trade union leaders within the relevant sectors/ministries. As one economy expert only allowed his or her responses to serve as background information, the total number of respondents is 44.
21. The total number of administrative unit types examined here is not 27 (3 * 9) as Norway's ministerial department for the Media area belongs under 'Culture and Education'.
22. Six basic variables—including three values—are applied on nine sectors, but as the ministry of the media sector belongs under 'Culture and Education', we end up with fifty-two (not fifty-four) measures of range. In about 60 per cent of these

instances, the experts fully agree and the range is 0, and in 16 per cent of the cases the range is 1.
23. In this sense, the results nearly echo the conclusion of a public report based on interviews with the secretary generals and director generals in the ministries in 2003–4 on appointments of top leaders in the state administration: that politicians are usually kept informed during the process, but that they seldom modify the nomination of the administration to regular civil service positions. This said, it seems as if the sector experts in our survey, to some extent, allow for a slightly more active role of politicians than the public report, even here (see Statskonsult, 2004: 17).
24. The results reported are simple frequencies, but I have checked whether means of sector scores (shares) produce different figures. Even though a few missing values are unevenly distributed across sectors (and there is only four respondents in the economy sector in sum) no significant differences were revealed.
25. Party representatives are nominated by the county councils/municipal councils.
26. The same largely applies to a category that was excluded from the analysis for comparative purposes: county governors (*fylkesmenn*). As of 2010, fourteen out of eighteen serving county governors were former politicians, but only a minority (six) were appointed by their 'own' party in government. Source: various official documents identified through <http://www. regjeringen.no>, <http://www.fylkesmannen.no> accessed April 2010, and *Store Norske Leksikon*, <http://www.snl.no>.
27. Since the early 1990s, the number of employees in the ministries' communication units has tripled (Statskonsult, 2007: 10). However, campaigning and communication with the minister's party organization or parliamentary group are not seen as administrative tasks (Innst. S. no. 175, 2000–1: 2–3). See also Mjelva (2011).

CHAPTER 15

Party Patronage in Portugal: Treading in Shallow Water

Carlos Jalali, Patrícia Silva, and Diogo Moreira

INTRODUCTION

It has become a cliché for students of Portuguese politics to note the country's status as the first 'third wave' democracy.[1] This is, however, less of a cliché when we examine party patronage, a trait frequently ascribed to third wave democracies and party systems across the globe (cf. Mainwaring, 1999 on Brazil; Rakner and van de Walle, 2009 on African democracies; O'Dwyer, 2006 on Central and Eastern Europe; or Chandra, 2004 on India). In this context, the Portuguese case becomes potentially relevant in the study of patronage, shedding light on its mechanisms and—given its longer democratic history, as compared to other third wave democracies—how these may evolve over time.

Portugal underwent considerable political change in the last century. In 1910, the Portuguese constitutional monarchy was overthrown. Its replacement, the so-called First Republic, was to prove an unstable and fractious regime. It gave way in 1926 to a short-lived military dictatorship, the prelude to the long-lived authoritarian New State regime of Salazar, formally established in 1933. The New State was to be overthrown in the 1974 'Carnation Revolution', and since then Portugal has gradually but surely established itself as a consolidated European liberal democracy. It joined the European Union in 1986, and has sought to be at the forefront of integration in Europe, most recently as part of the first wave of the Euro single currency. This latter outcome is also a reflection of the country's substantial modernization and development in the last four decades, which propelled Portugal to developed world standards.

Despite these changes, there remains one constant across these different regimes and socio-economic standards: the perception of pervasive patronage in Portuguese politics. Thus, patronage is singled out as a salient feature of the constitutional monarchy and First Republic (see, respectively, Magone, 2000: 341; and Opello, 1985: 87). It is perceived as persisting under Salazar, albeit under new guises (Wiarda,

1974), and enduring—if not expanding—in the post-1974 period (e.g. Lopes, 1997). Overall, then, patronage is seen as an entrenched and widespread characteristic of Portuguese politics and political culture—its roots potentially going as far back as the fifteenth century (Greenfield, 1977)—that has, if anything, 'retained or actually increased its strength during the twentieth century' (Diamandouros et al., 2006: 17).

This received wisdom merits further scrutiny, on at least three different levels. First, at a conceptual level: the oft-repeated notion of patronage in Portugal is only infrequently preceded by a careful definition of the concept. As such, the literature may be picking up different (even if related) phenomena to which it ascribes equally the patronage label. The second is the empirical dimension. Descriptions of patronage in Portugal derive from very distinct (if at all) empirical data sources, making it difficult to assess their wider validity. Third, even if we accept the notion of patronage as a prominent constant of Portuguese politics, its nature is unlikely to remain unchanged in the face of substantial political (as well as economic and social) change. As such, descriptions of Portugal as continuing to be characterized by patronage overlook the potential changes in the nature of patronage over time and institutional contexts.

This chapter analyses patronage in contemporary Portugal, taking into account these dimensions. First, it provides a precise conceptualization of patronage and, second, bases its assessment on a detailed empirical basis, which makes it comparable to the other cases analysed in this book. Third, and related, this chapter further specifies the dependent variable of patronage. Our departure point is a neo-institutional one, that the nature of patronage in Portugal is unlikely to remain unaffected by changes in the country's institutional context. As such, we assess not only the practice of patronage but also its scope, logic, and style, in order to better understand how democratization, the evolving nature of the Portuguese state and bureaucracy, as well as its parties and party system dynamics, have potentially impacted on the nature of patronage in Portugal.

Overall, we find that while patronage is a feature of the Portuguese political system, it falls short of being an all-pervasive one, with political parties more interested in colonizing the upper echelons of the civil service than in occupying the lower levels. Moreover, we find that patronage is largely perceived as a means of achieving greater control over the policy process, even if this can coexist with the more prosaic and traditional objectives of rewarding supporters and servicing party organizations. This policy rationale is also reflected in the criteria for patronage, with professional qualifications highly prominent, at the very least on a par with political and personal allegiances. Finally, our evidence points to a more 'consensual' form of patronage, with governing parties sharing appointments with the opposition rather than monopolizing them. In sum, then, our results point to a pattern of patronage in Portugal that is more complex than the existing literature tends to suggest, and confirm the need for a more nuanced view of patronage.

DEFINING PATRONAGE IN CONTEMPORARY DEMOCRACIES: PARTY PATRONS AND STATE BENEFITS

There is a long tradition to the concept of patronage. As Greenfield (1977) posits, the notion of a hierarchical relationship between patrons and clients—with the former providing benefits in exchange for the latter's support and loyalty—can be traced as far back as the fifteenth century, in the writings of the Infante D. Pedro of Portugal, if not even further (see the volume edited by Wallace-Hadrill, 1989). While the concept has been approached from different perspectives—be it anthropological, historical, or political—its various definitions invariably converge on the existence of patrons and clients engaged in a particularistic, non-commercial, and asymmetric exchange, with the former enjoying hierarchical superiority vis-à-vis the latter. In this relationship, patrons provide (divisible) benefits to clients, in return for the latter's loyalty and support (see Shefter, 1994: 21).

In the context of modern party democracies, the patron is generally seen as being the political party (Shefter, 1994). As for the benefits, these encompass a relatively broad range, including jobs, titles, contracts and licences, subsidies and grants, and legislation (Müller, 2000: 142–3). In this chapter, we focus on the first of these: indeed, the appointment to jobs is generally seen as the most important form of patronage (Müller, 2006b: 190). We are thus interested in party patronage, which we define here as party-driven appointments to positions in public and semi-public administration. This narrow conceptualization allows us to focus on the most prevalent form of patronage, permitting an empirical analysis of patronage that avoids generalizations based on imprecise or excessively broad definitions. A distinction also emerges here between 'service patronage' and 'power patronage'. The first refers to 'employment or promotion in exchange for the client's loyalty outside his or her job'; the second to 'the allocation of important positions' that allow the client to render services to the party once appointed to the specific position (Müller, 2006b: 190).

Why might parties resort to patronage, and what forms might this take? Strøm and Müller (1999) conceptualize parties as having three main objectives: policy, office, and votes. This triad of goals is helpful in understanding the rationales that underlie party patronage, as the degree to which parties seek these different goals is likely to have implications for the way they use patronage, be it as an instrument or as an objective.

Vote-seeking parties pursue votes primarily. While votes are a means to an end (be this achieving office, influencing policy, or even obtaining prestige), the active pursuit of votes can clash with policy or office objectives—e.g. if the policy goals or position in office prove to be vote-losers (Strøm and Müller, 1999: 9). Patronage has traditionally been seen as a resource in vote-seeking behaviour, as a means to attract 'voters, contributors, and activists' (Shefter, 1994: 21). Patronage may also be used to anchor nascent parties within the political system (Kopecký and Mair,

2006), maintain the support of party members (Blondel, 2002), or entrench party organizations in the face of weakening social anchorage (Katz and Mair, 1995).

This vote-seeking objective generates clear expectations in terms of the rationale and form of patronage. In terms of the former, patronage becomes a form of reward—be it *ex ante* or *ex post*—to party supporters, with the occupation of bureaucratic posts a form of inducing support and servicing party organizations. A high proportion of service patronage is expected, as jobs are given to bring about support in other arenas (notably, the electoral one). Equally, such jobs are likely to reach all levels of the civil service—with universal and equal suffrage, lower positions are a cost-effective way of generating wider electoral support. In this case, we would also expect clients to be selected primarily for their partisan and/or personal allegiance to the patron.

Patronage can also be a predominant feature of office-motivated parties. These seek to maximize the private benefits of holding political office, with appointments to governmental or subgovernmental positions (Strøm and Müller, 1999: 5). In this context, patronage becomes an end in itself (Andeweg, 2000), and subcabinet-level appointments to public and semi-public administration may even 'swamp the value of cabinet appointments' (Strøm and Müller, 1999). Under such conditions, one would again expect to find patronage to be granted largely on partisan and personal grounds; to centre on service patronage; and to be primarily motivated by reward considerations (Laver and Schofield, 1990: 166). The distinction between vote- and office-seeking motivations is expected to emerge in the depth of patronage, the latter generating substantially larger incentives to colonize the upper reaches of public administration.

While vote- and office-seeking motivations have traditionally dominated analyses of patronage, a more recent strand of literature has linked it to parties' policy-seeking objectives (e.g. Andeweg, 2000; Meyer-Sahling, 2006b). In this context, parties use appointments as an instrument to control the bureaucracy, in order to facilitate the implementation of their policy goals. Shaping, developing, and maintaining policies are increasingly bureaucratic activities, not least due to the gap that exists between policy formulation and implementation (Page and Jenkins, 2005). As such, policy-oriented parties are not only concerned with the allocation of government portfolios, but also with appointments to key positions in departments, so as to have some control over these and see their policy goals implemented (Andeweg, 2000). Indeed, as governance processes become increasingly fragmented and complex, appointments allow parties to access an important and potentially elusive territory of policy making (Montricher, 2003), allowing them to acquire 'a voice in, and gain feedback from, the various policy making that characterise modern multi-level governance systems' (Kopecký and Mair, 2006: 8).

This policy-seeking objective is expected to result in a substantially distinct nature of patronage. It will generate predominantly power patronage, with appointments centring on positions that can influence policy orientation and

TABLE 15.1 *Party goals and nature of patronage*

		Nature of patronage		
		Rationale of patronage	Depth of patronage	Criteria for selecting clients
Party goals	*Vote*	Reward	High	Partisan and personal loyalty
	Office	Reward	Low	Partisan and personal loyalty
	Policy	Policy control	Low	Professional, as well as political and personal

implementation, and the expected payback of appointees being directly related to the position they have been granted. The rationale for patronage is gaining additional leverage over (and information within) the policy process. Likewise, the archetypal appointee is predominantly characterized by professional competence—even if this may well coexist with partisan or personal considerations. This policy-seeking objective also suggests a normative reclassification of the concept of patronage. Patronage has long been associated (if not conflated) with rent-extracting behaviours such as clientelism and corruption, and perceived as generating agency loss in democratic contexts. Yet this policy-seeking rationale suggests that patronage may in fact serve to reinforce vertical accountability and reduce agency loss, to the extent that it facilitates the implementation of parties' policy preferences once they are in office.

Overall, we can expect to find different types of patronage according to distinct types of party goals, as summarized in Table 15.1. While these can coexist in reality—much as party goals are not necessarily exclusive—this classification allows a clearer assessment of the nature of patronage in different contexts, permitting a finer and more nuanced understanding of its mechanics and logic.

PATRONAGE IN PORTUGAL: STATE SUPPLY MEETS PARTY DEMAND?

In this section, we examine the supply- and demand-side of patronage in democratic Portugal. In particular, we examine three key aspects: first, the timing and mode of the country's transition to democracy; second, the evolution of the state and bureaucracy in democracy; and third, the nature of political parties and the party system in the post-1974 period. As will be outlined, all three potentially impacted on the development of patronage in Portugal, by expanding the opportunity structure for patronage, and generating potential demand for patronage on the part of political parties.

The nature of democratic transition profoundly shaped how political parties were to act in relation to the top civil servants, especially those who had worked with the previous regime. Portugal's *ruptura* with the authoritarian regime impelled the incoming post-Salazar elites to dismantle the former model of administration. As this process was led by actors that had, by and large, been excluded from Salazar-Caetano's political elite, a rupture from the previous regime also emerged at the administrative level. This was most visible with the 'cleansing' laws ('*leis de saneamento*'—Bermeo, 1987), which generated wholesale replacement of much of the authoritarian period's bureaucratic elite. While the conclusion of the 1974–5 revolutionary period put a gradual end to these purges, by then the upper tier of public administration had become an arena for partisan occupation. As one former minister, quoted in Lobo (2000a: 163), put it, 'After the revolution, public administration stopped being technical and became highly politicized.' While the notion of a merely 'technical' public administration under the New State is questionable—it may have been apartisan, but it was hardly apolitical—the quote reflects well the opening up of public administration to parties after the revolution.

At the same time, the democratic period saw a dramatic transformation of the Portuguese state. The Salazar regime had a minimal welfare state. The subsequent expansion of welfare provision, notably in the sectors of health, education, and social security, also generated a substantial growth in public employment. In 1968, the total number of public servants stood at 196,755; by 1979, it had virtually doubled, to 383,103; and had doubled once again by 2005, when it peaked at 747,880, before falling subsequently to a level that remains in excess of 600,000.[2] Such an expansion in public employment considerably widens the scope available for patronage, both at lower and upper echelons of the bureaucratic hierarchy. As Müller (2006b: 190) points out, 'the greater the public sector, the greater is the potential for patronage'.

Additionally, the leftwards tilt of the revolutionary period led to a considerable expansion of the state sector through a massive programme of nationalizations. The nationalizations and agrarian collectivization of 1974–5 led the state's role in the economy to expand, in a short period of time, to levels that were comparable to, if not higher than, other European countries with high levels of state interventionism (Lobo, 2000b: 623). The ensuing public business sector also considerably expanded the opportunities for patronage. While this was mitigated with the privatization process initiated in the 1990s, the possibilities for patronage in publicly-owned or publicly-participated companies remain considerable. The Portuguese state currently participates (directly or indirectly, through other state companies) in some 131 enterprises,[3] granting it the possibility of appointing to the board of directors. In several cases, the state also retained 'golden shares' in former state companies that were privatized, thus reserving special rights, including the right to appoint company directors and members of the board.[4]

This general expansion of the opportunity structure for patronage has changed in recent years. The need to restrain the growth of public expenditure, to respond to the decline in citizens' trust in political institutions—and, thus, the need to distance these agencies from party intervention (Pollitt et al., 2001)—and to improve the quality of services have led to attempts at reducing the public sector and changing its operation. In particular, a trend towards the delegation of authority to quangos has emerged. There were only twenty-two autonomous public bodies at the time of democratization, increasing to a total of thirty-three in the first years of the democratic period (1974–80). This number underwent sustained growth until the mid-1980s, when it reached a peak of ninety-nine quangos (Moreira, 2001). The number of quangos has, however, been slowly decreasing since the 1990s, and in 2006 there were seventy-two.[5] Despite this decreasing trend, the number of quangos has nevertheless stabilized at a considerably higher level than that of the first decade of democracy.

This move towards quangos was to a large extent a strategy to overcome the difficulties in dealing with conventional bureaucracies, perceived to be insufficiently responsive to the priorities of parties in government. However, these reforms did not substantially change the power of patronage, as ministers retained authority over the appointment of the management boards of these semi-autonomous bodies and maintained the possibility to intervene and constrain their decisions (Decree-law 105/2007).

Overall, then, the supply of available patronage positions expanded considerably in democratic Portugal. The question that remains is whether parties took advantage of this expanded opportunity structure, and, if so, how. As the literature on patronage highlights, parties and party systems are crucial variables in explaining the degree and nature of patronage (Shefter, 1994; O'Dwyer, 2006; Meyer-Sahling, 2006b). We thus analyse the nature of Portugal's parties and party system next, focusing on how these may influence patterns of patronage.

Portugal presents a strong party system with 'weak' parties. Both were shaped by the specificities of the country's protracted and complex transition to democracy. This was dominated by an intense conflict over the choice of regime to succeed the New State, which brought one of the oldest and most ethnically homogeneous nation states of Europe close to civil war. Regime choice thus became the central conflict in Portuguese politics in the revolutionary context of 1974–5.

Parties emerged in this revolutionary period, and developed as organizations in a context where establishing mass organizations was a secondary concern to the more immediate conflict over regime choice. This was to impact particularly on the centre-left Socialists (PS) and the centre-right Social Democrats (PSD), the two main parties of the democratic party system. In 1974–5, programmatic consistency was a luxury these parties could ill afford, given the Communist Party's (PCP) comparative strength in organizational terms. A broad (even if shallow) support, on the other hand, served to signal to the PCP the social upheaval it faced if it sought to take over power through force.

This genetic imprint of the revolution was to endure subsequently: parties—notably the PS and PSD—have relatively weak organizational bases, and never developed deep social anchors. This is also reflected in the nature of party membership, which is generally low and top-heavy, with 'more chiefs than indians' (Jalali, 2007). Indeed, even at their peak, the declared membership of the PSD and PS always stood at below 190,000 members per party, and below 275,000 members for the two combined. Moreover, while these numbers are low in comparative perspective (Mair and van Biezen, 2001)—and with regard to the size of public administration—they are almost certainly inflated by some 100,000–125,000 members.[6]

Nevertheless, parties have managed to consolidate their position and be 'the key political institutions' of democratic Portugal (Bruneau, 1997: 19)—in no small part thanks to their monopoly of political representation in parliament and their capacity to tap state resources. This is reinforced by the prevalence of the party in public office, a pattern that emerged early on. The first provisional government of May 1974 included the PSD, a mere nine days after the party was formed, when it had virtually no organizational structures. The case of the PS is not dissimilar, having been created in exile in 1973. The organizational structures of the parties thus emerged with the party already in office, rather than by building organizations to win power. The PS and PSD thus become a form of Shefter's (1994: 31–2) 'internally-mobilized' parties, despite the transition through rupture.

The parties' capacity to consolidate themselves is also reflected in the rapid structuration of the Portuguese party system, presenting a generally stable pattern of interparty interaction, and developing into a 'working' (moderate and centripetal) mould. The party system can be characterized as an 'imperfect bipartyism' (Magone, 2000) that has, if anything, seen a reinforcement of the position of the two centrist parties since the mid-1980s (Jalali, 2007). Since 1985, PS and PSD have almost entirely monopolized government, with both achieving single-party parliamentary majorities, as well as large pluralities, despite a proportional representation electoral system (for an overview of the parties and party system, see Jalali, 2007).

Against this backdrop, we expect to find widespread patronage in Portugal. Following Shefter (1994: 31–2), the internally mobilized nature of parties, combined with the fact that universal suffrage preceded bureaucratic professionalization, generates substantial incentives for party patronage. Given the lack of deep social anchoring, patronage became a potentially crucial resource for mobilizing support and developing party organizations. Likewise, this is consistent with Meyer-Sahling's (2006b) conclusion that patronage is positively associated with party system institutionalization.

In terms of motivations for patronage, we are interested in assessing the balance between reward and policy control objectives. The former played a crucial role in party development at the outset of democracy. Moreover, while Portuguese parties have never needed to mobilize large masses of supporters (consistent with their internally mobilized nature), a modicum of support is required even for such parties. At the same time, Portugal did not escape the general pattern of complexification of governance. As such, patronage is also likely to be used as a means to control policy.

Also of interest will be assessing to what extent professional qualifications feature in the criteria for recruitment. The work of Nunes (2003)—which finds that appointees to top administration positions in Portugal are highly qualified (more so than the generality of European countries)—suggests that professional criteria will be highly prominent. At the same time, these can well coexist with political and personal criteria—a pattern consistent with Nunes' (2003) assessment that appointments are also highly politicized.

Finally, we are interested in examining whether patronage is more majoritarian or consensual in nature. As highlighted earlier, the Portuguese party system has seen a considerable strengthening of the two main parties since the mid-1980s, with single-party majorities and wholesale alternations in power becoming commonplace. The question is then whether this has also generated a more majoritarian form of patronage use, or whether the strong cooperative patterns that emerged in the democratic transition and consolidation—especially between PS and PSD (Jalali, 2007)—have endured in the arena of patronage in spite of party system trends.

THE LEGAL FRAMEWORK OF PATRONAGE

As Shefter (1994: 27–8) points out, access to patronage is at least partly dependent on the legal framework regulating appointments, making this a necessary component of our analysis. The upper echelons of the Portuguese civil service are currently appointed through a process of free designation, in which ministers are free to choose top civil servants on the basis of political confidence, and civil servants in top positions can currently be replaced when a new minister is nominated, except for those that 'mainly perform technical functions' (art. 25, Law 51/2005).[7] Although individuals can still be appointed to these positions for considerable lengths of time—longer than the period of a four-year mandate[8]— Law 5/2005 abolished the need for substantial financial compensation if their replacement occurs when new parties enter government, thus reducing the costs of replacing a previous government's appointees.

One of the main depoliticization 'flags' has been the selection of middle management positions through a complex process of competitive and open selection. Different parties in government have argued that the professionalization of the top civil service will be achieved through this means. The first legal rule, approved in 1979, determined that intermediate posts of chief of services and chief of division were to be filled though political appointments. Open competitions were rarely used then.

This tendency was changed during a Socialist government, in 1997, which approved a law designed to implement compulsory competitive examinations for these posts, a Socialist electoral promise. The same government, however, two years later, passed new regulations creating an extensive set of exceptions to the use of competitive examinations.[9] In fact, in anticipation of these, almost 600 chiefs of services and chiefs of division were appointed regardless of the contests.[10] Thus, Law 49/99 widened the set of exceptions to the process of competitive examinations. In practice, exceptions were so wide that it was often possible to avoid the selection through open competitions.[11]

In 2004, the legislation stipulated that these posts were to be appointed by the hierarchically superior top civil servants (who were themselves appointed by the minister), suggesting the possibility of an indirect involvement in this process. Currently, Law 51/2005 determines the mandatory use of competitive and open selection procedures for these posts, with independent juries being responsible for the selection. However, ministers retained the authority to dismiss the selected civil servants.

There is a separate legal framework for the managers of public enterprises. Managers are appointed by the Council of Ministers, under the proposal of the finance minister and the minister responsible for the economic sector of activity of the enterprise. These managers are to perform their functions for periods of three years, potentially renewed up to a limit of three mandates. Additionally, the responsible minister can also appoint non-executive managers to these companies' management boards.

THE INDEX OF PATRONAGE IN PORTUGAL

The index of patronage (see Chapter 2) is a composite measure that reflects the range and depth of party patronage in each country, through an aggregation of the results of the survey in terms of range and depth of appointments in each institutional category and policy area.

As depicted in Table 15.2, the overall level of party patronage in Portugal is 0.29. The composite index evidences a decrease in the overall results as we move from ministries to executing institutions and non-departmental agencies and commissions (NDACs), with the former having a considerably greater influence of party patronage (0.40) than NDACs (0.20) or executing institutions (0.27). Although it is generally accepted that the growing fragmentation of governance processes and institutions is related to the increase in appointments, overall levels of party patronage are more salient in central public administration. This is

TABLE 15.2 *The index of party patronage in Portugal*

Policy area	Ministries	NDACs	Executing institutions	Policy area total
Economy	0.44	0.11	0.67	0.41
Finance	0.33	0.22	0.33	0.30
Judiciary	1.00	0.22	0.11	0.44
Media	0.67	0.22	0.33	0.41
Military and Police	0.22	0.11	0.22	0.19
Health Care	0.22	0.11	0.22	0.19
Culture and Education	0.22	0.17	0.03	0.14
Foreign Service	0.22	0.33	0.33	0.30
Regional and Local Administration	0.28	0.33	0.22	0.28
Total	0.40	0.20	0.27	0.29

consistent with a general conception that the various phases of the policy process are mainly performed by central public administration civil servants, a pattern that seems to be particularly marked in new democracies (Kopecký, Scherlis, and Spirova, 2007).

While the small number of interviews per policy area qualifies the validity of cross-sector comparisons, it is worth noting that the extent of patronage seems to vary substantially across policy fields. The Judiciary is the area in which party patronage appears to be most present (0.44), followed by the Economy and Media (both with 0.41), Finance, and Foreign Service (both with 0.30). Party patronage is less prominent in the sectors of Culture and Education (0.14), Military and Police, and Health Care (both with 0.19). However, as Blondel (1995) highlights, these differences may be due to differing policy-making processes in different sectors rather than the intrinsic nature of the policy area.

The area with the highest aggregate levels of party patronage is the Judiciary. This is due to the perception of depth and range of appointments in ministerial departments (being the only policy sector with a perfect score of 1 according to our experts). On the other hand, judicial NDACs and executing institutions (e.g. courts) have the lowest levels of party patronage (0.22 and 0.11, respectively). The same occurs in relation to the Media. In this case, patronage in the ministerial department reaches the second highest value (0.67), whereas party patronage practices in NDACs and executing institutions do not deviate from the national overall levels (0.22 and 0.33, respectively). These results are consistent with the desire to control media output by politicians, a pattern stressed by our respondents.

A starkly divergent pattern is evident in the case of the Economy. The high level of party patronage (0.41) is due mainly to patterns of patronage in the executing institutions—largely comprised of state-owned corporations—which have a patronage index value of 0.67, the highest of all the executing institutions. By contrast, the overall value of patronage practices in this policy sector in its ministerial department is close to the national level (0.44), and the value for the economic NDAC is among the lowest (0.11).

The index of patronage largely corroborates a tendency for parties to retain a grip on the selection of the core civil service and, to a lesser extent, on the composition of the semi-public sector management structures. The former is likely to be strategically more important for parties and ministers. But the overall results mask significant differences in party patronage practices in different policy sectors. This raises the question of the motivations and rationales of party patronage. It is interesting to note that jobs in management boards are usually associated with higher salaries and benefits, making these positions potentially more prone to be distributed as rewards for services and loyalty to the party (Kopecký, 2006a). However, such positions may also potentially fulfil an extractive function, serving to bolster party financing—for instance, through siphoning off a part of the salaries (which are substantially higher than in the public sector) for party campaigns and activities. This would certainly appear to be more consistent with the pattern of appointments to these positions in Portugal: the high salaries would lead us to expect these positions to reward more outstanding party supporters; instead, they often go to less prominent (but loyal) party members.

PRACTICE, RANGE AND DEPTH OF PATRONAGE

As previous chapters in this volume have demonstrated, we are not only interested in the aggregate levels of party patronage, but also in analysing the three separate dimensions of the concept of patronage: its practice, range, and depth. As such, we are not only interested in assessing whether parties appoint people, but also to what extent those appointments occur in all, or just some, institutions in a given policy area. Finally, depth attempts to quantify the hierarchical level at which party patronage occurs.

As Table 15.3 shows, party patronage practices occur in all institutional types: 89 per cent at the ministerial level, 91 per cent in the NDAC category, and 90 per cent in the executing institutions, largely confirming our expectation of widespread patronage. We can thus assume that the entire public sector is reachable by political parties as an arena for patronage. Nevertheless, according to our respondents, parties do not necessarily reach all parts of the state uniformly. Since no institutional framework impedes appointments in specific policy areas, the differences that seem to emerge may be correlated to the rationale for appointments, as certain functions may be more attractive for vote-, office-, and policy-seeking purposes than others. The pattern of the policy areas with highest overall patronage—Media and Foreign Service—is consistent with this. While parties have a strategic interest in state-owned media institutions, due to the importance of media

TABLE 15.3 *Party patronage practice, by institutional type and policy area in Portugal*

Policy area	Ministries	NDACs	Executing institutions	Policy area total
Economy	100%	80%	100%	93%
Finance	80%	80%	80%	80%
Judiciary	80%	80%	100%	87%
Media	100%	100%	100%	100%
Military and Police	80%	80%	80%	80%
Health Care	100%	100%	80%	93%
Culture and Education	100%	100%	67%	89%
Foreign Service	100%	100%	100%	100%
Regional and Local Administration	60%	100%	100%	87%
Total	89%	91%	90%	

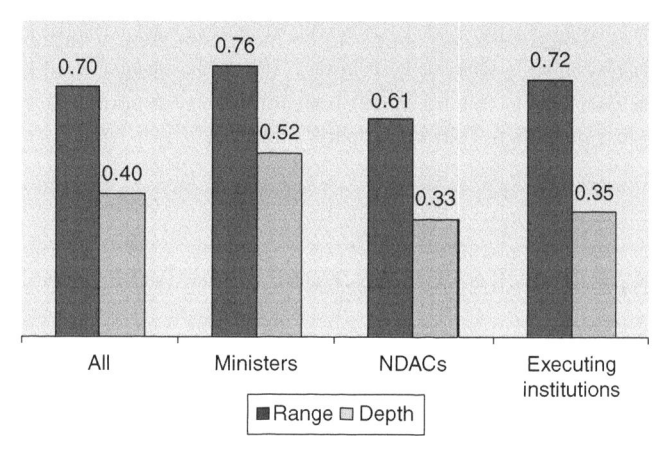

FIGURE 15.1 Reach and depth of party patronage, by institutional type

communication in reaching voters, positions in Foreign Service are, according to some respondents, highly valuable for the personal rewards associated with them.

The range of institutions targeted by party patronage is much wider than its depth (Figure 15.1). Overall, the range of institutions affected by party patronage reaches 0.70, while its depth is only 0.40. These results suggest that Portuguese parties attempt to 'colonize' a wide range of institutions but mainly appoint to the upper echelons of the civil service. Why might this be the case? In part, this reflects state supply. The purges in public administration after the fall of the New State focused primarily on higher-level positions, with greater continuity in lower-level administration. As such, the former became more pliable to patronage. At the same time, this also reflects partisan demand, be it motivated by policy control or reward objectives. With regard to the former, it is control of top administrative positions that generates greater leverage over policy. As for the latter, the small

Party Patronage in Portugal

and top-heavy nature of Portuguese parties is relevant here. With a narrow membership base that is largely drawn from the Portuguese elite, demand for the lucrative and more prestigious positions in the upper echelons of public administration is likely to outstrip that for lower-level positions.

Disaggregating the data by institutional categories, we find that the 'reach' and 'permeation' of parties is greater in central public administration, with the allocation of jobs in ministerial departments having a mean range of 0.76 and depth of 0.52. Parties' grip on the semi-public sector is relatively limited, with both the range and depth of party patronage in NDAC institutions being lower—0.61 and 0.33, respectively. Parties appoint to a wider range of executing institutions (0.72), but with a similar level of depth (0.35). Overall, ministerial departments appear to be the most patronage-prone institutional type, a trend that seems to be common in new democracies, where there is an enduring notion of traditional state bureaucracies being responsible for policy making (Kopecký, Scherlis, and Spirova, 2007). Overall, although extensive, party patronage practices are not pervasive. Parties do reach all institutions but the depth of patronage practices is, on the other hand, more limited. As such, our data suggests that parties seek primarily to appoint civil servants that are hierarchically closest to the political heads of the different ministries. Figure 15.2 displays the levels of party patronage range and depth in different policy sectors.

Policy Area	Range	Depth
Economy	0.67	0.56
Finance	0.89	0.33
Judiciary	0.67	0.56
Media	0.78	0.56
Military and Police	0.56	0.33
Health Care	0.56	0.33
Culture and Education	0.44	0.28
Foreign Service	0.89	0.33
Regional and Local Administration	0.83	0.33

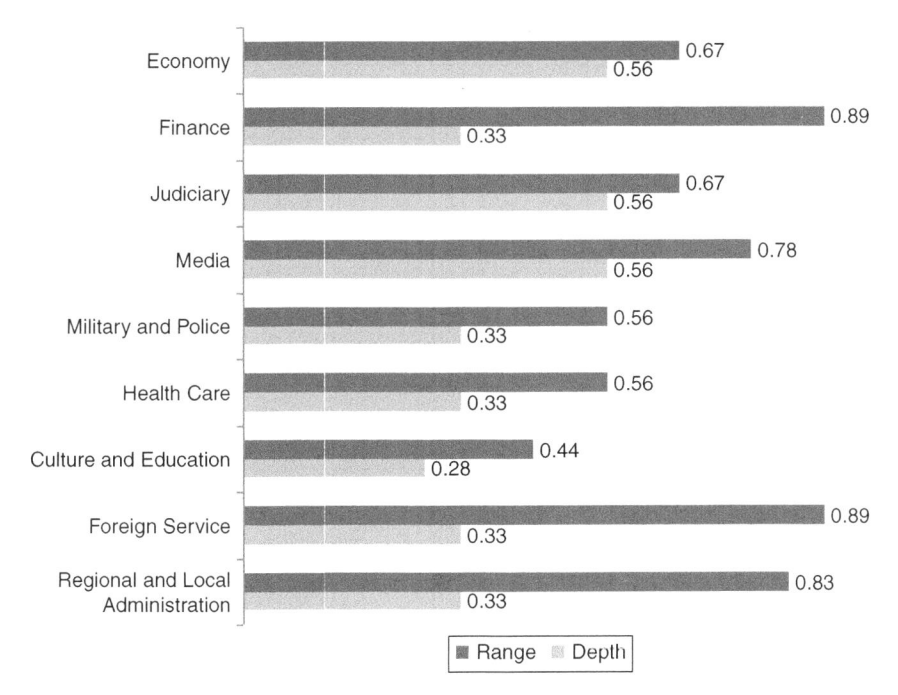

FIGURE 15.2 Reach and depth of party patronage, by policy area

308   *Carlos Jalali, Patrícia Silva, and Diogo Moreira*

Again noting the limitations due to the small N per policy area, substantial differences emerge between policy areas, both in terms of range and depth. The policy sectors that display the greater range of party patronage include Finance (0.89), Foreign Service (0.89) and Regional and Local Administration (0.83). The deepest levels of patronage appointments are reached in the Economy, Judiciary and the Media, where party patronage is capable of reaching lower levels of the civil service (all with 0.56). Culture and Education is the policy area with the lowest level of range (0.44) and depth (0.28) in Portugal.

MOTIVATIONS FOR PARTY PATRONAGE IN PORTUGAL

As previously demonstrated, two main motivations can underpin party patronage. Patronage may be used as a means of distributing selective goods to supporters, or as a means to strengthen control over particular sectors of the administrative system. Figure 15.3 reports the interviewees' perspective on the dominant motivation behind patronage appointments in Portugal.

The largest cohort of our experts highlighted that parties' motivation can be both reward and control. As one interviewee put it, when parties form a government, their members expect to be rewarded. A dual motivation for patronage can thus be perceived, allowing for the reward of loyal members while, at the same time, enhancing control of sensitive policy sectors. As described by one former minister, appointments combine the willingness to be appointed and the party's

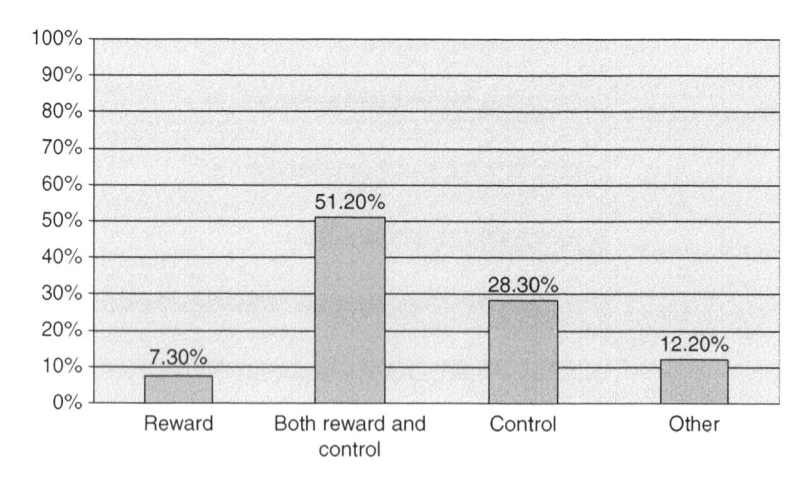

FIGURE 15.3 Motivations for party patronage in Portugal

Motivation	Percentage
Reward	7.30%
Both reward and control	51.20%
Control	28.30%
Other	12.20%

need for someone of political confidence in a key position, corroborating the coexistence of policy and reward dynamics.

At the same time, this dual motivation can occur not only in specific appointments, but also through the aggregation of appointments. Several of our interviewees with a background in public administration pointed to a pattern of combining reward and control-motivated appointments to public or quasi-public administration structures. Thus, individuals appointed with a reward rationale to a specific body were accompanied by others appointed with a policy control motivation to the same body. This combination thus allows rewards to coexist with effective policy control, with the latter appointees ensuring greater supervision of performance within the body concerned.

When comparing the balance between control and reward motivations, the former emerges as the strongest according to the majority of our experts. As mentioned earlier, Portugal did not elude the general trend of a growing complexity in governance processes. Indeed, if anything, it saw this occur at a more rapid pace than other West European countries, as the previously restricted participation, limited state, and closed economy of the authoritarian regime gave way to a vibrant democracy, a massive expansion of welfare, an open economy, and active supranational integration. Our results indicate that the incentives to use patronage to maintain control of policy are particularly intense. This is likely to reflect pressures to improve public sector efficiency since the mid-1980s. These have been particularly visible in the new millennium, with membership of the single currency. Portugal has been largely unable to remain below the 3 per cent budget deficit ceiling since 2001,[12] making control of public finances a key priority for successive governments, be they of the left or of the right. In such a context, patronage seems to constitute an important instrument to gain leverage over the public sector, especially in the face of reforms that are unpalatable to most civil servants. Indeed, the use of appointments as an instrument of control is also associated with the 'inertia' or the 'resistance' of public administration, as highlighted in several of our interviews. As one interviewee—a former minister—put it, patronage serves as a means to circumvent civil servants' capacity to 'boycott the decisions made by the political authority', especially in those policy sectors where a strong *esprit de corps* exists.

Respondents admit that the selection of top administrative posts takes into account government priorities, but also how certain policy areas can be important for the 'popularity of the executive'—i.e. people are selected according to their ability to establish good relationships with the major stakeholders of key policy areas. Respondents also associate this need for *ex ante* control through appointments with the increasing difficulties in monitoring civil servants' activities, as some respondents report the weakness (if not absence) of *ex post* monitoring instruments. To a certain extent, at least, controlling the recruitment process releases ministers from tight monitoring activities. Indeed, one respondent—also a former minister—readily admitted to a lack of time and resources to invest in monitoring activities.

While the logic of 'appointment for reward' may not be discarded, it is far from dominant. As highlighted earlier, patronage by reward was crucial in party development. The lack of material, human, or even ideological resources impelled parties—particularly during the democratic transition—to attract and absorb pre-existent local and regional networks through patronage (Jalali and Lisi, 2009: 450–1). However, our data suggests a relatively minor role for strict reward motivations in contemporary patronage. According to respondents, patronage for reward is most visible in lower-ranking positions and specific positions in ministerial offices and regional structures, although this can also coexist with some more lucrative positions (such as certain positions in embassies or in the management boards of state companies).

The issue of the motivations underlying appointments is also necessarily linked to the criteria used in the appointment of top civil servants. Figure 15.4 summarizes the perspective of interviewees on the relative importance of professional qualifications and political or personal allegiances.

While all the criteria are relevant in the selection of top civil servants, the most important criterion is their educational and professional background. This is consistent with our results vis-à-vis motivations, as parties' policy-seeking objectives tend to require high levels of expertise. As respondents indicated, these professional criteria are associated not only with technical competences to perform the job, but also management skills, and preferably knowledge of the policy sector where the individual is to perform their functions. Indeed, some respondents considered more 'technical' policy domains with a larger impact on public

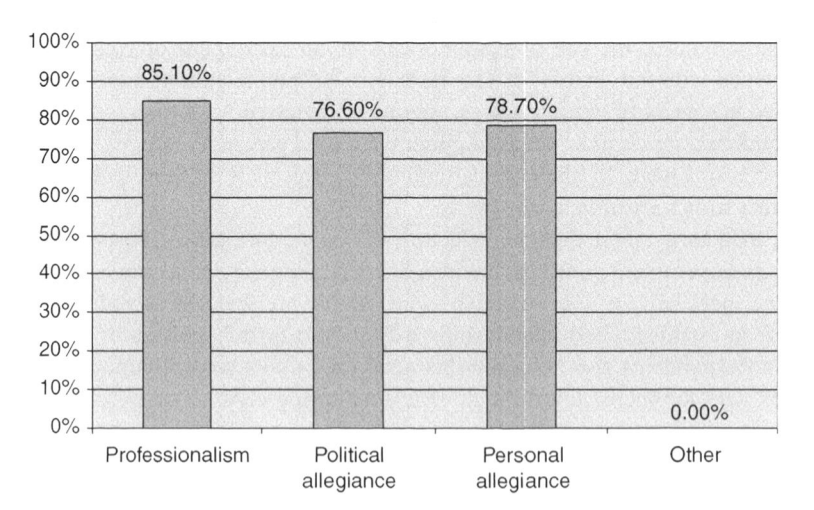

FIGURE 15.4 Qualifications of appointees in Portugal

accounts—such as health, finances, and labour—to be more strongly associated with recruitment based on professionalism, due to the specialization and the learning costs associated with these functions.

The question that then emerges is by what criteria to select from within the pool of qualified professionals, assuming that this cohort is larger than the number of positions to be filled. Interestingly, personal allegiances play a significant role in appointments, and even exceed political links as a reason for being appointed. This personal dimension is consistent with the personalization of government found in earlier studies, with a strong role for ministerial cabinets in policy formulation (Portas and Valente, 1990; Lobo, 2000a). In our study, respondents highlight personal knowledge of an individual as the best way to assess their professional qualifications, and this is also perceived as the safest method of selecting top civil servants. The role of personal ties indicates an important role for personal networks in appointments, seemingly more so than the party network.

Indeed, the least relevant dimension is the political/partisanship connection, albeit by a small margin. Again, our respondents indicate that this is likely to vary from sector to sector. When policy sectors or institutions are involved in deep reforms, selection based on political allegiances is more likely to occur. However, as several respondents put it, the partisan connection may partly be a cipher for personal networks. As one respondent clarified, belonging to a political party tends to create 'strong solidarities' and, additionally, creates the perception of political allegiances. Likewise, if a minister has a strong partisan experience, the range of recruitment to positions in the senior civil service tends to be biased towards other party members. Consistent with this comparatively weaker role of partisanship for appointments, several respondents mentioned a weakening capacity of parties to attract qualified individuals as accounting for the relative unimportance of the party in selecting individuals to perform these functions.

Overall, then, although a high level of partisanship is not unusual at the upper echelons of the civil service (Peters and Pierre, 2004b), not all appointments are based on political grounds. Moreover, to the extent that party patronage is distributed in a 'proportional' manner (cf. Figure 15.5 below), this potentially accounts for the relative unimportance of partisanship criteria in appointments. Personal allegiances to the party or faction leader are thus more important than the more abstract concept of party loyalty or influence. For technocratic ministers, or those that are not members of the party, personal allegiance is likely to be all the more important.

Finally, given the tendency to a 'majoritarian' pattern of party government alluded to earlier, we are interested in assessing the style of patronage distribution in Portugal.

As Figure 15.5 depicts, the majority of our respondents share the perception that parties outside the government have an influence over party patronage appointments. Respondents do, however, highlight that only a minority of the appointments are distributed (an often cited example is that of the state-owned bank) and

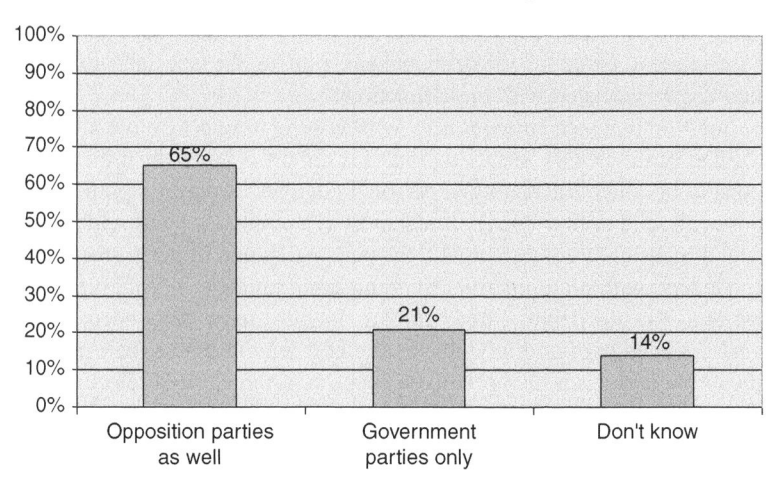

FIGURE 15.5 Party patronage style

that this 'proportional' style in patronage distribution is largely restricted to the main opposition party. In addition, certain positions in the state apparatus also require some consultation of the largest party in the opposition, particularly regarding some posts at NDAC institutions and in executing institutions.

Why does this occur? On the one hand, this cooperation ensures the mutual survival of the main parties. Withdrawing benefits from the state is crucial for party survival, but that does not mean the party in government attempts to 'starve' the opposition of resources (Grzymala-Busse, 2006). In the Portuguese case, the cooperation between the two main parties during the early years of democracy—perceptible not only during the revolutionary period but also in the crucial 1982 constitutional revision and the 1983–5 grand coalition—has generated a coordination-game Nash equilibrium: incumbent parties have an incentive to share patronage appointments with the opposition, to avoid wholesale purges of their appointees once they lose power. Moreover, consistent with this equilibrium, the sharing of patronage resources does not occur with all parliamentary parties alike, but rather is more evident with the main opposition party, which can lead a subsequent government.

Granting opposition parties patronage appointments may also be a crucial strategy for obtaining the necessary political support for effective policy control. In this case, then, appointments help to 'co-opt' support to the policy-making process (Gordin, 2002: 521). While the exclusion of the Communist Party from national-level appointments is largely confirmed—a pattern consistent with the Communists' systematic exclusion from constitutional governments since democratization—our evidence points to their involvement in appointments at the subnational level in regions where the PCP has a strong presence in local power. As our experts pointed out, this was aimed at facilitating greater consensus at the regional level in decisions

Party Patronage in Portugal 313

that involve both the central state and local power. This type of bargaining also occurs at the national level with the rightist CDS-PP (Party of the Democratic Social Centre—Popular Party), the occasional (but increasingly infrequent) coalition partner of PS and PSD. As one respondent put it, the CDS-PP was able to 'put some of its pieces on the board' in terms of appointments, in exchange for the party's support on specific policy issues in parliament.

CONCLUSION

Consistent with its 'third wave' nature, Portugal not only presents a long tradition of patronage, but also parties that have weak social roots and where state structures seem to be particularly prone to party colonization. Likewise, the expansion of the state's role after democratization considerably enlarged the opportunities for patronage. Yet, despite these factors, Portuguese parties seem to be treading in shallow waters when it comes to patronage, being primarily interested in the top levels of public administration. Such a pattern is consistent with a policy-seeking rationale for party patronage, with appointments to top positions a means for parties to gain leverage over fragmented governance processes. Indeed, the control of policy emerges as the most salient motivation for patronage appointments in Portugal.

The Portuguese case also illustrates that policy goals can coexist with the rewarding of supporters for office- or vote-seeking reasons. In some cases, the two logics can coexist in one appointment; more frequently, however, certain positions become the preserve of 'patronage as reward'. The use of patronage for parties' policy goals is also reflected in the qualifications of those appointed, with professional aptitudes featuring prominently alongside personal and political allegiance. Finally, patronage is not an exclusive instrument of governing parties, despite the increasingly majoritarian nature of the party system. Incumbents share patronage resources with the opposition, especially with the main opposition party, allowing parties to preserve their position in the political system.

In a sense, then, the cartel thesis of Katz and Mair (1995) is extensible also to patronage, at least in the Portuguese case, where parties act as a cartel in the distribution of patronage resources, confirming Katz and Mair's assessment that being in opposition 'rarely implies a denial of access to the spoils of the state, nor to at least some share of patronage appointments' (Katz and Mair, 1995: 17). Yet this cartelization of patronage does not necessarily limit itself to bolstering party organizations. In the Portuguese case, the sharing of appointments reflects policy objectives as well, with the distribution of patronage helping to facilitate policy consensus with the opposition. Moreover, our results help detail Katz and Mair's assessment that with cartelization there is an 'enhancement of the partyness of government' (reflected inter alia in a strengthening of appointments) despite a 'dissolution of the partyness of society' (Katz and Mair, 2009: 760). In part, we find confirmation of this: parties certainly retain a central role in appointments. Yet the criteria for appointments that emerge in Portugal reveal a more nuanced picture. Thus, political criteria play a relatively weak role in appointments, a pattern in part explained by the weakening pull of parties among qualified individuals (itself a manifestation of the 'dissolution of the partyness of society'). As such, the Portuguese case suggests that the weakening 'partyness of society' can also feed back through to the 'partyness of government' in spite of cartelization, at least with regard to patronage. The pattern that emerges is one of political criteria—traditionally associated with party networks—being supplanted by personal networks (which can also emerge within parties) in deciding appointments. As such, the Portuguese case suggests that, with regard to patronage, the greatest challenge to the 'partyness of government' may come from personalization. Moreover, this can occur not only in terms of government but also within parties—at the limit, weakening the very 'partyness' of parties.

Overall, then, we find that traditional accounts of Portugal as a high-patronage country need to be revised. While patronage is pervasive, its nature is now considerably more nuanced that previous accounts suggested, with patronage emerging as a relevant instrument of parties' policy-seeking goals, even if these can coexist with more prosaic vote- and office-seeking objectives. The implications of this for other third wave democracies are not inconsiderable: by generating a stronger partisan grip on policy and public administration, patronage can potentially serve to reduce agency loss and generate greater accountability in terms of policy. This is all the more relevant in the context of increasing fragmentation and complexity of governance processes, which all contemporary democracies currently face. The question that remains, however, is whether such gains are recognized by a citizenry that is increasingly mistrustful of parties.

NOTES

1. This research was funded by the Portuguese Foundation for Science and Technology (FCT) under grant PTDC/CPO/65419/2006.
2. See Pordata: Base de Dados sobre Portugal Contemporâneo [available at: <http://www.pordata.pt/azap_runtime/> accessed August 2010].
3. The Public Entrepreneurial or Business Sector (*Sector Empresarial do Estado*) includes all public companies (see Portuguese Ministry of Finance, 2011).
4. These golden shares and special rights were abolished in 2011 (see Decree-law 90/2011, 25 July), as a result of the EU/IMF-Portugal Financial Aid Agreement.

However, the early evidence suggests that this may not entirely remove de facto government influence in appointments to these companies.
5. Data for 2006 compiled by authors from Decree-law 204/2006, 27 October.
6. Both parties updated their membership files at the turn of the millennium: for the PSD, this led membership to fall from its peak of 183,000 in 1996 to 77,000 in 1999; for the PS, from over 120,000 in 2001 to 66,000 in 2002 (Jalali, 2007). Party membership in 2009 and 2010 is below 80,000 in each case.
7. Law 51/2005 calls for a subsequent regulation that should distinguish those posts that ceased functions with government and those that didn't. Two years later, the government withdrew in this intention. So, intermediate posts do not cease their functions if government changes, but we do not know which top civil servants are meant by those who 'mainly perform technical functions' (art. 25).
8. Service commissions (which have, since 1979, a duration of three years) could be renewed, at a minister's discretion, several times without a limit. Law 2/2004 was the first to limit the service commission to a maximum of nine years, and Law 5/2005 widened this period to twelve years.
9. Art. 4, Law 49/99.
10. The Portuguese Audit Court considered these appointments illegal and demanded their annulment (Sentence 33/98, Official Publication, II series, no. 98, 28 April 1998, 5621–5).
11. Even when contests were mandatory, the selection criteria often seemed to have been defined according to the profile of the preferred candidates (see 'Guterres trava "jobs for the boys" na hora da despedida', Público online, 26 December 2001. Available at: <http://www.publico.pt/Pol%C3%ADtica/guterres-trava-jobs-for-the-boys-na-hora-da-despedida-56075> accessed March 2010).
12. The budget deficit has been in breach of the 3 per cent ceiling for five of the nine years of the period 2001–9.

CHAPTER 16

Party Patronage in Spain: Appointments for Party Government

Raúl Gómez and Tània Verge

INTRODUCTION

As in the rest of the countries included in this book, the use of party patronage, understood as the appointment of party activists and supporters in the public sector, has not produced much empirical evidence in Spain. Its use and type is blended to the evolving political and administrative structure, as political parties do not operate in a vacuum but in a context that both constrains and provides resources for agency (Perkins, 1996: 368; Gordin, 2002). In the Spanish case, several facilitating conditions for party patronage can be identified. First, the creation, reconfiguration, and growth of Spanish political parties took place when the boundaries of the state and the public administration were growing due to the launching of welfare state programmes during the 1980s. A weak membership pushed parties to use public administration patronage resources in order to extend their rank and file. Second, regional administrations were created through a deep political decentralization process, increasing the chances for multilevel party patronage.

This chapter examines Spanish political parties' access to patronage since the transition to democracy. Although we will concentrate on current practices of party patronage, we are also interested in potential patterns of change over time and across parties. The chapter is structured as follows. The first two sections present the traditional reach of the parties in Spanish society and the civil service traditions in Spain. The third section analyses the scope and reach of patronage practices, parties' motivations, the role of the party in central office in making appointments, and the degree to which patronage appointments are shared among the (governing and opposition) parties. It also compares, when applicable, current patronage practices to those of previous periods. The final section presents the main findings and discusses the importance of patronage for the organization of Spanish parties and for the performance of party government.

THE REACH OF PARTIES WITHIN SOCIETY

Unlike most European countries, political competition and universal suffrage were simultaneous events in Spain's recent democratic history, reducing both the need and the opportunity for the creation of extraparliamentary mass organizations dependent on organizational resources (Gunther, Montero, and Wert, 2000). In the late 1970s, as the Francoist regime was languishing, political parties were either heavily restructured as catch-all organizations, or created anew, engaging in electoral mobilization before having consolidated their grass-roots organizations. As a result, the ratio of party members to the electorate in Spain falls below the European mean, although it has consistently grown—in both relative and absolute terms—since the transition to democracy (van Biezen, Mair, and Poguntke, 2012).[1]

The Spanish political system was designed to confer a high degree of stability on the party system. The proportionality of the electoral system was limited by the introduction of the D'Hont allocation method, coupled with small-sized provincial districts (averaging 6.7 seats), a small number of MPs in the lower chamber—the Congress of Deputies—and a 3 per cent electoral threshold. This majoritarian twist works to the advantage of the two larger parties, the Spanish Socialist Workers' Party (*Partido Socialista Obrero Español*, PSOE) and the People's Party (*Partido Popular*, PP), but less so for small state-wide parties such as the left-wing coalition United Left (*Izquierda Unida*, IU), the successor of the Communist Party of Spain (*Partido Comunista de España*, PCE). Regionalist-nationalist parties, whose votes are concentrated in a few constituencies, are better off, though (Magone, 2004: 80), such as the Catalan Convergence and Union (*Convergència i Unió*, CiU) and the Basque Nationalist Party (*Partido Nacionalista Vasco*, PNV).

Despite some other regionalist-nationalist parties being represented in the Congress of Deputies, the effective number of parties is 2.5. Usually, the two main parties hold about 80 per cent of the seats, the rest being mostly shared among several regionalist parties. This has led to single-party cabinets headed by one of the two main parties, and occasionally supported by some of the minor parties. The PSOE governed between 1982 and 1996 (1993–6 as a minority government) and between 2004 and 2011 (in a minority status again), and the PP between 1996 and 2008 (1996–2000 as a minority government) and from 2011 onwards.

The stability of the party system is also granted by generous public funding allocated according to the votes and seats obtained in the last election, thus reducing the incentives to create a more structural relationship with civil society (van Biezen, 2000b: 337). Over 80 per cent of PSOE's and PP's total revenues come from public funding, whereas membership dues represent less than 10 per cent (Court of Audit, 2006). Besides, closed party lists and highly centralized selection procedures have reinforced the dependence of MPs on the party organization and made a political career outside parties nearly impossible (Matuschek,

2003: 341). Therefore parties have been able to effectively control electoral processes and representation.

Parties have managed to penetrate both state and society. They perform a gatekeeping role towards interest groups, controlling their access to the decision-making arena, and virtually monopolizing the position of intermediary actors between the political system and society (Morlino, 1998: 227; Matuschek, 2003: 349). In addition, weak membership has inclined parties, particularly in the 1980s and 1990s, to seek other sources of linkage with society and to deploy different strategies towards social organizations, such as sponsoring the creation of collateral social groups and co-opting social activists into their ranks to serve as public officers (see Verge, 2012).

CIVIL SERVICE TRADITION

With both the reforms of 1852 and the passing of the Civil Service Act of 1918, the open spoils system that had been introduced by the first democratic constitution of Spain (1812) was substituted by a Weberian-inspired model of bureaucracy. The public service has since then been characterized by a tenure-of-office logic and the existence of different autonomous bodies of civil servants—the so-called corps, which date back to the nineteenth century (Jiménez Asensio, 1992).

Although initially Francoism reintroduced open spoils system criteria, the defeat of fascism in the Second World War led the authoritarian regime to seek its own institutionalization by turning into a bureaucratic regime, particularly from the end of the 1950s when power was transferred to a group of high-level technocrats. Several administrative reforms were carried out, based on the Weberian ideal of hierarchy and neutrality of the bureaucracy, aimed at building a sort of 'rule of law' without democracy. The new Civil Service Act of 1964 established a system largely managed by the bureaucratic corps and informed by the principles of efficiency and governance (Parrado, 2000, 2001). The bureaucrats' power became so large that even the main political bodies of the regime were populated by them: 80 per cent of the ministers, 92 per cent of the undersecretaries, and 90 per cent of the directors general belonged to the major corps of the civil service (Álvarez, 1984). Their presence was also pervasive in both public and private companies (Baena, 1977). The bureaucratization of the regime and the pre-eminence of administrative criteria prevented to a large extent the expansion of clientelism (Villoria Mendieta and Huntoon, 2002).

Democratization brought about two main processes. On the one hand, from 1982 political parties extended the number of political appointments they were legally entitled to make, and attempted to limit the power of the major administrative corps. The transition government and its successor party, the Union of the

Democratic Centre (*Unión de Centro Democrático*, UCD), which won the first democratic elections in 1979, did not make major changes in the public administration, arguably because the party was itself colonized by technocrats (Román Masedo, 1997). Although the 1978 constitution guaranteed both the principle of civil service impartiality and the prohibition of political layoffs, some timid partisan criteria were introduced with the progressive expansion of certain discretionary posts, especially by means of two political offices: the minister's cabinet and the junior ministers. The victory of the Social Democrats in 1982 triggered further reforms. As usually happens in new democracies, parties needed to replace the personnel from the previous regime in order to implement new policies and legitimate the public administration. Yet the institutional representation of the heterogeneous parties that opposed Francoism, along with the consensual constitutional and decision-making process in the first years of democracy, ensured a high horizontal accountability in the definition of party patronage positions, which defused the potential politicization of the intermediate and lower levels of the public administration (di Mascio et al., 2010: 14).

In 1984, the Public Service Act was basically aimed at undermining the power of the corps, which had self-financing and self-management capacity and could veto proposals of politicians in personnel matters (Parrado, 2000). Although the corps system was not eliminated, and in fact its influence persisted, a more open system was established. Job positions were broken down into thirty different grades that could be assigned to civil servants regardless of the corps they belonged to. The reform was also characterized by a clear attempt to develop a labour regime more similar to that of the private sector (Villoria Mendieta and Huntoon, 2002). In 1987 the Constitutional Court determined that regular vacancies should be filled with civil servants only, unless otherwise stated by an explicit statutory law containing the exceptional cases. Nonetheless, the increase in the number of political appointees was significant at the highest level. Whereas eighty-eight direct political appointments were made in 1973 at the top level of the central administration—excluding ministers—by 1986 the number had trebled (Parrado, 2004: 240).

Political posts in the Spanish public administration can be divided into several tiers (see Figure 16.1). The first tier includes the minister, whereas the second one includes junior ministers, undersecretaries and secretaries general, and the third is composed of directors general, general technical undersecretaries, the chief of the minister's cabinet and equivalent posts. In general terms, political appointments are circumscribed to these three tiers, and civil servant status is required for all posts below this.

A new reform came about with the People's Party victory in 1996, including a clearer distinction between politically oriented and technical posts. Among the abovementioned three tiers of political appointees, the undersecretaries (tier 2) and general technical undersecretaries (tier 3) must since then be chosen on the basis of their professional experience among tenure civil servants belonging to Group

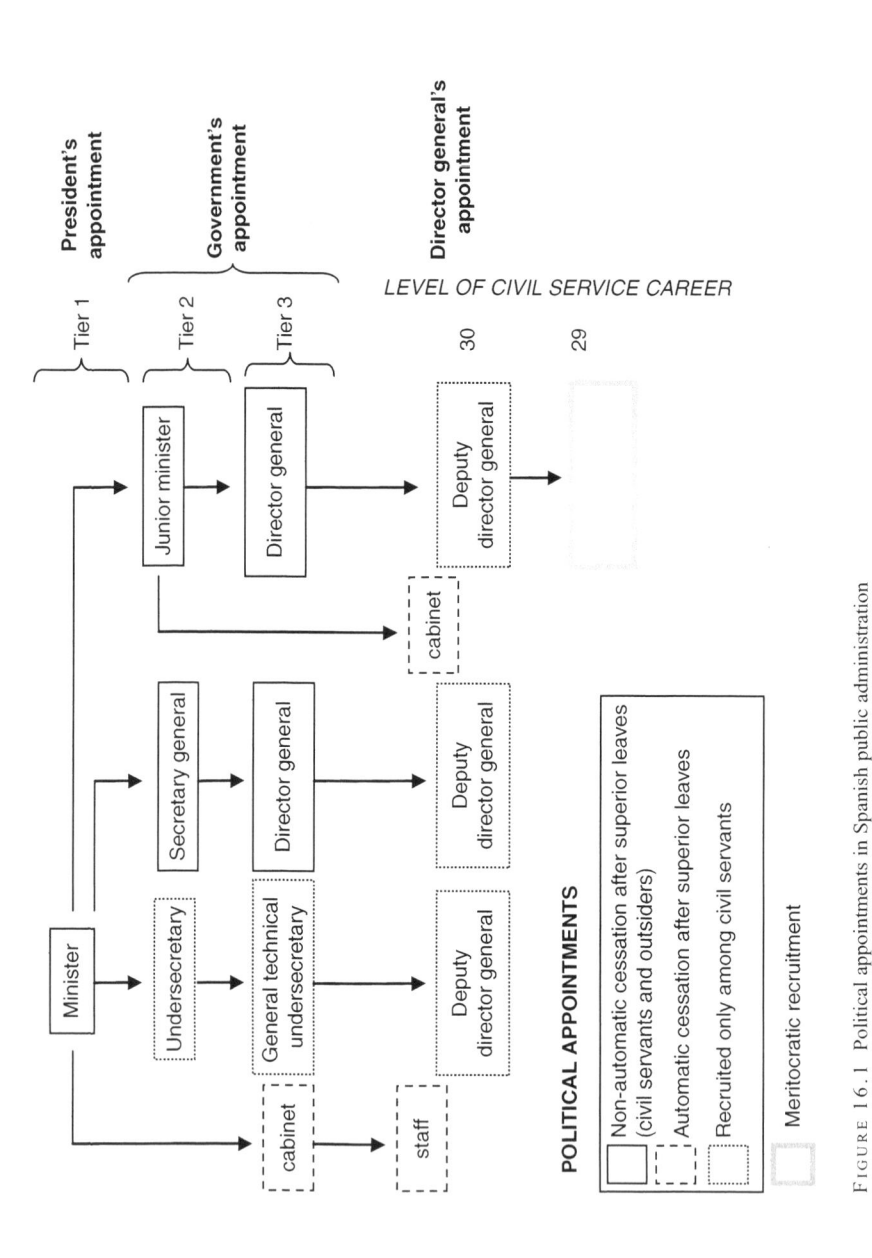

FIGURE 16.1 Political appointments in Spanish public administration

Source: Parrado, 2004: 233

A (which requires a bachelor's, engineering, architectural, or equivalent degree). Civil servant status is also required for directors general (tier 3), although exceptions may be made in view of the required appointee's specific characteristics by means of a government decree. Regarding civil service careers, the system remained virtually the same. Civil servant status is required for all posts below tier 3. However, access to the highest posts below this tier (levels 26 to 30) is not always meritocratic in practice. Candidates are preselected and their profile is published in the official diary so that the concours is already shaped beforehand and based on the discretionary criteria of those in charge of making the appointment (Parrado, 2004).

On the other hand, the devolution process implied the development of autonomous administrations at the regional and local levels. Although intended to accommodate the so-called historical regions (Catalonia, the Basque Country, and Galicia), which demanded recognition for their different cultural and historical traditions and their own legislative codes, it was eventually implemented throughout the whole country in an asymmetrical fashion—the historical regions automatically acquiring a higher degree of self-government. However, by 1999, all regions had basically attained the same fundamental competences (Beltran, 2002: 71). The creation of seventeen autonomous communities[2] redistributed financial and human resources from the centre to the periphery. Between 1982 and 2008, the proportion of civil servants in the central administration was sharply reduced (from 81 per cent to 23 per cent), whereas the regions increasingly expanded their personnel (from 4 per cent to 52 per cent)—the rest being found at the local level.

Despite having full autonomy to create and structure their administrations, regions mimetically followed the hierarchical structure of the central administration. The explanation is twofold. First, the central administration imposed de facto its structure when its personnel were transferred to the regional administrations; and, second, regions could not implement their own civil service policy before the central government had passed a common law on public administration—which was eventually passed in 1984 (Castells, 1988: 76–7).

Regional administrations multiplied the number of freely appointed directive levels, limiting the professionalization of managerial administrative personnel and reducing the career expectations of civil servants, albeit with dissimilar intensity in different regions.[3] Cabinet advisory boards proliferated too in both departmental and non-departmental agencies (Jiménez Asensio, 1992: 89). The desire of regional cabinets to count on loyal personnel meant that bureaucracies rapidly increased in size (Tornos, 1983: 125). Besides, as regional administrations had neither institutionalized civil service corps (such as finance inspectors, diplomats, or trade technicians), nor any previous civil service tradition, possibilities for political patronage were greater. Overall, this level presents a considerable 'organic inflation', irrespective of range of devolved competences, civil service size, and governing party (Hopkin, 2001: 127; Matas, 1995: 6; Ramió and Subirats, 1996: 158).

EMPIRICAL ANALYSIS

Scope and reach of patronage within the state

Spain has been included by some authors in the category of medium-level use of party patronage (Müller, 2006b: 189). The data collected in this research will help us know more about the current situation of patronage practices in the country. The fieldwork was carried out in 2008 and 2009, when the PSOE was in central government.

Before proceeding to the analysis of patronage across policy areas, some clarifications should be made. The Media area in Spain is regulated by an executing institution that fell under the responsibility of the Ministry of Industry when this research was conducted. No specific ministry or non-departmental agency or commission (NDAC) has been created for that area so far, so the only place where patronage can occur in the Media sector is at the executing level. We therefore took it out from the Ministry of Industry and considered it as one area, with only one level, the consequence being that absolute indicators will have less potential variation than originally intended.

When measuring the opportunity for party patronage across policy areas, both our reading of the formal situation and that of the experts' coincided. In Spain, political appointments are actually allowed by the law in every single institutional type. Furthermore, there is no discrepancy either between measures of opportunity and current practice of patronage. Thus, parties make use of all the existing opportunities to fill positions with political appointees.

Range values are rather high in general, which indicates that parties can reach almost all institutions in Spain. However, the depth of these practices is much more restricted. Parties are generally interested in the positions that control the functioning of the administration—i.e. top-level positions—but not in the rest. Besides, competitive civil service examinations can be, and frequently are, scrutinized by the courts, making political intervention risky. Thus, political patronage is rare at the lowest levels, while the degree to which political appointments are made at intermediate levels is quite dissimilar across different areas. The results barely change when the regional administration is excluded from the analysis. Arguably, this is so because regional administrations actually reproduce the same patterns found at the national level.

Table 16.1 shows the index of patronage across different policy areas. It reaches its highest degree at the ministerial level (0.50), but goes down when it comes to NDACs (0.42), and is even lower for executing institutions (0.30). This is reproduced across most policy areas: the ministries are commonly populated by politicians, while in most NDACs it is only the head of the institution or a small directive group who is freely appointed. By contrast, when it comes to executing institutions, parties' room to manoeuvre is limited, and for some of them, such as

TABLE 16.1 *The index of party patronage in Spain*

Policy area	Ministries	NDACs	Executing institutions	Policy area total
Economy	0.67	0.33	0.33	0.44
Finance	0.33	0.33	0.33	0.33
Judiciary	0.67	0.67	0.11	0.48
Media	n/a	n/a	0.28	0.28
Military and Police	0.33	0.33	0.33	0.33
Health Care	0.67	0.67	0.67	0.67
Culture and Education	0.33	0.33	0.22	0.30
Foreign Service	0.33	0.33	0.22	0.30
Regional and Local Administration	0.67	0.33	0.22	0.41
Total	0.50	0.42	0.30	0.40

school or university boards, common courts, etc., parties do not appoint people at all.

Of the policy areas, Health Care is by far the most exposed to party patronage (0.67), followed by the Judiciary (0.48), Economy (0.44), and Regional and Local Administration (0.41). Indeed, the degree of patronage in the Judiciary is striking, and it is probably related to its current intense level of politicization. Patronage is extremely limited in judicial executing institutions, since political appointments to lower courts and tribunals are not possible, but that is not the case for other institutional types. Politicization is clear in the Supreme Court, the Constitutional Court, and the General Council of the Judiciary (*Consejo General del Poder Judicial*, CGPJ). At the time this research was conducted, disagreement between the two largest parties had completely blocked the renewal of both the Constitutional Court and the CGPJ. We therefore suspect that politicization might have led parties to increase their influence over institutions that were easily accessible within this policy area.

At the other extreme, we can find policy areas such as Foreign Service, and to a lesser extent, Finance, where patronage is generally low. This pattern holds for the Military as well, although it is more difficult to fully appreciate here, given that it was put together with an extremely patronaged area—the Home Office—in order to facilitate cross-country comparisons. Culture and Education are often highly politicized areas but, according to our index, they show a low degree of patronage. However, since Education has been to a large extent devolved, it might be possible that institutions in which more party patronage is found are now in the hands of regional governments.

Although the index does not allow for distinguishing this, political appointments always tend to be restricted to top-level positions, so depth is much more limited than range, whichever policy area we look at.[4] In contrast with Education, the Health Care sector displays the deepest level of patronage, despite being one of the areas where devolution has been developed further. Arguably, the difference may lie in the profile and the number of institutions left in the hands of the central government, which in the case of Education involved a high number of scientific and technical institutions.

As already mentioned, party patronage is quite similar at both the national level and the regional level. Although the data show that range is higher in the national administration, respondents considered that patronage practices are more widespread at the regional level. However, regional administrations involve a very broad range of policy areas, and so it would be interesting for further research to look more deeply into them.

Motivations of patronage appointments

Party patronage in Spain seems to be guided by the desire to ensure that the decisions made by top rank public officers are not at odds with the government's criteria (see Figure 16.2). Thus, control is the single most relevant motivation, according to our experts (40 per cent). It definitely appears to be much more predominant than reward (4.4 per cent), although most interviewees pointed to a combination of both (51.1 per cent). Respondents noted that politicians need to appoint someone they can trust, so that their goals can be easily pursued with no major obstacles. Most interviewees posited that partisanship is not a *sine qua non* condition for the use of reward as it is also distributed across trustworthy and professional officials.

Concerning the criteria parties use when selecting people (Figure 16.3), professional criteria rank first (93.3 per cent), irrespective of the inclusion or exclusion of

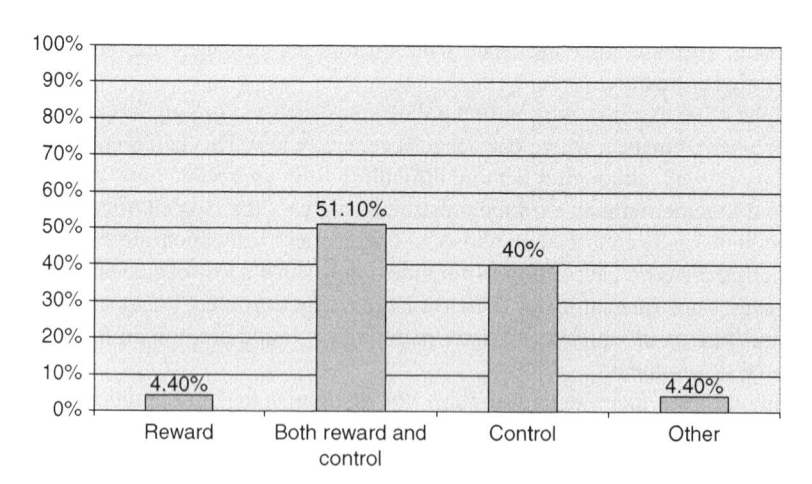

FIGURE 16.2 Motivations for party patronage in Spain

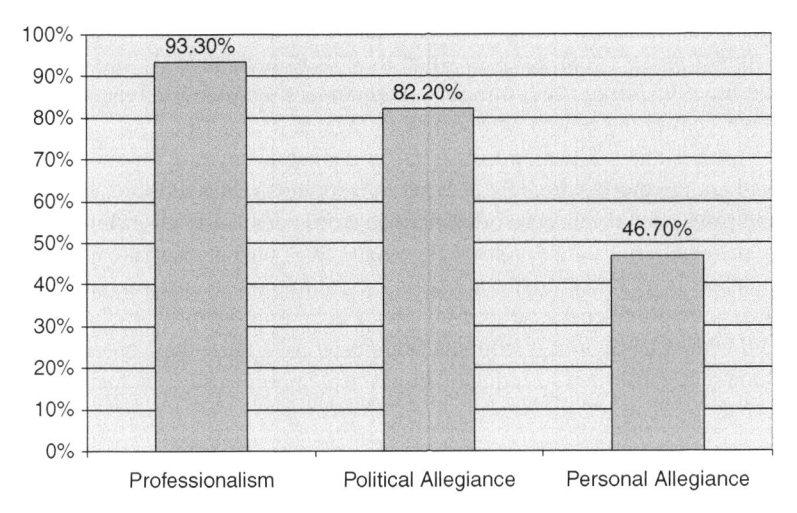

FIGURE 16.3 Qualifications of appointees in Spain

the regional level. It is followed by political criteria (82.2 per cent), and personal motivations rank last (46.7 per cent). Experts stated that there is a prize to loyalty when it comes to advisers, but expertise or professionalism is the main criterion for other positions. Thus, ministers often appoint people considered suited to the tasks, regardless of party membership. This does not mean that political sympathy is completely irrelevant, but, as some experts argued, professionalism is a necessary condition while political criteria are not. Experts suggested that political criteria have to do with political closeness, and not strictly with party membership. The appointee is usually required to show some degree of sympathy with the party in government and/or no active political connections with opposition parties. Interestingly enough, although some of the interviewees had been appointed on political grounds—either alone or alongside professional criteria—they stressed that they had never been required to render accounts to the party.

Differences between professional and political criteria are relatively small. In fact, both of them have the same weight in several areas (Economy, Media, Military, Foreign Service, and Regional Administration). Professional criteria are far more relevant for appointments at the NDAC and executing levels, irrespective of the area. Experts argued that the lower the level, the lower the importance of political criteria and the greater the relevance of personal links in free appointments. This is found to be especially true for executing institutions. The use of political criteria over professionalism is more extensive at the regional level. Indeed, party membership is much more common among regional rather than national high officials (Villoria Mendieta and Huntoon, 2002: 177). In this vein, a recent study on the Catalan public administration (Matas, 2001: 54) found that regional ministers themselves considered political criteria to have clearly outweighed professional grounds when they were appointed. In this very same region, by 1995, 40 per cent of political appointees were civil servants compared to 75 per cent in the central administration (Matas, 1995: 10).

The truth is that political, professional, and personal criteria commonly interrelate and are therefore extremely difficult to distinguish. Furthermore, some political and professional links are often derived from personal relationships. In some areas, personal criteria rank remarkably high. Thus, in Finance and Welfare they equal the score of political criteria and rank close to professionalism. According to many experts, this is because ministers tend to appoint people they have already worked with in a previous institution. Simultaneously, these appointees reproduce the same practices when selecting other political appointees below them (Parrado, 2001).

Role of the party in making appointments: the clear predominance of the party in public office

Even though most respondents denied the role of parties in political appointments, during the interview they pointed to government members as the people who decided. Experts claimed that the prime minister—and his office—appoints ministers, and the latter choose top positions in the ministry, agencies, and executing institutions, although the Council of Ministers has to ultimately ratify all those appointments. Ministers do enjoy a high degree of autonomy, but in no case can they ignore political guidelines from above, especially from the prime minister, who has veto power and occasionally makes direct recommendations—in particular for the position of junior minister. Such recommendations, as well as some other exceptional appointments directly proposed by the prime minister, affect the most politically relevant offices. For instance, regarding embassies, the prime minister usually exerts a strong influence on the most important ones, given that foreign policy is directly concerned. The former prime minister, José Luis Rodríguez Zapatero, also intervened in the selection of senior officials in order to guarantee general criteria such as gender and generational balance. Clearly, respondents referred to the leading role of the party in public office with respect to political appointments, which confirms the relevance of this face of the party in new democracies, as previous research has indicated (van Biezen, 2003: 157–9).

Whereas the party on the ground has no stake at all in party patronage, the party in central office does play a more meaningful role. Besides, since all Spanish prime ministers (Adolfo Suárez from the UCD, Felipe González from the PSOE, José M. Aznar from the PP, José L. Rodríguez Zapatero from the PSOE, and, last, Mariano Rajoy from the PP) have also been the party leader, the attribution of responsibilities with respect to appointments is a fuzzy task. For instance, under the PP's governments (1996–2004) all deputy prime ministers were simultaneously party deputy leaders. As for the PSOE government (2004–11), the deputy leader of the party was a cabinet member from 2008 to 2011.

Respondents clearly identified the party leader, along with his closest team from within the party executive board, as the elite intervening in the nomination process. These include the organization secretary and the sectoral secretaries (health, economy, defence, labour, etc.). Nonetheless, the role of the party in central office mainly consists in making recommendations rather than imposing names on those who must decide.[5] Yet, the party in central office provides some criteria that the party in public office usually respects. The most prominent criterion is the territorial quota that is informally applied following the electoral performance of party regional branches in legislative elections. This is particularly relevant for the PSOE, as regional leaders, particularly those who simultaneously head the regional party branch and the regional government (the so-called *barones*), have been very influential when the party's dominant coalition was either divided (during the 1990s) or had not yet consolidated its power within the organization (2000–4).

Alternatively, on those occasions when appointments must be agreed on with opposition parties, the party apparatus exerts a greater influence. Actually, the party in central office exerts a great deal of influence over the parliamentary groups in Spain (Strøm, Müller, and Bergman, 2003; van Biezen, 2000a). After all, it controls public funding and establishes voting discipline—enforced through economic sanctions and, eventually, expulsion from the party. The party in public office has no say in the elaboration of candidate tickets in elections, and the permanence of MPs depends on an array of mandate limitations and incompatibilities (Verge, 2007: 302–16). In this vein, it is not surprising that, on average, three-quarters of the ministers appointed between 1977 and 2004 were already party members before being in office, and 56.8 per cent had responsibilities within the party—67.8 per cent of them at the national level, and the rest at either the regional or the local level (Rodríguez Teruel, 2009: 11). As has been remarked by some scholars, in cases of bipolar competition between two main parties which alternate in office, the accession to government generally leads to the fusion of the party elite and the ministerial elite (Blondel, 2000: 105). Nevertheless, it is worth noting that 50 per cent of the ministers were experts in the area they were appointed to (Rodríguez Teruel, 2009: 35), which is partly due to the legacy of a technocratic conception of the public administration dating back to the Francoist regime.

Change over time

Political patronage in Spain is extensive but not pervasive. Parties can and do generally appoint people to most institutions, but restrict themselves to the top level—which, for many NDACs and executing institutions, only involves the head of the institution. However, a large number of politically appointed positions change hands with government replacement.

Turnover rates after government changes were especially dramatic during the first decade after the transition to democracy, when the new socialist government swept away a large proportion of the appointments made by the incumbent. Political appointments were four times higher in 1982 than in 1973: 76 per cent of high officials were removed and new appointments made (Parrado, 1996).

The development of the welfare state in the 1980s also sharply increased the opportunities for political patronage. Between 1982 and 1994, more than half a million new jobs in the central administration were established, and the government could directly appoint an important share of the highest positions in the new departments (Beltran, 1996). Although public employment may have contributed to PSOE's organizational development, it was not a significant feature of the party's electoral mobilization. Besides, government spending did not follow clientelistic patterns but democratic ones, focusing on social protection and economic modernization (Hopkin, 2001: 127).

Change was also significant when the PP ousted the PSOE from government in 1996. After fourteen years of socialist government, the conservatives considered that they needed to populate public administration with their own personnel in order to adequately control its functioning. Turnover rates reached about 90 per cent of free appointments at the top level of the political-administrative structure and high-ranking administrative levels in 1996 (Magone, 2004: 74).[6] Many of these positions were filled by appointees from the most elitist administrative corps (Villoria Mendieta and Huntoon, 2002: 183).

On both occasions, 1982 and 1996, there was a need to ensure civil service loyalty while bearing full ministerial responsibility. The PSOE did not trust the cadres who had taken part in the previous transition government and in Franco's dictatorship, and the PP mistrusted most political appointees from PSOE governments (Parrado, 2001: 11). Again, it is important to note that the effects of party change are concentrated at the top level, affecting the political-administrative structure (junior ministers, undersecretaries, and directors general) and high-ranking administrative levels—which go from level 26 to 30—such as deputy directors general and equivalent, many of whom are often reassigned to different positions.

Access to government by the different parties has provided them with an excellent opportunity to reinforce their presence on the ground (Hopkin, 2001: 126). Between 1982 and 1986, the PSOE incorporated over 73,000 new members, and between 1996 and 2000, 97,000 new members joined the PP. However, this sharp trend did not come about after the PSOE reached public office again in 2004 (Verge, 2007: 113).

According to the experts interviewed, turnover rates in public administration have attained similar proportions in Zapatero's cabinets (2004–11). Many of the new recruits (half the ministers and a similar proportion of high-ranking officials) had already been political appointees under the socialist governments led by Felipe González.

Government replacements have also brought about large turnover rates at the regional level. When the PP first won the presidency of Galicia in 1990, 97 per cent of the free designation public servants were removed. In 2005, the bipartite coalition between the Socialists and the Galician nationalists changed 60 per cent of the political-administrative structure during its first two years in government.[7] In Catalonia, over 1,000 political appointees, advisers, and freely designated high-rank civil servants lost their jobs when the nationalist party federation Convergence and Union was replaced by a tripartite left-wing coalition.[8] In the Basque country, the Socialist government elected in 2009 removed 655 political appointees who had served under the cabinets led by the Basque Nationalist Party.[9]

The two main national parties differ in that the major corps—i.e. tax inspectors, engineers, public prosecutors, etc.—are far more represented among PP high-ranking officials. The very same prime minister, José María Aznar, belonged to one of them (as a tax inspector) before he became the party leader.

The number of high-ranking officials has steadily increased at both national and regional levels. It is remarkable that there has been no reduction at the national level despite the devolution process, as Table 16.2 reports. The debate on the number of political appointees and advisers has always been on the electoral agenda, the challenger blaming the incumbent for its large numbers. It has been observed that the second cabinet a party forms tends to inflate its numbers. The increase in cabinet advisers was particularly large with the last PSOE government until the economic crisis forced the central cabinet to apply a significant reduction.[10] It should be noted that, in 2008, the vast majority of the advisory staff was concentrated at the Ministry of Public Administration (160) and the Ministry of the Presidency (254), the rest of the ministries having an average of fourteen advisers (ranging from 0 to 33).

TABLE 16.2 *Top-level political appointees and advisers (1999–2008)*

	PP		PSOE	
	1999	2000	2004	2008
Top-level appointees[a]	333	350	367	409
Cabinet advisory staff[b]	374	394	582	674
Number of ministries	14	15	16	17

Source: Intervención General del Estado, *Personal al servicio del sector público estatal* (1999, 2000, 2004, 2008, 2010).

[a] Includes junior ministers, undersecretaries, secretaries general and directors general, and political appointments at top positions of NDACs.

[b] Includes not only externally hired staff but also top civil servants who eventually integrate into these cabinets. Disaggregated data for these two categories has been impossible to obtain.

Sharing patronage appointments among parties: the predominance of majoritarian appointments

Political relations in Spanish democracy are conceived as adversarial rather than accommodative politics (Field, 2006). This is so although democracy was installed through a pacted transition (*reforma pactada*) led by the elites and based on multilateral compromises which could well have given rise to a corporative or consociational democracy (Karl and Schmitter, 1991). However, the main political actors did not have a consensual political culture that could facilitate negotiation and compromise once democracy had stabilized (Hopkin, 2005: 23).

Spain has a democratic parliamentarian regime with majoritarian rule, as the executive power is heavily concentrated. Since 1977, there have been no coalition governments, even when the winning party has not reached a majority of seats in the lower house. All single-party majority governments have excluded opposition parties from patronage positions to a great extent. Appointments are basically made by the party in government, and opposition parties only get a share when either the law or the constitution dictates that they have to be consensually decided at the lower house or at both the lower and the upper houses (Congress of Deputies and Senate), as Figure 16.4 shows.

Consensual appointments are mainly concentrated at the NDAC level, although shared appointments can also be found in executing institutions. Most of the appointments in which government and opposition participate affect regulatory agencies or constitutional bodies whose aim is to control state institutions. In these cases, government and opposition parties have to agree on the proposed candidates, whose professional qualifications and experience are publicly scrutinized. That is the case for the Court of Auditors (Finance), the Constitutional Court (Judiciary), the General Council of the Judiciary (Judiciary), and the members of

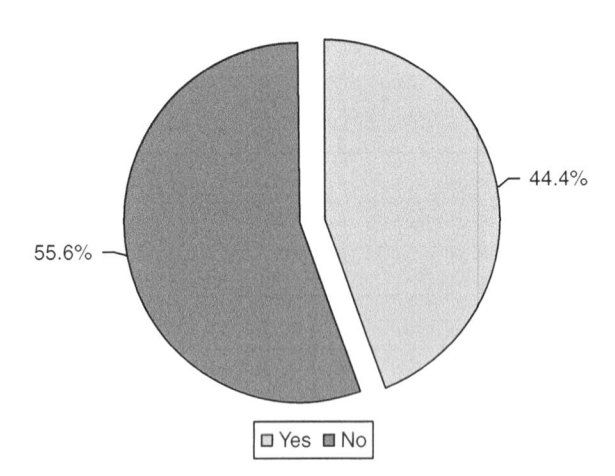

FIGURE 16.4 Sharing of patronage appointments among parties

the council of the state-owned television and radio network *RTVE* (Media). Additionally, a qualified majority is required for most of them.

A small number of positions in the management board of some regulatory agencies are also reserved to the opposition in the Industry/Economy area (National Committee for Energy, *Consejo Nacional de la Energía*, and Committee for Nuclear Security, *Consejo de Seguridad Nuclear*) and the Finance area (Bank of Spain and Stock Market National Committee, *Comisión Nacional del Mercado de Valores*).

It is normally the main opposition party (either the PSOE or the PP) which gets the largest share of such appointments. Participation of minor parties in the distribution of political appointments depends on the parliamentary arithmetic. Minority governments (1993–6, 1996–2000, 2004–11) have been more generous with small parties that helped ensure the government's investiture and that supported the most important pieces of legislation, including the annual budget. On these occasions, supporting parties have influenced nominations at the intermediate level and even obtained some second-level positions, though this is very rare.

CONCLUSION

Our empirical analysis has confirmed that Spain can in fact be included in the category of medium-level use of party patronage, as previous research had established. Party patronage is extensive but not pervasive, generally restricted to high-ranking officials, for whom meritocratic forms of recruitment based on a civil service career are not legally required. However, parties' room to manoeuvre narrows down when it comes to lower levels. Although parties have attempted to open up the public administration to more flexible hiring criteria, reforms have always faced some restrictions due to the constitutionalization of Weberian-inspired principles and the influence of the bureaucratic corps.

At the top level, political parties exert a great deal of influence over the selection of personnel, sometimes making it hard for observers to distinguish between the party in public office and the highest echelons of the public administration. Political parties are mostly the parties of public office, and make use of patronage not in order to develop clientelistic practices or networks of support but to ensure their control over the state. In this sense, patronage has become a mode of governing (see Kopecký and Mair, 2006).

In Spain, the number of political appointees has considerably increased since the transition to democracy, which comes as no surprise given that parties were keen to replace the personnel from the previous regime in order to implement new policies and legitimate their administration. The devolution process has also provided parties with new opportunities for patronage through the creation *ex novo* of regional public administrations in the seventeen autonomous communities, where no previous public service tradition existed and the degree of flexibility was, therefore, somewhat larger. Indeed, decentralization, together with new management practices, may in principle have led to more dispersed patterns of governance. And yet, parties have used patronage as a way to reach almost all institutions, no matter if they are public or semi-public, or the level they belong to.

On the other hand, Spain seems to follow the same path found in other new democracies, characterized by political parties with weak social anchoring but strong presence within the state institutions (van Biezen, 2003; Mainwaring and Scully, 1995; Salih, 2003; van Biezen and Kopecký, 2007). The legal opportunities for patronage expand to virtually all the areas of public administration under study and, indeed, parties have made extensive use of them. At the top levels of the administration, the influence of political parties reaches most institutions: political appointments and high turnover rates are the rule, especially in areas where less expertise is required. Otherwise, parties try to restrict themselves to favouring more neutral appointments, although political sympathy is always an asset.

However, the depth of patronage is clearly much more limited than its range, leading to the coexistence of a patronage system for the top ranks of the administration with a more protective civil service system for the rest. This is arguably explained by the nature of patronage. Since it is mostly seen as a means to achieve coherence, it is by and large concentrated at the top of public administration—that is, positions aimed at the design of public policies.

Spain's parliamentary system is characterized by adversarial politics, patronage being virtually monopolized by the governing party, which is always reluctant to share appointments. As some scholars have pointed out, patronage seems more likely to occur under conditions of polarized competition (Meyer-Sahling, 2006c), since incentives for parties to ensure the political control of public administration are much higher. Thus, in Spain opposition parties are generally excluded unless the constitution establishes a consensual appointment. Minority governments have been more generous with minor parties, giving them the opportunity to make some political appointments in exchange for their support. The collusion of different parties in the distribution of patronage is much more common at the regional level because many regions are ruled by coalition governments, but still the main opposition party tends to be excluded whenever its inclusion depends purely on the governing party/ies' decision.

Adversarial politics also explains why turnover rates are so high at the top level of the administration. Although some exceptions can be found, most political appointees do not survive different ministers of the same party, let alone the election of a new party. Parties pursue the control of the administration, which leads politicians to seek trustworthy professionals on the basis of their political views and/or personal links.

The party in public office clearly stands as the more influential face of political parties in Spain with regard to patronage appointments, to the extent that, as mentioned above, it is often utterly entwined with the top level of the administration. The participation of the party in central office in party patronage is limited to the proposal of some names and of regional and gender quotas. Ministers are autonomous when it comes to appointments, but the prime minister and his cabinet do have a significant influence over the overall design, which ends up being the by-product of the loose coordination of a reduced number of political leaders.

Yet this does not mean that the party in central office is completely subordinated to the party in public office. Indeed, the former tightly controls the parliamentary group with strict discipline and is exclusively in charge of drafting candidate tickets, so political careers outside parties are virtually impossible. In addition, the fact that all Spanish prime ministers have also been the leader of their party makes the attribution of responsibilities a fuzzy task.

Finally, although the opportunities for party patronage in the public and semi-public sphere have helped parties develop their organization to some extent, particularly by widening their membership, this has not been a significant feature of electoral mobilization; nor has it entailed clientelistic practices. Occasionally, in the context of factional disputes, parties have used patronage resources to promote intraparty cohesion and organizational loyalty. But, in general, party patronage follows a pattern that is related to governance rather than to any specific form of exchange.

Thus, party patronage in the Spanish context should be seen as part of party government, as 'a way of governing rather than as a way of generating favours' (Kopecký and Mair, 2006: 7). In other words, it must be regarded as an instrument of governance that helps political parties implement public policies and allows them to distinguish from each other in terms of managerial and policy-solving capacity.

NOTES

1. The ratio of party members to the electorate increased from 1.82 in 1980 to 3.42 in 2000, and to 4.36 in 2008 (van Biezen, Mair, and Poguntke, 2012).
2. Besides two autonomous cities, Ceuta and Melilla.
3. The catalogue of politically designated posts at the regional level uses slightly different denominations. See Ramió and Subirats (1996) and Mesa del Olmo (2000) for the equivalences with the central administration.
4. If we calculate the median values of all policy sectors for each institutional level, we obtain that, in a 0–1 scale, range is at 0.89 and depth 0.33.

5. However, in the 1980s, in the context of factional disputes among *guerristas* and *renovadores*, it has been documented how both factions, and especially the former, widely used patronage as a means to reward loyalty to their supporters (Gillespie, 1994).
6. Appointments of ambassadors, government delegates in provinces and the like are not included.
7. *La Opinión Coruña*, 4 March 2009.
8. *El País*, 10 December 2003.
9. *El Correo Digital*, 9 March 2009.
10. By 2010, top-level appointees had been reduced to 340, although cabinet advisory staff increased to 717.

CHAPTER 17

Party Patronage in the United Kingdom: A Pendulum of Public Appointments

Matthew Flinders and Felicity Matthews

INTRODUCTION

> Over the Labour years these groups have swelled from an irritant into a state within a state. With 700,000 employees and boards that read like a who-was-who of the Blair/Brown era, the quangos will represent Labour's stay-behind fifth column. Not only are the quangocrats implacably opposed to the Conservatives' reform programme, but they are better placed than even the wiliest Sir Humphrey to thwart change and mount a guerrilla insurgency against public spending controls... The public are thoroughly fed up too with the smug, preachy, arrogant, and largely unaccountable class who are in day-to-day command of so much of national life.
>
> Dennis Sewell, *The Spectator,* October 2009.

The UK is widely regarded as a classic example of 'party government', in which the governing political party has very few, if any, restrictions on its capacity to appoint individuals within the civil service and wider state sector. This power-hoarding dynamic stems from the nature of a majoritarian polity based on a 'winner takes all' approach to power at the national level and a commitment to 'strong' government, both of which are manifestations of the overarching two-party system (see Lijphart, 1984). Yet, since the mid 1990s the distribution of power in the UK has altered significantly, and as a result the UK is no longer a classic example of pure majoritarianism but is better understood as a form of 'modified majoritarianism' (Flinders, 2009). The argument of this chapter is that a central element of this modification has occurred in relation to party patronage, wherein the power of government actors has been gradually—and consciously—diluted or transferred over to non-partisan actors. Recognizing the existence and extent of these changes in the UK is critical, and there is a significant disjuncture between the increasingly limited capacity of ministers to influence senior public appointments and widely-held opinion regarding corruption and cronyism. This tension has been driven and reinforced by a range of factors, including the lack of recent detailed and theoretically informed research into party patronage in the UK, and a national media that portrays every appointment as a partisan decision (see the quote at the head of this chapter).

Political analysis in relation to party patronage is, however, by no means a straightforward endeavour for scholars, as 'most governments are reluctant to admit patronage practices due to the negative connotation the notion of partitocracy has on public opinion' (Kopecký and Scherlis, 2008: 361). In Britain, the notion of 'sleaze' generally shadows any discussion of party patronage and therefore makes ministers and their officials extremely reluctant to discuss the topic, which has contributed to the dearth of scholarship (for notable exceptions see Denton, 2006; Pyper and McTavish, 2007). This chapter therefore seeks to address this lacuna within the literature, and draws upon over sixty semi-structured interviews and the analysis of parliamentary, legislative, and scholarly documents in order to discuss the reality of party patronage in the UK. The outcome is a body of work that challenges both academic stereotypes and public perceptions of party patronage in the UK. Party patronage still exists. Ministers still wield significant powers. However, the capacity and discretion of ministers in the sphere of party patronage has been reduced significantly since 1995, and this process shows few signs of waning. Ministers will only get personally involved in a very small number of the public appointments for which they are constitutionally responsible. In turn, the scope of party patronage is narrow, and the dominant motivation is control rather than reward (cf. Kopecký and Scherlis, 2008). Furthermore, the shift towards regulated appointment practices suggests that it is senior civil servants and members of appointing bodies who wield the most power in relation to public appointments, which has led to concerns regarding the accountability and legitimacy of those arenas to which responsibility for appointments has been passed. Finally, in the UK the link between party affiliation and party patronage is not always a positive one, and close personal relationships with the party of government are likely to act against a candidate, because ministers and their officials are aware that the appointment would become the focus of accusations of cronyism, sleaze, and corruption in parliament and the media.

PARTY GOVERNMENT AND PUBLIC APPOINTMENTS IN THE UK

The extent to which political parties are engaged in British society is largely a product of the party system and the electoral system that sustains it, and the UK has been characterized as having a two-party system, based on a 'party *duopoly* of parliamentary seats and a party *monopoly* of the executive government' (Finer, 1980: 3). The existence of a two-party system in the UK has been reflected in the oscillation of power between two main parties, a phenomenon that Finer termed 'the party pendulum' (Finer, 1980: 6). In the nineteenth century, governmental power swung back and forth between the Conservative and Whig parties, the latter being absorbed into the Liberal party in 1859. After the First World War, the two-party system focused upon the Conservative party and the Labour party—which was established in 1900, and enjoyed two brief spells as a minority government in 1924 and 1929–31. The period that followed 1931 saw the suspension of the two-party system, as from 1931 to 1940 the country was governed by the National government (although Finer described this as 'a Conservative party under a fancy name' (Finer, 1980: 8)), and during 1940–5 was governed by an all-party wartime coalition. The two-party system resumed in the post-war period, and since 1945 has centred on competition between the Labour and Conservative parties as the Liberal party was finally consigned to the role of a minor player. The dominance of the two-party system has been reinforced, possibly even created, by the 'first past the post' electoral system, which has the effect of disproportionately exaggerating aggregate movements of public opinion. The result of the electoral system is to produce decisive shifts in government—a 'winner takes all' alternation of power between the two main parties (Sartori, 1976), and it has been suggested that the British electoral system 'makes voters prisoners of parties' (Rose, 1980: 9). The Labour landslide of 1997, for example, which saw the party win 63.4 per cent of available seats in the House of Commons, was based on only 42.3 per cent of the votes cast within a turnout of 71.5 per cent—the lowest national level of turnout since 1935. The disproportional electoral system therefore creates what Rae calls 'manufactured majorities' (Rae, 1967: 74), which afford the party in power significant—and disproportionate—control over a range of state resources.

The work of Lijphart offers a sophisticated way of understanding the interrelationships between political parties, democratic traditions, and, in turn, the character of executive power. He highlights a number of characteristics that feed into the conception of the UK as a power-hoarding polity, including the concentration of executive power in one-party cabinets; cabinet dominance; a two-party system; and majoritarian and disproportional systems of elections (Lijphart, 1999: 10–21). In terms of shedding light on the reach of political parties in the UK, Lijphart's analysis therefore demonstrates that in the British context 'government' acts as shorthand for 'political party in power'. In turn, a minister is essentially an agent of the ruling party, since cabinet ministers are, by long-standing convention, obliged to be parliamentarians, which have been almost entirely party political representatives. Indeed, since 1950 there have only been three members of parliament (MPs) who have entered the House without any party political affiliations. The effects of the electoral and party systems therefore afford the party in government substantial executive powers, enabling it to reach deep into society through its capacity to command legislative, executive, and financial resources. Such evidence led Webb to conclude that 'there is little difficulty in concluding that public policy can still generally be clearly identified as the policy of a given party' in Britain (Webb, 2000: 261).

While political parties have the potential to reach into British society through the exercise of governmental power, they remain distinct from other state and civil organizations. There has, for example, been a long-standing separation between the civil service and government, with a series of reforms introduced in the nineteenth century to safeguard the neutrality of the civil service, as discussed below. It is also important to note that British political parties have always been formally separate from organized interest groups. In some respects, the Labour party's relationship with the trade unions could be seen as an exception; yet, even in this instance, Finer suggested that 'even this is best seen as an interpretation of two functionally distinct and independent organizations' (Finer, 1980: 142). And while the unions remain the largest funder of the party, there has been a gradual loosening of the ties between Labour and the unions since the early 1990s (Alderman and Carter, 1994). The main way in which political parties permeate British society is therefore through their control of legislative and executive power while in government, and although this affords limited reach to those out of power, the scope and reach of the party in government is expansive and deep.

This short overview thus indicates that in power, parties have a range of resources at their disposal to drive their political agenda across society. One key resource is the capacity of government ministers, as party representatives, to make appointments across the state. Debates regarding party patronage and the implementation of transparent, merit-based systems have a distinguished history in the UK. In the early nineteenth century, the emergent British state was largely based around independent appointed boards, often beyond the immediate sphere of ministerial control. The purchase or distribution of sinecures form a central element of this process, and allowed individuals to draw a wage from the state (for life) for very little or no actual work (see Gorman, 2001). However, a shift in attitudes towards the appointed state was driven by the publication of the North-cote-Trevelyan Report in 1854, which recommended a clear distinction between staff responsible for routine work and an administrative class of staff responsible for policy formulation. Following the Report's recommendations, the Civil Service Commission was created in 1855, which was responsible for the recruitment, selection, and training of civil servants, based upon the overriding principle of appointment on merit. The creation of the Civil Service Commission thus fundamentally circumscribed the ability of ministers to make appointments to the civil service.

Despite the reforms enacted within Whitehall, there remained a large swathe of administrative functions exercised beyond the immediate auspices of central government, as the rapid growth of the state from the late nineteenth century onwards increased ministerial reliance upon semi-autonomous public bodies as vehicles for day-to-day policy delivery. By the mid-1970s, ministers were responsible for over 10,000 public sector appointments to a disparate penumbra of public bodies; and the absence of any transparent appointment procedures created a concern that a form of 'new corruption' was emerging, based around the distribution of positions on public boards among party loyalists or sympathizers in return for political support or favours. Labour ministers, in particular, were charged with 'succumb[ing] to the temptation of making unashamedly political appointments' to push their policy preferences through (Holland and Fallon, 1978: 19). This led Goldston to lament that a 'new kind of insidious patronage' had developed, which was 'just as reprehensible as a Jacksonian "spoils" system' (Goldston, 1977: 82). Evidence suggests that both Conservative and Labour governments increasingly adopted patronage practices, as the 1970s witnessed the over-representation of trade union leaders on the boards of public bodies, and the 1980s and early 1990s favoured pro-business appointees, reflecting the traditional power bases of each of the two main parties (Cole, 2005).

In theory, the formal reach of ministers vis-à-vis arm's length bodies was relatively extensive and pure, as they enjoyed total discretion in choosing and appointing individuals. This was justified on grounds of individual ministerial accountability which not only allowed, but actively encouraged, ministers to deploy their patronage powers, while interpreting calls for these powers to be limited as unconstitutional. In practice, however, the reach of ministers was so extensive that in all but the most senior appointments ministers could not play a personal role, but would instead either select from a shortlist provided by their department, or simply sign-off a single candidate. This, in turn, suggests that patronage was often exercised as a bureaucratic—rather than party political—resource.

Despite the implications of such ministerial discretion in terms of accountability and propriety, the system remained largely stable and unchallenged. However, a series of events in the mid-1990s conspired to bring the issue of public appointments under intense political and public scrutiny, in turn creating a 'window of opportunity' to implement far-reaching reforms. Allegations of sleaze and corruption dogged the Conservative government following a series of high-profile scandals regarding the personal and professional impropriety of several senior ministers. These events led then prime minister John Major to establish the Committee on Standards in Public Life (CSPL), with broad terms of reference 'to examine current concerns about standards of conduct of all holders of public office' (HC Deb. col. 758, 25 October 1994). In relation to the abuse of party patronage, the CSPL's first report stated that 'although the perception of bias has become quite widespread, the evidence is circumstantial and inconclusive'. Nonetheless, acknowledging the 'considerable powers of patronage' exercised by ministers, the report recommended that 'an Independent Public Appointments Commissioner be established to regulate, monitor and report on public appointments'. The CSPL advocated that all appointments be 'governed by the overriding principle of appointment on merit', although it sought to maintain the enduring convention of individual accountability, recommending that 'ultimate responsibility for appointments should remain with ministers' (Cm. 2850-I, 1995: 76–7). These recommendations were accepted by the government, and the Office of the Commissioner for Public Appointments (OCPA) was established six months later.

'New Labour' and party patronage

The establishment of OCPA represented a move from pure reach to constrained selectivity, which was a stark shift from a patronage-based system to a public appointments framework. Indeed, the creation of OCPA can be seen as a critical juncture: a significant departure from the British political tradition, which marked the start of a series of reforms—even a process of 'regulatory creep'—through which the reach and permeation of ministers was gradually but consistently reduced, and often transferred to bureaucratic, non-political actors. Of particular significance has been the creation of a plethora of independent appointment commissions, which exist beyond the sphere of influence of party actors. The NHS Appointments Commission, for example, was established by the government in 2000 in response to a critical report which suggested the existence of patronage practices (Commissioner for Public Appointments, 2000). Rather than simply regulating appointments, the Commission assumed responsibility for making all appointments across the spectrum of NHS boards. As a result, it is arguably a critical reference point for studies of party patronage in the UK, because it marks the complete end of ministerial capacities in one specific policy area. Developments in the Health Care sector resonated with later developments in the Judiciary, and in 2005 the Constitutional Reform Act formally delegated judicial appointments from the Lord Chancellor to the new Judicial Appointments Commission (JAC). The creation of the JAC therefore represents a fundamental erosion of ministerial reach as, for the first time in over 900 years, the Lord Chancellor no longer has the sole power to select which judge to appoint, and is limited to either accepting the JAC's selection, rejecting a name, or asking for reconsideration.

In addition to these specific institutional innovations, two key broader changes have occurred to allay public concerns regarding corruption by reinforcing the merit-based framework. The first has been the ongoing extension in the organizational jurisdiction of the Commissioner for Public Appointments (CPA), which in 1998 was expanded to nationalized industries, public corporations, utility regulators, and advisory non-departmental public bodies (NDPBs), bringing an additional 6,500 appointments under her remit (Commissioner for Public Appointments, 1998: 5). The CPA's jurisdiction was once again expanded in 2002 to cover all reappointments made in the name of ministers, and in 2004 to encompass all appointments to tribunal NDPBs. Such developments led the CPA to be praised by the CSPL as being 'undoubtedly an improvement on the pre-existing arrangements of unfettered ministerial patronage' (Cm. 6407, 2005: 21). The second has been the formal role of the House of Commons in relation to a specified range of senior appointments (Cm. 7170, 2007). This formalized role has so far taken two forms. First, in relation to around fifty of the most senior ministerial appointments, an affirmative vote procedure has been introduced within the House of Commons. Secondly, for around fifty senior public sector positions, pre-appointment hearings have been introduced whereby select committees are invited to interview the minster's intended appointee (see Flinders and Matthews, 2009). These are not intended to be confirmation hearings, and the government has gone to great lengths to emphasize that, although the views of the committee will be taken into account by the relevant minister, they are formally 'non-binding' (see HC 384, 2007). In terms of its impact upon political parties, the involvement of the legislature in scrutiny does provide backbench and opposition members with an opportunity to be involved in an area of governance from which they had been previously excluded. However, problems of instituting a form of legislative scrutiny within a highly adversarial, two-party majoritarian polity have been illustrated by a stand-off in October 2009 between Ed Balls, the Secretary of State for Children, Schools and Families and the Children, Schools and Families Committee over the appointment of Maggie Atkinson as Children's Commissioner. Balls disregarded the Committee's conclusion that it was 'unable to endorse her appointment' (HC 998, 2009: §18).

Beyond Westminster, a range of reforms have been undertaken in the regions of Northern Ireland and Scotland, in accordance with their devolved competencies. In parallel with the creation of OCPA, a Commissioner for Public Appointments for Northern Ireland (CPANI) was established in 1995, with similar powers and responsibilities to those exercised by its UK-wide counterpart. Covering a total of eighty-four public bodies, it exists to provide guidance for government departments on appointments procedures; to audit those procedures and report on them annually; and to investigate complaints about appointment processes. Whereas the CPANI exercises similar functions to the CPA, a different trajectory has been followed in Scotland. Devolution has offered the new Scottish political institutions the opportunity to develop their own system of regulation, and in 2003 a separate Commissioner for Public Appointments in Scotland (CPAS), with responsibility for regulating sixty-seven public bodies, was established under the Public Appointments and Public Bodies Act (Scotland). Crucially, this legislation has led to a far more robust regulatory system than exists in the rest of the UK. Firstly, the CPAS is formally independent from the politicians it regulates. It is appointed by the Crown on the recommendation of the Scottish Parliament, and receives its funding from the Scottish Parliament rather than a department of the Scottish Executive. Secondly, the CPAS has a much stronger array of compliance mechanisms at its disposal than the CPA—notably the whistle-blowing capacity to inform the Scottish Parliament if the appointments code has been breached, which is reinforced by the CPAS's power to direct Scottish ministers to delay making the appointment in question until the Scottish Parliament has been able to consider the case. In both instances, it must be noted that the CPANI and CPAS are only responsible for appointments that fall within the competencies of the devolved administrations, and that the CPA is still responsible for many 'reserved' appointments that fall within her remit as Commissioner for Great Britain.

Northern Ireland and Scotland also have separate statutory arrangements for judicial appointments. In Scotland, the Judicial Appointments Board for Scotland

(JABS) was established in 2002 as a 'recommending commission'. It is charged with providing ministers with a ranked list of candidates for each judicial vacancy, and the first minister has the narrow discretion to reject the Board's recommendation and require a new list to be drawn up. The politics of judicial appointments assumes an added saliency in Northern Ireland, due to the history of sectarian tension and conflict. In June 1998 a Criminal Justice Review Group was established as part of the commitment to review the criminal justice system, as agreed in the Good Friday Agreement (officially entitled the Belfast Agreement 1998). In 2000, the Review Group recommended that political responsibility for judicial appointments should lie with the first minister and deputy first minister, who should take over responsibility from the Lord Chancellor. The Review Group also recommended the creation of a judicial appointments commission, and the Northern Ireland Judicial Appointments Commission (NIJAC) was subsequently established under the Justice (Northern Ireland) Act 2002. The NIJAC is a 'recommending commission' with a similar role and status to the JABS; it is responsible for recruiting and selecting judges and making a final recommendation to the first minister and deputy first minister. The executive may invite the NIJAC to reconsider its recommendation but, ultimately, are obliged to appoint or recommend for appointment candidates selected by the commission.

EMPIRICAL ANALYSIS

The politics of party patronage and reform in the UK

So far, this chapter has shown that—in simple terms—the capacity and discretion of ministers in the sphere of party patronage has been reduced significantly since 1995, and this process shows few signs of waning. The aim of this section is to use qualitative and quantitative research data to engage with the common themes of this volume, and to determine the extent to which the public appointments system in the UK is a product of party politics. To do so, a series of interrelated themes will be considered, including: the extent to which government ministers are engaged in making appointments, both formally and informally; the factors that influence appointment decisions; and the broader role of political parties in the appointment process. Through this analytical framework, a series of important findings will be set out, including the fettering of the link between party politics and public appointments, which has meant that the scope of party patronage is narrow. The constriction of ministerial reach has in turn meant that a focus on 'party patronage' risks veiling the role and power of what might be termed 'bureaucratic patronage' (i.e. the capacity of senior civil servants to control and dominate appointment processes). Finally, an unintended consequence of the desire to 'clean up' appointments has, arguably, been the wholesale devaluation of political engagement, which has meant that the link between party affiliation and patronage is not always a positive one, and can actually be prejudicial to potential appointees.

The shrinking reach of ministers

As discussed above, the popular perception of public appointments is of government ministers being driven by a desire to fill public bodies with party sympathizers to repay past debts, or to colonize the state with loyalists. Indeed, prior to the establishment of the CPA in 1995, evidence suggests that such a crude caricature was, in many respects, a relatively fair portrayal of appointment practices in the 1970s and 1980s. The prevalence of such practices was highlighted by several interviewees:

> All the previous Chairmen [of the BBC] were appointed entirely by the decision of the prime minister... There was no interview process, no public process, no accountable process to parliament, nothing of that type (interviewee in the Media sector).
>
> I remember speaking to one terribly senior judge who said that he took no part in it, because it was just promotion on the basis of gossip and rumour... The criticism was that it was almost jobs for the boys. If you weren't in the inside track, or the exclusive network, you weren't going to have a chance (interviewee in the Judicial sector).

To counter such practices, the raft of reforms instigated since 1995 have sought to limit—even, in the instances of the Health Care and Judicial sectors, to remove—the capacity of ministers to engage in public appointments, although the principle remains that ministers are formally accountable for all public appointments made in their name.

The net effect of these changes has been to heavily circumscribe formal ministerial reach, whilst limiting the opportunities for the exercise of informal ministerial reach. This was reflected by the interview data, which resulted in the UK scoring 0.09 overall in terms of the scope and reach of patronage (see Table 17.1). Indeed, 87 per cent of respondents thought that institutions were formally reachable by ministers, but only 24 per cent of respondents thought that ministers played a large role in making appointments. The 13 per cent of respondents who thought that institutions were not formally reachable by ministers were all drawn from the Health Care sector, which is something of an outlier in the British context, as it is the only field where party involvement in appointments has been eradicated, reflected in the score of 0.00 in Table 17.1. Indeed, a former member of the NHS Appointments Commission stated:

TABLE 17.1 *The index of party patronage in the United Kingdom*

Policy area	Ministries	NDACs	Executing institutions	Policy area total
Economy	0.00	0.22	0.00	0.07
Finance	0.00	0.22	0.22	0.15
Judiciary	0.00	0.22	0.33	0.19
Media	0.00	0.33	0.33	0.22
Military and Police	0.00	0.17	0.06	0.07
Health Care	0.00	0.00	0.00	0.00
Culture and Education	0.00	0.11	0.00	0.04
Foreign Service	0.00	0.06	0.06	0.04
Regional and Local Administration	0.00	0.22	0.00	0.07
Total	0.00	0.17	0.11	0.09

> My great pride that I have is that when [I was involved in] the Appointments Commission, I had three Secretaries of State during that time, and I never talked to any of them about any appointments. I talked to them about other things, but not about appointments. And they scrupulously avoided talking to me about appointments.

Beyond the field of health, there is some evidence of inconsistencies in public appointments, as a small number of interviewees suggested that government ministers had, at times, attempted to exceed their formal powers:

> It's probably no great secret that some ministers take more of an involvement behind the scenes than they do formally ... I know long lists and shortlists are often given to ministers for a view, and that is then fed back into the process (interviewee from the Culture sector).

Despite such anomalies, the overwhelming majority of interviewees stressed that ministers did act in accordance with their formal powers, which again demonstrates the extent to which the regulation of appointments has served to curb ministerial reach, and validates the low scores detailed in Table 17.1. Indeed, one interviewee in the Foreign Service sector suggested that the British experience in relation to diplomatic appointments stood out, as 'colleagues in other government departments [are] just gobsmacked at the political neutrality of the process', as it is often 'a question of which political party's turn is it to get the job'.

With the exception of Health Care, the extent of ministerial involvement across the sectors focused upon in this volume has been relatively constant. Yet it is also important to distinguish between different 'levels' of appointments within sectors. While ministers remain formally accountable for all appointments made by their department, in accordance with the convention of individual ministerial responsibility, in reality they are only actively engaged in a relatively small number of key appointments, such as the very senior or politically sensitive, with civil servants or appointing bodies exercising a leading role in the remainder. Again, this was reflected in the interview data, with 98 per cent of respondents believing that ministers made top-level appointments, compared to just 2 per cent who thought that ministers made appointments at the middle and bottom levels. With an estimated 30,000 public appointments falling under the remit of government ministers, prioritization and delegation to civil servants or appointing bodies is inevitable, as ministers often lack the time and knowledge to play a role in the large majority of appointments:

> I was to some extent involved in at least having a glance at... but it was a phoney exercise. I used to get a box every night that had forty names that had applied to be the junior ambassador to Mogadishu or something... and you kind of thought I don't know any of these characters, so how can I make a sensible comment? (interviewee in the Foreign Service sector).

Furthermore, the rapid turnover of ministers in Whitehall—averaging 18 months in each portfolio—means that ministers are often unable to get a full steer regarding the scope of public bodies within their remit. This led one interviewee to suggest that the involvement of ministers was a hollow gesture:

> I think there's a huge amount of exaggeration about ministerial responsibility. It's a very good excuse to say 'we want to control ourselves'. But virtually every appointment that is made spans several Secretaries of State and umpteen different ministers, so whose ministerial responsibility is it? I think it's a load of junk... Nobody is going to tell me that a minister is (a) going to spend the time, or (b) has the time, to go through the process of interviewing all the candidates. They don't... What are they adding to the system? Absolutely zero (interviewee in the Health Care sector).

The inability to have a strong grip on appointments renders ministers increasingly reliant on officials in their department, and an unintended consequence is the disproportionate empowerment of civil servants through their control of the sifting and shortlisting processes. This was highlighted by several interviewees, who talked of being unable to 'even get a look in... [because] civil servants did it'; of 'one very senior civil servant [who] thought that the whole thing was in his hands'; and of civil servants acting like 'control freaks who want to control from the centre'. Together, such evidence points to a shift away from party patronage and the emergence of a system of 'bureaucratic patronage', with power being exercised by officials one step removed from transparency and accountability.

The motivations of ministers in making decisions

In a complex governing terrain, the power to appoint individuals to key leadership positions within the bureaucracy provides a critical form of control capacity. Party patronage can therefore be interpreted as a type of risk-reduction exercise that enables ministers to appoint individuals in whom they have confidence due to

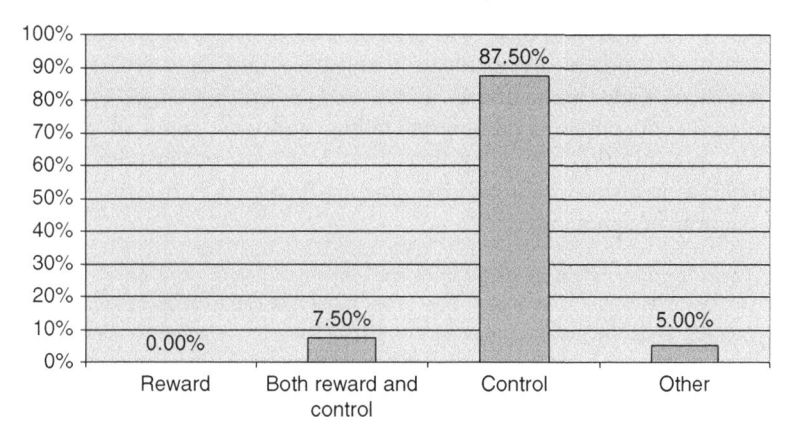

FIGURE 17.1 Motivations for party patronage in the United Kingdom

personal, party, or ideological affiliations. Indeed, in the UK the main driver for making appointments is 'control capacity', with appointment on merit representing a key expression of control, as highlighted by a total of 95 per cent of respondents (Figure 17.1)

The majority of interviewees believed that this shift in emphasis was desirable, and that the principle of merit has been firmly embedded in practice: 64 per cent of respondents believed that the principle of merit was the key motivating factor for ministerial decisions, with 84.4 per cent of respondents citing 'professional qualification' as a reason for why appointees got their jobs. Indeed, some respondents suggested that the failure to appoint on merit would serve to undermine the government's credibility and command in important policy areas:

> I think the important thing for monetary policy, here and everywhere, is credibility. The policy-making group have to be credible. It's not interest rates that contain inflation, it's the thought that the committee or governor is a credible person, who is solely interested in monetary objectives, and has no other motive. Therefore it would be seriously damaging for the credibility of the monetary policymakers if the markets thought that someone was acting with vested interests (interviewee from the Finance sector).

Reflecting the extent to which the principle of merit has been accepted, evidence suggests that ministers are generally willing to follow the advice of appointment panels:

> There were very few [departmental recommendations] which [ministers] rejected outright, and I would have said never on political grounds (interviewee from Military and Police sector).
>
> Certainly in practice to date, the Lord Chancellor had not questioned any name put forward (interviewee from the Judicial sector).

It should be noted that ministers have not passively acquiesced to selection panels, and have on occasion challenged the recommendations they are given. However, there is little evidence to suggest that, in challenging the recommendations made, the principle of merit has been compromised, or that party political considerations have affected their judgement:

> On one occasion, the candidate that we recommended was not outstanding enough, and we were asked if we could re-advertise the vacant board position... and actually got a better candidate, so it was absolutely the right decision (interviewee in the Media sector).
>
> We then put up a recommendation, but it is within the power of ministers to change the choice... It happened once. We had two very finely balanced candidates. To be honest, there was very little in it, and ministers went for the other one (interviewee in the Economy sector)

Moreover, there are suggestions that, in the pursuit of appointment on merit, the pendulum has swung too far in favour of political neutrality, which could actually serve to undermine the principle of merit. Concerns were raised that wholly capable candidates were being excluded from public life because of their political allegiances or previous political activity. This position was particularly marked in the observations of former ministers:

> I accept entirely that nepotism and jobs for the boys and girls should not exist. I accept entirely that what ministers do should be transparent. I'd just like it to apply all the way through the process, and instead of having politicians excluded and bureaucrats revered, we should have a balance that ensures that on every major public appointment we actually have a good spread of people with very different experiences (former minister in the Culture and Education sector).
>
> I think we undermine the legitimacy of the political process. It should be neither favour, but it shouldn't be a disadvantage either. It should be regarded as a perfectly legitimate and honourable occupation (former minister in the Health Care sector).

Such evidence suggests that an unintended consequence of the drive to 'clean up' politics and eradicate cronyism has been the denigration of political activity, which led one former minister to suggested that 'we're moving in the opposite direction, where we're shovelling accountable politics out of the window as fast as we can'. Such evidence suggests that a grey area has emerged, and in the pursuit of objectivity and neutrality the key principle of appointment upon merit may become undermined while also hollowing out the leadership capacity and role of ministers.

The majority of evidence suggests that appointment on merit has been embedded as a key principle, which was also borne out by interview data. However, whilst 84.4 per cent of respondents stated that appointments are made on the basis of professional qualification, 24.4 per cent of respondents also highlighted 'political links', and 15.6 per cent highlighted 'personal allegiances' as reasons why appointees were chosen, as detailed in Figure 17.2.

Several respondents acknowledged that there were occasions when it could be desirable to appoint people with similar political perspectives. One former minister in the Health Care sector stated that: 'political parties want their people there... because of certain ethos, and things which are important to them. It's your way of making sure that your values are represented all over the place... to control the political process.'

Furthermore, a chair of a major public board suggested that political considerations were wholly relevant in a small number of appointments 'where you need the right sorts of sensitivities for those jobs to be done well. So, inevitably, an element of judgement about somebody's political nouse comes into the selection process.' Indeed, an interviewee associated with OCPA stated that it would be 'naive to think that if a minister has a long-standing, respected relationship through a party with an individual, they're not going to get a better chance'. Nonetheless, they stressed that as long as transparency and openness was maintained, they had 'no problem with that'.

Several recent high-profile appointments have attracted criticism for being influenced by party political considerations. Such incidents included the appointment of former Labour ministers Lord Smith as Chair of the Environment Agency in May 2008; Baroness Andrews as Chair of English Heritage in June 2009; and Lord Rooker as Chair of the Food Standards Agency in July 2009. These appointments attracted criticism from the other political parties—for example, Norman

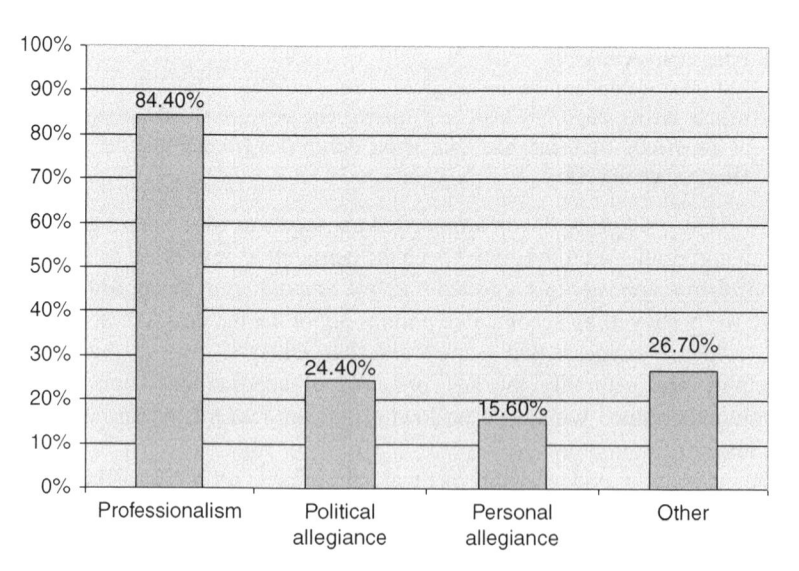

FIGURE 17.2 Qualifications of appointees in the United Kingdom

Lamb of the Liberal Democrats stated that 'I am not comfortable with this trend of appointments as it looks like jobs for Labour's boys and girls.' He went on to suggest that the principle of merit had been compromised, stating that 'if we are looking for the best people for these public jobs it is remarkable the number of ex-ministers who appear to be getting into these positions' (*The Times*, 2009). Indeed, one interviewee spoke candidly about these instances:

> If you look at the fact that the Chairman of the Environment Agency is an ex-Labour minister, the Chairman of the Food Standards Agency is an ex-Labour minister... I think there are some aspects of appointments that are moving in that direction and I regret it... I'd be surprised in both cases if there weren't candidates that had more obvious qualities.

A further irregularity is the phenomenon of the recycling of board members, which can be seen as an unintended consequence of the way in which 'merit' is defined in terms of previous experience:

> I would say that more of an issue is that people get appointed if they've already had appointments. I think there is a coterie of people who get these appointments and once you've got one, it's easier to get the next one (interviewee in the Judicial sector).
>
> I think that these bodies have now got a life of their own, which means they're almost self-perpetuating (interviewee in the Culture and Education sector).

Together, such evidence suggests that whilst the principle of merit has been broadly accepted, pockets of anomalies do exist, and that partisan considerations may be an influencing factor when ministers choose between candidates who are deemed 'above the bar'. The phenomenon of the recycling of board members also suggests that 'merit' has been interpreted in a way that favours certain groups of appointees, such as those with extensive experience of the public sector, which may in turn lead to an over-representation of certain political viewpoints. However, in both instances it must be noted that there was no evidence of favour or reward, or that the successful candidates were not of an appointable standard.

The role of the broader party and of other parties in making appointments

The overriding majority of public appointments in the UK are made by government ministers, and whilst their formal reach has become significantly limited, it is important that ministers retain the capacity to make the final decision in order to uphold the convention of individual ministerial responsibility. The net effect of this convention, coupled with the adversarial, power-hoarding culture of party politics, is that non-government political actors—backbenchers and opposition members—have had limited involvement in appointment decisions. Some exceptions do exist, however, particularly where a balance of political engagement and representation is important to achieve an organization's goals. Half of the members of the Westminster Foundation for Democracy (WFD), for example, are constituted on a cross-party basis, and while appointments are formally made by the Secretary of State for Foreign and Commonwealth Affairs, in practice the parties decide upon their nominees (through an interview with a WFD board member). Political parties also have the right to nominate a single person to the board of the Electoral Commission. However, the final appointments are formally made, not by ministers or parties, but by the Speaker's Committee in the House of Commons. Moreover, such appointments must be subject to a confirmation vote in the House of Commons.

Despite power-hoarding at the central level, the devolved and local tiers of administration provide examples of more consensual, power-sharing approaches to public appointments. Appointments to individual police forces, for example, are made and governed by local police authorities, which typically comprise of nine councillors, three magistrates, and five independent members. Councillors are drawn on a representative basis, to reflect the political make-up of the councils within the authority. Police force interviewees stated that, in theory, policing appointments are 'very reachable by politicians' and therefore 'it's not inconceivable' that party politics could be an influencing factor, although they stated that in practice merit remained the overriding principle. There have also been experiments with different appointment procedures in the devolved regions. For example, the CPAS has a more direct relationship with the Scottish parliament and has greater powers of scrutiny than its UK-wide counterpart, as discussed above. Alternative forms of legislative scrutiny have also been implemented—for example, the whole of the National Assembly for Wales has been engaged in making public appointments to the bodies within its remit, through debates and votes on the floor. A former member of the Assembly praised this process, stating that: 'one of the beneficial consequences was that, as the whole Assembly had to agree to appointments, there was a need to find a system which involved all the parties, and therefore all the parties owned the process of appointment'.

Yet, when asked whether similarly consensual arrangements were workable in the national context, interviewees appeared doubtful, citing concerns regarding the vast scope of public appointments across the UK. Interviewees were also doubtful of the capacity to utilize Westminster's select committees as decision-making vehicles, suggesting that this would be at odds with their scrutiny function. This suggests that while individual examples of successful consensual working exist, greater engagement in decision making is unlikely on a UK-wide basis. The challenge, being compounded by the adversarial, power-hoarding nature of party politics in Westminster, means that there is little appetite amongst government members to relinquish any of their powers to opposing political actors.

Despite the power-hoarding associated with the two-party system, there are increasing opportunities for MPs from all political parties to be involved in the scrutiny of key appointments, as detailed above. Since the introduction of pre-appointment hearings, there has been a wide debate regarding their added value. It has been argued, including by the CPA, that the process of pre-appointment hearings will deter many potential candidates (HC 152, 2008: § 9–13). However, this perspective was rejected by the majority of interviewees:

> I wouldn't have been averse, as someone who was appointed Chairman... to some kind of public airing. I think it could be quite positive really (interviewee from the Judicial sector).
>
> If you're not tough enough to go through that process, you're not tough enough to do a job like that in the first place... It's like being England cricket captain and not like appearing in public playing cricket. It's a bit crazy (interviewee from the Media sector).

In terms of their effectiveness at holding the government to account, it has been argued that denying select committees the powers to veto appointments risks the process of pre-appointment hearings being little more than superficial. Furthermore, some interviewees suggested that the introduction of such hearings could lead to serious tensions between ministers and select committees in the event of a negative hearing:

> I think it's very dangerous ground... to have been appointed by the Secretary of State where all [the Committee] can say is 'we think you're inappropriate'. I think there's a dangerous rhythm to that... and [there] is a huge constitutional issue about the relationship between the appointing minister and the Select Committee (interviewee from the Education and Culture sector).
>
> I know they're not formally confirmation hearings, but in fact if a Committee says they're not in favour of a person then that would be the end. So in practice they are confirmation hearings (interviewee from the Foreign Service sector).

Indeed, the public row between Ed Balls and the Children, Schools and Families Committee, as detailed in the previous section, is stark evidence of tensions created by empowering select committees with enhanced powers of scrutiny within a crudely adversarial and partisan political culture.

THE UNFOLDING DIRECTION OF PARTY PATRONAGE IN THE UK

> Mr Cameron will find, as [Thatcher] did, that a significant proportion of national expenditure is not decided by the government or even the local authorities, but by quangos. Many of these are neither transparent nor accountable. He will also find, as Mrs Thatcher did, that Labour has used appointments to senior quango jobs both as patronage and to spread its ideas of what is politically correct.
>
> Lord Rees-Mogg, *The Times*, October 2009.

As demonstrated throughout this chapter, majoritarian polities tend to exhibit a 'winner takes all' mentality, which emphasizes governing capacity and stability above more democratic values like representation, fairness, and inclusivity. In this context, control of appointments to public bodies in the UK has often been perceived as a 'spoils system': a gift of the party in power to reward party loyalists and to ensure the implementation of its political will. Yet, since the creation of OCPA in 1995, the story of party patronage in the UK has been based on a narrative of a conscious fettering of ministerial reach and capacity, as there has been a decisive shift towards standardized and regulated public appointment procedures, which have gathered pace.

The creation of the OCPA can therefore be seen as constituting a critical juncture in the politics of patronage, heralding a shift in attitudes and practices, which over time have gradually widened and deepened to effectively curb the patronage capacity of ministers, as the logic of reform in one sphere spills over to stimulate demands for similar reforms or intensified measures elsewhere. This has been evidenced throughout this chapter in relation to the creation of bodies to regulate appointments in other sectors, for example the NHS Appointments Commission and the JAC. Indeed, this spillover is far-reaching, as recent reforms in the UK have stimulated pressure for similar measures to be introduced elsewhere. For example, concerns about cronyism forced the recent Rudd government in Australia to introduce the National Broadcasting Legislation Amendment Bill 2009, which sought to remove politicians from an active role in the recruitment process and impose a transparent and merit-based framework based on OCPA. Edwards (2010: 16) notes that '[t]here is no question that the process set out in the Bill is a paradigm shift from the position up until now... Cronyism should be significantly reduced. The power of ministers will be significantly constrained.' Thus, while it is critical not to overstate the extent or pace of change—the executive has not afforded legislative committees a veto capacity, and it remains reluctant to increase the powers of the CPA—it is at the same time necessary to acknowledge the extent and direction of change that has occurred.

In many respects, the creation of OCPA in 1995 was a rational act for the outgoing Conservative government, enabling it to utilize a scandal of its own making to constrain the appointment powers of its successor, and reflects the adversarial political culture created by the two-party system. Explaining the pace of change since that point is more difficult. In opposition, the Labour party made great political capital out of attacking the Conservative governments' use of their patronage powers during 1979–97, and having made a number of explicit commitments in their 1997 election manifesto they arguably had little room for manoeuvre in terms of implementing those pledges. The subsequent creation of other appointing bodies such as the NHS Appointments Commission and JAC can be seen as reflecting the Labour government's acceptance of the concept of depoliticization as a rational response to the challenges of modern governance, as well as its awareness of increasing public disenchantment with politics, political processes, and political institutions. In 2003 the then Lord Chancellor acknowledged this situation when he noted:

> What governs our approach is a clear desire to place power where it should be: increasingly not with politicians, but with those best fitted in different ways to deploy it... Interest rates are not set by politicians in the Treasury but by the Bank of England, membership of the House of Lords will be determined not in Downing Street but in an independent Appointments Commission. This depoliticizing of key decision-making is a vital element in bringing power closer to the people (Quoted in Hay, 2007: 5).

Driven by a desire to 'clean up' politics, and to mitigate accusations of cronyism and nepotism, the politics of patronage in the UK has therefore become associated with the shrinking reach and diluted permeation of ministerial powers, which is counter-intuitive to what might be expected in a highly majoritarian polity (Flinders, 2008).

However, evidence suggests that the pendulum has swung too far away from party involvement in public appointments, in effect sanitizing politics and removing a critical tool of political control. This sanitization—and particularly the severing of the relationship between ministers and appointments in some sectors—is particularly at odds with the power-hoarding logic of the UK's party political and electoral norms. This was echoed by interview evidence from former government ministers:

> I was down to ensuring that I suggested to people that I thought would be very competent that they should apply, but that's no more or less than other people could have done, in the know, knowing that an appointment was coming up. I didn't want free, gratis to simply say 'that's the person I've met over the years who seems to me to be the best person'. I didn't want that power. But I wanted to have a handle on the shortlist recommendation (former minister in the Education sector).
>
> What are we doing as politicians? We're elected to make decisions, not to run away from them (former minister in the Culture sector).

Further unintended consequences of the government's programme of reforms have also arisen, including the apparent exclusion of appointees with a history of partisan or political activity, which one former minister described as being 'a kind of dishonourable badge', the prejudicial connotations of which are compromising the principle of appointment on merit.

These unintended consequences were recognized by the Public Administration Select Committee (PASC), whose current stance on public appointments has undergone a fundamental sea change since its 2003 enquiry:

> Ministers have themselves reduced their freedom to influence appointments, perhaps more radically than was initially intended... We do not wish to return to a situation in which patronage prevails, either in the civil service itself or in

other public service bodies. However, in the urge to avoid patronage, it is worth asking whether the balance between ministerial control and ministerial accountability is now struck in the right place (HC 122-I, 2006–7: 26).

The extent to which the government recognizes the challenges that have been created by its programme of reforms is ambiguous. Certainly, the government has continued to express its commitment to the traditional principles that underpin the UK constitution, and has pledged to uphold the principle of ministerial accountability as the cornerstone of public appointments. The rhetoric in recent publications suggested that the government is keen to 'increas[e] democratic scrutiny of public appointments' (Cm. 7342, 2008), despite the emergent disjuncture between the appointments regime and individual ministerial responsibility. However, some ministerial actions—such as the appointment of party loyalists to key public appointments, or the rejection of the advice of select committees—suggest that a degree of party political assertiveness is identifiable. The reasons for this embryonic 'patronage creep' are unclear. It could represent a reaction to the increasingly circumscriptive regulation that surrounds ministerial appointments; it could also represent a conscious attempt by a government, which was aware of the likelihood of leaving office in 2010, to ensure that its political supporters were on key bodies. What is clear is that the trajectory being followed represents a conscious fettering by government actors of a critical political and governing tool, which in turn poses a fundamental challenge to the traditional interpretation of the adversarial two-party system that has characterized the British polity, and raises key questions about the emerging party political culture in the UK.

NOTE

On 6 May 2010, a general election was held in the United Kingdom, which threw many of the assumptions of this chapter into sharp relief. Despite the existence of a majoritarian electoral system, no single party was returned with a majority of parliamentary seats; and following a frenetic five days of negotiations, the Conservative Party and Liberal Democrats came together to form a Coalition Government, underpinned by a Coalition Agreement. Amongst the many policy commitments in the Agreement was a pledge to strengthen the power of select committees to scrutinise public appointments. Moreover, as part of the Coalition's wider programme of political and constitutional reform, the posts of Civil Service Commissioner and Commissioner for Public Appointments were brought together, with Sir David Normington being appointed to this dual role in April 2011. A year later, Sir David introduced a new Code of Practice, which is intended to be more proportionate and risk-based; and in many respects this new Code recognizes the concerns expressed in this chapter. Whilst the Code is in its infancy, it is clear that the pendulum of public appointments has begun to swing in a different direction.

Part 3: Conclusion

CHAPTER 18

Conclusion: Party Patronage in Contemporary Europe

Petr Kopecký and Peter Mair

In preparing this book, we have sought to accomplish two distinct goals. In the first place, we have sought to restore attention to the topic of party patronage, while at the same time linking it more closely to theories of party government rather than to those of exchange politics and clientelism. For this reason, we have focused mainly on party patronage as an organizational and governing resource rather than as an electoral resource, or as a form of linkage between citizens and parties. This latter aspect remains important, to be sure, but, in common with much of the theoretical literature in the field, we anticipated that it would have become less important to parties and to their supporters as democracies matured and as societies modernized. Patronage as an organizational resource, on the other hand, was anticipated to have become more important with time, and to have become more central to the process of party government.

Second, we have sought to explore the role of parties in contemporary governing and policy-making processes—not, as noted in the introduction, in the sense of the familiar 'do parties matter?' literature, which is more concerned with the impact of party preferences on policy outcomes, but rather in the sense of the management and organization of policy making. Hence we adopted an empirical focus, researching the capacity and willingness of parties to control appointments to the key policy-making institutions of the state—including, obviously, the central institutions and ministries, but also the autonomous agencies and executive bodies.

This also meant that we have tried to link two literatures that normally remain at quite a remove from one another: that on public administration and public management, on the one side, and that on party organization and party models, on the other. Throughout this volume, and across all the various national studies, our chief concern has been with the role of parties as institutions in twenty-first century democracies, and with the way in which they organize and act within systems of modern governance. The study of patronage as an organizational resource has offered an important avenue for exploring this concern and for substantiating it with extensive cross-national data.

All of the original data that have been employed in this book, and the overall data set that has been created, which is now publicly available,[1] have been compiled through extensive, in-depth expert surveys in each of the countries included in the volume. In each polity, some five experts in each of nine policy areas were interviewed about patronage practices within these policy areas, and asked about the extent and reach of party patronage, the motivations that were likely to lie behind the use of patronage appointments, the degree to which the practice of party patronage was competitive or consensual, majoritarian or proportional, and the extent to which current practices differed from those in the past. Based on about forty-five to fifty expert interviews in each of fifteen countries, and therefore on 647 expert interviews in total, the result is a unique and relatively standardized cross-national data set on party patronage that marks a major milestone in the empirical study of party government in contemporary Europe.

However, it is not just the innovative data that mark this project out. As will be immediately apparent to anyone reading even a selection of the fifteen national studies included in this volume, the capacity to build on perspectives drawn from both party politics and public administration has yielded substantial insights into the working of party government in the various national polities. In this sense, the national studies tell us not only about patronage and party government, but also party systems and party competition, and, in particular, changing party organizations. In this chapter we return to the central themes identified in the introduction to the volume. Using the insights from the national studies we, in turn, focus on the declining role of political parties in organizing patronage, on the changing style of party patronage, and on the scale and location of party patronage in contemporary Europe. We conclude with a note on the notion of the party as network.

THE DECLINING ROLE OF THE PARTY IN CONTROLLING PATRONAGE

As stated in the introduction, party patronage is defined for the purposes of these analyses as the power of parties to appoint people to positions in public and semi-public life, with the scope of the patronage then being considered to be the range of positions so distributed. One of our concerns has therefore been to establish how far within a given political system the allocation of jobs and other important public and semi-public positions is in the gift of, or is controlled by, political parties. We deal with this concern below. As has become apparent in many of the national studies, however, the term 'party patronage' is difficult to evaluate, in that in practice it is often hard to distinguish whether an appointment is made by the party as such, or by an individual politician; and, if the latter, as often proves to be the case, it is often hard to know to what extent the party as such is involved. Indeed, one of the most striking conclusions to be drawn from this study is the extent to which party organizations have lost cohesiveness in recent years, fragmenting not only in terms of vertical linkages, with each of the different levels of party organization often acquiring substantially greater autonomy than in the past, but also within the same levels, with individual leaders and government ministers in particular increasingly seeming to operate as independent actors, disconnected from and relatively unbeholden to the broader party apparatus.

The Italian case, which, since the collapse of the old regime and the dominance of Berlusconi, may well be an extreme case, shows this trend more than most. As Di Mascio points out, patronage in Italy has become highly personalized in recent years, with public managers no longer likely to be recruited through parties as organizations, but being nominated instead by individual political actors who draw on personal networks embedded in the professional world. It is also in the Italian case that we see the most pronounced stratarchy, with subnational notables offering the national leaders an organizational base for use in national political competition, in exchange for a lack of interference in their own local operations and in their own use of local public resources. In this case, it seems that the party as such, except in its role as coordinator, almost disappears.

There are counter-examples, of course. Bulgaria and Spain are two of the very few polities where this research indicates that the party as such plays a more prominent role in the appointment process than the individual ministers and leaders. To become a patronage appointee in the Bulgarian case, for example, it is not enough to be part of the personal network of a minister or local party leader. Rather, as Spirova argues, at least some form of party identity and allegiance is necessary. In contrast to the Czech case, where the party as such barely constrains the choices of the ministers, and where personal networks feed into party-building, this also suggests that party identity actually precedes the creation of the networks of supporters. In Spain the party also plays a prominent role, exemplified in this case by the power of the party in central office in recommending appointments. The unusually strong position of the party in central office in the Spanish case has already been noted in earlier literature on the development of party organizations (van Biezen, 2003). And in the patronage context, Gómez and Verge suggest that this can be linked to the decentralized character of Spanish politics, which helps to privilege the party in central office as the organizational guardian of territorial quotas in the public appointment process.

An emphasis on the role of party over that of the individual leaders or ministers is also evident in the Hungarian and Dutch cases. In Hungary, the individual ministers can play an important role, but, as Meyer-Sahling and Jáger attest, this role is shared with the prime minister and general party leadership. In the Netherlands, where party patronage is more evident than is often assumed to be the case, it is again the party as such which plays a crucial role. Individual ministers and their networks matter, but, as van Thiel emphasizes, it is striking to see how each of the parties designates one of its MPs—known as 'the party lobbyist'—as the person whose job it is 'to keep track of vacancies and select potential candidates from the party network'. This is clearly a pronounced party filter, but for less obvious reasons than in Bulgaria, Spain, and Hungary, where patronage also plays an important role in party-building (see below).

In the other democracies, ministerial discretion is more in evidence. In Iceland, for example, as Kristinsson argues, 'political appointments usually take place through personal networks rather than the party hierarchy or party apparatus'. Indeed, when ministers seek to gain control of and manage a policy sector for which they are responsible, this is usually an individual effort, where the party is of limited help. As a result, the 'informal control networks of different ministers from the same party may interconnect, but the "principal" is usually the minister rather than the party'. This more personalized or individualized process is emphasized throughout the analyses of the established polities, and, as in the Irish case, for example, seems to have become more pronounced over time. Indeed, in the Irish case, as O'Malley, Quinlan, and Mair conclude, there is very little of the party *qua* party that remains visible in the wider political process. At local level, personal networks and candidate appeals appear to be more important than party loyalties, while at elite level personal networks and relations are also more important in building networks of power. In these circumstances, they argue, parties get squeezed from both sides, and while patronage might remain as important as ever in Ireland, in terms of both reward and control, it might not be something that is exercised in any meaningful sense by the parties as such. In Germany, as John and Poguntke argue, despite the importance of party both legally and constitutionally, one of the main findings of the analysis is that party patronage is largely the result of strategic decisions by different individual party politicians at different levels of the state, and is not driven or organized by a coordinating party body such as the party central office: as also seems to be the case in many other polities, 'parties as unitary or corporate actors are less important than the individual leaders who carry the label'. In Portugal, personal allegiances also play a significant role in appointments and even exceed political links as a reason for being appointed, a pattern that is consistent with the evidence of a personalization of government that can be found in earlier Portuguese studies. As Jalali, Silva, and Moreira conclude, 'personal allegiances to the party or faction leader are more important than the more abstract concept of party loyalty or influence'.

Although personal loyalties can prove more important than party loyalties or identities in appointment processes, it is precisely through party patronage that these types of networks can be developed as a means of party-building. As Scherlis (2010) has shown in the case of Argentina, the fact that the personal network precedes the party (rather than vice versa) means that it can also be used to strengthen the party and to help foster subsequent organizational loyalties (see also Kopecký and Spirova, 2011). In the Czech case, for example, as Kopecký suggests, giving MPs positions on the boards of companies is often done with the intention of cementing their loyalties to the party—something which is particularly crucial in nascent party systems, which are often subject to frequent party splits. In such a context, as Kopecký goes on to argue, it is not uncommon to observe that it is the party that emanates from the practice of patronage, rather than patronage emanating from the party, with some of the professionals who are placed by the parties in important state offices being then courted by the party leadership. Some of these individuals eventually decide to join the party and pursue a career in politics, thereby guaranteeing a renewal at the party elite level that otherwise might be difficult to achieve in the standard bottom-up intraparty process.

A similar process is visible in Bulgaria, where, as Spirova argues, parties sometimes even 'headhunt'—seeking to locate people with good professional standing who they then attempt to incorporate in the party with promises of future appointments in the state structure. Irish parties also headhunt, sometimes promising candidacies or contracts to those who can bring resources to the party.

FROM ELECTORAL RESOURCE TO ORGANIZATIONAL RESOURCE

There has been less ambiguity in finding answers to our second major concern, which involves the motivations for patronage. Here, as the chapters make clear, the trend is more or less unequivocal, in that there has been a substantial shift away from patronage as reward and an increasing resort to patronage as control. The aggregate data in Figure 18.1 confirm this finding: control was seen as the most important motivation for parties to make patronage appointments by nearly 43 per cent of all respondents, while reward on its own was mentioned by only 7 per cent. As outlined in the introduction to this volume, reward is generally associated with the use of patronage for electoral purposes, while control is associated with the use of patronage as an organizational resource. In other words, the national case studies and the aggregate data clearly confirm our initial expectation that party patronage has become an organizational rather than an electoral resource.

There are a variety of reasons for this change, some of which are common to many of the countries included in this volume. In the Icelandic case, for example, Kristinsson offers four strong reasons why the use of patronage as reward became more difficult and more contested following the 1960s, reflecting developments that are also often cited in the other national analyses. The first is the impact of the privatization and divestment of many state assets that followed the Thatcher–Reagan initiatives in the mid to late 1980s. This not only meant that there were fewer positions available with which to reward party supporters, but it also fostered a more independent business community that was probably less keen to do favours for the party organizations.

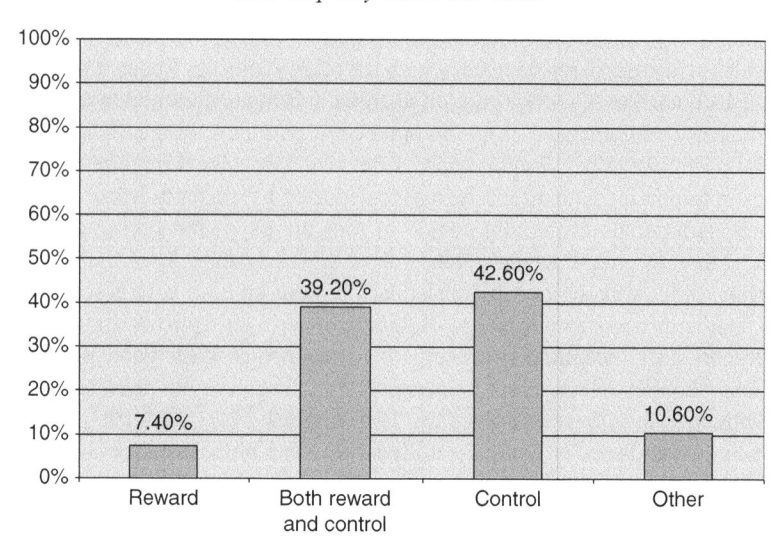

FIGURE 18.1 Motivations for party patronage, European averages

The second has been the increased professionalization of public administration, which has helped to close down the opportunities for non-qualified office holders. This is also true in other polities. At the same time, however, this may have opened other doors for the more professional appointees who came to be appointed for control purposes. Professional administrations were vulnerable to the new forms of patronage in two ways: on the one hand, it became more difficult for the civil service to resist the appointment of party nominees who were also professionally qualified and who therefore 'fitted in'; on the other hand, by emphasizing the sheer professionalism and political neutrality of the administration, the bureaucracy itself encouraged the appointment of politically sensitive nominees, who could offer a useful interface with the politicians—people with political 'nouse' as one of the UK respondents put it, or, as in the Czech case, the people who could be designated as 'politically connected professionals'. What is interesting to note here is the perhaps paradoxical impact of the 'new public management' principles within the bureaucracy, which may also have enhanced the opportunities for party patronage as control. In Austria, as Treib suggests, citing also Liegl and Müller (1999: 101), the new system reduced the party political shadow of history in ministerial departments, offering ministers many more opportunities to change the personnel of heads of sections according to their party political tastes, while also strengthening their powers of reorganization.

The third reason suggested by Kristinsson for the decline of patronage as reward, and a factor that is also cited by many of the other analyses, is the impact

Conclusion: Party Patronage in Contemporary Europe 363

of media scrutiny and transparency. Both features—especially when tied to growing legal restrictions—ensure that appointments cannot be hidden from public view, and often have to be publicly justified and defended. In the Irish case, for example, one respondent referred to this as the 'Joe Duffy effect', referring to a radio broadcaster who presents a popular daily phone-in programme dealing with the major controversies of the day. In the British case, as Flinders and Matthews suggest, media scrutiny is such that having close personal relationships with members of the party in government can actually damage the prospects of potential appointees. In this context, it is also interesting to note the Bulgarian pattern, where we see relatively weak evidence of patronage in institutions subject to substantial external control (including European controls), such as financial institutions, and much stronger evidence in institutions in policy areas that are free of external controls, such as in cultural policy and welfare policy.

The fourth factor refers to the demand side, in that in Iceland, as elsewhere, there are fewer party volunteers that need rewarding, or, as in the Irish case during the boom years, fewer that need rewarding in the way that parties can manage. There are, to be sure, exceptions to this trend. The Greek case remains dominated by reward-oriented patronage—Pappas and Assimakopoulou refer to their country as a 'party patronage democracy' rather than as a 'party democracy'—and exchange motivations also continue to be evident in some of the other polities at the lower levels of the appointments ladders. In Austria, on the other hand, a polity long dominated by exchange practices, patronage as reward has declined, with access to community housing, for example, being organized on a more objective and transparent basis so as to prevent political parties from using it as an instrument of clientelism. That said, some of the patronage-heavy sectors in Austria, such as the Military and Police in particular, continue to be marked by more traditional forms of reward-oriented exchange politics.

One of the most obvious problems in Austria, as elsewhere, is that the experts who we have interviewed often claim to find it difficult to draw a precise distinction between motivations of reward and control, and hence often judge party appointment strategies to be a combination of both. This is clearly demonstrated in Figure 18.1, where both reward and control was, with 39 per cent of respondents, nearly as large a category of answers as control. What matters here, however, is the relative infrequency with which experts almost everywhere judge appointments to be based on reward motivations alone. If a party supporter can get a pay-off through an appointment, well and good, but this usually only happens, at least at the middle and upper levels of the ladder, when there is also an organizational advantage to be gained by the party or minister involved. In Portugal, for instance, as Jalali and his colleagues attest, it is important for the parties that their appointees can serve as a means to circumvent civil servants' capacity to 'boycott the decisions made by the political authority', especially in policy sectors where there is a strong bureaucratic *esprit de corps*. Hence, even when being rewarded, the appointees must also be skilled. A similar pattern is evident in Spain, where Gómez and Verge point out that patronage is sometimes guided by the desire to ensure that the decisions made by top-ranking public officers do not run counter to the approach adopted by the government—in this case, 'professionalism is a necessary condition while political criteria are not'.

There are also other interesting patterns here. While Spain, Bulgaria, and Germany are among the few countries where reward on its own continues to be emphasized, John and Poguntke argue that the intent to reward party members in Germany through promoting their civil service careers should not be seen as a dominant factor driving party patronage. In this case, indeed, the evidence of patronage instead reflects a considerable demand-side element, with middle-ranking civil servants tending to use their party membership as a resource in their efforts to further their own careers. In both Bulgaria and Spain, the pattern is more conventional. In the former case, new governments have frequently created new positions in the public and semi-public sector with which to reward supporters. One telling example cited by Spirova was the newly created Ministry of State Administration, a government department that was officially justified by citing the need to build a strong bureaucracy because of the EU accession process, but which, following media reports, was believed to have been created specifically to satisfy the demand for positions from the three newly incumbent parties. In the event, the new ministry led to the creation of 140 new staff positions, all filled by the three coalition partners. In the Spanish case, a change of government tends to provide a boost for the newly incumbent party's membership levels, suggesting that rewards are likely to become available. There has also been extensive reshuffling of top administrative positions following changes of government at the regional level in Spain, although this might reflect the intent by the new incumbents to put their partisan stamp on the policy-making process. Here, also, reward and control motivations are mixed.

There are also efficiency requirements here. When parties, or their ministers, engage in patronage they do so by appointing people that are professionally qualified to do the job. As Figure 18.2 shows, professionalism was the single most frequently mentioned reason for appointees to obtain the job, significantly exceeding both political and personal allegiances. This is, of course, not to say that political considerations play no role when parties make an appointment: political allegiance is still mentioned by nearly 70 per cent of all respondents. The crucial question is what exactly does the political allegiance mean, and how does it square with traditional notions of partisanship? And here again one of the most striking conclusions to be drawn from this study is the extent to which 'political allegiance' can no longer easily be equated with strong partisan purpose, not least because the people that get appointed by parties are often not party members or even members of wider party networks, but rather come from the personal networks of ministers or from other non-partisan institutional settings.

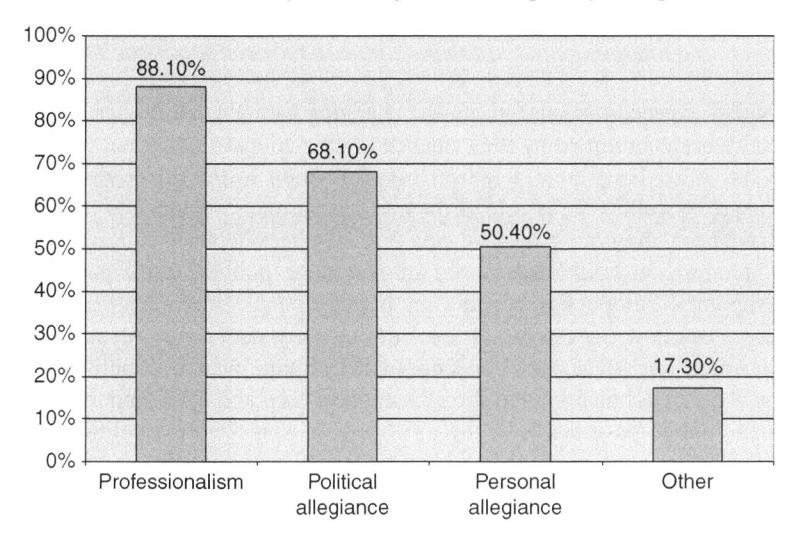

FIGURE 18.2 Qualifications of appointees, European averages

- Professionalism: 88.10%
- Political allegiance: 68.10%
- Personal allegiance: 50.40%
- Other: 17.30%

Furthermore, when parties or their ministers exercise patronage in an effort to enhance their control over policy making, it is also often without strong ideological intent. As is evident from many of the national analyses, the exercise of patronage is often less concerned with bringing party preferences to bear on policy outcomes, and is more directed towards the efficient management and organization of decision making. It is also a strategy of blame avoidance, at least in the sense that it seeks to ensure that mistakes will not be made. This is also why, as Treib points out for the Austrian case, we can witness the transformation of party patronage in public and semi-public institutions from a mass phenomenon oriented to rewarding supporters to an instrument that often targets leadership positions. In Denmark, for example, as Bischoff notes, when there are so-called 'control appointments', it is not so much about pushing policy as it is about needing well-functioning boards. In Ireland, when parties or their ministers are concerned with patronage as control, this is more likely to be about controlling performance and output rather than policies and input. Since the decision-making process is subject to increasing public scrutiny, those appointed must be able to provide safe pairs of hands and ensure that things don't go wrong. In the UK case, as one former minister put it to Flinders and Matthews, patronage can be justified in cases 'where you need the right sorts of sensitivities for those jobs to be done well. So, inevitably, an element of judgement about somebody's political nouse comes into the selection process.' In Norway, as Allern notes, even if many of the respondents refer to efficient policy formulation and implementation, some also argue that politicians need trustworthy appointees simply 'to prevent administrative mistakes from being made'.

PARTY PATRONAGE IN CONTEMPORARY EUROPE

Our initial expectations concerning the changing nature of party patronage have generally been confirmed by the evidence of the national studies, suggesting that there has often been quite a radical transformation in the underlying logic of patronage, as well as in the role of the party as patron. In contrast to the patterns that have been observed in the past, and that have been depicted extensively in the vast literature on traditional modes of patronage politics, party patronage in contemporary Europe has become an organizational rather than an electoral resource. But how widespread is this form of party patronage? As stated in the introduction, one of the key concerns of the volume was to establish how far within a given political system the allocation of jobs and other important public and semi-public positions is in the gift of, or is controlled by, political parties. Indeed, this is a concern that has long preoccupied empirical studies of patronage politics in Europe and elsewhere (see Chapter 2 for more details). Moreover, in addition to investigating the scale and depth of party patronage, we were also interested in mapping out the precise institutional location of patronage appointments within each political system, including not only the core civil service, but also institutions that are not part of the civil service but are under some form of state control, such as public hospitals, various regulatory agencies and commissions, and state-owned companies.

Figure 18.3 reports the values of the index of party patronage in the fifteen European countries covered in this volume. The index is a measure designed to estimate the scale and depth of party patronage, and the specific values are also reported and analysed in each individual national study. As can be seen from these data, the United Kingdom records the lowest level of patronage, with an index of 0.09, while Greece leads the rankings with a score of 0.62. These values are to a large extent consistent with other estimates of patronage in Europe. This is especially true if we look at countries showing the highest levels of party patronage, with Greece, Austria, and Italy long being considered as the patronage heartlands of Europe (e.g. Müller, 2007b). In other words, while the underlying logic of patronage may have changed quite dramatically in at least the latter two of these countries, the scale is still particularly pronounced. Not all cases with extensive patronage in the past reveal similarly high levels of patronage in the present, however, as evidenced most notably by the cases of Iceland and, to a lesser degree, Ireland. These two countries, which are often treated as patronage-ridden political systems in the literature (e.g. Piattoni, 2001a), reveal values of this party patronage index that are well below the European mean.

Most of the new democracies included in this study—the three post-communist countries as well as Spain—are grouped together at or slightly above the mean for Europe as a whole. This is also consistent with many predictions about the predispositions of democracies emerging during the third wave of democratization

Conclusion: Party Patronage in Contemporary Europe 367

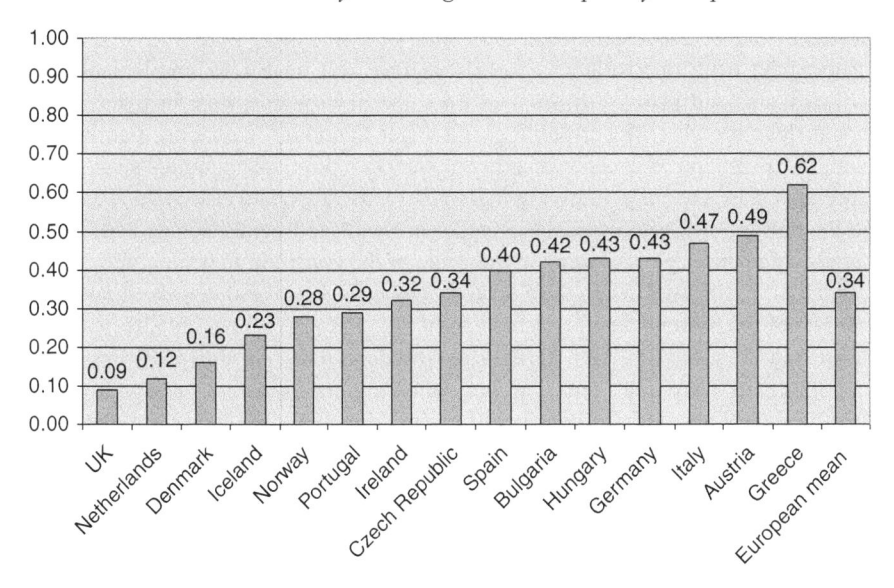

FIGURE 18.3 The index of party patronage in fifteen European democracies

to be relatively prone to party patronage (e.g. Shefter, 1994; O'Dwyer, 2006). Indeed, the most evident cases of patronage being specifically used for party-building are in the more recently democratized polities—Bulgaria, the Czech Republic, and Hungary in Central and Eastern Europe (CEE), and Portugal and Spain in the south. The imperatives in the former group of countries are clear. Following the transition to democracy, the new parties in power devoted considerable efforts to clearing out and counteracting the extensive patronage appointments which had been inherited from the former communist regimes. Indeed, at a stretch, it seems plausible to consider the old *nomenklatura* practices in CEE as an extreme form of party patronage conceived as an organizational and governing resource, with the new democratic governments then being obliged to sweep away the old appointees and to put others in their place in order to cement the democratic transition. In their discussion of the Hungarian case, for example, Meyer-Sahling and Jáger note that 'the literature on party patronage in Central and Eastern Europe tends to assume that the mere presence of laws and regulations establishes breaks on the ability of parties to make political appointments in the public sector', and argue that the Hungarian case in particular, and the other CEE cases more generally, show that such an assumption is untenable. The imperatives of party-building, and the need to counteract the *nomenklatura* legacies, can help to explain why. As Spirova notes in the case of Bulgaria, the need to replace the 'oldtimers'—including people in various state institutions such as ministries, schools, and hospitals—became part of the democratization process. In the words of one of her respondents, the Union of Democratic Forces (SDS), representing the main opposition to the old regime, felt unable to 'implement new policies with old people'. Moreover, once the new people were in place, there could develop what Meyer-Sahling and Jáger define as 'cascading patronage', with the allocation of decision-making powers to a political appointee such as the specialist state secretary, implying that party patronage could cascade downwards to the bottom of the ministerial hierarchy. In Spain, following Gómez and Verge, large-scale patronage also came in the wake of the transition to democracy, and in particular at the point when the Socialists came to power and displaced not only the last of the power-holders associated with the Franco regime, but also many of those put in place by their centre-right predecessors. As they note, political appointments were four times higher following the Socialist victory in 1982 than in the 1970s, with 76 per cent of high-ranking officials being removed and replaced.

Denmark, the Netherlands and Norway offer the most contrasting examples to these often highly politicized patronage practices. Denmark, as is more than evident from Bischoff's study, is a case apart—being, as Bischoff calls it, a 'negative' case with virtually no evidence of party patronage. There are some small signs of relevant undercurrents, of course. Political colour can matter, especially as far as appointments to the advisory boards that offer policy advice are concerned, and as one of Bischoff's respondents observed, 'it is part of the ordinary political process when you appoint to councils and committees etc. . . . these people are selected on their qualifications, network and political profile'. But even then, political colour is more a matter of broad ideological orientation and political sensitivity than party loyalty as such. As Bischoff reports, ministers making appointments will often canvass opposition parties for suggestions of names. As in the Netherlands, such appointments are thereby also intended to foster cross-party consensus, and to broaden the sources of political input. Citing Larsen (2003), Bischoff suggests that the key to Danish exceptionalism is the combination of a strong and independent—even proactive—bureaucratic culture, on the one hand, and a tendency towards the appointment of minority governments, on the other. As is sometimes also the case elsewhere, a strong bureaucracy can resist political interference, while minority governments are usually too weak to push against such resistance and, were this to be driven by partisan considerations, would be unlikely to win support from the opposition parties on whose votes they depend. As Larsen (2003: 75) originally noted, it seemed no coincidence that the initiation of the process leading to the introduction of politically appointed 'special advisers' in 1993 coincided with the first majority government in twenty-two years in Denmark.

The Norwegian and Dutch cases offer more evidence of party patronage, but often in a form that is relatively depoliticized and consensual. In Norway, for example, Allern argues that appointments to important positions in the state administration are more likely to be related to government as such rather than to *party* government in particular. Political allegiance is seen to matter surprisingly often in the appointment process, but this seems less for party purposes than for the value attributed to political sensitivities and awareness. As Allern suggests, the administration in Norway has in general become more politicized, and political skills are increasingly valued in the policy-making process. This blurring of the lines between politics and administration is 'due to intensified political-administrative leadership teamwork, and due to a growing number of public relations officers working closely with ministers', resulting in a greater demand for the appointment of people with political experience—not least, as Allern points out, in the Foreign Service, where a background in politics is seen as a professional qualification in its own right. In other words, party patronage can be important, but not necessarily in the sense of partisan patronage.

This also tends to be true in the Netherlands. In this case, the frequency of coalition government, often with three or even more parties involved, together with the strong consociational and accommodationist tradition, effectively requires the inclusion of all substantial parties in the appointments process. In the individual ministries, for example, multiparty patronage allows all the parties to have a voice in the relevant policy fields rather than having the ministry dominated by the particular party from which the senior minister is drawn. The process is depoliticized, to be sure, as in Norway, but, as van Thiel points out, this is achieved not by removing parties but by incorporating them. This also explains why Dutch ministers often appoint top civil servants with a different party political background to their own: as many of her respondents pointed out, 'Not only are pure partisan appointments rare and frowned upon, but ... a strong minister will appoint candidates *from other parties* to create a system of checks and balances.'

Scholars of public administration might be interested in the fact that, as Table 18.1 demonstrates, in all but two countries, the core civil service is the most patronage-ridden institutional type. The index of party patronage is often twice to three times higher in the ministries than it is in the non-departmental agencies and commissions, or in the executing institutions that are charged with policy delivery in relevant policy areas. Only in the UK and in the Netherlands does the score of the index for the other institutional types exceed that for the ministerial bureaucracy. These are also countries in which, as our national studies indicate, civil servants enjoy particularly strong protection by civil service legislation and traditions, much like in Norway, Denmark, and Iceland—all three countries where ministries turn out to be also less politicized than similar institutions in other European countries. With a score of zero, the UK actually appears to be a textbook example of separation between civil service and government. Indeed, as Flinders and Matthews argue in their chapter, this separation is a result of a series of reforms introduced in the nineteenth century to safeguard the neutrality of the civil service, further reinforced by reforms introduced by Tony Blair's Labour governments, which also seriously undermined party or ministerial involvement in public appointments outside of the core civil service.

TABLE 18.1 *Party patronage in different types of institutions*

	Ministries	NDACs	Executing institutions	Country total
Austria	0.63	0.31	0.52	0.49
Bulgaria	0.61	0.34	0.32	0.42
Czech Republic	0.67	0.25	0.14	0.34
Denmark	0.33	0.11	0.11	0.19
Germany	0.68	0.25	0.21	0.43
Greece	0.73	0.54	0.58	0.62
Hungary	0.65	0.30	0.34	0.44
Iceland	0.25	0.20	0.23	0.23
Ireland	0.36	0.29	0.31	0.32
Italy	0.63	0.40	0.38	0.47
Netherlands	0.14	0.15	0.07	0.12
Norway	0.33	0.28	0.23	0.28
Portugal	0.40	0.20	0.27	0.29
Spain	0.50	0.42	0.30	0.40
UK	0.00	0.17	0.11	0.09

Note: light shaded = least patronage; dark shaded = most patronage

As Table 18.1 shows, the pervasiveness of patronage in general also decreases as we move from non-departmental agencies and commissions to the executing institutions—although in several countries the pattern in the two institutional types is similar, and with one major exception, Austria, patronage seems to be much more widespread in the executing institutions than in the agencies. The general trend can at least partly be explained by the huge diversity and sheer number that both groups of institutions represent in each national context. Some of the agencies are highly technical bodies that will be of little interest to political actors. In other cases, where institutions will be the subject of partisan interest—as, for example, is often the case with state-owned companies or with schools and their governing boards—it is enough to appoint a director or a CEO in order to control the entire institution. This said, the exception of Austria is important in this context because it leads us to another important variation, documented in Table 18.2— variation among policy areas.

As Table 18.2 shows, there is no one single policy area that would seem to be highly politicized in all European countries. The media, which could plausibly be expected to feature high on the wish list of political parties as an object of political control through appointments, comes closest to such characterization: the data in Table 18.2 show that Media is the most politicized policy area in four out of fifteen European countries, and the least politicized in only one of them. In a similar vein,

TABLE 18.2 *Party patronage in different policy areas*

	Economy	Finance	Judiciary	Media	Military and Police	Health Care	Culture and Education	Foreign Service	Regional and Local Administration
Austria	0.67	0.59	0.39	0.33	0.63	0.52	0.30	0.41	0.56
Bulgaria	0.44	0.37	0.33	0.44	0.33	0.48	0.52	0.56	0.31
Czech Republic	0.37	0.30	0.37	0.33	0.37	0.30	0.30	0.39	0.39
Denmark	0.11	0.22	0.00	0.17	0.13	0.19	0.15	0.33	0.17
Germany	0.26	0.35	0.58	0.56				0.50	0.44
Greece	0.56	0.56	0.46	0.83	0.30	1.00	0.78	0.56	0.67
Hungary	0.48	0.32	0.26	0.58	0.36	0.44	0.23	0.44	0.41
Iceland	0.30	0.19	0.22	0.24	0.30	0.30	0.11	0.22	0.17
Ireland	0.22	0.28	0.52	0.30	0.22	0.42	0.26	0.33	0.29
Italy	0.44	0.37	0.37	0.67	0.26	0.44	0.41	0.39	0.89
Netherlands	0.22	0.07	0.07	0.22	0.13	0.08	0.07	0.11	n/a
Norway	0.30	0.30	0.26	0.33	0.31	0.30	0.22	0.26	0.24
Portugal	0.41	0.30	0.44	0.41	0.19	0.19	0.14	0.30	0.28
Spain	0.44	0.33	0.48	0.28	0.33	0.67	0.30	0.30	0.41
UK	0.07	0.15	0.19	0.22	0.07	0.00	0.04	0.04	0.07

Note: light shaded = least patronage; dark shaded = most patronage

there is also no one single policy area which would be uniformly least politically controlled by partisan actors in the European context. More interesting is to see that there are countries, like the Czech Republic and Norway, where the index shows very little variation and hence where differences in policy areas influence the overall extent of patronage much less than in other countries. In most European cases, by contrast, we clearly see certain policy areas that, as Meyer-Sahling and Jáger put it, are 'partially insulated' from patronage and others that can be deemed to have been 'captured' by the parties. We suspect that these variations, both within and between countries, are likely to be of substantial future research interest to scholars in public policy and public administration, as well as in the field of party politics.

THE PARTY AS A NETWORK

Although these variations tell us much about the changing world of party politics, as well as about the changing relations between parties and the state, they are far from offering a conclusive or uniform picture of contemporary party organizational life. Nor do they offer a distinct image of the emergence of some new party model or of a definitive transformation of party government. In this sense, the picture, though revealing, remains unclear. That said, the unique empirical perspective adopted in this volume does provide yet more evidence documenting the erosion of the traditional mass party model and pointing to the more generalized decline of partisanship in contemporary structures of government. This can be seen in at least three aspects of the role of party patronage in party organizational life.

In the first place, party patronage in the past was dominated by the party's central office or a central committee, which steered the distribution of jobs and controlled most of party organizational life. Within such a framework, patronage resources were largely in the hands of the extra-parliamentary institutions that acted on behalf of the party on the ground. What we most often see in the evidence in this volume, by contrast, is the tendency for appointments to be sourced from the party in public office without much evidence of any major constraints being imposed by the party apparatus beyond these confines. Patronage resources therefore appear to be increasingly concentrated in the hands of a relatively narrow group of partisan elites, usually occupying positions in the public sphere. However, it is also interesting to observe that even the party in public office often appears to lack cohesion and coordination capacity, with individual ministers assuming an increasingly dominant and quite autonomous role in appointments within their own policy areas.

Second, party patronage in the past was predominantly used as an inducement to build and sustain the infrastructure of the party, including the mobilization of large networks of activists on the ground and a party bureaucracy at the centre (see e.g. Key Jr., 1964; Sorauf, 1969). Party patronage also helped in the efforts to sustain the cohesion of the party by ensuring that positions were distributed among the multiple factions or tendencies that made up mass parties. The Italian DC (Christian Democrats), the Japanese LDP (Liberal Democratic Party), and the Austrian SDAP (Socialist Party) and ÖVP (People's Party) are among the most commonly cited examples in this regard (Leonardi and Wertman, 1989; Park, 2001; Müller, 1989). Today, however, this is less likely to be the case, and instead it seems that parties are more likely to emphasize appointments that can help them to manage the infrastructure of government and the state.

Third, while the recipients of party patronage in the past were primarily party members coming from within the large party organizations or their affiliate groups, appointees of the contemporary parties are often drawn from other channels and from outside the party as such. Indeed, while a party membership card used to provide the leaders with decisive clues regarding the potential trustworthiness of their appointees, those appointed today are more likely to have been recruited on the basis of their professional expertise as well as on the basis of a very broad notion of political allegiance and ideological affinity.

All of this tends to point to parties that are increasingly open, network-like organizations, with a flexible set of programmatic goals represented and implemented by individual politicians and ministers, and operating within a dispersed and complex multilevel system of government. These are parties which may lack substantial vertical or horizontal coherence in organizational terms, but which work through relatively loose and fragmented teams of leaders. These teams themselves develop in different ways, emerging from inside the party in some cases, coming together through the very process of being appointed in other cases, or constituting a mix of personal, professional, and partisan coteries in yet other. The party apparatus, which itself is increasingly professional and managerial, often lacks a strong partisan identity, and, as in the cartel party model, will be more inclined to cater to the needs of these teams of leaders when in public office rather than to those of the (often shrinking) party on the ground. In this case, moreover, the principal task of the party apparatus, whether located in the party headquarters, in parliament, or in government offices, becomes one of coordination and linkage, coordination itself being one of the main functions carried out by parties in contemporary democracies (Bolleyer, 2011).

The party in this sense is a network two times over. It serves as the coordination mechanism for a network of policymakers in government, integrating and communicating decisions, and providing the glue for what Tony Blair liked to call 'joined-up government'. At the same time, it is also a network in itself, in that the absence of a strong and coherent hierarchical party organization leads to a situation in which the party is constituted by its leaders and their personal and political hinterlands. In specifying the conditions for effective party government in his classic essay from the 1980s, Richard Katz (1986: 43) argued that in such a system 'positions in government must flow from support within the party rather than party positions flowing from electoral success', and that the highest positions in public office needed to be selected from within parties and to be held responsible through parties. With the ascendancy of the party in public office, however, these flows risk being reversed. The leaders may be selected within the party, but they then come to define the party. Rather than representing the party and being responsible to it, the leaders become the party, and the party becomes the leaders, or the teams of leaders, that are themselves constitutive of a party network. In this new configuration, party patronage plays a central and formative role.

NOTES

1. The data are available at: <http://www.socialsciences.leiden.edu/politicalscience/research/research-data/party-patronage.html>.

Appendix 1

PROCEDURE FOR DATA AGGREGATION AND COMMON INDICATORS

1. Data aggregation: explanation of common data reported in each chapter:
    a. Composite index (index of party patronage): The index is calculated based on the *median* values for the range and depth of patronage in each of the nine policy areas and three institutional types, and following these steps:
        i. The two values are multiplied to produce a value with a maximum of 9 that reflects the extent of patronage in each institutional type in each policy area (a total of 27 values for each country).
        ii. The values are added across the three policy areas to produce a value reflecting the extent of patronage in that policy area, with a maximum score of 27 (9 values for each country).
        iii. The values are also added across institutional types to produce a value for each of the three institutional types, with a maximum score of 81 (3 values per country).
        iv. A total score for each country is calculated by adding the three to produce a value with a maximum score of 243.
        v. As final output the index is presented in standardized values with a range of 0 to 1.
    b. Motivations of patronage:
        i. For each country—percentage of respondents giving possible categories of answers.
    c. Nature of appointees:
        i. For each country—percentage of respondents giving possible categories of answers.
    d. Additional data: role of the party and sharing of patronage:
        i. Role of the party: percentages of respondents saying small or large.
        ii. Sharing of appointments: percentages of respondents saying yes or no.

Appendix 2

QUESTIONNAIRE FOR THE EXPERT INTERVIEWS

Q1. Is this institution formally reachable by political parties, i.e. do parties have legal power to appoint individuals to jobs in . . . ? (asked of the researcher himself/herself)

Q2. In your opinion, is the [name of the institution(s)] formally reachable by political parties, i.e. in general, do people linked to political parties have legal power to appoint individuals to jobs in these institutions?

Q3. In your opinion, do such individuals (ministers, prime minister, president, party chairman) actually appoint individuals to jobs in the [name of institution(s)]?

Q4. If yes, what role do political parties play in these appointments?
   – large role
   – small role

Q5a. If yes, would you say that political parties appoint (choose the one that applies):
   – in a few institutions
   – in most institutions, or
   – in all institutions.

Q5b. If yes, would you say that political parties appoint (choose the one that applies):
   – at the top managerial level
   – at the middle level: employees
   – at the bottom level: technical and service personnel

Q6. In your opinion, why do political parties actually appoint people to these jobs? Are they interested in rewarding their loyal party activists and members with state jobs or do they want to control these sectors and institutions by having personnel linked to the party appointed in them?

Levels	Ministerial	NDACs	Executing institutions
Top level	Ministers, deputy ministers, political cabinet secretaries (state, permanent), chief directors	Directors of agencies Deputy directors of agencies	Directors Board members
Middle level	Directors, heads of departments, section heads, national directors, general directors, coordinators, heads of directorates	Managers of lower-level sections	Managers
Bottom level	Experts, specialists, secretaries (administrative), maintenance and security personnel	Employees	Employees

Appendix 2

Q7. Now, we want to ask you a question about the people appointed by political parties to these positions. Would you say that they have gotten their jobs because they are professionally qualified for them, or because of their political link, or because of their personal allegiance, or any other allegiance?

Q8. Do you think that the current practices of appointments differ substantially from previous periods, say in the last fifteen to twenty years? If so, how and why?

Q9. In reality, who within the parties is responsible for making these appointments?

Q10. In general, when political parties make appointments, are these appointments done only by parties currently in government, or do opposition parties also get a share of appointments in state institutions?

Q11. Additional comments, questions and clarifications, e.g. potential explanations for the scope and extent of party patronage.

Appendix 3

INSTITUTIONS COVERED BY THE ANALYSIS IN GERMANY

Policy sector	Ministerial department		Non-departmental agencies and commissions		Executing institutions	
	National level	Land level*	National level	Land level*	National level	Land level*
Economy	Federal Ministry of Economy and Technology	Ministry of Economic Affairs and Energy	Federal Network Agency German Competition Law: Federal Anti-Trust Agency Monopolies Commission The German Council of Economic Experts	—	Deutsche Telekom AG Deutsche Bahn AG Deutsche Post AG	Several energy providers at the local level Several housing societies
Finance	Federal Ministry of Finance	Ministry of Finance	Federal Reserve Bank Federal Financial Supervisory Authority (BAFIN) Federal Audit Court	—	KfW Banking Group Federal Reserve Bank	Westdeutsche Landesbank (WestLB) Savings banks (Sparkassen)
Judiciary	Federal Ministry of Justice	Ministry of Justice	—	—	Federal Constitutional Court Federal Fiscal Court Federal Court of Justice The Federal Administrative Court of Germany	Constitutional Court Finance Courts Higher Regional Courts District Courts Local Courts Higher Administrative Court NRW Administrative Courts Higher Social Court and Social Courts Higher Labour Courts and Labour Courts Public Prosecutors General and Public Prosecutor's Offices

Continued

Policy sector	Ministerial department		Non-departmental agencies and commissions		Executing institutions	
	National level	Land level*	National level	Land level*	National level	Land level*
Media	–	–	–	–	–	–
Military and Police	Department of Home Affairs	Department of Home Affairs	Federal Secret Service Military Secret Service Federal Agency for Constitutional Protection Federal Criminal Police Office	State Criminal Police Office	–	Central Land Agency for Policy Services Police
Health Care	Department of Health	Department of Labour, Health and Social Affairs	–	–	Peak organizations of General Local Health Insurance (N=16) Charity organizations	Hospitals
Culture and Education	Department of Education and Research	Department of Schooling and Further Education Ministry of Innovation, Research, Science and Technology	–	Agency for Further Education of Teachers	–	The State Agency for Civic Education NRW Different school types: basic primary school, secondary school, grammar school Universities

Foreign Service	Foreign Office	There are 228 German foreign missions:
	Federal Ministry for Economic Cooperation and Development	- 148 embassies
		- 62 general consulates or consulates
		- 12 permanent representations
		- 6 other foreign representations
		German Academic Exchange Service (DAAD)
		Foreign Aid: Gesellschaft für technische Zusammenarbeit (GTZ) GmbH
		Technisches Hilfswerk (THW)
		KfW Entwicklungsbank
		DEG (Deutsche Investitions- und Entwicklungsgesellschaft)
		DED (German Development Service)
		InWEnt (Capacity Building International)

*example: Nordrhein-Westfalen (NRW)

Bibliography

Aarts, K. and J. Thomassen (2008). 'Dutch Voters and the Changing Party Space'. *Acta Politica* 43: 203–34.

Abercrombie, N. and S. Hill (1976). 'Paternalism and Patronage'. *British Journal of Sociology* 27 (4): 413–29.

Act Relating to Limited Liability Companies (Aksjeloven).

Aftenposten (2006). 'Fall for eget grep', by Håvard Narum. Morning edition, 3 June 2006.
—— (2008). 'Irritasjon i UD over Støres utnevnelser', by Morten Fyhn. Morning edition, 26 May 2008. Available at: <http://www.aftenposten.no/nyheter/iriks/politikk/Irritasjon-i-UD-over-Stores-utnevnelser-6564775.html> accessed 10 November 2008.
—— (2009): 'Politiske holdninger kan avgjøre dommen', by Robert Gjerde. Morning edition, 1 October 2009.

Ágh, A. (1997). 'Defeat and Success as Promoters of Party Change: The Hungarian Socialist Party after Two Abrupt Changes'. *Party Politics* 3 (3): 427–44.

Albæk, E. (2004). 'Ekspertvælde?', in J. G. Andersen, P. M. Christiansen, T. Beck Jørgensen, L. Togeby, and S. Vallgårda (eds.), *Den Demokratiske Udfordring*, pp. 227–47. Copenhagen: Hans Reitzels Forlag.

Alderman, K. and N. Carter (1994). 'The Labour Party and Trade Unions: Loosening the Ties'. *Parliamentary Affairs* 47 (2): 321–37.

Alivizatos, N. (2001). Ο αβέβαιος εκσυγχρονισμός και η θολή συνταγματική αναθεώρηση [The uncertain modernization and the obscure constitutional revision]. Athens: Polis.
—— and P. Eleftheriadis (2002). 'The Greek Constitutional Amendments of 2001'. *South European Society and Politics* 7 (1): 63–71.

Allern, E. H. (2010a). 'Parties as Vehicles of Democracy in Norway: Still Working After All These Years?', in K. Lawson (ed.), *Political Parties and Democracy: Europe*, ii. Westport, Conn.: Praeger.
—— (2010b). *Political Parties and Interest Groups in Norway*. Colchester: ECPR Press.
——, C. Bischoff, and G. H. Kristinsson (2012). *Bureaucratic Autonomy or Political Control? A Comparison of Public Appointments in Denmark, Iceland and Norway*. Paper prepared for presentation at the Third International Conference on Democracy as Idea and Practice, Oslo, 12–13 January 2012.

Álvarez, J. (1984). *Burocracia y poder político en el régimen franquista*. Madrid: INAP.

Amato, G. (1979). 'Le istituzioni per il governo dell'economia', in L. Graziano and S. Tarrow (eds.), *La crisi italiana*. Torino: Einaudi.

Andersen, J. G. (2004). *Et ganske levende demokrati*. Aarhus: Aarhus Universitetsforlag.

Andersen, L. B., J. G. Christensen, and T. Pallesen (2008). 'The Political Allocation of Incessant Growth in the Danish Public Service', in Hans-Ulrich Derlien and B. Guy Peters (eds.), *The State at Work: Public Sector Employment in Ten Western Countries*, pp. 249–67. Northampton: Edward Elgar Publishing Limited.

Andeweg, R. (2000). 'Political Recruitment and Party Government', in J. Blondel and M. Cotta (eds.), *The Nature of Party Government*, pp. 119–40. Wiltshire: Palgrave.

Bibliography

Andeweg, R. B. and G. A. Irwin (2005). *Governance and Politics of the Netherlands*. Basingstoke: Palgrave MacMillan.
Arnold, B. (2009). *The Irish Gulag*. Dublin: Gill and Macmillan.
ASEP (2003a). *Annual Report 2002* [Ετήσια έκθση 2002]. Athens: National Printing Office.
—— (2003b). *Annual Reports for the Years 1994–2000* [Ετήσιες εκθέσεις για τα έτη 1994–2000]. Athens: National Printing Office.
—— (2005). *Annual report 2004* [Ετήσια έκθεση 2004]. Athens: National Printing Office.
—— (2007). *Annual Report 2006* [Ετήσια έκθση 2002]. Athens: National Printing Office.
—— (2009). *Annual Report 2008* [Ετήσια έκθεση 2008]. Athens: National Printing Office.
Baakman, N. (2004). 'De nomenklatoera in Nederland. Over het verschijnsel van partijpolitieke benoemingen', in G. Voerman (ed.), *Jaarboek DNPP 2003*, pp. 173–97. Groningen: DNPP.
Baena, M. (1977). 'El poder económico de la burocracia en España'. *Información Comercial Española* 522: 12–21.
Balázs, I. (1993). 'Creation of the Personal Conditions of the New Machinery of Public Administration', in T. M. Horváth (ed.), *Public Administration in Hungary*, pp. 54–67. Budapest: Hungarian Institute of Public Administration.
Bátory, A. (2002). 'Attitudes to Europe: Ideology, Strategy and the Issue of European Union Membership in Hungarian Party Politics'. *Party Politics* 8 (5): 525–39.
Bax, M. (1970). 'Patronage Irish Style: Irish Politicians as Brokers'. *Sociologische Gids* 17 (3): 179–91.
—— (1976). *Harpstrings and Confessions: Machine-Style Politics in the Irish Republic*. Assen: Van Gorcum.
Bearfield, D. A. (2009). 'What is Patronage? A Critical Re-examination'. *Public Administration Review* 69 (1): 64–76.
Beltran, M. (1996). 'La administración pública', in J. Tusell et al. (eds.), *España entre dos siglos*, pp. 265–94. Madrid: Alianza.
—— (2002). 'L'administration espagnole depuis la fin du franquisme'. *Pôle Sud* 16: 65–77.
Bergman, T. (1993). 'Formation Rules and Minority Governments'. *European Journal of Political Research* 23: 55–66.
Bermeo, N. (1987). 'Redemocratization and Transition Elections: A Comparison of Spain and Portugal'. *Comparative Politics* 19 (2): 213–31.
Berlingske Tidende. Daily newspaper. Copenhagen.
Biehl, H. (2006). 'Wie viel Bodenhaftung haben die Parteien? Zum Zusammenhang von Parteimitgliedschaft und Herkunftsmilieu'. *Zeitschrift für Parlamentsfragen* 37 (2): 277–92.
Bille, L. (1997). *Partier i forandring*. Odense: Odense Universitetsforlag.
——, J. Elklit, K. Pedersen, B. Hansen, H. J. Nielsen, and R. Buch (2003). *Partiernes medlemmer. Magtudredningen*. Aarhus: Aarhus Universitetsforlag.
Björnsdóttir, M. (2006). 'Lög um fjárreiður stjórnmálastarfsemi?'. *Morgunblaðið*, 12 January 2006.
Blakeley, G. (2001). 'Clientelism in the Building of State and Civil Society in Spain', in S. Piattoni (ed.), *Clientelism, Interests, and Democratic Representation: The European Experience in Historical and Comparative Perspective*, pp. 77–100. Cambridge: Cambridge University Press.
Blok, A. (1969). 'Variations in Patronage'. *Sociologische Gids* 16 (6): 365–78.

Blondel, J. (1995). 'Toward a Systematic Analysis of Government–Party Relationships'. *International Political Science Review* 16 (2): 127–43.

—— (2000). 'A Framework for the Empirical Analysis of Government-Supporting Party Relationships', in J. Blondel and M. Cotta (eds.), *The Nature of Party Government: A Comparative European Perspective*, pp. 96–116. New York: Palgrave.

—— (2002). 'Party Government, Patronage and Party Decline in Western Europe', in R. Gunther, J. R. Montero, and J. Linz (eds.), *Political Parties: Old Concepts and New Challenges*, pp. 233–56. Oxford: Oxford University Press.

Bogumil, J. and W. Jann (2009). *Verwaltung und Verwaltungswissenschaft in Deutschland: Einführung in die Verwaltungswissenschaft*. 2nd, completely revised, edition. Wiesbaden: VS Verlag für Sozialwissenschaften.

Boissevain, J. (1969). 'Patrons as Brokers'. *Sociologische Gids* 16 (6): 379–86.

Bolleyer, N. (2008). 'The Organizational Costs of Public Office', in K. Deschouwer (ed.), *New Parties in Government: In Power for the First Time*, pp. 17–44. London: Routledge.

—— (2009). 'Inside the Cartel Party: Party Organization in Government and Opposition'. *Political Studies* 57: 559–79.

—— (2011). 'The Influence of Political Parties on Policy Coordination'. *Governance: An International Journal of Policy, Administration and Institutions* 24 (3): 467–92.

Bozóki, A. (1997). 'The Ideology of Modernization and the Policy of Materialism: The Day after the Socialists'. *Journal of Communist Studies and Transition Politics* 13 (3): 56–102.

Bruneau, T. (1997). 'Introduction', in T. Bruneau (ed.), *Political Parties and Democracy in Portugal*, pp. 1–19. Boulder: Westview Press.

Brusco, V., M. Nazareno, and S. Stokes (2005). *The Electoral Consequences of Particularistic Distribution in Argentina*. Paper prepared for the conference, Poverty, Democracy, and Clientelism: The Political Economy of Vote Buying, Stanford, 28 November–2 December 2005.

Burstein, P. (1976). 'Political Patronage and Party Choice Among Israeli Voters'. *The Journal of Politics* 38: 1024–32.

Business Post (2007). '17 Years of the Movement for Rights and Freedoms'. 4 January 2007. Available at: <http://www.bpost.bg/story-read-9307.php>.

Caciagli, M. (2006). 'The Long Life of Clientelism in Southern Italy', in J. Kawata (ed.), *Comparing Political Corruption and Clientelism*, 157–170. Aldershot: Ashgate.

Calvert, R., M. Moran, and B. Weingast (1987). 'Congressional Influence over Policy Making: The Case of the FTC', in M. D. McCubbins and T. Sullivan (eds.), *Congress: Structure and Policy*, pp. 493–522. Cambridge: Cambridge University Press.

Calvo, E. and M. V. Murillo (2004). 'Who Delivers? Partisan Clients in the Argentine Electoral Market'. *American Journal of Political Science* 48 (4): 742–57.

Campbell, J. K. (1964). *Honour, Family, and Patronage: A Study of Institutions and Moral Values in a Greek Mountain Community*. Oxford: Oxford University Press.

Carty, R. K (1981). *Party and Parish Pump: Electoral Politics in Ireland*. Ontario: Wilfried Laurier University Press.

—— (2004). 'Parties as Franchise Systems: The Stratarchical Organizational Imperative'. *Party Politics* 10 (1): 5–24.

Cassese, S. (1993). 'Hypotheses about the Italian Administrative System'. *West European Politics* 16 (3): 316–28.

Cassese, S. (1999). 'Italy's Senior Civil Service: An Ossified World', in E. C. Page and V. Wright (eds.), *Bureaucratic Élites in Western European States: A Comparative Analysis of Top Officials*, pp. 55–64. Oxford: Oxford University Press.

Castells, J. M. (1988). 'Las administraciones autonómicas en la nueva fase'. *Revista Vasca de Administración Pública* 22: 69–86.

Chandra, K. (2004). *Why Ethnic Parties Succeed: Patronage and Ethnic Head Counts in India*. Cambridge: Cambridge University Press.

Christensen, J. G. (1999). *Bureaucratic Autonomy as a Political Asset*. Aarhus: Department of Political Science.

—— (2000). 'Efter almindelige administrative principper: Efterkrigstidens centraladministration', in Peter Bogason (ed.), *Stat, forvaltning og samfund efter 1950*, pp. 67–106. Copenhagen: Jurist- og Økonomforbundets Forlag.

—— (2001). *Political Responsiveness in a Merit Bureaucracy*. Paper prepared for the 14th annual PATNET conference, Leiden University, 21–3 June.

—— (2004). 'Det tidløse ministerstyre', in J. G. Andersen, P. M. Christiansen, T. Beck Jørgensen, L. Togeby, and S. Vallgårda (eds.), *Den Demokratiske Udfordring*, pp. 185–205. Copenhagen: Hans Reitzels Forlag.

—— (2006). 'Politik og organisation, organisation og politik', in H. F. Hansen (ed.), *Den organiserede forvaltning*, pp. 35–61. Copenhagen: Forlaget Politiske Studier.

Christensen, T. (2005). 'The Norwegian State Transformed'. *West European Politics* 28 (4): 721–39.

—— and P. Lægreid (2002). *Reformer og lederskap: Omstilling i den utøvende makt*. Oslo: Universitetsforlaget.

—— —— (2009). 'Living in the Past? Change and Continuity in the Norwegian Central Civil Service'. *Public Administration Review* 69 (5): 951–61.

Christoffersen, H. (2000). 'Den udvidede forvaltning', in P. Bogason (ed.), *Stat, forvaltning og samfund efter 1950*, pp. 21–66. Copenhagen: Jurist- og Økonomforbundets Forlag.

Chubb, B. (1963). 'Going About Persecuting Civil Servants: The Role of the Irish Parliamentary Representative'. *Political Studies* 10 (3): 272–86.

Citroni, G. (2009). 'Governo SpA: Pubblico e privato nelle società partecipate degli enti locali'. *Rivista Italiana di Scienza Politica* 1: 87–112.

Civil Service Act (Tjenestemannsloven).

Clancy, P. and G. Murphy (2006). *Outsourcing Government—Public Bodies and Accountability*. Dublin: Tasc.

Clapham, C. (ed.) (1982). *Private Patronage and Public Power: Political Clientelism in the Modern State*. London: Pinter.

Cm. 2850-I (1995). *Standards in Public Life*. First Report of the Committee on Standards in Public Life. London: HMSO.

Cm. 6407 (2005). *Getting the Balance Right—Implementing Standards of Conduction in Public Life*. Tenth Report of the Committee on Standards in Public Life. London: HMSO.

Cm. 7342 (2008). *The Governance of Britain—Constitutional Renewal*. London: HMSO.

Cm.7170 (2007). *The Governance of Britain*. London: HMSO.

Cole, M. (2005). 'Quangos: The debate of the 1970s in Britain'. *Contemporary British History* 19 (3): 321–52.

Commissioner for Public Appointments (1998). *Third Report 1997–1998*. London: OCPA.

Commissioner for Public Appointments (2000). *Fifth Report 1999–2000*. London: OCPA.

The Constitution of the Kingdom of Norway (Grunnloven).
Conway, M. M. and F. B. Feigert (1968). 'Motivation, Incentive Systems and the Political Party Organization'. *American Political Science Review* 62 (4): 1159–73.
Cooney, J. (1999). *John Charles McQuaid: Ruler of Catholic Ireland.* Dublin: The O'Brien Press.
Cotta, M. (1996). 'La crisi del governo di partito all'italiana', in M. Cotta and P. Isernia (eds.), *Il gigante dai piedi d'argilla: La crisi del regime partitocratico in Italia*, pp. 11–52. Bologna: Il Mulino.
Court of Audit (*Tribunal de Cuentas*) (2006). *Informe de Fiscalización sobre la Contabilidad de los Partidos Políticos: Ejercicio 2003*, No. 713. Madrid: Tribunal de Cuentas. Available at: <http://www.tcu.es/uploads/713%20%20PARTIDOS%20POLÍTICOS%202003.pdf>.
Crampton, R. J. (1987). *A Short History of Modern Bulgaria.* London: Cambridge University Press.
Csanádi, M. (1997). *Party States and their Legacies in Post-Communist Transformation.* Cheltenham: Edward Elgar.
Daalder, H. (1966). 'Parties, Elites, and Political Developments in Western Europe', in J. LaPalombara and M. Weiner (eds.), *Political Parties and Political Development*, pp. 43–77. Princeton: Princeton University Press.
Dagbladet (2009). 'Presset til ekstrarunde om PST-sjef', by Harald S. Klungtveit. 10 September 2009. Available at: <http://www.dagbladet.no/2009/09/10/nyheter/politiets_sikkerhetstjeneste/justisdepartementet/knut_storberget/8034961/> accessed 25 September 2009.
D'Alimonte, R. (2005). 'Italy: A Case of Fragmented Bipolarism', in M. Gallagher and P. Mitchell (eds.), *The Politics of Electoral Systems*, pp. 253–76. Oxford: Oxford University Press.
Daly, M. E. (1997). *The Buffer State: The Historical Roots of the Department of the Environment*. Dublin: Institute of Public Adminstration.
Damgaard, E. (2003). *Folkets styre. Magt og ansvar i dansk politik*. Aarhus: Aarhus Universitetsforlag.
Danmarks Statistik (2010). *Beskæftigelse i offentlig forvaltning og service 2002–2008*. Available at: <http://www.dst.dk/pukora/epub/Nyt/2010/NR036.pdf.
Deegan-Krause, K. and T. Haughton (2010). 'A Fragile Stability. The Institutional Roots of Low Party System Volatility in the Czech Republic, 1990–2009'. *Politologický časopis* 3: 227–41.
della Porta, D. and A. Vannucci (1999). *Corrupt Exchanges: Actors, Resources, and Mechanisms of Political Corruption*. New York: Aldine De Gruyter.
———— (2007). *Mani impunite: Vecchia e nuova corruzione in Italia*. Roma-Bari: Laterza.
Denton, M. (2006). 'The Impact of the Committee on Standards in Public Life on Delegated Governance: The Commissioner for Public Appointments'. *Parliamentary Affairs* 59 (3): 491–508.
Derlien, H. (2001). 'Personalpolitik nach Regierungswechseln', in H. Derlien and A. Murswieck (eds.), *Regieren nach Wahlen*, pp. 39–57. Opladen: Leske + Budrich.

Derlien, H. (2002). 'Öffentlicher Dienst im Wandel', in K. König (ed.), *Deutsche Verwaltung an der Wende zum 21. Jahrhundert*, pp. 229–53. Baden-Baden: Nomos Verlagsgesellschaft.

—— (2003). 'German Public Administration: Weberian Despite "Modernization"', in K. K. Tummala (ed.), *Comparative Bureaucratic Systems*, pp. 97–122. Lanham: Lexington Books.

—— and R. Mayntz (1988). *Einstellungen der politisch-administrativen Elite des Bundes 1987 (Comparative Elite Study II)*. Bamberg: University of Bamberg.

Der Spiegel (1965). 'Große Koalition: Kungeln und Rangeln', *Der Spiegel*, No. 36, pp. 70–80.

Devlin, L. St. J. (1970). *Report of the Public Services Organisation Review Group 1966–69*. Dublin: Stationery Office.

De Winter, L. (2006). *Sixty Years of Party Patronage in the Belgian Partitocracy: Quantitative and Qualitative Transformations*. Paper prepared for the ECPR Joint Sessions of Workshops, Nicosia, Cyprus, 25–30 April 2006.

Dexter, L. A. (1970). *Elite and Specialized Interviewing*. Evanston, IL: Northwestern University Press.

Diamandouros, N. P., R. Gunther, D. A. Sotiropoulos, and E. E. Malefakis (2006). 'Introduction: Democracy and the State in the New Southern Europe', in R. Gunther, N. P. Diamandouros, and D. A. Sotiropoulos (eds.), *Democracy and the State in the New Southern Europe*, pp. 1–41. Oxford: Oxford University Press.

Di Mascio, F., C. Jalali, T. S. Pappas, T. Verge, and R. Gómez (2010). *Southern European Party Patronage in Comparative Perspective*. Paper presented at the PSA 60th Anniversary Conference, Edinburgh, 29 March–1 April 2010.

Dimitrov, V., K. H. Goetz, and H. Wollmann (2006). *Governing After Communism: Institutions and Policy Making*. Langam: Rowman and Littlefield Publishers, Inc.

Dimitrova, A. L. (2002). 'Enlargement, Institution-Building and the EU's Administrative Capacity Requirement'. *West European Politics* 25 (4): 171–90.

—— (2005). 'Europeanization and Civil Service Reform in Central and Eastern Europe', in F. Schimmelfennig and U. Sedelmeier (eds.), *The Europeanization of Central and Eastern Europe*, pp. 71–90. Ithaca: Cornell University Press.

Di Palma, G. (1979). 'The Available State: Problems of Reform'. *West European Politics* 2 (3): 149–65.

Di Virgilio, A. (2006). 'Dal cambiamento dei partiti all'evoluzione del sistema partitico', in L. Morlino and M. Tarchi (eds.), *Partiti e caso italiano*, pp. 173–206. Bologna: Il Mulino.

Division for Public Administration and Development Management and Department of Economic and Social Affairs, United Nations (DPADM and DESA) (2003). Republic of Bulgaria. Public Administration. Available at: <http://unpan1.un.org/intradoc/groups/public/documents/un/unpan023210.pdf> accessed 17 July 2009.

DNPP: Documentatiecentrum Nederlandse Politieke Partijen. Rijksuniversiteit Groningen. Available at: <http://www.rug.nl/dnpp;.

Döhler, M. (2002). 'Institutional Choice and Bureaucratic Autonomy in Germany'. *West European Politics* 25 (2): 101–24.

Döhler, M. (2007). 'Vom Amt zur Agentur? Organisationsvielfalt, Anpassungsdruck und institutionelle Wandlungsprozesse im deutschen Verwaltungsmodell', in W. Jann and M. Döhler (eds.), *Agencies in Westeuropa*, pp. 12–47. Wiesbaden: VS Verlag.

Dooney, S. and J. O'Toole (2009). *Irish Government Today*. 3rd edition. Dublin: Gill and Macmillan.

Duverger, M. (1976). *Political Parties: Their Organization and Activity in the Modern State*. London: Methuen.

Ebinger, F. and L. Jochheim (2009). 'Wessen loyale Diener? Wie die große Koalition die deutsche Ministerialbürokratie veränderte'. *Dms—der moderne staat—Zeitschrift für Public Policy, Recht und Management* 51 (1): 335–53.

Eckhoff, T. and E. Smith (2006). *Forvaltningsrett*. Oslo: Universitetsforlaget.

Edwards, M. (2010). 'Board Games: Our 'Independent' ABC', *The Public Sector Informant*, February 2010.

Egeberg, M. (1998). *Causes of Bureaucratic Autonomy: The Impact of Organizational and Cultural Factors*. Working Paper 98/15. Oslo: Arena, Centre for European Studies, University of Oslo.

Eggertsson, D. (2000). *Steingrímur Hermannsson. Ævisaga III*. Reykjavík: Vaka-Helgafell.

Eichbaum, C. and R. Shaw (eds.) (2010). *Partisan Appointees and Public Servants: An International Analysis of the Role of the Political Adviser*. Cheltenham: Edward Elgar.

Eisenstadt, S. N. and R. Lemarchand (eds.) (1981). *Political Clientelism, Patronage and Development*. London: Sage.

—— and L. Roniger (1980). 'Patron–Client Relations as a Model of Structuring Social Exchange'. *Comparative Studies in Society and History* 22 (1): 42–77.

El Correo Digital (2009). 'Más de 650 altos cargos temen por su puesto si el PNV sale del Gobierno vasco'. 9 March 2009.

Eleftheriadis, P. (2005). 'Constitutional Reform and the Rule of Law in Greece'. *West European Politics* 28 (2): 317–34.

Eleftherotypia. Daily newspaper. Greece.

El País (2003). 'Más de mil altos cargos perderán su puesto en la Generalitat'. 10 December 2003.

Epstein, L. (1980). *Political Parties in Western Democracies*. New Brunswick: Transaction Books.

Eschenburg, T. (1961). *Ämterpatronage*. Stuttgart: Curt E. Schwab.

European Commission (2005). *Bulgaria: 2005 Comprehensive Monitoring Report*. Available at: <http://ec.europa.eu/enlargement/archives/pdf/key_documents/2005/sec1352_cmr_master_bg_college_en.pdf> accessed 30 January 2011.

Evans, G. and S. Whitefield (1998). 'The Structuring of Political Cleavages in Post-Communist Societies: The Case of the Czech Republic and Slovakia'. *Political Studies* 46 (1): 115–39.

Farnham, D., S. Horton, J. Barlow, and A. Hondeghem (eds.) (1996). *New Public Managers in Europe: Public Servants in Transition*. London: Macmillan.

Ferraro, A. (2006). 'Una idea muy precaria. El nuevo servicio civil y los viejosdesignados políticos en Argentina'. *Latin American Research Review* 41 (2): 165–86.

Field, B. (2006). 'Transition Modes and Post-Transition Inter-Party Politics: Evidence from Spain (1977 82) and Argentina (1983–89)'. *Democratization* 13 (2): 205–26.

Finansministeriet (1998a). Betænkning no. 1354. *Forholdet mellem ministre og embedsmænd.* Copenhagen: Schultz.
—— (1998b). *Borgerne og den offentlige sektor.* Copenhagen: Finansministeriet.
—— (2004). *Betænkning no. 1443—Embedsmænds rådgivning og bistand.* Copenhagen: Schultz.
Fine Gael (2008). *Streamlining Government.* Dublin: Fine Gael.
Finer, S. (1980). *The Changing British Party System.* New York: American Enterprise Institute.
Fink, M. (2006). 'Unternehmerverbände', in H. Dachs, P. Gerlich, H. Gottweis, H. Kramer, V. Lauber, W. C. Müller, and E. Tálos (eds.), *Politik in Österreich: Ein Handbuch*, pp. 443–61. Wien: Manz.
Flinders, M. (2008). *Delegated Governance and the British State: Walking Without Order.* Oxford: Oxford University Press.
—— (2009). 'The Politics of Patronage and Public Appointments: Shrinking Reach and Diluted Permeation'. *Governance* 22 (4): 547–70.
—— and F. Matthews (2009). *Party Patronage and Legislative Scrutiny.* Mimeo. Sheffield: University of Sheffield.
Flynn, S. (2010). 'Nine Out of 10 Primary Schools are under Catholic Patronage'. *Irish Times*, 30 January 2010.
Fowler, B. (2004). 'Concentrated Orange: Fidesz and the Remaking of the Hungarian Centre-Right, 1994–2002'. *Journal of Communist Studies and Transition Politics* 20 (3): 80–114.
Fry, G. K. (2000). 'The British Civil Service System', in H. A. G. M. Bekke and F. M. van der Meer (eds.), *Civil Service Systems in Western Europe*, pp. 12–35. Cheltenham: Edward Elgar.
Gabriella, R. M. and R. W. Jackman (2002). 'Sources of Corruption: A Cross-Country Study'. *British Journal of Political Science* 32: 147–70.
Gajduschek, G. (2007). 'Politicisation, Professionalisation, or both? Hungary's Civil Service System'. *Communist and Post-Communist Studies* 40 (3): 343–62.
Gallagher, M., M. Laver, and P. Mair (2006). *Representative Government in Modern Europe: Institutions, Parties and Governments.* 4th edition. New York: McGraw-Hill.
Gammeltoft-Hansen, H. J. A., K. Larsen, K. Loiborg, M. Engberg, and J. Olsen (2002). *Forvaltningsret.* Copenhagen: Jurist- og Økonomforbundets Forlag.
Garry, J. and L. Mansergh (1999). 'Irish Party Manifestoes', in M. Marsh and P. Mitchell (eds.), *How Ireland Voted 1997*, pp. 82–106. Boulder: Westview.
Garvin, T. (1998). 'The Strange Death of Clerical Politics in UCD'. *Irish University Review* 28 (2): 308–14.
Geddes, B. (1994). *Politician's Dilemma: Building State Capacity in Latin America.* Berkeley: University of California Press.
Georgiev, B. (1999). *Civil Services and State Administrations (CSSA): Country Report: Bulgaria.* SIGMA.
Georgiev, P. K. (2008). *Corruptive Patterns of Patronage in South East Europe.* Wiesbaden: VS Research.
Gibbon, P. and M. Higgins (1974). 'Patronage, Tradition and Modernisation: The Case of the Irish Gombeenman'. *Economic and Social Review* 6 (1): 27–44.

Gillespie, R. (1994). 'The Resurgence of Factionalism in the Spanish Socialist Workers' Party', in D. S. Bell and E. Shaw (eds.), *Conflict and Cohesion in the Western European Social Democratic Parties*, pp. 50–69. London: Printer Publishers.

Gleerup, A. et al. (2002). *An Introduction to Danish Law*. 1st edition. Allingaabro: Forlaget Drammelstrupgaard.

Goetz, K. H. (2001). 'Making Sense of Post-Communist Central Administration: Modernization, Europeanization or Latinization?'. *Journal of European Public Policy* 8 (6): 1032–51.

Golden, M. A. (2003). 'Electoral Connections: The Effects of the Personal Vote on Political Patronage, Bureaucracy and Legislation in Postwar Italy'. *British Journal of Political Science* 33: 189–212.

Golden, M. and E. C. C. Chang (2001). 'Competitive Corruption: Factional Conflict and Political Malfeasance in Postwar Italian Christian Democracy'. *World Politics* 53 (4): 588–622.

Goldston, R. S. (1977). 'Patronage in British Government'. *Parliamentary Affairs* 30 (1): 80–96.

Gordin, J. (2002). 'The Political and Partisan Determinants of Patronage in Latin America 1960–1994: A Comparative Perspective'. *European Journal of Political Research* 41: 513–49.

Gorman, F. (2001). 'Patronage and the Reform of the State in England, 1700–1860', in S. Piattoni (ed.), *Clientelism, Interests, and Democratic Representation: The European Experience in Historical and Comparative Perspective*, pp. 54–76. Cambridge: Cambridge University Press.

Graziano, L. (1976). 'A Conceptual Framework for the Study of Clientelistic Behaviour'. *European Journal of Political Research* 4: 149–74.

Greek Ministry of Interior (2009). Δελτίο στατιστικών στοιχείων ετήσιας απογραφής του δημόσιου τομέα [Statistical Bulletin of Annual Public Sector Census]. Athens: National Press.

Greek Ombudsman (2006). *Special Report. Appointments in the Public Sector. Processes beyond ASEP's Jurisdiction* [Ειδική έκθεση. Προσλήψεις στο δημόσιο τομέα. Οι εκτός του ελέγχου ΑΣΕΠ διαδικασίες]. Athens: The Greek Ombudsman.

Greene, K. (2010). 'The Political Economy of Authoritarian Single-Party Dominance'. *Comparative Political Studies* 43 (7): 807–34.

Greenfield, S. (1977). 'The Patrimonial State and Patron-Client Relations in Iberia and Latin America: Sources of "the System" in the Fifteenth-Century Writings of the Infante D. Pedro of Portugal'. *Ethnohistory* 24 (2): 163–78.

Grendstad, G., W. R. Shaffer, and E. N. Waltenburg (2010). 'Revealed Preferences of Norwegian Supreme Court Justices'. *Tidsskrift for Rettsvitenskap* 123 (1): 73–101.

Greskovits, B. (2001). 'Brothers-in-Arms or Rivals in Politics? Top Politicians and Top Policy Makers in the Hungarian Transformation', in J. Kornai, S. Haggard, and R. Kaufman (eds.), *Reforming the State: Fiscal and Welfare Reform in Post-Socialist Countries*, pp. 111–41. Cambridge: Cambridge University Press.

Grzymala-Busse, A. (2003). 'Political Competition and the Politicization of the State in East and Central Europe'. *Comparative Political Studies* 36 (10): 1123–47.

—— (2006). 'The Discreet Charm of Formal Institutions: Postcommunist Party Competition and State Oversight'. *Comparative Political Studies* 39 (3): 271–300.

Grzymala-Busse, A. (2007). *Rebuilding Leviathan: Party Competition and State Exploitation in Post-Communist Democracies.* Cambridge: Cambridge University Press.

Guarnieri, C. (2003). *Giustizia e politica: I nodi della Seconda Repubblica.* Bologna: Il Mulino.

Günes-Ayata, A. (1994). 'Clientelism: Premodern, Modern, Postmodern', in L. Roninger and A. Günes-Ayata (eds.), *Democracy, Clientelism and Civil Society*, pp. 19–28. Boulder: Lynne Rienner.

Gunther, R., J. R. Montero, and J. L. Wert (2000). 'The Media and Politics in Spain: From Dictatorship to Democracy', in R. Gunther and A. Mughan (eds.), *Democracy and the Media: A Comparative Perspective*, pp. 28–84. Cambridge: Cambridge University Press.

Gwiazda, A. (2008). 'Party Patronage in Poland. The Democratic Left Alliance and Law and Justice Compared'. *East European Politics and Societies* 22 (4): 802–27.

György, I. (1999). 'The Civil Service System of Hungary', in T. Verheijen (ed.), *Civil Service Systems in Central and Eastern Europe*, pp. 131–58. Cheltenham: Edward Elgar.

Hanretty, C. (2010). 'Explaining the De Facto Independence of Public Service Broadcasters'. *British Journal of Political Science* 40 (1): 75–89.

Hansen, H. F. and Beck Jørgensen, T. (2009) 'Den danske forvaltningsmodel og globaliseringens udfordringer', in M. Marcussen and K. Ronit (eds.), *Globaliseringens udfordringer: Politiske og administrative modeller under pres*, pp. 36–64. Copenhagen: Hans Reitzels Forlag.

Hardiman, N. and M. MacCarthaigh (2008). 'The Segmented State: Adaptation and Maladaptation in Ireland'. Discussion Paper Series on the research project, 'Mapping the Irish State'. Dublin: Geary Institute, University College Dublin.

Haughton, T. (2008). 'Parties, Patronage and the Post-Communist State'. *Comparative European Politics* 6 (4): 486–500.

Hay, C. (2007). *Why We Hate Politics*. London: Polity.

Hazelkorn, E. (1986). 'Class, Clientelism and the Political Process in the Republic of Ireland', in P. Clancy, S. Drudy, K. Lynch, and L. O'Dowd (eds.), *Ireland: A Sociological Profile*, pp. 326–43. Dublin: Institute of Public Administration.

Healey, J. F. (1999). *Statistics: A Tool for Social Research*. Belmont, CA: Adsworth.

HC 122-I (2006–7). Politics and Administration: Ministers and Civil Servants. Fourth Report of the Public Administration Select Committee, Session 2006–7. London: HMSO.

HC 152 (2008). *Parliament and Public Appointments: Pre-Appointment Hearings by Select Committees*. Third Report of the Public Administration Select Committee, Session 2007–8. London: HMSO.

HC 384 (2007). *Pre-Appointment Hearings by Select Committees*. First Report of the Liaison Committee, Session 2007–8. London: HMSO.

HC 998 (2009). *Appointment of the Children's Commissioner for England*. Eighth Report of the Children, Schools and Families Committee, Session 2008–9. London: HMSO.

Heidar, K. (1991). 'Should the Parties be Incorporated in the Written Constitution?', in *The Role of Constitutions in a Changing Society*, pp. 299–315. Oslo: Norwegian Academy of Science and Letters.

—— (2005). 'Norwegian Parties and the Party System: Steadfast and Changing'. *West European Politics* 28: 807–33.

Heinisch, R. (2003). 'Success in Opposition—Failure in Government: Explaining the Performance of Right-Wing Populist Parties in Public Office'. *West European Politics* 26 (3): 91–130.

Hloušek, V. (2010). 'Seeking a Type: The Czech Party System after 1989'. *Politics in Central Europe* 6 (1): 90–109.

Holland, P. and M. Fallon (1978). *The Quango Explosion: Public Bodies and Ministerial Patronage*. London: Conservative Political Centre.

Hopkin, J. (2001). 'A "Southern Model" of Electoral Mobilisation? Clientelism and Electoral Politics in Spain'. *West European Politics* 24 (1): 115–36.

—— (2005). 'From Consensus to Competition: The Changing Nature of Democracy in the Spanish Transition', in S. Balfour (ed.), *The Politics of Contemporary Spain*, pp. 6–26. London: Routledge.

—— (2006). 'Clientelism and Party Politics', in R. S. Katz and W. Crotty (eds.), *Handbook of Party Politics*, pp. 406–12. London: Sage.

—— and C. Paolucci (1999). 'New Parties and the Business Firm Model of Party Organization: Cases from Spain and Italy'. *European Journal of Political Research* 35 (3): 307–39.

Huber, J. and R. Inglehart (1995). 'Expert Interpretations of Party Space and Party Locations in 42 Societies'. *Party Politics* 1 (1): 73–111.

Íbúalýðræði (2009). Data from research project on local democracy in Iceland, 2009.

Indenrigsministeriet (2007). *Kommunalreformen—Kort Fortalt*. Available at: <http://www.im.dk>.

Indenrigs- og sundhedsministeriet (2004). *Betænkning no. 1434. Strukturkommissionens betænkning*. Available at: <http://www.im.dk>.

Indriðason, I. (2005). 'A Theory of Coalitions and Clientelism: Coalition Politics in Iceland 1945–2000'. *European Journal of Political Research* 44 (3): 439–64.

INE [Institute of Labour] (2009). *Η ελληνική οικονομία και η απασχόληση 2009* [The Greek Economy and Employment: Annual Report 2009]. Athens: INE/GSEE-ADEDY.

Information. Daily newspaper. Copenhagen.

Innst. S. no. 175 (2000–1). *Innstilling fra familie-, kultur- og administrasjonskomiteen om forholdet mellom embetsverket, departementets politiske ledelse og andre samfunnsaktører*.

Innstillingsrådet for dommere (2009). *Innstillingsrådets praksis/policynotat*.

Intervención General del Estado (IGAE) (1999, 2000, 2004, 2008, 2010). *Personal al servicio del sector público estatal*. Madrid: IGAE. Available at: <http://www.igae.pap.meh.es/sitios/igae/es-ES/ClnPublicaciones/ClnPublicacionesLinea/paginas/personalalserviciodelsectorpublicoestatal.aspx> accessed 1 February 2012.

Jacobsen, K. D. (1960). 'Lojalitet, nøytralitet og faglig uavhengighet i sentraladministrasjonen'. *Tidsskrift for samfunnsforskning* 1: 231–48.

Jalali, C. (2007). *Partidos e democracia em Portugal (1974–2005)*. Lisbon: Instituto de Ciências Sociais.

Jalali, C. and M. Lisi (2009). 'Weak Societal Roots, Strong Individual Patrons? Patronage and Party Organization in Portugal'. *Revista Enfoques* 7 (11): 411–70.

Jensen, H. (2002). *Partigrupperne i Folketinget*. Copenhagen: Djøf, Jurist- og Økonomforbundet.

Jensen, H. N. and P. L. Olsen (2000). 'De nye topembedsmænd: Topchefers Karriereforløb og ministeriers rekrutteringsmønstre', in T. Knudsen (ed.), *Regering og embedsmænd: Om magt og demokrati i staten*, pp. 151–78. Århus: Forlaget Systime.

Jensen, T. K. (2000). 'Party Cohesion', in P. Esaiasson and K. Heidar (eds.), *Beyond Westminster and Congress: The Nordic Experience*, pp. 210–36. Columbus, Ohio: Ohio State University Press.

Jiménez Asensio, R. (1992). 'Política y Administración: los puestos de designación política en las administraciones públicas'. *Revista Vasca de Administración Pública* 32: 73–101.

Jónsson, J. (1952). *Komandi ár*. Reykjavík: Ísafoldarprentsmiðja.

Kalyvas, S. N. (1997). 'Polarization in Greek Politics: PASOK's First Four Years, 1981–1985'. *Journal of the Hellenic Diaspora* 23 (1): 83–104.

Kapital (2005). 'Split up and Conquer'. 2005 (43). 22 October 2005, p. 15.

—— (2006). 'Political Sweeps Hurt the Taxpayers'. Available at: <http://www.capital.bg/show.php?storyid=234609>.

Karanatsis, H. 'Curse for the NHS the Transfers of Nurses' (Πληγή του ΕΣΥ οι μετατάξεις νοσηλευτών), *Kathimerini* (daily), 1 November 2009.

Kárason, E. (2005). *Jónsbók: Saga Jóns Ólafssonar athafnamanns*. Reykjavík: Mál og menning.

Karl, T. L. and P. Schmitter (1991). 'Modes of Transition in Latin America, Southern, and Eastern Europe'. *International Social Science Journal* 43 (2): 269–84.

Karlhofer, F. (2001). 'Österreich: Zwischen Korporatismus und Zivilgesellschaft', in W. Reutter and P. Rütters (eds.), *Verbände und Verbandssysteme in Westeuropa*, pp. 335–54. Opladen: Leske + Budrich.

—— (2006). 'Arbeitnehmerorganisationen', in H. Dachs, P. Gerlich, H. Gottweis, H. Kramer, V. Lauber, W. C. Müller, and E. Tálos (eds.), *Politik in Österreich: Ein Handbuch*, pp. 462–79. Wien: Manz.

Kathimerini. Daily newspaper. Greece.

Katz, R. S. (1986). 'Party Government: A Rationalistic Conception', in F. G. Castles and R. Wildenmann (eds.), *Visions and Realities of Party Government*, pp. 31–71. Berlin: De Gruyter.

—— (1987). 'Party Government and its Alternatives', in R. S. Katz (ed.), *Party Governments: European and American Experiences*, pp. 1–26. Florence: EUI, and Berlin: de Gruyter.

—— (1990). 'Party as Linkage: A vestigial function?'. *European Journal of Political Research* 1: 143–61.

—— and P. Mair (1995). 'Changing Models of Party Organization and Party Democracy. The Emergence of the Cartel Party'. *Party Politics* 1 (1): 5–28.

———— (2002). 'The Ascendancy of the Party in Public Office', in R. Gunther et al. (eds.), *Political Parties: Old Concepts and New Challenges*, pp. 113–35. Oxford: Oxford University Press.

Katz, R. and P. Mair (2009). 'The Cartel Party Thesis: A Restatement'. *Perspectives on Politics* 7: 753–66.

Key, V. O. (1935). 'Methods of Evasion of Civil Service Laws'. *Southwestern Social Science Quarterly* 15 (4): 337–47.

Key, Jr. V. O. (1964). *Politics, Parties, and Pressure Groups*. New York: Crowell.

Kitschelt, H. (2000). 'Linkages between Citizens and Politicians in Democratic Polities'. *Comparative Political Studies* 33 (6/7): 845–79.

——(2007). 'The Demise of Clientelism in Affluent Capitalist Democracies', in H. Kitschelt and S. I. Wilkinson (eds.), *Patrons, Clients and Policies*, pp. 298–321. Cambridge: Cambridge University Press.

——(2009). *Expert Survey on Citizen–Politician Linkages: Initial Findings for Greece in Comparative Perspective*. Mimeo. Durham, NC: Duke University.

——, Z. Mansfeldova, R. Markowski, and G. Tóka (1999). *Post-Communist Party Systems: Competition, Representation, and Inter-Party Cooperation*. Cambridge: Cambridge University Press.

—— and S. I. Wilkinson (eds.) (2007). *Patrons, Clients, and Policies: Patterns of Democratic Accountability and Political Competition*. Cambridge: Cambridge University Press.

Klieve, F. (2003). 'Parteipolitische Ämterpatronage'. *Verwaltungsrundschau—Zeitschrift für Verwaltung in Praxis und Wissenschaft* 49 (6): 183–9.

Klisurova, L. (2005). 'They Split the Ministries on the 8:5:3 Principle'. *24 Chassa*, 15 August 2005.

Kloepfer, M. (2001). 'Politische Klasse und Ämterpatronage'. *Zeitschrift für Beamtenrecht* 6: 189–94.

——(2002). 'Schutz vor Ämterpatronage', in C.-E. Eberle, M. Ibler, and D. Lorenz (eds.), *Der Wandel des Staates vor den Herausfoderungen der Gegenwart—Festschrift für Winfried Brohm zum 70. Geburtstag*, pp. 683–92. München: Verlag C.H. Beck.

Knudsen, T. (1995). *Dansk statsbygning*. Copenhagen: Jurist- og Økonomforbundets Forlag.

——(1997). *Politiseres/Policieres centraladministrationen?* Demokratiprojektet, working paper, August 1997. Copenhagen: Institut for statskundskab.

——(2000). *Regering og Embedsmænd: Om magt og demokrati i staten*. Århus: Århus systime.

——(2002). 'Hjælp til overbebyrdede ministre søges'. *Kristeligt Dagblad* (daily newspaper), 9 January 2002.

Knutsen, O. (2004). 'Voters and Social Cleavages', in K. Heidar (ed.), *Nordic Politics: Comparative Perspectives*, pp. 60–80. Oslo: Universitetsforlaget.

Komito, L. (1984). 'Irish Clientelism: A Reappraisal'. *Economic and Social Review* 15 (3): 173–94.

——(1985). 'Politics and Clientelism in Urban Ireland: Information, Reputation, and Brokerage'. PhD thesis. Pennsylvania: University of Pennsylvania.

König, K. (1992). 'The Transformation of a "Real Socialist" Administrative System into a Conventional West European System'. *International Review of Administrative Sciences* 58: 147–61.

Koole, R. A. (1994). 'The Vunerability of the Modern Cadre Party in the Netherlands', in R. S. Katz and P. Mair (eds.), *How Parties Organize: Change and Adaptation in Party Organizations in Western Democracies*, pp. 278–303. London: Sage.

Kopecký, P. (2004). 'Czech Republic: Entrenching Proportional Representation', in J. M. Colomer (ed.), *The Handbook of Electoral System Choice*, pp. 347–58. Basingstoke: Palgrave.

Kopecký, P. (2006a). 'Political Parties and the State in Post-Communist Europe: The Nature of Symbiosis'. *Journal of Communist Studies and Transition Politics* 22 (3): 251–73.

—— (2006b). 'The Rise of the Power Monopoly: Political Parties in the Czech Republic', in S. Jungerstam-Mulders (ed.), *Post-Communist EU Member States: Parties and Party Systems*, pp. 125–46. Aldershot: Ashgate.

—— (2007). 'Building Party Government: Political Parties in the Czech and Slovak Republics', in P. Webb and S. White (eds.), *Party Politics in New Democracies*, pp. 119–46. Oxford: Oxford University Press.

—— (2011). 'Political Competition and Party Patronage: Public Appointments in Ghana and South Africa'. *Political Studies* 59 (3): 713–32.

—— and P. Mair (2006). *Political Parties and Patronage in Contemporary Democracies: An Introduction*. Paper prepared for the workshop on 'Political Parties and Patronage', ECPR Joint Sessions of Workshops, Nicosia, Cyprus, 25–30 April 2006.

—— and G. Scherlis (2008). 'Party Patronage in Contemporary Europe'. *European Review* 16 (3): 355–71.

—— —— and M. Spirova (2007). *Party Patronage in New Democracies: Concepts, Measures and the Design of Empirical Inquiry.* Paper presented at the party patronage workshop, Florence.

—— —— —— (2008). *Conceptualizing and Measuring Party Patronage*. Working Paper No. 25. Mexico: IPSA Committee on Concepts and Methods, CIDE.

Kopecky, P. and M. Spirova (2011). 'Jobs for the Boys: Patterns of Party Patronage in Post-Communist Europe'. *West European Politics* 34 (5): 897–921.

Kopsini, C. (2005) 'Trade of Hope for a Place in the Public Sector through the Stages Programs' (Εμπόριο ελπίδας για μια θέση στο Δημόσιο με προγράμματα stages). *Kathimerini* (daily), 25 October 2009.

Körösényi, A., C. Tóth, and G. Török (2009). *The Hungarian Political System*. Budapest: Demokráciai Kutatások Alapítv.

Kosiara-Pedersen, K. (2010). *Partiernes medlemstal 2010: Aktuel graf nr. 6*. Copenhagen: Center for Valg og Partier, Institut for Statskundskab, Københavns Universitet.

Kotchegura, A. (2008). 'Civil Service Reform in Post-Communist Countries. The Case of the Russian Federation and the Czech Republic'. Dissertation. Leiden University Press.

Krammer, J. and G. Hovorka (2006). 'Interessenorganisationen der Landwirtschaft: Landwirtschaftskammern, Präsidentenkonferenz und Raiffeisenverband', in H. Dachs, P. Gerlich, H. Gottweis, H. Kramer, V. Lauber, W. C. Müller, and E. Tálos (eds.), *Politik in Österreich: Ein Handbuch*, pp. 480–92. Wien: Manz.

Kristinsson, G. H. (1996). 'Parties, States and Patronage'. *West European Politics* 19 (3): 433–57.

—— (2001). 'Clientelism in a Cold Climate: The Case of Iceland', in S. Piattoni (ed.), *Clientelism, Interests, and Democratic Representation: The European Experience in Historical and Comparative Perspective*, pp. 172–92. Cambridge: Cambridge University Press.

—— (2006). *Patronage and Public Appointments in Iceland*. Paper prepared for the ECPR Joint Sessions of Workshops, Nicosia, Cyprus, 25–30 April 2006.

—— (2007). *Íslenska stjórnkerfið*. 2nd edition. Reykjavík: Háskólaútgáfan.

—— (2010). *Íbúalýðræði*. Unpublished manuscript.

Kristmundsson, O. H. (2003). *Reinventing Government in Iceland: A Case Study of Public Management Reform*. Reykjavík: University of Iceland Press.
Kristmundsson, Ó. (2005). 'Bakgrunnur aðstoðarmanna ráðherra: Þróun 1991–2005'. *Stjórnmál og stjórnsýsla* 1 (1): 53–72.
—— (2007). *Könnun á starfsumhverfi ríkisstarfsmanna*. Reykjavík: Ministry of Finance.
Krnáčová, A. (2006). 'Financování politických stran v ČR', in D. Ondráčka et al., *Transparentní Procesy v Politickém Rozhodování*, pp. 63–126. Prague: Transparency International Czech Republic.
Kroken, N. (2006). 'Kvalifikasjonsprinsippet ved offentlige ansettelser'. Thesis. Oslo: Department of Public Law, University of Oslo.
Krouwel, A. (2006). 'Party Models', in R. S. Katz and W. J. Crotty (eds.), *Handbook of Party Politics*, pp. 249–69. London: Sage.
Krusekamp, H. (2004). 'Die Bestenauslese wird ihrem Anspruch nicht gerecht: politisch oder persönlich motivierte Ämterpatronage versus Objektivität'. *Innovative Verwaltung* 4: 31–4.
Landé, C. H. (1977). 'Introduction: The Dyadic Bases of Clientelism', in S. W. Schmidt, L. Guasti, C. H. Landé, and J. C. Scott (eds.), *Friends, Followers, and Factions: A Reader in Political Clientelism*, pp. xiii–xxxvii. Berkeley: University of California Press.
La Opinión Coruña (2009). 'El cambio en la Xunta supondrá el relevo de 400 altos cargos y personal de confianza'. 4 March 2009.
Larsen, M. (2003). 'Politiske embedsmænd i Danmark, Sverige og Norge—En forklaring på den beskedne udbredelse af politiske embedsmænd i Danmark'. Thesis. Aarhus: Aarhus Universitet.
Lauber, V. and D. Pesendorfer (2006). 'Wirtschafts- und Finanzpolitik', in H. Dachs, P. Gerlich, H. Gottweis, H. Kramer, V. Lauber, W. C. Müller, and E. Tálos (eds.), *Politik in Österreich: Ein Handbuch*, pp. 607–23. Wien: Manz.
Laver, M. and N. Schofield (1990). *Multiparty Government: The Politics of Coalition in Europe*. Oxford: Oxford University Press.
—— and K. A. Shepsle (1994). 'Cabinet Government in Theoretical Perspective', in M. Laver and K. A. Shepsle (eds.), *Cabinet Ministers and Parliamentary Government*, pp. 285–310. Cambridge: Cambridge University Press.
Lawson, K. (2007). 'When Parties Dedemocratize', in K. Lawson and P. H. Merkl (eds.), *When Parties Prosper: The Uses of Electoral Success*, pp. 353–66. Boulder: Lynne-Rienner.
Legg, K. (1969). *Politics in Modern Greece*. Stanford: Stanford University Press.
Leonardi, R. and D. Wertman (1989). *Italian Christian Democracy: The Politics of Dominance*. Basingstoke: Palgrave.
Lewanski, R. (1999). 'Italian Administration in Transition'. *South European Society & Politics* 4 (1): 97–131.
Lewis, P. (2006). 'Party Systems in Post-Communist Central Europe: Patterns of Stability and Consolidation'. *Democratization* 13 (4): 563–83.
Li, B. and A. Walder (2001). 'Career Advancement as Party Patronage: Sponsored Mobility into the Chinese Administrative Elite, 1949–1996'. *American Journal of Sociology* 106 (5): 1371–408.

Liegl, B. and W. C. Müller (1999). 'Senior Officials in Austria', in E. C. Page and V. Wright (eds.), *Bureaucratic Élites in Western European States: A Comparative Analysis of Top Officials*, pp. 90–120. Oxford: Oxford University Press.
Lijphart, A. (1984). *Democracies: Patterns of Majoritarian and Consensus Government in Twenty-One Countries*. New Haven: Yale University Press.
—— (1999). *Patterns of Democracy: Government Forms and Performance in Thirty-Six Countries*. New Haven: Yale University Press.
—— (2007). *Verzuiling, pacificatie en kentering in de Nederlandse politiek*. Amsterdam: Amsterdam University Press.
Litova, M. and L. Klisurova (2005). 'Simeon Surprise Choice of Ministers'. *24 Chassa*, 16 August 2005.
Lobo, M. C. (2000a). 'Governos partidários numa democracia recente: Portugal, 1976–1995'. *Análise Social* 35: 147–74.
—— (2000b). 'Portugal na Europa, 1960–1996—uma leitura política da convergência económica', in A. Barreto (ed.), *A Situação Social em Portugal 1960–99*, ii, pp. 611–43. Lisbon: Instituto de Ciências Sociais, Universidade de Lisboa.
Local Government Act (Kommuneloven).
Lopes, F. (1997). 'Partisanship and political clientelism in Portugal (1983–1993)'. *South European Society and Politics* 2 (3): 27–51.
Lupo, N. (2003). *Dalla legge al regolamento: Lo sviluppo della potestà normativa del governo nella disciplina delle pubbliche amministrazioni*. Bologna: Il Mulino.
Luther, K. R. (2006). 'Die Freiheitliche Partei Österreichs (FPÖ) und das Bündnis Zukunft Österreich (BZÖ)', in H. Dachs, P. Gerlich, H. Gottweis, H. Kramer, V. Lauber, W. C. Müller, and E. Tálos (eds.), *Politik in Österreich: Ein Handbuch*, pp. 364–88. Wien: Manz.
Lyons, F. S. L. (1973). *Ireland Since the Famine*. Glasgow: Fontana.
Lyrintzis, C. (1984). 'Political Parties in Post-Junta Greece: A Case of "Bureaucratic Clientelism"?'. *West European Politics* 7 (2): 99–118.
MacCarthaigh, M. (2005). *Accountability in Irish Parliamentary Politics*. Dublin: Institute of Public Administration.
MacDermott, E. (1998). *Clann na Poblachta*. Cork: Cork University Press.
McAuley, Adam, Robert Elgie and Eoin O'Malley (2012). *The (Surpricing) Non-Partisanship of the Irish Supreme Court* Working Papers in International Studies (Paper No. 2012-4). Dublin City University.
McGauran, A., K. Verhoest, and P. C. Humphreys (2005). *The Corporate Governance of Agencies in Ireland: Non-Commercial National Agencies*. CPMR Research Report 6. Dublin: Institute of Public Administration.
McNamara, K. (2002). 'Rational Fictions: Central Bank Independence and the Social Logic of Delegation'. *West European Politics* 25 (1): 47–76.
Magone, J. (2000). 'Political Recruitment and Elite Transformation in Modern Portugal 1870–1999: The Late Arrival of Mass Representation', in H. Best and M. Cotta (eds.), *Parliamentary Representatives in Europe, 1848–2000: Legislative Recruitment and Careers in Eleven European Countries*, pp. 341–70. Oxford: Oxford University Press.
Magone, J. A. (2004). *Contemporary Spanish Politics*. London: Routledge.
Mainwaring, S. (1999). *Rethinking Party Systems in the Third Wave of Democratization: The Case of Brazil*. Stanford: Stanford University Press.
—— and T. R. Scully (eds.) (1995). *Building Democratic Institutions: Party Systems in Latin America*. Stanford: Stanford University Press.

Mair, P. (1987). *The Changing Irish Party System: Organization, Ideology and Electoral Competition*. London: Pinter.

——(2008a). 'The Challenge to Party Government'. *West European Politics* 31 (1–2): 211–34.

——(2008b). 'Dutch Voters and the Changing Party Space 1989–2006'. *Acta Politica* 43: 235–53.

——and I. van Biezen (2001). 'Party Members in Twenty European Democracies, 1980–2000'. *Party Politics* 7 (1): 5–21.

Majone, G. (2001). 'Two Logics of Delegation'. *European Union Politics* 2 (1): 103–22.

Manow, P. (2002). 'Was erklärt Politische Patronage in den Ländern Westeuropas?'. *Politische Vierteljahreszeitschrift* 43 (1): 20–45.

——(2005). 'Die politische Kontrolle der Ministerialbürokratie des Bundes: Die Bedeutung der Landesebene', in S. Ganghof and P. Manow (eds.), *Mechanismen der Politik: Strategische Interaktion im deutschen Regierungssystem*, pp. 245–75. Frankfurt a. Main: Campus Verlag.

——(2006). *Parliamentary Elections and Party Patronage—An Empirical Study of the German Top Ministerial Bureaucracy at the Federal and State Level, 1957–2005*. Paper prepared for the workshop on 'Political Parties and Patronage', ECPR Joint Sessions of Workshops, Nicosia, Cyprus, 25–30 April 2006.

——and P. Wettengel (2006a). 'Ämterpatronage in der leitenden Ministerialbürokratie der Länder'. *Die Verwaltung—Zeitschrift für Verwaltungsrecht und Verwaltungswissenschaften* 39 (4): 553–70.

————(2006b). *Party Patronage and the Ministerial Bureaucracy—an Empirical Analysis of Job Growth in the Ministerial Bureaucracy of the German States, 1958–2004*. Paper prepared for the ECPR Joint Sessions of Workshops, Nicosia, Cyprus, 25–30 April 2006.

Markowski, R. (1997). 'Political Parties and Ideological Spaces in East Central Europe'. *Communist and Post-Communist Studies* 30 (3): 221–54.

Marsh, M. (2006). 'Party Identification in Ireland: An Insecure Anchor for a Floating Party System'. *Electoral Studies* 25: 489–508.

——(2007). 'Candidates or Parties? Objects of Electoral Choice in Ireland'. *Party Politics* 13 (4): 500–27.

Martz, J. D. (1997). *The Politics of Clientelism: Democracy and the State in Colombia*. New Brunswick: Transaction Publishers.

Matas, J. (1995). *Public Administration and the Recruitment of Political Elites: Formal and Material Politicization in Catalonia*. Working Paper No. 104. Barcelona: Institut de Ciències Polítiques i Socials.

——(2001). 'El control político de la Administración en Cataluña', in J. Matas (ed.), *El control politico de la Administración*, pp. 33–76. Barcelona: Institut de Ciències Polítiques i Socials.

Mathieson, A., B. Weber, N. Manning, and E. Arnould (2007). *Study on the Political Involvement in Senior Staffing and on the Delineation of Responsibilities Between Ministers and Senior Civil Servants*. Paris: OECD.

Matuschek, P. (2003). 'Spain: A Textbook Case of Partitocracy', in J. Borchert and J. Zeiss (eds.), *The Political Class in Advanced Democracies*, pp. 336–51. Oxford: Oxford University Press.

Mavrogordatos, G. Th. (1997). 'From Traditional Clientelism to Machine Politics: The Impact of PASOK Populism in Greece'. *South European Society and Politics* 2 (3): 1–26.

Mavrogordatos, G. Th. (1983). *Stillborn Republic: Social Coalitions and Party Strategies in Greece, 1922–1936*. Berkeley: University of California Press.

Mayntz, R. and H. Derlien (1989). 'Party Patronage and Politicization of the West German Administrative Elite 1970–1987—Toward Hybridization?'. *Governance: An International Journal of Policy and Administration*, 2 (4): 384–404.

MBMD (2005). *Survey of the Bulgarian State Administration*. Available at: <http://mbmd.net/AnonymousActivityPage?param=78cdf2495f4cd92024a61bce5b279ee2>.

MD (2005). *Retningslinjer for karantene og saksforbud ved overgang til ny stilling m.v. utenfor statsforvaltningen*. Moderniseringsdepartementet.

MDAAR (Ministry of the State Administration and Administrative Reform) (2006). *Annual Report 2006*. Sofia: MDAAR.

MDAAR (Ministry of the State Administration and Administrative Reform) (2007). *Annual Report 2007*. Sofia: MDAAR.

MDAAR (Ministry of the State Administration and Administrative Reform) (2008). *Annual Report 2008*. Sofia: MDAAR.

Mediapool (2006). 'The DPS Congress'. 2 April 2006. Available at: <http://mediapool.bg/show/?storyid=115974&srcpos=5&p=4>.

Mesa del Olmo, A. (2000). *Administración y altos cargos de la Comunidad Autónoma Vasca*. Madrid: Centro de Investigaciones Sociológicas.

Meyer-Sahling, J.-H. (2001). 'Getting on Track: Civil Service Reform in Post-Communist Hungary'. *Journal of European Public Policy* 8 (6): 960–79.

——(2006a). 'Civil Service Reform in Post-Communist Europe: The Bumpy Road to Depoliticisation'. *West European Politics* 27 (1): 71–103.

——(2006b). 'The Institutionalisation of Political Discretion in Post-Communist Civil Service Systems: The Case of Hungary'. *Public Administration* 84 (3): 693–716.

——(2006c). 'The Rise of the Partisan State? Parties, Patronage and the Ministerial Bureaucracy in Hungary'. *Journal of Communist Studies and Transition Politics* 22 (3): 274–94.

——(2008). 'The Changing Colours of the Post-Communist State: The Politicisation of the Senior Civil Service in Hungary'. *European Journal of Political Research* 47 (1): 1–33.

——(2009). *Post-Accession Sustainability of Civil Service Reforms in Central and Eastern Europe*. SIGMA Paper No. 44. Paris: OECD Publishing.

——, L. Vass, and V. Vassné (2012). 'Rewards for High Public Offices: Hungary', in M. Brans and B. G. Peters (eds.), *Rewards for High Public Office in Europe and North America*, pp. 209–28. London: Routledge.

Meynaud, J. (1965). *Les forces politiques en Grèce*. Paris: Etudes de Science Politique.

Mills, M. (2005). *Hurler on the Ditch: Memoir of a Journalist who Became Ireland's First Ombudsman*. Blackrock, Co. Dublin: Currach Press.

Ministeransvarlighedsloven (1964). LOV nr. 117 af 15/04/1964. Justitsministeriet: Lovtidende A.

Ministerie BZK (2009). *Trendnota Arbeidszaken 2008*. Tweede Kamer, parliamentary year 2009–2010, 32 124, No. 1–2.

Ministry homepages (2010). Information gathered from the homepages of relevant ministries in May 2010.

Ministry of Finance (2000). *Ábyrgð, valdsvið og stjórnunarumboð forstöðumanna ríkisstofnana*. Reykjavík: Fjármálaráðuneytið.
Mjelva, S. U. (2011). 'I spenningsfeltet mellom forvaltning og politikk. En studie av departementenes kommunikasjonsenheter'. MA thesis. Oslo: Department of Political Science, University of Oslo.
Montricher, N. (2003). 'Politics and Administration', in B. G. Peters and J. Pierre (eds.), *Handbook of Public Administration*, pp. 293–9. London: Sage.
Moreira, V. (2001). *Relatório e proposta de lei-quadro sobre os Institutos Públicos*. Lisbon: Ministério da Reforma do Estado e da Administração Pública.
Morlino, L. (1998). *Democracy Between Consolidation and Crisis: Parties, Groups, and Citizens in Southern Europe*. Oxford: Oxford University Press.
Mossialos, E. and S. Allin (2005). 'Interest Groups and Health System Reform in Greece'. *West European Politics* 28 (2): 420–44.
Mouzelis, N. (1978). 'Class and Clientelistic Politics: The Case of Greece'. *The Sociological Review* 26 (3): 471–97.
Müller, W. C. (1989). 'Party Patronage in Austria: Theoretical Considerations and Empirical Findings', in A. Pelinka and F. Plasser (eds.), *The Austrian Party System*, pp. 327–56. Boulder: Westview.
—— (2000). 'Patronage by National Governments', in J. Blondel and M. Cotta (eds.), *The Nature of Party Government: A Comparative European Perspective*, pp. 141–60. Basingstoke: Palgrave.
—— (2006a). 'Die Österreichische Volkspartei', in H. Dachs, P. Gerlich, H. Gottweis, H. Kramer, V. Lauber, W. C. Müller, and E. Tálos (eds.), *Politik in Österreich: Ein Handbuch*, pp. 341–63. Wien: Manz.
—— (2006b). 'Party Patronage and Party Colonization of the State', in R. S. Katz and W. Crotty (eds.), *Handbook of Party Politics*, pp. 189–95. London: Sage.
—— (2007a). 'The Changing Role of the Austrian Civil Service: The Impact of Politicisation, Public Sector Reform, and Europeanisation', in E. C. Page and V. Wright (eds.), *From the Active to the Enabling State: The Changing Role of Top Officials in European Nations*, pp. 38–62. Houndmills: Palgrave.
—— (2007b). 'Political Institutions and Linkage Strategies', in H. Kitschelt and S. I. Wilkinson (eds.), *Patrons, Clients and Policies*, pp. 251–75. Cambridge: Cambridge University Press.
——, W. Philipp, and B. Steininger (1996). 'Austria: Party Government Within Limits', in J. Blondel and M. Cotta (eds.), *Party and Government: An Inquiry into the Relationship between Governments and Supporting Parties in Liberal Democracies*, pp. 91–109. Houndmills: Macmillan.
Müller-Rommel, F. (1997). 'Federal Republic of Germany: A System of Chancellor Government', in J. Blondel and F. Müller-Rommel (eds.), *Cabinets in Western Europe*, pp. 171–91. 2nd edition. London: Palgrave Macmillan.
Narud, H. M. (2008). 'Partienes nominasjoner. Hvem deltar? Og spiller det noen rolle?'. *Tidsskrift for samfunnsforskning* 49: 543–73.
Nerland, S. (1997). *Toppledere i sentralforvaltningen med politisk bakgrunn: En studie av toppledernes karrieremønster med utgangspunkt i årene 1936, 1956, 1976, 1996*. Oslo: Department of Political Science, University of Oslo.

NHD (2005). *Retningslinjer for arbeidet i valgkomiteer.* Oslo: Nærings- og handelsdepartementet.
NHD (2006). *Instruks for forberedelse av valg til styrer i heleide selskaper i NHDs eierskap.* Oslo: Nærings- og handelsdepartementet.
NHD (2007). *Statens eierberetning 2007.* Oslo: Nærings- og handelsdepartementet.
NHD (2008a). *Regjeringens eierpolitikk.* Oslo: Nærings- og handelsdepartementet.
NHD (2008b). *Statens eierberetning 2008.* Oslo: Nærings- og handelsdepartementet.
Nielsen, H. J. (2002). 'De mange gode partier at vælge imellem', in E. Albæk, P. Munk Christiansen, and B. Møller (eds.), *Demokratisk set: Festskrift til Lise Togeby*, pp. 69–84. Aarhus: Aarhus Universitetsforlag.
Nieuwenkamp, R. (2001). 'De prijs van het politieke primaat: Wederzijds vertrouwen en loyaliteit in de verhouding tussen bewindspersonen en ambtelijke top'. Dissertation. Delft: Eburon.
Nissen, C., H. H. Brydensholt, O. Zacchi, I. Thygesen, and J. Ottosen (2010). *På ministerens vegne—at styre og lede i statens tjeneste. Bidrag til fortællingen om styring og ledelse i statens departementer, styrelser og institutioner i sidste halvdeaf det 20. Århundrede.* Copenhagen: Handelshøjskolens Forlag.
Noordegraaf, M. (2000). 'Attention! Work and Behavior of Public Managers Amidst Ambiguity'. Dissertation. Delft: Eburon.
Novotný, V. (2004). 'The Creation of Regional Government in Czechia in the 1990s'. Dissertation. Glasgow: University of Strathclyde.
Nunes, F. (2003). 'Os directores-gerais: a elite administrativa portuguesa durante o XIV Governo Constitucional', in A. C. Pinto and A. Freire (eds.), *Elites, sociedade e mudança política*, pp. 97–129. Oeiras: Celta.
O'Byrnes, S. (1986). *Hiding Behind a Face: Fine Gael Under Garret FitzGerald.* Dublin: Gill and Macmillan.
O'Carroll, J. P. (1987). 'Strokes, Cute Hoors and Sneaking Regarders: The Influence of Local Culture on Irish Political Style'. *Irish Political Studies* 2: 77–92.
O'Dwyer, C. (2004). 'Runaway State Building: How Political Parties Shape States in Postcommunist Eastern Europe'. *World Politics* 56: 520–53.
——(2006). *Runaway State-Building: Patronage Politics and Democratic Development.* Baltimore: Johns Hopkins University Press.
OECD (2002). *Distributed Public Governance.* Paris: OECD.
OECD (2005). *Modernising Government: The Way Forward.* Paris: OECD.
OECD (2008). *Ireland: Towards an Integrated Public Service.* OECD Public Management Reviews. Paris: OECD.
OECD (2009). *Government at a Glance 2009.* Paris: OECD.
OECD (2010). *Factbook—Ecomomic, Enviromental and Social Statistics.* Available at: <http://www.oecd-ilibrary.org>.
Oosterwaal, A. and R. Torenvlied (2010). 'Politics Divided from Society? Three Explanations for Trends in Societal and Political Polarization in the Netherlands'. *West European Politics* 33 (2): 258–79.
Opello, W. (1985). *Portugal's Political Development: A Comparative Approach.* Epping: Bowker Publishing Company.
Østerud, Ø., F. Engelstad, and P. Selle (2003). *Makten og demokratiet.* Oslo: Gyldendal Akademisk.

Ot. prp. (parliamentary bill) no. 84 (2004–5). *Om lov om visse forhold vedrørende de politiske partiene.*

Outrata, E. (2007). 'Civil Service in Dysfunction'. *The New Presence,* September 2007: 15–16.

Page, E. and B. Jenkins (2005). *Policy Bureaucracy: Government with a Cast of Thousands.* Oxford: Oxford University Press.

Page, E. C. and V. Wright (eds.) (1999a). *Bureaucratic Élites in Western European States: A Comparative Analysis of Top Officials.* Oxford: Oxford University Press.

—— —— (1999b). 'Conclusion: Senior Officials in Western Europe', in Page, E. C. and V. Wright (eds.), *Bureaucratic Élites in Western European States: A Comparative Analysis of Top Officials,* pp. 266–79. Oxford: Oxford University Press.

Pagoulatos, G. (2005). 'The Politics of Privatization: Redrawing the Public–Private Boundary'. *West European Politics* 28 (2): 358–80.

Pakulski, J. (1986). 'Bureaucracy and the Soviet System'. *Studies in Comparative Communism* 19 (1): 3–24.

Panebianco, A. (1988). *Political Parties: Organization and Power.* Cambridge: Cambridge University Press.

Papadopoulos, Y. (2003). 'Cooperative Forms of Governance: Problems of Democratic Accountability in Complex Environments'. *European Journal of Political Research* 42 (4): 473–501.

Pappas, T. S. (1999). *Making Party Democracy in Greece.* London: Palgrave/Macmillan.

—— (2003). 'The Transformation of the Greek Party System Since 1951'. *West European Politics* 26 (2): 90–114.

—— (2009a). *Το χαρισματικό κόμμα: ΠΑΣΟΚ, Παπανδρέου, εξουσία* [The Charismatic Party: PASOK, Papandreou, Power]. Athens: Patakis.

—— (2009b). 'Patrons Against Partisans: The Politics of Patronage in Mass Ideological Parties'. *Party Politics* 15 (3): 315–34.

Park, C. H. (2001). 'Factional Dynamics in Japan's LDP Since Political Reform'. *Asian Survey* 41 (3): 428–61.

Parrado, S. (1996). 'Flexibility of Staffing and Personnel Systems in Central Administration in Spain', in H. van Hassel, M. Högye, and G. Jenei (eds.), *New Trends in Public Administration and Public Law, EGPA Yearbook,* pp. 131–62. Budapest: EGPA and Center for Public Affairs Studies Budapest.

—— (2000). 'The Development and Current Features of the Spanish Civil Service System', in H. A. G. M. Bekke and F. M. van der Meer (eds.), *Civil Service Systems in Western Europe,* pp. 247–74. Cheltenham: Edward Elgar Publishing.

—— (2001). *Spanish Civil Service: A Career System without Career Perspectives.* Paper prepared for the Conference, Status and Role of Top Civil Servants in Europe Today, Université de Picardie, Amiens, 15 June 2001.

Parrado, S. (2004). 'Politicization of the Spanish Public Service: Continuity in 1982 and 1996', in B. G. Peters and J. Pierre (eds.), *Politicization of the Civil Service in Comparative Perspective: The Quest for Control,* pp. 227–56. London: Routledge.

Pasquino, G. (1995). 'La partitocrazia', in G. Pasquino (ed.), *La politica italiana: Dizionario critico 1945–1995,* pp. 341–53. Roma-Bari: Laterza.

—— (2002). *Il sistema politico italiano.* Bologna: Bononia University Press.

Pedersen, K. (2003). *Party Membership Linkage: The Danish Case*. PhD serien. Copenhagen: Institut for Statskundskab, Københavns Universitet.

Pedersen, O. K. and P. Lægreid (1999). 'Fra opbygning til ombygning', in P. Lægreid and O. K. Pedersen (eds.), *Fra opbygning til ombygning i staten*, pp. 345–71. Copenhagen: Jurist- og Økonomforbundets Forlag.

Pelinka, A. (2009). 'Das politische System Österreichs', in W. Ismayr (ed.), *Die politischen Systeme Westeuropas*, pp. 607–41. Opladen: VS Verlag für Sozialwissenschaften.

Perkins, D. (1996). 'The Role of Organizations, Patronage and the Media in Party Formation'. *Party Politics* 2 (3): 355–75.

Personalhåndbok for Oslo kommune (2010).

Personalreglement for Bergen kommune (2008).

Reglement for personalforvaltningen i utenrikstjenesten med kommentarer (2003). Accessed from intranet on 25 November 2008.

Peters, B. G. (1988). *Comparing Public Bureaucracies: Problems of Theory and Method*. Tuscaloosa: University of Alabama Press.

——(2002). *Governance: A Garbage Can Perspective*. Vienna: Institute for Advanced Studies.

——(2008). 'The Napoleonic Tradition'. *The International Journal of Public Sector Management*, 21 (2): 118–32.

——(2010). *The Politics of Bureaucracy: An Introduction to Comparative Public Administration*. 6th edition. London: Routledge.

——and J. Pierre (eds.) (2004a). *Politicization of the Civil Service in Comparative Perspective: The Quest for Control*. London: Routledge.

————(2004b). 'Politicization of the Civil Service: Concepts, Causes, Consequences'. In B. G. Peters and J. Pierre (eds.), *Politicization of the Civil Service in Comparative Perspective: The Quest for Control*, pp. 1–13. London: Routledge.

————(2004c). 'Conclusion: Political Control in a Managerialist World', in B. G. Peters and J. Pierre (eds.), *Politicization of the Civil Service in Comparative Perspective: The Quest for Control*, pp. 283–90. London: Routledge.

Piattoni, S. (ed.) (2001a). *Clientelism, Interests, and Democratic Representation: The European Experience in Historical and Comparative Perspective*. Cambridge: Cambridge University Press.

——(2001b). 'Clientelism in Historical and Comparative Perspective', in S. Piattoni (ed.), *Clientelism, Interests, and Democratic Representation: The European Experience in Historical and Comparative Perspective*, pp. 1–29. Cambridge: Cambridge University Press.

——(2001c). 'Clientelism, Interests, and Democratic Representation', in S. Piattoni (ed.), *Clientelism, Interests, and Democratic Representation: The European Experience in Historical and Comparative Perspective*, pp. 193–212. Cambridge: Cambridge University Press.

Poguntke, T. (1994). 'Parties in a Legalistic Culture: The Case of Germany', in R. S. Katz and P. Mair (eds.), *How Parties Organize: Change and Adaptation in Party Organizations in Western Democracies*, pp. 185–215. London: Sage.

——and P. Webb (eds.) (2005). *The Presidentialization of Politics*. Oxford: Oxford University Press.

Politiken. Daily newspaper. Copenhagen.

Pollitt, C. (2003). *The Essential Public Manager.* UK: Open University Press.
——, K. Bathgate, J. Caulfield, A. Smullen, and C. Talbot (2001). 'Agency Fever? Analysis of an International Policy Fashion'. *Journal of Comparative Policy Analysis* 3 (3): 271–90.
—— and G. Bouckaert (2004). *Public Management Reform: A Comparative Analysis.* 2nd edition. Oxford: Oxford University Press.
Portas, P. and V. P. Valente (1990). 'O primeiro-ministro: estudo sobre o executivo em Portugal'. *Análise Social* 107 (3): 333–49.
Portuguese Ministry of Finance [Ministério das Finanças] (2011). *Sector Empresarial do Estado: Relatório de 2011.* Lisbon: Direcção-Geral do Tesouro e Finanças. Available at: <http://www.dgtf.pt/ResourcesUser/SEE/Documentos/Relatorios/2011-Boletins_Trim/Relatorio_SEE_2011.pdf>.
Prime minister's report (2005). *Skýrsla forætisráðherra um fjárframlög til stjórnmálastarfsemi og stjórnmálaflokka á Íslandi.* 131. löggjafarþing, þskj. 1169.
PUMA (2003). *Managing Senior Management: Senior Civil Service Reform in OECD Member Countries.* Background note GOV/PUMA 17. Paris: OECD.
Putnam, R. (1973). *The Beliefs of Politicians: Ideology, Conflict and Democracy in Britain and Italy.* New Haven, CT: Yale University Press.
Putnam, R. D. (1976). *The Comparative Study of Political Elites.* Englewood Cliffs: Prentice-Hall Inc.
Pyper, R. and D. McTavish (2007). 'Monitoring the Public Appointments Process in the UK—Issues and Themes Surrounding the use of Semi-Independent Commissioners'. *Public Management Review* 9 (1): 145–53.
Radaelli, C. (2002). 'The Italian State and the Euro: Institutions, Discourse, and Policy Regimes', in K. Dyson (ed.), *European States and the Euro: Europeanization, Variation, and Convergence,* pp. 212–37. Oxford: Oxford University Press.
Rae, D. W. (1967). *The Political Consequences of Electoral Laws.* New Haven, CT: Yale University Press.
Rakner, L. and N. van de Walle (2009). 'Opposition Weakness in Africa'. *Journal of Democracy* 20 (3): 108–21.
Ramió, C. and J. Subirats (1996). 'Los aparatos administrativos de las Comunidades Autónomas (1980–1995): Entre el mimetismo y la diferenciación'. *Revista Vasca de Administración Pública* 45 (2): 151–81.
Randeraad, N. and D. J. Wolffram (2001). 'Constraints on Clientelism: The Dutch Path to Modern Politics, 1848–1917', in S. Piattoni (ed.), *Clientelism, Interests, and Democratic Representations: The European Experience in Historical and Comparative Perspective,* pp. 101–22. Cambridge: Cambridge University Press.
Rannsóknarnefnd Alþingis (2010). *Aðdragandi og orsakir falls íslensku bankanna 2008 og tengdir atburðir.* Reykjavík: Rannsóknarnefnd Alþingis.
Reglement for personalforvaltningen i departementene (1998).
Remmer, K. (2007). 'The Political Economy of Patronage: Expenditure Patterns in the Argentine Provinces, 1983–2003'. *The Journal of Politics* 69 (2): 363–77.
Rodríguez Teruel, J. (2009). *Reclutamiento y carrera ministerial de los ministros en España (1976–2005).* Working Paper 273. Barcelona: Institut de Ciències Polítiques i Socials.

Rokkan, S. (1967). 'Geography, Religion, and Social Class: Crosscutting Cleavages in Norwegian Politics', in S. M. Lipset and S. Rokkan (eds.), *Party Systems and Voter Alignments: Cross-National Perspectives*, pp. 367–444. New York: Free Press.

Román Masedo, L. (1997). 'Burocracia e transición política. Algúns apuntamentos sobre o caso español (1975–1982)'. *REGAP: Revista galega de administración pública* 17: 165–87.

Rommetvedt, H. (2003). *The Rise of the Norwegian Parliament*. London: Frank Cass.

—— (2005). 'Norway: Resources Count, But Votes Decide? From Neo-Corporatist Representation to Neo-Pluralist Parliamentarism'. *West European Politics* 28 (4): 740–63.

Roness, P. G. and V. Rolland (2010). 'Mapping Organizational Units in the State: Challenges and Classifications'. *International Journal of Public Administration* 33 (10): 463–73.

Rose, R. (1980). *Do Parties Make a Difference?* Chatham, NJ: Chatham House.

Rouban, L. (2007). 'Politicization of the Civil Service', in B. G. Peters and J. Pierre (eds.), *Handbook of Public Administration*, pp. 199–211. Concise paperback edition. London: Sage.

Sacks, P. M. (1976). *The Donegal Mafia: An Irish Political Machine*. New Haven: Yale University Press.

Salih, M. A. (ed.) (2003). *Political Parties in Africa*. London: Pluto.

Salomonsen, H. (2003). 'Embedsmænds fornemmelse for politik: Institutionaliseringen af danske embedsmænds politiske rådgivning'. Ph.d. afhandling afleveret ved Institut for økonomi, politik og forvaltning, Aalborg Universitet.

Sartori, G. (1976). *Parties and Party Systems: A Framework for Analysis*. Cambridge: Cambridge University Press.

—— (2005). 'Party Types, Organisation and Functions'. *West European Politics* 28 (1): 5–32.

Sbragia, A. (2001). 'Italy Pays for Europe: Political Leadership, Political Choice, and Institutional Adaptation', in M. Green Cowles, J. Caporaso, and T. Risse (eds.), *Transforming Europe: Europeanization and Domestic Change*, pp. 79–96. Ithaca: Cornell University Press.

Scarrow, S. (2000). 'Parties without Members?', in R. Dalton and M. Wattenberg (eds.), *Parties without Partisans*, pp. 79–101. Oxford: Oxford University Press.

Scherlis, G. (2010). 'Patronage and Party Organization in Argentina: The Emergence of the Patronage-Based Network Party'. Unpublished PhD dissertation. Leiden University.

Schöpflin, G. (1994). *Politics in Eastern Europe, 1945–1991*. Oxford: Basil Blackwell.

Schwanke, K. and F. Ebinger (2006). 'Politisierung und Rollenverständnis der deutschen Administrativen Elite 1970 bis 2005—Wandel trotz Kontinuität'. *Politische Vierteljahresschrift*, Special Issue 37, Politik und Verwaltung: 228–49.

Scott, J. (1969). 'Corruption, Machine Politics, and Social Change', *American Political Science Review* 63 (4): 1142–59.

Seip, J. A. (1963). *Fra embedsmannsstat til etterpartistat og andre essays*. Oslo: Scandinavian University Press.

Shefter, M. (1977). 'Party and Patronage: Germany, England and Italy'. *Politics and Society* 7 (4): 403–52.

—— (1994). *Political Parties and the State*. Princeton: Princeton University Press.

Shoylekova, M. (2004). *Building Capacity for Policy Making: Experience from the Bulgarian Administrative Reforms*. Paper presented at the 12th NISPAcee Annual Conference, Vilnius, Lithuania, 13–15 May 2004. Available at: <http://unpan1.un.org/intradoc/groups/public/documents/nispacee/unpan018698.pdf>.

Sickinger, H. (2006). 'Politische Korruption', in H. Dachs, P. Gerlich, H. Gottweis, H. Kramer, V. Lauber, W. C. Müller, and E. Tálos (eds.), *Politik in Österreich: Ein Handbuch*, pp. 561–76. Wien: Manz.

—— (2009). *Politikfinanzierung in Österreich*. Wien: Czernin.

Sikk, A. (2006). 'From Private Organizations to Democratic Infrastructure: Political Parties and the State in Estonia'. *The Journal of Communist Studies and Transition Politics* 22 (3): 341–61.

Šmíd, M. (2000). *Média, internet, TV Nova, a já*. Praha: ISV.

Sorauf, F. (1959). 'Patronage and Party'. *Midwest Journal of Political Science* 3 (2): 115–26.

Sorauf, F. J. (1969). 'The Silent Revolution in Patronage', in E. Banfield (ed.), *Urban Government: A Reader in Administration and Politics*, pp. 376–86. New York: The Free Press.

Sørensen, R. J. (2005). 'Et folkestyre i fremgang: Demokratisk kontroll med brannalarmer og autopiloter'. *Nytt Norsk Tidsskrift* 22: 258–70.

Sotiropoulos, D. A. (1996). *Populism and Bureaucracy: The Case of Greece under PASOK, 1981–1989*. Notre Dame: University of Notre Dame Press.

—— (2004a). 'A Description of the Greek Higher Civil Service', in E. C. Page and V. Wright (eds.), *Bureaucratic Élites in Western European States: A Comparative Analysis of Top Officials*, pp. 13–31. Oxford: Oxford University Press.

—— (2004b). 'Southern European Bureaucracies in Comparative Perspective'. *West European Politics* 27 (3): 405–22.

Spanou, C. (1996). 'Penelope's Suitors: Administrative Modernisation and Party Competition in Greece'. *West European Politics* 19 (1): 97–124.

—— (2008). 'State Reform in Greece: Responding to Old and New Challenges'. *International Journal of Public Sector Management* 21 (2): 150–73.

Sperl, G. (2003). *Die umgefärbte Republik: Anmerkungen zu Österreich*. Wien: Zsolnay.

Spirova, M. (2008). 'The Communist Successor Party in Bulgaria: The Long Road to Europe'. *Communist & Post-Communist Studies* 41 (3): 481–95.

—— (2009). 'Bulgaria'. *European Journal of Political Research* 48 (7–8): 913–16.

Stanev, E. (2005). 'The Coalition is Sinking in Bureaucracy'. *Kapital*, 1–7 October 2005.

Stanishev, S. (2005). *Political Report at the 46th Congress of the BSP*. Available at: <http://www.bsp.bg/shownews.php?id=648>.

Starfshópur forsætisráðuneytisins (2010). *Viðbrögð stjórnsýslunnar við skýrslu rannsóknarnefndar Alþingis*. Reykjavík: Forsætisráðuneytið.

Statens personalhåndbok (2010). Oslo: Ministry of Government Administration, Reform and Church Affairs.

Statistik Austria (2010). *Statistisches Jahrbuch 2010*. Wien: Österreichische Staatsdruckerei.

Statistisches Bundesamt (2008). *Statistisches Jahrbuch 2008 für die Bundesrepublik*. Germany: Wiesbaden.

Statskonsult (2003). *I kongens navn: Den norske regjeringen i europeisk perspektiv.* Oslo: Statskonsult.

—— (2004). *Toppledere i staten—Rekruttering.* Report 2004: 9. Oslo: Statskonsult.

—— (2007). *Ja vel, statsråd? Om departementenes utfordringer i rollen som sekretariat for politisk ledelse.* Report 2007: 27. Oslo: Statskonsult.

St. meld. no. 11 (2000–1). *Om forholdet mellom embetsverket, departementets politiske ledelse og andre samfunnsaktører.*

St. meld. no. 10 (2006–7). *Embedsutnemningar m.m. 1. juli 2005–30. juni 2006.*

Štička, M. (2006). 'Depolitizace ústřední státní správy v ČR: nedokončený úkol', in D. Ondráčka et al., *Transparentní Procesy v Politickém Rozhodování*, pp. 127–56. Prague: Transparency International Czech Republic.

Strøm, K. (1994). 'The Political Role of Norwegian Cabinet Ministers', in M. Laver and K. A. Shepsle (eds.), *Cabinet Ministers and Parliamentary Government*, pp. 35–55. Cambridge: Cambridge University Press.

—— and W. C. Müller (1999). 'Political Parties and Hard Choices', in W. C. Müller and K. Strøm (eds.), *Policy, Office, or Votes: How Political Parties in Western Europe Make Hard Choices*, pp. 1–35. Cambridge: Cambridge University Press.

—— —— and T. Bergman (eds.) (2003). *Delegation and Accountability in Parliamentary Democracies.* Oxford: Oxford University Press.

—— —— —— and B. Nyblade (2006). 'Dimensions of Citizen Control', in K. Strøm, W. C. Müller, and T. Bergman (eds.), *Delegation and Accountability in Parliamentary Democracies*, pp. 651–706. Oxford: Oxford University Press.

—— and H. M. Narud (2006). 'Norway: Virtual Parliamentarism', in K. Strøm, W. C. Müller, and T. Bergman (eds.), *Delegation and Accountability in Parliamentary Democracies*, pp. 523–51. Oxford: Oxford University Press.

——, H. M. Narud, and H. Valen (2005). 'A More Fragile Chain of Governance in Norway'. *West European Politics* 28 (4): 781–6.

Suiter, Jane and O'Malley, Eoin (2012). *Yes, minister: The Impact of Decision-Making Rules on Geographically Targeted Particularistic Spending.* Working Papers in International Studies (Paper No. 2012–1). Dublin City University.

Suleiman, E. (2003). *Dismantling Democratic States.* Princeton: Princeton University Press.

Sundberg, J. (1994). 'Finland: Nationalized Parties, Professionalized Organizations', in R. S. Katz and P. Mair (eds.), *How Parties Organize: Change and Adaptation in Party Organizations in Western Democracies*, pp. 158–84. London: Sage.

Tavits, M. (2009). 'Geographically Targeted Spending: Exploring the Electoral Strategies of Incumbent Governments'. *European Political Science Review* 1: 103–23.

Ten Velde, H. and G. Voerman (2000). *Ten geleide* [introduction to Jaarboek DNPP 2000]. Groningen: DNPP online.

't Hart, P. et al. (2002). *Politiek-ambtelijke verhoudingen in beweging.* Amsterdam: Boom.

Thatcher, M. and A. Stone Sweet (eds.) (2002). 'The Politics of Delegation: Non-Majoritarian Institutions in Europe'. *West European Politics*, special issue 25 (1).

The Times. Daily newspaper. UK.

Toole, J. (2000). 'Government Formation and Party System Stabilization in East Central Europe'. *Party Politics* 6 (4): 441–61.

Torchia, L. (ed.) (2009). *Il sistema amministrativo italiano nel XXI secolo*. Bologna: Il Mulino.
Tornos, J. (1983). 'La función pública en las Comunidades Autónomas: Condicionantes previos y marco normativo de la potestad legislativa autonómica'. *Revista Vasca de Administración Pública* 7: 117–46.
Toshkov, D. (2003). 'There and Back Again: Organizational Changes in the Bulgarian Core Executive'. Unpublished MA thesis. Leiden Universiteit.
Treisman, D. (2007). 'What Have we Learned about the Causes of Corruption from Ten Years of Cross-National Empirical Research?'. *Annual Review of Political Science* 10: 211–44.
Trifonova, P. (2005). 'From the Hairdresser's to the Ministry'. *24 Chassa*, 9 December 2005.
Tsebelis, G. (2002). *How Political Institutions Work*. Princeton: Princeton University Press
Ucakar, K. (2006). 'Sozialdemokratische Partei Österreichs', in H. Dachs, P. Gerlich, H. Gottweis, H. Kramer, V. Lauber, W. C. Müller, and E. Tálos (eds.), *Politik in Österreich: Ein Handbuch*, pp. 322–40. Wien: Manz.
Ugebrevet A4. Weekly magazine of LO, Confederation of trade unions in Denmark.
Valen, H. and S. Rokkan (1974). 'Norway: Conflict Structure and Mass Politics in a European Periphery', in R. Rose (ed.), *Electoral Behavior: A Comparative Handbook*, pp. 315–70. New York: Free Press.
van Biezen, I. (2000a). 'On the Internal Balance of Party Power. Party Organizations in New Democracies'. *Party Politics* 6 (4): 395–417.
—— (2000b). 'Party Financing in New Democracies'. *Party Politics* 6 (3): 329–42.
—— (2003). *Political Parties in New Democracies: Party Organization in Southern and East-Central Europe*. Basingstoke: Palgrave Macmillan.
—— (2004). 'Political Parties as Public Utilities'. *Party Politics* 10 (6): 701–22.
—— (2005). 'On the Theory and Practice of Party Formation and Adaptation in New Democracies'. *European Journal of Political Research* 44 (1): 147–74.
—— and P. Kopecký (2007). 'The State and the Parties: Public Funding, Public Regulation and Rent-Seeking in Contemporary Democracies'. *Party Politics* 13 (2): 235–54.
——, P. Mair, and T. Poguntke (2009). *Going, Going . . . Gone? Party Membership in the 21st Century*. Paper prepared for presentation to the workshop on 'Political Parties and Civil Society', ECPR Joint Sessions of Workshops, Lisbon, 14–19 April 2009.
———— (2012). 'Going, Going . . . Gone? The Decline of Party Membership in Contemporary Europe'. *European Journal of Political Research* 51 (1): 24–56.
van der Meer, F. M. (2004). 'Dutch Government Reform and the Quest for Political Control', in B. G. Peters and J. Pierre (eds.), *Politicization of the Civil Service in Comparative Perspective: The Quest for Control*, pp. 206–26. London: Routledge.
—— and G. S. A. Dijkstra (2000). 'The Development and Current Features of the Dutch Civil Service System', in H. A. G. M. Bekke and F. M. van der Meer (eds.), *Civil Service Systems in Western Europe*, pp. 148–87. Cheltenham: Edward Elgar.
—— and J. C. N. Raadschelders (1999). 'The Senior Civil Service in the Netherlands: A Quest for Unity', in E. C. Page and V. Wright (eds.), *Bureaucratic Élites in Western European States: A Comparative Analysis of Top Officials*, pp. 205–28. Oxford: Oxford University Press.

van der Steen, M., M. van Twist, and R. Peeters (2009). *Political Strategists? Making Sense of the Work of Political Assistants in Dutch Government*. Paper presented at 25th EGOS colloquium, Barcelona, 2–4 July 2009.

van Thiel, S., B. Steijn, and M. Allix (2007). '"New Public Managers" in Europe: Changes and Trends', in C. Pollitt, S. van Thiel, and V. Homburg (eds.), *New Public Management in Europe: Adaptation and Alternatives*, pp. 90–106. Basingstoke: Palgrave MacMillan.

Velinova, R., V. Bozhidarova, and V. Kolcheva (2001). 'Politico-Administrative Relations in Bulgaria', in T. Verheijen (ed.), *Politico-Administrative Relations: Who Rules?*, pp. 64–85. Bratislava: NISPAcee.

Verge, T. (2007). *Partidos y representación política: Las dimensiones del cambio en los partidos políticos españoles, 1976–2006*. Madrid: Centro de Investigaciones Sociológicas.

—— (2012). 'Party Strategies towards Civil Society in New Democracies: The Spanish Case'. *Party Politics* 18 (1): 45–60.

Verheijen, T. and A. Kotchegura (eds.) (2000). *Civil Service Systems in Central and Eastern Europe*. Cheltenham: Edward Elgar.

Verzichelli, L. (2009). 'Italy: The Difficult Road Towards a More Effective Process of Ministerial Selection', in K. Dowding and P. Dumont (eds.), *The Selection of Ministers in Europe: Hiring and Firing*, pp. 79–100. London: Routledge.

—— and M. Cotta (2000). 'Italy: From "Constrained" Coalitions to Alternating Governments?', in W. C. Müller and K. Strøm (eds.), *Coalition Governments in Western Europe*, pp. 433–97. Oxford: Oxford University Press.

Vibert, F. (2007). *The Rise of the Unelected*. Cambridge: Cambridge University Press.

Villoria Mendieta, M. and L. Huntoon (2002). 'Transitions from Authoritarianism: The Case of Spain', in R. Baker (ed.), *Transitions from Authoritarianism: The Role of the Bureaucracy*, pp. 165–88. London: Prager Publishers.

Voerman, G. (1995). 'De ledentallen van politieke partijen 1945–1995', in G. Voerman (ed.), *Jaarboek DNPP 1995*, pp. 192–206. Groningen: Rijksuniversiteit Groningen.

von Arnim, H. H. (2004). 'Institutionalized Political Unaccountability and Political Corruption in Germany', in E. Bohne, C. F. Bonser, and K. M. Spencer (eds.), *Transatlantic Perspectives on Liberalization and Democratic Governance*, pp. 371–85. Münster: Lit-Verlag.

——, R. Heiny, and S. Ittner (2005). 'Politik zwischen Norm und Wirklichkeit: Systemmängel im deutschen Parteienstaat aus demokratischer Perspektive'. FÖV Discussion Papers No. 35. December 2006 edition. Speyer: Deutsches Forschungsinstitut für öffentliche Verwaltung Speyer.

Voulgaris, Y. (2001). Η Ελλάδα της Μεταπολίτευσης 1974–1990 [Post-Authoritarian Greece 1974–1990]. Athens: Themelio.

Wallace-Hadrill, A. (1989). *Patronage in Ancient Society*. London: Routledge.

Walle, N. van de (2003). 'Presidentialism and Clientelism in Africa's Emerging Party Systems'. *Journal of Modern African Studies* 41 (2): 297–321.

Ware, A. (1996). *Political Parties and Party Systems*. Oxford: Oxford University Press.

Warner, C. (1998). 'Getting out the Vote with Patronage and Threat: The French and Italian Christian Democratic Parties, 1944–58'. *Journal of Interdisciplinary History* 28 (4): 553–82.

Webb, P. (2000). *The Modern British Party System*. London: Sage.

Webb, P. and S. White (2007). 'Political Parties in New Democracies: Trajectories of Development and Implications for Democracy', in P. Webb and S. White (eds.), *Party Politics in New Democracies*, pp. 345–70. Oxford: Oxford University Press.

Weber, M. (1922/1978). *Economy and Society*. Berkeley: University of California Press.

Weeks, L. (2009). 'Parties and the Party System', in J. Coakley and M. Gallagher (eds.), *Politics in the Republic of Ireland*, pp. 137–67. 5th edition. Abingdon: Routledge.

Weingrod, A. (1968). 'Patrons, Patronage, and Political Parties'. *Comparative Studies in Society and History* 10 (4): 377–400.

Whyte, J. H. (1980). *Church and State in Modern Ireland 1923–1979*. Dublin: Gill and Macmillan.

Wiarda, H. J. (1974). 'Corporatism and Development in the Iberic-Latin World: Persistent Strains and New Variations'. *Review of Politics* 36 (1): 3–33.

Wichmann, M. (1986). *Parteipolitische Patronage: Vorschläge zur Beseitigung eines Verfassungsverstoßes im Bereich des öffentlichen Dienstes*. Frankfurt a. Main; Bern; New York: Verlag Peter Lang GmbH.

Wilson, J. Q. (1973). *Political Organizations*. New York: Basic Books.

Wilson, W. (1887). 'The Study of Administration'. *Political Science Quarterly* 2 (2): 197–222.

World Bank (2007). *EU-8: Administrative Capacity in the New Member States—The Limits of Innovation?* Washington: World Bank.

Wright, V. (1994). 'Reshaping the State: The Implications for Public Administration'. *West European Politics* 17 (3): 102–37.

Zuckerman, A. (1979). *The Politics of Faction: Christian Democratic Rule in Italy*. New Haven: Yale University Press.

Index

agencification 12, 22
  in Ireland 225
Austria
  administrative tradition in 35–7
  Alliance for the Future of Austria (BZÖ) 33–5, 46–7, 50
  Austrian People's Party (ÖVP) 31–5, 46–8, 50
  control (patronage as control) 44–5, 49–50
  elite patronage 49–50
  Freedom Party of Austria (FPÖ) 33–35, 47, 49–50
  grand coalition 33,36, 40, 46–7, 49–50
  Haider, Jörg 49
  index of party patronage in 37
  mass patronage 34, 48–50
  motivations for party patronage in 44–5
  New Public Management 39
  party mechanisms of patronage in 46–8
  political parties in 33–5
  proportional patronage 47
  Proporz system 36, 40, 49–50
  qualifications of patronage appointees in 44–5
  reward (patronage as reward) 44–5, 49–50
  Social Democratic Party of Austria (SPÖ) 33–4, 40, 46–7, 50
  Weber, Max and administrative tradition in, 35

brokerage 4–6, 209
Bulgaria
  political parties in 55
  index of party patronage in 58
  consensual (shared) patronage appointments in 69–71
  Movement for Rights and Freedoms (DPS) 55, 58, 68–70
  National Movement Simeon the Second (NDSV) 55, 58, 67, 69–71
  Law on the State Administration 56
  Law on the Civil Servant 56
  European Union and patronage in 54, 62, 67–8, 71
  the administrative tradition in 56–7
  motivations for party patronage in 63–4
  qualifications of patronage appointees in 65–7
  party mechanisms of patronage in 67–9
  Bulgarian Socialist Party (BSP) 55, 57–8, 67–8, 72

case selection 15, 23
consensual patronage practices 15, 358, 368, *see also* within countries
control patronage 8, 10–16, *see also* within countries
core civil service 21, 369
Czech Republic
  administrative tradition in 77–9
  Civil Service Act 78
  CSSD 76–8, 88
  deputy ministers 80–1, 85, 88
  index of party patronage in 80–4
  KDU-ČSL 76, 81, 85, 89
  klientelismus 74–5, 90
  KSČM 76–7, 89,
  Labour Code 78, 81
  motivations for party patronage in 84–7
  ODS 75, 82, 88
  party mechanisms of patronage in 88–9
  political parties in 75–7
  qualifications of patronage appointees in 86
  regional and local administration 83–4
  SZ 76–7, 87
  trafika 74–5, *80*, *90*

Denmark
  administrative tradition in 92–94, 98–102
  consensual (shared) patronage appointments in 94, 109, 112
  index of party patronage in 102–106
  motivations for party patronage in 107–8
  party mechanisms of patronage in 93–4, 115
  political parties in 106–107, 117
  qualifications of patronage appointees in 110–115
depolitization 368–9, *see also* politicisation
expert interviews 20–1, 24–5, 376–7

Germany
  administrative tradition in 122–5
  Bund 122
  Bundesländer / Länder 121, 132–4
  federal ministries 122–3, 130–1, 135, 139, 141
  federalism 125–6
  index of party patronage in 127–9
  motivations for party patronage in 136–7
  North-Rhine Westphalia (NRW) 123, 126, 128–9, 132–4, 136, 142
  partisan networks 130–4, 139–41
  party mechanisms of patronage in 138
  political civil servants 123, 131–3
  political parties in 122
  qualifications of patronage appointees in 137–8
  staff council for civil servants 129–30
Greece
  administrative tradition in 147–9
  bureaucratic clientelism 145
  consensual (shared) patronage appointments in 157–8
  index of party patronage in 150–4
  machine politics 145–6
  motivations for party patronage in 154–5
  New Democracy (ND) 146–7, 149, 155, 159

Panhellenic Socialist Movement (PASOK) 146–7, 149, 151, 18–9
party democracy 144, 146, 363
patronage democracy 144, 363
polarization 146, 160
political parties in 145–6
qualifications of patronage appointees in 156–7
state centralism 146–7
Supreme Council for Personnel Selection (ASEP) 147–9, 152–3, 157, 159
two-party politics (also twopartyism) 146, 160

Hungary
  administrative tradition in 167–8
  motivations for party patronage in, 182–3
  captured sectors 164, 172–5, 184
  consensual (shared) patronage appointments in 183–4
  index of party patronage in 171–3
  partially disciplined sectors 176–7, 184
  partially insulated sectors 164, 172, 177–9
  party mechanisms of patronage in 179–80
  patterns of patronage 172–9
  political control 175, 182, 185
  political discretion 168–9, 171, 179
  political parties in 164–6
  politicisation 173–5, 177
  qualifications of patronage appointees in 179–81

Iceland
  administrative tradition in 188
  clientelism 186–7, 191, 195
  consensual (shared) patronage appointments in 204
  constituency for bureaucratic autonomy 186, 190
  control appointments 186–7, 188, 190, 192–5, 197, 200–1, 203–5
  index of party patronage in 192–195

motivations for party patronage
  in 200–201
party mechanisms of patronage
  in 201–203
party rule (flokksræði) 191
political parties in 189–190
professionalization 190
qualifications of patronage appointees
  in 201–204
rewards appointments 186–7, 189,199,
  200, 203
Shefter 186–7
index of party patronage, *see also* within
    countries
  defined, 26
  in Europe, 366–9
  calculation of, 375
institutional types
  defined, 21
  patronage by, 370
Ireland
  administrative tradition in 213–4
  candidates 208–9
  consensual (shared) patronage
    appointments in 224
  Fianna Fáil 206–10, 214, 227
  Fine Gael 206–209, 216–7, 224, 227
  franchise model 208
  index of party patronage in 214–218
  Labour Party 206–7, 338
  motivations for party patronage
    in 219–222
  party mechanisms of patronage
    in 218–220, 226
  political parties in 208–210
  qualifications of patronage appointees
    in 222–4
  Social Partnership 217, 222, 226
  Taoiseach 207, 215, 217, 222
  The 'Battle of Baltinglass' 206
Italy
  administrative reform 231, 237, 243
  administrative tradition in 232–3
  colonization 230
  consensual (shared) patronage
    appointments in 241–3

entourage 241
fragmented bipolarism 231
index of party patronage in 234–7
lottizzazione 244–5
motivations for party patronage in 237–9
Napoleonic tradition 229
partitocracy 230–1, 234, 243, 246–7
party mechanisms of patronage in
  243–4
personalization 240–1, 243, 247
polarized pluralism 230, 240
political parties in 231–2
privatization 231–2, 237, 243, 246
qualifications of patronage appointees
  in 239–41

maps of states
  defined 21
  availability, 28
multi-level governance 4, 11, 373

Netherlands
  administrative tradition in 252–5
  coalition government 250–2, 255–6, 267
  consensual (shared) patronage
    appointments in 267
  consensus (consociationalism) 251–2,
    267, 270
  distribution of appointments (distributive
    system) 269, 271
  electoral volatility 252, 274
  index of party patronage in 256–60
  motivations for party patronage in 264–5
  New Public Management 252, 362
  party lobbyist 267–8, 270–1, 360
  party mechanisms of patronage
    in 267–70
  pillarization 250–2, 260–1, 267
  political parties in 250–2
  professionalization of appointment
    procedures 269, 287–9
  qualifications of patronage appointees
    in 265–7
  responsive competence 255, 266
  senior civil service 253–4, 256
  water boards 256, 262–4, 271

Netherlands (cont.)
    Weberian civil service tradition 252–3
network
    party as a, 7, 10–3, 359–60, 372–4
    ministerial, 18, 364
nomenklatura 54, 57, 74, 77, 367
non-majoritarian institutions 13, 240
Norway
    administrative tradition in 274–7
    cabinet meetings 275, 278
    Council of State 278
    embedsmenn 278
    index of party patronage in 279–82
    ministerial accountability 275
    monarchy 274
    motivations for party patronage in 284–5
    Office of the Prime Minister 275, 281
    parliament 273–5. 278, 283
    party mechanisms of patronage in 282
    political parties in 273–4
    qualification principle 279, 285
    qualifications of patronage appointees in 284–7
    senior civil servants of the Crown 278
    Stortinget 273, 275, 278, 284

party competition 12, 358, *see also* parties within countries
party government 3–4, 10–4, 357–9, 372–3
    in Austria 32–3
    in the Czech Republic, 75, 86–7, 91
    in Spain 331–3
    in the UK 336–9
party organization 7–10, 358–361, 372–373
    in Ireland 208–10
    in the Netherlands 252
patronage
    definition 3–4
    as an organizational resource 7–10
    as an electoral resource, 4–7
    and clientelism, 9
    and corruption, 8–9

policy areas 21–3
politicization 26, 36, 50, 56, 79–80, 82, 125, 146, 160, 163–4, 173–5, 177. 236, 238, 243–4, 255–6, 273, 280, 287–8, 319, 323, 352
pork barrel 17, 27
Portugal
    administrative tradition in 302–3
    cartel thesis 313
    CDS-PP 313
    consensual (shared) patronage appointments in 311–312
    democratization 295, 300, 312–3
    index of party patronage in 305–8
    internally mobilized parties 301
    motivations for party patronage in 308
    nationalization 299
    office-seeking 297, 314
    party goals 298
    party mechanisms of patronage in
    party system institutionalization 301
    partyness of government 314
    partyness of society 314
    PCP 300, 312
    policy-seeking 297–8, 305, 310, 313–4
    political parties in 300–301
    power patronage 296–7
    privatization 299
    PS 300–302, 313, 315
    PSD 300–302, 313, 315
    qualifications of patronage appointees in 310–311
    service patronage 296–7
    third wave democracies 294, 314
    transition through rupture 301
    Vote-seeking 296–7, 313

reward patronage 8–11, 14, 26

Spain
    1984 Public Service Act 319, 321
    Administrative corps 318, 328
    administrative tradition in 318–319
    Basque Nationalist Party (PNV) 317
    consensual (shared) patronage appointments in 330–1

Convergence and Union (CiU) 317
Council of Ministers 326
Felipe González 326, 328
index of party patronage in 322–4
José Luis Rodríguez Zapatero 326, 328
José María Aznar, 326, 329
Mariano Rajoy 326
motivations for party patronage in 324–5
party mechanisms of patronage in 326–7
People's Party (PP) 317, 326, 328, 329, 331
political parties in 316–7
qualifications of patronage appointees in 325–6
Spanish Socialist Workers' Party (PSOE) 317, 322, 326–329, 331
Union of the Democratic Centre (UCD) 317, 319, 326
United Left (IU) 317

United Kingdom
administrative tradition in 338–9
Civil Service Commission 328, 338, 354
Commissioner for Public Appointments (CPA) 340
Commissioner for Public Appointments for Northern Ireland (CPANI) 341
Commissioner for Public Appointments in Scotland (CPAS) 341
Committee on Standards in Public Life (CSPL) 339
Judicial Appointments Board for Scotland (JABS) 341
Judicial Appointments Commission 340, 342
majoritarianism 335
ministerial reach 340, 342–4, 352
modified majoritarianism 335
motivations for party patronage in 345–6
NHS Appointments Commissions 340, 343, 352
Northern Ireland Judicial Appointments Commission (NIJAC) 342
Office of the Commissioner for Public Appointments (OCPA) 339, 340–1, 348, 352
party mechanisms of patronage in 349–350
political parties in 336–8
pre-appointment hearings 340, 357
qualifications of patronage appointees in 347–9
index of party patronage in 343–5, 351–3
select committees 350–1, 354
consensual (shared) patronage appointments in 349–351